The Government Machine

History of Computing

I. Bernard Cohen and William Aspray, editors

Jon Agar, *The Government Machine: A Revolutionary History of the Computer*

William Aspray, *John von Neumann and the Origins of Modern Computing*

Charles J. Bashe, Lyle R. Johnson, John H. Palmer, and Emerson W. Pugh, *IBM's Early Computers*

Martin Campbell-Kelly, *From Airline Reservations to Sonic the Hedgehog: A History of the Software Industry*

Paul E. Ceruzzi, *A History of Modern Computing*

I. Bernard Cohen, *Howard Aiken: Portrait of a Computer Pioneer*

I. Bernard Cohen and Gregory W. Welch, editors, *Makin' Numbers: Howard Aiken and the Computer*

John Hendry, *Innovating for Failure: Government Policy and the Early British Computer Industry*

Michael Lindgren, *Glory and Failure: The Difference Engines of Johann Müller, Charles Babbage, and Georg and Edvard Scheutz*

David E. Lundstrom, *A Few Good Men from Univac*

René Moreau, *The Computer Comes of Age: The People, the Hardware, and the Software*

Emerson W. Pugh, *Building IBM: Shaping an Industry and Its Technology*

Emerson W. Pugh, *Memories That Shaped an Industry*

Emerson W. Pugh, Lyle R. Johnson, and John H. Palmer, *IBM's 360 and Early 370 Systems*

Kent C. Redmond and Thomas M. Smith, *From Whirlwind to MITRE: The R&D Story of the SAGE Air Defense Computer*

Raúl Rojas and Ulf Hashagen, editors, *The First Computers—History and Architectures*

Dorothy Stein, *Ada: A Life and a Legacy*

John N. Vardalas, *The Computer Revolution in Canada: Building National Technological Competence*

Maurice V. Wilkes, *Memoirs of a Computer Pioneer*

The Government Machine

A Revolutionary History of the Computer

Jon Agar

The MIT Press
Cambridge, Massachusetts
London, England

Set in Baskerville by SNP Best-set Typesetter Ltd., Hong Kong.

Library of Congress Cataloging-in-Publication Data

Agar, Jon.
The government machine : a revolutionary history of the computer / Jon Agar.
p. cm.—(History of computing)
Includes bibliographical references and index.
ISBN 978-0-262-01202-7 (hc. : alk. paper), 978-0-262-53388-1 (hc.)
1. Computers—Government policy—Great Britain—History. 2. Public administration—Great Britain—Data processing—History. 3. Civil service—Effect of technological innovations on—Great Britain—History. I. Title. II. Series.

QA76.9.G68A33 2003
004'.0941—dc21 2003042121

Contents

Contents

Acknowledgements

When I started this project I knew that I wanted to write about computing in a different way, but beyond that I only had some rather disconnected ideas concerning machines and metaphor. If these ideas have been sharpened over the years it is because I have benefited from many formal and informal discussions with colleagues.

At Manchester University I was lucky enough to work at the Centre for History of Science, Technology and Medicine, the home of the National Archive for the History of Computing. My Mancunian colleagues probably heard more versions of *The Government Machine* than was good for them, and I say a hearty *thanks* to them: Jeff Hughes, John Pickstone, Roger Cooter, Jack Morrell, Penelope Gouk, Carsten Timmermann, Aya Homei, Simone Turchetti, Helen Blackman, Alison Kraft, Jon Harwood, Paolo Palladino, Ian Burney, Vladimir Jankovic, Roberta Bivins, Chandak Sengoopta, Sam Alberti, David Cantor, Lyuba Gurjeva, Jay Kennedy, Joan Mottram, Helen Valier, Abigail Woods, Rebecca Herzig, Lyn Schumaker, Patrick Joyce, Penny Harvey, and Sarah Green. On moving to London, I found an equally congenial intellectual atmosphere at the Department of Science and Technology Studies, UCL.

Others to whom I have incurred a debt of gratitude include Ben Marsden, Stephen Twigge, Thomas Kaiserfeld, Ian Miles, Andrew Warwick, David Edgerton, Mats Fridlund, Graeme Gooday, Marc Berg, Geof Bowker, Simon Schaffer, Doron Swade, Robert Bud, Tim Boon, Stephen Johnston, Rhodri Hayward, Iwan Morus, Will Ashworth, Adam Tooze, Jane Caplan, John Torpey, Sally Wyatt, Stephen Brown, Steve Woolgar, John Krige, Delphine Gardey, Michael Allen, David Vincent, Jim Bennett, Arne Kaiser, Thomas Hughes, Tom Haigh, Charlie Gere, Dorothy Porter, Andrew Hodges, Ludmilla Jordanova, and staff of the Public Record Office, BT Archives, and the British Library. For help with the illustrations and photographs of this book I would like to also thank Philip Hoare, John Jensen, and Emily Lewis.

My study certainly benefited from the hospitality, interest, and sense of community of historians of computing. In the UK, Martin Campbell-Kelly offered me much useful advice, while his colleagues Mary Croarken, Steve Russ, and Ross Hamilton have made the University of Warwick a campus I am always happy to visit. In the United States, I particularly want to thank Bill Aspray, Bob Seidel, and Janet Abbate.

Finally, I would like to recommend The MIT Press to aspiring authors. Larry Cohen is a patient and wise editor, the copy editing is diligent, and the books are always beautifully designed and produced.

The Government Machine

Introduction
The State of Knowledge

Sitting in the reading rooms of the Public Record Office in London, a historian is in the center of a museum of organization. Copies of the catalogue to the museum fill several walls (although these are now complemented by online versions). The catalogue lists are dominated by references to objects of one kind: the file. The file has in its lifetime been registered at least twice: once by the government body that produced it and once by the Public Record Office when, after surviving many reviews considering its historical worth, it was selected as worthy of being kept for posterity. If the file is more than 30 years old, the historian notes the latter number, types it into a computer terminal, and waits a while for the pager to beep, indicating that the file has arrived at the collection desk. Although it might be weeded for duplicate or sensitive papers, the file the historian sees is usually the same artefact handled by civil servants and politicians. Typically the file has a card cover, its ruled jacket bearing the signatures of those who have handled it. Inside are notes, letters, minutes, memoranda, or reports, often ordered chronologically and annotated as work was done. At this point nearly every historian forgets about the form of the file and reads the content.[1] This historian did not, and the book that follows is the result.

However, this book is not just about files. (Even though I have argued elsewhere that what society designates as uninteresting makes for rich sociological study, I would not write solely on filing systems.[2]) But what files *do* leads to the concerns of this book. Consider the following points. First, files are information technologies: they are material artefacts that store and organize information. A file is a part of a technological system: its number refers to its place in a registry. The efficient organization of registries for a particular department at a particular time was never a trivial problem. And the file, as an information technology, would not work without a range of associated devices: ink pens, typewriters, standardized paper, Treasury tags. The civil servant, certainly in this crude sense but also in others ways that are explored in this book, has always been a technophile. But the academic specialty of history of technology has not centered its study on the office as often as it should. Second, consider again the historian of the state confronted with a file and avidly reading the contents. The encounter is pre-structured to a profound degree: the material form is shaped by choices in information technology, and the text is shaped by the rules and models of writing—civil servants are skillful literary practitioners. The file being examined is the end product of a massive expenditure by the state of "paperwork" that gives the text much of its meaning. To put such work aside and consider the file as objective evidence is, to say the least, a leap of faith by the unwary historian. This problem is felt with even greater force when the historian lifts official statistics, also produced by the state, for use in his or her arguments. The temptation to use the statistics is understandable, since only governments have the powers, resources, and geographical reach to manufacture much statistical knowledge. But such knowledge has been produced under conditions dependent not only on the bureaucratic technologies mentioned above but also on techniques developed—and made sense of—within government. As the influential early-twentieth-century statistician Arthur Bowley emphasized, understanding what a statistic says requires knowledge of the state's "methods of collection and compilation."[3] Prior to such historical facts is the practice of government.

However, the historian is not alone. Perhaps the most commonplace encounter between citizen and state is the filling out of a standardized form. Again notice that the encounter is already mediated by an information technology of a simple but important kind. Indeed, the modern state is not, and never has been, encountered in "raw" form, directly. The paper trail is a long one: standard mass questionnaires were used in 1798 by local officials in Britain to interrogate all eligible males as to their willingness to take up arms in the event of a Napoleonic invasion, standardized forms were used in the fourth British census of population in 1831, and other bureaucratic genres have much longer histories.[4] However, since the middle of the nineteenth century there has been an intensification of involvement between citizen and state, a topic well studied within political and social history. This entanglement was mediated by skills, sometimes embodied in inspectors, sometimes embodied in the techniques and practices that were an integral part of the material culture of bureaucracy. Either way, the politics of expertise came to possess crucial significance.

With this preamble the purpose of this book can be stated. It is a study of the mechanization of government work in the United Kingdom, with a focus on the changing capacities of government, from the early nineteenth century to the beginning of the twenty-first, a period in which the "size" of the state peaked. The story is about humans and machines, but particularly about humans who promoted machines. However, it is not a comprehensive story. That would be a lifelong project. Instead, I will propose an argument about the relationship of humans and machines that emphasizes the importance of groups and relates to a peculiarly important machine: the general-purpose computer. Expert movements—communities that based their authority on expertise but also had to persuade outsiders of the legitimacy of this claim, and which often championed the introduction of new techniques—provide the prism through which this social, political, cultural, and technological history is viewed. I will argue that the apotheosis of the civil servant can be found in a place unfamiliar to most historians and in a form that will surprise them: the computer. Such a statement will, I hope, discomfort many readers enough to make them want to read on.

This book attempts to bridge two areas of scholarly and popular interest. It aims to convince political historians and historians of public administration that they would profit from understanding the history of technology and the material culture of bureaucracy. (Indeed, "bureau" should be put back into studies of "bureaucracy.") The following points should be highlighted:

- The changing capacities of government depended on the implementation of new technologies.
- The British Civil Service contained technocratic movements of experts. To fully grasp the implications of this claim requires rejecting the received "negative" historiography of the Treasury.
- A distinct solution to the problems of "surveillance" raised by the expanded state, congruent with articulations of "Britishness," was enacted.

Conversely, this book should provoke historians of science and technology to re-examine the role of government. In particular, it suggests the following:

- The uptake of office technology depended on a vision of government, even if it was often commercial business that formed the main market.
- The state provided a model of organization so fundamental that considerations of "order," "framework," "structure," and "machine" are inextricably linked with understandings of "state" or "government." This last point can be considered as asserting, in its extreme form, that to study the history of technology is to study the state, and vice versa.
- The Civil Service, cast as a general-purpose universal machine, framed the language of what a computer was and could do.

If this book succeeds in its aims, then when a political historian or a historian of public administration discusses, say, the mobilization of scientists in World War II or a prediction of economic growth on which a crucial policy turns, the historian will immediately ask "What techniques were at hand to allow this style of government?" (The answer here might be "Lowly information technologies such as registers or more sophisticated methods such as computerized models of the economy.") Likewise, a historian of technology faced by some device or artefact, whether it be a punched card or a Ferranti Mark I electronic computer, should immediately ask "How was this used and what difference did such use make to organization or government?" "The power of governments," Brewer has noted, "has always been and always will be in large part dependent upon their capacity to order and manipulate different sorts of information."[5] Schellenberg, in his classic account of the growth of archives, noted that there was an official need for the ordered preservation of public records:

> Records, even the older ones, are needed by a government for its work. They reflect the origins and growth of a government and are the main source of information on all its activities. They constitute the basic administrative tools by means of which the work of government is accomplished. They contain evidence of financial and legal commitments that must be preserved to protect the government. They embody the great fund of official experience that the government needs to give continuity and consistency to its actions, to make policy determinations, and to handle social and economic as well as organizational and procedural problems. In short, *they are the foundation upon which the governmental structure is built.*[6]

And that foundation is one of knowledge organized by material, if simple, information technologies. The mechanization of government work therefore is also of epistemological interest.

Whitehall: An Odd Place for a Historian of Technology

If the historian gets back on the train at Kew Gardens and travels east along the Thames into the center of London, after a few miles of leafy suburbia the train will plunge underground; half an hour later the historian can emerge at Westminster. This is the heart of British politics, captured by two names, both taken from old royal palaces: Westminster and Whitehall. "Whitehall" now signifies the buildings that house government departments populated by thousands of civil servants. The buildings have a strangely organic feel: it is hard to tell where one stops and the other starts. It is impossible to know for sure which government department inhabits which. The most important departments cluster around Parliament Square, onto which the underground entrances empty pedestrians, but civil servants are housed along many of the criss-crossing streets in the surrounding area. Despite imperial flourishes, the architecture is one of discretion, of a turning away from the public light.[7] In complete contrast, Westminster is unmistakable. The scene, dominated by Big Ben, is instantly familiar as the tourist image of Britain, but it is also one created by the public sector's first information technology disaster. Charles Dickens tells the story:

> Ages ago a savage mode of keeping accounts on notched sticks was introduced into the Court of the Exchequer; the accounts were kept, much as Robinson Crusoe kept his calendar on his desert island. In the course of considerable revolutions of time, the celebrated Mr. Crocker was born and died; Mr. Walkinghame, of the Tutor's assistant, and a terrible hand at figures, was born, and died; a multitude of accountants, book-keepers, actuaries, and mathematicians, were born, and died; and still official routine clung to the notched sticks, as if they were pillars of the constitution, and still the Exchequer accounts continued to be kept on splints of elm wood, called "tallies." Late in the reign of George III, some restless and revolutionary spirit originated the suggestions, whether, in a land where there were pens, ink, and paper, slates and pencils, and systems of account, this rigid adherence to a barbarous usage might not possibly border on the ridiculous? All the red tape in the public offices turned redder at the bare mention of this bold and original conception, and it took till 1826 to get the sticks abolished.[8]

Then, in 1834, when these sticks were thrown in the furnace used to heat the House of Lords, the resulting conflagration burned down the Palace of Westminster. The new Houses of Parliament were built in its place.

Dickens poked fun at the Exchequer tallies for a serious purpose. He related the story of their fiery fate in an 1855 speech to the Administrative Reform Association, which he supported passionately. He was accusing the British government of being archaic, unreformed, and deeply reluctant to change its techniques. Even before Dickens, it was a commonplace that British administration had been slow to modernize and hostile to new technology and to technically minded entrepreneurs. The shabby treatment by civil servants of the source of the country's wealth, the inventor, was also a theme of one of Dickens's most powerful novels. In *Little Dorrit* (1857), the sickliness of the civil servants in the Circumlocution Office, all appointed through corrupt patronage and many from the same family, is contrasted with the vigor of the inventor Daniel Doyle. The collapse of Doyle's business is a foundational cultural moment, associating the decline of science and engineering in Britain with an inefficient and technophobic Civil Service.

Whitehall is an odd place to find a historian of technology. The British Civil Service is assumed to be the preserve of gentlemen, and gentlemen and machines are not presumed to mix. (See figure I.1.) But the Administrative Reform Association's target was already undergoing profound change begun before Dickens had lent his considerable rhetorical power to the attack on Whitehall. The Northcote-Trevelyan report of 1854 provided a template on which the Civil Service was to be reorganized. The slow, piecemeal, incomplete reorganization that was to ensue would have considerable technological ramifications. This book is about mechanization within a Civil Service organized by Trevelyan's principles. It is inspired by Campbell-Kelly's accounts of

Figure I.1
A cartoon (undated; probably from the late 1920s or the early 1930s) produced by a British punched-card company. Can the "master of the house," a gentleman, be mechanized? Note the punched-card "data." (source: National Archive for the History of Computing, University of Manchester)

"Victorian data processing."[9] The sheer size of the Civil Service, alone, would be enough to justify a historian of technology's interest (40,000 were employed in the 1850s, more than 750,000 a century later). But there is an additional justification: I suggest that several of the most important moments in the history of information technology revolve, rather curiously, around attempts to capture, reform, or redirect governmental action. Two such attempts were the justly famous projects of Charles Babbage and Alan Turing, which will be freshly interpreted in the following chapters.

Alan Turing's "universal machine" was the imaginary device he used to demonstrate the unprovability of Hilbert's *Entscheidungsproblem*. (See chapter 2.) Turing wrote his paper on computable numbers while at Cambridge in the mid 1930s and published it in 1936. Because Turing was deeply involved during the Second World War with the secretive code-breaking project at Bletchley Park and after the war with computers at the National Physical Laboratory and at Manchester University, and occasionally for chauvinistic reasons, Turing's universal machine has been retrospectively claimed as a computer manqué. Indeed, formally there is a logical equivalence between the stored-program computer idea, as articulated by the ENIAC team in 1945, and the universal Turing machine. But no real stored-program computer can ever approach the ideal: limited by finite memories and finite storage capacities in peripherals, as well as by application, real machines in the real world are *always*, strictly speaking, special-purpose machines. Therefore, the good historical question to ask is not "Are stored-program computers universal Turing machines?" but "Why have electronic stored-program computers been cast as universal, as general-purpose machines?"

In chapter 1 I consider why machine-like characteristics have been attributed to governments or parts of governments. I borrow and extend Otto Mayr's arguments concerning the interplay between metaphorical machines and styles of government. In chapter 2 I examine the British general-purpose "government machine," the permanent Civil Service, paying close attention to the interplay of discursive and material technologies. The outcome of the events discussed in chapters 1 and 2 was an immense repertoire of mechanical language concerning government. What fascinates me is how, and why, this became a resource for an expert movement of mechanizers.

During the nineteenth century, many aspects of British governance came to depend not on appeals to gentlemanly codes of conduct but on rational, professional, mechanically objective routines of specialist expertise (what Habermas, in *Toward a Rational Society*, called the "scientization of politics"). Royal Engineers constructed sewers, highways, and public buildings, and staffed the new Ordnance Survey. Medical Inspectors of Health wrote statistics-laden reports on industrial urbanization, sanitation, and cholera. Elsewhere, statisticians, chemists, veterinarians, and physicists gained positions of authority on various boards and in various departments and inspectorates. The historiography of this shift has been admirably summarized by MacLeod, who places great emphasis on the model proposed by historian Oliver MacDonagh.[10] Taking as a point of departure the early-twentieth-century analyses of A. V. Dicey, MacDonagh's model proposed five stages in the rise of the expert: The exposure of an "intolerable situation" (often, as with cholera, an "evil" of urbanization) by means of reports and "blue books" led Parliament to pass permissive or enabling legislation, which, without means of enforcement, proved inadequate.[11] This failure was opportunistically grasped by special officers or experts appointed to enforce the legislation. The experts then pressed for further compulsory legislation and for a superintending central body to oversee it. As these moves often did not lead to substantial alleviation of the problem, the officials often sought to intervene directly, or sought preventative measures instead of mere cures; both scenarios enlarged the area of applicability and the influence of their expertise. The self-interest of experts therefore gave "momentum" to administrative change.

MacLeod argues that the influence of experts peaked during Dicey's second period, the "flowering of the spirit of enquiry" (1832–1870). During this period, specialists such as Robert Angus Smith, John Simon, Henry Thring, and to a lesser extent John Tyndall enjoyed considerable influence predicated on their expertise. The apotheosis of the expert, Edwin Chadwick, flourished briefly before ambition and rancor ended his project to drain London and systematically recycle its filth.[12] After 1870, MacLeod claims, there was a "gradual submersion of the mid-century specialist into watertight departmental structures which compelled him to rely on secretarial sanction, formal procedures and codes, and which constrained him to terms of reference not of his choosing or design," a restriction MacLeod labels "departmentalism."[13] The Permanent Secretaries, presiding over larger and larger departments, were distanced from the experts in the ministry, to the detriment of the power of the specialist. Furthermore, MacLeod claims that "an intensified preoccupation with "making no mistakes" implied longer hours for specialists in the office—hours devoted to the completion of minutes and memoranda, usually without sufficient clerical assistance, and affording less contact with the public": participation in the meetings of professional societies, for example, dropped.[14] According to this standard historiography the experts, now mere specialists, were reined in, demoted as the generalist products of the Northcote-Trevelyan reforms secured an ever-tighter grip on the Civil Service.[15]

I do not think that this influential phased model of specialists in the Civil Service is accurate. In chapter 3, I show how the Royal Statistical Society continued to be a forum in which civil servants played an important role. Indeed, the expert movement of statisticians was marked by an interdependence of official and non-official experts. Moreover, in the case of office mechanization, examined in detail in chapters 5 and 8, close attention to routine was the very basis on which new claims to expert authority were based. The late nineteenth century may have seen the demotion of the largely autonomous government expert championed by MacDonagh and MacLeod, but it did not see the demise of the expert movement within government. It would be more accurate to say that as the style of government mutated, so did the opportunities for expert organization and the forms that expert movements took.

What I propose is that there have been overlapping expert movements active in the nineteenth and twentieth centuries: statisticians, economists, the Organization and Methods movement, operational researchers, even the media-savvy "spin doctors" of the turn of the millennium. These movements often exhibit the pattern of rise, flowering, and reining in described by MacDonagh and MacLeod; however, they do not rise and fall together, and important expert movements—specialist economists for example—have no such clear trajectory. At any one moment there may be several movements active; however, the fortunes of the expert movements examined in this book can be summarized as follows: After the power of the nineteenth-century expert was curtailed late in that century, there was, contra MacLeod, a period in which expert statisticians enjoyed peculiar influence. (See chapter 3.) When control over the statisticians was reasserted, another expert movement—the mechanizers—arose (although not at the statisticians' direct expense—the politics of expertise was never so simple). The mechanizers' power, at its height in post-Second World War Whitehall, was curtailed by the early 1970s.

Expert movements have many sociologically familiar characteristics: group identities reinforced by professional names, journals, meeting places, heroes, stories of successes and failures, and so on.[16] The "social movements" that the sociologist Rob Kling insists are crucial to American computerization should be seen as the most recent manifestation of this historical pattern, albeit for a different country.[17] Each movement developed some degree of disciplinization in academia and in other public institutions and used it to promote its views. Some institutions, in particular the London School of Economics and Political Science and the Institute of Public Administration, accommodated experts—both experts of the narrow "movement" kind and (if the grotesque neologism can be excused) "generalist-experts" such as Harold Laski and Richard Burdon Haldane. Indeed, for some experts application within government was a minimal concern; industry, commerce, or academia took up far greater attention. However, the experts that interest me—and from here on when I refer to "expert movement" I do so to indicate this role—are those with a vision of government reformed through the uptake or application of specialized techniques. As such they deserve the label "technocratic," strictly meant.[18]

If the above arguments are taken seriously, they imply a necessary shift in future writing on the British Civil Service. The history of the Civil Service is still written from the top down. The values of a huge organization's elite generalists are still taken to represent the values of the whole.[19] Generalists—the "intellectuals" of Northcote-Trevelyan—are portrayed as hostile to specialists, hostile to quantification, and hostile to modern mechanization and industry, and as such are regular villains in the histories of British decline.[20] The addition of the history of expert movements provides the means to upset this picture. The full implementation of the Northcote-Trevelyan report left a Civil Service with an intellectual generalist First Division (after 1920 the "Administrative Grade"), a lower army of mechanical supplementary clerks, and a middle class of Second Division employees. The pivotal expert movement was composed of the proponents of office mechanization, which appealed to the middle ranks (the executive officers) but whose technocratic vision had deep implications both for the generalists and the lowly supplementary clerks. Histories of the Civil Service (e.g. Hennessy's *Whitehall* and Chapman and Greenaway's *Dynamics of Administrative Reform*), though excellent in many respects, pass over information technologies, even office machinery.[21] The misreading of the British twentieth century Civil Service, including the identification within it of an anti-quantification bias, is largely informed by the viewpoint of a few high-level administrators, and it cannot be sustained against empirical research focusing on the everyday practices of expertise. Expertise, promoted at middle levels, was profoundly important throughout the Civil Service.

Though the main focus of this book is the expert movement of mechanizers, which took up the message of American systematic management and incorporated it into a vision of British public administration, chapter 3 examines the work of the expert movement of statisticians in the nineteenth century and the early years of the twentieth. There are several good reasons for doing so. First, in the context of changing styles of administration, statisticians campaigned for vastly greater quantities of information to be collected by the regulatory state, and for new centralized bodies to organize such work. In this campaign, an image of "chaotic" Britain was often opposed to images of other nations. The spread and popularization of this language provided a discursive opening for other protagonists of order, in particular mechanical order. Second, the technocratic vision of some of the statisticians was revealed by controversies and conflicts with others in government (in particular over centralization and over "informative" statistics). Finally, statistical knowledge was brought together with other government knowledge systems, notably the registers that are the subject of chapter 4, in recognizably contemporary computer projects. Chapter 4 analyzes several ambitious schemes, all proposed during the First World War and all to a greater or lesser extent failures, to bureaucratize the British subject. Unlike information provided by a census, schemes such as the National Register provided knowledge of the individual not the aggregate, a dossier culture not often associated with British political history—indeed, an explanation of *why* this association was not made, and why partial (not universal) registers became a hallmark of British government is an important corollary of the chapter.

Although both chapter 3 and chapter 4 deal with government techniques of information processing, neither features many machines. The growth of the experts' office-mechanization movement is the subject of chapter 5. Although punched-card machinery was introduced before 1914 to handle the Census of Population and clerical work associated with National Insurance, the experience of war profoundly reshaped attitudes to office machinery in Whitehall. Put crudely, a deal was struck between the higher administrators of the Treasury (who sought techniques to fully implement the Northcote-Trevelyan and Haldane recommendations and to cement its control over the Civil Service) and an expert movement of mechanizers (who argued that the "aim of every alert organization should be mechanization"). Treasury control secured over the Civil Service by a more architectural, panoptic solution was not a feasible option in a Whitehall composed of unplanned buildings and converted old palaces, private mansions, and hotels.[22] Mechanization was thus an ideology of middle-level "executive officers" that flourished in a Treasury that appreciated the benefits that flowed from possessing a mechanizing Investigating Section that could survey other Whitehall departments. Putting these developments together: If one searched interwar Britain for a "general-purpose machine" governed by a "code" made explicit in the form of "programmes," one would be led to His Majesty's Treasury.

Chapters 4–7 deal with the relationship between warfare and changing informational techniques. My main claims on this subject are to be found in chapter 6, where I argue that an apparent informational crisis in the 1930s was met by the establishment of a number of dedicated organizations: the Telecommunications Research Establishment at Malvern (where radar development was later housed); the massive Government Code and Cypher School at Bletchley Park; a second long-lasting National Register; a Social Survey; Mass Observation, a deepened state capacity to calculate manifested in numerous bureaus; and a Central Statistical Office. Most of these are well known to historians, but no one has brought them together and asked why so many information-collecting and information-processing organizations emerged for such diverse purposes at the same historical moment. To answer this question we will need an understanding of different forms of expertise and how they fitted in the culture of the wartime command economy.

The first stored-program electronic computer, built at Manchester University and prompted by American theory, was possible only because parties from two of the wartime governmental organizations, the Telecommunications Research Establishment and Bletchley Park, briefly came together. Max Newman brought the concept of a computer from the code-breaking project, and F. C. Williams brought the practical methods of electronic data storage from Malvern. In chapter 7 the early British computers, and how they were applied to military tasks, are discussed. In chapter 8 we move back to the mainstream of this book's argument: the relationship between government administration and office mechanization. In the years after 1945 the Treasury mechanizers, now the center of a burgeoning "Organization and Methods" (O&M) movement with satellites in nationalized and private industry, were at their most influential. Treasury O&M (a section of Treasury that led the wider O&M movement) oversaw an ambitious program of computerization, accelerated when the Labour Party returned to power under the statistician Harold Wilson. For many reasons, the landscape changed again in the 1970s. Treasury O&M lost its broad scope and thus its vision. Government computer projects became controversial: either they failed to deliver (a recurring feature in the 1980s and the 1990s) or they became entangled in the panic over privacy. Chapters 9 and 10 discuss these debates in the context of attacks on "big government."

Information technology is important to government (the only similar case is aircraft) because of the number of ways the two interact: government has always been a gatekeeper of information and a major user. Also, either as a large-scale buyer of machines or by intervening and setting industrial policy, government has significantly shaped the development of information technologies. However, insofar as definitive historical studies of the government's industrial policy are soon to be completed, I restrict my interest to changes *in* Whitehall.

Though this is not often emphasized, an office of civil servants can be regarded as an information-processing entity. My aim is to produce a *historical* analysis of government that places centrally the collection and use of data, and to show how this conception of the state differs from other approaches. However, taking recent historiography of science and technology as my exemplar, my aim is not to reify and essentialize "information." Instead, information—what it meant and how it was collected and used—must be understood in terms of its context. Straws in the wind suggest that an informational history is emerging. Historians of an older generation, including Alfred Chandler Jr. and Robert Darnton, are re-emphasizing informational aspects of their own work to reinterpret business and cultural history.[23] Chandler (with Cortada) has edited a book that suggests the United States was "a nation transformed by information." Information serves as a way of dressing up studies of postal systems or histories of Enlightenment publishing, but it also provides a means of bringing troublesome new technology into national narratives, thus domesticating it. There is potential in a new informational history, but "information" must be treated sensitively.

In the case of the Civil Service, for example, "information" changes radically between its regulatory, social services and its nationalization/welfare-state periods—not least in the sheer quantity collected.[24] Nor can information be separated from its techniques. And mechanization (from standardized forms and clerks' desks, through punched-card installations, to electronic computers) is a continuous theme. I intend to criticize and even undermine two enduring accounts of information technology. First, the proponents of an "information revolution" routinely claim that information technologies have brought about some fundamental social discontinuity. They tend to identify a contemporary break (most recently, one associated with computer networks), and there are commercial or political motives for doing so. I therefore have sympathy with the handful of historians who have claimed that a transition occurred near the end of the nineteenth century. The latter, generally American scholars, attribute the chief role to the demands of big corporations, and I am interested in knowing quite how necessary is the commitment to business in information historiography.[25] It may be as persuasive, for example, to hitch the history of information to the rise of professional society as Perkin has conceived it.[26] We should also be wary of thinking that recent impressions of "information overload" are new. Nearly a century ago Graham Wallas argued that the stock of knowledge had grown too vast for successful use, and earlier pessimists can be found.[27] Quantities of information may have increased, but the form of information has also been simplified: as Scott argues the decisive act of state power is one of simplification, and of course information technologies are deeply intertwined with this process.[28] In general, I am skeptical about "information revolutions"—my impression is one of continuity (despite great growth), and I suggest that a comparative study would illuminate this major issue of twentieth-century history: how, for example, does the situation change when attention focuses on Britain, where government plays a relatively more important role than business? The second enduring trope of writings on information technology is the alleged link with authoritarianism and state power. However, how can a balanced inquiry into this claim be made in the absence of a general history of government techniques of information?

1

The Machineries of Government

Metaphor

Metaphor is at one and the same time a revealing and slippery historical resource. When metaphors are fresh they are striking and surprising, a sign of the creative insight of the poet. But it is when a metaphor is a commonplace, when it has struck a deep contextual chord, or when it has become the organizing principle for a way of thinking that it draws the attention of the historian. Within history of technology, interest in metaphor has come in waves. Four decades ago, analyses of the relationships between literary cultures and industrialism gave us two brilliant texts: Raymond Williams's *Culture and Society* (1958) and Leo Marx's *The Machine in the Garden* (1964). The latter is a foundational work of American history of technology; the former unfortunately failed to launch a British equivalent. Something of the style of each perhaps smacks of unfashionable history of ideas, but this would be to miss the point: they are books about the relationship of language and technology and about mediation by metaphor. What at first glance looks literary is actually of burning importance to the new history of technology. Metaphor is important, but how can it be safely handled? More recently there has been a linguistic turn across the academy, many historians included. But the poststructuralist tools are not ideal to our purpose, at least initially when a big picture needs sketching.

The argument of this book will turn on claims about a particular and large metaphorical cluster: government as a machine. Much of this chapter will seek to establish the genealogy of the metaphor of government as machine as it was mobilized, deployed, attacked and derided.

But what can the status of a historical argument concerning metaphor be? In particular, to what extent does the metaphor associated with an entity contribute to the nature of that entity? At one extreme, it has been argued that the language that takes an entity as its object thoroughly *constitutes* that object—

either in a strong form that states that the textual is all there is, or in a significantly weaker form that emphasizes that, though the entity may be real, access to it is forever mediated by language. In either case, the historian would be compelled to pay attention to all figures of language, metaphor among them. At the other extreme, it has been claimed that the nature of an entity is entirely independent of the language used to describe it. A historian of clocks, say, could happily proceed with a description of the development of timepieces without once worrying about the metaphorical baggage that accompanies the entities—the moral or political overtones of "to run like clockwork," for example.

I would like to move from a crude dichotomy to something subtler. Metaphor presents peculiar problems for the historian in that, whatever position the historian subscribes to as to its constitutive qualities, metaphor has a certain secondary quality: though a particular metaphor might be used to describe an entity in four cases out of five, there are always other metaphorical constructions that can be used in the fifth case. Otto Mayr expressed this problem succinctly:

> If one compares the genealogy of metaphors with those of concepts and ideas, there is a basic difference. Concepts like *trinity* or *momentum* live in history as subjects of continuing discourse. Anyone wishing to participate in this discourse is expected to be knowledgeable about the concept's previous history and to express himself in the terminology of the preceding discussion, no matter whether he wishes to approve of the concept or criticize it. Such constraints on behalf of focus, cohesion, and homogeneity are notably lacking in the use of metaphors. Metaphors, by their nature, are not the *subjects* of the discourse but only auxiliary devices adduced for emphasis and illustration, upon which neither author nor audience will concentrate much attention.[1]

I would argue that concepts and ideas are also discursive; however, that is a quibble, and I accept Mayr's main point: that metaphors are auxiliary. (The point will be illustrated below through a demonstration that other metaphors of government were current and sometimes popular.) If metaphor was solely constitutive of an entity this multiplicity could not be the case. Yet metaphor is—if you will excuse the metaphor—like scaffolding. It is auxiliary, but it *lends shape* to the entity. And if neither author nor audience much attends to the scaffolding, it is because both assent to its giving such shape—and it therefore tells the historian much about the assumptions and commitments of both. The Scottish essayist Thomas Carlyle said of the metaphor of government as machine: "Considered merely as a metaphor, all this is well enough; but, here, as in so many cases, the 'foam hardens itself into a shell' and the shadow we have wantonly evoked stands terrible before us and will not depart at our bidding."[2] What once had been mere froth became a constraint on thought and action.

For these reasons, arguments that depend on metaphorical evidence alone are difficult to sustain. A skeptic can easily point out a few counterexamples and rest his or her case. But to do so would, I think, be unfair. Metaphorical evidence invites such objections by its very nature, but the insights it provides into the assumptions and commitments of the user of the metaphor are important enough to at least ask for a sympathetic reading. Both Marx and Mayr presented us with deep arguments, concerning the relationship of technology to culture, that are dependent on metaphorical evidence. Mayr in particular suggests that two major metaphorical clusters—that of clockwork and of self-regulating mechanisms—should be related to the two rival political traditions of authoritarianism and liberalism. On the Continent, where the metaphor of clockwork found favor, it was aligned to an authoritarian concept of political order.[3] In Britain a liberal concept of order correlated to a preference for metaphors of self-regulating machines. But when the crunch came, Mayr did the honest scholarly thing and summarized the relationship as speculative (but note the *importance* of the claim, an argument about Britain and the industrial revolution):

> About the details of the causal nexus between the advent of the liberal conception of order and the rise of the self-regulating machines we are reduced . . . to speculation. Quite firmly established, however, is the fact of the simultaneous appearance in Britain of these two phenomena, which in itself is forceful evidence of the interdependence of the socio-intellectual with the technological activities of a culture.[4]

My book can be read as an extension of Mayr's arguments into later periods of history, during which both political order and technologies change. Again I think I have convincing evidence, like Mayr, of the prevalence of a particular metaphor, and I think it has profound consequences for the technologies of the nineteenth and twentieth centuries.

I was first struck by the prevalence of mechanical metaphors of government in recent studies of the British Civil Service. Take for example this sample from Whitehall's foremost contemporary commentator: "The Civil Service is a bit like a Rolls-Royce—you know it's the best machine in the world, but you're not quite sure what to do with it" (the Tory politician R. A. Butler in 1962, quoted by Hennessy on p. 15), "a creaking inherited machine" (p. 20), "an alternative machine" (p. 20), the "bureaucratic engine room" (p. 22), "central government machine" (pp. 23, 26), "levers of public power" (p. 33), "government machine" (pp. 46, 60), "the only machine so far invented for changing the orientation of a national society in a fairly short time-span" (quoting Eric Hobsbawm on the remedial properties of central government and the state), "the great technician of the machinery of government" (p. 59), "Whitehall machine" (p. 65), "machine-minding" (about arch-civil servant Hankey, who had "an incredible memory . . . an official brand which could reproduce on call the date, file, substance of every paper that ever flew into a pigeonhole," pp. 65–66), "desiccated calculating machinery" (an old ritualized insult, p. 70), "machine" (p. 74), "static penny-pinching state machine" (p. 82), "state machine" (p. 84).[5] Nor is the machine metaphor confined to popular analyses: one of the most academically respected of theorists on political strategies organizes his work by the metaphor of the "tools of government."[6] Here was clearly a metaphor that both recent authors and audiences were comfortable with.

There are three aspects of what I shall call the mechanical discourse of government, and it is important to attend to each one. First, as a dominant set of metaphors the mechanical discourse guided and constrained thought and action. To describe the state as a "machine" immediately begged questions concerning control, routine, remorselessness of action, efficiency, simplicity, motive power, the identity of the machine operators, and so on, which would not be so immediately present, or as immediately expressible, if another discourse had been used.[7] Not only was the government, and especially the civil service, a "machine" as an actors' category, but it has also become a ubiquitous analytical one, from seemingly untheoretical familiar examples such as the "well-oiled machine" to more apparently deliberate choices such as Hood's "tools of government."[8] Alternative discourses did exist, and even flourished at certain stages: the most common being that of the "organism"—which begged questions of sickness, vigor, and moral comparisons drawn from nature, and, literally, the "body politic."[9] Indeed there is often a mix: John Stuart Mill accompanied his proposed "central organ of intelligence" with the, by then familiar, mechanical metaphor.[10] Take for example this extract from his "third and most cogent reason for restricting the interference of government": that following Northcote-Trevelyan "the evil would be greater, the more efficiently and scientifically the administrative machinery was constructed—the more skillful the arrangements for obtaining the best qualified hands and heads with which to work it."[11] The thrust of the mix here—which is a moral order, in Woolgar and Grint's usage—is that the organic controls the machine.[12] Mill therefore used both metaphors but kept them separate too. A further complication is that with the rise of the mechanical vision of the body, the two discourses could—although not often in Britain—become completely intertwined.[13] Furthermore, "society" which by the middle of the nineteenth century did not refer just to polite society but to a more enveloping universal concept, was increasingly discussed in organismic terms especially by the late-nineteenth-century British Idealists, with Spencer in particular basing his evolutionary sociology explicitly on the analogy.[14] Government "machinery" could therefore be embedded in many bodies.

What were the historical causes and consequences of the machine metaphor for political organization? And, following Mayr, were political organization and technology therefore interdependent? If so, what sort of machines were implicated? What follows is a historical analysis in three stages. First I briefly outline the spectrum of alternative metaphors for aspects of government. Then I turn to a genealogy of government as a whole (the state) as a machine. Finally, I examine how the British Civil Service, in particular, was cast as a machine, during which a division of labor was confirmed that, I claim, has a peculiar significance. Later in the book I will ask how metaphorical construction of aspects of government as mechanical related to mechanization, but in this chapter, in two case studies, I will immediately reflect on "real" machine projects, those associated with Charles Babbage and Alan Turing. I will argue that, in Babbage's own words, his greatest mechanical project, the Analytical Engine, was a political machine with the power to control both the legislative and the executive—a revolutionary claim. Likewise, Turing's greatest paper, "On computable numbers, with an application to the *Entscheidungsproblem*," can be read, indeed should be read, as being informed by the organization of civil service "machines." Other chapters will deal with the details of mechanization projects and with less well-known figures, but the moral of this broad-brush chapter should be plain: that mechanical metaphors of government and seminal computing machines were intimately interrelated.

Other Metaphors

Besides mechanical metaphors of government, a range of other metaphors have been deployed. What they meant in particular circumstances, even for the same metaphor, varied immensely from author to author and from audience to audience. But I cannot attend to such matters here, for reasons of space.[15] What I offer is merely a quick tour.

Organic metaphors of the body could supplant or complement mechanical metaphors. I take as my illustrative author the poet, intellectual, and Germanophile Samuel Taylor Coleridge. The British constitution as a body was worked out at length in Coleridge's *On the Constitution of Church and State* (1830): ". . . the right idea of a STATE, or Body Politic; 'State' being here synonymous with a *constituted* Realm, Kingdom, Commonwealth, or Nation, *i.e.* where the integral parts, classes, or orders are so well balanced, or interdependent, as to constitute, more or less, a moral unit, an organic whole; and as arising out of the Idea of a State I have added the Idea of a Constitution, as the informing principle of its coherence and unity."[16] So the state was a holistic body—the metaphor of the "body politic" was an old one, with the constitution not some sort of supporting structure (a skeleton) but a unifying principle.[17] All metaphors invite extensions. By casting the state as a body, Coleridge could ask, by extension, what were medical or physiological understandings of the state, or what parts of the state corresponded to body parts (head, arms, trunk) or the bodily functions. For example, he took contemporary theories about the imponderable vital fluids and energies of the body and stated:

> The first condition then required, in order to a sound constitution of the Body Politic, is a due proportion of the free and permeative life and energy of the Nation to the organized powers brought within containing channels. What those vital forces that seem to bear an analogy to the imponderable agents, magnetic, or galvanic, in bodies inorganic, if indeed, they are not the same in a higher energy and under a different law of action—what these, I say, are in the living body in distinction from the fluids in the glands and vessels—the same, or at least a like relation, do the indeterminable, but yet actual influences of intellect, information, prevailing principles and tendencies (to which we must add the influence of property, or income, where it exists without right of suffrage attached thereto), hold to the regular, definite, and legally recognized Powers, in the Body Politic.[18]

When the "body politic" metaphor became this complex it was often intertwined with medical understandings of the body, including mechanistic aspects. (Even the most idealist or vitalistic of physicians understood the frame of the body mechanically.) This is illustrative of the difficulty of deciphering metaphors of government: the two most important metaphorical clusters are of body and machine, yet they interact in necessarily complex ways. Coleridge, writing to thank John Rickman, the first British census taker, prophesied: "In whatever part of Christendom a genuine philosopher in Political Economy shall arise, and establish a system, including the laws and the disturbing forces of that miraculous machine of living Creatures, a Body Politic, he will have been in no small measure indebted to you for authentic and well guarded documents."[19] A second example is the socialist mill owner Robert Owen of New Lanark, who spoke of how "dead machinery" was in competition with "live machinery." Or, authors could embrace both organic and mechanical metaphors: the "body politic" need not be a body metaphor opposed to a material one. Carlyle, for example, cast it as mechanical, playing on the Cartesian opposition, in his aside: "Thus is the Body-politic more than ever worshipped and tended [like a machine]; but the Soul-politic less than ever."[20] But the body metaphor of government could also be simple and straightforward, and it is certainly more often encountered in formations less complex than those given by Coleridge or Carlyle. A nineteenth-century commonplace, for example, was that country gentlemen were the "very nerves and ligatures of the body politic," and that what they naturally felt so did the nation.[21] Organic metaphors were, at heart, conservative: helping to protect supposedly long-grown traditions and the "natural" order rather than brash new invention. Coleridge was a great influence on conservative thought, as was his forebear, Edmund Burke, who had warned that the French revolution was an attack on the organic principles of society.

Other metaphors used for aspects of government were minor, but not unimportant. The British constitution, which being unwritten invited attributions of metaphorical meaning, was, besides being occasionally mechanical (see below) or an organic life-giving principle (Coleridge), a building or fabric. In the 1790s, the radical Horne Tooke, reacting to the French Revolution, claimed that the "main timbers" of the British constitution were sound even if dry rot had got into the superstructure. "Fabric" was a favorite constitutional trope: "the work of infinite wisdom," stated Prime Minister Lord North, "the most beautiful fabric that had ever existed since the beginning of time."[22] The constitution as fabric was intricately woven, a robe of splendor for Britannia. But the building and fabric metaphors differed from the organic metaphor in a crucial sense: whereas organisms naturally grow, buildings and fabrics must be made. The former did not need human intervention, the latter did. Likewise mechanical metaphors of the constitution allowed, by extension, the existence of machine makers and tenders. So when the jurist William Blackstone called the British constitution a "vast and intricate machine of voluminous family settlement," he was both commenting on its development as an intricate accumulation of common law, made by judges (like himself) over the centuries, but also saying that engineers—lawyers—were needed to make it work.

Government as a Machine

"If a technological innovation displays in structure and functioning an unmistakable analogy to the structure that a society prefers to give its various practical and theoretical systems," Mayr concluded, "if it reflects the various mentalities that shape public life, in short, if it matches and reinforces the prevailing conception of order, it will be received more warmly, regardless of its technical merits, than other inventions." This is to say that the prevailing concept of order—government—is a factor in the selection of technologies. Furthermore, if the use of technologies shapes government, there must be a dynamical relationship between the two wherein one helps re-imagine the other. Often, however, the particular technology that was in mind when an

Table 1.1
Metaphorical technologies and styles of government.

Technology	Government	Representative author	Reference
Clockwork	Authoritarian	Frederick II	Mayr
Balance	Liberal	Montesquieu	Mayr
Engine	Representative democracy?	Bagehot	Wise and Smith
Universal computer	Generalist-mechanical bureaucracy	Turing	

analogy was drawn between government and machine is not clear. In these cases we must think of the general characteristics attributed to machines: regularity, repetition, connection to sources of power, and so on.

Neither Niccolò Macchiavelli, in *The Prince*, nor Francis Bacon, in *New Atlantis*, used mechanical metaphor to describe government. Though the "balance of power" was central to Macchiavellian thought, the metaphor did not depend deeply on references to mechanical balances, and certainly did not possess the liberal connotation of later centuries. Bacon deployed "mechanic" twice, both in reference to the mechanical arts, with no strong political implications.[23] It might seem that Jean Bodin, the French political theorist, in *Les Six Livres de la République* (1576), mobilized "machinery" to make a foundational distinction: "It is very important that a clear distinction be made between the form of the state, and the form of government, which is merely the machinery of policing the state, though no one has considered it in that light."[24] Thus, Rome had been, for Bodin, a democracy governed aristocratically, the true state distinguished from how it was "merely" governed. France, England, and Spain were monarchies governed democratically. "Machinery" here acts to bracket off that part of the state that the reader was invited to forget. Certainly, for Bodin, what mattered was not how the state was governed but what the form of the state was—and that should be an undivided sovereign power, a monarchy. But machinery was not the metaphor originally used by Bodin. "Machinery" appears only in much later translations—mechanical government did not exist in the sixteenth century.[25]

Mechanical imagery of the state became highly politically charged in the seventeenth and eighteenth centuries, when the metaphors appealed to particular types of machine. In particular, as Mayr has shown, early modern natural and political philosophy can be seen as "authoritarian" or "liberal" according to whether they were organized by clockwork or balance metaphor. For example, the late-sixteenth-century analyst of absolutism Justus Lipsius drew on the analogy between parts of a clock and parts of the state: the hidden internal mechanisms were akin to the inscrutable inner workings of government while, in Mayr's words, "the conspicuous visibility of the ruler's public life" followed the "simplicity of the action of the clock hand."[26] The clockwork state was authoritarian because of its model of power, with forces expressed mechanically and without question from the top:

> For a king or some Potentate operates in far distant places as if he were present, by power derived from himself, which he confers upon the Laws and Judges . . . viz., Of Watches, Clocks, and Engines wherein many Wheels are orderly moved in the absence of the Workman, yet by a virtue imprinted upon them by the first direction of the Artist.[27]

Likewise for the English materialist philosopher Thomas Hobbes, submission to authority was essential if humans were to avoid the "nasty, brutish and short" life characteristic of the state of nature. The most powerful expression of mechanical political philosophy can be found in the famous opening paragraph of *Leviathan* (1651), although its metaphorical interpretation is far from straightforward:

> Nature, the art whereby God hath made and governs the world, is by the *art* of man, as in many other things, so in this also imitated, that it can make an artificial animal. For seeing life is but a motion of limbs, the beginning whereof is in some principal part within, why may we not say, that all *automata* (engines that move themselves by springs and wheels as doth a watch) have an artificial life? For what is the *heart*, but a *spring*; and the *nerves*, but so many *strings*; and the *joints*, but so many *wheels*, giving motion to the whole body, such as was intended by the artificer? *Art* goes yet further, imitating that rational and most excellent work of nature, man. For by art is created that great LEVIATHAN called a COMMONWEALTH, or STATE, in Latin CIVITAS, which is but an artificial man . . . .[28]

Tangled together, deliberately, were a mechanical philosophy of nature (the body as machine) and a political philosophy that emphasized the state as being artificial but necessarily ruled with absolute power.[29] The merger of body and machine metaphors allowed Hobbes great play with specific analogies: "sovereignty" was the "artificial soul," magistrates the "artificial joints" (transmitters of power), "reward and punishment" were "nerves," "wealth and riches" were "strength," "salus populi" (people's safety) was the "business" of the state, "counsellors" were the memory, "equity and law" were "artificial reason and will," "concord" was "health," "sedition" was "sickness," and "civil war" was "death."[30] Having boldly set out the analogies, Hobbes does not once return to "automata" by name in the following pages, although the whole text was animated by the metaphor.

Any reader of Hobbes's introduction—even if that reader turned no further pages—would have subsequently thought of the state when thinking of a machine, and vice versa. For Mayr, the fate of clockwork or automata metaphor in English political thought followed that of Hobbes himself: abhorred at home and exiled to the continent; if a state was clockwork, argued William Penn in his *Frame of Government of Pennsylvania*, then it was so in a negative sense: "Governments, like clocks, go from the motion men give them; and as governments are made and moved by men, so by them they are ruined too."[31]

In Prussia and France the clockwork state came to dominate political thought in the eighteenth century. Frederick II of Prussia consistently wrote of the state through both clock and body politic metaphors, using them to support his powerful vision of enlightened despotism. As Mayr has summarized: "The two analogies of clock and body expressed two different principles that were both essential for Frederick's conception of the state: on the one hand, the body analogy, which likened the prince to the head or heart, served to defend the central and supreme place of the prince in the hierarchy of the state. The clockwork analogy, on the other hand, expressed the ideal of a state where all problems, now and hereafter, could be solved by appropriate administrative mechanisms that were programmed in advance to take care of any eventuality."[32] "Program" is well used, since as Goethe reported, the prince was like the control drum of a musical automata or barrel organ: ". . . from the huge clockwork that unrolls before you, from the movement of the troops, you can deduce the hidden wheels, especially that big old drum, signed FR [Fredericus Rex], with its thousand pins which generates these tunes, one after another."[33]

The Prussian vision was attractive in France, where the metaphor of the state builder as engineer flourished in the writings of Étienne Bonnot de Condillac and Jean-Jacques Rousseau, and it reappeared elsewhere in Germany, where it underpinned Kameralism, the theory of the control of economy and society by the state articulated by writers such as Johann Heinrich Gottleib von Justi. To quote Mayr again: ". . . roughly between 1740 and 1780, many and perhaps most German and French political thinkers were in the habit of visualizing the state, the government, and the body politic primarily in terms of clockwork."[34] The metaphor highlighted the need for a statesman-engineer who would predict and repair glitches, emphasized the advantages of central coordination or control, made the smooth running of clockwork the counterpart of the ideal political order, and supported a hierarchical conception of functions and authority. If there was a difference between German and French political thinking about the state machine, it was that the Germans viewed it positively while for the French it was a necessary evil.[35]

But, and here is Mayr's central claim, the clockwork state was rejected in favor of the "liberal" balance after the late eighteenth century. Balances had already become an increasingly powerful metaphor in many domains: the balance of power between states became the techniques through which to articulate foreign policy, which in turn spilled over into seventeenth century English economic policy. The balance of trade was the central concept of mercantilism (albeit ensuring that the balance tipped heavily in favor of the home country). The balance differed from clockwork because of its properties of self-regulation: equilibrium maintained through the opposition of forces. Newtonian dogmas of attraction and repulsion, integral to the identity of eighteenth century English natural philosophy, justified self-regulation in the natural realm. Political philosophies, especially those favored after the Whig ascendancy that followed the Glorious Revolution of 1688, justified self-regulation in the political realm. That constitutional settlement rested on a separation and balance of power within the state among a circumscribed monarchy, an aristocracy, and an assertive "People" (in fact the Whig constituency of a prosperous and expanding middle class).

The most influential eighteenth-century argument for the separation of powers within the state was articulated not by an English Whig but by a French aristocrat, Charles de Secondat, Baron de Montesquieu, in *Des l'esprit de loix* (1748, translated nearly immediately into English by Thomas Nugent as *The Spirit of the Laws*). Harking back to the clockwork state, Montesquieu first noted that the direct transmission of power from an absolute monarch made for the simplest machine: "In monarchies, policy effects great things with as little virtue as possible. Thus in the nicest machines, art has reduced the number of movements, springs and wheels."[36] But his main thrust was a critique of such simple mechanics, and in a review of Roman political history he sought to establish the importance of a balance of powers between legislative, executive and judicial parts of government.[37]

One generalization that can be made about the use of metaphorical machines of government is that they were a means of making constitutional connections explicit, often at moments of tension (a point to which I will return). The language of checks and balances was famously taken up with gusto by the engineers of the American constitution, who "constructed a government as they would have constructed an orrery."[38] Delegates at the

Convention held in Philadelphia in 1787 spoke of the "admirable mechanism of the English Constitution," and the mechanical metaphor became a commonplace, for both Federalists and Anti-Federalists in the debates over ratifying the constitution in 1787–88.[39] Alexander Hamilton, John Jay, and James Madison's *Federalist Papers*, the foundational collection of essays written between 1787 and 1788, drew repeatedly on analogies between material and political machines. Moreover, it allowed them to celebrate the application of Enlightenment science in the New World.[40] If a Parliament acted "to keep the machine from running into disorder," then new knowledge would lead to still further improvement:

> If Europe has the merit of discovering this great mechanical power in government [of representative democracy], by the simple agency of which the will of the largest political body may be concentred, and its forces directed to any object which the public good requires, America can claim the merit of making the discovery the basis of unmixed and extensive republics. It is only to be lamented that any of her citizens should wish to deprive her of the additional merit of displaying its full efficacy in the establishment of the comprehensive system now under her consideration.[41]

In particular:

> The science of politics . . . like most other sciences, has received great improvement. The efficacy of various principles is now well understood, which were either not known at all, or imperfectly known to the ancients. The regular distribution of power into distinct departments; the introduction of legislative balances and checks; the institution of courts composed of judges holding their offices during good behavior; the representation of the people in the legislature by deputies of their own election: these are wholly new discoveries, or have made their principle progress to perfection in modern times.

Indeed, the authors of *The Federalist Papers* copied Montesquieu and rhetorically foregrounded the liberal interpretation of balances by deploying clockwork and automata metaphors during passages of criticism. Thus, on the effect of increasing the number of representatives, the reader was told: "The countenance of government may become more democratic, but the soul that animates it will be more oligarchic. The machine will be enlarged, but the fewer, and often more secret, will be the springs by which its motion is directed." Likewise, on the proposal for a separate court for trial of impeachments, the authors demur: "To some minds it will appear a trivial objection, that it could tend to increase the complexity of the political machine, and to add a new spring to government, the utility of which would at best be questionable."

There is a sharp difference between the mechanical government envisaged by Montesquieu, the American constitutionalists, and the English Whigs and the sleek efficient machine deduced by a later generation from their Utilitarian science of politics. The influence of the Utilitarians on early-nineteenth-century reforms in suffrage, police, education, church, and economic policy has been exhaustively debated by historians.[42] Here I will only emphasize their sanction for the production of knowledge, their emphasis on making things—from constitutions to minds—visible, and the accusations from their critics of a desire for mechanical government. While the Whigs emphasized the importance of a balance of powers, in particular that the British Constitution was a compromise based on a balance of monarchical, aristocratic, and democratic forces and a proper separation of the executive, legislature, and judiciary, Bentham's Utilitarianism was critical.

Jeremy Bentham, a weak child of precocious intellect, was resentfully forced through school by his father. He arrived at Oxford's Queen's College at the age of 12. After being trained in law, he rejected what he found at the bar, aiming instead to replace the unruly organic growth of common law with a mechanical code deduced from principles. His "fundamental axiom" was, famously, that "the greatest happiness of the greatest number is the measure of right and wrong." Conduct would be ruled by a calculation of the balance of pains and pleasures. Stephen, in his collective biography of the utilitarians, drew out the natural philosophical inspiration:

> This embodiment of the general doctrine of utility or morality had been struck out by Hutcheson in the attempt (as his title says) "to introduce a mathematical calculation on subjects of morality." This defines the exact reason which made it acceptable to Bentham. For the vague reference to utility which appears in Hume and other writers of his school, he substituted a formula, the terms of which suggest the possibility of an accurate quantitative comparison of different sums of happiness. In Bentham's mind the differences between this and the more general formula was like the difference between the statement that the planets gravitate towards the sun, and the more precise statement that the law of gravitation varies inversely as the square of the distance. Bentham hoped for no less an achievement than to become the Newton of the moral world.[43]

An early formulation of the principle appeared anonymously in Bentham's *Fragment on Government* in 1776, the year he started work on *Introduction to the Principles of Morals and Legislation* (finally published in 1789), which he hoped would stand in relation to his later studies as pure mathematics did in relation to applied mathematics.[44] Bentham's subsequent science of government eschewed the abstract—he loathed the vagueness of the declaration of rights of man—in favor of the concrete and the rational code. In the French Revolution he saw the opportunity, not to execute, but to codify and legislate.[45] The plan for the Panopticon prison, that "mill for grinding rogues honest, and idle men industrious," which Bentham presented to the revolutionary government in 1790, is now his best-known concrete project. With his brother, the inventor Samuel Bentham, he designed the prison to the last detail, producing maps, models, and specimens of technologies of restraint. As Foucault reminded us, in the Panopticon the prisoners, ordered and arranged around the circumference, have to assume they are under constant surveillance from the central watchers, the arrangement creating relations of knowledge and power. More practically, Bentham's attempt to realize his scheme at Millbank in London, pursued for two decades until its abandonment unfinished in 1811, seems to have drawn Bentham's attention to the fact that officials and politicians could be evasive and irrationally refuse to adopt plans.[46]

The death of the Panopticon led Bentham to seek to rearrange political organization so that, next time, it would act rationally. He had, in the calculus of pleasure and pain, the instruments to measure the worth of legislation, which to be wielded only needed the collection of knowledge and the calculation of the balance. Why did governments not legislate according to his advice? He analyzed the problem: instead of governments acting to secure the greatest happiness for the greatest number, they sought the greatest happiness of the governors. If the interests of the governors could be made to coincide with the interest of the governed, then the problem of responsibility was solved. Bentham proposed a representative democracy, an answer that was to be propagated in a toned-down but succinct form by his utilitarian disciple James Mill. The master's deductions were more radical: an explicit written constitution enshrining universal suffrage, annual parliaments, vote by ballot, officials appointed by competitive examination, and law based on the "Pannomium" or universal code, rather than "judge-made" tradition.[47]

The Scot James Mill moved from Edinburgh to London in 1808, where he became a disciple—and soon a neighbor—of Bentham. Mill's prose is brutally compact and logical where his master's was prolix. Taking Bentham's principles, James Mill viewed his task in his *Essay on Government*, completed in 1820 as a supplementary chapter to the fifth edition of the *Encyclopaedia Britannica* and subsequently published in pamphlet form, as an exercise in clear and explicit language, in total the "science of Government."[48] The form of excellent government would not merely be "supposed," but, after "analysis," be given a "proof."[49]

The "end of government" was simple: the utilitarian greatest happiness for the greatest number. The substantive question concerned the means by which the end was to be achieved. Each of the three pure forms of government—democratic, aristocratic, and monarchical—suffered debilitating faults. By the "universal" law of human nature, perhaps given specific piquancy in a society driven by unheralded consumption, if given the chance, anyone would seek to deprive others of their "objects of desire."[50] Democracy, government "by the community itself, which alone is free from motives opposite to those ends, is incapacitated by its numbers from performing the business of Government; and that whether Government is intrusted to one [monarchy] or a few [aristocracy], they have motives which will carry them, if unchecked, to inflict the greatest evils."[51] (Thus even the English gentlemen, when granted absolute aristocratic power in the West Indies, were "led . . . not only to deprive their slaves of property of their fellow-creatures, but to treat them with a degree of cruelty, the very description of which froze the blood of their countrymen."[52]) One might think that, following Burke, perfection in government must be sought from a balanced combination of the three, exemplified by the tradition of "British constitution."

However, Mill's perfect combination was not found through a simple balance. Take any mixture of forms of government, he argued. "If one is slightly stronger than the other, the stronger will take from the weaker, till it engrosses the whole." And on exact balance: "How is it to be established? Or by what criterion is it to be ascertained? If there is no such criterion, it must, in all cases, be the result of chance. If so the chances against it are as infinite to one. The idea, therefore, is chimerical and absurd."[53] To the balance must be added proper a check, in particular via "the grand discovery of modern times, the system of representation, the solution of all the difficulties, both speculative and practical, will be found."[54] A "Representative body" must have an "identity of interest with the community," and must have "sufficient power successfully to resist the united power of both King and Aristocracy."[55] Mill thought he had argued from first principles, via a "chain of deduction" to indubitable conclusion: the Representative Body (which was the legislative)—must have powers at least equal to those of the King (under whom lay the administrative component of the executive) and the aristocrats, combined. Ideally, in the British Constitution the House of Commons did indeed have that power over the King and the House of Lords, but to truly possess it, it must be strengthened by extending the system of representation, at least to include the "intelligent and virtuous" men of the "middle rank": "There can be no doubt that the middle rank, which gives to science, to art, and to legislation itself, their most distinguished ornaments, the chief source of all that has exalted and refined human nature, is that portion of the community of which, if the basis of Representation were ever so far extended, the opinion would ultimately decide."[56]

Of course there remained the issue of whether through the mechanism of representation the people would truly *know* their own interest. For Adam

Smith, individuals—and capitalists better than country gentlemen—not only could know their interests, but their free pursuit of it would underpin a rational, laissez-faire economy. Could the Utilitarians extend self-knowledge to the community as a whole? Despite arguments from principle that "the community cannot have an interest opposite to its interest," it may still "act wrong from mistake."[57] The Utilitarian solution was forthright:

> The evils which are the produce of interest and power united, the evils on the one side, are altogether incurable: the effects are certain while that conjunction which is the cause of them remains. The evils that arise from mistake are not incurable; for, if the parties which act contrary to their interest had a proper knowledge of that interest, they would act well. What is necessary, then, is knowledge. Knowledge on the part of those whose interests are the same as those of the community, would be an adequate remedy. But knowledge is a thing which is capable of being increased: and the more it is increased the more the evils on this side of the case would be reduced.[58]

Knowledge made explicit was therefore a crucial component of the Utilitarian project. It should be seen as part of the wider profound Utilitarian theme of making things visible. Bentham's Constitutional Code was motivated by the desire to make law visible through explicitness and clarity. His Panopticon prison, likewise, depended on making its prisoners visible. Even James Mill's psychological theory, expressed in his *Analysis of the Phenomena of the Human Mind* (1829), aimed to "make the human mind as plain as the road from Charing Cross to St. Paul's."[59] Their sanction encouraged the production of knowledge—especially in its explicit thing-like *factual* form, and confirmed their love of statistics. It also encouraged its diffusion. Mill sat on the committee for Henry Brougham's Society for the Diffusion of Useful Knowledge, launched in 1827, happy to suspend his suspicions of the flashy brilliant Whig in the name of the greater cause. The SDUK circulated many thousands of popular publications in its 20-year history. Mill drew on the Utilitarian concerns for visibility and mechanical explicitness in his essay "Education." Using the term to cover not only ordinary "technical" (school) education but also the "social education" by which members of a society learn from each other, he came to the "keystone of the arch": "political education." The means by which the "grand objects of desire may be attained" depend "almost wholly upon the political machine," which must be engineered so that such objects are "the natural prizes of just and virtuous conduct, of high services to mankind and of the generous and amiable sentiments from which great endeavors in the service of mankind proceed." Mill continued: "It is natural to see diffused among mankind a generous ardor in the acquisition of those admirable qualities which prepare a man for admirable action, great intelligence, perfect self-command, and over-ruling benevolence."[60] The Utilitarian political machine would thus be an educational mill to grind men virtuous.[61] Its success, guaranteed by following explicit rules, would be visibly displayed in good liberal conduct.

Utilitarian advocates of mechanical government still followed the model of checks and balances, but they were contemptuous of the Whig separation of powers.[62] When given imaginative free rein, for example in proposals for the reconstruction of Indian government, they rearranged powers in a hierarchy, with the legislature sovereign and the judiciary and executive directed along predictable mechanical paths. There was still a separation of powers, but the powers were arranged vertically rather than horizontally, and they were under mechanical control. This, we shall see, has surprising echoes in the work of Charles Babbage.

The transition from checks and balances to dynamic machines as metaphors of government machines is most clearly seen in the work of Walter Bagehot (figure 1.1). Bagehot wrote concise, sharp prose, a skill he honed as a journalist and later as editor of the free-trade *Economist.* Three of his books went through many editions and translations: *Lombard Street* (1873), on the money market, *Physics and Politics* (1872), an "attempt to apply the principles of natural selection and inheritance to political society," and *The English Constitution* (1867), used as an Oxford textbook and now most often recalled for emphasizing the value of a dignified spectacle of monarchy.[63] The move to *The English Constitution* elegantly parallels Norton Wise's thesis that there was a shift from the balance to the steam engine as a cultural mediator in natural philosophy and political economy.[64] Indeed, Bagehot's text can be read as a thorough commentary on the formal theory of checks and balances.[65] He divided institutions, such as the constitution, into two: "first, those which excite and preserve the reverence of the population—the dignified parts . . . ; and next, the efficient parts—those by which it, in fact, works and rules."[66] The whole is a "machine," by inference an engine, since the "dignified parts of government are those which bring it force—which attract its motive power. The efficient parts only employ that power."[67] The metaphor of government as engine suggested extensions: Bagehot talked both of a "regulator" (the power to dissolve the "sovereign chamber," Parliament) and of a "safety valve" (the ability of the executive—the Cabinet—to choose new Lords).[68] The motive power stemmed from the monarch. Indeed, here Bagehot equated Queen Victoria with nature: the "reverence that she excites is the potential energy—as science now speaks—out of which all minor forces are made, and from which lesser functions take their efficiency." If she were to make use of her full power, "it would terrify . . . like a volcanic eruption from Primrose Hill."[69] Reverence played an important role in Bagehot's text. In addition to the natural power of the queen,

Figure 1.1
Walter Bagehot, editor of *The Economist* and author of *Lombard Street*, *Physics and Politics*, and *The English Constitution*. *The English Constitution* made repeated use of a dynamic steam-engine-as-government metaphor that can be contrasted with the static equilibria of the earlier checks-and-balances model. (source: National Portrait Gallery, London)

by the "theatrical show of society" the mass would defer to efficient rule: "As a rustic on coming to London finds himself in the presence of a great show and vast exhibition of inconceivable mechanical things, so by the structure of our society he finds himself face to face with a great exhibition of political things which he could not have imagined."[70]

Bagehot therefore made great use of the following analogies:

government	:	machine (engine)
monarch	:	nature
society	:	body or theatre.

In doing so, he was extending a distinction that had been published a few years earlier in John Stuart Mill's *Representative Government* (1861). There were, James Mill's son wrote, two ways of talking about government. The first was a parody of his own early Benthamite views:

> To some minds, government is conceived as strictly a practical art, giving rise to no questions but those of means and end. Forms of government are assimilated to any other expedients for the attainment of human objects. They are regarded as wholly an affair of invention and contrivance. Being made by man, it is assumed that man has the choice to make them or not, and how or on what pattern they shall be made. Government, according to this conception, is a problem, to be worked like any other question of business. They look upon the constitution in the same light . . . as they would upon a steam plough or a threshing machine.[71]

This view, therefore, assimilated government "to a machine," and it was opposed by those who held an organic view that government was

> a sort of spontaneous product, and the science of government as some sort of natural history. According to them, forms of government are not a matter of choice. . . . Governments cannot be constructed by premeditated design. They are "not made, but grow." Our business with them, as with the other facts of the universe, is to acquaint ourselves with their natural properties, and adapt ourselves to them. The fundamental political institutions of a people are considered by this school as a sort of organic growth from the nature and life of that people.[72]

Mill labeled both extremes "absurd." Although his radical scorn was directed toward the organic position, he also criticized the purely mechanical view, branding it as a belief in perpetual motion, a thermodynamic impossibility: ". . . political machinery does not act of itself. As it is first made, so it has to be worked, by men, and even by ordinary men." As this quotation suggests, in his discussion Mill preserved the image of the structures of government as a machine. This allowed him to exclude such issues and focus on the crucial question of nineteenth-century politics: "In politics, as in mechanics, the power which is to keep the engine going must be sought for outside the machinery."[73] But what was this "power" to be? We have already seen that for Bagehot the power was the natural force of the monarch. For Mill, writing between the Reform Acts and the rising tide of the mass franchise, it was "an open question what actual functions, what precise part of the machinery of government, shall be directly and discharged by the representative body"—and it was the "good qualities of the governed" that provided the "motive force to [the] machinery." Representative democracy would provide the controlling mind in the machine, without which the state was a dead bureaucracy. Although a bureaucracy "accumulates experience, acquires well-tried and well-considered traditional maxims, and makes provision for appropriate practical knowledge in those who have the conduct of affairs. . . . It is not equally favorable to individual energies of mind. The disease which afflicts bureaucratic governments, and which they usually die of, is routine. They perish by the immutability of their maxims; and still more, by the universal law that whatever becomes a routine loses its vital principle, and having no longer a mind acting within it, goes on revolving mechanically. . . ."[74]

Enemies of the Government Machine

Opposition to mechanical government could take two forms: one could deny that civil government could be likened to a machine, or one could attack government for machine-like faults. I present Thomas Reid as an example of the first, and Alexis de Tocqueville, Henry David Thoreau, and Thomas Carlyle as instances of the second.

The Scottish common-sense philosopher and divine Thomas Reid succeeded Adam Smith in the chair of moral philosophy at the University of Glasgow in the 1760s. If he is remembered today, it is for his answer to Hume's skepticism, presented in his *Inquiry into the Human Mind* (1764), including an argument, before Kant, that perception, of space for example, cannot be constructed only from the empirical sensations of sight and touch. After retiring from academia in 1780, Reid produced two more notable works, on human "intellectual powers" and "active powers." It was in *Essays on the Active Powers of Man* (1788) that Reid addressed government in a broad sense, the word encompassing natural, animal, individual, civil, and divine kinds. "There are two kinds of government very different in nature," he wrote. "The one we may, for distinction's sake, call *mechanical* government, the other *moral*. The first is the government of beings which have no active power, but are merely passive and acted upon; the second, of intelligent and active beings."[74] His examples of mechanical government were nature, puppetry, and a ship at sea. "Reason teaches us to ascribe to the Supreme Being a government of the inanimate and inactive part of his creation, analogous to that of mechanical government which men exercise, but infinitely more perfect," this, thought Reid, was "what we call GOD's *natural* government of the universe."[76] In mechanical government, the governed must follow the governors instructions, so "praise or dispraise . . . belongs solely to the author."[77] In puppetry, the "puppets, in all their diverting gesticulations, do not move, but are moved by an impulse secretly conveyed, which they cannot resist. If they do not play their parts properly, the fault is only in the maker or manager of the machinery."[78] Reid wonders aloud what we might call the puppets if we grant them "understanding and will, but without any degree of active power": ". . . this will make no change in the nature of their government. . . . They might, upon this supposition, be called *intelligent machines*; but they would be machines still as much subject to the laws of motion as inanimate matter, and therefore incapable of any other than mechanical government."[79] Reid's point was that humans have higher active powers (such as those springing from passion or reason), and are moral agents, so "civil government among men is a species of moral government."[80] Government, meaning government of people, *must* be moral not mechanical. To deny this would be a falsehood, and indeed an impiety (since liberty under moral government is related to free will under God).

Before moving on to authors who happily ignored Reid's distinction and launched attacks on the government machine, I want to record a subtle but significant elision in Reid's evidence. Take the case of the ship, his first example of mechanical government:

> An instance of mechanical government may be that of a master or commander of a ship at sea. Supposing her skillfully built, and furnished with every thing proper for the destined voyage, to govern her for this purpose requires much art and attention: And, as every art has its rules, or laws, so has thus. But by whom are those laws to be obeyed? not by the ship, surely, for she is an inactive being, but by the governor. . . . The sailor, perhaps, curses her for not obeying the rudder; but this is not the voice of reason, but of passion, like that of the losing gamester, when he curses the dice. The ship is as innocent as the dice.[81]

My point is merely that in this example of mechanical government the two potential actors are the governor (the "master or commander") and the ship itself. The crew are missing, and they must be considered to be part of the machine. Yet humans are moral agents, and therefore, simultaneously, are not. The cause of this invisibility, I suspect, goes beyond mere convenience of argument, since it was typical of published writings on government (the missing mechanicals are the civil servants of the executive) before the later nineteenth century and indeed resembles the disappearance of the operators of scientific instruments from published accounts.[82]

Though Reid could not, philosophically, accept the existence of a mechanical government of people, others in the following century protested against its presence. Some critics noted with alarm the hidden dangers of an American bureaucratic machine—the multiplication of secret springs. Tocqueville, the insightful outsider who toured the United States in the early nineteenth century, recorded the alarm with which Americans regarded centralized federal power (he considered such fears to be "purely imaginary" and instead thought that federal government was "visibly losing strength").[83] But he also noticed something curious about American administration: to European eyes, it seemed not to exist at all! "Nothing is more striking to an European traveler in the United States than the absence of what we term the Government, or the Administration." But bureaucracy *was* present, if hidden, and Tocqueville used mechanical language to describe it. He mobilized a particularly powerful metaphorical machine to support his observations regarding the paradoxical invisibility of the administrative part of the state, a device that was imaginary and uncanny, an affront to enlightened reason, yet also seductive: the perpetual-motion machine.[84] "Written laws exist in America," Tocqueville argued, "and ones sees that they are daily executed; but although everything is in motion, the hand which gives the impulse to the social machine can nowhere be discovered."[85] (In particular, the law of inheritance, the institutionalized means by which "man acquires a kind of preternatural power over the future lot of his fellow creatures," was a "machine once put in motion will go on for ages and advance, if self guided, towards a given point."[86]) The state machine was presented as autonomous technology, a democracy uncontrolled by the *demos*.

Two decades after Tocqueville's analysis, Thoreau wrote fervently to advocate disobeying the state when disobedience was necessary and justified. A mechanical metaphor of government was central to his rhetoric: the state was a machine and an individual's life under it became more subservient, more mechanical, weaker and poorer. In his essay on civil disobedience, Thoreau echoed Tocqueville's baleful analysis of inheritance—that the state was a machine that reproduced itself:

> This American government—what is it but a tradition, though a recent one, endeavoring to transmit itself unimpaired to posterity, but each instant losing some of its integrity? It has not the vitality and force of a single living man, for a single man can bend it to his will. It is a sort of wooden gun to the people themselves. But is not the less necessary for this; for the people must have some complicated machinery or other, and hear its din, to satisfy that idea of government which they have. . . . The mass of men serve the state thus, not as men mainly, but as machines, with their bodies. . . .[87]

The metaphor of the government machine gave Thoreau his great simile for civil disobedience: friction. Sparks flying signified complaint and righteous anger, but also injustice. "All machines have their friction. . . . But when the friction comes to have its machine, and oppression and robbery are organized," Thoreau implored, "I say, let us not have such a machine any longer."[88] It was precisely because injustice was the grit in the mechanism, that there was reason for hope and a justification for civil disobedience:

> If the injustice is part of the necessary friction of the machine of government, let it go; perchance it will wear smooth—certainly the machine will wear out. If the injustice has a spring, or a pulley, or a rope, or a crank, exclusively for itself, then perhaps you may consider whether the remedy will not be worse than the evil; but if it is of such a nature that it requires you to be the agent of injustice to another, then, I say, break the law. Let your life be a counter friction to stop the machine.

In the British context, opposition to mechanical government—indeed mechanism generally—was most powerfully expressed by the Scottish historian, essayist, and prophet Thomas Carlyle. This critique stemmed from Carlyle's life-changing conversion in 1821, when he rejected the materialist vision of a universe "void of Life, of Purpose, of Volition, even of Hostility . . . one, dead, unmeasurable steam-engine, rolling on in its dead indifference, to grind me limb from limb."[89] As one prophet eyes a rival, he assailed one source of mechanism. However, although Carlyle was a natural enemy of "gross steam-engine Utilitarianism," he also praised its rigor and lack of "cant," and he was a friend of the younger Mill.[90] In the remarkable essay "Signs of the Times," published anonymously in the *Edinburgh Review* in 1829, Carlyle announced: "Were we required to characterize this age of ours by an single epithet, we should be tempted to call it, not an Heroical, Devotional, Philosophical, or Moral Age, but above all others, the Mechanical Age. It is the Age of Machinery, in every outward and inward sense of that word."[91] The "great art of adapting means to ends," he noted sarcastically, encompassed everything: "Nothing is now done directly, or by hand; all is by rule and calculated contrivance." Carlyle's complaint, therefore, was directed not only at changing methods of work and the mechanical conquest of nature, but also at "internal" mechanization: of Education, of Religion, of Science.[92] Here he was at his most scathing: inward mechanization—the metaphysics, psychology, and philosophy of mind stemming from Locke and Hume, and the materialism of the body of Joseph Hartley, Erasmus Darwin, Pierre-Jean-Georges Cabanis, or the virtuoso maker of automata Jacques Vaucanson—had either failed or been replaced by sciences of the exterior, as if "to the inward world (if there be any) our only conceivable road is through the outward; that, in short, what cannot be investigated and understood mechanically, cannot be investigated and understood at all."[93]

"Nowhere," insisted Carlyle, was "the deep, almost exclusive faith we have in Mechanism more visible than in . . . Politics." But, although "civil government does by its nature include much that is mechanical," it "includes much also that is not mechanical, and cannot be treated mechanically."[94] Indeed, "we might note the mighty interest taken in *mere political arrangements*, as itself a sign of a mechanical age. The whole discontent of Europe takes this direction. The deep, strong cry of all civilized nations—a cry which, every one now sees, must and will be answered, is: Give us a reform of Government! A good structure of legislation, a proper check upon the executive, a wise arrangement of the judiciary, is *all* that is wanting for human happiness!" The influential political philosophers were not those, like Plato, who emphasized "the necessity and infinite worth of moral goodness, the great truth that our happiness depends on the mind which is within us," but those—and Carlyle accuses Adam Smith, Jean Louis de Lolme, and Jeremy Bentham directly—for whom "happiness depends entirely on external circumstances; nay that the strength and dignity of the mind within us is itself the creature and consequence of these. . . . Thus it is by the mere condition of the [government] machine, by preserving it untouched, or else by reconstructing it, and oiling it anew, that man's salvation as a social being is to be insured and indefinitely promoted."[95]

Now, I am not so much concerned with Carlyle's prescription, which was to reassert the secondary importance of the external and mechanical by fostering and strengthening the inward "infinite" qualities—the "mysterious springs of Love, and Fear, and Wonder" that owed nothing to institutions. (A call for the "Dynamical" to follow the "Mechanical" that, perhaps deliberately and not ironically, mirrored Bentham's procedure of starting with static classification ("pathology") before moving to "dynamics."[96]). Nor does my interest lie merely in his dominant metaphor. Indeed, he used "machine" so generally—for anything institutionalized—that it was in danger of losing force—although I think it is the root of his insight: that the there was deep similarity between changing methods of education or religious organization and industry. Carlyle, in his rush of words, could certainly be inconsistent and even incoherent.[97]

What Carlyle did was contribute substantially to machine as a metaphor of government and cast it as a term of opprobrium. He was heralding (or reasserting) a moral order: an expression of longing for the future day when "mechanism is not always to be our hard taskmaster, but one day to be our pliant, all-ministering servant."[98] So "government machine" was, perhaps primarily, the language of its *critics*. For the "Codemaker" Bentham, government was indeed thought of as a machine—but he himself rarely made use of the metaphor. His enemies, however, did: in their anxiety they labeled it—putting their metaphor in others' mouths—a machine. Again, it made things *explicit*: ". . . men have lost their faith in the Invisible, and believe, and hope, and work only in the Visible."[99] But once, among other things, government was "made mechanically visible," it was a short step—and a major theme of this book—to take the metaphor literally. It is no surprise, as we shall see, that Carlyle loathed Charles Babbage.

Babbage's Revolution

In the late 1820s and the 1830s, Charles Babbage was seriously interested in Whig politics. He chaired the election committee for William Cavendish in the contest for the Cambridge parliamentary seat in 1829. In 1832, Babbage attempted to find a seat for himself, but failed, after proving, notes one historian, "too much of a prima donna for selection committees."[100] He stood again, unsuccessfully, 2 years later. The first, direct approach to political power had failed. In the next chapter, we will see how Babbage, rather than turning his back on seeking political influence, mobilized an expert movement of statisticians, as if control could be gained through institutionalizing the human agents of statistical knowledge. Babbage later described the target to Adolphe Quetelet as "the influential class comprised of civil servants, members of Parliament—all the men who are involved in public affairs."[101] As the statistical attack faltered by the late 1830s, I will now argue that Babbage launched a third attempt at seizing power, the result being a profound revolution in which mechanization and the "influential class" were conflated.

Babbage had failed as a parliamentary candidate because he put people's backs up. With Carlyle the personality clash had been extreme, and he recorded his hatred: "Babbage continues to be eminently unpleasant to me, with his frog mouth and viper eyes, with his hidebound, wooden irony, and the acridest egotism looking through it."[102] The core beliefs of these prophets of mechanism and anti-mechanism stood opposed. Whereas Carlyle rejected mechanism as a proper route to internal understanding, Babbage embraced it: his model of the intellect, characterized by the mechanical following of explicit rules, had not been pushed far enough. Likewise, whereas Carlyle mocked those who sought human happiness in a "good structure of legislation, a proper check on the executive, a wise arrangement of the judiciary," for Babbage it was precisely in separation, mechanization, and control of the governing powers that political progress lay.

Separation of the governing powers was embedded in a form very familiar to historians of computing: the Analytical Engine. Babbage had witnessed, with his astronomer and reformist friend John Herschel, the way attention to division of labor had made the manufacture of mathematical tables an efficient process in post-revolutionary France. On his return to British shores, Babbage had brought this idea together with a second obsession, the automatism and industry of steam, to propose a radical machine: a brass-and-wood Difference Engine that would automate mathematical calculation. Babbage's conflicts with government and engineers during the 12-year period in which he attempted to have the Engine built are now familiar to historians of science and technology to the point of cliché. Toward the end of the affair, Babbage became increasingly distracted by a second project, one which promised to do

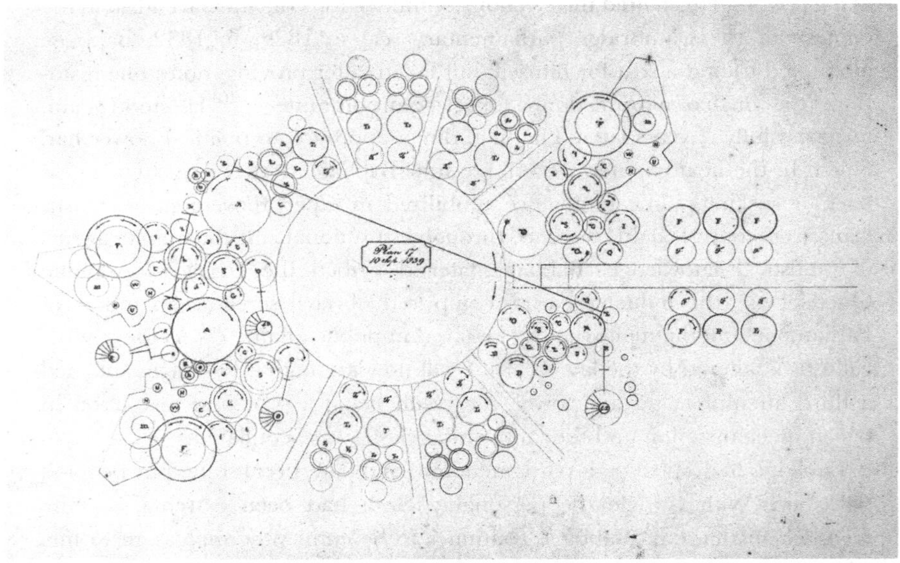

Figure 1.2
A diagram of the Analytical Engine showing the separation of "store" (memory, right) and "mill" (site of calculation, left). Babbage was drawing on his extensive expert knowledge of factory governance, and the industrial inspiration can be seen clearly inscribed into the design of the machine. Babbage wholeheartedly agreed with the description of the Analytical Engine that it would "give us the same control over the executive which we have hitherto only possessed over the legislative department." Parliamentary seats for factory cities, such as Manchester and Birmingham, had only been awarded in the previous decade. This gave factory masters some influence on the legislative, but, as yet, the industrial party could not be said to control the executive. (source: Science & Society Picture Library, Science Museum, London)

anything the Difference Engine could do, and much more besides. The Analytical Engine (figure 1.2) was a design for an automatic universal calculating machine, with numbers kept in a "store" and processed in a "mill." This was to be no liberal balance, a Whig separation of powers, since the store and the mill would be under direct mechanized command. Like a Jacquard Loom, the Engine was to be controlled not by human intervention but by instructions stored in the form of holes punched into cards—the materialization of thought separated from labor. Furthermore, Babbage imagined the Analytical Engine by first inventing a strict language to specify the work of the machine—an achievement Babbage considered to be as important as the Engine itself, and without which no "machinery of equal complexity [could] ever be contrived." The Mechanical Notation was a "system of signs for the explanation of machinery . . . by which the drawings, the times of action, and the trains for the transmission of force" were expressed in a "language at once simple and concise" (complex and precise might be better).[103] The grammar and syntax of the mechanical work—and thought—preceded mechanization.[104]

In popularizations of Babbage's life story, he is like John Harrison in Sobel's *Longitude*, cast as the scientific genius working against the obstacles of bureaucrats. This is a complete misconception: not only did the Difference Engine receive unprecedented government funding, but in a profound way the Engines must be seen as materializations of state activity. My best evidence for this interpretation comes from Babbage himself. In his autobiography he repeats the encapsulation of the Analytical Engine by an Italian friend, Giovanni Plana, in a letter dated 1840: "Hitherto the legislative department of our analysis has been all-powerful—the executive all feeble. Your engine seems to give us the same control over the executive which we have hitherto only possessed over the legislative department." As cast by the Piedmontese astronomer, the Analytical Engine was a thoroughly and profoundly political machine, literally a mechanical revolution in which control over the process of government would be seized. And Babbage agreed:

> Considering the exceedingly limited information which could have reached my friend respecting the Analytical Engine, I was equally surprised and delighted at his exact provision of its powers. Even at the present moment I could not express more clearly, and in fewer terms, its real object.[105]

This statement suggests that, if we take Babbage at his own word, the Analytical Engine must be seen as a political machine.[106] Plana's letter has not survived in the voluminous Babbage correspondence, but it clearly circulated to other key figures. This deeper context reveals that Babbage had left for Italy thinking of the Analytical Engine as a mathematical machine. The Italians, viewing the engine refracted through the turbulent Risorgimento politics of the 1840s, added the politically loaded word "executif," so that when writing of the "executif of analysis" they made a direct connection between political power and rule-following mathematics. The Kingdom of Piedmont-Sardinia had in 1836 instituted the Regia Commissione Superiore di Statistica (Royal High Committee on Statistics), and 2 years later held its first census.[107] At issue in 1840 was whether the collection and knowledge of the statistics should be open—the liberal position—or restricted to the use of Royal (executive) bureaucratic power. Control of the executive was desired by both sides.

On the pretext of congratulating Babbage on an honor awarded by the king of Piedmont-Sardinia, collected while visiting Italy, the political economist Jean Charles Léonard Sismonde di Sismondi wrote: "If the King of Sardinia had conferred on me a decoration of the first rank, such a mark of his approval would have been without doubt of great consequence in my land, and would have been likely to open the way to the construction of this machine that, as Plana has written, grasps the entire executive of mathematical analysis [comprend tout l'executif de l'analyse]."[108] Babbage agreed: ". . . the great object of my visit to Turin was to convey to Plana and some analysts of Italy the principles on which I had contrived an engine to perform as he has beautifully expressed it 'the whole Executive of Analysis.'"[109]

For Sismondi, a completed Analytical Engine would not merely "help raise science in England"; dwelling on the political nature of the machine, and picking his words carefully, was "destined to change the aspect of modern analysis" ("modern society" was his first expression, but he crossed it out).[110] Babbage had hoped that Plana would back the Englishman's plans by writing a glowing report on the Engine for the Royal Academy of Turin, which in turn could be used to shame authorities at home. "The discovery is so much in advance of my own country," Babbage echoed Sismondi, "and I fear even of the age, that it is very important for its success that the fact should not rest in my own unsupported authority."[111] With Plana reluctant, or more likely genuinely ill, one of the other "Italian analysts" stepped in. In October 1841, Babbage, passing through Florence and somewhat mollified, conceded to Plana: "I must be content with the description drawn up by M. Menabrea with which I am well satisfied because he seems to have penetrated completely the principles on which it rests." (Indeed, Luigi Frederico Menabrea's description, alongside the extensive notes of Ada Lovelace, were to comprise the most complete description of the Analytical Engine available.)

In the following decade, Babbage applied the insights of the Analytical Engine, not least the Mechanical Notation, to improve the design of his earlier machine. In June of 1852, armed with drawings of Difference Engine No. 2, he mobilized his contacts for a further assault on government. His plea, which went through many drafts before being printed, was placed in the hands of the Anglo-Irish astronomer and aristocrat Lord Rosse, who gave them to the prime minister, Lord Derby. "I have sacrificed time, health and fortune," Babbage wrote, "in the desire to complete these calculating Engines. I have also declined several offers of great personal advantage to myself. But, notwithstanding the sacrifice of these advantages for the purpose of maturing an Engine of almost intellectual power, and after expending from my own private fortune a larger sum than the Government of England has spent on that Machine, the execution of which it commenced [but not finished!—was it any wonder Babbage wanted control over the executive?], I have received neither an acknowledgement of my labors, nor even the offer of those honors or rewards which are allowed to fall within the reach of men who devote themselves to purely scientific investigations."[112] The plea, despite the careful drafting, was not well composed: in what should have been a statement of the advantages of Difference Engine No. 2, Babbage frequently reverted to dwell on the powers of the Analytical Engine. At a "period when the progress of physical science is obstructed by that exhausting intellectual and manual labor, indispensable for its advancement, which it is the object of the Analytical Engine to relieve," Babbage argued that he thought "the application of machinery in aid of the most complicated and abstruse calculations, can no longer be deemed unworthy of the attention of the country. In fact there is no reason why mental, as well as bodily Labour, should not be economized by the aid of machinery."

The failure of government to build the Difference Engine had been, for Babbage, a failure of the executive. Plana's vision of the Analytical Engine was that it would pass control over the executive to the machine, and therefore the expert speakers of the Mechanical Notation. Babbage in 1852 had laid before the prime minister, should he choose to pick it up, the extension of mechanization to include the "intellectual" as well as the routinely mechanical actions of mere "bodily labor." Within months, the Northcote-Trevelyan report would make the same split, complementing the previously automatic status of intellectual gentlemen with the accolade of passed examinations (making merits explicit, like the Mechanical Notation) and casting the remainder of the civil service as mere mechanicals. The crucial ambiguity of the Northcote-Trevelyan report was whether the gentlemen were part of the machine—a useful vagueness, since senior civil servants could be portrayed as part of the machine when necessary (on matters of trust) or not if the label proved delicate (they were, after all, gentlemen). Babbage's proposal, with its assertion that the intellectual should certainly be thought of as mechanizable, was far too blunt.

Babbage waited for Derby's response. (He filled time by having, to his amusement, a phrenological reading.[113]) But the prime minister was distracted by more pressing matters. Derby, who of course was the real executive political power was in no position to offer deals, since he had lost control of the real legislative (i.e., a majority in the House of Commons) in a general election in July 1852.[114] Thus, when Derby's reply arrived in August, it was not welcome news. Despite the fact that Ada Lovelace was at that moment in a "state of painful suffering," Babbage launched into a final defense of the Engines. "My first impression on reading Ld D's letter," he wrote immediately to Rosse, "was that I ought to make no further attempt to force a generous offer upon a reluctant country, in fact it appears that I have thrown pearls before swine." But on consulting another ally, Hawes, "who shares with you fully in the perception of vast importance of the substitution of mechanical for mental labor," he was convinced that Derby's reply would backfire. The prime minister had refused the offer of Difference Engine No. 2 on four grounds: "indefinite expense," "problematic success," "expenditure *certainly* large," and "*utterly incapable* of being calculated." (How bitter that line must have been to Babbage!) But, thought Hawes and Babbage, these were merely "bold assertions" made by "an unprofessional man about a machine the drawings of which no professional person would venture to give an opinion upon without having first seen and fully studied them." Politicians were not experts, they were not professionally positioned to rule on the Engines. Despite wishful thoughts of exposing the correspondence to the public gaze ("it would be most injurious to the reputation of the Chancellor of the Exchequer both for prudence and for sagacity"), the matter rested and no Engines left unfinished. Babbage's revolution had failed.

A few months later, Babbage received a letter in the hand of the Assistant Secretary to the Treasury. Sir Charles Trevelyan, in the midst of composing the Report on the Organization of the Permanent Civil Service, had taken time to contact the would-be mechanizer of intellectual work. Did Babbage, asked Trevelyan, have any advice on the scale to be used on Ordnance Survey maps? If Babbage had hoped for a reprieve for his Engines, only to be disappointed by the cartographical query, he did not show it. Instead he replied calmly that a universal scale based on numerical ratios—say 1/2,500 for rural maps and 1/500 for urban—was preferable to a scale relative to national measures.[115] The complete rebuff from Lord Derby only months earlier had made another attempt at political lobbying inconceivable. Indeed, Trevelyan, as a senior civil servant, was, in his mind, an interest-free component of a neutral machine.

2

"The Parent of a Totally Different Order of Things": Charles Trevelyan and the Civil Service as Machine

Many of the great departments of state were in place by the eighteenth century. The two "money ministries," the Board of Trade and the Treasury, could both trace their modern roots to the restoration turmoil of the previous century. The Board of Trade's beginnings can be found in the eighteenth-century mercantilist Committee for Trade and Plantations (although the Board was abolished for four years between 1782 and 1786 after a withering attack by Edmund Burke). It started as a small consultative body, but it had many other functions charged to it in the early to mid nineteenth century, including the collection of statistics and the supervision of railway acts. The Treasury meanwhile added to its ancient accounting responsibilities the new decisive role of controller of both revenue and overall departmental expenditure in Whitehall—that name beginning to refer not to the old royal palace but to the huddle of government buildings between St. James's Park and the River Thames. By the 1780s two more great departments had appeared: the Foreign Office, which quickly developed an elite culture of its own, and the Home Office, responsible for internal—and miscellaneous—affairs. What must be emphasized is the difference, both qualitative and quantitative, between Whitehall of this period and that of the twentieth century. For example, the number of civil servants in 1982 was 675,000, whereas in 1801 the war-inflated figure was 39,000 and the nascent Home Office employed only 30.[1]

Employees were unevenly distributed across departments. Within the Civil Service, two public offices, later combined, were the dominant employers, in terms of numbers: Customs and Excise, which in 1797 employed 6,004 and 6,580 persons respectively—three-fourths of the entire Civil Service. Excisemen were armed with slide rules.[2] Moreover, the eighteenth-century administrative burden fell mainly on individuals *outside* the Civil Service: the numerous Justices of the Peace, usually country gentlemen, untrained but self-governing and therefore independent. ("The discharge of his duties by an independent gentleman was thought to be so desirable and so creditable to him that his

Table 2.1
Numbers of civil servants employed, 1797–1999.

		Sources and comments
1797	16,267	Cohen 1941, p. 23
1801	39,000	Padfield and Byrne 1981, p. 152
1850s	40,000	
1902	107,782	Cohen 1941, p. 164. Excludes industrial staff.
1911	135,721	Cohen 1941, p. 164. Excludes industrial staff.
1920	368,910	Cohen 1941, p. 164. Excludes industrial staff.
1929	306,154	Cohen 1941, p. 164. Excludes industrial staff.
1938	376, 491	Cohen 1941, p. 19. Excludes industrial staff.
1951	425,000	Theakston 1995, p. 78.
1960	380,000	Theakston 1995, p. 79. Excludes industrial staff. Total: 643,000.
1976	751,000	Britain 2001, p. 61. Includes industrial staff. This was the peak in total staff numbers.
1979	566,000	Theakston 1995, p. 123. Excludes industrial staff. Total: 730,000.
1982	675,000	Hennessy 1989, p. 28
1992	504,000	Theakston 1995, p. 123. Excludes industrial staff. Total: 565,000.
1999	460,000	*Britain 2001*, p. 61

want of efficiency must be regarded with consideration."[3]) They administered the Poor Law (until 1834), regulated the police, and ruled on local finance and trade. They were opposed to the growing centralized power, as incarnated in custom-house officers, excise officers, stamp distributors and postmasters and other tax gatherers. Parliament was the meeting place of the country gentlemen, and they opposed a centralized hierarchy of officials. (This opposition had implications for the technological infrastructure of the country, a comparison between the bad roads in England and the good roads of France was a favorite among contemporaries.)

Despite the presence of some vigorous counter-examples, the stereotypical civil servant of the eighteenth century was a well-connected gentleman, even an aristocrat, who regarded his job, often secured through patronage, as a sinecure.[4] However, the post-industrialization swelling of the middle classes, which desired jobs and influence, and increasing criticisms of Civil Service inefficiency, created pressure for reform. The expense of the American war of independence led to criticisms of financial control of administration and, beginning in 1780, the appointment of Commissioners of Inquiry to examine shortcomings and make recommendations. Their reports give detailed insights into the practices of British administration and list numerous abuses. Many of these were later seen as absurdities, and were cited, retrospectively, as clear evidence of the need to reform: the use of Latin accounts in the Exchequer of Imprest (which we saw mocked by Dickens in the first chapter), and the sale of offices, especially those—the sinecures—that generated an income for no work. Although the Commissioners' proposed changes were postponed by the French Revolution—when reformist firebrands like Burke switched to become staunch supporters of old British traditions—some of the "worst excesses" were curtailed.[5] But we must be careful not to fall into the teleological trap of spotting inevitable progress. Changes were indeed made: accounting techniques were revised and standardized (in particular, there was an end to accounts organized according to whether they had been generated by individuals, and a continuous account was introduced[6]); civil servants were less often paid individually according to services provided—for example, being paid tuppence for every land-tax pound raised; and sinecures became a rarity. But notice that these changes were all marked by moves from the personal to the impersonal, from practices contingent on the individual to the systemic. Trust in the gentleman was being transferred, partially, to trust in the system. This, not an end to corruption, was the main effect of administrative reform.

Indeed, when reform did come, it was a sublime act of accommodation, preserving elite power just as this itself was shifting as a result of reforms of the universities and the franchise. The process was slow, but its definitive moment—in the memory of the Civil Service and in the view of most historians—was the submission of the Northcote-Trevelyan report to both Houses of Parliament in February of 1854. I, too, claim that the report was seminal, not because of its role in administrative reform, of which it was a symbol rather than instigator, but because of the language its authors used and a division of labor that they sought to impose on the depersonalized system, or "machine."

Reform of the home Civil Service was decisively shaped by two other reforming movements, one aimed at the administration of India and the other at the universities of Oxford and Cambridge.[7] The three movements involved overlapping social networks of people and ideas. Oxford had no "genuine" degree examinations before 1800. At Cambridge, persons of noble birth or members of King's College were excused from taking the tough disputations in modern philosophy and mathematics and the Mathematical Tripos.[8] In the early nineteenth century, both Oxford and Cambridge came to rely more and more on examinations to test the proficiency of students or to award Fellowships. The system of competitive examinations gained adherents, such as Robert Lowe, who would later support a similar means of selecting civil servants. Likewise, in the case of India, direct appeal was made to Cambridge experience.[9]

The instrument of policy in India was the East India Company, established in 1600, making government in the subcontinent a private venture, but one of immense political consequences and impact on public affairs. Company regional policy, which was fairly decentralized and strongly influenced by the indigenous pattern of political organization, meant that India was subdivided into many administrative regimes. This factor, plus the distance of the subcontinent from Britain, made India a hothouse of institutional innovation and experiment in government.[10] However, two main styles of East India Company government can be identified. Centered on Madras was the Munro system. Heavily influenced by romanticism, which validated an immersion in Indian culture and especially an intense interest in language and custom, Sir Thomas Munro (and fellow colonial heavyweights John Malcolm, Montstuart Elphinstone, and Charles Theophilus Metcalfe) co-opted native patterns of government, grounded in personal authority, and put them to work on behalf of the Company. Under the Munro system, English rulers would simply supplant existing Mughal rulers. Less attention to overhauling government meant more time for generating immense wealth. Opposing Munro's template was the Cornwallis system, based in Bengal: the imposition of supposedly English styles of government, an anglicization that excluded Indians from power and imported English missionaries in an attempt to fundamentally change Indian cultures.

This opening of possibilities attracted experimenters from home, who were viewed with distaste from Madras. The followers of Munro rejected the Cornwallis "cult of administration," took a stand against "impersonal, mechanical administration," and loathed "automatic" rule.[11] In particular, India attracted utilitarians. Bentham, recalling the ancient framer of the Athenian constitution, dreamed of being the "Indian Solon."[12] He had grand hopes for his chief disciple, James Mill: "Mill will be the living executive—I shall be the dead legislative of British India."[13] Mill was certainly well placed, employed as an examiner at the Company's India House office from 1819 until his death in 1836. He saw no contradiction in his belief that he was ideally placed to push Indian reform despite never having been to the subcontinent, since it was perfectly in his accord with the depersonalized utilitarian ideal of government, in which what governed was the symbolic abstraction of writing and the surveillance of facts: " . . . as you know that the government is carried on by correspondence and that I am the only man whose business it is, or who has the time, to make himself master of the facts scattered in a most voluminous correspondence." (He was what his son, John Stuart Mill, would later call a "central organ of information," although we should contrast Mill's attitude toward Bayly's conclusion that in India "the British were forced to master and manipulate the information systems of their Hindu and Mughal predecessors."[14])

A touchstone of the English style of government imposed under the Cornwallis system was clearly defined personal property rights, especially of land. Mill, thousands of miles away, threw his weight behind a massive project of gathering data, sweeping away existing complex claims, and introducing the *ryotwar*, a Domesday compilation of landholdings in which land was measured and rights were visibly assigned in written documents and enforced by laws designed to be "efficient and swift, clear and easily intelligible, simple and readily available," and (significantly) "automatic."[15] Utilitarian experimentation in government was allied to Ricardian experiment in economics: David Ricardo viewed rentiers as parasites, and the aim of the Cornwallis system was to break local landowners—who by Ricardian theory could never share the interests of the rest of the community—and replace them with the state. This boost to bureaucracy was, not coincidentally, very lucrative: taxation of land made up half of the Indian revenue. That the new system was administratively disastrous in practice, the simplified view of the state being no replacement for complex, opaque, but locally understood assignments of land rights, will not detain us. What concerns us is that Mill subscribed to values of depersonalized and systematic administration.

The Indian Civil Service expanded, and its expansion raised questions about its organization, in particular about training and entry by nomination. From 1714, appointments in Indian administration had been solely made by nomination of the East India Company, conferring on its directors immense powers of patronage. Though the process of nomination had been tightened (the outright sale of positions, for example, was forbidden), appointment and promotion followed this pattern well into the nineteenth century. However, when the Company's charter came up for renewal in 1833, the young Secretary to the Board of Control, Thomas Babington Macaulay, introduced into the legislation a provision for examinations (four candidates to be nominated, best chosen by examination), and though the company won a reprieve, a further Charter Act of 1853 removed the patronage of directors and made examinations (open to British subjects only) compulsory.[16] After the Indian Mutiny in 1857, the East India Company was relieved of its administrative functions, and the bureaucracy became a formal extension of the British Civil Service.

Adherents of both the Munro and Cornwallis systems could agree that some training was beneficial to young administrators, and this overlap allowed Haileybury College to be established in 1806. The new College could be packed with utilitarian sympathizers. Thomas Robert Malthus, an enthusiast for statistics, became the first professor of history and political economy.[17] Although the rule was subsequently modified, four terms at Haileybury became compulsory for Company servants in 1813.

One figure shaped by evangelicalism, its shared ideology with utilitarianism, and by the experience of India was Charles Edward Trevelyan.[18] Born the fourth son of Archdeacon George Trevelyan and Harriet (née Neave) in 1807, Trevelyan attended Taunton Grammar School (where he showed great linguistic ability) and Charterhouse before his four terms at Haileybury.[19] With colonial training under his belt, he entered the East India Company's Bengal service, the spiritual home of the Cornwallis system. For a while he was assistant to Sir Charles Theophilus Metcalfe. In 1831 he was appointed deputy secretary in the political department of Calcutta in 1831. In Calcutta he married Hannah Moore, sister of Lord Macaulay, in December 1834 (the font of a dynasty that included his son, the politician George Otto Trevelyan, and his grandsons, the politician Charles Philips Trevelyan and the historian G. M. Trevelyan). Macaulay and Trevelyan became intimate friends. Together they made plans for the introduction of competitive examinations into the Indian Civil Service.[20] At Calcutta, in the Cornwallis tradition of anglicization and the utilitarian tradition of making things visible (in this case, to make Indian culture clear to the colonial rulers), Trevelyan devised a "plan of expressing the language of the East in the English character" that, he claimed, offered "the best and nearest prospect of fixing and enriching the Native Dialects, and of establishing a common medium of communication, epistolary as well as oral, between the people and their rulers."[21] However, Trevelyan left India at the end of 1839. In 1859 (two years after the Indian Mutiny) he returned, briefly, as governor of Madras. (A scandal over an open telegram led to his recall.) He returned for a final time in 1862, as Indian finance minister. Back in Britain in 1865, he wound down to retirement, occupying himself with matters of army reform and social questions—calling, for example, for the "systematic visitation of the poor in their homes" (another alien culture made visible to British administration).[22] Trevelyan died in London in 1886.

Trevelyan imbibed a certain administrative experience of India, and this influenced his thoughts during his first sojourn at home. Between 1840 and 1859, Trevelyan was an assistant secretary at the Treasury, a job secured for him—perhaps hypocritically—through the influence of Macaulay, who wanted his "beloved sister" in England.[23] To a modern eye Trevelyan's tenure at the Treasury was one of dreadful ironies: his single-minded drive for efficiency now seems to contrast with his pitiless management of Irish famine relief and Crimean War supplies (he was held responsible for both), but in his own context there was no paradox. Irish famine relief, which employed 734,000 men between 1845 and 1847 (and for which Trevelyan was knighted the following year), provided him a second experience of large-scale organization. In particular, the "Irish business" strained the civil servants of the Treasury to the breaking point. Trevelyan told a parliamentary select committee how he got up early, spent 3 hours before breakfast reading papers, then worked at the Treasury until late in the evening, returning home too exhausted for anything except sleep.[24] He had to work like this, he claimed, because civil servants were not interchangeable: no one else could step in, resulting in a "degree of precariousness in the transaction of the public business which ought not to exist."[25] Indeed, Trevelyan's three immediate predecessors had broken under the strain.[26]

Trevelyan's solution was to depersonalize the Civil Service. In 1853, he and Sir Stafford Northcote signed the Report on the Organization of the Permanent Civil Service. Trevelyan was the main author of this exceptional piece of rhetoric in which illness and laziness served metaphorically as foils to administrative and bodily efficiency:

> Those whose abilities do not warrant an expectation that they will succeed in the open professions, where they must encounter the competition of their contemporaries, and those whom indolence of temperament, or physical infirmities [have made] unfit for active exertions, are placed in the Civil Service, where they may obtain an honorable livelihood with little labor, and with no risk; where their success depends upon their simply avoiding any flagrant misconduct, and attending with moderate regularity to routine duties; and in which they are secured against the ordinary consequences of old age, or failing health, by an arrangement which provides them with the means of supporting themselves after they have become incapacitated.[27]

Trevelyan portrayed typical civil servants as "sickly youths" who were "obliged to absent themselves from their duties on account of ill-health, and afterwards [retired] with their pensions . . . on the same plea." "The character of the individuals influences the mass," he wrote, and the outcome was a sick Service. If that was not enough, the character of the work, when it was done, enervated the body further:

> Many of the first years of [a civil servant's] service are spent in copying papers, and other work of an almost mechanical character. In two or three years he is as good as he can be at such employment. The remainder of his official life can only exercise a depressing influence on him, and renders the work of the office distasteful to him.

> Unlike the pupil in the conveyancer's or special pleader's office, he not only begins with mechanical labor as an introduction to labor of a higher kind, but often ends with it.[28]

With work routine, and progression "merely departmental promotion," the effect was "to cramp the energies of the entire body." Trevelyan's cure was the introduction of examinations and a division of labor. As Andrew Warwick has shown in the case of the reform of the Cambridge Mathematics Tripos in this period, bodily vigor was profoundly intertwined with the apparently meritocratic action of examinations.[29] Trevelyan's suggestion was that there should be "in all cases a competing literary examination," alongside "careful previous inquiry into the age, health and moral fitness of the candidates." "We see," he wrote, "no other mode by which . . . the double object of selecting the fittest person, and of avoiding the evils of patronage." As for the natural world Darwin would later replace the patronage of God with the competitive examination of competition between species, so Trevelyan hoped examinations would provide a new grounding for the administrative order. Subjects should include "history, jurisprudence, political economy, modern languages, political and physical geography . . . besides the staple of classics and mathematics."

Trevelyan's program of entry to the Civil Service by examination could not have succeeded without directly appealing to three constituencies for support. First, university reformers such as Reverend Dr. Benjamin Jowett, Fellow and Tutor, and later Master, of Balliol College, Oxford, immediately spotted the market a reformed Civil Service would provide for the gentlemanly output of Oxford's liberal education. Trevelyan's list of topics met with approval from Jowett, who outlined an examination scheme in a letter that accompanied Northcote and Trevelyan's original minute. The Oxbridge bias of the Civil Service examination later became a frequent target for critics (the short-lived Administrative Reform Association opposed the tests for being too "academic," with no room for "practical" business attitudes). Likewise, as we have seen, Trevelyan's brother-in-law Thomas Babington Macaulay saw examination as a lever to prise open the Indian Civil Service to competitive entry and administrative reform. (Open competitive examination had been accepted in principle for the ICS in 1854.) For Macaulay the proposed examinations would serve as a ideal model for mobilization in other battles. Finally, Trevelyan's mentor, Chancellor of the Exchequer William Ewart Gladstone, enthused that the examination would legitimate rather than threaten the power of the elite: it "would strengthen and multiply the ties between the higher classes and the possession of administrative power. I have a strong impression that the aristocracy of this country are even superior in natural gifts, on the average, to the mass: but it is plain that with their acquired advantages . . . they have immense superiority. This applies in its degree to all those who may be called gentlemen by birth and training."[30] This strange, indeed contradictory, hybrid, "gentlemen by birth *and training*," would prove a rather important bridge, spanning the gap between the periods when professional regulation rather than birth determined patterns of authority—and one as significant in the Civil Service as in the sciences.

Equally congenial to Gladstone was the second of Trevelyan's proposals, a division of labor which is to prove extremely important to the concerns discussed in following chapters. Though examinations would underwrite a fit gentlemanly civil servant (and establish a meritocracy of sorts among them), this group must be split away, argued Trevelyan, from the supplementary clerks below: there must be "a proper distinction between the intellectual and mechanical labor."[31] No longer would civil servants have to start from the bottom rung, as Trevelyan's predecessor, Sir Alexander Spearman, had done, enduring the routine of copying minutes for years before promotion by seniority led to slow elevation. The "superior" class would begin immediately on intellectual and managerial tasks. "A great deal of [mechanical] work of various kinds," noted Trevelyan, "such as copying, registering, posting accounts, keeping diaries, and so forth, may very well be done by supplementary clerks of an inferior class under the direction of a small number of superiors." The proposal for a division of labor must be understood in the context of changes in office work. "Extra-clerks" were already employed for "mechanical" routine work—especially copying—at the fringes, and on an ad hoc basis. They received low wages and had no expectations of promotion. Moreover, this growth was part of a background of increase in cost of public administration: aside from extraordinary events such as the Irish famine, government had undertaken the supervision of Poor Law administration (1834), the inspection of factories (1835), and the encouragement of education. Bigger government led to pressure to economize, and, as Trevelyan argued, in comparison with salaries in private concerns (e.g. East India Company, Bank of England, the big mercantile houses), superior employees were not overpaid, but routine work could definitely be done more cheaply.

The typical movements of the mechanical supplementary clerk and the intellectual gent were to be horizontal and vertical, respectively. For clerks, Trevelyan raised the possibility of a giant centralized copying office, a manufactory of memoranda, "common to the whole or most of the departments in the neighborhood of Whitehall, at which all of them might get their copying work done at a certain rate of payment by the piece," but dropped the idea in favor of clerks—like interchangeable parts—moving smoothly sideways

Figure 2.1
The information technology of the male Victorian clerk c. 1880: quill pen, brass inkwell, paperweight, candle. (PRO STAT 20/443)

between departments as demand arose: "a proper system of transfers according to fixed rules in each office, and insured by periodical reports to the chief."[32] In contrast, the paper trail for the intellectual gentleman began with the examination and would trace the progress of his career:

> A Book should be kept in every office, in which should be entered the name and age of each Clerk or other officer, at the time of his appointment, the dates of his examination, first appointment, and subsequent promotions, together with notes of all the reports made upon him from time to time, either on the occasions afforded by the occurrence of vacancies, or at other times, in consequence of some special instance either of good or ill behavior.[33]

Such a dossier would inevitably record progress as training and experience molded the pliable youth ("it is found that the superior docility of young men renders it much easier to make valuable public servants of them, than those more advanced in life"). It is most unusual to find docile gentlemen.

Charles Trevelyan appeared in caricature as Sir Gregory Hardlines in Anthony Trollope's novel *The Three Clerks* (1857), a dossier of the progress of three civil servants that was read by millions. The dull but dependable Harry Norman and his younger colleague, the energetic but flawed Alaric Tudor, are employed in the respectable Weights and Measures department. Alaric's poorer cousin labors in the degenerate Internal Navigation Office—the "Navvies." Hardlines dreams of reform, of countering sloth and inefficiency, first in his own department and then elsewhere:

> . . . if he could promote a movement beyond the walls of Weights and Measures; . . . if he could introduce conic sections into Custom House, and political economy into the Post Office . . . , what a wide field for his ambition would Mr. Hardlines then have found!
>
> Great ideas opened themselves to his mind as he walked to and from his office daily. What if he could become the parent of a totally different order of things! What if the Civil Service, through his instrumentality, should become the nucleus of the best intellectual diligence in the country, instead of a byword for sloth and ignorance![34]

Hardlines's—and of course Trevelyan's—proposal is that, in order to "revivify, clarify and render perfect the Civil Service of the country," invigorating competitive examination should be introduced.[35] He is assisted by Mr. Jobbles, "a worthy clergyman from Cambridge," clearly a cipher for the Oxonian Jowett. Trollope satirizes the topics under test: Jobbles asks "Could you tell me now, how would you calculate the distance in inches, say from London Bridge to the nearest portion of Jupiter's disc, at twelve o'clock on the first of April?"[36] One by one the elder or better clerks, including the bovine Harry Norman, drop out, and Alaric Tudor leaps ahead by passing the new examination, and becomes the protégé of Hardlines. Trollope lets us know that this upsetting of the natural Victorian order—Norman is clearly more of a gentleman that Tudor—leads to private misery, first in the young clerks' relationships with the Woodward girls (the love interest that leavens the bureaucratic chapters) and then, as mere cramming is shown to be no indication of character, when Tudor is tempted into stock-jobbery and corruption. Trollope also gestures toward deeper Victorian horrors that might be unleashed if meritocracy were to be taken to its logical limit: the fanatic Jobbles is described as "enthusiastically intent on examining the whole adult male population of Great Britain" as having "gone so far as to hint that female competitors might, at some future time, be made subject to his all-measuring rule and compass."[37] Such opening up of the Civil Service did indeed upset the order of things.

Trollope wrote as an insider—he began as a junior clerk in London in 1834 and worked up to be a Post Office Surveyor in Ireland and west England—and he was furious at what he saw as Trevelyan's treacherous attack from within. "How is the Civil Service spoken of by men behind the scenes," he asked, "who are themselves in authority therein, who are considered specially qualified to give opinion on the matter, and who, it will be thought, are not likely to foul their own nest unnecessarily?"[38] Trollope then lifted and reprinted whole sections of the Northcote-Trevelyan report.[39] The unintended effect was to bring the contents and arguments of the report to a much broader audience, and with it a deeper cultural impact. *The Three Clerks* has not survived as a classic of Victorian literature. Nevertheless, in its own time it was regarded as a triumph, a "really brilliant tale of official life" according to the *Times*, and an improvement on the (now more popular) *Barchester Towers*.[40] *The Three Clerks* was a direct intervention into a hot political debate, and as the debate has cooled so has the novel—which in truth has a clunky narrative—fallen in critical esteem.[41]

Trollope's fictional assault was matched in the clubs and offices around Whitehall. Macaulay recorded the reaction in one club: "I went to Brooks and found everybody open-mouthed, I am sorry to say, against Trevelyan's plans."[42] Reaction to the Northcote-Trevelyan report was threefold: objection to the language of the report (especially the slur of indolence), vigorous opposition to the proposals for open competitive examinations, and qualified support from a handful of commentators. An anonymous civil servant, frothing with indignation, published a collection of hostile editorials against the "stigma cast upon the whole body of the Civil Servants of the Crown."[43] The *Morning Post* argued that open competitive examinations would not be meritocratic: who would choose the examiners? "The entire patronage of the Crown is to be swept away for ever; and the appointment of all officers who do the work of the Government departments, and are responsible to the Executive, is to be handed over to examiners in scientific and general attainments," the paper noted, "who, as all patronage is abrogated, must, of course, drop from the clouds or grow in their places like mushrooms."[44] The *Morning Post* explicitly expressed the fear that political patronage would be replaced by technocratic patronage:

> Professor Faraday and Mr. Babbage are very eminent for their scientific attainments; yet it would hardly be satisfactory to the Sovereign or to the Country that they should select and appoint the Prime Minister or the Chancellor of the Exchequer, both of whom must be among the sixteen thousand [chosen through examination].

The imposition of examinations was seen as an attempt to gain control over the political process by specialists, in particular scientists, despite the fact that

Jowett's proposals were based squarely on the existing university curriculum. Examinations tested the wrong thing. The successful clerk, mocked the *Morning Herald*, would be "the fortunate clodhopper who could best solve a quadratic equation," but "our first-class men are not so much distinguished by their knowledge of crabbed sciences and abstruse learning as by the quickness of their judgment, the charm of their manners, and their intimate acquaintance with man in his social relations"—the last two characteristics possessed only by gentlemen.[45] Examinations were seen by their proponents as mechanically meritocratic—automatic even, since the human hand of patronage was absent. The choice of Babbage was, therefore, particularly apt, in view of his summary of the Analytical Engine as a machine to control the legislative (Parliament) and the executive (Prime Minister, cabinet, and Civil Service). Enemies of the examination noted that the human hand, the "men of letters and . . . men of science," would in fact be handed political control.

The *Daily News* repeated the *Morning Post*'s sentiments and added a further warning:

> It seems that, in addition to the regular army, navy, and police, we have in London an official army 16,000 strong!—paid out of the taxes—to fill public offices, and there perform those laborious duties of red-tapery which do so very much good to the nation. The Russian despotism has won its success, and holds its fatal power over the people it enslaves, by doing precisely what we are now requested to sanction in England—by enlisting a mass of clever rather than scrupulous men in its service, and then by drilling them into a perfect machine for controlling the nation upon whose industry they subsist in comparative idleness.[46]

Here Trevelyan's scheme was seen as an attempt to engineer a bureaucratic "machine" on the continental model, and therefore as a threat to English liberty. "To support any scheme for converting the 16,000 clerks in public offices into a Prussian or Austrian phalanx of red tapists would be a most dangerous error." Technocracy threatened liberty, a simple point that the *Daily News* repeated over and over:

> If we are to have technically educated officials, the public must become their slaves, and cease to take part in the national administration. If we establish the service of the Government as a profession we shall become, like the Prussians and Austrians, the menials of a bureaucracy. No one man makes a despotism. It is a system, and the perfection to which the system of Government has attained in Austria and Prussia, by having vast bodies of well-trained civil servants, is there fatal to liberty.

Three useful remarks can be made about this argument. First, it admitted that to make government the work of professionals meant that government became rule through the possessors of specialist knowledge. Yet this would lead to strains in the relationship with Parliament, for whenever "a class of men are educated to perform the functions of Government, for other men to interfere with them is for ignorance to dictate to knowledge." Professional, technically educated civil servants would be masters of the paperwork of democracy,[47] and Parliament would not have the competence to compete and would have to concede power. Although "Parliament is the representative of the ignorance as well as the knowledge of the nation," and although ignorance of official matters would increase as the electoral franchise widened, the *Daily News* was forthright in its preference for democratic ignorance over professional knowledge. The choice was between control of the executive through representative democracy and automatic control of the executive on lines set out by Babbage or Trevelyan. Second, the opponents of Trevelyan too cast the Civil Service as a "machine," all the more so in its supposed aim to follow continental models. Since both sides of the debate labeled the Civil Service a machine, albeit for different reasons, the effect was to reinforce the metaphor. Third, the position taken by the critics made the division of labor proposed by Trevelyan doubly important, since the separation of the superior intellectual gentlemanly generalists from the inferior mechanicals assuaged anxieties that the traditional social order would be threatened. Again both sides could agree on the benefits of such an organization, and the division of labor—rule-giving generalists and rule-following mechanicals uniting to make a machine—gave the British Civil Service a distinctive trajectory.

Few voices expressed support. Rowland Hill, Secretary to the Post Office, and inventor of the penny post, suggested that examinations be tried as an experiment in some of the higher offices.[48] Only John Stuart Mill, the builder of public health systems Edwin Chadwick, educationalists such as Jowett, the *Times*, and the Dean of Hereford published expressions of enthusiasm in 1855. Non-official support also appeared in print as private individuals sort to hitch the reforms onto their own hobby-horses. One striking example was the Honorary and Reverend Samuel Best, who, in a resonant metaphor that others, including Walter Bagehot, would immediately recognize, likened advancement by examination to the operations of the steam engine: "First, the safety-valves may they be called for the outlet of superabundant energy; and, secondly, for the appropriation of the power the system had generated."[49] A flurry of support for Trevelyan followed the disasters of the Crimean War, which led in May of 1855 to the establishment of the Administrative Reform Association and the Civil Service Commission, charged with responsibility for overseeing change. But the commissioners largely stalled. Therefore, it was against immense opposition that the reforms articulated in the Northcote-Trevelyan report slowly percolated through Whitehall, and were achieved only on a department-by-department basis, for lower and higher posts in the Service, until 1870, when Prime Minister Gladstone's new chancellor of the exchequer, Robert Lowe, issued a Civil Service Order that gave his Treasury greater controlling powers and enabled the introduction of examinations and the intellectual-mechanical split across the whole Civil Service (with the exceptions of the Foreign Office and the Home Office).[50] A new industry accompanied the changes: study aids were now sold in all the subjects under examination: history, bookkeeping, geography, French, arithmetic and mathematics more generally (trigonometry, coordinate geometry, mechanics, calculus, "tots"), précis writing, spelling, and dictation.[51] Journals such as the *Civil Service Competitor* and the *Civil Service Aspirant* offered tips to "men, boy and female clerks." King's College, in London, held evening classes.[52]

Not incidentally, the same year that Lowe and Gladstone extended the reform also saw the most significant indication that the state was developing and taking on new roles: the private telegraph operators were nationalized under the Controller of the Post Office, bringing into state ownership an entire industry and into state employment tens of thousands of employees (including, for the first time, female clerks).[53] Adding to its traditional functions of repelling external aggression and maintaining internal law and order, the boundaries of the state began to expand, dramatically so in the years around the turn of the century. A Victorian multiplicity of inspectors and boards, in areas from public health to factories to education, was an early sign of change. The implementation of collectivist notions of state education and social insurance led to a jump in the size of the Civil Service: from 40,000 in the 1850s, to 80,000 in the 1890s and a further tripling by the year of National Insurance, 1911. Other key welfare measures were the Liberal government's introduction of old age pensions (1908) and William Beveridge's Labour Exchanges (1909). Finally, to its regulatory and welfare roles, the state added industrial ownership, although there is a big gap between telegraphy in 1870 and the extensive nationalizations of the twentieth century.

Some of the reasons behind the growth of central government and the accompanying swing away from local government were internal, some external.[54] The latter were heterogeneous: increased military and naval commitments on the Continent and in the Empire strained the budget at a time of, if not depression, then certainly flat economic performance. The unique tensions in Ireland between nationalists and Anglo-Irish landlords justified public projects of a qualitatively new kind, while a panoply of new pressure groups, from the Fabians to the Tariff Reformers, as well as New Liberal political thought, raised expectations of the role of government. Internally, the giant miscellenea departments—such as the Home Office—ceded ground to new specialized bodies, often spearheading government intervention: the telegraphy acts (1868 and 1869) nationalized an industry, the Education Act (1870) enforced compulsory schooling, the Local Government Board (1870) expanded bureaucratic control over sanitation and public health (while paradoxically trying to limit and privatize relief to paupers), and the establishment Board of Agriculture (1894) meant that a single government body was actively concerned with that sector.[55] The growth of central government, and the reasons given above, are standard social and political history.

Growth meant more paperwork and an expanding Civil Service. The strain generated was particularly noticeable in the difficulties presented by the civil servants who used machines. In the wake of Lowe's imposition of the Northcote-Trevelyan reforms, there now existed a single service "machine," led by the Treasury and consisting of an upper echelon that did not use real machines (thought it did direct them) and a lower echelon that increasingly did use real machines. The most mechanical of work was, as Trevelyan had pointed out, copying. Copying presses were used, but their distribution was patchy. The earliest seems to date from 1786, since a legible copy made on a copying press of that year was brought before an official committee in 1860.[56] In 1850 the Board of Trade, in response to a shortage of copyists, had introduced a press, and found them very satisfactory, so that by 1873 most of the board's copying was mechanized. Other departments followed (the War Office, the Admiralty, the Customs Office, the Education Office), but the Treasury had not used them and had not advocated their general introduction. As the state grew, more and more copyists were needed. But the status of the armies of copyists, poles apart from the gentlemen at the top yet still civil servants, created discomfort. Furthermore, since 1870 boys as young as 14 had been employed in an attempt to cope with the paperwork.

In 1871 a move was made to create an unestablished class of "writers," who would be paid at a uniform low rate (10 pence an hour) and would have no sick pay or leave. The existing copyists were aggrieved and indignant. The Playfair Commission, set up in 1874 to inquire into the condition of the Civil Service and in particular that of the copyists, made a compromise. Leaving the upper strata alone, Lyon Playfair noted the degenerative effect of routine on the lower ones, with men becoming "mere machines, . . . incapable of the exercise of higher qualities."[57] His commission therefore recommended that the division of labor proposed by Trevelyan be enforced strictly, with an Upper Division clearly demarcated from a Lower Division, which in turn would be sealed off from an underclass undertaking the only work extensively done with machines: copying, which would become the task of boys paid at piece rates.

The proposals were implemented in 1876. Alongside Lowe's 1870 order, they mark the application of Trevelyan's principles to create a unified service. However, what looks like a dispute over pay and conditions can equally well be read as moves to exclude real machines (and machine operators) from the Civil Service machine.

But the position of copyists remained intensely troublesome, and it was only resolved with the introduction of typewriters operated by women. This transition reveals much about the politics of class, gender, and mechanization in late-Victorian offices. I noted above that the first introduction of women came after the nationalization of the telegraph system in 1870. The former Electric and International Telegraph Company, for example, employed 201 female Morse operators at its central station.[58] The following year, the Postmaster-General, Frank Ives Scudamore, set out the arguments for extending the employment of female labor to clerical work, noting the virtues they demonstrated as telegraph operators. Though his first reason—that "they have in an eminent degree the quickness of eye and ear, and the delicacy of touch, which are essential qualifications of a good operator"—did not transfer to general clerical work, it would apply to typewriting.[59] His second reason certainly applied to the chair-bound clerks: "They take more kindly than men or boys do to sedentary employment, and are more patient during long confinement to one place." But it his third reason that is most revealing: "The wages, which will draw male operators from but an inferior class of the community, will draw female operators from a superior class." Scudamore confidently expected that women would cost less, since they would retire upon marriage. Not only would female clerks be cheaper; employing women would resolve the difficulties of having to draw on men and boys of ever-lower class as the state bureaucracy expanded. The superior virtues of women as clerks were spelled out:

> Female operators thus drawn from a superior class will, as a rule, write better than the male clerks, and spell more correctly; and, where the staff is mixed, the female clerks will raise the tone of the whole staff.
>
> They are also less disposed than men to combine for the purpose of extorting higher wages, and this is by no means an unimportant matter.

All in all, female clerks would be more trustworthy than males from an "inferior" class. Scudamore began with "forty ladies" in the new Telegraph Clearing House Branch, where telegrams were inspected for numbers of words and the requisite payment by stamps. (Again supposed female virtues came into play: "The work which consists chiefly of fault finding is well within the capacity of the female staff.") Encouraged, female clerks were introduced in a second Post Office branch, one dealing with returned letters. The backlash began. Criticisms were couched in moral terms: forwarding a returned letter required opening it and reading its contents. Patrick Comyns, a first-class clerk reporting evidence to the Playfair Commission, suggested that the women had difficulties when confronted with the "signatures of bishops or peers."[60] Boy clerks were, in Comyns's experience, "far better adapted for returning letters than girls, as letters of a very objectionable nature sometimes fall into their hands." The delicate, corruptible moral temperament of women made them necessarily specialist, since they could not be asked to read all correspondence. Opposition to employment of women came particularly from the lower-status clerks, with whom women competed for employment. Certainly witnesses were polarized; whereas some statements attested to the good health retained by female clerks, others emphasized the weakness of the sex: for example, cross-entry acknowledgements had to be written "with heavy pressure by means of very hard pens and carbonic paper," and this was too tiring for women. However, the efficiency, trustworthiness, and cheapness of women clerks persuaded other departments to follow the Post Office: the Board of Education (1899), the Registrar-General's office, and a whole Women's Branch for the National Health Insurance Commission in 1912.

With the propriety of employing women in the Civil Service established, albeit uncertainly, the problem of the copyists was revisited. The reproduction of memoranda and minutes was increasingly in the hands, literally, of untrustworthy men. The solution was typewriters with female operators. With the Sholes patent machine, reliable typewriters, faster than the pen and producing text easier to read, had emerged in the United States around 1871–72.[61] The Remington factory began producing cheap machines in 1874, and in 1878 a model with capital letters became available. The 1880s saw the beginning of the typewriter revolution in American offices and increasing interest across the Atlantic. A few typewriters were already in place in the British public bureaucracy: the Treasury allowed the Convict Prisons Office to buy one already "long in use" in 1876, but prevented the Stationery Office from placing typewriters on the list of supplies until a glacially slow committee of inquiry reported.[62] In 1877, the Admiralty, as an "exceptl. case," was granted leave to purchase Papyrographs for HMS *Excellent* and HMS *Minotaur*. The Board of Trade purchased a typewriter, but had payment of the bill forbidden by the Treasury.[63] Small numbers of machines began to infiltrate other public offices: one in the Meteorological Office (1877), three for the Probate Registry (1879, withdrawn in 1881), one for the Wreck Commissioners (1881, returned in 1883 with a finding of "no practical use").[64]

It was in the Inland Revenue that a champion of the scheme was found. Sir Algernon West, against Treasury opposition, demonstrated how "typewriting women" could take the place of "men copyists."[65] The Stationery Office was allowed to supply machines to departments beginning in 1885. The work was not mere copying, since it could involve turning a third-person memorandum into a first-person letter; it was this kind of activity that depended on trust. West reported in 1888 that he looked forward to the complete abolition of copyists.[66] Indeed trust in the upper- and middle-class women typists was such that even the introduction of Isaac Pitman's phonographic shorthand—which was inscrutable to the higher-ranking civil servants, and which complemented the efficiency gains made by the typewriter—was deemed acceptable.[67] (Pitman's invention, a project for the "conscious control" of language, is discussed further in the conclusion.)

However, the employment of women created moral dangers. Although the Postmaster-General had introduced the "hazardous experiment" of having men and women in the same room, this was not the typical arrangement of early female employment. The Board of Agriculture placed its one female typist in a dingy basement closet, and the chief clerk issued an "imperative order that no member of the staff over the age of fifteen was to enter the room."[68] Another department locked its two typists, supplied by the typewriter firm and "regarded as part of the machinery," in a room "in the upper part of the building and their work and meals were served to them through a hatch in the wall. They left a quarter of an hour before the men, and no man was allowed to take work to them without a special permit from a responsible official—only granted with great difficulty."[69] Generally, typists and shorthand typists worked under female supervisors. Whatever the arrangement, seven departments employed female typists by 1892, and typists numbered 600 by the outbreak of the First World War (when there were 4,000 in clerical grades, excluding the 60,100 by then employed by the state as nurses, cleaners, and so on).[70] Male copyists were extinct.

Trust in the Machine

The language of government as machine had an old history, but it was deepened considerably in the nineteenth century. We have seen that the metaphor was sustained because it was useful both to proponents and enemies of "mechanical" government.[71] Critics, for example, mobilized the metaphor administrative machinery as a means of drawing contrasts with Continental regimes and, by doing so, reasserting traditions of individualism and English liberty.[72] Another attraction to critics was that the metaphor of machinery could be used to suggest that their opponents were too concerned with means rather than ends. This was central charge of Carlyle's polemic. Likewise, Matthew Arnold wrote: "When I began to speak of culture, I insisted on our bondage to machinery, on our proneness to value machinery as an end in itself, without looking beyond it to the end for which alone, in truth, it is valuable."[73] For Raymond Williams such sentiments provided evidence of the construction in the nineteenth century of an opposition between culture and mechanism (and therefore industrialism) that stained British society. Mechanical could be equated with mere means because "mechanical," in the hands of influential authors, notably Charles Dickens, meant the unthinking following of rules.[74] But this was precisely the advantage seen by many attempting the reform of the Civil Service, and a further profound twist on thinking mechanically would be provided by Alan Turing.

Most significant, during the nineteenth century "machine" increasingly did not refer to all of government, but was reserved for one part of the executive: the Civil Service. Accompanying the Northcote-Trevelyan settlement, a new code of conduct was adopted through the Civil Service, led by the Treasury. Civil servants fell silent in public. In return, ministers took full responsibility for departmental actions.

Vincent has given a succinct analysis of this compromise, which he labels "honorable secrecy."[75] We saw above how Gladstone enthusiastically backed the Northcote-Trevelyan reforms because they preserved the status of higher civil servants as gentlemen. Vincent notes that this was part of a broader debate. With the fading of aristocratic power, gentlemanly status could not be linked unequivocally to social rank. In response, a set of ideals became more explicit, including "courage, truthfulness, honesty, unselfishness, generosity, modesty, composure, thoughtfulness, and a self-denying lack of ambition for external recognition."[76] Demonstrative behavior approaching these ideals could complement, even substitute for, rank. But more was needed. In Germany a similar crisis led to the prominence of dueling as a means of maintaining elite values. Vincent argues that military codes were not strong enough in Britain for this to be an answer. Instead, the prime indicator of a gentleman became "reserve," a discreet lack of openness rooted in self-control.[77] The Northcote-Trevelyan settlement could exploit this new resource. The deal was that politicians would not interfere with a Permanent Secretary's organization, and in return the civil servants would not write publicly. Politicians would protect the Civil Service through the adoption of the principle of ministerial responsibility, but civil servants would renounce any rights to publicly criticize their political masters. They could be relied upon to stick to the deal because, via the separation of the generalists from the mechanicals, higher civil servants were gentlemen, and gentlemen were discreet. Through this embrace of honorable secrecy, Vincent argues, civil servants became anonymous.

I can now state three reasons why the Civil Service—including even the gentlemen generalists who would normally have resisted the label—was cast as a machine. The first reason is that it supported this crucial distinction to be drawn between politicians (the operators of the machine) and a supposedly *interest-free, neutral* Civil Service that would *operate identically* under both Liberal and Tory governments.[78] This made use of an important aspect of the nineteenth-century mechanical metaphor: that the Civil Service machine, once set in motion, would follow a single, predictable path. Since the generalists were included, the whole was a *general-purpose machine*. Second, the Civil Service was labeled a machine because, as the state grew, people were employed whom the gentlemanly elite could not *automatically* trust: lower-class clerks and even women. Trust in the upper echelons was secured by the appeal to honorable secrecy and gentlemanly discretion. Casting the "mechanical" groups as components of a "machine" helped resolve these issues of trust by extending to the lower echelons a metaphorical reliability. This was important, not least because increasingly the government underwrote the truth status of knowledge, especially statistics, produced by the state. Finally, labeling the Civil Service a machine appealed to a growing technocratic element in British government. This was not foreseen by the proponents of the Northcote-Trevelyan settlement. The work of expert movements is important in understanding aspects of the history of British technology and government. In particular, the metaphorical language of the government machine was willfully and creatively reinterpreted by an expert movement of mechanizers, which gained influence during the First World War and grew to a peak of influence after the Second. It is this group's appropriation of the mechanical discourse of government that turns the history of ideas into social history.

The question around which this book is centered concerns the relationship between mechanical discourse and mechanization. To answer this question, the narrative has to briefly split. In one direction, I want to discuss the final metaphorical embellishment of the Civil Service as machine: an analysis, provided by Richard Burdon Haldane, that connects the development of the metaphorical government machine, outlined above, to the mechanizers discussed in chapter 5. In the other direction, I want to discuss a parallel route by which the government machine materialized: the startling proposals made by Alan Turing.

National Efficiency and Haldane's Machinery of Government

The two most striking and connected examples of mechanical metaphor that were mobilized as ideological resources around 1900 can be found in the increasingly frequent derogatory comparisons of Great Britain with other nations and in the "national efficiency" movement, the latter the subject of a ground-breaking analysis by Searle.[79] The disasters of the British wars against the Boers (blamed on undue Treasury control and on a disregard for the "intellectual" side of war—there was no general staff, and the advice of the tiny Intelligence Division was ignored) brought to a head criticisms of government that had been brewing for decades. According to Searle, the Boer crisis brought to the surface an "ideology of national efficiency," a cross-party movement with many targets which, although Searle does not say this, could not have been possible without the prior conception of government as machine. Drawing on insecurity about national economic performance, the proponents of "national efficiency" compared Britain unfavorably to Germany and even Japan: there was "an attempt to discredit the habits, beliefs and institutions that put the British at a handicap in their competition with foreigners and to commend instead a social organization that more closely followed the German model": model Armies, Bismarckian social insurance, highly organized education with links to science-based industries, and the idea of the state as a creative force.[80] (Of course Prussia, and now Germany, had been labeled a "war machine."[81]) The ideology fed into fin-de-siècle concerns about deterioration of the "national physique," which in turn boosted interest in various programs, from eugenics (the informational aspects of which feature in the next chapter) to Scouting.[82] Most important for the purposes of this book, proponents of "national efficiency" targeted "machinery of government" in its second, more specialized sense: the distribution of functions within the structure of government. Searle shows how, for example, the size of the Cabinet was criticized as too large, too inefficient, and perhaps not centralized enough. Some called for the importation of more authoritarian structures, such as those found in the Indian Civil Service—a reminder of the importance of imperial experience.[83] For models of better government, the "national efficiency" ideologues looked to science and business, which in combination formed part of the wider interest at the turn of the century in technocracy and a science of government.

There was real overlap between such discourse and the process of mechanization—the replacement or supplementation of humans by machines. "Real" mechanization dovetailed with discursive constructions of the state as machine. One link in this history is the report on Machinery of Government brought on by the experience of the First World War, bearing the name of the man attributed with coining the slogan "national efficiency." Richard Burdon Haldane (figure 2.2) came from an evangelical, naval, and military background, although the Haldane family produced the celebrated scientific dynasty too. Richard Haldane was professionally a lawyer, politically a Liberal Imperialist, and philosophically an idealist—commitments that grounded his work as Lord Chancellor, his promotion of higher education (he was a co-founder of the London School of Economics and Political Science), and his analysis of administration. After a remarkable tenure as Secretary of State for War (from which he had been hounded out for alleged German sympathies), Haldane was appointed by the Minister of Reconstruction in July 1917 to head a Committee on the Machinery of Government. The committee's report of December 1918, primarily the work of Haldane and the Fabian leader Beatrice Webb, was recalled by Charles Wilson in the 1956 Haldane Lecture as having "had a central place in the technical literature of the subject from that day to this. . . . Many of its formulations . . . have passed into the common language of the subject, rather as those of Bagehot once formed the standard descriptions of our Constitution."[84] The Haldane Report is important not merely because it rooted discussion of government in a comprehensive mechanical metaphor but also because of the systematic principles expounded in it, and their creative appropriation by an expert movement of mechanizers.

The mechanical metaphors of administrative efficiency were a favorite Fabian trope, as is shown by examples from H. G. Wells (the great fictionalizer of middle-class British technocracy) and from Beatrice Webb.[85] Haldane himself equated his belief in the possibility of finding rational principles by which to reconfigure public bodies with his idealist philosophy: a Hegelianism that viewed government and law as the building of reason into the world.[86] However, as Wilson points out, this profession of rational empiricism is rather undermined by the fact that Haldane always discovered the same "three central regulative principles of administrative efficiency—specialization of function, organization of intelligence and command, and sound financial control." In a proposal by Haldane that was met with incomprehension by the Army Council in 1906, these principles had translated as a "Hegelian Army" divided by function, with a General Staff—thinking separated from action again. In the Report on the Machinery of Government the principles became distribution of work to ministries by function (old age, health, and so on), the duty of investigation and thought as preliminary to action—that is to say the separation, institutionalization and expansion of intelligence from administrative action, and the strengthening of Treasury control. The organization of

Figure 2.2
A sketch (by Sir Francis Carruthers Gould) of Lord Richard Burdon Haldane, who brought German idealism into the study of the "machinery of government" of British public administration. (source: National Portrait Gallery, London)

thought and its separation from action—the Babbage model—on one trajectory led from Haldane to the setting up of the proto-research council, the Department of Scientific and Industrial Research. (The nineteenth-century separation was also the model of the managerial revolution of late-nineteenth-century America and interwar Britain.) Crucially for this account, Haldane's recommendations provided a powerful resource for the mechanization movement in the Treasury, a materialization of Haldanian ideals.

The simple argument that mechanization realized Haldane's metaphorical machinery is far too simple. Close examination of the 1918 report suggests that Haldane viewed government not as a machine but as a whole that should be functionally reordered for efficient operation. Such an emphasis was driven by his idealist vision. His separation of thought from action, like that of the brain from the mechanical body, supports this interpretation. Indeed, he explicitly wrote of the Army as a body "a real whole, complete with a due proportion of various arms" with an "effective thinking" General Staff.[87] But his call for greater Treasury control, and a group to be given power to investigate and improve the efficiency of the mechanical limbs, gave a powerful platform to those within the Treasury who might wish to promote the mechanization of the Civil Service. However, the implicit hierarchy of thought over action meant that some of Haldane's mechanical metaphors of government had to be creatively misunderstood by an expert movement if a radical mechanization project was to be pursued.

Turing's Universal Machine

Both Babbage's Analytical Engine and the description of a "universal computing machine" by the English mathematician Alan Turing have been claimed as computers before their time. Historians are uneasy about such claims and have rightly warned against the sin of retrospectivism. The Analytical Engine and Turing's Universal Machine were devices of their own contexts, not forecasts of later developments. But it is not retrospective to assert that both have features—important, similar features—that stem from similarities of context. I argued above that we should take Babbage at his word when he described the power and mechanism of the Analytical Engine as a machine for gaining control over the legislative and the executive. I will show that Turing's theoretical Universal Machine should also be read as inscribed with political references. If the Analytical Engine, the Universal Machine, and the computer are similar, it is because they were imagined in a world in which a particular bureaucratic form—an arrangement of government—was profoundly embedded.

As a boy, Alan Mathison Turing was immersed intermittently in Civil Service culture. He was conceived in Chatrapur, near Madras, where his father, Julius Mathison Turing, was employed in the Indian Civil Service. He was born in London in 1912, after which his mother stayed in England while his father traveled back to the subcontinent. His mother rejoined Julius, leaving Alan in the hands of guardians. This pattern, in which the family was separated and reunited, marked Alan's early life. By 1921, dedication to a Civil Service career had made Julius Secretary to the Government Development Department of Madras, which by this time was governed not by the romantic Munro system but, as in the rest of India, along utilitarian lines.[88]

Our best account of Turing's life and work is the biography by Andrew Hodges. He traces Turing's long interest in machines and the mind to the traumatic experience of losing a very close friend, Christopher Morcom, to bovine tuberculosis in 1930, when both were attending Sherborne School and preparing for Cambridge University. The hope, prompted by intense remorse, that Morcom's mind might linger after death, expressed in a paper on the "Nature of Spirit" written for Christopher's mother, was an early exploration of the relationship of mind and thought in a material world, elements of which later appeared in "Computing machinery and intelligence" (1950). Hodges's thesis is convincing. What I add here is an emphasis, hinted at but not developed in Hodges, on a conceptual and metaphorical resource available to Turing.

Hodges recounts, as a curious aside, the remark by Robin Gandy, a friend and Cambridge and wartime colleague, that Turing was a "J. S. Mill man."[89] Hodges takes the reference to be to Mill's argument in *On Liberty* that legal penalties merely strengthen social stigmas, such as that against heresy or—more pertinently in this case—that against homosexuality. The association between Mill and Turing also provided a clue in my investigations. John Stuart Mill (1806–1873) was the son of James Mill, who subjected him to an experimental upbringing. He learned Greek by the age of 3. In his *Autobiography* he accepted, unwillingly, the barbed description aimed at the Benthamites of being a "mere reasoning machine."[90] By maturity, John Stuart Mill was recognized as one of the intellectual leading lights of Victorian England; he also (at age 20) had suffered a nervous breakdown, after which he "began to find meaning in things which I had read or heard about the importance of poetry and art as instruments of human culture." Like his father, John Stuart Mill joined the administration of the East India Company, but he left when the administration passed into the hands of the British government after 1857. The younger Mill can fairly be said to have wrestled with his father's inheritance, a motivation that led in his own science of government to attempt to

Figure 2.3
Alan Mathison Turing. The organization of the Civil Service provided Turing with a resource for thinking about the operation of his own "universal machines." He was later employed by the British government, at Bletchley Park and at the National Physical Laboratory. (Source: National Archive for the History of Computing, University of Manchester)

reconcile James Mill's version with the critiques launched by Macaulay and Carlyle.[91]

Let me take the liberty of considering Turing as a "J. S. Mill man" in the sense of responding to a father's inheritance. While a fellow of King's College, Cambridge, in the mid 1930s, Turing had begun to attack the decidability problem—the *Entscheidungsproblem*—set by David Hilbert. The celebrated Göttingen mathematician had pinpointed several outstanding questions, the solution of which would, he hoped, place mathematics on a sound foundation. Hilbert hoped that mathematics could be proved to be complete, consistent, and decidable. It would be complete if every mathematical statement could be shown to be either true or false, consistent if no false statement could be reached by a valid proof starting from axioms, and decidable if there could be shown to be a definite method by which a decision could be reached for each statement as to whether it was true or false. But to Hilbert's chagrin, the Czech mathematician Kurt Gödel demonstrated in 1930 that arithmetic, and therefore mathematics, must be incomplete. Gödel constructed examples of well-formulated mathematical statements that could not be shown to be either true or false. Starting with any set of axioms, there always existed more mathematics that could not be reached by deduction. This was an utterly shattering conclusion, an intellectual high point of the twentieth century.

There remained the possibility that mathematics could still be kept respectable. Perhaps, even if there existed statements that could not be proved true or false, there might still exist a method that would show (without proof) which statements were true and which were false. If mathematics was decidable but incomplete, the troublesome parts could still be cut out or contained. This was the problem that fired Turing's imagination in the summer of 1935. What is remarkable about his solution, written during a sojourn at Princeton and published in the *Proceedings of the London Mathematical Society* in 1937, was that Turing not only answered the decidability question (with a "no") but in doing so presented the theoretical Universal Computing Machine.[92]

The inspiration seems to have come from Turing's mentor at Cambridge, Max Newman, who wondered aloud whether the Hilbert problems could be attacked by a "mechanical" process.[93] By "mechanical" Newman meant by "routine," a process that could be followed without imagination or thought. The start of Turing's insight was to willfully allow a slippage of meaning and treat "mechanical" as meaning "done by machine." (Note the parallel between labeling a part of the Civil Service "mechanical" because it was supposedly routine and without thought and the creative rereading of such language by the expert movement of mechanizers.) Turing defined a "computing machine" as "supplied with a "tape" (the analogue of paper) running through it and divided into "squares," each square capable of bearing a "symbol."[94] The computing machine could scan a symbol and move up and down the tape, one square at a time, replacing or erasing symbols. The possible behavior of a computing machine was determined by the state the machine was in and the symbol being read.[95] Turing argued that such machines, differing only by their initial *m*-configuration, could start with blank tape and generate numbers of a class he called "computable." Although the route to answering Hilbert's question from there is interesting, it is rather involved and beside the point of this book. What matters is Turing's description of a "universal computing machine" capable of imitating the action of any single computing machine.

To justify his definition of "computable" numbers, Turing had to show that they encompassed "all numbers which would naturally be regarded as computable"—that is to say, all numbers expressible by a human computer. ("Computer" most commonly referred to a human, not a machine, before the Second World War.[96]) Crucially, to make his case, Turing conjures up two types of human computer. They appear in an important section in the logical structure of "On computable numbers with an application to the Entscheidungsproblem" that bridges the gap between the demonstration of the existence and restrictions of a universal computing machine and its application to Hilbert's problem. In the first type, much of the information of how to proceed was contained in many "states of mind," equivalent to many m-configurations of a machine. This was a model of a generalist: work proceeds by the manipulation of symbols on paper, but with the emphasis on the managerial flexibility contained in the large number of states of mind. This interpretation is justified by Turing's second type:

> We suppose, as in [the first type], that the computation is carried out on a tape; but we avoid introducing the "state of mind" by considering a more physical and definite counterpart of it. It is always possible for the computer to break off from his work, to go away and forget all about it, and later to come back and go on with it. If he does this he must leave a note of instructions (written in some standard form) explaining how the work is to be continued.[97]

Here is the generalist-mechanical split, the generalist leaving the office and ensuring that the mechanical clerk will be trusted to follow the routine instructions. The "state of progress of the computation at any stage" is "completely determined by the note of instructions and the symbols on the tape."[98] Turing's point is that such work is equivalent to the actions of a computing machine (in which case both generalist and mechanical would be part of the machine), and, in particular, that any such work would be replicable by a universal computing machine. "Alan had proved," Hodges notes, "that that there was no 'miraculous machine' that could solve all mathematical problems, but in the process he had discovered something almost equally miraculous, the idea of a machine that could take over the work of any machine. And he had argued that anything performed by a human computer could be done by a machine."[99] It helps us understand the seemingly miraculous if we remember that government—especially the Civil Service—had previously been constructed as a machine capable of general-purpose action. As Turing would state explicitly later, in the design for the Automatic Computing Engine: "The class of problems capable of solution by the machine can be defined fairly specifically"; they were "those problems which can be solved by human clerical labour, working to fixed rules, and without understanding."

I do not think we should be surprised that Turing's figure of a human computer is positively bureaucratic, not only in its attention to instruction following and the manipulation of symbols on paper but also in its mobilization of the generalist-mechanical split. If he knew anything about what his father did at work, then the pattern would have been a resource at hand to think by. But I do want to emphasize that this is the second time we have found that a description of a universal machine was shaped by a bureaucratic context. Turing's machine and Babbage's engines are examples of how political history—the metaphor of government as machine, mobilized for quite different reasons during the modern period—intermeshed with the history of technology. This interpretation of Turing's theoretical research of the 1930s will help us reinterpret the work of Bletchley Park in the 1940s and Turing's own attempt to give the universal machine a material form.

3

"Chaotic England" and the Organized World: Official Statistics and Expert Statisticians

Statistics has a reputation as a dry and dull subject. In the nineteenth century, Benjamin Disraeli could score jokes at the expense of a gathering of the Statistical Society of London. However, statistics was—and is—among the most powerful tools of information management: complex, multi-faceted entities like an economy or a country's population have been summarized, made manipulable, even in a sense constituted, by the invention of their indices.[1] An immense amount of physical and intellectual work is needed to create even the most simple statistical fact—indeed, the simpler a fact is, the more refinement, and therefore the more effort, is necessary. This aspect was noticed early on in the history of statistics, not least by Charles Babbage: facts have to be *manufactured*, with all the implications of process, organization, quality, and product that the metaphor of the factory involves. In this chapter I examine the organization behind the fact: how statisticians grouped together and came to form a professionalizing expert movement. I will argue that they formed a particular vision of how expertise and government could work together, with implications for both the politics of Whitehall and the politics of knowledge.

Owing to the effort and the expense associated with making and maintaining simple statistical facts, only bodies with particular characteristics can compete. First, statistics, as expensive products, required a considerable source of funding. Second, most statistics gain their value by forming part of a time series, therefore some institutional structure is needed, insofar as institutions are bodies that can carry values over time, such as rules about collection or comparison. The state possessed both of these characteristics: it had a steady revenue stream through taxation, and it had complex but stable institutional structures. However, a third factor places the state in an unbeatable position: compliance with the process of statistical production can, in principle, be enforced, since the state has a defining characteristic of seeking—and often gaining—a monopoly of the means of violence. In the United Kingdom, as in many other countries, individuals and firms were legally compelled to complete census forms. However, this capacity was often not granted, and it should not be overemphasized. Voluntary, not compulsory, statistical returns were typical. G. Udny Yule, a highly influential British statistician of the early decades of the twentieth century, explained: the "mass of . . . voluntary information is a feature of our statistics not always sufficiently remembered."[2] At the same moment, Arthur Bowley, an academic statistician prominent at the new London School of Economics, complained that the "compulsory powers of collecting statistics are too few and too seldom applied," while too much reliance was placed on "a few sympathetic employers . . . and we tend to get a biased selection."[3] "If the method of samples were employed with compulsory powers," Bowley argued, "we could . . . by a rapid and abridged investigation get a great deal of unbiased information." In this way the power of the state could be harnessed to underwrite objective knowledge produced by expert professionals.

This position did not go uncontested. While would-be professionalizers, such as Bowley, emphasized the benefits of broad and deep knowledge of the country through statistics, others were suspicious. Miners, for example, rejected efforts by the Board of Trade ("Your schedules are of a prying nature and calculated to do the working class more harm than good").[4] The same government department could be told by an industrialist that "it was an utterly futile return. . . . Some idiot is hard up for employment and has hit upon this brilliant idea to give overpaid and underworked officials a chance of wearing out government pens and filling government foolscap with rubbish. Your department is the last refuge of the decrepit trade union official or the out at elbows socialist orator."[5] The rise of the professions upset both labor and capital. A typical act of resistance was sullen misleading compliance: one statistician, a civil servant in fact, recalled that a manufacturer, faced with a deluge of compulsory schedules to fill, put "any kind of figure . . . into his return. There was no certainty, therefore, that the granting of compulsory power would elicit truth."[6] This tension between the power of the state and the rights of individuals, a common opposition but one with British idiosyncrasies, and how it was managed by professional expert movements within government, marks this and the remaining chapters.

Another interesting feature of the British case is that, until the Second World War, official statistics remained decentralized: instead of a central statistical office, each department made arrangements for making the statistics that it wanted. This feature immediately suggests similarities to the registers considered in the next chapter. In particular, it is interesting to ask whether parallel arguments could be made, for example about maintaining the appearance of lack of surveillance through not creating a central focus. First, however, the growth and operation of decentralized British statistics must be examined, in particular in connection with campaigns to create a central body where all statistical facts would pass. In what follows I first account for the growth of statistics in the nineteenth century, which takes a decentralized departmentalized form in the United Kingdom. Intertwined with this growth is the formation of a professional consciousness among statisticians, marked by societies, organizations, journals, techniques, and an articulated public purpose. As professionals, statisticians had interests that flowed over departmental boundaries. The nature of these interests was revealed when they conflicted with those of other groups. I therefore examine a series of confrontations, paying special attention to what sorts of knowledge each side valued. Professional statisticians were committed to a concept of "informative" official statistics: government-produced information that was general enough to allow effective intervention by statisticians into issues of the day, but which also required validation by their expertise. The Census of Production, an innovation of 1907, provides one example, as do two campaigns to centralize the manufacture of official statistics: the lobbying over many decades for a central statistical office in Whitehall and the global vision of a British Empire Statistical Bureau.

Departmentalized Knowledge? Non-Official and Official Statistics, 1832–1914

The link with government is commemorated in the etymology of "statistics": in German, "Staat" denotes a state, a government, or a body politic.[7] However, a feature of statistics, as the product of an expert movement, has been a symbiotic relationship between official and non-official statisticians. I will concentrate on official statistics, but there are several aspects of the institutions of non-official statistics, the statistical societies, that are of great interest. Indeed it is an interdependence between official and non-official statisticians that marks the expert movement, and, among other things, is a cause of the notable "avalanche of printed numbers" in Western Europe (statistical knowledge was kept discreet in the East): government-made knowledge was brought into the public realm, and officials judiciously borrowed knowledge from civil society.[8] In Britain the statistics movement flourished from the 1830s, although it could, and did, claim a tradition back to the seventeenth-century political arithmetic of John Graunt, William Petty, and to a much lesser extent Gregory King.[9] The mid-nineteenth-century practitioners of statistics were generally not professional statisticians: professionalization was an outcome, not a resource, of their activities. Instead they saw statistics as a step in attaining their political target of urban reform. As doctors, commissioners, or inspectors, investigators such as James Kay in Manchester or the utilitarian Edwin Chadwick in

London collected information on social questions with the expectation that, if the facts were clearly presented, reform would follow and social unrest would be averted. To further such projects of building order in the world, the Manchester Statistical Society was set up in 1833, and the Statistical Society of London in 1834.[10] Both these societies would last until the present day (the London group transforming into the Royal Statistical Society in 1886–87), but many other local societies also flourished in the years of political reform and unrest.

The formation of the Statistical Society of London is particularly interesting for its connections with events I discussed in the preceding chapter. At the third meeting of the British Association for the Advancement of Science in 1833, the presence of the eminent Belgian statistician Lambert Adolphe Jacques Quetelet gave Charles Babbage an excuse to break the rules. Without seeking any sanction, Babbage announced the existence of an extra section of the British Association—a section devoted to statistics.[11] A small gathering was held, with Thomas Malthus in the chair and Quetelet the star guest. Babbage packed it with allies, including Richard Jones (a professor of political economy at King's College, London), John Elliot Drinkwater (a Home Office civil servant), and William Henry Sykes (a former Statistical Reporter to the Government at Bombay). All these men were liberal in politics, and both Jones and Sykes had special interest (and, in Sykes's case, experience) of statistics collected through the Indian Civil Service. Babbage's intention, with his own failed attempt at election as a member of Parliament fresh in his mind, was that scientists should exert influence on government through the production of statistical facts. He was opposed by the president of the British Association in 1833. Conceding the existence of the new section, the geologist Adam Sedgwick warned: "If we transgress our proper boundaries, go into provinces not belonging to us, and open a door of communication to the dreary world of politics, [in] that instant will the foul Daemon of discord find his way into our Eden of philosophy."[12] This opening was, of course, precisely what Babbage desired. The politicization of statistics was a continual bone of contention within the expert movement of statisticians.

The statistical section of the British Association of 1833 provided the springboard for the establishment of the Statistical Society of London in 1834. Despite Babbage's intention, the society needed to *appear* politically neutral. Tories, as well as Liberals and Whigs were invited to join, and it was declared that the "first and most essential rule of [the society's] conduct" was to "exclude all *opinions*." (Of course, this did not make the society any less political: it underlined the authority of statisticians to speak because of their control over statistical *fact*.) But as others joined, Babbage's control within the society began to slip away. (We saw in the chapter 1 what would be his third, most radical assault on political power that followed this failure.[13]) Though the early governing committees of the London society contained Babbage's allies, they were diluted by newcomers. In the following years, the Statistical Society of London may not have fulfilled Babbage's hopes, but it did settle into the central institutional locus of the expert movement of statisticians. It was there, guided by George Richardson Porter, that non-official and official statisticians met. The Society provides good reason for thinking of statisticians as a movement (working both inside and outside government) rather than a pressure group. Society members could be either official or non-official statisticians, but together they called for government to expand the scope of its statistics.[14]

The movement's aims were inherited by the great projects to know the contours of poverty associated with Henry Mayhew, B. Seebohm Rowntree, and Charles Booth—private philanthropists who should be placed just outside the expert movement of statisticians.[15] As statistics developed they also changed. In particular there was a profound shift from enumeration (How many poor are there?) to analysis (What regularities, laws even, are revealed in the statistics of the poor?). This shift was highly significant for the history of science, since it was not confined to the social sciences but shaped the physical sciences too, where statistical theories of gases, thermodynamics, and, later, matter (quantum mechanics) appeared.[16] Across the spectrum statistics became more theorized, the projects of Adolphe Quetelet and Francis Galton being mathematized in the hands of Karl Pearson and others. Sophisticated technique reinforced the movement toward professionalization, since it tended to exclude amateurs.

Within British government, statistical production was increasing, but not smoothly. The regular publication of national criminal statistics by the Home Office began in 1810 and has continued to the present day.[17] This was not the pattern with agricultural figures. In 1793, the Scot Sir John Sinclair, in return for support for Pitt, had successfully begged for the foundation of a Board of Agriculture. Sinclair was president of the board, and Arthur Young , a charismatic proponent of agricultural improvement, was secretary. Sinclair had previously organized, at his private expense, the *Statistical Account of Scotland*, which appeared in 21 volumes between 1791 and 1799. These books had popularized the word "statistics" in the English language, although its meaning was still far from stable: only in the following decades did "statistics" refer to quantitative data only.[18]

The leg work for Sinclair's *Statistical Account* was done by parish ministers, to each of whom Sinclair had sent an identical list of queries and "begged, bullied, made jocular threats."[19] The Board of Agriculture, which Stephen aptly described as a "rather anomalous body, something between a government office and such an institution as the Royal Society," set out to replicate the Scottish project; this time, however, the project of producing knowledge would be backed by the state rather than privately financed.[20] The aim was highly political: the statistical account would encourage enclosure, that seizure of common land that Sinclair often toasted ("May commons become uncommon"). However, the clergy, representatives of the country interest and therefore at first sight a group one would expect to be sympathetic, rebelled, suspecting an attack on their tithes, and the grand statistical survey was scaled down. The board died in 1822.

The appearance of the statistical societies in the 1830s was accompanied by the establishment within Whitehall of the first statistical department: the Board of Trade's in 1832. The prompt was an acknowledgment by central government of a disturbing ignorance of provincial conditions at a time of economic troubles and destabilizing discontent surrounding electoral reform (the franchise was extended that year, a great turning point of British politics). For example, here is William Jacob, comptroller of corn returns, and proponent of establishing the new department:

> A more general diffusion of accurate knowledge regarding the state of public affairs would tend to check that excitement and party spirit which has often been created by misrepresentation or exaggeration, and has produced an annoyance to the government, and at least a temporary disaffection of the public mind.[21]

The activities of George Richardson Porter bound the official and the nonofficial wings of the expert movement of statisticians together. Porter, a failed sugar broker turned statistician, was invited by the president of the Board of Trade, Lord Auckland, to make a digest for the board of the increasing amounts of information generated by parliamentary reports and papers.[22] Auckland must have been impressed by the order brought to the figures. In 1834, Porter became supervisor of the board's statistical department, while simultaneously seeing his promotion of a Statistical Society of London come to fruition. He was also active in Section F (Statistical) of the British Association for the Advancement of Science, and his marriage to Sarah Ricardo, the sister of the Benthamite economist, further strengthened his position at the center of mid-nineteenth-century British statistical institutions. Porter set about organizing a massive compendium of statistics, published as *The Progress of the Nation* between 1836 and 1843, in which he aimed to show, among other things, that, despite the upheavals of industrialization and the Napoleonic wars, the weekly wages of most artisans and manual workers had increased, or at least had greater spending power.[23] He was a liberal free-trader, and these values, too, suffused through *The Progress of the Nation.* The very title of the work boasted of what an institution could achieve with dynamic knowledge of the country in the form of time series. Previous private commentators had either presented static quantitative pictures of the country (as in John Ramsay McCulloch's 1839 *Statistical Account of the British Empire*) or exploited the institutional capacities of government by borrowing official statistics. Joseph Lowe's *The Present State of England in Regard to Agriculture, Trade and Finance, with a Comparison of Prospects of England and France* gave the first chronological series of national income figures, but depended on data from the 1821 census and other official reports.[24] Indeed, by the time the first statistical societies were set up, the decennial census of population had already been carried out four times (1801, 1811, 1821, and 1831), initially an exercise in national survival, as Colley has most recently reminded us, assessing whether Britons had the will to fight a Napoleonic army.[25]

Nineteenth-century official and non-official statistics were interdependent, despite a shift of informational power toward the center.[26] On the one hand it was the power and reach of government that non-official statisticians coveted. On the other, official statisticians had to rely on the willing collaboration of outside investigators to amass the statistical knowledge they desired. Porter acknowledged this interplay in *The Progress of the Nation*, emphasizing that government, especially after liberal reform, would demand and generate masses of information. In particular, the dynamic relationship between the legislature (Parliament) and the executive (e.g. Porter's department) expanded the state's appetite for statistical knowledge.[27]

Further evidence of both the interdependence of official and non-official sources and the increasing role of government in the production of facts is given by another of Porter's contributions. In 1849, a fat instruction book, *A Manual of Scientific Enquiry*, was published, a collection written by the elite of British science and edited by Sir John Frederick William Herschel. The Lords Commissioners of the Admiralty had informed the astronomer that articles should be "generally plain, so that men merely of good intelligence and fair acquirement may be able to act upon them" and should be neither displays of "very deep and abstruse research" nor accounts of methods requiring the "use of nice apparatus and instruments."[28] The hope was to exploit the presence in the empire of thousands of inquisitive sailors of the Royal Navy, as well as the many other British subjects—from missionaries to engineers to doctors—and to turn them into an efficient scientific reporting network.

Readers were instructed on how and what to observe on subjects of interest, including astronomy (by Sir George Biddell Airy), magnetism (Lieutenant-Colonel Edward Sabine), tides (Rev. Dr. William Whewell), hydrography (Captain F. W. Beechey), mineralogy (Sir Henry De La Beche), zoology

(Richard Owen), botany (Sir William Hooker), medicine (Dr. Alexander Bryson), ethnology (Dr. J. C. Prichard), and geology (Charles Darwin). George Porter wrote the instructions on statistics.[29] He spelled out the categories of information a keen observer should be collecting, starting with population numbers and proceeding through rates of mortality, employment in agriculture or trade and manufactures, the numbers of factories and sizes of farms, the quantities of products and amounts consumed, the mineral resources, the restrictions on employment of women, the expenditure of families, the incomes of the clergy, the degree of instruction of children, the state of crime, the provision made for the indigent, the length and condition of public and private roads, and the foreign commerce through the ports, as well as descriptions and quantities of goods imported and exported, the flow of currency, and the weights and measures in operation. Everywhere maps should be bought. The tips Porter gave were practical. In particular he urged the traveling Briton to tap into official sources abroad: ". . . the actual numbers of any population can never be so satisfactorily ascertained as by the interference of the government," so look there first. Likewise, only someone with the "authority of government" could succeed in knowing with "minuteness" the breakdown of industry by sector or employment numbers by branch. (In the absence of foreign official figures, Porter advised whom to approach, such as "intelligent merchants" for imports and exports, or "men of intelligence" for the reliability of local maps.) Finally, Porter urged that "no fact shall be disregarded as without value by reason of its incompleteness of the information it yields, since it may well be that this very fact may supply a link in the chain that will give value and completeness to former or to future observations." At the center, where Porter sat, a complete statistical picture of the empire could be constructed, a product of public-private collaboration.

Reliable statistics were seen to depend also on disciplining techniques of collection. Porter's tips to travelers and the navy on reporting useful information should be seen as part of an attempt to regulate what data were collected, and how. Other techniques were also innovated. We have already seen that identical questionnaires provided John Sinclair with the means to attempt to condition his clerical informants in survey of Scotland in the 1790s. Frederick Morton Eden copied Sinclair's method in *The State of the Poor* (1797).[30] In the 1831 Census of Population, standardized forms were introduced. The first four censuses had been organized by John Rickman, a clerk of the House of Commons, and carried out locally by overseers of the parish and clergymen.[31] "The documents and instructions were issued to the Overseers of every parish, town or place whom, or in default, some 'substantial Householder,' had to proceed from house to house and to ascertain and record the prescribed particulars, aided in this task, where necessary, by 'Church Wardens, Chapel Wardens, Sidesmen, Parish and Vestry Clerks, Constables, Tything-men, Head Boroughs and other Peace Officers.' "[32]

Under Rickman, a trusted confidant of a literary and largely Tory political coterie (he was a friend of the essayist Charles Lamb, the poets Samuel Taylor Coleridge and Robert Southey, and the engineer Thomas Telford; he was a disputant with the Greek scholar Professor Richard Porson, the radical lecturer John Thelwall, and George Dyer), the work of producing a digest of the Census of Population was a strikingly informal affair.[33] It is significant that when an exhibition of registration was put together in 1937, no original records could be shown that illustrated Rickman's work: they were destroyed as soon as they were used.[34] Permanence was not necessary if the authority of the figures was based on gentlemanly trust. But this changed with the introduction of the a new, more bureaucratic census. In 1841, following Rickman's death the year before, responsibility for the census passed to the General Register Office (GRO), the government department responsible for the upkeep of the registers of births, deaths and, later, marriages (an innovation in 1836, and in themselves forming a significant new database). Now records would be centralized and kept permanently (figure 3.1). Statistical facts about the population could be checked by retracing the calculation through the enumerators' schedules and tables.

Under the influence of the doctor William Farr, another leading light of the Statistical Society, a considerable amount, and in his eyes a coherent structure, of statistics were produced at the GRO from the 1840s to the 1870s.[35] Farr's arguments were also influential, for example being recycled in Edwin Chadwick's *Sanitary Report on the Condition of the Labouring Population of England* of 1842.[36] The GRO's interest covered the spectrum of "moral statistics"—data concerning crime, education, and religion[37]—as well as quantitative measures of the population. In 1851, for example, ambitious education and religious censuses were undertaken. Both faced fierce opposition, and after a compromise they were made voluntary rather than compulsory—a reminder of the checks on the power of government. On 30 March 1851, attendance at churches was counted and summarized by the GRO official Horace Mann. His shock at finding a far larger than expected number "destitute of spiritual teaching"—"laboring myriads" indifferent to church attendance—was shared by many Victorians.[38]

The Board of Trade and the GRO were joined by other houses of statistical production in Whitehall. Furthermore, the pattern of interdependence between official and non-official statistician continued. For example, when in 1842 Prime Minister Robert Peel introduced the first peacetime income tax,

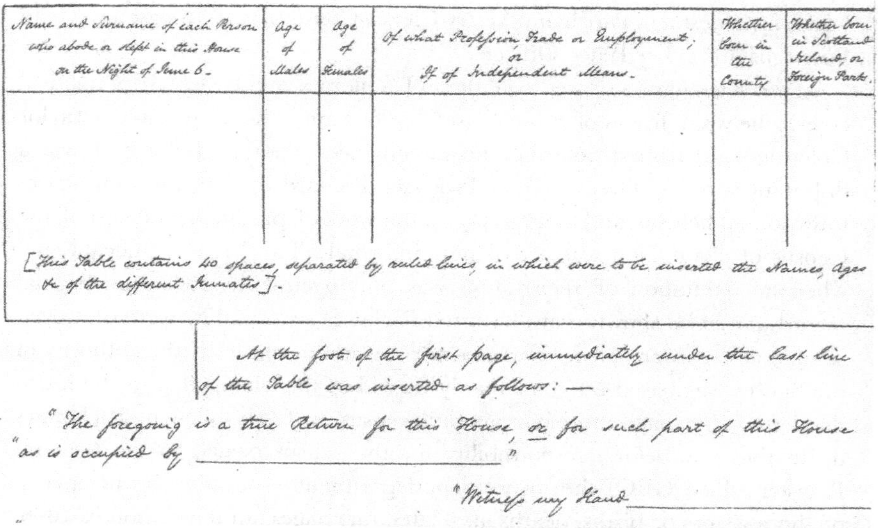

Name and Surname of each Person who abode or slept in this House on the Night of June 6.	Age of Males	Age of Females	Of what Profession, Trade or Employment; or If of Independent Means.	Whether born in the County	Whether born in Scotland, Ireland, or Foreign Parts.

[This Table contains 40 spaces, separated by ruled lines, in which were to be inserted the Names, Ages &c of the different Inmates].

At the foot of the first page, immediately under the last line of the Table was inserted as follows: —

"The foregoing is a true Return for this House, or for such part of this House "as is occupied by ____________"

"Witness my Hand ____________

Figure 3.1

A standardized form used in the Census of Population of England and Wales, 1841. The first four censuses (1801, 1811, 1821, and 1841) had relied on the integrity of John Rickman and a network of assistants. Standardized forms were used in 1831, but from 1841 the Census, managed by the new General Register Office, was marked by bureaucratic rather than personal authority, and permanent records of how the data was collected and digested would be kept. Forms such as these can be understood as information technologies that provide an informational interface between state and individual, configuring both to some degree. Forms have three important characteristics: (1) Forms can be mass produced and thus identical. (2) By directing any response to be made in particular place or in a particular form, a form acts as a pre-processor of information, taking a messy, complex world and simplifying it. Despite the fact that the information is simplified, expertise is needed to make use of it. (3) Forms are always part of a power structure, of asker and asked. All the forms filled out by ordinary people have been destroyed. The one shown here is a copy made in 1841. (PRO/RG/27/1) supposedly as a temporary measure following the repeal of the corn laws but re-enacted annually and finally permanently in 1874, a vast new set of data on individuals was compiled within Whitehall. An active member of the Statistical Society of London, Robert Dudley Baxter, exploited the resource, combining the income tax information with figures culled from the 1861 Census of Population to provide a statistical breakdown of income in Britain.[39] Baxter's work was subsequently extended by other statisticians. The point is that a change in the style of government had implications for the type of information collected, which was subsequently analyzed by a non-official statistician, the results being fed back—via the Statistical Society—into official deliberations.

Similarly, the independently wealthy Charles Booth relied on official 1891 Census of Population figures to guide his investigations of poverty (including the definition of the "poverty line"), which culminated in the publication of the seventeen-volume *Life and Labour of the People of London*. Booth's spiritual successor, Seebohm Rowntree, spent his time and wealth organizing the investigation of the poor of York, but, when called, would also work for the state as director of the Welfare Department of the Ministry of Munitions.[40] However, there was no attempt to centralize or even systematize the statistical production of government departments or private bodies. On the official side, the improvised arrangement stuck, and the British pattern became one of separate statistics being prepared by separate departments. Though the production rate was high (many of the departments poured their statistical knowledge into print, producing the "blue books" beloved by historians), the vision was not unified.

The example of labor statistics, drawn from the detailed historical investigations of Roger Davidson, provides an excellent case study of the politics of official statistics in this period, but also raises issues of general interest to the arguments of this book. Davidson examined the establishment of the Board of Trade's Labour Statistical Bureau (1886)—subsequently the Labour Department (1893)—in the context of a twentieth-century historiographical debate that interpreted the increasing welfare provision of the late nineteenth century and the early twentieth as either progressive action or acts of social control by the state.[41] Though Davidson, on balance, suggests indirect social control as the correct interpretation of the work of the Labour Statistical Bureau, it is the empirical substance of his work rather than his conclusions that interests me here.[42] What was collectively labeled the "Labour Problem"—an increase in industrial unrest, underemployment and unemployment at unprecedented highs, and low-income destitution—rose to the top of the political agenda in the 1880s and the 1890s. Even today the causes are a subject of historical debate.[43] In the last decades of the nineteenth century, the causes of the Labour Problem were seen as either unknown or contested. That the official knowledge of labor was deficient, chaotic, and unmanageable became a commonplace.[44]

The campaign for the ordering of official knowledge of labor was a typical effort of statisticians as an expert movement. While the Board of Trade pressed the Treasury for action (and money), private statisticians, such as Rawson W. Rawson, called for a thorough reappraisal, shaming the government with examples drawn from the United States and Continental Europe.[45] The two aspects of the movement coordinated actions through the (now Royal) Statistical Society, of which Rawson was president. In 1885 the society sponsored a conference, attended by official and non-official statisticians and by sympathetic politicians (such as A. J. Mundella, a member of the society) to further press the issue. With a Liberal election victory in 1886, Mundella was appointed president of the Board of Trade, and a Labour Statistical Bureau was created. (Helping to concentrate minds on the need for increased production of information, 20,000 unemployed dock and building worker led 2 days of rioting and looting across the West End of London in February of 1886.[46] The order of statistical information would stand against chaos.) The Bureau had four objectives : to chart "progress" of wage earnings since 1830, using blue books and "reputable unofficial sources"; to "provide regular and full returns on wages"; to publish information of "immediate practical use" on matters relating to conditions of the working classes; and to provide comparable data with conditions abroad.[47] These categories addressed the severe informational anxieties of late-nineteenth-century Britain, whether it was lack of knowledge leading to fears of mob violence stemming from "outcast London" or economic competition from Germany or the United States.[48]

The Bureau received a grander title, the Labour Department, after the general election of 1892, a sop to those, such as the Fabians, calling for a full-fledged Ministry of Labour.[49] There were benefits: a network of fee-paid local investigators, distributed throughout the country and reporting to statisticians well placed within the Board of Trade, was instituted. An extraordinary collection of statistical talent was attracted to the Department, not least William Beveridge, later one of the architects of the British welfare state. Davidson notes that they can be divided into two groups, by political philosophy. The "conservatives" included Robert Giffen, the most eminent official statistician of his time, and other traditional free-traders who "regarded the prime function of labor statistics as being to 'educate' the Labour Movement, on the assumption that accurate data on employment, on the costs and benefits of strike action, and on the cost structure of British industry, would rehabilitate the consensus tactics of mid-Victorian craft unionism and serve to preserve industrial peace."[50] Davidson divides the "progressives" (generally more sympathetic to state intervention) into social innovators and technical innovators.

Social innovators typically passed through the obligatory passage points of late-nineteenth-century middle-class left-leaning social radicalism: the University Settlement Movement (which brought young academic improvers into the slums), the Charity Organization Society (which visited, and spied on, working-class homes), Toynbee Hall (the center of such activity in East London), or involvement with the philanthropic surveys of poverty of Charles Booth. The belief of this group, which included Hubert Llewellyn Smith, Clara Collet,and David Frederick Schloss, was that "careful, minute, systematic observation of working-class life as affected by environment, heredity, and habit . . . would provide an impartial data base for debate on labor issues."[51] They shared with their "conservative" colleagues a distaste for unprofessional "investigatory sensationalism," the paradigmatic case being Andrew Mearns and W. C. Preston's *Bitter Cry of Outcast London* (1883), which they regarded as "seriously deficient in the scientific sense"—or, in other words, produced by people outside the expert movement of statisticians. The social innovators, although they favored state intervention (such as progressive taxation or unemployment exchanges), shared with the conservatives a rejection of an essential antagonism between classes. Expert management of information was therefore, for them, a tool against class war.

Also among Davidson's progressives were the "technical innovators." Some, including Arthur Bowley and George Wood, were similar in political philosophy to the social innovators. Others (such as G. Udny Yule, who had trained in German physics laboratories and had been eugenicist Karl Pearson's demonstrator in the 1890s, yet rejected eugenics) were far more reticent to pin their ideological colors to the mast. This group, notes Davidson, "derived their inspiration from the rise of sociometrics and mathematical statistics at the turn of the century, associated in part with Social Darwinism and in part with more pragmatic demands for quantitative information generated by the Tariff Reform debate."[52] Though attached to the Board of Trade, they were also academics, and were among the most celebrated statistical theoreticians of their day. Yule, for example, generalized and expanded the statistical tools developed for Pearson's eugenic investigations, providing formulas for multiple-regression analysis and measurements of association between sets of data.[53] The group were united in bemoaning the lack of sophistication of official statisticians. Bowley argued that the government faced an intense informational crisis: the Labour Problem appeared intractable because of lack of knowledge. Bowley described the task as "to measure the inaccessible" and "to describe the animal from the single bone, to make firm observations from a shifting base."[54] The solution was partly full use of the institutional resources of government (adequate time series, for example) and partly mobilization of the new theoretical tools of professional statisticians, in particular sampling. Key developments in the practices of statistics were encouraged by the involvement of statisticians such as Bowley in governmental work—which in turn took directions from social and economic anxieties.

The Treasury loathed this expansion of the Board of Trade. Partly, the opposition stemmed from the former's traditional function, interrogation of proposed public expenditure. Partly, it came from suspicions of creeping state intervention.[55] However, it also partly arose from a commitment to a certain structure of the Civil Service. I argued in the last chapter that the generalist-mechanical split had been accepted, and was being promoted, by the Treasury after 1870. The statisticians in the Board of Trade—specialists in high-level posts, appointed without competitive examination—contradicted this policy. Statistics, insisted the Treasury, was the work of low-grade "mechanicals," and proper funding for the Board of Trade's labor statistics department—at least in the opinion of the expert movement of statisticians—was always withheld. At stake in this argument was whether government should produce statistical knowledge purely for its own administrative necessity (a purpose the Treasury approved), or whether it should go further, be "informative" (or "promotional" or "speculative" according to the Treasury). What sort of national knowledge could or should be known? Riding on the outcome of this conflict was the adoption of statistical practices, since only statisticians of the caliber of Bowley or Yule could introduce the methods needed to make sense of the broader and deeper statistical data. As we shall see, a compromise was brokered.

Let us pause to consider what the Treasury's actions meant for expert movements within government. Insistence on the generalist-mechanical split meant implacable Treasury opposition to high-ranking specialist professional statisticians within government, but it served to reinforce the Treasury's own commitment to the mechanical language. In turn, this gave support to the creative reading of "mechanical" taken by the expert group of mechanizers that grew powerful within the Treasury. Furthermore, the Home Office and the Treasury's other allies on this issue, which also were jealous of the Board of Trade's growing strength in statistics, echoed the Treasury's specific argument that statistical work was "mechanical."[56]

By the time of the First World War a daunting list of the myriad Whitehall statistical projects that led to publications distributed could be compiled.

The Campaign for a Central Statistical Office

The message of table 3.1 is that statistical production within Whitehall by the early 1900s was voluminous and decentralized. Visitors from abroad commented on this odd organization. In 1882, M. Cheysson, director of the French

Table 3.1
Principal statistical information published by departments. Source: Cd. 7351 and other documents.

	Principal subjects upon which statistical information is published
Board of Trade	Trade and industry of the UK, foreign trade, navigation and shipping, emigration and immigration, railway capital and traffic, railway accidents, wrecks and casualties to shipping, census of seamen employed, tramways, insurance companies, bankruptcy, labor exchanges and unemployment insurance, wages and hours of labor, trade unions, strikes and lockouts, Census of Production
Board of Customs and Excise	Imports and exports (with BoT), customs and excise, revenue and administration
Board of Agriculture and Fisheries for England and Wales, Board of Agriculture for Scotland	Agriculture in England and Wales and in Scotland, agricultural holdings, area under and produce of crops, livestock, sea and inland fisheries of England and Wales, corn sales and prices
Board of Agriculture and Technical Instruction for Ireland	Agriculture, agricultural holdings, area under and produce of crops, livestock, the trade of Ireland
Fishery Boards for Scotland, Ireland	Sea and inland fisheries of Scotland and Ireland
Lunacy Commissioners for England and Wales, Scotland, Ireland	Lunacy, lunatics, asylums
National Debt Office	National debt
Registry of Friendly Societies	Industrial, provident, and cooperative societies, building societies
War Office	Regular Army and Army Reserve, the territorial forces
Admiralty	Health of the Navy
General Register Offices for England and Wales, Scotland, Ireland	Census of the respective divisions of the UK: population, births, deaths, marriages
Boards of Education for England and Wales, Scotland, Ireland	Educational matters, primary schools, school attendance, educational results, revenue and expenditure in connection with education
Home Office	Criminal and judicial statistics (mines and minerals, industrial accidents, factories, prisons, reformatories, aliens)
India Office	Various

Ministry of Public Works and vice-president of the Paris Statistical Society, wrote of his surprise at finding in the United Kingdom "a total absence of any central or general supervision over official statistics."[57] Cheysson's arguments were not neutral: he was in the midst of campaigning for a French central statistical body, a goal he reached 3 years later with the formation of the Conseil Supérieur de Statistique (modeled on that of Belgium, where Quetelet's central statistical office had existed since 1841). Cheysson's comments were grist to the mill of like-minded statisticians in Britain. The Statistical Society of London translated and reprinted Cheysson's Statistical Society of Paris article in its own journal within months.

Why did the Statistical Society do this? This question gets to the heart of understanding statisticians as experts in relation to government and power. Statisticians bucked the trend of government-expert relations outlined by MacLeod, the "gradual submersion of the mid-century specialist into watertight departmental structures which compelled him to rely on secretarial sanction, formal procedures and codes, and which constrained him to terms of reference not of his choosing or design."[58] The alliance between official and non-official statisticians—the expert movement of statisticians—continued well after MacLeod's date for the onset of "departmentalism," 1870. Just to give one example, albeit an outstanding one: In 1876 Robert Giffen moved from journalism (he was assistant editor of *The Economist* under Bagehot and later a co-founder of *The Statist*) to the Board of Trade, where he successively accumulated leadership of the statistical, commercial, and labor departments before retiring in 1897. During this period he was also editor of the *Journal of the Statistical Society of London* (which became Royal during his tenure) and president of the society in 1882–1884. Giffen was one of a number of men who could move effortlessly between government department and professional society. As a grouping of officials, professionals or amateurs, the statisticians constituted a potential expert movement: they could claim positions of influence through being mediators and interpreters of information. But in order for this claim to translate into real power the pattern of statistical production tied tightly to the administrative needs of departments had to be broken up and reconstituted as a more autonomous central body. Therefore, in order to understand statisticians as prime movers in a movement of experts we must turn to the arguments for and against centralization, and to connected controversies (in particular, controversies over whether statistical knowledge should be produced purely to guide administration or whether it had broader, more public, and more political uses—the question of "informative" statistics).

In 1871 Frederick Purdy presented a paper before the Statistical Society of London. Purdy was an exemplary case of the combination of government expert and professional statistician, being both Principal of the Poor Law Board's Statistical Department and an Honorary Secretary of the Statistical Society. With an air of studied weariness he told his audience that he had "traveled for many years, as part of my official duty, the same statistical road, not . . . without duly looking about, for the way is rugged, strewn here and there with deceptive fragments, or broken up with ugly pitfalls."[59] (It is probably not a coincidence that the imagery suggests the Scottish Highlands of McCulloch.) Purdy could list numerous examples of the fragmentary nature of parliamentary statistics, "on collating different series of these documents, we find time, space and mode severely clashing." For example, there were many different official "years": the financial year ended on 31 March, trade returns on 31 December, and emigrations on Lady Day. The Poor Rate Year in England and Wales ended on 25 March; in Scotland and Ireland the dates were 14 May and 29 September respectively. The English criminal year (like the year of Oxbridge students) began with Michaelmas, whereas Scottish and Irish criminals were counted in a year ending on the 31 December. Spatially, similar clashes could be found. Many statistics were counted by administrative areas, and these often differed according to where in government they were being collected: Ashton-under-Lyne, for example, a settlement east of Manchester, was a parish of 66,801, a poor law union of 134,753, a town of 29,791 inhabitants, a petty sessional division (i.e. a judicial district) of 41,597, a municipal borough of 34,886, and a parliamentary borough of 33,917. "Here, then," remarked Purdy, "we employ an identical mark to represent six disparate things." Such absurdities became a stock-in-trade of the proponents of centralized statistical knowledge.[60]

Passage through this statistical landscape should, Purdy argued, be smoothed, and the "chaotic mass of parliamentary statistics might, with great public advantage and at a cost of production less than the present, be brought into more serviceable order." The crisis afflicted the head of the body politic: Parliament was unable to bring together coherently the flows of information directed toward it. In such a situation, decision making would be flawed at best, catastrophic at worst. Purdy's proposed solution was the establishment of "a department which should be an intermediary between Parliament and the various Government Departments." He listed the capacities of the new department: it should "make itself master of as soon and as fully as possible of all clues to statistical and tabular matter printed throughout the sessional papers," it should "index all the statistical returns and principal papers upon some comprehensive and intelligible system"; it should possess "all forms, accounts, and books used in the ordinary business of the different Government offices," and thereby oversee the flow of information. A statistician running such a meta-department would, of course, wield considerable power.

Although the Treasury recognized the "chaotic conditions" of official statistics, its response to calls such as Purdy's was measured. No action was taken until a fierce row broke out between the Board of Trade and the Board of Customs & Excise. In 1877 W. H. Smith was Secretary to the Treasury (he was also a "Son" in W. H. Smith & Sons, and largely responsible for establishing, via the burgeoning railway system, the familiar—and lucrative—chain of booksellers and newsagents). That year, in response to the controversy between the boards, Smith appointed a Statistical Committee with a remit to consider "defects then existing in the organization and scope of official statistics."[61] This group heard a substantial and detailed argument from Giffen, who pressed for centralizing statistics under his own department, the Board of Trade.[62] The Third Report of the Committee made two recommendations on "future conduct and control." First, "while each of the statistically important departments should continue to be responsible for its own statistics, a small Central Statistical Department, subordinate to the Treasury (not Giffen's board), should be set up with functions such as the preparation of annual abstracts, the compilation of an annual index or guide to official statistics and the editing of a miscellaneous volume containing statistical returns from the smaller departments." Second, a "small permanent Board or Commission should be formed to carry on the supervision of statistics and to secure a continuance of "order and harmony" in the general body of returns presented to Parliament."[63]

T. H. Farrer, Secretary of the Board of Trade, perhaps the most important department for the production of statistics, opposed the first recommendation. The problem, he argued, lay not with the lack of central coordination, but in the unevenness of Britain: "It would be sanguine to hope that [the differences of law and customs in the several parts of the United Kingdom] could be removed in order to render statistical records uniform."[64] In other words, to make orderly statistics the nation would first have to be ordered.[65] (This sentiment is powerfully reminiscent of the recent argument of James C. Scott that the state has only been able to "see" clearly after acts of radical simplification.[66]) Farrer regarded as slim the chances of success of this disciplining transformation: "Human life and habits can seldom be altered in order to make records perfect." Behind Farrer's objection lay both Whitehall interdepartmental politics and divergent ideological commitments. The Board of Trade had built up a considerable organization for making and commenting on statistics, and was very unwilling to cede control to the Treasury. Likewise, the Treasury was unsympathetic to Farrer's counter-proposal that the board take on responsibility for statistical production from other parts of Whitehall. With the powerful departments at loggerheads, the Chancellor of the Exchequer could resist the call for a central statistical office: the liberal Gladstone suspected anyway that the office would grow "beyond the limits required by economy and expediency."[67] Farrer would have been sympathetic to this argument: as a committed free-trader, he would not have regarded such an extension of government as legitimate.[68] Compare and contrast Purdy and Farrer on statistical topography: for the former the rugged highlands should be smoothed and standardized by the action of government, whereas for the latter this was anathema. Such differences symbolized the difficulties presented to the professionalizing statisticians when they sought to argue for a central statistical office.

The second proposal of the Official Statistical Committee, for a "small permanent Board" to ensure "order and harmony," fared slightly better. The Treasury set up a Statistical Enquiry Committee to review Whitehall statistics, but its work was hampered by opposition from other departments and it had no statutory powers to enforce cooperation. With its second and final report the Statistical Enquiry Committee threw in the towel, recommending that the Treasury postpone the appointment of a permanent formal Supervising Committee and proceed only "tentatively and informally" in the face of departmental opposition. In 1907 the president of the Royal Statistical Society, Sir Charles Wentworth Dilke, noted that little had changed since 1871, and that "permanent statistical control" was still lacking.[69] Though he presented one argument in favor of the decentralized status quo,[70] the weight of his evidence supported the opposite case. "The most pressing need," Dilke argued, "is that we should hand over to a Statistical Department those statistics which are collected by various Departments in the course of administrative work, and of which the publication is not necessary fro the purposes of administration." "Permanent statistical direction" under the Treasury, was required, certainly not a "mere meeting of statisticians . . . to constitute an advisory committee."

Dilke was in the chair 7 months later when the academic Arthur Bowley robustly re-stated Dilke's case for a central statistical office. Bowley, who had been briefed by Board of Trade civil servants, repeated the argument on several fronts, addressing the British Association soon after the Royal Statistical Society.[71] He outlined seven criteria for good statistics: rigorous definition of units, homogeneity, universality, stability (over time), comparability (rules about comparing like with like), relativity (rules about comparing unlike quantities), and accuracy.[72] These criteria addressed the "nature and conditions of statistical measurement" and should be read in professionalizing terms. For example, Bowley argued that "the statistical unit is extremely complex, that it is an entity possessing a great number of attributes, and that these attributes need very careful definitions and explanations." A "gardener" includes "'fern decoration artist,' orchid grower, herb grower, horticulturist, propagator, bulb importer, bouquetist, flower farmer, ornamental rock worker . . . market gardener, . . . mushroom spawn manufacturer, cropper, seed picker . . . ," and so on. Only an expert statistician could handle such categories with safety. Likewise, the scientific ideals of homogeneity, universality and accuracy were products of the exertions of experts rather than givens. Universality provides a particularly good example: "the general method of attempting to secure universality is to count all that is practicable and ignore the rest," but, Bowley stated, this would not do: an error of unknown magnitude would be introduced. Instead, careful corrective methods, either by estimating maximum and minimum differences or by sampling, should be applied. The fear was, quite literally, of the "residuum," an important concept in late-Victorian social science: "In the population census an estimate can be made for the travelers and homeless on the census night. . . . For the national income maximum and minimum values could (but have not been) estimated. . . . Such estimates of the residuum are sometimes difficult . . . but nothing is gained by ignoring them."[73] Indeed, what was gained was the extension of disciplinary prestige by bringing such a troublesome category under potential administrative supervision. Sampling, too, was a new technique being pushed by expert statisticians—who theorized what a true random sample should be—although some (even G. Udny Yule) were skeptical and others (including Giffen) were hostile.[74] Thus, Bowley's paper can be read as a professionals' plea, combining codes of correct behavior (e.g., the criteria of good statistics) with the possession of technical expertise, all directed toward the provision of socially useful services (in the last case, a statistical handle on delinquent groups).

One response to Bowley's claim to special expertise on behalf of statisticians was the anger of politicians and newspaper editors. Both groups had been accused of misusing statistics (in other words, of not having the statistical training to understand them properly). Leo Chiozza Money—a remarkable character who added his extra last name "Money" in 1903 when pursuing a complete revision of the Board of Trade returns—suffered on both accounts: he was a Labour MP and had been editor of *Commercial Intelligence.* He objected to the "destructive" criticism made by Bowley. The mixed audience of the Royal Statistical Society, a strength in most respects in that it gave statisticians a very clubbable access to power, could therefore also create problems. At worst such discord might scupper Bowley's familiar project: the establishment of a "Central Thinking Office of Statistics" that "must have cognizance of all the statistics, of more than departmental importance, which are published officially" and "must act with, or direct, or supplant, the statistical officers of the various departments." (As with Purdy in the 1870s, the affliction was with "thinking," the head of the body politic.) Unless the professionalization message had been mistaken, Bowley underlined, "appointments in the office should only be open to those who show the possession or promise of statistical ability, and the Civil Service Commission's examinations should be modified for this purpose."

However, professional statisticians had an even trickier relationship with the "general public." Their anxieties had five roots. First, statisticians needed members of the public to answer their returns, whether on a compulsory or voluntary basis. Second, even as a professional interest group they needed to recruit the public as an ally to press for their centralizing project. Bowley himself later wryly recorded that he "did not think that owing to public opinion the front pages of the halfpenny press would be devoted to the advocation of a Central Statistical Office."[75] "The essential need," Bowley concluded, "was to get the public and political opinion in such a position that the reform would become practical politics." Third, if the politicians were accused of willfully misunderstanding statistics, the public also did not have the training or disposition to grasp them. As Josiah Stamp (who, like Bowley, had attended the new London School of Economics, where his dissertation had awed Graham Wallas) remarked, there were "no statistics without tears," and the "public must not expect that they were going to produce volumes from which anyone could skim off their inferences or their generalizations without any effort or thought on their part." Stamp continued: "You will never say anything worth listening to about these figures until you go away and get a headache over them. . . . The more it was rubbed into people that statistics is to some extent an esoteric science, and not a thing consisting only of tabular statements and collections of figures, the more respect they would have for it."[76] This quotation from Stamp contains the fourth root of anxiety: professional status did not only rest on internal regulation (exams, entry to societies, and so on); it also had a public component, formulated in terms of "respect." Indeed, the disrespectful public could be actively hostile, both in regard to filling in forms and in regard to statisticians' authority. More than one statistician bemoaned "the distrust of all statistics which pervades the public." Finally, the public was more interested in "informative" statistics than in purely "administrative" statistics.

The preceding discussion is relevant to the purposes of this book on two fronts. First, as I have argued, the act of filling in a form, whether it be a farmer totaling his livestock or a householder a census schedule, represents an informational interface between state and individual. (See figure 3.1.) Second, the statisticians aimed to form a powerful expert movement within and without government, bearing comparison to other movements considered in this book.

The rest of this chapter focuses on three episodes, the first only a partial success and the other two failures. The fact that they were failures is significant: they illustrate how an expert movement can fail in its attempt to gain control—or at least extend influence—within government, with the outcome that the group becomes subsumed and specialized. First I examine the Census of Production, a new technique of knowing the economy introduced in the midst of the centralization campaign discussed above. This census had its roots in a concrete case of "abuse" by politicians. Second, I turn to the last years of the Great War, when the centralizing tide reached its high-water mark before receding until further times of intense conflict. Finally, many of the issues come together in an even more ambitious project: centralizing knowledge not merely of the United Kingdom, but of the Empire as a whole.

A "Revolution in Official Statistics": The Census of Production and Inquisitive Government

It is difficult to realize how short a time it is since questions for which we now rely entirely on official statistics were discussed by the ordinary political methods of agitation and advocacy. . . . At least ten million people must, since 1903, have taken part in the Tariff Reform controversy; and that controversy would have degenerated into mere Bedlam if it had not been for the existence of the Board of Trade Returns, with whose figures both sides had at least to appear to square their arguments.

—Graham Wallas, *Human Nature in Politics* (1948 Constable reprint of 1920 edition; first edition published in 1908), p. 259

The first decade of the twentieth century was "a time when the scientific collection of economic data with no immediate and specific administrative object had become politically possible."[77] The crucial question to ask is "Why was this so?" A government collecting knowledge beyond that needed for administration demonstrates that the style and the capacity of government were transmuting, and we should look for changes in technique that accompany any such change. Furthermore, we should look for the groups within and without government that would press for it. The focus of the following case study may be on the minutiae of early-twentieth-century British politics, but at stake is something more important: the possibility and propriety of government's producing general-purpose facts.

The cause of tariff reform split the Conservative party in 1903. The elderly Joseph Chamberlain's vision was of a British Empire transformed into a unified trading bloc protected from the rest of the world by high import taxes. When the Conservative Party remained unpersuaded, Chamberlain resigned as Colonial Secretary and led his Liberal Unionists out of alliance to pursue his goal through a Tariff Reform League. The 1906 election was lost to the Liberals. Tariff Reform was, as Searle rightly points out, a prime example to the ideologues of "national efficiency" of how the state should be active rather than passive: "Economic progress . . . must depend on the conscious purpose and efficient action of the State itself. Government, in a word, should be the brain of the State, even in the sphere of commerce."[78]

Out of this context sprang the Census of Production.[79] It did so in two senses. First, both tariff reform and the census raised the questions of the proper arena of government action and the benefits of free trade. Tariff reform was a direct attack on free trade and appealed to a collectivist, rather than an individualist, conception of government.[80] The Census of Production, likewise, was an extension of government—asking questions of private businesses which had never been asked before, and which an earlier generation of statisticians, such as Giffen and Farrer, both staunch free-traders, would have regarded as iniquitous. Second, tariff reform and the Census of Production connected because of the stresses and opportunities the former created for statisticians. Despite Graham Wallas's assertion in the passage quoted above that only Board of Trade statistics had prevented the political process becoming Bedlam (a madhouse of Commons), statisticians were highly uncomfortable about the use to which statistics were put during the tariff-reform controversy. The feeling was summarized by the Australian statistician T. A. Coghlan before a sympathetic Royal Statistical Society in a discussion following a paper by Yule, in which the latter praised the Census of Production for ending the era during which "we have suffered for so long under the dearth of information as to the real state of the industry and internal trade of the United Kingdom":

> They [the society] had all observed the dishonesty with which men approached the examination of economical questions, affecting controversial politics, such as those affecting Free Trade and Protection. . . . It is a matter of common knowledge that in order to establish certain conclusions, different years were taken as the point of comparison, one year to show progress and another to show depression, as it suited the arguments sought to be enforced.[81]

However, tariff reform also created opportunities for statisticians, since both sides needed statistics for their rhetoric. Arguments centered on the growth or decline of trade, the levels of import and export of goods, and the impact that protectionism would have on labor utilization and welfare, and consequently raised questions about the working class's consumption patterns.[82] The statistics, insisted the statisticians, needed careful, expert handling that could be provided only by professionals. Consider, for example, this 1907 suggestion by Dilke: "The grouping of commodities has led to misconception as to the growth or decline of particular branches of trade. Change and finality are both difficult to procure. New trades develop and old trades are split up; but statistical supervision would have lessened the difficulty. . . ."[83]

Statisticians could carve a niche in which they produced, so they argued, reliable facts for both sides. "In 1903," noted Bowley, "statisticians rather suddenly found their neglected wares in demand."[84] They diagnosed the cause of controversy as a lack of information, and they presented themselves as dispensers of a remedy.

The revolutionary aspect of the Census of Production was that it marked the beginning of the routine generation by the government of statistical information that was not of direct administrative utility—precisely the "informative" statistics that were at issue. Although, in the words of the biographer of A. W. Flux, the census's first organizer, the survey "made possible the quantitative study of the structure and interrelations of British industry," it was not self-evident to many that it fell within the proper remit of government.[85] A tussle ensued over the scope of the census legislation. The Census of Production Bill, introduced in 1906, proposed that wide powers be given to government to obtain information about industry. Yule records that these powers were substantially curtailed during passage through the House of Commons.[86] Though this is true, David Lloyd George, as president of the Board of Trade, managed to negotiate a surprisingly strong census through a sustained charm offensive aimed at Members of Parliament sympathetic to manufacturers' interests. At a meeting on 25 October 1906, Lloyd George listed and discounted the manufacturers' objections. Was the census "too sweeping"? Did it "demand the minutest details about the way in which a man carries on his business"? Did it "demand information with regard to the secrets of a man's trade"? Lloyd George assuaged these anxieties with reassurances that the census was producing aggregate knowledge and that trade secrets would be kept. He even offered solace to the monopolists: where "three or four trades [were] so much in the hands on one man, that to publish aggregate output . . . would mean really to divulge the business [of those firms]," then they would be lumped under "miscellaneous"! Members of Parliament representing manufacturers' interests offered little resistance. The final word was an appeal to transatlantic practices, in this case on the demand to state total horsepower in each factory:

The President: What manufacturer will object to that . . . ?

Mr. Llewellyn Smith: It is given in America, I believe.

The President: Oh yes; America is very much more inquisitive.[87]

Lloyd George was right. In the United States, beginning in 1899, the quinquennial Census of Manufactures, produced by the Bureau of the Census, generated immense quantities of information, which was tabulated by state, by city, and by industrial sector.[88] There were surprisingly few American qualms about asking owners of industry—private citizens—details about salaries, staff numbers, capital invested, and power deployed. (It is how we know, for example, that 77 times as much capital was invested in making typewriters as in making airplanes in 1914.[89])

The Census of Production Act, 1906, driven through Parliament by Lloyd George and over the objections of manufacturers, specified what information could be obtained:

> . . . the nature of the trade or business, and particulars relating to the output, the number of days on which work was carried on, the number of persons employed, and the power used or generated and relating to such other matters of a like nature, except the amount of wages, as may be necessary for the purpose of enabling the quantity and value of production to be ascertained [and] the aggregate estimated value of the materials used and the total amount paid to contractors for work given out to them.

The information to be collected was limited in detail and scope. Agriculture, although not specifically proscribed, was not covered by the census. (Farmers had submitted Agricultural Returns to government voluntarily since the 1860s. Such Returns were compulsory only between 1918 and 1921 and after 1926). However, the limited nature of the first Census of Production is partly a construction of later statisticians, to whom the usefulness of the project was a given. Yule, in 1907, while noting that the Bill had been watered down, called the limitations "minor points" and summarized that, overall, the census was a "valuable . . . addition to the statistical organizations of the United Kingdom."[90] The first census schedules were completed in 1907 by all owners of factories and workshops, by owners, managers, and agents of mines, by builders and construction workers, by persons "who by way of trade or business gives work out to be done elsewhere on his own premises," and by some other specifiable traders. Organization and tabulation of the census was largely the work of H. Fountain at the Board of Trade.[91] By 1908 the Board of Trade could claim to be generating more than 1,000 extra pages of published statistics compared to 1903 when tariff reform agitation had begun. Greeted as a success, the Census of Production was envisaged as a quinquennial event.[92] The audience at the Royal Statistical Society even rubbed their hands at the thought of a biennial census.

The second quinquennial Census of Production was taken in 1912. Work to reduce the raw data to usable statistics was stopped when members of the staff joined the armed forces or were transferred to other departments during the First World War. No census was taken in 1917 for the same reason. By 1919, A. W. Flux, who inherited responsibility for the census from H. Fountain in 1911, was pushing for resumption, but his efforts were rebuffed. A year later he proposed to the Treasury in December that a partial census be taken in 1921, arguing that "it is considered to be of the highest importance in these times of fluctuating trade and values that more adequate information than is presently available . . . should be at the disposal of the Government."[93] Flux could cite several recent examples where government business had been hampered by a lack of information: only a very rough estimate had underpinned the Foreign Dyestuffs (Import Regulation) Bill, tariff reform was based on uncertain figures, and when the Cabinet had asked for an analysis of the effect on industry of a major strike (it was a time of considerable unrest in the docks, mines, and railways) "the lack of recent production figures was seriously felt."[94] Statistics could therefore be tools of social control. The Treasury, however, held that the parlous and rapidly fluctuating economy provided a very good reason *not* to hold an expensive and potentially misleading census. Gentlemanly intuition was a better guide than formal facts. This reasoning overcame the Treasury's own intense need for up-to-date statistics: a "new complete set of statistics showing the postwar situation [would] be really valuable." (The Treasury had no faith in a partial census: it would be "absolutely valueless. . . . No one but Mr. Flux or some similarly minded statistician out of touch with life would have pressed for such a ridiculously useless extravagance."[95])

Pressure mounted on the Treasury to change its policy. The Federation of British Industry and the Army Council joined the call in 1921, but not until 1924, when Sidney Webb, president of the Board of Trade in Ramsay MacDonald's administration, appealed directly to Chancellor of the Exchequer Philip Snowden, were funds granted: ". . . we are crippled without it, and the country . . . will look to us for it and complain if we do nothing."[96] (It is characteristic of the arch-bureaucrat Webb that he foresaw complaints resulting from *not* filling in forms.) For 17 years, because of wartime disruption, reliable detailed knowledge of British business was not available to politicians. Webb could list many questions having an important bearing on policy and on which a Census of Production would throw light: ". . . the relation of our foreign trade to our home production; whether the output has increased or decreased in proportion to the number engaged; the real effects of the price changes since the War . . . ; the amount of the National Income." An article in the *Board of Trade Journal*, written either by Webb or by one of his underlings, picks up the theme:

> For ourselves, we need to see where we stand after the disorganization of a great war, which has made all previous standards antiquated. We need to have a datum-line from which we can measure afresh the progress on which we hope our industries are again entering . . . to all these questions only a Census of Production can give an answer.[97]

The filling in of forms was made a patriotic issue, and manufacturers were called upon to make the Third Census of Production a success.

Censuses of Production followed that of 1907 in 1912, 1924, 1930, and 1935. Beginning in 1933, these roughly quinquennial censuses were supplemented by inquiries made under the Import Duties Act of 1932. By the 1930s, the Board of Trade was compiling various Imperial Statistics, publishing annual and monthly returns of foreign trade, and collecting information from the Home Office and the Ministry of Labour to complement its own censuses for the purpose of preparing an annual Survey of Industrial Development, as well as gathering regular statistics on shipping, navigation, taking an annual census of seamen, compiling lists of casualties to ships and deaths at sea, and publishing a *Board of Trade Journal*, which included an annual estimate of the balance of payments of the United Kingdom.[98] After a brief discussion of contested national centralization, I will turn to the general organization of Imperial Statistics.

Skirmishes over Centralization

Further opportunities for statisticians were created by claims (such as those emanating from Sidney Webb at the Board of Trade) that the aftermath of the Great War was marked by vast and critical gaps in information. In particular, the goal of a central statistical office could be resurrected. The proposals made in the first decade of the twentieth century by Bowley and Dilke had led to little institutional change, although they were significant as expressions of professional ideals. In December 1916, Geoffrey Drage rose to address the Royal Statistical Society. Drage's eye was firmly fixed on postwar opportunities. Again he complained of "the want of a proper system," and he noted that members of the society had "long been pressing for a remedy, namely, a Central Direction."[98] "A new department," he concluded, "is urgently required." His words stirred the audience. They were well aware that the extension of government during wartime meant that the bounds of the politically possible had expanded. Josiah Stamp, a bright academic prospect emerging from the London School of Economics and already in "constant contact" with the Chancellor of the Exchequer and financial secretaries to the Treasury, argued: ". . . anything that was to be done must be done early, and the earlier the better, at the conclusion of the war. . . . It was a propitious time, because a break had to be made with the traditions of the past. . . . That would all be gone, and from that point of view, through the natural break that had occurred . . . there arose an opportunity of starting this scheme. . . ."[100]

Even those who "affected to despise statistics" would have to admit that reconstruction was needed if it they were not to be "chaotic." The suggestion by one John Baker that a deputation be taken to ministers was seconded by Sir Bernard Mallet, the president of the society and the Registrar General—a particularly good example of the close links between statisticians and government: here was the society's president and a senior civil servant instrumental in creating a directly political appeal. As soon as conflict ended—many of the audience to Drage's paper were deeply immersed in war work—the statistical campaign began. In July 1919 an Official Statistics Committee of the Royal Statistical Society met, including Drage, Stamp, and Herbert Samuel (a Member of Parliament).[101] A letter, outlining plans for a petition, along with offprints of Drage's paper, were sent to learned societies, newspapers and prominent members of the establishment. It appeared in the *Times* and the *Morning Post* and offers to sign the petition were already rolling in by the second meeting of the committee held only six days later. Further letters were sent to MPs, large councils and selected financial, insurance and industrial companies. By October, 100 copies of the petition had been printed and sent out, and a question arranged to be asked in the House of Commons, inquiring after the prime minister's response. The petition was presented to the Government, signed by both businessmen and statisticians, requesting a Royal Commission or Parliamentary Committee to investigate the case for a central statistical office. Official statistics, as the foundation of a proper system of civil intelligence, the petitioners argued, must be reorganized. Although Prime Minister Bonar Law had tersely described the scheme as not "practicable" in July, he met the petition with a more guarded answer.[102] Indeed, the petitioners appeared to get what they had asked for. A Committee of Enquiry, appointed by the Cabinet in 1920, was instructed to report on "the specific question of appointing a Committee to enquire into the defects alleged in the Petition . . . and to constitute a Permanent Consultative Committee on the statistical work of Government Departments."

The Committee of Enquiry, chaired by the country's leading actuary (he was both Government Actuary and president of the Institute of Actuaries) Sir Alfred Watson, saw both financial and constitutional difficulties in the petitioners' call for a central statistical office. First, in 1920 the economy was in a parlous state after the Great War, which had not only been cripplingly expensive but had also triggered the loss of key markets. The constitutional problem was more subtle. The Committee distinguished "administrative" statistics, which a department needed to pursue its immediate ends, from "informative" statistics, which were "collected or compiled and issued to meet public demands for information touching the progress and welfare of the community." Informative statistics were therefore those which enabled the community to be beheld as a whole. Each minister was responsible for the departmental budget, which, uncontroversially, would support the production of administrative statistics. A central statistical office, though it "would not interfere with the statistics prepared by a department for its own internal purposes, . . . might wish to secure for national informative purposes, extended or additional statistics which would impose upon that Minister's officers a burden which [the minister] might regard as unreasonable."[103] This constitutional disadvantage—interference with ministerial responsibility—the Committee concluded, outweighed the advantages gained, such as the ability of a central office to regularize statistics across departments and make partial statistics more complete. Support for this position came from a congregation of Whitehall statisticians, which nevertheless emphasized the need for a unified vision:

> The object to be aimed at is the collection and presentation of statistics by each Department in such form, and, so far as the limits of the powers exercised permit, covering such ground, that when they are all brought together, they should constitute a harmonious group, dovetailing at every essential point, so that the statesman, the publicist and the student may have before them a coordinated index of the national life and welfare drawn from the past and serving as a guide for the problems of the future.[104]

Watson's Committee therefore supported the idea of the president of the Board of Trade that interdepartmental cooperation could be encouraged through a Permanent Consultative Committee on Official Statistics (PCCOS)—the emphasis being on "consultative" since it had no powers of recommendation of its own, nor indeed could it receive representations from non-government bodies (such as the Royal Statistical Society). PCCOS could however initiate discussion, consider matters put to it by departments and make suggestions, and was charged with editing an annual index to published government statistics. PCCOS, with members drawn from 23 departments, first met in 1921 and elected Watson as it chair.[105]

The fear, refracted through interdepartmental tensions, that led to the rejection of the central office in favor of the toothless PCCOS was of the growth—and power—of informative statistics. The petitioners considered that a "proper system of civil intelligence," that is to say statistics that went beyond mere administrative by-product, was the responsibility of government, whereas, for their opponents, Watson included, "that proposition has never been accepted in this country." In effect, in a still largely liberal country, there was no mandate for the state to control one of the key means of representation. The episode is a good example of the debates over where the proper boundaries of the state lay: the Royal Statistical Society, and allies the Institute of Actuaries, wanted the state to accept the duty of producing the statistical picture of the nation—a true nationalization. The government, counterintuitively but in line with similar reluctance in other areas, refused to extend its responsibilities, at least publicly. But "informative statistics," a collective representation and public good, still grew. Informative statistics also provide the tool to link the various sections of this chapter: they had special significance for professional statisticians, since they gave them political clout while being produced from within central government. The Census of Production was an early revolutionary example of their prominence, and they were at the heart of discussions over centralization. All these issues reoccurred, with extra vehemence, in the most ambitious project to centralize the production of statistical knowledge: the parallel campaign for an Empire Statistical Bureau.

Knowing the Empire

The public character of informative statistics meant that its producers, the statisticians, were exposed to political controversy. The statistician could take a variety of attitudes to this visibility: from frank admission of the political character of statistical fact, to a stance of scientific objectivity and neutrality. The latter position, of course, would still permit and justify involvement in political debate, since statisticians could argue that objectivity, founded on sound scientific method, was a rational, optimal approach to politics. Such a position is a technocratic one. The fierce controversy over the establishment of a British Empire Statistical Bureau provides a concrete historical episode in which the possibilities and limitations of an imperial statistical technocracy were raised in a series of stark and fascinating exchanges between the opposing camps.

In 1885, Joseph Körösy, the municipal statistician of Pest, Hungary, whose work was regularly read and praised at the Royal Statistical Society, proposed in a paper published by the society's journal a "unification of census record tables" on an international scale. The idea was picked up in Britain by the historian and ethnographer of India, Sir J. Athelstane Baines, who publicized the proposal made at the 1897 St. Petersburg meeting of the International Statistical Institute, in the same journal.[106] For the census of 1901, held in many Empire countries, some coordination was achieved, after the suggestion of Joseph Chamberlain, and the Registrar General compiled a volume of population statistics of the British Empire. "But," noted Baines, "the work was based on material necessarily sporadic, and not prepared with any regard to Imperial comparison [and] lent itself, accordingly, but grudgingly to the statistical handling by which the dry bones of the tables could be brought to life."[107] Baines maintained the pressure of the previous decade, bemoaning in 1901 that each national census "works upon its own system with an eye to its own statistical requirements—too often reduced by financial considerations to their lowest terms, and without regard to their ultimate coordination with those of the rest of the Empire."[108] He saw hope in the Registrar-General's plan to hold a conference of census officials "of this country and the Britains beyond the Seas."

Overall, argued Baines, "it is not that information is lacking, or that there are not means of obtaining more, but each unit is kept, statistically speaking, isolated from the rest. We have here not the greatest variety of race to be found under any single rule, but our own kin living under the most varied climatic and economic conditions: yet it is a constant source of wonder amongst foreign statisticians that so little effort should be made to present those who, presumably, are most interested in the matter any succinct and comprehensive view. . . ." Baines wanted "in all but the wilder tracts a minimum demand in the way of information regarding the native communities," and this information "uniformly made" was to be "compiled into identical tables." ("Fuller detail, no doubt, will be collected regarding the British and other white population, to be separately dealt with.") Baines's arguments were received sympathetically, with Archer Bellingham of the Statistical Department of the GRO urging that the Under Secretaries of State for the Colonies and for Foreign Affairs impress on the authorities of colonies the "desirability and importance of taking a census in 1911" and that each previous Colonial Report be scrutinized for defects, and standardized: "the Colonies should thus be asked to supply tables on lines suggested and prescribed by this

Office."[109] The pressure was for imperial statistics to be more coordinated, and thereby comparable.

Limited statistics relating to imperial trade had been collected and published by the Board of Trade, and, of course, by the administrations of the various countries of the Empire. Though intermittent calls for an Empire Statistical Bureau had been made in the first decade of the twentieth century, the first concrete proposal emerged from the Dominions Royal Commission, set up in 1913 and which made its final report in 1917. The representatives from the United Kingdom, Canada, New Zealand, South Africa, and Newfoundland examined issues of trade, but found that its enquiry was severely hampered by either "defective" or incomparable statistics, and after raising the possibility of a Bureau concluded "we are of the opinion that the creation of some office of the kind is eminently desirable."[110] This call led to a conference of Empire statisticians, who were guided by the pronouncement of the Imperial War Conference, where ministers from all the five countries above, plus Australia and India, had met in 1918. These ministers at first passed a resolution proposed by the Canadians, agreeing "in principle to the establishment of an Imperial Statistical Bureau under the supervision of an Inter-Imperial Committee," but later changed this wording, allowing the suggested conference of statisticians to consider the arguments for and against a Bureau.

To ease understanding, I will label the two camps "pragmatists" and "technocrats." For the gentlemanly pragmatists, statistics were by their nature political: statistics did not have a distinct, superior status separate from other sorts of knowledge brought to bear in negotiation. If they appealed to authority, it was to an experiential or constitutional rather than expert form (witness Watson's earlier insistence on ministerial responsibility). The statistical technocrats, on the other hand, argued that since statistics were grounded in the scientific method they could be politically neutral. Indeed, as we shall see, the technocrats went further, claiming that interpretation of statistical facts, as well as the facts themselves, could be objective. As such statistics were stable artefacts that could appear to travel and speak for themselves. The pragmatists disagreed: statistics were fragile and interpretation contingent on local imperial politics. The pragmatist model of imperial authority was the local human administrator, who, although trained at college in Britain, embodied skills and knowledge of governance gained through experience.[111] The technocrats, on the other hand, were confident that the stability of statistics meant that power could be centralized: on the basis of statistics someone in London, say, could reliably guide policy in the imperial periphery. The technocrats often repeated and amplified comments by foreign statisticians, apparently amazed that so few statistics were centrally collected about the British Empire—recalling

Baines's phrase, a "constant source of wonder," above. This attitude is revealing, since a number of explanatory models to account for the imperial statistical movement can be proposed: if large quantities of statistics were *not* needed to coordinate an Empire, then an explanation of imperial statistics projects by appeal to instrumental utility is undermined. Other possibilities are opened up: were statistics an expression of hopes of coordination—holistic visions of unity—rather than administrative need? Was there perhaps a requirement for the *appearance* of control rather than control per se?[112] A way of approaching such questions is to ask who would be interested in conjuring complete statistical pictures of empire? More narrowly, differences over the nature of knowledge therefore would shape attitudes to plans for a British Empire Statistical Bureau. The statistical technocrats, confident about the objective collection and interpretation of imperial statistics, demanded a strong Bureau. The skeptical pragmatists wanted a weak Bureau, if at all, and one restricted to mere collection of data. The pragmatists were mostly senior civil servants—generalists—from the large Whitehall departments. The technocrats were a more motley collection: some Whitehall civil servants, usually of middle rank, dominion ministers and academic statisticians. There is some evidence that many of the technocrats were more interested in eugenics than the pragmatists—which might help explain why they were keen on interpreting, as well as collecting, imperial statistics.

On 13 February 1920 the British Empire Statistical Conference considered a draft memorandum written by the technocrat Herbert Vincent Reade, Assistant Secretary at the Board of Customs and Excise, outlining a British Empire Statistical Bureau. Reade's draft report took inspiration from George Handley Knibbs, an Australian working at the Commonwealth Bureau of Census and Statistics, part of the Department of Home and Territories at Melbourne. As early as 1910, Knibbs, then president of Section G1 of the Australian Association for the Advancement of Science, had eulogized the increased spread of statistics in public life.[113] (He also looked forward hopefully to future eugenic possibilities, quoting Punnett approvingly: "Permanent progress is a question of breeding rather than pedagogics," arguing "we should do well in this young country, where we have the British race transplanted, to watch the evolution of the people in an appropriate [statistical] manner, and a beginning . . . will shortly be made by the systematic examination of school children from an anthropometric and hygienic point of view.") In 1918, emerging from war, Knibbs could still see threats to the Empire "arising from monopolistic tendencies, or from a deliberately hostile people whose methods are assiduous and thorough."[114] This thinly veiled characterization of corporate America and militant Germany, respectively, the perceived threat from which

I think is key to grasping why the issue of strengthening ties—or control, even—of the empire was raised—was contrasted with a British imperial identity disadvantaged by liberty:

> The free spirit of the British people has expressed itself in relation to the statistical effort of various parts of the Empire, by great independence of action, often resulting in the focusing of attention on the immediate requirements of the individual parts, to exclusion of attention to the more or less intimate connection between one part and another. Not only was this element of interdependence insufficiently studied, but very often the statistical data necessary to disclose the trend of the affairs of the Empire as a whole—and indeed also of individual parts thereof—left much to be desired.

Only by comprehending the Empire "in detail and as a whole, but also in regard to the mutual relations of its several members," through a British Empire Statistical Bureau, "can a hope be founded of that State being sufficiently informed" to avert crisis. The Bureau would be staffed by experts in statistical theory, technique of collection and compilation, pure and applied mathematicians, statistical editors, linguists and people skilled in draftsmanship and graphics. A Director headed the hierarchical structure, the base of which had compilers who "would in their turn direct and control the clerical and computational effort of a large number of clerks and computers." While even Knibbs considered the imposition of "*identical* methods of collection and compilation" impracticable, the Bureau would ensure "such a degree of *uniformity of method*" that statistics of trade, production, transport, communications, population, labor, industry, finance (and later education, legislation, public justice, hospitals, social insurance, public hygiene and naval and military defense), would all be viewed under a single imperial gaze. Knibbs regarded the benefits of extensive use of calculating machines through the Empire Bureau as self-evident.[115] This was the model which inspired Reade's draft report which lay for discussion before the conference.

The leading member of the pragmatist faction, Sir Alfred Watson (the government actuary who pulled the teeth of the PCCOS) was unhappy. Watson incisively focused on a proposal of Reade's that "such a Bureau would not merely assemble the records, but would apply the analytical [statistical] methods which have been developed," or, in other words, would go beyond aiming merely to "coordinate statistics and to publish a year book" and instead "investigate and criticize the enormous number of social phenomena which will come before [the bureau's director] from all parts of the British Empire."[116] This stronger bureau raised, for Watson, several potential areas of conflict. First, the proposal marked an encroachment of government on the statistical work of individuals. It was "something in the nature of the disestablishment of the private investigator, and the substitution for him of a public official." This nationalization would "never eliminate" the private individual statistician, a desirable outcome anyway since "many private investigators can speak with authority quite as great as that which any public official can possess." We have seen above that the interdependence of official and non-official statisticians characterized British statistics, but, in Watson's reading, was challenged by the arguments of the technocrats. Furthermore, it was not "as though these analytical methods which have been developed by the advances of statistical science in recent years are all absolutely agreed." The result of diversity, different "statistical schools" as well as the public-private split, would be a "great deal of violent dissent outside and a good deal of friction within." Worse still, there would be an ungentlemanly descent into "quite unscientific language." Sir Alfred Watson felt he did not want to be "involved in that sort of thing." He was ready to exploit differences within the theoretical commitments of the expert movement of statisticians to dispose of the proposed bureau. Reade, the technocrat who had drafted the memorandum could not deny that there would be conflict, but refused to accept that the Bureau should "leave the field entirely to private persons." Indeed, "in statistics, as in everything else, controversy is very healthy: it is a necessary condition of advance."

The second area of potential conflict stemmed from the Bureau's Director relations with other outlying parts of imperial administration. The technocrat faction envisaged the Director to be a "super-statistician," able to understand both statistics and their scientific interpretation, and therefore claim a legitimate rational authority. Watson struck at the foundations of this authority. By offering broad interpretations the Director would "begin to rub up sores." Imagine, Watson argued, the local reaction:

> It would be said at once that [the director] could not know the local conditions, he was a theorist sitting in London thousands of miles away from where things were going on, and it would [be] utterly out of place for him with his limited range of comprehension of local difficulties to attempt to draw conclusions, from mere figures, as to the particular social and economic conditions of the people whose ire he had excited. They would say of course that figures can prove anything . . . and they would certainly say it in the more distant parts of the Empire, with the comment that figures done by some fellow in London were not worthy for a moment of local consideration.[117]

To support his argument for the fragility of statistics as a strategy of communication over distance, Watson cited an example from his own experience. His Irish representative, James Gray Kyd, Actuary to the Irish Insurance Commission, had written a "perfectly sound" report on infant mortality in Dublin that "did not please the political people." The local politicians did not challenge the findings of the young actuary, but because he was a "Scotsman and a representative of a Government Department centered in London" they rejected them forthwith, because, quoted Watson, he was "out of sympathy with the aspirations of the Irish people."[118] Sylvanus Percival Vivian, one of the architects of National Registration, supported Watson on this point. Even if the Bureau initially only advised the countries of the Empire, it would gradually encroach: "a body which, in the first place is under the liability to give advice . . . tends to become a body which has a right to advise . . . , and such a body imperceptibly develops into one which entertains the expectation that its advice will be taken."[119] The technocrats did not agree that this would be a problem, since Dominion statisticians would be integrated in the Bureau: Cousins, a statistician from South Africa and a member of the technocratic tendency, foresaw "cordial cooperation" based on a common ground of agreed modern statistical method. Just as in the imperial case, if the Bureau's findings conflicted with the interests of another domestic government department, and questions were asked in Parliament, the relevant minister would be compelled to defend their own civil servants, against the Bureau which "would at once be in trouble." The political nature of statistics meant that the Director would inevitably be drawn into conflict.

The technocrats' counter-argument rested on the particular qualities of the Director. Although not a "super-man," noted Knibbs, the Director "must be a professional statistician, with a commanding knowledge of statistical method, who has in addition common-sense and administrative ability." Just as a captain must know engineering—the basic mechanics—to fully control a ship (engineering qualifications were, by 1920, compulsory for Naval Commanders), "it requires knowledge [of all levels] to direct," an almost cybernetic epigram. "The characteristic," said Knibbs, "of progress in control is that we are realizing the necessity of the more difficult and higher function being associated with the easier one." Robert Hamilton Coats, the Canadian delegate, listed the attributes of the super-statistician: alongside Reade and Knibbs's gentlemanly "discretion, tact and common-sense" and indisputable mathematical expertise, he added an appreciation of the "broad economic and social drift of his time." With facts tempered by political understanding, but speaking from an authority founded on objective statistical method, how could such a super-statistician be gainsaid? In any controversy the Bureau Director would win through rational expertise. The pragmatists gave such technocratic sentiment short shrift. As Watson bluntly responded: "where any central Bureau tabulates views based on its investigations as to the social conditions prevailing . . . in any particular part of the Empire which views are inconvenient to the politicians concerned, or obnoxious to them" they will be challenged "promptly." In other words, the pragmatists thought the technocrats were politically naive.

Third, Watson argued that statistician-led technocracy would not be *transparent*, although not quite in our sense of the word. Though "we," meaning his fellow experts, "can understand and follow the very valuable mathematical demonstrations which are produced . . . on statistical subjects but when we talk to the general public or to members of Parliament or even to Cabinet Ministers, about skew curves and variants and correlation . . . we are simply talking to the air." The non-expert "will listen to what you say but it will make no impression on their minds because they do not understand it." Until the statisticians possessed a transparent, widely comprehensible language they could not claim legitimate authority in a democracy. Crucially, although Watson did not—perhaps could not—express the point in this way, the generalists already *did* share the language of (most) politicians, a language of shared assumptions inculcated at private schools and university. The division was therefore also between two sorts of universalism: the pragmatist's generalist gentlemanly language and the technocrat's objectivity claimed through possession of specialist technique.

The technocrats won the vote, and in April 1920 the Cabinet decided to put the question to the same committee, chaired by Watson, which had unanimously rejected the proposal for a central statistical office within Whitehall. Interdepartmental politics had stalled that idea, but the idea of a British Empire Statistical Bureau opened up wider options, some of which would not necessarily founder because of opposition from powerful departments of state. After a year's prolonged deliberations the two factions found it impossible to agree, and two reports were issued. The position of the pragmatists formed the Majority Report, signed by Watson, J. George Beharrell (Director-General of Finance and Statistics, Ministry of Transport), Michael Heseltine [later at the Ministry of Health], James Rae (Assistant Secretary, Treasury), Percy Jesse Rose (probably representing the Secretary of State for Scotland) and Vivian. The technocrats submitted a Minority Report, signed by William H. Coates (Director of Statistics and Intelligence, Inland Revenue Department), Alfred William Flux (Assistant Secretary of the Statistics Department, Board of Trade), John Hilton (Assistant Secretary and Director of Statistics, Ministry of Labour), and Reade.

The central point at issue between the pragmatists and the technocrats was the nature of interpretation: "What does it mean and how is it to be exercised?"[120] "Statistics," the technocrats argued, "may be called the science which measures the social organism, regarded as a whole; or the science of averages. The primary business of the statistician is to furnish facts, to collect, arrange and describe, to present and weigh evidence. The word 'interpretation' signifies the explanation of what the figures mean, and of the statistical inferences which can be properly drawn from them."[121]

Whereas the pragmatists in the Majority Report claimed that interpretation involved "critical powers in regard to any policies of which the tendencies may be statistically illustrated"[122], that is to say interpretation was not neutral with regard to policy, the technocrats denied this. How they did so is important. Science formed part of the solution: "the interpretations furnished will be directed towards explanations of [the data's] characteristics, their limitations, and their comparability . . . a sifting of the information presented. . . . A Scientific examination of the data published will content itself with an impartial statement of all the points emerging, and will not attempt to arrive at any conclusions, much less to issue authoritative and didactic pronouncements, on thorny or controversial issues of a political character."[123] This might be read as a self-imposed limitation, by the technocrats, of the sorts of investigations made by the Bureau. But interestingly, this reading would be wrong: the technocrats believed that through apolitical representation political controversy would not be encountered. It was not the case that science would guarantee objectivity up to, but no further than, the point of political controversy. Instead the scientific application of statistical expertise—and therefore uncontroversial interpretation—would be "ensured" by the right constitution of the Bureau.[124] "Representation" therefore had a deliberate double sense: political and pictorial. When the signatories of the Minority Report wrote that "the development of organizations and machinery representing the Empire as a whole is in its infancy" they meant it in the political sense—of making manifest the interests of the member states of the Empire—but they deployed it to make the case for the pictorial: to construct a statistical image of the Empire as a whole.

The differences over interpretation therefore stemmed from differences over the political underpinnings of knowledge. The technocrats considered science and apolitical representation to go hand in hand, making uncontroversial interpretation possible. They therefore, for example, saw no problem in regarding the three existing Imperial bureaus (Entomology, Mycology and Mineral Resources) as precedents for the much more ambitious British Empire Statistical Bureau.[125] The pragmatists began from a different foundation: statistical knowledge drew meaning from the political contexts of its creation or deployment. The study of the fungi of the Empire rarely raised political problems between nations or departments. An Imperial Bureau of Mycology might therefore operate safely. But the nature, scope of the subject matter and functions of a Statistical Bureau were "a different matter" and the pragmatists rejected the analogy. Similarly because the pragmatists assumed that conflicts in interpretation would inevitably arise, only a Council of the Bureau chaired by the Prime Minister of the United Kingdom and drawing its membership from High Commissioners of the Dominions would be suitable. The Bureau would therefore wastefully duplicate existing political structures. Worse still the Prime Minister bearing responsibility, on the ministerial model, for the Bureau would lead to constitutional problems:

On the one hand the Prime Minister, as the Chairman of the Council of the Bureau, would presumably have to accept responsibility for the decisions of a majority of the Council. On the other hand, the Prime Minister would be responsible to the Imperial Parliament for bringing to the notice of the Council the views of the Home Government in regard to any proposed publications. In a dispute between the Home Government and the Bureau the Prime Minister would apparently be committed to representing the views of both the contending parties.[126]

The Minority Report ridiculed this idea, since, again, interpretation was not political.

Before moving in it is worth considering what was at stake in knowing the Empire. Remember that the campaign for a British central statistical office was contingent on Whitehall politics. This factor was far less important in the imperial case: although, for example, the Board of Trade, in favor of an Empire Statistical Bureau, preferred it to be under their administration, in line with the board's domestic strategy. Likewise other British departments of state either welcomed the proposal (e.g. the Home Office) or accepted it while raising reasonable queries: the Board of Education argued that the severity of the task of collating educational statistics had been underestimated. Only the Ministry of Health and the Ministry of Agriculture and Fisheries objected vehemently, both raising the "interpretation" argument characteristic of the pragmatists. (Also, only the Ministry of Health pointed out that there was potential overlap with the international statistical offices of the new League of Nations.) In general Whitehall departments were willing to pass to the Bureau all their published statistics, most of their unpublished ones, advise on technical issues and requested consultation in the event of Bureau interpretation. The overall attitude was, however, lukewarm: the push for producing detailed statistical summaries of the Empire came from elsewhere. An argument from narrow utility to government departments will not explain the movement for Imperial statistics. I argue that it was an alliance between technocrats (the technocrats in the home departments), and Dominion Ministers motivated by trade issues and economic anxieties, and an "imperial holism" shared by both. This vision of Empire, imagined as an potentially efficient whole, can be found most clearly expressed in the Minority Report:

The main purpose of the establishment of an Empire Bureau of Statistics is the circulation throughout the Empire of full, accurate and comparable information as to its population, its natural resources, its capacity for production and manufacture, its communications, labor, finance, etc. The collection of information, sifted, analyzed and coordinated, is designed to solve one of the great difficulties of the past, namely, the absence of that knowledge of facts brought into their proper shape, which is the essential preliminary to action. The objects sought are the promotion of trade, the closer unity of the Empire, a clearer comprehension of mutual difficulties, a knowledge of the problems that present themselves in various parts of the Empire, their magnitude, their peculiarities and the methods being adopted for their solution.[127]

This was the assessment of technocrats in the home departments: that a clear detailed statistical representation of the Empire was both a means of unification but also a prerequisite to political action. The political action envisaged—technocratic, rational, efficient and information-intensive—was to mutate in Britain and elsewhere into "planning," but in 1918 it had already gained socialistic overtones, as Joseph Cook, the Australian Minister of the Navy, explained to the Imperial War Conference:

I can see the function which this Imperial Bureau will fulfill and it is a very useful one. . . . It is in the direction of forecasting the Empire's requirements. . . . That is to say, not only ascertaining the facts from time to time, but so shaping these facts as to be of use to the traders, the producers of the Empire, and even to suggest suitable employment for the capital of the Empire. At present we are . . . haphazard in those higher spheres of State action. It seems to me that a little socialism would not be a bad thing at all as it applies to this question of ascertaining the Empire's requirements, the Empire's resources. . . .

With their majority on the home committee investigating the proposed British Empire Statistical Bureau the pragmatists defeated the technocrats. No Bureau was set up. (Perhaps the Empire Marketing Board, started in 1926, provided an alternative route—propaganda—to picturing the Empire.[128] Perhaps, as satirized in Kipling's short story "Pig," the tensions between imperial statisticians were too great.[129]) There was, however, some consolation for the imperial statisticians: the fact that they were able to meet afforded the opportunity to plan and coordinate their census work.[130] The Registrar-General was able to report that "agreement was reached with regards to the major points upon which uniformity of action within the Empire is desirable, and plans were concerted to secure that common Imperial requirements were, as far as possible, observed in the results of the separate censuses of the several Dominions, Colonies, and Protectorates."[131] (The only cloud on this statistical horizon was Ireland, where conflict had made such improved coordination "impracticable.")

Conclusion

The campaign for an imperial statistical bureau revealed tensions within the expert movement of statisticians. I have noted that the movement was marked by interdependence between official and non-official statisticians. But in the early to mid nineteenth century this alliance would be best likened to a gentlemen's club, with the Statistical Society of London, and its journals, as its center. From the late nineteenth century there was an increasing emphasis on statisticians as professionals-in-government, as a center for statistical production, as a provider of resources and coordination, and government as a guarantor of the good status of statistical knowledge. (The middle-class professional values embedded in statistics help explain why many statistical returns were greeted with hostility by representatives of labor and commerce.) The appearance of the Labour Statistical Department, the Census of Production, and the technocrats' position in the imperial debate all provide evidence for this shift. In the last case, the role of the private investigator was defended by the pragmatists (that is, the generalists), while the technocrats failed to make their case that government statisticians could be trusted to speak impartially and objectively.

It was partly this lack of consensus, but also a hostile economic context that led to the collapse of the imperial scheme. While the global economic challenge felt by the British empire from America and Germany created the prospect of an Empire linked and strengthened by coordinated statistical knowledge, the economy immediately following the First World War was extremely turbulent—many government services were cut by the "Geddes axe," for example, making a commitment to an expensive empire bureau far less likely. Finally, tensions within the Empire, with the dominions in particular pulling away from London influence, contributed to the demise of an Imperial statistical center. However, the lack of consensus within the expert movement of statisticians was profound, because, I shall argue below, a movement that appealed to technocratic specialism was irreconcilable with the founding organizational principle of British public service.

Statisticians such as Bowley and Yule urged the Board of Trade to adopt the most sophisticated techniques available, in particular random sampling and index numbers—techniques that could handle the greater amount of incoming data and be used to go beyond mere descriptive statistics to offer deeper analysis. I have argued that these demands should be interpreted as claims to professional authority, and MacKenzie has shown that a professional consensus on the validity of the new mathematical theory of statistics was contested throughout the period discussed.[132] They were certainly opposed by the Treasury, which feared a challenge to the generalist-mechanical split, in this spirit. The fact that statisticians such as Bowley and Yule had less and less influence within the Civil Service suggests that the Treasury-imposed regime seriously interrupted and *limited* the achievements of statisticians as an expert movement within government. But the problem of expertise within government was not reducible to mere interdepartmental politics, since the generalist ideal was accepted, internalized and became part of the self-rationalization of non-Treasury officials. For example Hubert Llewellyn Smith of the Board of Trade argued that the use of sophisticated statistical theory made labor intelligence appear the "monopoly of a professional clique" and unintelligible to other users, including policy makers.[133] Such arguments were echoed by Watson in the debate over the empire statistical bureau. In both cases, coherence, relevance, and intelligibility were judged more important than methodological rigor. Statistical innovation was sacrificed to the generalist philosophy. But it also had to be adapted to the other side of the split: the mechanicals. As the economist Alfred Marshall complained to Arthur Bowley of the London School of Economics courses that trained official statisticians, they were "designed for officials in public employment whose province is the faithful execution of orders rather than a profound investigation of the principles on which those orders should be based. . . . The training emphasizes mechanical methods of investigation, i.e. those in which highly specialized calculating machines—whether made of cog-wheels or of torpid flesh and blood can be set to tunes based on formulae to grind out results which are officially pure and above reproach."[134]

Glimpsed here is the subjection of one expert movement (statisticians), but also the beginning of a second (the mechanizers). The latter was much better adapted to the fundamental organizational principle—the generalist-mechanical split—of the Civil Service.

In 1916, at the same moment as Drage addressed the Royal Statistical Society, Alfred Flux was being questioned by a Select Committee on Publications. The Chair of the Committee wondered aloud about the mass of statistics that flooded from Whitehall departments, after quizzing Flux, whether there was not a "brain big enough to assimilate the whole of them." He asked another witness this question:

> Before the war, you know this subject was very much under discussion; the avalanche of statistics that was issued every year was so great that it was quite evident that

there must be some sort of reorganization in their preparation and presentment, or else we should be snowed under, spending our lives as Members of Parliament in reading an infinity of undigested details. It seems to me a necessity that there should be a very skilled and very capable Department of Government to control the issue of statistics?[135]

The idea of an "avalanche" of numbers is a familiar one to historians of science and technology: it was an abiding image of Ian Hacking's *The Taming of Chance*, who located the deluge in the middle of the nineteenth century, and it is also recognizable in modern anxieties about "information overload."[136] All claims of this sort have their historical specificity, and one must always ask: who has to gain from assertions that information is chaotic, overwhelming and out of control? The answer is usually found in the expert groups who offered solutions.

The expert group examined in this chapter was of statisticians, who drew on strong links with government from the nineteenth century. "Gradually," around the 1830s, concludes Eastwood, "central government exchanged a partnership with the localities for a partnership with experts."[137] Although they were professionalizing, the boundaries within statistical institutions remained fluid: audiences at the Royal Statistical Society heard papers from civil servants, politicians, barristers, academics and other members of the elite. As a professional movement in the late nineteenth and early twentieth century, the statisticians were deeply intertwined with the profound changes in the nature of government. Statistics were shaped, and were shaped by, the growth of government and the assumption of new administrative responsibilities. There was a reinforcing, circular relationship: the growth of the state depended on increased capacities for knowing, which in turn required more employees to generate knowledge. Some statisticians set their face against the changes—we have seen how Farrer and Giffen remained committed to laissez-faire. However, even Giffen, perhaps prompted by inter-departmental rivalries, made arguments that statistical production by government could, and should, be centralized and expanded. The growth of government therefore presented opportunities that the statisticians could exploit: they could claim that their expertise was crucial to the success of the new state, and three examples were examined above: the failed campaigns to centralize national statistics, the successful innovation of the Census of Production, and failed proposal for a British Empire Statistical Bureau.

The shift from the night-watchman state of the early and mid nineteenth century to the regulatory state of the later decades had statistical consequences: trade statistics and criminal statistics, for example, were substantially reorganized, but also transformed. The process was two-way: early statistical accounts of crime provided crucial resources for proponents of reforming and reorganizing the police.[138] Historians have noted that the nature of statistics changed in this period from enumerative to analytic. Criminal statistics are exemplary: numbers of crimes were pored over in the expectation that patterns—natural laws—would emerge: the "recidivist" was found.[139] Analytical statistics were tied to the centralizing campaign—institutional and epistemological aspects locked together. For example, in discussion after Bowley's proposal for a Central Thinking Office of Statistics, Coghlan remembered "having to look into the work of a department dealing with criminal statistics, and he found that when a person was accused, every appearance of the accused and every application made on his behalf was counted as a new case. Consequently, the statistics were greatly swollen; and perhaps the same man . . . appeared 20 times as a "criminal." Was that sort of thing to be continued?"[140] The statisticians' answer was, of course, "no," not if they were given custody of a central statistical office.

It was the context of tariff reform, the key regulatory issue of early-twentieth-century politics, that provided a clear example of statistics and the regulatory state: both the Census of Production and, because issues of imperial preference arose, imperial statistics were shaped in this context. (The subsequent shift from a regulatory state to a welfare state had even deeper implications for the British politics of information, as is discussed later in this book.) To some contemporaries there was new significance to the politics of numbers in the early twentieth century: Graham Wallas's remark that official statistics had only lately replaced the "ordinary political methods of agitation and advocacy" is a provocative one. In fact, as we see in the next chapter when Cabinet arguments centered on figures of conscriptable men became, numbers and agitation were more often complementary than opposites. However, that such a claim could be made in an influential book provides ample illustration of the opportunities available to the statisticians.

What is the significance of this chapter for the argument of this book? There are four interconnected aspects which answer the question: one social, one epistemological, and two are part discursive and part technological. First, the statisticians were a social movement of experts which aimed to transform government. They claimed a special expertise and sought influential positions in government: the super-statistician possessing an interpretative gaze over the British Empire was perhaps the most ambitious. As such the statisticians were a technocratic movement in the strict sense of their desire for government by experts. However, reality did not match their ambition: no central statistical office was established (until, as we see in chapter 6, the Second World War) and imperial statistics remained merely "coordinated." The expert movement of statisticians did not fit easily into a Civil Service organized by the principle of the generalist-mechanical split. The movement faltered at precisely the moments when this principle was appealed to. Unlike the central expert movement of this book, the proponents of mechanized business efficiency, the statisticians were always hampered by the fact that to claim special expertise in government they were open to being labeled as specialists. However, as we see below the relative failure of the statisticians created peculiar conditions, ones which later movements would exploit. Furthermore, statistical production would increasingly depend on the application of machines: the Registrar-General in 1910, for example, insisted to the Treasury that only arithmometers "made it possible for the Department to cope with the increasing requirements for statistics."[141] We will see shortly why the Treasury might be receptive to such a stance.

The second argumentative thread which links this chapter to the book's thesis concerns what kinds of knowledge were produced. The politics of Whitehall shaped the important distinction between administrative and informative statistics. Administrative statistics were made merely to guide the day-to-day activities of departments. Informative statistics, according to the protagonists, broke over these boundaries: they needed, so it was argued, to be brought together to provide a unified picture of the nation—a picture even the public should be allowed to appreciate. Just as the encounter between subject and government became a more everyday occurrence, so government statisticians had a greater hand in providing a coordinated image of the nation. It is no coincidence that the timing of this shift is well known to historians as a period of intensification of nationalism and imperialism.[142]

The drive for late-Victorian and Edwardian nationalism came from economics and threat to British interests from Germany and the United States. Here the third argumentative thread appears, one woven tightly with the last: Britain's data was repeatedly labeled as "chaotic," a word with negative overtones: New Liberalism regarded old liberal laissez-faire as inefficiently organized. Order was also associated with Prussian militarism (the engine of unified Germany), and corporate America. "Chaos" therefore had specific and contingent historical meanings. The importance for this book is that British "chaos" marked a discursive opening that could be filled by protagonists of "order." There were many contenders. The "national efficiency" movement offered one solution; the statisticians, with their proposal for centralized institutions of knowledge, offered another. (In other countries, other solutions predominated, for example—put incredibly crudely: militarism in Germany, the corporation in the United States and sociology in France.[143]) It will be argued in the following chapters that mechanizers made the most of this discursive opportunity. References to machines formed a relatively unimportant corollary to the arguments presented by the centralists. Bowley in 1908, for example, noted that "part of the expense of more elaborate tabulation could be avoided by the use of machinery. It is surely rational to employ intelligent persons where intelligence is needed, and machinery where the work is mechanical."[144] Eight years later, he expanded on this division of labor:

> He pictured [the Central Statistical Office] as a machinery office, and thought there would have to be a considerable number of machines in it. There were very few in the Government service at the present time. There should be every aid to calculation, and then we should be able to get our returns more quickly as well as more adequately.[145]

We will see in chapter 5 what happened when this invitation was taken up.

Finally, the critics argued that it was the "head" of government which was afflicted: in the 1870s this was Parliament and by the 1900s this meant the great departments of Whitehall (this move in itself was significant in that it marked the shift of political, if not constitutional, power). The remedy proposed by the statisticians was centralization: a "Central Thinking Office." At present this is left as an observation—one of political neurology perhaps—but in chapter 6, we will see how under radically different political conditions, such a remedy would be seen as necessary.

4

"One Universal Register": Fantasies and Realities of Total Knowledge

In the middle of the First World War, a committee of bureaucrats, including Beatrice Webb, could list with disapproval eighteen *disjointed* registers of people, held for administrative purposes. Some were collected by the lowest tier of local government bodies and mapped by medical area: the Urban and Rural Sanitary Districts. These registers included Notification of Births, the Housing Register, the Food Control Register, the Notification of Infectious Diseases, as well as the new leviathan, the National Register, of which more below. Maternity and Infant Welfare Records, a TB Register, a Mentally Deficients Register, the School Attendance Lists, each had their own geography based on locations of institutions such as dispensaries or local government offices. Three other registers were organized by parish, but by different officers: the Electoral Register managed by Registration Officers, the Rate Books by overseers of parishes or Urban District Council, and the Valuation Lists by a Poor Law Assessment Committee. The Poor Law generated further lists of people, such as that of recipients of Poor Law Relief. The relatively ancient Registers of Births, Deaths and Marriages was also now under the authority of the Poor Law Boards of Guardians.[1] Finally, new and extensive records of persons had accompanied the introduction of welfare provisions in the 1910s. A trio of registers formed a safety net of files: Old Age Pension records and the National Health and Unemployment Insurance Registers. The model technique of government—the registry—had been turned from managing bureaucratic objects, such as files, to the problem of managing the people in a welfare state.[2]

Many of this list of lists were new, the product of late-nineteenth-century medical and political movements. Their implementation and use were often highly local, indeed only one register authority was a central Whitehall department rather than a local body: the Unemployment Register controlled by the Ministry of Labour. Even then the practical use was local, at the labor exchanges that had very recently spread across the country. What upset the committee of bureaucrats was that these lists did not join up. One of their number, the Registrar-General Sir Bernard Mallet, argued that what was needed was "one universal register" in which the administrative information needed by central and local government would be held together and cross-referenced. This chapter examines the fate of this scheme, alongside other appeals to list and know the nation's subjects. The tension was between a totalizing fantasy, invoking a myriad of possibilities afforded by a central register, and the pragmatics and politics of administration. It is just as essential to understand the thought and actions of a civil servant such as Mallet in a wider cultural context that encouraged fantasies of total knowledge, as it is to view his schemes in the familiar Whitehall environment.

This wider cultural context was military, museological, imperial and in crisis. In the nineteenth century the British Museum was perhaps the most important ideological institution of empire. Founded in 1753 on the death of Sir Hans Sloane, the Museum had begun with three collections (Sloane's eclectic possessions, and the libraries of the Cotton and Harley families), but even then the classificatory policy encompassed all the secular world: books, manuscripts and "Natural and Artificial Productions." In the eighteenth century, a monstrous collection of objects was donated: Egyptian mummies (the first in 1756), a hornet's nest found in Yorkshire "more compleat than are usually met with," part of a tree gnawed by a beaver, a Chinese bowl fire-damaged in the Lisbon earthquake, an unburnt brick supposedly from the Tower of Babel, a chicken with two heads and a "monstrous pig from Chalfont St. Giles."[3] To such oddities were added weighty collections, such as the Royal Library, or the artefacts gathered by Captain James Cook on his Pacific voyages, as well as uniquely important objects, such as the Rosetta Stone (a spoil of war, in 1802). In the early nineteenth century, order was brought to the collection. Unclassifiable monsters were expelled (they went to the Hunterian), leaving everything else—in principle—classifiable within a universal system of knowledge, the encyclopaedic ideal. In principle at the Museum knowledge and material sent back from the periphery were classified, ordered, made known and displayed to visitors. Objects helped form imperial subjects. But the Museum did not contain *knowledge of the subjects, themselves.*

For Thomas Richards, such institutions are an important cultural resource for imagining empire, and in particular for imagining schemes of *comprehensive* knowledge.[4] His interest is primarily in how these fantasies were reworked in literature: the museums and networks of intelligence in Kipling's *Kim*, or the comprehensive knowledge of the sea as surveyed from Captain Nemo's *Nautilus*. (The paranoid early-twentieth-century spy thrillers, featuring networks of Germans preparing the invasion of Britain, of William Le Queux can be read similarly.[5]) However what makes Richards's work highly relevant to the study undertaken here is that he argues that the plans for comprehensive knowledge traveled effortlessly between literary and political fields. His remarks on the latter are only made in passing, but the examples discussed below should be seen as just such political cases.

Three schemes for total centralized registers are considered here, one by an outsider, Noel Pemberton Billing, and the other two by insiders: Sylvanus Percival Vivian's National Register and Mallet's scheme for a peacetime universal register. All three failed, indeed only one, the National Register, got off the ground at all, and lasted for five years before collapsing. How and why they failed is very revealing for the historian for several reasons. First, they show again how the experience of the First World War strained the traditional organization of British politics and authority. In the Pemberton Billing case the war can be seen as creative—at least for furthering the right-wing maverick's agenda, whereas for the National Register the war was destructive and entropic of orderly bureaucracy. Second, mechanization haunts the debates. The registers were unmechanized, at first at least, but the ideal of an interlinked database of subject information immediately suggests to the more recent observer anxieties over computerized data. Slightly whiggish, but perfectly valid, questions are prompted: was it possible to hold centralized records without machines? Were technological solutions imagined? How period-specific were anxieties about collated personal knowledge? The answers to these questions turn on a specific context of time and place, but also illuminate contemporary debate.

A Mechanical Experiment on the Diseased Social Organism: Pemberton Billing's Plan for National Bookkeeping

> An un-numbered, un-recorded and un-measured nation presents a spectacle somewhat akin to that of a museum containing a vast number of valuable specimens, no catalogue of which has been constructed and no systematic tabulation attempted.
>
> —PRO RG 28/110 (untitled and undated memorandum by Noel Pemberton Billing)

Noel Pemberton Billing was a maverick. He was a troublesome MP, sitting as an Independent for East Hertfordshire. He was an aviator, a modernist pioneer celebrated for his "Supermarine" flying boats. He was a right-ring conspirator and libelist, scourge of what he saw as a decadent and effete elite through his incendiary pamphlet, the *Imperialist*. As an outsider, his account of his imagined totalizing register was sent from the fringes of political life. In 1911, Austen Chamberlain received a scheme devised by "PB" the previous year.

The Unionist thought it "impracticable owing to the fact that the people of this country would fiercely oppose any system of registration," but also probably paid it little attention, coming at the time of his bruising failure to seize Conservative party leadership after Balfour's resignation.[6] The plan resurfaced, however, in 1917, by which time a system of National Registration had indeed been introduced. War had changed expectations of the art of the possible.

Billing's proposal was for a "system of National Book-keeping," by which he did "not refer to . . . the Government's income and out-go, its assets and liabilities, but . . . in its widest sense to the Nation's income and out-go, its assets and liabilities . . . we require machinery by which we may effect an annual national stocktaking and thence deduce a measure of our progress."[7] The accounts would be comprehensive and of more than merely an individual's name and address. The "function of this register is that of measurement . . . to represent numerically the value of the life to which it refers." Each individual would be scored annually against a "permanent standard" according to four categories: "moral standing," "economic ability," "health," and "family responsibility." The task of compilation of this new "Domesday book," although difficult given the "complexity of the social organism," would make for efficient legislation. As Billing argued in a passage that is worth quoting in full:

> It is essential to remember that the nation is composed of units exercising volition, under perhaps the influence of ambition or maybe indifference, and the greatness of the nation depends upon the economic welfare of these units. National expansion is the direct outcome of individual aspiration, as national decay is the result of individual indifference. In other words the history of a nation or empire is only the combined history of its individuals. To pursue this argument must lead us to the conclusion that if the historical study of a nation's past growth can give any indication of its future destiny, the history of the individual character and economic efficiency is a still more direct indication of the national tendency. Our object then is continually to weigh the national units morally and economically year by year to ascertain any improvement, or shall we say profit, that may be the result of incentive provided by some legislative measure. The latter must often be experimental and its vindication will rest with the subsequent result derived from the national statistics. At the outset the problem of weighing and measuring these elusive qualities of character and efficiency, must appear a difficult one, needing delicate machinery which certainly does not exist at the present time. Its solution is possible however, and lies in the adoption of a complete life register for every person composing the nation, tabulating those facts which are of paramount importance on national progress.

The nation is composed of individuals, each of which could be measured and tracked by the compilation of "a complete physical, moral and financial balance sheet." The ills of the "social organism"—inefficiency, degeneration, and decay—could only be cured by legislative "experiment" requiring "delicate machinery," following tabulation of symptoms. Only those with a "good record" would be beneficiaries of legislation—here perhaps we can see the context of Billing's initial draft: a reaction against the sweeping National Insurance measures of 1911, what Billing would have seen as socialism. Several comments can be made about Billing's proposals. First, note the tension between organismic and mechanical language: inefficiencies are diseases of the social "organism," the cure is mechanical: "The position has to be grasped in all its details, statistically measured, and then with certain knowledge in our possession we may proceed to apply the remedy, watching carefully the result upon the diseased organism, and modifying our methods as circumstances demand." The metaphor of government machine is multivalent: as surgeon's scalpel, as source of efficiency, and as a symbol of order—mechanical order and direction versus organic "society . . . a somewhat chaotic muddle of valuable forces." Having presented himself as a heroic aviator (he was driven through the streets in an airplane during election campaigns), he was strongly identified with the machine as an icon of modernism and efficiency. Second, his radical right ideology featured the distinctive contradiction between his own libertinism and centralized control for the greater good of the whole:

> The conception of a system of National Book-keeping is the logical outcome of a sincere belief in the unity of a nation. A "whole" implies the correct placing and tabulation of the parts, their sphere of action, their ability to carry out their allotted duties, and generally their interrelationship. The conviction that one has a significant position in this "whole" produces popular manifestations of patriotism, and civilization itself is only a stumbling progression along a road toward national unity.

Finally, Pemberton Billing's bookkeeping proposal should be seen in the context of the radical right agenda pursued during the First World War. As Philip Hoare has recently described, Billing and his Vigilante Society's project was to attack what he saw as corrupt, decadent, and aristocratic ruling elite symbolized in life by Prime Minister H. H. Asquith and socialite Margot Asquith, and in death by Oscar Wilde. This campaign exploded on the home front in Billing's sensational claim, made through his *Imperialist* in January 1918, that the German Secret Service possessed a "Black Book of sin" in which the names of 47,000 "Privy Councillors, wives of Cabinet Ministers . . . diplomats, poets, bankers, editors, newspaper proprietors, and members of His Majesty's Household."[8] (Not surprisingly, Billing announced, from the dock, that the Book included the name of germanophile Lord Haldane.[9]) The dynamite implication was of a blackmailed elite holding back from efficient warfare.

Pemberton Billing made no explicit connection between national bookkeeping and his assault on the 47,000, but the coincidence in time welds the two projects. A further reason then for each individual to be measured financially, physically, and *morally* was to pinpoint the perverted 47,000. The irony is that, while (as Hoare points out) "the notion of the Black Book . . . drew on the popular conception of Teutonic efficiency in matters of cataloguing," Billing was planning a population survey of Teutonic proportions.

Pemberton Billing had mock Registers printed, and even architectural drawings of "the building for accommodating and facilitating the working of the system." However, central government was unimpressed, although the rejection was not because of his political allegiances. Christopher Addison, the reforming Minister of Reconstruction, referred the proposal to Hayes Fisher, President of the Local Government Board and therefore the person responsible for reconsidering National Registration. Hayes Fisher's civil servants were dismissive:

> . . . although the experience of the war may have prepared the average Englishman for a fuller registration system than he knew before, it is difficult to imagine that he would tolerate such a system as this, with its never ceasing entries and its almost daily handling of the registration record by employers, schoolmasters and workmen alike.[10]

It was deemed unlikely that "workmen would acquiesce in the proposed continuous recording of their character by employers . . . or that employers would submit to the imposition of the time and labor involved in making the records." As well as being un-English, there were practical problems: how would casual workers or the self-employed fit in? How would it graft on to existing insurance and pension schemes? More important, Hayes Fisher and his civil servants were already deep into re-imagining a comprehensive means of knowing subjects, a recast National Registration, and their time "could not be very profitably spent in investigation of brand new schemes."

The Rise and Fall of the National Register

Pemberton Billing's plan for measuring the morals of subjects was mechanical without real machines. It is a crucial argument of this book that the imaginative and metaphorical use of machines preludes—or at least creates the conditions for—mechanization. Furthermore, the imaginary machine works by its accompanying metaphors: efficiency, speed, or directed order versus an unknown or a chaotic diffusion. The "chaos" of the First World War was the crisis of stressed institutions. Whereas for the maverick Pemberton Billing the seeds of chaos lay in the corrupt elite, for the civil servants with rival plans of comprehensive registration the crisis was of government much more generally. The state knew little of itself. Mobilization and demobilization had made the 1911 census results meaningless. Novel government plans, from national insurance to plans for an expanded electorate, required new sorts of knowledge. It was in this context that Sir Bernard Mallet envisaged a second universal register, one which would he hoped would build on the real administrative experience of the National Register.

In 1914 recruitment for the British Expeditionary Force was on a voluntary principle. Men were encouraged to join up, often in "pals" or "comrades" battalions, urged on by either civic or aristocratic authorities. By the end of the year the gulf between the demands for "manpower" (a telling neologism), both on the front and in industry, and the numbers produced by voluntary recruitment was becoming stark. The War Cabinet split between those willing to consider compulsory national service—a radical realignment of relations between government and the people—and those who resisted such a draconian move. There were further disagreements: what should the balance be between military and industrial manpower. Should manpower allocation be planned? The arguments centered on numbers, and here there was confusion. For example, through 1915 the discussions between the War Office and the Board of Trade on export trade and army size were "meaningless" because the statistics of each side, collected on different bases, were incomparable.[11] Even the potential number of recruits was unknown, making arguments over the possible size of the army (General Kitchener's aim was 70 divisions, or 1,200,000 men) irresolvable.

In 1913 a compulsory register of all persons was politically unthinkable. However, by 1915 the President of the Local Government Board and proponent of compulsion Walter Long, was able to pass the National Registration Bill. Like the Defence of the Realm Act, which gave the government sweeping powers to organize industry, break strikes, censor the press, protect secrets (and restrict drinking hours), the National Registration Bill was justified by war. And like DORA its provisions were meant to last only as long as the hostilities. Long's Bill ordered that a "register shall be formed of all persons male and female, between the ages of fifteen and sixty-five."[12] Long's organization of the Register followed that of the decennial census, with local councils and the Registrar General as local and central registration authorities respectively. Each local registration authority was to compile their register and tabulate the contents for the Local Government Board. Personal data collected under National Registration were name, place of residence, marital status, number of dependents, occupation, name address and business of employer, nationality, and a series of questions keyed to recruitment: was the registrant employed in work for war purposes? was he or she skilled and willing to work? The Act made provision for this list of questions to be expanded indefinitely. Only prisoners, "certified lunatics or defectives," inmates of Poor Law institutions and hospitals, interned prisoners of war, and those already recruited were exempt, although, of course, registers already existed of such people. The aim was therefore a complete register, locally held but accessible from the center, of the inhabitants of England, Wales, Scotland and Ireland.

While the Northcliffe press (the *Daily Mail*, the *Daily Mirror*, the *Daily Times*) was satisfied, the liberal left was up in arms against Long's Bill.[13] The *Nation* considered it hasty: "if in the midst of a tremendous war we are to devise machinery for changing the spirit of our institutions, would it not be well to apply some serious thought to the process?."[14] The *Nation* doubted that the information was needed, and hinted that the National Register represented "merely a preparatory scheme for bringing pressure to bear on the men and women of the working classes—pressure secured through local dignitaries or bodies—to enlist or to change their occupations." The freedom of private life—but not, note, any right to privacy—of the British subject was outraged:

> Are the volunteers who will compile the returns to be sworn to secrecy, as are the census officials? And if not, by what right will they ask, under penalty, such questions as whether a woman is married or has had children? Mr. Long invokes the aid of local schoolmasters. Are these people the proper recipients of the private secrets of their neighbors? and why should we confer a roving power of inquiry as to people's concerns . . . ?

National Registration, from this viewpoint, was a "clumsy steam-hammer for crushing nuts."[15]

Assistant Secretary of the National Health Insurance Commission, Sylvanus Percival Vivian, was also dismayed. He had direct experience of the only similar enterprise, the listing of one third of the population necessary for the introduction of national insurance, and was therefore called in to advise on the Register. He was "a past master," "you are in the position of the designer of a Dreadnought called upon to advise as to the construction of a coracle!," flattered his colleague, Violet Carruthers.[16] Vivian diagnosed the problem: the Local Government Board's reliance on the censal model for what was in fact a radically different project:

> A census is solely directed to the compilation of statistics as regards the number and classification of the population on a given day. It is concerned with any person not as an individual but as a unit comprised in a total in a particular category; and for this reason it is not concerned with any particular person when he has once been reckoned

in his appropriate category. The fact, therefore, that census returns are very largely incorrect on the day after that upon which they were made does not appreciably invalidate the statistics prepared at leisure on the basis of those returns.

But in the case of a register of population the whole object and theory is different. The purpose of a register is presumably to secure information at any time as to the actual personnel of any given district. Changes therefore in the residence and status of individuals, which would leave the value of a census entirely unimpaired, are of vital importance to a register, and any scheme for the organization of a register must necessarily provide adequate machinery for recording, not merely a statistical summary of the population, but its actual personnel, which is of course, in a constant state of flux.[17]

National Registration was a system "diametrically opposed" to a census, the informational task more difficult, and different "machinery" was therefore needed, or else the scheme would collapse. Indeed the first national insurance registration had ended in disaster. The business had been put out to private insurance companies and in 1913 the London Insurance Committee received 600,000 notices of "removals": the insured population (1,450,000) of the metropolis was too mobile, and registration broke down. Yet here was a proposal for an even larger scheme on the same flawed principles! Nor would the threat of legal sanctions help: "the most radical fallacy of the whole system is the assumption that the individual members of the population can be brought to perform even the simplest operation by being subjected to a legal obligation to do so." The cause, for Vivian, was "not due to any lack of patriotism of respect for the law," but lay in the liberal British subject:

. . . deep down in the genius of the nation, the freedom of its private life from bureaucratic incursions, its unfamiliarity with and distaste for formalities or procedure and "red tape." Such a system [of legal sanctions] could only be successful when enforced, as in Germany, by a rigorous and ubiquitous police system upon a nation accustomed to be regulated in all minor matters of life. Any system of registration which is intended top operate successfully in this country must be based on different principles.

Prussification was to be rejected, and British identity performed by opposition to continental forms of registration, although there is a strong irony in the argument being made by one of British bureaucracy's key architects. What were the alternatives compatible with the free British subject? The techniques of advertising had no purchase: for national insurance a few years earlier "millions of leaflets" aimed at the "masses" had been released "with little or no apparent effect." For National Registration the problem was doubled: not only was it larger, but the "registered person has no interest in the notification and will not recognize its point or importance." Therefore, as in fact happened after the breakdown of the state insurance system if the "mountain would not come to Mahomed, Mahomed must go to the mountain," there must be a "point d'appui": "Just as Insurance machinery could be brought into touch with insured persons at the point of choice of doctor through the doctor, so the [National Registration] machinery can be brought into touch with *employed* registrable persons at the point of employment through the employer by means of placing any necessary obligations upon him."[18] The solution to the informational crisis was to build on existing modes of authority, the (near) universal one being that of the workplace.

Walter Long's bill was swiftly revised along these lines, published on 9 July 1915, and swung into action within the week. The "coracle" was afloat, and the closing date for the forms was a mere month later. The Register symbolized the new informational relationship between government and people. But the fate of the material artifacts of National Registration demonstrates how industrialized warfare strained bureaucracy. For example, industrialized warfare overwhelmed standard paper as the method of storing information. Due to the scale of National Registration "a box of papers under the ordinary process of vertical sorting [would] become waste paper in a week." The forms were therefore specially strengthened and made durable. The sturdy returns could be regimented in ways that ordinary paper could not easily be: once divided by different colors for men and women, cards could be rapidly sorted by employment block (there were 45 occupation categories), then by age group, then by surname. Red cards marked employment in special "war work" to warn off recruiting officers. A central clearing house coordinated the local boxes and would oversee the system. In Neville Chamberlain's Birmingham—and this achievement demonstrates conclusively what was technologically possible, but generally and deliberately unchosen—the National Register was compiled using Hollerith tabulating and sorting machines. There was "no better means of handling such a problem" than to use punched cards, argued the General Manager of British Tabulating Machines.[19] Several local authorities followed progressive Birmingham's example, but the national government decided against the universal adoption of punched cards, not because of cost but because of the "impossibility of obtaining enough cardboard."[20] Such mundane resources were needed elsewhere, for, as part of National Registration, and symbolizing the new relations between state and individual, Identity Cards were issued for the first time in Britain.

By now the demand within the War Cabinet for manpower figures was intense, and, despite Vivian's earlier plea that National Registration was more than a Census of Population, its main impact during the Great War was just that. The steam-hammer had crushed the nut. With returns from 90 percent of the population, the Registrar-General estimated that 1,413,900 men in England and Wales were still available for military service, the arrival of the figure welcomed, as Vivian sourly expected, "like the first fruits of ju-ju."[21] The number was used immediately by Lord Derby in his last-ditch defense of voluntary service. Under the "Derby scheme," men between the ages of 18 and 41 were encouraged to offer a "pledge" that they would join the army if necessary. However set-backs on the front-line and the failure of the Derby scheme to produce the recruits expected, meant that the end of the voluntary principle was near.

For Vivian, the "first fruits of ju-ju" were merely a censal spinoff from the greater project: an ongoing register of the location and status of individuals in the population. To the annoyance of the administrators once National Registration had, apparently, clarified the number of recruitable men and the political battle in the War Cabinet been won, the government's commitment to the Register fell away. Criticisms were aimed at the Local Government Board who had, in the eyes of the Vivian, administered National Registration incompetently, and at the politicians who, it was alleged, had no understanding of what are well-run registration could achieve. Violet Carruthers, writing to Vivian, expressed the mood eloquently: "I shall strictly charge my Secretaries that all reference to any connection with the National Registration Committees is to be kept out of my tomb stone. I am most heartily ashamed of the whole business, which for futility and ineptitude has been hard to beat—even in this war."[22]

Vivian likened the effect of the hasty and politically driven implementation of National Registration to that of the "Bandar-log" (Kipling's crass monkey troop from *The Jungle Book*): touching "nothing which they do not disadorn: their path is strewn with shreds and patches":

> . . . they have taken the germ of a system which we hoped and believed might have been the basis of a real working register, and monstrously perverted and misapplied it. . . . This has finally queered the pitch . . . for the purpose of building up any clean and coherent system. I doubt if the evil can be undone, and that is why I think our efforts are at an end.[23]

Within months, however, the gloom had lifted and a clean coherent comprehensive register was again being imagined. This campaign's ambition, and the reaction of Whitehall, are very revealing of attitudes to surveillance and fantasies of comprehensive knowledge in Britain.

The scheme was the proposal of Sir Bernard Mallet, Registrar-General of England since 1909, President of the Royal Statistical Society for the latter half of the Great War, and a future President of the Eugenics Society. As the Registrar-General, Mallet was familiar with the shortcomings of the systems of registration: deaths were sometimes registered without a certificate of the cause of death and were public documents (an obstacle to compiling official statistics, particularly of venereal disease[24]), stillbirths went unrecorded, and procedure as regards burials was "lax" at best. Two problems resulted: informational problems of *production* and *representation*. First, the patchy data hampered the production of official statistics making them "insufficient to meet the growing demands upon my office for information as to the facts of natality, fertility and mortality."[25] Second, the record failed to mimic the population: "insufficient in that it either fails to identify with completeness the person to whom it relates, or to point to the next step in tracing the family history." That is to say, the failure lay in both correspondence between representation and object, and between elements of the representation (certificate to certificate). The origin of these problems lay in the growth of the state, but warfare made them more urgent. The "dislocation of the population caused by war—the withdrawal of the men of military age from civil life and the movement of the civil population in consequence of the demand for munition and war services" made the census of 1911 "largely worthless as a guide to local populations" and the National Register unreliable:

> It has to all events demonstrated the utter inadequacy of our pre-war arrangements in these respects and the need for some permanent organization for obtaining, at frequent intervals, information as to individuals in addition to the purely statistical information afforded by a decennial census of population.[26]

Mallet's proposal had two parts: First, standardize the creation of registers at local level. The Poor Law Guardians, for example, who oversaw the Registers of Births and Deaths, would pass their informational responsibilities to the tiers of local government which already managed public health.[27] One local body would manage all lists: registers for elections, vaccinations, school attendance, infectious diseases, mental deficients, marriages, deaths, births, the payment of rates, and so on. This simplified structure would be "linked up to a Central Authority which could enforce uniformity and exercise effective control."

This uncontroversial part was a means to a radical end: he put the case for a new, more ambitious National Register (remember the 1915 Act had stated that NR would end with the conclusion of hostilities):

> . . . the ideal to be aimed at . . . is that of one universal Register . . . which would serve all purposes for which registration is required. . . . The substitution of a single complete register by extraction from which all purposes involving the registration of sections of the population could be served, for the present system of independently compiled ad hoc registers for each such purpose.

The benefits Mallet envisaged from a universal register were fourfold. The first two stemmed from war: refugees and conscription. The refugee, when categorized by the state, became an "alien" and was therefore listed in registers which were the responsibility of the police. There were at least five disconnected lists of aliens maintained in 1916. Lists of aliens also intersected with the lists of spies and possible spies held by the secret service, and had only began a few years earlier.[28] Mallet, as Registrar-General had some direct experience here, despite alien registers being a Home Office matter. The registration of the floods of Belgian refugees had convinced him that only a centralized register was practicable "from the point of view of police supervision"—and therefore if a universal register was to handle aliens it must too be centralized. Flows of refugees would perhaps peak with the Armistice. However, though the war might end, the state should be left on a war footing:

> Whatever the shortcomings of the National Registration . . . it proved to demonstration that no orderly system of recruiting for the army, at all events on a compulsory basis, is possible without it. Can we safely assume that nothing of the kind will be required in future? Even if no form of universal compulsory service results from the war the maintenance of a register which would enable such a system to be re-instituted in case of need at the earliest possible moment would seem to be a measure of obvious prudence.[29]

And if a register of males of military age was deemed necessary, then it would be wasteful not to extend it. The third of Mallet's projected benefits was a saving of both time and money: "much economy should result . . . of expense and labor, and it may be added, of trouble to the public." Finally, the public's life would be eased by their own individual tie to the universal register, an ID card: "one form of certificate might be made to serve all purposes involving evidence of identity or age which would supersede the present bewildering variety of certificates issued and fees paid for the same services for different Government purposes." Mallet had a highly sanguine view of the population's response: a "document so generally useful and so easily obtained," he thought, would be "preserved as a matter of convenience . . . with the result that in time every individual could be expected to possess documentary evidence of his identity."

Securing Surveillance, Preserving Britishness

Like Pemberton Billing's project of a moral archive, Mallet's universal register was also rejected. Unlike Billing, however, Mallet was an insider: as Registrar-General he was in a strong position to argue for informational reform. He also had allies within and without Whitehall. A committee chaired by Mallet, with members Sir Arthur Newsholme, Dr. T. H. C. Stevenson, and Beatrice Webb, met and recommended that a "General Register should be compiled and maintained" at local government level, connecting to a "Central Index." The register would record name, address, sex, date of birth, place of birth, marital status, possibly occupation, and "references to any special registers upon which any individual is borne."[30] By linking up to the special registers, the universal register would hold basic knowledge of the all the population but be expandable in the categories of special interest: deviance, illness, welfare, contact with state institutions, and so on. This recommendation was made despite a rather lukewarm response from local authorities regarding the utility of a permanent register.[31]

Furthermore there were contextual pressures for knowing the population at a finer—even individual—level. The spread of the franchise, the biggest leap yet being the inclusion of women over the age of 21, meant that a truly "mass" polity now existed. The consequences were manifold, but one interests us particularly: the mechanism of electoral registration provided a tempting Trojan horse to smuggle in a universal register, since Whitehall was interested in breaking down the "mass" into knowable parts—*representation* of the people in more ways than one. The growth of the state, especially through welfare measures such as public health, national insurance and associated taxation also contributed both a cause and means for informational reforms. Indeed each of these measures provided smaller registers out of which a universal one might be knitted. Finally, the experience of the Great War transformed the state and changed people's expectations of what the state could, or should, do. As Sir H. Munro wrote to the President of the Local Government Board in September 1916 (echoing, as we have seen, a similar response to Billing's proposals):

> It is no doubt worth considering whether after the war public opinion will tolerate a system of universal registration, which involves the continual reporting of removals etc. and a considerable amount of interference with individuals. Two years ago this would have been regarded as a "Prussianizing" institution, but we have got used to various things since then and it is quite possible that it would not be viewed with so much hostility now.[32]

This ratcheting effect of war, in which the postwar administration can pursue policies that would have been unthinkable before the conflict because the population had become accustomed to the extension of state powers, is a well-known effect in political history.[33] The irony of the greater acceptability of "Prussian" institutions after the war's end is what is significant for this argument: it is a clue to why Mallet's scheme failed—or seemed to.

The problems facing a universal register were rightly anticipated in terms of a clash between certain performances of national identity and a perceived foreign-style institution, in this case "Prussian" bureaucracy. Parts of the press would certainly have spoken strongly against a universal register, just as they had against the wartime necessity, National Registration. It was this tight situation, where changes in the nature of government pressed for greater knowledge of the nation but where changes faced a powerful obstacle in ideas of national character, that a very clever compromise was agreed. Here is one expression of it:

> . . . just as the Representation of the People Act has provided machinery which will fill one gap in the existing facilities for securing information, so future legislation [e.g. an extensive Unemployment Act, or any legislation for the restriction of aliens], may fill others, with the quite possible result that without taking any express new powers for national registration as such, all the necessary facilities for information may become available, which would render a national registration system feasible. If so, all that would be necessary would be creation of a coordinating authority, and not new powers expressly for registration purposes which would be bound to be invidious.[34]

So no special powers were needed to secure the information which Whitehall needed to work, and from there it was a short step to deciding that, so long as registers could be informally cross-checked, then surveillance of the population could be achieved without that symbol of oppressive bureaucracy, a universal register. Surveillance would take place without *visible* conflict with national identity. Likewise, statistical knowledge was obtainable without taking the final step of tracking everyone individually. The following comment on Pemberton Billing's National Book-Keeping, also applies to the universal register: "Would any statistics founded on the records be likely to be as valuable or as reliable as the statistics of the same kind now obtained through the various services themselves, whose records are capable of expansion and are no doubt continually expanding?"[35] The paradox of anti-red tape rhetoric coming from the architects of an expanding and more bureaucratic state can be resolved when it is understood that they sought the surveillance and accurate knowledge of the state needed for the provision of government services while preserving an outward image of Englishness.

The deliberate unobstrusiveness of the national surveillance was, for Vivian, best captured by the words of Jeremy Bentham. It was essential, Bentham had written, "to avoid shocking the national spirit," but there were many advantages to be gained from a "new system of nomenclature . . . so that each individual in a nation should have a peculiar name, borne by no one but himself." Vivian agreed: ". . . tempering any restrictive machinery to the character of the population under control is extremely sound; and for my own part the three years' experience of National Registration has taught me that the social structure and psychology of the population must be treated as the background of the machinery."[36] The great political philosopher had eulogized on the subject of liberty and sailors' tattoos:

It is a common usage among English sailors to trace their family and baptismal names upon the wrist, in distinct and indelible characters. It is done that they may be recognized in case of shipwreck. If it were possible for such a practice to become universal, it would furnish a new aid to morals, a new power to the laws, an almost infallible precaution against a multitude of offenses, especially all kinds of fraud, for the success of which a certain degree of confidence is necessary. Who are you? Who am I dealing with? There would be no room for prevarication in the answer to this important question.

This means, by reason of its very energy, would favor personal liberty, by permitting the rigors of procedure to be relaxed. Imprisonment, where it has no object except securing the person, would be less often necessary, if men were thus held as it were by an invisible chain."[37]

Vivian was particularly struck by the phrase "invisible chain." "It corresponded well," he wrote, to "the less restrictive term "invisible net" which I used . . . as the best general description of National Registration."[38] It also serves as a fitting metaphor for twentieth-century British policy on registers of individuals.

Choosing Partial Registers

The National Register was, of course, not "machinery" in our everyday sense, but its history during the Great War proves an important, if Whiggish, point: centralized, interlinked records were materially realizable, and pre-date by many years the computerized data banks discussed in chapter 9. Furthermore their meaning was highly contextual: whereas in the later twentieth century the discourse was firmly centered around "privacy" and individuals' rights, in the early to mid century the emphasis was subtly but crucially different: privacy understood in terms of collective national identity, "freedom," and "liberty." (Note also the echo from chapter 3 and George Handley Knibbs's peroration on the "free spirit of the British people" in relation to national and imperial statistical programs.)

The choice whether or not to build pervasive universal information systems of individual records in peacetime was a political one, not driven by technological possibility. (Recall that a National Register based on punched cards was a proven and available alternative.) The political choice, a judgment of what would not shock the national spirit, was for many "invisible" partial specialized registers of information, and not a peacetime National Register, although it remained in the Whitehall "War Book" and was promptly reintroduced in 1939, as we shall see in chapter 6.[39] Partial registers preserved Britishness. The specialized registers accumulating in twentieth-century Britain were of several types. The oldest were the registers of births, deaths and marriages, their form largely unchanged since the Benthamite 1836 Act (stillbirths were added 90 years later). However, while the form remained stable, the quantity steadily increased. While each local Registration District recorded the vital information, copies of all certificates were also forwarded to the General Register Office. In the vaults of Somerset House, 160 million entries had accumulated by 1931, and alphabetical indexes of births and deaths were kept. Mechanization, using punched cards, of processing the information found in the registers of deaths, is considered in the following chapter. The emergence of the Welfare State added many more to these foundational specialized registers—Beatrice Webb's wartime list provides ample evidence.

The Interconnection of Technological and Information Systems

The most important means of identifying British subjects in the twentieth century was not the identity cards of the National Register, but the simple automobile driver's license. The register of driver's licenses satisfied all the characteristics of a successful partial register acting as a surrogate for a universal register. The documents of identification were part of a wider information system, which also included vehicle registration and licensing, and which in turn was "parasitical," in Vivian's sense (see chapter 6), on a new, popular technological system of cars and roads.

Vehicle registration was introduced in the Motor Car Act (1903), and vehicle licensing in the 1920s.[40] Under the 1903 Act, local councils were charged with maintaining registers of vehicles sold in their areas, and were told to make them freely available for inspection by the Inland Revenue, other councils or the police.[41] The latter requires an explanatory note. Cars provoked a crime wave: burglars previously located in the large towns suddenly found rich pickings in the surrounding countryside which was now only minutes away—the graph of break-ins outside urban areas closely matches that of car ownership; the velocity of cars meant that the number of accidents, including "hit-and-run" accidents, increased; cars themselves were stolen; and with the introduction of further legislation, driving infringements became criminal offenses in their own right.[42] One effect was that the criminal statistics became dominated by car-related crime. The "register of mechanically propelled road vehicles" was therefore largely maintained for the police "for the purpose of readily tracing persons involved in accidents, offenses and crimes connected with the use of motor vehicles on the public roads."[43] Quite quickly, the registers relating to motoring had become a central tool in police work.[44]

Personal data leaked from these early information systems. As well as the police, local councils and the Inland Revenue, individuals, too, had limited access to the information: "While no unnecessary obstacle should be placed in the way of a person who requires to identify a car for the purpose of taking proceedings, the entries in the Register ought not to be made public for the gratification of curiosity or for any other insufficient reason."[45] The "reasonable cause" test allowed insurance companies to access information concerning claims on stolen cars, but refused, for example, the manufacturers of the "Controlograph" the addresses the firm wanted for advertising. Likewise a request for information from a woman seeking her husband's address to serve him divorce papers was turned down.[46] During the interwar period—and the temporary absence of National Registration—the general reticence to divulge information was related, in the eyes of civil servants and politicians, to national tradition:

> In determining his attitude in the matter generally, the Minister has been guided by the fact that this country, unlike some continental countries, maintains no general system of registration of names and addresses and, in ordinary circumstances, as he understands, no one has a right to require a person to disclose his address, or to require anyone to disclose the address of any other person, and so, as far as he is aware, no compulsion can be applied.
>
> Registration is only required in special cases, and under Acts of Parliament where its purposes are obvious, and it is suggested that these Acts should be construed strictly in favor of the person registering, and that in respect of matters unconnected with the cause of object of registration he should not be put in a worse position by the disclosure of the registration particulars to third parties than a person who had not been required to register. Indeed, the Minister feels that any other course would tend to bring the registration system into disfavor and to make the administration of the legislation in regard to motor vehicles more difficult. For the smooth working of that legislation, the goodwill of the motoring community is important.[47]

The 1903 act required that the license number be displayed on a plate attached to the automobile. In the 1920s, following further legislation, a Registration Book had to be kept with the vehicle (to the advantage of vendors of cars hawking hire-purchase schemes: they would keep the Book so the car could not be sold on).

As the names suggest, vehicles licenses were attached to vehicles, while driver's licenses were carried by individuals. The licensing of drivers was tightened in response to deaths on the roads, since as the number and speed of motor cars increased so did the figures of road casualties. Though every driver needed a license under the 1903 Act, "anyone," explained a lord introducing the new 1930 Traffic Act Bill, "could obtain a license for the mere asking. It was not necessary to have any arms or legs and the most defective mental case could be licensed to drive a car to the danger of everybody—himself included" (the defective driver, not the peer).[48] Reluctance on the part of the state to define and assess "good driving" was confirmed by a Royal Commission in 1905.[49] After 1930 drivers had to make a declaration of physical fitness. Certain disabilities constituted an "automatic bar" to driving; individuals with other disabilities had to pass a test of competence before being granted a license. However, as a civil servant ruefully recorded, "this was a great step forward but it did not prevent the road casualty figures from soaring upwards." In fact casualties had soared after the speed limit had been removed by the 1930 Act, after pressure from a road lobby which powerfully reflected commercial and middle-class interests.[50] In 1934 a new Road Traffic Act reintroduced the speed limit and required that, beginning 1 June 1935, all novice drivers be tested. On the grounds of road safety, therefore, the state undertook to assess driver competence, and record it through personal licenses—necessitating, of course, a register to mirror the licenses held by individuals. Later, after the collapse of the Second World War National Register, the driver's license would become a de facto British identity card. By then, paper was as essential to running a car as petrol.

A Secret Epilogue

A final clutch of partial registers, so far unconsidered, appeared and prospered in the twentieth century: lists increasingly central to policing, law and order, and national security. The emergence of the "new" police force, "paid, uniformed and bureaucratically controlled," is no longer viewed by historians as a straightforward achievement of enlightened reform.[51] Instead, geographical unevenness and complexity of change is emphasized. However, all authors agree that the model of the Metropolitan Police, as reformed by the middle of the nineteenth century, was deeply influential. The aspect most relevant here was the development of Scotland Yard as a center of information exchange and as a repository of partial registers. A local register of "burglars, housebreakers, receivers, etc." had begun at Bow Street, London, as early as 1755, as a response to increased organization and mobility of the criminal community.[52] However little attempt was made at a national, or even London-wide, register until the establishment of a detective force in the Metropolitan Police in 1869. Even then the project to list all "habitual criminals" capsized due to weight of numbers, and had to be re-launched in 1877. Three years later the setting up of the Convict Supervision Office of the plainclothes detective Criminal Investigation Department (CID), prompted Scotland Yard to develop a "record system of its own, with photograph albums and registers in which were recorded biographical details, peculiarities of method, physical marks, etc.," a system amalgamated with the habitual criminals register in 1896, when simultaneously card indexes replaced book registers.[53]

In chapter 3 it was noted that the reform of criminal statistics helped create the category of the recidivist. But although statistics and registers might reveal a minimum number of habitual criminals, this in turn provoked anxieties over the unknown total number. Both facts and fears were mobilized to justify new methods of identifying criminals. For six years from 1894 the French anthropometric Bertillon system, which depended on bodily measurements such as length of the head, middle finger and foot, was imported. The rival to the Bertillon system was one based on fingerprints. The eventual success of fingerprinting at Scotland Yard, once a method of classification had been added, has usually been ascribed to its technical superiority over Bertillon, indeed the criminal statistics could, and were, placed opposing each other: 410 identifications by the Bertillon Method in 1901, 1,722 by fingerprints in 1902.[54] However, in the crucial year of decision, 1900–01, such a statistical "objective" case could not be made. The complex and culturally loaded history of the "English finger-print method" should be borne in mind. Though Darwin's cousin, the eugenicist Francis Galton, had proposed the use of fingerprints, the all-important method of categorization was forged in (or appropriated from) India, where colonial administrators Sir William Herschel and Edward Henry had sought means to identify the native non-English-speaking population.[55] This device of distrust found its way to the center of Empire when Henry returned from Bengal to Scotland Yard at a critical moment in late-Victorian society. The history is further clouded by vicious, ongoing priority disputes waged by Henry Faulds against Herschel and Galton.[56] I argue that the cultural resonances that the English fingerprint method invoked swung the case against continental Bertillon anthropometry. By 1909, 140,000 fingerprints were on file.

In 1903 Henry was promoted to Commissioner of Police of the Metropolis, a post he held until 1918, and was therefore in a position to build up Scotland Yard as a center of information. The central Finger Print Bureau, alongside the criminal registers, provided the basis for the Criminal Record Office. A modus operandi list, called the Crime Index, was added later. A telegraph network with its hub at the Yard—there was a strange reluctance to introduce telephones[57]—kept the London and provincial forces in touch, the "telegraph office is engaged throughout the day and night sending and receiving messages, by telegraph and automatic recording instruments. . . . By this means and by wireless the two hundred police stations, and the thousands of police scattered over the seven hundred square miles of Greater London, can be apprised within a very short time of, say, a criminal whose arrest is desired."[58]

The Metropolitan Police connected through its Special Branch to the secret service, with which it sometimes cooperated in matters of national security. The Secret Service Bureau—the fledgling MI5—was set up under ex-CID administrator Vernon Kell in 1909 following German spy scares. Home Secretary Winston Churchill gave Kell permission to collect the first register of aliens (mostly Germans) in 1910.[59] By spring 1917 MI5 this Central Registry had expanded to encompass "suspicious persons" and contained 250,000 names and 27,000 personal files, classified from AA ("Absolutely Anglicized") to BB ("Bad Boche").[60] The Register, MI5's "great standby and cornerstone" proved particularly useful in policing entry to the country through its thorough inter-connection with the work of Passport Control Officers.[61]

Out of the partial registers of the police came one more proposal for a universal register, which is of interest since it ties together the themes of this chapter. In 1917 Major J. Hall-Dalwood, Chief Constable of Sheffield, wrote to the Under Secretary of State for the Home Office of his deep concerns over subversion. "The present need," he wrote, was for a "highly organized system to deal scientifically and swiftly with undermining movements, whether affecting naval, military or industrial activities."[62] The failure of National Registration, "an imperfect copy of the German system" in Hall-Dalwood's eyes, was due to lack of "machinery to ensure its proper working," or in other words a powerful, centralized executive that could use a universal register to combat Bolsheviks and other subversives. He proposed a new "state department": "the organization of the system would be uniform for all counties, relevant facts and statistics in each case being collected and transmitted to Central Headquarters without delay. Beginning in Great Britain, but extending to the colonies and British Possessions, the outcome would be "greater efficiency," "unified control," and "financial economy." Though Andrew has shown that Sir Basil Thomson, chief of CID, supported Hall-Dalwood's scheme and, on the back of a wave of serious strikes—including one by police in 1918, secured a new Directorate of Intelligence with himself at its head, the immediate fate of Hall-Dalwood's scheme foundered on familiar shoals.[63] Even the Chief Constable of Sheffield had to preface his proposal with reference to national identity:

In submitting a scheme for the inauguration of a National Intelligence Service, the word "secret" has been carefully avoided for the reason that in this country one of the most highly prized liberties has been freedom of the individual. Under normal conditions State Control has been regarded as repugnant to the spirit and genius of the British Race and any such encroachment upon the liberty of the subject would have been met with general opposition.[64]

However, in peacetime—as with the National Register—the political preference was for the invisibility of uncentralized organization, through the existing police forces, central coordination not direction. Hall-Dalwood's scheme sank, like the National Register, because of a reluctance, given meaning by appeals to national identity, to give the *appearance* of state surveillance.

This chapter has dealt with plans for universal registers, and ended with the history of growth of partial ones. The next chapter examines the spread of machines, especially punched-card mechanization, in the Civil Service. However, the reader will notice that technique and machinery has already become a recurring motif: Pemberton Billing and Hall-Dalwood's schemes, as well as the National Register, were metaphorical machines—and materially, through paper and card, information technologies. At Scotland Yard the registers were intimately tied to the organization of information and its communication through telegraph and photograph-facsimile machine. I want to end with a vivid image of resistance to machines. The figure is that of a suffragette in Holloway Prison in north London in 1913. CID demanded fingerprints and photographs for the files, but

. . . because of the resistance such prisoners would no doubt offer to the taking of their finger prints and because any resistance to their photographs being taken by a Prison Officer in the ordinary way would of course make the attempt useless. Having regard to the increasing gravity of the offenses committed by this class of prisoner, the [Prison] Commissioners see no reason why force should not be used to secure their finger prints in all cases where their offenses have been serious; while as regards the photographs, the Commissioner of Police is prepared, in cases where the prisoner has refused to be photographed in the ordinary course, to send an expert photographer to the Prison who would take the photograph on the exercise ground or elsewhere without the prisoner's knowledge.[65]

Force largely failed—the pictures came out blurred and fingerprints smudged. The prison's response was further reliance on machines: the fastest camera exposures, purchasable from Covent Garden scientific instrument makers Messrs. Newton & Co., caught—and thereby registered—the suffragette image.

5

The Office Machinery of Government

The great registers showed that large-scale information systems, though cast metaphorically as "mechanical," were built and run largely without machines. How then do we explain mechanization, which swept through government offices in the early twentieth century? The answer will be seen to lie in the rise of another expert movement, which could, unlike the statisticians, find a means of managing the defining generalist-mechanical split that organized the Civil Service. Remember from chapter 2 that the growing Civil Service had been decisively split into two, generalists on top and mechanicals below, with the whole, to ensure trust, referred to as a machine. What follows depends on a creative and deliberate misreading of "machine" by a new expert movement. The expert movement of mechanizers aimed at a transformation of the practices of offices, partly through inspection and analysis of British departments, but also by inspiration from the United States, where the modern business creed of "systematic management" had been articulated by the late nineteenth century. I will first consider the historiography of office mechanization in the two countries, before turning my attention to examine the expert movement in Whitehall in detail.

Campbell-Kelly argues that, whereas in the United States the emergence of large-scale offices was correlated with the use of office machinery (although the causality is disputed), in Britain "the large-scale office developed much earlier and mechanized much later," raising the question of just how Victorian data were processed. He finds the answer in organization and highly subdivided clerical labor. The Railway Clearing House, which was formed in 1842, had by 1876 a clerical staff of 1,440, organized functionally into three large divisions, and thence into sections, and so on.[1] The colossal task of handling many low-cost transactions—such as passenger ticket receipts—was met in the Victorian office by organizing many clerks rather than by mechanization. The national contrast is explicit: "The office-machine revolution that swept across the United States in the 1880s and the 1890s largely passed by

British offices leaving them unaffected."[2] The difference between the two countries was the appearance in the United States of systematic management, the ideological managerial component to the big corporations that displaced and replaced small, informal family firms. Systematic management, which began in 1870s engineering circles before becoming a broader managerial credo, was a vastly influential program—more so, for example, than its more well-known contemporary, scientific management, which, as Yates and others rightly insist, should be seen as a mere offshoot from the trunk of systematic management.[3]

Systematic management was distinguished by two principles: "a reliance on systems mandated by top management rather than on individuals" and "the need for each level of management to monitor and evaluate performance at lower levels."[4] The first principle, "the need to transcend reliance on individuals," was, in a profound sense, the metaphorical mechanization of the organization, since it directly appealed to the engineering tenet of interchangeable parts: just as a machine was made more efficient by the degree to which spare parts could be standardized and ordered off the peg, so too could a largely human organization be made more efficient if the system—explicit rules, communications, and functions—rather than the individual was considered first. The conversion to systematic management preceded the widespread introduction of office machinery, and therefore illustrates for the private American firm what this book attempts to show for the British public bodies: that the imaginary reconstruction of organization as like a machine was prior to "real" mechanization—prior to but not preceding, since systematic management enabled technological change, and, vice versa, technological change reinforced the position of systematic management. For example, systematic management's principles implied an expansion in reporting and communication between levels in the organization—in other words, much more "information" (a word defined by proponents as "recorded communication") was collected, made explicit and displayed.[5] This proliferation of reports, memos, notes, and other documents was helped greatly by innovations in production technologies (pre-eminently the typewriter in the 1880s), in reproduction technologies (the rolling copier, carbon paper, and much later the photocopier), and in storage systems (vertical filing after 1893). Take the typewriter. Not only did it allow fast production of documents and better copying through carbon paper; it also helped to separate the production of documents, largely by new female "typists," from their creation, which remained largely in hands of male managers—a functional distinction in full accord with the spirit of systematic management.[6]

In Yates's account, systematic management first found expression in mid-nineteenth-century American railroad companies before spreading throughout other large corporations in succeeding decades. Managerial theory and technological change mutually reinforced each other with revolutionary effect in the decades around 1900. Innovation in management ideology and technique is therefore firmly located at a particular time and in a particular place: the American private sector in the mid to late nineteenth century. The historiography of the mechanization of the American office is, explicitly in the case of Yates, indebted to Alfred Chandler's account of the rise of the corporation. (And, with its focus on business history, much history of computing is likewise Chandlerian.) There are, of course, many good reasons why we should not be surprised that office mechanization developed most speedily in the context of large private corporations, but Yates's account should, I feel, be complemented and extended by comparing her case studies to those of a country in which public bodies were relatively more important.

The corporation did not innovate techniques from scratch. Yates herself gives examples where the new corporations imported data-handling and data-processing techniques from government (although typically, through initiatives such as the Keep Commission of 1906 and the Taft Commission of 1910–1913, the movement of techniques in the United States was in the opposite direction).[7] Numerical registration of incoming correspondence was learned by American railroad companies from Whitehall registry practices.[8] However, private business and public bodies had very different interests, which go some distance toward explaining the different patterns of implementation of office technologies: firms motivated by the pursuit of profit were likely to be more interested in speed of processing than the state (except, crucially, in times of war); likewise, firms with an eye on margins were made to concentrate on economy, whereas for government bodies this pressure, though present, operated in a different manner, for example through negotiations with the Treasury; furthermore, governments differed in attitude toward permanence of records—a factor that, Yates notes, predisposed government more than business to carbon paper.[9]

The Chandlerian highlighting of innovation by business can be problematized as follows: What models did businesses have when developing into vertically integrated, hierarchical, managerial corporations? What else was around that had developed complex organizational solutions to problems of geographically dispersed control, or that separated ownership from management, or that sought to banish market uncertainty by establishing hierarchies from resource extraction up? The answer is, of course, the state. We should not forget that much of the rise of the corporation was achieved through imitation of government, in particular the import of lessons of bureaucracy as a means of coping with geographically dispersed problems of control: hierarchy, tiers of management, centralized power and depersonalized authority. In parallel to Alder's recent claim that many of the supposed innovations of the American modes of manufacture can be found in revolutionary France[10]—or, indeed, to Merritt Roe Smith's longer-standing arguments regarding organizational innovations in the federal armories—a second revisionist question can be put: Can all the chief characteristics of the Chandlerian corporation be found earlier in, say, the Indian Civil Service? Unfortunately, this is not the place to answer such a question, the point here being merely that the related historiographies of office mechanization and managerial movements consists almost entirely of literature on the private sector. Yet a fuller account must discuss the flow of techniques to and from, and within, the state. After the managerial revolution, when big business became far more similar to government, such flow became easier—yet contingent on the remaining differences in interest noted above. Take the copying of copying as an example: Yates informs us that duplicating and addressing machines were business innovations (an assessment with which the British government agreed[11]), but within a few years the same machines were used by the British Home Office as instruments of policing and social control. What is needed, then, is a history of use. What was office machinery used for, and why?

In this chapter I examine mechanization in offices of the public sector, in a country, the United Kingdom, where the state has taken on more diverse roles than in the United States, and therefore where the differences made by the mechanization of governmental data processing are more evident. A wide range of machines appeared in late-Victorian and Edwardian offices: slide rules, mechanical calculators, adding machines, typewriters, combined typewriter-adding machines, cash registers, accounting and tabulating machines, rotary copying machines, rotary duplicators, Motabradors, envelope-closing and franking machines, Electrical Blue Printers, Gammeters, Roneotype machines, Dictaphones, Linotypes, improved printing presses, litho presses and litho machines, wire stitching machines, guillotines, telephones, Addressographs, photostats. To trace and explain the innovation of all of these would be confusing. I will therefore concentrate, although not exclusively, on one technology: punched-card data processing. There are several other good reasons for this focus: It was a later symbol of business efficiency. Punched-card systems were precursors to computers (and an important point of this book is to help us understand why this should not be a surprise). Punched-card systems were expensive, so their introduction had to be justified in detail.[12] Most important for our purposes here, punched-card systems were championed by the expert movement of mechanizers.

Punched-Card Data Processing

Herman Hollerith developed punched-card office machinery in response to a severe data-processing problem encountered by the US government.[13] The late nineteenth century was marked by immense growth of industry and by a population changing rapidly through immigration and internal migration. Without up-to-date information, effective governance was threatened. However, the same factors that made knowledge of the population essential also overwhelmed the decennial census through which such knowledge could be gained. The 1880 census took 7 years to tabulate, and the more complex 1890 census was expected to take even longer.[14] The Director of the Census, the British-born Robert P. Porter, announced a competition and invited the submission of schemes to speed up tabulation. A former instructor in mechanical engineering at the Massachusetts Institute of Technology, Hollerith offered a technical solution based on his own patents: mechanization of the process of tabulation by storing the information in the form of holes punched into standardized machine-sortable cards. Porter, impressed by the speed of the Hollerith system, chose it over rival hand-sorting methods for the 1890 census.

Despite the publicized success of the census, completed in 2 years and celebrated on the front page of *Scientific American* in August 1890, the following years were difficult for Hollerith as he struggled to make a business of his invention. The decennial census was too infrequent a job to support the nascent punched-card industry, and it was not until the breakthrough of regular data-processing applications in the offices of railroads (acceptance by the New York Central Railroad in 1895–96 was particularly important) that some measure of stability and growth could be brought to Hollerith's enterprise. Punched-card machinery sold steadily to the large corporations of turn-of-the-century America, where a market in office machines was already flourishing. In Chandler's analysis of this history, vertical integration and the accompanying growth of middle management were encouraged by economies of scale forced by competition in the massive American market and the challenge of organizing technological systems, such as railroads, of wide geographical spread. (It has already been noted that, because of contextual factors felt with force in the nineteenth-century United States, businesses were borrowing the state's bureaucratic techniques.) With the American market healthy, the promoters of the Hollerith system looked to expand in Europe. The earliest attempt recorded by Martin Campbell-Kelly was Porter and Hollerith's presentation of the punched-card system to the Royal Statistical Society in December of 1894.[15] In chapter 3 I argued that the RSS played an important role in the late nineteenth century as a forum for the technocratic interests of statisticians within the Civil Service, academia, journalism, and industry. The RSS was the center of a professional movement that, justified by a claim to expertise, had its sights on reform of government. Porter and Hollerith's choice of the RSS as the venue for the first British demonstration of the possibilities of punched cards was therefore canny, as was Porter's appeal to the RSS's old enthusiasm, the international organization of statistics.[16] The chairman of the debate, G. B. Longstaff, agreed that "as a theatre of statistical investigation at the present time, no country in the world was so interesting as the United States," and warmly thanked Hollerith and Porter, expressing the hope that the punched-card system might be applied to the London County Council census of 1896. In advising the government in preparation for the 1901 census, the Royal Statistical Society began to mention and encourage the use of punched-card machinery. Though I have noted tensions between the respective expert movements of statisticians and mechanizers, here their interests coincided.

In 1901, after the assassination of President McKinley, Porter's political fortunes nosedived. He returned to Britain to a career in journalism and a sideline as a promoter of the Hollerith system. Porter, given approval by Hollerith's Tabulating Machine Company to negotiate a British outlet, soon met Ralegh Phillpotts, secretary of the British Westinghouse Company, who agreed to act as the company's general manager. Phillpotts, recognizing his own technical limitations, decided to share the work and passed operational matters on to a Cambridge engineering graduate, Christian Augustine Everard Greene.[17] The company was first incorporated as The Tabulator Limited in 1904. A reflotation in 1907 led to the name by which British Hollerith operations would be familiar for 50 years: British Tabulating Machine Company (BTM). Work for the arms manufacturers Vickers, Sons and Maxim from 1905 and an early contract from a railway company, the Lancashire and North Yorkshire Railway, saw BTM through its early years. As Campbell-Kelly shows, the history of BTM was decisively shaped by the settlement with its American parent (which, after a series of mergers, had emerged as IBM): large cash payments as well as 25 percent of royalties for the Hollerith rights in the British empire—a "permanent millstone" around the neck of BTM.

By the First World War, BTM had a competitor in Britain. The Russian-born James Powers had by 1911 followed the same path as Hollerith out of the US Census Bureau into his own punched-card business. Despite the glaring infringement of copyright, Hollerith's company remarkably chose to reach a license agreement with Powers rather than prevent manufacture completely.[18] In 1915 the British Powers agency, now named the Accounting and Tabulating Machine Company of Great Britain—"the Acc and Tab" for short—became a wholly owned subsidiary of the American company. As Campbell-Kelly argues, the later entry of Powers into the British market assisted the company, since punched-card machinery had begun to lose its strangeness and wartime sales were brisk.[19] The decisive force in Powers's British history was the involvement of the Prudential insurance firm, guided by its principal actuary, Joseph Burn. In 1918, impressed by the success of its own massive Powers installation and the potential of mechanized offices to bring down the costs of insurance policy administration, Burn persuaded the Prudential to acquire outright the manufacturing and selling rights from the American parent, probably for £20,000. Campbell-Kelly notes that the insurance firm preferred Powers's system over BTM's because the former printed results, crucial in accounting.[20] The choice of Powers machines for the 1921 Census of Population was, Campbell-Kelly writes, the "first wind of competition" felt by BTM, and thereafter the two companies competed for contracts.[21]

This potted history of Powers completes my sketch of the early British punched-card industry. With this background knowledge, let me now turn to application within government departments. I will argue that in early-to-mid-twentieth-century Britain there existed a growing expert movement, which eventually was to find its center and heart in, of all surprising places, His Majesty's Treasury. This Whitehall department has received much critical opprobrium, and this and following chapters should be seen as a radical reinterpretation of the Treasury as being, in parts at least, a technophilic body sympathetic to technical specialists. Crucially, the expert movement of mechanizers sought to connect good administration to the project of office mechanization.

A Whitehall Experiment with Punched Cards: The 1911 Census

The historian of medicine Edward Higgs has provided a compelling account of the introduction of the first full implementation of punched-card methods into government work.[22] The General Register Office (GRO) was a Victorian center of calculation and a data-processing powerhouse. Quietly, after the famous wrangles between the irascible Charles Babbage and the government, William Farr had introduced the Edvard Scheutz difference engine in the 1860s to calculate life tables.[23] The complex Swedish machine proved troublesome, but calculation in the GRO was soon assisted by a string of smaller devices: simple analogue slide rules, Burroughs Adding Machines, and arithmometers, which were now being marketed with vigor.[24] The GRO was an enlivened organization in a dynamic context: the old Registrar General, Brydges Henniker, had retired, and the vigorous Bernard Mallet was his replacement. Henniker had been ill when the methods of the 1901 census had been drawn up, and Higgs suggests that this "bad timing," combined with the Stationery Office's reluctance to spend, is enough to explain why Hollerith methods were not applied to the decennial Census of Population at the first opportunity.[25]

BTM was marketing Hollerith-based machines in the United Kingdom by 1911, but availability alone does not explain the introduction of punched-card methods into Whitehall, although it was a necessary condition for mechanizing that year's census. By the late nineteenth century, depression and foreign competition—particularly American and German—had created a harsh social environment in British cities. Middle-class anxieties stoked fears of the "residuum," liable to riot, unionism, and overbreeding. In what is a familiar pattern, the construction of an informational "unknown" allowed the subsequent introduction of information-technology "solutions." The link in this case is not entirely straightforward, because the professional classes were split. One side, dwelling on failure in the Boer Wars against an "inferior" enemy and a perceived dearth of middle-class babies, foresaw the degeneration of the "British race." Their answer was eugenics. But many public-health professionals could not easily adopt selective breeding. Instead they believed that the root to amelioration lay in nurture, not nature: urban environmental improvements would unclog the social pressure valve via clean streets and safe housing. They were therefore representative of the second response: welfarism. Attitudes to government intervention had changed, owing partly to the death of old liberalism and partly, with Bismarck's Prussia an inspiration, to a political decision to contain social violence through social expenditure. Both welfare and eugenic models of the state encouraged government intervention.

Statistical facts, underwritten by government authority, could bolster either side's arguments. It was therefore crucial how the facts were solicited. The Local Government Board, a department staffed with public health professionals, had contacts within Whitehall. The Royal Statistical Society added to the pressure. In 1909 the GRO agreed to provide statistics on marital fertility broken down by occupations (and hence by social strata).[26] In a 1910 memorandum, Mallet, a future president of both the Royal Statistical Society and the Eugenics Society, linked the new census questions to future eugenic options:

> . . . for the first time enquiries [will be made] into the duration of existing marriages and the number of children born to these marriages. This enquiry is pressed by the Royal Statistical Society, and forms part of the Census of Australia, of the United States of America and of France. A detailed scheme for utilizing the results of this enquiry has been prepared and it is believed that it will furnish data of the very highest value

> for the study of certain social problems (the importance of which is now increasingly being recognized) such as the comparative fertility of married couples in different social positions, and of different occupations, and the bearing of social position, occupation and ages of parents upon infantile and child mortality.[27]

George Handley Knibbs—a proponent of eugenics, a statistician-led technocracy, and an Imperial Statistical Bureau—stated "emphatically" to Mallet that "these questions have not been found inquisitorial in Australia."

The inclusion of questions regarding occupational status made for a much more complex enumeration in 1911. Victorian censuses had been processed by the "ticking system": a clerk worked through the schedules, deciding for each question which category each person fell under ("coding"), and adding "ticks" on a large piece of paper under appropriate headings. When the pile of schedules had been worked through, the accumulated ticks gave the figure required. Ticking was arduous and slow. Victorian censuses had therefore been kept simple.[28] The most onerous task of the 1901 census, the preparation of tables showing occupations of individuals by sex and age, and in females by condition of marriage, required sheets of paper 40 inches by 261/2 inches, ruled and cross-ruled into more than 5,000 compartments—the sheets used in 1881 had contained less than half that number.[29] Different sheets were needed for each cross-tabulation, with the effect that the statistical information extracted tended to be minimized. A GRO statistician, Archer Bellingham, stated the problem as part of an exhaustive plan for the 1911 census: "If . . . any alteration in the form of the returns, any considerable increase in the scope of the Census inquiry, or any greater detail on the presentation of results were required, it might be found that the ticking system would be inadequate."[30]

Card systems offered several advantages over ticking. We know that the immediate concern in the 1911 census was the added complexity of the family fertility questions, and there is no doubt that card systems were seen by the protagonists as the solution. "The ticking system is admitted by its warmest advocates to have reached the limit of its practicable application" in the 1901 census, said Bellingham's colleague T. H. C. Stevenson.[31] However, and more important in the long run, cards offered other advantages. When a tick was made upon a sheet the identity of the entry was lost, whereas on a card (whether written and hand-sorted or punched and machine-sorted) it was retained: it was "possible therefore with cards to obtain a complete check of the workers' accuracy, as well as that of the tabulating machines."[32] Cards offered a *permanent* record, already noted as a bureaucratic virtue. Such checks were particularly useful when the replacement of male clerks with women and boys raised issues of trust in the Victorian office.[33] Card systems were more flexible: with ticking, once a plan of tabulation had begun it had to be completed and no deviation was allowed. Furthermore, "with a card system, if the cards [were] preserved, and if any subsequent time it [was] desired to obtain information, for any area greater in detail than it was taken out at the time of the census this can be done at trifling cost, whereas the ticking system the cost renders it impossible to undertake such work on any considerable scale."[34] Cards, especially punched cards, were the solution that appealed to a state that was anticipating a need to process and remember far more information than previously. The choice of punched-card machinery for the 1911 census was a momentary eugenic spasm, but it was also an anticipation of greater and continuous future data processing by the state.

A punched-card system was not incontestable. Disadvantages were also noted. In particular, the reliance on machines was troublesome in three ways. First, holes in cards were more inscrutable than tabling sheets and would "not afford such a ready means of reference in the post-censal period." Second, the GRO would be "dependent on an external agency for the compilation of our tables," since the Office would be tied to the commercial provider of card punches and tabulating equipment. Finally, and the converse of an advantage noted above, the "checking of the work would involve absolute reliance on the correctness of the machines and the accuracy of the manipulators." The standing of early Victorian government statistics had been tied to the gentlemanly status of Victorians. Professionalization and mechanization disturbed this link. Mechanization allowed the employment of unskilled boys and even women, but Whitehall hesitated to trust either on their own. The combination of women and boys with machines, as we saw the replacement of the copyists in chapter 2, was a different matter. There is no doubt that the mechanization of the 1911 census—employing part of the masses to survey the masses—was the GRO's "leap in the dark," a reform in which "it appears to be necessary to have recourse to actual experiment": "In advocating a change of system . . . of such magnitude . . . it must be shown that the alteration will be such an undoubted improvement as to justify the risk attendant on departure from known and tried methods." Like franchise reform, informational reform was slow. Mechanization was acceptable in 1908 in Britain only after "a card system of one kind or another has already been adopted by the Census Authorities of practically all civilized countries, in some cases having displaced the ticking system in use here; it may therefore be taken for granted that there is no impracticability in introducing it for Census purposes in this country."[35] A punched-card system, however, sped up one half of the process: each return would have need to coded, but the information on the cards could be sorted, and cross-tabulated, in any number of ways. What BTM machines promised to the GRO was the possibility of asking more complicated questions (for example, on occupation and fertility), performing ambitious analyses, and producing vastly more statistics for immediate deployment in departmental dispute and public debate. As Higgs has argued, the analyses the GRO had in mind were medical, although the GRO was also under intense pressure from the demands for more statistics coming from the Home Office, the Board of Trade, the Institute of Actuaries (which publicly encouraged the government adoption of card systems in 1900), and the Royal Statistical Society.[36] For years the Local Government Board had encouraged the GRO to change the unit of area for tabulation from the registration district (or subdistrict) to the administrative sanitary area. Under this change, geographical statistics of death would reflect where people lived rather than where people died. (More and more people were dying in institutions, and local rate payers resented the increased taxes stemming from skewed statistics.) Mechanization, with its flexibility in sorting cards, finessed this adjustment of administrative area, requiring neither wholesale local reorganization nor change in law.[37] It seems that it was acceptable that some of the expected efficiency gains of mechanization were to be used up in this fudge, another compromise that preserved Britishness while securing surveillance.

The use of the punched-card system may have been a bureaucratic fix, but it also tied one informational center of government (the GRO) closer to another (the Ordnance Survey). Bellingham, in his description of the forthcoming census, reported the sharp remarks of Mr. Harper, the Statistical Officer of the London County Council (LCC). London presented particularly intense local informational problems, and the LCC, a vehicle of Fabianism and the public health movement, was in a good position to experiment. Rather than use written "plans of division" to guide the London census enumerators in 1901, Harper (a former surveyor) had equipped them with Ordnance Survey maps. He was "astonished to find that practically no use" was made of maps for the national census of population. So was the GRO, and Bellingham included visual rather than written means of dividing up England and Wales in the 1911 methodology. The wider significance is of the enmeshing of governmental informational projects. In this case, databases of change through time and space were increasingly interlinked.

The GRO was awakening and becoming interested in informational reform, including mechanization of both census work and routine work. Before 1908 no GRO official had traveled to inspect the organization of foreign censuses (not even a "visit [to] the cities of Edinburgh or Dublin," Bellingham noted ruefully). By 1911, both T. H. C. Stevenson and his superior, Registrar-General Mallet, had witnessed the classicompteur—the cheap cards-without-punched-holes system devised by M. Lucien Marc, Director of the Bureau de Statisque Generale, and already used by other governments. One indication of how seriously the GRO now took new mechanical methods was that Stevenson traveled to America by steamship to question the US Census Bureau on Hollerith methods. Although BTM's machines were based on the Hollerith patent, British and American punched-card systems differed in some details. A trip to Washington would enable Stevenson not only to compare differences between the Washington and London systems but also to "see and study the general system of tabulation by electro-magnetic machine sorting of punched cards, getting particulars as to accuracy, speed and flexibility, and especially as to weaknesses inherent in the system of which we naturally hear little from the British company."[38] Furthermore, the GRO was puzzled by some developments across the Atlantic. BTM was offering "the latest type of Hollerith machine," one "not used in Washington." Hollerith had quarreled with the US Census Bureau, and the GRO was keen to hear the great man's version of events.[39]

With the census year fast approaching, the GRO was under severe pressure: it had promised the inclusion of extra questions, and BTM's Hollerith machines seemed the only solution. The pressure sparked a fascinating exchange within Whitehall between the Registrar-General and the body responsible for purchasing office machinery, His Majesty's Stationery Office (HMSO). Bailey, the HMSO official responsible for negotiating with BTM, was outraged by the cost of the machines, and a fierce argument between government and firm ensued. BTM was threatened with the Patents Act, which would allow the government, on grounds of national interest, to ignore Hollerith's patent and copy the design directly.[40] Across the Atlantic, the US government, which was already designing improved machines, expressed willingness to supply the British government with drawings. Hollerith, the owner of BTM's patents, stood by. (Bailey also felt that the Great Western Railway could be induced to allow their BTM machine to be copied, although the arms-manufacturers Vickers, Sons & Maxim "were unable to entertain the idea.")[41] All that prevented this radical move—which would have broken the patent and established an independent British punched-card machine industry—was the imminence of the 1911 census: the federal offer was "useless now for want of time."

Registrar-General Mallet was sympathetic to the company, especially the firm's secretary, the "invaluable" C. A. Everard Greene, who had given advice and assistance "freely before there was any certainty that his Company would be employed." BTM had offered, as an experiment, to produce the statistics needed for the GRO's 1910 Annual Report. Under this special offer, BTM provided the machines for free, and the GRO merely had to arrange staff ("one second division clerk and three or four boys") and spend £40 on 250,000 cards.[42] Therefore, by November 1910, in the midst of the Patents Act threats, Mallet reported to the Treasury that the situation had been "completely changed by the success of the experiments" and requested sanction to mechanize the 1911 census.[43] To HMSO's mortification, Mallet was successful.[44] Employees were trained, cards and punches purchased, and sorting and counting machines hired. In 1911 the GRO processed 42 million cards (36 million "personal" and 6 million "fertility" cards). BTM made a profit, not on machine rental, on which it paid substantial royalties back to Hollerith, but on the sale of cards. Figure 5.1 shows an example of a punched card.

Mechanization had allowed the GRO to reorganize the geography of its statistics and to speed up its census processing; it also provided a cover for introducing a new nosology (the International List of Causes of Death) and the tabulation of deaths of infants "according to parents' occupation, thus providing valuable information hitherto lacking as to differential occupational and social rates of fertility and infant mortality." (The eugenic question was an indication of the possible new extensive role of the state.[45]) More important, stores of machine-sortable information began to build up in Whitehall, and departments had their first experience of the expertise required by and the possibilities afforded by punched-card mechanization.

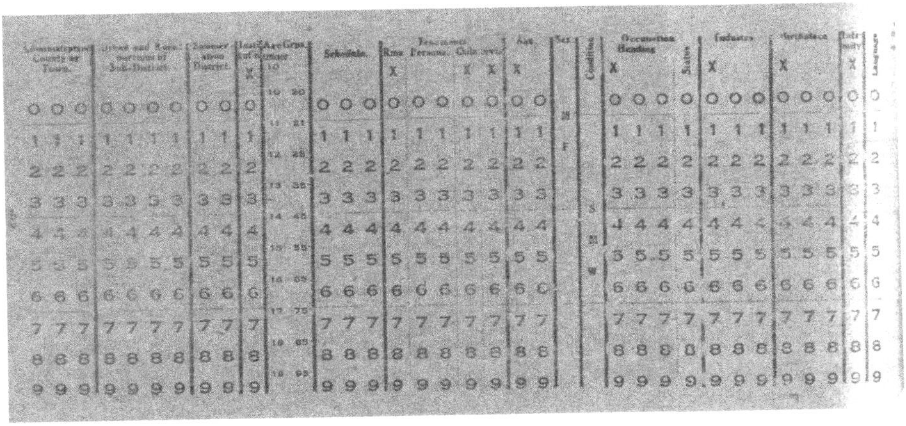

Figure 5.1
A punched card used in the 1911 Census of Population of England and Wales. (source: Public Record Office)

Further Trials: Powers vs. Hollerith

HMSO had negotiated with BTM the rental of the punched-card machines on behalf of the GRO. However, the government department responsible for all material aspects of Civil Service work, from paper supplies to large machines, was "not satisfied" with the terms offered and actively sought competitors to the Hollerith system. Other office-machinery companies were keen to demonstrate their wares. The American Consulate in London passed word of the potential market across the Atlantic, and two companies quickly responded. One, the Spicer Tabulating Machine Company, based in Washington, contacted HMSO in September 1912, but it was outflanked by more aggressive marketing from its New York rival, the Powers Accounting Machine Company. The Powers system was already being used by American railroads, and Thomas Felder, a member of the Powers Company's board of directors, made sure to visit HMSO when passing through London in October. Felder intimated that Powers would be prepared to demonstrate its mechanical system for free in London. (Spicer made no free offer.) As it turned out, an investigating party journeyed to Berlin in December 1913 to witness Powers's first European installation at the company's offices on Potsdamerstrasse. Four days were spent "examining, testing and experimenting with the machines."[46]

HMSO was in a buyer's market: both Powers and BTM offered to install machines in Whitehall for a full-scale experiment. The tabulating machine companies regarded HMSO as both a potential high-volume customer and a prestigious one. Like the 1911 census, HMSO's new interest was directly linked to the expanding boundaries of the state. In 1911 the National Insurance Act had introduced two state-sponsored welfare schemes. First, there was to be compulsory insurance for medical treatment and financial benefits for sickness, disablement, and maternity for nearly all manual workers between the ages of 16 and 70 and for low-earning employees—16 million persons in total. Second, for workers in certain industries, unemployment benefits would be payable for up to 15 weeks per year. These state measures replaced the provisions under the Poor Law (the traditional "workhouse" form of relief for paupers) and, to a certain extent, displaced reliance on Friendly Societies, charities, and the family.[47] The legislation was a compromise between the Liberal government, which was in favor of fully state-organized social insurance on a Bismarckian model, and its opponents, in particular, the private insurance societies, including the Friendly Societies. Certain "Approved Societies" were therefore charged with administering the benefits, and the immense data-processing demands entailed by the welfare bureaucracy fell on both private and

Figure 5.2
A BTM three-bank counting machine, used in the 1911 Census of Population of England and Wales. (source: National Archive for the History of Computing, University of Manchester)

public bodies. In 1911, the driving force behind the National Insurance Act, Chancellor of the Exchequer David Lloyd George, asked the Prudential Assurance Company, the largest of the Approved Societies, to manage the data processing.[48] HMSO installed in London first BTM's Hollerith machines for a 3-month trial (in early 1914), then Powers's machines for a 3-month trial.[49] The result of the experiment was recorded as "conclusively in favor of Powers," probably because, as a later report noted, the Powers tabulator was "able to print all the entries on the cards passed through it . . . and simultaneously to add selected columns."[50] By 1915, the Prudential, impressed by the Berlin installation but also certainly knowing the results of HMSO's experiments, had installed Powers machinery (40 card punches, seven tabulators, and seven sorters, all supplied by Accounting and Tabulating Machine Company of Great Britain). This was the beginning of a close relationship between Powers and "the Pru."

However, it was not just the private insurance houses that changed under welfare-state reorganization and mechanized data processing. The other half of the National Insurance Act, dealing with unemployment, placed intense demands on the human bureaucracy. The Board of Trade received 1.1 million Unemployed Register Cards in 1913–14 , and it was estimated that the number could rise to more than 1.5 million in bad years. These cards had to be sorted into age groups in each occupation and then tabulated. The manual method was tabulation by superimposition; however, the numbers strained the system. William Beveridge (then Assistant Secretary at the Board of Trade, later to be the architect of the post-1945 welfare state) wrote in January 1915:

> After experience of the nature and volume of the work . . . the Board consider that the task is essentially one that can be done with far greater efficiency and economy by substituting sorting and tabulating machines for labor. . . . To deal with these returns three Punching machines, one Sorting machine and one Tabulating machine will be required permanently. A supply estimated at 1,350,000 per annum of special cards will also be required [in addition to] twenty filing cabinets specially made to hold the punched cards in the various stages of work.[51]

Beveridge, aware of the HMSO experiment and of the Prudential's choice, asked for Powers equipment, citing "an all round superiority over . . . the Hollerith system." The parts of Whitehall concerned with social insurance had begun to adopt punched-card machinery for accounts and statistics; however, it is significant that mechanization came after the political decision—indeed, after a year's difficult experience with manual methods. Technological and organizational change, in this case, followed political change.

HMSO had begun to investigate punched-card machines because it anticipated the growth in bureaucracy that would be entailed by the provision of welfare services. For two reasons, HMSO officers were well positioned before 1914 to claim authority as experts: they had managed the experiments comparing Powers and Hollerith systems, and all government departments had to order equipment through their office. Sorting and tabulating machines joining the long list of devices for which, for government departments, HMSO was the sole agent. However, HMSO officers did not become the recognized experts or potential proponents of further Civil Service mechanization, and the reason lies in the impact of the First World War on the politics of technological expertise in the Civil Service. In the early months of the war, HMSO noted with relief that its experimental Powers accounting machines had been installed just in time:

> The test of the Powers machines was just concluded when the War broke out. The accounting and statistical work on which the machines had been tried was complete . . . and in consequence of the great strain thrown on the Department generally by the loss of a number of experienced clerks who were called to their regiments (Territorial) on mobilization and the enormous increase in the work of the Department caused by the supplies required by the Naval and Military Services, the old system of account keeping was dropped and the work transferred to the machines.[52]

Mechanization was introduced for the welfare state but confirmed through war. The census innovations at the GRO and the beginnings of mechanization under social insurance legislation would have remained isolated governmental experiments with punched cards were it not for the outbreak of war. The First World War is crucial to understanding the early spread of punched-card machines in government departments because it saw the rise of machine enthusiasts needed to trumpet this cause.

The Experience of the First World War

The First World War has long been understood it terms of the industrialization and mechanization of warfare: a "killing machine" with components such as the machine gun, the tank, and the airplane. Technological change was not, however, restricted to the battlefield. Less visibly, but equally important, administration was also stretched and transformed by the scale of the conflict. Government offices began to exploit the power of desk calculating machines, at first by mobilizing university laboratories.[53] Filing systems were dismembered under stress and attrition, and punched-card machinery spread through wartime offices. As Campbell-Kelly notes, "if one had to single put the point at which office machines 'took off' in Britain, it would have to be the years 1916–1917."[54] In administration, as on the front, machines supplemented or replaced humans. Furthermore, it was the experience of administration just behind the front lines, on the periphery rather than in Whitehall, that was to shape postwar attitudes toward the mechanization of Civil Service work.

Government departments used BTM punched-card equipment for accounting, statistical, and census work. The scale of government use should be compared to those of other organizations. This can be done for the period July 1916 to December 1919 because detailed accounts have survived for BTM, showing rental charges made and numbers of cards sold. This comparative assessment throws up some surprises.

First of all, consider table 5.1, where the aggregate figures are roughly allocated by sector. This table covers the 42 months from the middle of the First World War through to the end of 1919. BTM sold 153 million cards, of which more than one-third went to industrial concerns. Growing from nothing in 1907, BTM now received more than £20,000 per year in rental charges for sorting and tabulating machines. The British government's use of punched cards was roughly equal, measured by number of cards ordered, to railway companies and—surprisingly—sales to foreign governments. Commercial

Table 5.1

Use of BTM punched cards by sector, July 1916–December 1919. Cards per year and rental per year are adjusted for part-years. Source: BTM order book in National Archive for the History of Computing, University of Manchester.

Organization type	Number	Number of cards	Cards per year	Rental of sorters and tabulators (£)	Rental per year (£)
Commercial	9	11,637,300	3,834,000	4,189	1,568
Foreign government	4	24,548,000	12,862,000	4,327	2,509
Foreign railway	2	8,390,000	3,154,000	2,297	1,311
UK government	14	19,886,500	18,351,400	4,590	3,163
Government-industry	6	3,597,000	1,357,000	2,059	845
Industry	37	55,656,550	26,032,000	23,424	8,844
Local government	6	6,857,000	1,973,000	2,158	616
Railway	8	22,439,000	7,391,000	6,634	1,946
Total	86	153,011,350	74,954,400	49,678	20,802

use (dominated by insurance firms) and local government trail by this score, although many insurance companies were of course taking up the rival Powers system led by the Prudential. Going into the figures in more detail, the significance of a few large-scale users becomes immediately apparent. Out of 86 organizations, only 14 used two-thirds of all the cards produced by BTM and each ordered more than 3 million cards.[55] The largest individual user was, in fact, the Egyptian government, where the British colonial administration processed 15 million cards (a tenth of all sales) during a census. The pressures of war undoubtedly underlay some of the sales. The Chief Surgeon of the American Expeditionary Force, for example, needed nearly 7 million cards, and national munitions factories and private armaments firms (e.g. Vickers) were also major users.

No Whitehall department used so many cards during the First World War. The stress of demobilization, however, led to rapid mechanization. Punched-card installations allowed equipment and stores to be tracked and accounted for, and processed the records, especially pension calculations, of returning soldiers and sailors. The effect of this can be seen in figure 5.4, which plots BTM card sales against time. The peak in early 1917 was due to the Egyptian census, whereas the second peak was the effect of massive orders

Figure 5.3
Hollerith machinery in Egypt, c. 1920. (source: National Archive for the History of Computing, University of Manchester)

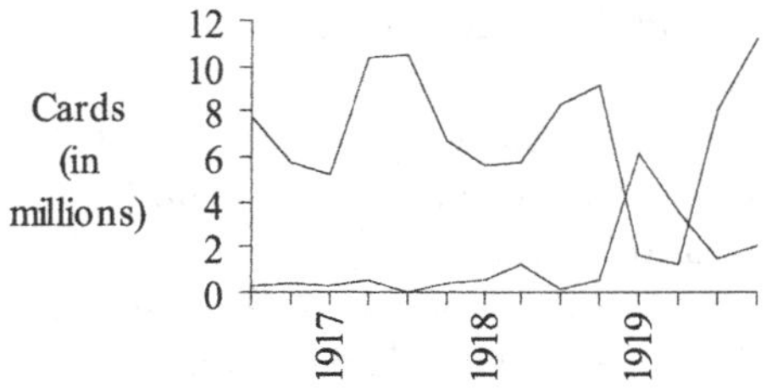

Figure 5.4
BTM's card sales (thousands per quarter-year), July 1916–December 1919. Upper line: total numbers of cards sold per quarter-year. Lower line: major sales to Whitehall departments. (source: BTM order book in NAHC)

from the War Office Mobilisation Directorate, the Admiralty Demobilisation Department, the Ministry of Labour (who took over responsibility for national service), and the Ministry of Pensions.

Central government departments were a minor user of such machines until demobilization. Other large organizations found punched-card equipment equally, or more, desirable. Unfortunately, such data do not reveal how this use of new technology connected to innovations in organization, or new accounting techniques, or intensified information collection. To understand how mechanization became institutionalized we must turn to see how a cadre of mechanizers formed out of the experience of First World War military bureaucracy.

"The Aim of Every Alert Organization": Institutionalizing Investigation and Mechanization

The experience of 18 months at General Headquarters (GHQ) in France turned Major Sydney George Partridge, a War Office civil servant from 1901, into a proselytizer for mechanization. In 1916 Partridge composed a memorandum and forwarded it to the Adjutant General. "In every organization," he argued, "the replacement of the human agent by the mechanical should be sought for and developed to as great an extent as possible, owing to the economy and efficiency which results from the use of the latter agent. . . . It is the aim of every alert organization seeking efficiency and economy in office administration to strike the balance between the 'human' and the 'mechanical,' and the more efficiently a Department is organized the greater will be the tendency for 'mechanical' to encroach on 'human' territory." This was not a report requested from above. It was entirely motivated and composed from below: from direct experience of the massive circulation of paper, munitions, and supplies behind the front. To support this striking mechanical manifesto, Partridge evoked the inevitability of technological change:

> The written message has replaced the verbal message; the duplicator and typewriter have eliminated altogether the group of "copyists"; the Sun-printing Apparatus has reduced the number of draftsmen; the "Addressograph" has cut down the "Despatch Room" by 90 percent; the "Dictaphone" has replaced the shorthand writer, and the Calculator and Comptometer have revolutionized the Counting House.

This list is reminiscent of one provided by the writer Henry Higgs, a friend and ally of many influential experts, including the statisticians Robert Giffen and George Udny Yule and the economist and logician William Stanley Jevons. Higgs's forte was the articulation and popularization of the programs of expert movements. In his Newmarch Lectures of winter 1916 and his 1917 book *National Economy* he enthusiastically reported to a British audience the recommendations of President William Howard Taft's Commission on Economy and Efficiency (1911–1913). (The implications of this influence will be considered further in chapter 11.) Higgs wrote fervently of how "the old-time clerk, who mended his quill, copied a document word by word, compared it with the original, and fastened his letters with wax, taper, and seal, has given way to the modern clerk with the steel nib, the fountain pen, and the gummed envelope." He continued: "The copying press, the carbon paper, the typewriter, the gelatine process give instantaneous mechanical copies which of necessity conform to the original. Short-hand has been revolutionized. The telegraph, the telephone, calculating machine, addressograph, vertical file, card index and loose-leaf ledger, electrical tabulating machine, automatic tell-tale time-keeper, and cash register are saving the work of armies of clerks."[56]

Higgs's overarching metaphor was of government as an army, which in turn was a machine. This should not be a surprise, in view of the context in which he was writing. The ideal arrangement of the "armies of clerks" would be a pyramidal army-style organization, which must, he argued, be "equipped with up-to-date appliances." Through this metaphor, contemporary attacks on the ill-equipped army were then made into apparently valid calls for the introduction of new technology in the home government. Once the "army is accoutred . . . it has to march," but "the machinery is too cumbrous and heavy to be set lightly in motion."[57] Again, Higgs appealed to the military model: discipline and ruthlessness were essential. For example, a "dead-head of exemplary character" must be dismissed early rather than at retirement: "Like a useless machine, the unserviceable official, if nothing better can be done with him, should be scrapped at once." Once the new model had been achieved, further change could be guided by the application of "scientific administration." Higgs's public appeal was therefore very similar to Partridge's discreet internal call for thorough mechanization of the office in the name of "economy and efficiency" (recalling the name of Taft's commission). Higgs's lectures came months after Partridge's memorandum, so although the former could not have directly influenced the latter, they were both reading from the same script, and Higgs's high-profile intervention must have helped create the conditions within which Partridge's arguments would be sympathetically heard.

Significantly for postwar developments, Partridge's aim was not merely further mechanization but coordination: the "provision of these two agents [human and machine] should be controlled by one Department." Indeed, a second and more comprehensive lobbying effort in December 1918 secured Partridge's project. This time he was joined by two junior officers. Norman G. Scorgie had studied natural sciences and Part II law at Trinity College, Cambridge, and had remained at the university as a Whewell Scholar in international law before volunteering in 1915. Along with R. A. Grieve, who had been a manager in industry, by 1918 Scorgie served below Partridge when the latter was a Colonel and Director of Army Printing and Stationery Services, GHQ. Civil servants had had room and justification to experiment in France: tinkering with office organization, redesigning forms, abolishing duplication of work where they could find it, even partly mechanizing aerial reconnaissance after the disastrous Somme offensive.[58] On demobilization the trio forwarded a detailed scheme for the coordination and mechanization of Civil Service work.

The trio's pitch played on Treasury anxieties anticipated in the period of reconstruction: the "office organization of government departments which has swollen during the war even more, proportionately, than the armed forces of the Crown, will offer the most favorable target for public criticism."[59] It would "therefore devolve upon the Treasury to justify every step and every delay in the reconstruction of government departments by irrefutable proof that the most efficient and economical methods are used"; otherwise "some of the best features of British civil administration may succumb in a general attack on bureaucracy based on its minor defects." Specifically they targeted the "subordinate staff"—the "mechanicals" of Northcote-Trevelyan as opposed to "the small proportion of staff . . . charged with the formulation and direction of policy." It was the mass of mechanicals that had "increased heavily during the war owing to the introduction of large numbers of untrained or partially trained clerks, both male and female, the enormous increase of routine work, the breakdown of much office organization and machinery which was perhaps adequate to cope with a smaller burden, and the hasty improvization of uneconomical organization and machinery in new branches and departments by those who had neither the time nor the expert knowledge to devote to the task of achieving the result in the best way."

The "problem" was therefore chaotic wartime growth and breakdown, and a system in which there was little contact between the government bodies responsible for provision of clerks (the Civil Service Commission) and machines (HMSO). The trio's solution was that "the necessary coordination between the human and mechanical sides of the problem . . . should be effected for all departments under the direct control of the Treasury itself, and that a small inspectorate of office administration, responsible to Their Lordships [of the Treasury], should be formed as a provisional experiment." The "primary function" of this inspectorate, "necessarily consisting of men who have expert knowledge based on experience," would be "by enquiry and impartial knowledge, to put the Treasury in possession of all the facts when information is required upon any proposal to expend public money in the provision of extra clerks or office machinery." Not immodestly—in view of their experience attempting promoting mechanization within British Expeditionary Force's administration—the trio suggested themselves as the inspectorate.

The Partridge-Scorgie-Grieve memorandum hit the Treasury at a critical and tumultuous moment in its history. Through internal reorganization it was being reorganized along Haldanian functional lines—Finance, Supply, and Establishments—and a further innovation could easily be incorporated. Indeed, the Inquiry into the Organization and Staffing of Government Offices, under permanent secretary Sir John Bradbury, which forced these changes and which was according to Hennessy "a *locus classicus* for those who delight in tracing the imprint of the alleged dead-hand of Treasury orthodoxy," had included a recommendation that the Treasury Establishment Division "have attached to it two or three specialists with expert knowledge" in "labor-saving" machinery.[60] More important, it was after 1918 that the Treasury's power, control, and influence over other departments surged, justified by the cost of reconstruction and the new proto-welfare-state responsibilities of government. In this context a proposal for a Treasury "in possession of all the facts" and a Treasury-controlled inspectorate coordinating humans and machines in other departments fell on fertile ground.

This context is crucial to understanding the growth of mechanization, since a number of factors opposed it. First, as Scorgie complained in 1948, "the average Treasury officer of [the 1910s] would be inclined to regard an office machine as a grubby thing beneath his notice."[61] Indeed there were good reasons for preferring no change: "Where . . . the official is old-fashioned and does not believe in new-fangled ideas, no harm, and also no good, is likely to arise but where misdirected enthusiasm is given free play, expensive machinery may be ordered, where no real economy can be effected."[62] Only the work of officers "who have devoted considerable time and labor to the question of labor-saving devices" would lead to real economies. Therefore the push of experienced machine enthusiasts was a necessary condition for extensive mechanization. Second, Civil Service generalists—perhaps especially the upper echelons of the Treasury—would be suspicious of creating an important role for expert specialists. The generalist creed of the Civil Service was, and is, a unique obstruction to would-be professionalizers. Therefore, a second set of necessary conditions were arguments that would sway the Treasury. In the hands of Partridge and other middle-ranking officers, the expert movement of mechanizers had a program that fitted the ideology of the generalist-mechanical split, casting the former as rule givers and the latter as rule followers and machine minders. And, since the Civil Service as a whole had been represented as a general-purpose machine, mechanization promised what the Treasury's generalists (and Charles Babbage) wanted: control over the executive. Tying mechanization to the aggressive Treasury campaign to coordinate and extend control over other departments, justified by economy, was one such argument: "It was difficult to find people who had any real interest or belief in mechanization. But economy did interest them [the Treasury]."[63] Mechanization gave the middle-ranking officials influence, since investigation and recommendation required expertise, *and* promised effects desired by the generalists.

Furthermore, the Treasury's conversion to mechanization was hastened by a turf war with HMSO, which was responsible for the provision of machines and which indeed had set up a small inspectorate after witnessing Partridge, Scorgie, and Grieve's operations in 1916.[64] HMSO's attitude toward expensive office machinery had been transformed by the experience of wartime administration:

> Prior to 1914, the SO had established at Princes Street a small duplicating and addressing department with the object of giving facilities for these services to the departments of Whitehall. On the outbreak war, certain departments decided they must have such machines and services in their own buildings. . . . Immediately after, the SO opened Underwood Street, which was on a very large and ambitious scale. During the first war the demand for typewriters, duplicating, addressing machines and relatively few other types of machines developed very rapidly.[65]

Moving men and machines to the front depended on a growing bureaucracy—and therefore a growing HMSO—which required reports typed, copied, and transported. HMSO is often regarded as of peripheral importance in Whitehall—the "department of paper clips"—but at this moment of mechanization a ministry of machines was potentially a real threat to the Treasury. A turf-war account of the Treasury's subsequent seizure of responsibility for machines was later given by Scorgie: the Establishment control of staff numbers, the keystone of the Treasury's control of the public service, "via office machinery procedure," was "in danger of slipping from their hands" to HMSO—"the only place that had hitherto shown any awareness of the relationship [between mechanization and human organization] or any willingness to trade machines for men."[66] Mechanization must be understood in the context of the politics of the internal control of Whitehall. The Treasury took it up because it preserved, extended, and eventually symbolized and materially expressed its grip on and its vision of the Civil Service.

Partridge, Scorgie, and Grieve were unsuccessful in their efforts to be appointed en bloc as the Treasury Investigating Section. Partridge, probably already too senior, became Deputy Controller of Information in the new Department of the Controller-General of Civil Aviation in 1919. Scorgie returned from the war to be Deputy Controller of HMSO, but the Treasury tried to poach him for the new section: "I would have gone but [Codling, Controller of SO] refused to release me."[67] Both Scorgie and Codling proposed Grieve. As it turned out, of the original trio only Grieve became a Chief Investigating Officer. He was joined by two assistants: H. J. Biggs, an expert on registries, and Walter Desborough, "a minor staff clerk in the Home Office" whom Scorgie "had never heard of except as the author of a small book on office machinery." Desborough was to become the foremost promoter of Civil Service mechanization in the interwar years.

"Desborough's Toys"

Walter Desborough joined the Home Office Statistical Branch as a lowly Boy Clerk around 1903, assisting in the preparation of "the Civil Judicial Statistics, the Licensing Statistics, the Statistics of Workmen's Compensation, and various Parliamentary Returns."[68] By 1914, having progressed through positions as Assistant Clerk and Second Division Clerk, he was earning a meager £85 per annum. To supplement his official income Desborough turned to lecturing to London County Council evening classes. The transfer of a colleague (a Mr. Stringer) to the Foreign Trade department left Desborough in charge of the Branch's various arithmetical, typewriting and duplicating machines at the beginning of the war. His superior, W. J. Farrant, pressing for a pay raise for the industrious clerk, recalled Desborough's wartime efforts:

> [He] devoted himself most zealously to the development of the [duplicating machine] process, and his perseverance and ingenuity have enabled him to make very considerable improvements in the machines, and more particularly in the accessories and supplies—waxed sheets, ink, and the various solutions &c.—and thereby to eliminate practically all the drawbacks of the process. . . . He has also enormously extended the scope of the application of the process, in directions never contemplated by the makers of the machines, e.g. bookwork printing, diagrams, &c. His improvements have been generally adopted by the Stationery Office and by other Government Departments. His mechanical skill enables him to execute most repairs and adjustments of the great variety of machines in use for different purposes.[69]

The Home Office was particular pleased with Desborough's "zeal, knowledge and intelligence." His deft use of Addressograph and duplicating machines enabled "instant and constant instructions be given to the police and other local authorities"—handy for the law and order department faced with uncertain knowledge of the wartime population.[70] Meanwhile, Desborough continued the evening lectures, conducting very large classes, nearly entirely of women, on business training and office procedure. The number of women employed in public service had jumped: in 1914 there were 65,000 (58,000 of which were in non-clerical Post Office grades—letter sorters, etc.). By 1919, 170,000 women were employed, many in central government departments which had previously showed reluctance. (This opportunity led Desborough to draft syllabi for the Home Office Committee on the Employment of Women, including one on subjects to be taught in women's commercial training classes.) Desborough therefore emerged from the First World War an expert in the mechanization of office work and the employment of women, which, as we saw in chapter 2, were closely interconnected.

With encouragement from their superiors, particularly Controller of Establishments Sir Russell Scott in the early 1920s, and with the Treasury's realization of its institutional interest in mechanization as a means of control of Civil Service staff and economy, the members of the Investigating Section busied themselves around Whitehall. Desborough led hundreds of civil servants around the annual Business Efficiency Exhibitions to introduce them to the potential of office machinery.[71] While appealing to "national efficiency" was a technique employed by the machine manufacturers (for example, a Comptometer Company pamphlet sent to the Treasury began with the phrase "At a time like the present when efficiency is a prime necessity not only for prosperity but for the very existence of the country, from a commercial point of view"), "efficiency" was understood within Whitehall as largely a matter of replacing expensive male clerks with a cheaper combination of machines and female operators.[72] The machines introduced into Whitehall in the 1920s to prune back departmental spending estimates were jocularly named

Figure 5.5
Walter Desborough. (source: National Archive for the History of Computing, University of Manchester)

Figure 5.6
Christmas dinner at Powers, 1944. Walter Desborough is seated at the far end of the table, on the right. (source: National Archive for the History of Computing, University of Manchester)

"Desborough's Toys" by Chancellor of the Exchequer Winston Churchill.[73] Work increased so much that Desborough, by the mid 1920s in sole charge of the Treasury Investigating officers, requested a deputy. ("He must at least be keen. He must have considerable knowledge of routine office work, preferably accounting or statistical, and he must have a good understanding of machine working. Above all, he must have a good personality and he must be able to preserve a real sense of proportion in dealing with suggestions for the use of machines. We don't want machines to be used as toys, but only where real staff economies will result."[74]) The Treasury approved: "There is so much done under this head and the savings are so substantial that it is a false economy to 'starve' this particular branch of Government activity."

But was there "so much done"? Many government concerns certainly retooled in a similar manner to the Royal Arsenal at Woolwich, which in 1921 requested office machinery "so as to bring the system more into line with modern practice; and to enable the Management . . . to be provided with the necessary information with a view to securing efficient and economic control."[75] However, many files from the 1920s and the 1930s, even those dealing with extensive reorganization through the introduction of office machinery, did not survive to be placed in the Public Record Office. The first full-scale mechanization project overseen by the Treasury section took place in the mid 1920s at the Post Office Savings Bank's clearinghouse at Blythe Road in London, where 15,000 post offices often sent information on 60,000 deposits per day.[76] In a paper discussing the history of this project, Campbell-Kelly describes the mechanization of the bank, which ended the use of hard-bound ledger books and introduced custom-made card-ledger equipment.[77] Campbell-Kelly ascribes what he sees as the bank's slowness to mechanize to "bureaucratic inertia and resistance to mechanization in the Post Office, and in the British Civil Service generally, . . . reinforced by a culture that tended to oppose gadgetry and ideas coming from outside the organization or the country."[78] Was this a typical pattern throughout Whitehall?

Desborough encouraged the use of punched-card machinery to make statistics. The Census of Production provides an interesting case. Burroughs adding machines had aided the calculation of statistics from the 1924 census. In the following years the Census of Production came to the attention of the Treasury investigators, led by Walter Desborough. As discussion began on arrangements for a survey in 1930, Desborough was keen to see further use of machinery. In June 1929 he proposed a punched-card system that would "not only enable the figures to be produced within a few days or weeks of the final examination of the schedules for any trade, but more detailed figures could be produced at no extra cost."[79] (At that very moment, across London at the Admiralty's Nautical Almanac Office in Greenwich, L. J. Comrie was pioneering the use of Hollerith machines in large-scale scientific calculation, generating positions of the moon.[80]) In the event, a Powers rather than a Hollerith system was given the nod. Either would result in "considerable speeding up of the work and [offer] much greater flexibility" compared to the Burroughs machines.[81] Powers required 715,000 cards, of five different types, to tabulate the census, in combination with a machine similar to one already in use for processing shipping statistics at the Board of Trade after "certain attachments were fitted."[82] Powers in turn mobilized the prestigious government commissions in its advertising, listing many government departmental users in an early 1930s pamphlet, headlined "Use this key to disclose the hidden facts of your business," in which readers "through the experience of [other "representative British houses"] may see the savings of a system of mechanical accounting which provides daily business 'X-rays' with hitherto unattained speed and accuracy," thereby unlocking "hidden business facts, [aiding] executives in securing information about their business, in time to make use of it."[83]

Desborough returned to his roots with his brief involvement in a third set of projects: mechanization within the Home Office. Desborough and his Treasury investigators recommended that punched-card techniques replace the old way of constructing criminal statistics—the "bar and gate" method in which figures were built up with "much mental and physical drudgery" on large ruled tabulating sheets (which got larger and more unwieldy as new crimes were categorized—new categorization went hand-in-hand with changes in data processing).[84] However, the Statistical Branch as a whole should not be seen as "backward" and was proud of its mechanizing history. Criminal statistics had been reported to the Home Office in an organized fashion since 1856, and a separate department initially collecting judicial statistics was formed within the Office in 1876.[85] Accusations of the statistical department's "notoriously inefficient manner"—which must be seen against the background of 1890s crime panics among the middle classes—were answered in 1893 by the construction of methods of preparing criminal statistics which emphasized completeness and "accuracy."[86] Likewise, civil judicial statistics were reformed "chiefly in the direction of uniformity and better arrangement." Accuracy was produced—in manner precisely analogous to contemporary transformations of physical laboratories—through disciplinary regimes. The Criminal Statistics Committee, for example, reported in 1893 that "care and accuracy both in the preparation of the individual returns and in the compilation of the final tables, are wasted unless the Central Department issues instructions which enable the police or the prison officers to work on uniform lines and exercises constant watchfulness to see that these instructions are carried out."[87]

At the same time, criminals were coming under greater and greater scrutiny, and the quantity and depth of criminal and judicial statistics expanded rapidly around the turn of the century. Licensing statistics were added as an extra burden in 1910, further expanding the cross-referential generation of knowledge: "the relation between the consumption of drink, and drunkenness and other social phenomena (trade, unemployment, etc.) . . . studied," knowledge which was therefore to hand when the First World War provided an opportunity to restrict the sale and consumption of alcohol.[88] Envious eyes were turned to the Continent, where greater standardization (in method and in law) and centralization suggested to the Home Office a potential path forward.[89] The Home Office therefore was motivated by a need to shake off what it saw as an undeserved past reputation for inefficiency, and was looking for a means to *display* efficiency. Furthermore, the Office's central role of coordinating techniques of *control* within British society, through the police and prisons, increased demands for more and fresher statistical information. Together these factors provide a context within which the Home Office's relative enthusiasm for mechanization can be explained. The work of statistical production in the Home Office, having been rationalized and disciplined through standardized methods, was then progressively mechanized: the "increase of work" after 1893 "immediately met in part by obtaining a calculating machine." In 1917, Desborough's boss, W. J. Farrant, boasted: "I have carefully inquired into and noted the capabilities and merits of the various mechanical labor saving appliances as they have become available, and from time to time, as the needs of the department have grown, I have procured the adoption, to the fullest extent to which they could be profitably utilized, of a variety of machines for arithmetical and other purposes."[90] The Home Office introduced electrical adding machines, duplicating machines, and the Addressograph (for printing addresses) ahead of the rest of the Civil Service, and both the latter machines soon proved themselves in expediting centralized social control:

> The fortuitous existence upon the outbreak of war of the duplicating and addressing machines in the Statistical Branch enabled instant and constant instructions to be given to the police and other local authorities [so that these bodies could be rapidly advised from the center]. The machines have been in constant use ever since.

Desborough, visiting on inspection in the 1920s, was therefore returning home in many senses: not only to where he gained his apprenticeship but also to where he developed his enthusiasm for machines and where there remained a culture receptive to mechanization. Desborough and his investigating colleague D. G. Robertson were pushing at an open door when they recommended the introduction of punched-card techniques. "Systems," such as those supplied by Powers or BTM, were, argued the Treasury section, "capable of providing all the statistics now obtained and with great economy. In fact all the necessary machine processes would barely occupy one girl operator full time. . . . The whole of this [Statistical] Branch should therefore be done by three clerks and a girl operator." Desborough and Robertson were, however, keen to point out that qualitative changes in the production of statistics could also be effected by the introduction of punched cards: additional statistics could be made cheaply and quickly.

Desborough and Robertson recommended further mechanization elsewhere in the Home Office. In the mid 1920s the Home Office's payroll—a large one because of the police service—had been prepared by the traditional method of noting in pencil any variations on the previous week's payroll before inking, checking, and counter-checking. The Treasury duo suggested a centralized system, with "girl operators in place of Police Sergeants" and with Adrema Electric Printing Machines and Burroughs Double Sterling Motor Control Carriage machines (which typed and calculated) in place of pencils, pens and paper. However, Home Office mechanization may have been interrupted when Desborough left the Civil Service in 1931 to become general manager of Powers—a "surprising choice," if we agree with Campbell-Kelly that he was a "career civil servant without any commercial or selling experience whatever," or not, if we note, as Campbell-Kelly also does, his "instrumental" role in mechanizing the British Civil Service.[91]

Even when statistical production within the Home Office was mechanized, the initial information was written up and submitted by police officers as an annual return. This situation changed in the late 1930s when the organization of criminal statistics was again reviewed by the Treasury and further introduction of punched-card machines implemented. The investigators reported that the police found the annual written return an "intolerable burden." "It has even been stated that Police Officers engaged in the work of annual tabulation were in a habit of shutting themselves away in a room for some days, although," joked a Home Office official. "The tale that some of them folded a wet towel round their head is somewhat exaggerated."[92] Moreover, complaints had been received from "various Parliamentary, other administrative, and outside sources" of delays—typically more than 2 years—in publishing the annual Criminal Statistics. The response was further disciplining of the reporting police officers: beginning in January 1937 they were required to fill out dual-purpose punched cards, which were then subsequently, and speedily, processed by the Home Office on Powers-Samas three-bank "punching-counting-sorting" machines. The scheme was indeed popular with the police and did speed up publication. But there were also other advantages to the Home Office. The card library on crime that the Home Office built up was far more flexible: figures within the month could be issued quickly "for detective purposes," and police forces could obtain "on request . . . particular figures relating to their own area." The diffusion of punched-card techniques from the center therefore led to the provision of fresh, more locally specific criminal information and helped the growth of detective work.

Punched Cards and the Expansion of the State

Policing has always been problematic in London, a sprawling capital city with by far the highest urban population in the United Kingdom. Likewise, the capital's Metropolitan Police encountered data-processing predicaments earlier and in a more intense form than the provincial forces. The Office of the Commissioner of the Metropolitan Police at New Scotland Yard, a body which was part Whitehall department and part police headquarters, mirrored many of the Home Office's developments in mechanization. While Colonel Partridge, now at the Statistical Office of the Criminal Investigation Department, recommended to his superiors in 1924 after due investigation that the time was not ripe for a BTM "Electrical Sorting Machine" (a conclusion the company agreed with), extensive mechanization in the Commissioner's Office was begun in the following decade.[93] The scheme to mechanize the S.2 (statistical) branch at Scotland Yard was composed "in his own time" by a member of the branch, S. J. Hobson, "in close collaboration with a machine expert," probably from the Treasury.[94]

Hobson's enthusiastic proposal provides a good illustration of an important pattern: mechanization appealed particularly to civil servants of Executive Officer level—middle managers, sandwiched between generalists and mechanicals—who were willing to devote time to such a technical project if it brought them career rewards, such as recognition by superiors, and because mechanization resonated with how they viewed the Civil Service: an organization that should value efficiency and explicit procedure. All the machine enthusiasts—Desborough, Partridge, Hobson—emerged from these middle layers of the hierarchy. The reason their superiors were inclined to listen, and even approve, schemes to mechanize the Civil Service, was because external and internal pressures prompted them to consider means of speeding up and expanding the state's capacities in data processing—a solution facilitated by the prior characterization of the Civil Service as a machine. In the case of Hobson's proposal the external pressure on the Metropolitan Police was the rise in vehicle accidents and new associated crimes—the beginnings of a close link between two technological systems, car culture and police data processing, that deepened through the century and is reconsidered in chapter 9. The rise in car ownership after the First World War and the introduction in 1935 of a 30-mph urban speed limit created a deluge of extra police work: 97,000 extra summonses for motor traffic offenses had to be reported to the Home Office or the Metropolitan Police Commissioner in the first year of the limit's operation alone.[95] Hobson emphasized in his proposal for punched-card mechanization at New Scotland Yard how cards alone could contain such an increase in work:

> . . . in order to exploit to the full the material now available (including also accidents which involve no personal injury) . . . the present method of recording the facts although more informative than in the past, is not sufficiently flexible and . . . the only

way of doing it is to record all salient particulars of each accident daily on a machine card.[96]

Hobson also promised acceleration of production of criminal statistics through the replacement of the bar-and-gate (sometimes called "barred-gate") manual methods, and in his words "abolishing the cumbersome and expensive "abstractor's" registers, of which there are 23 different types, some as wide as 3′6″ across, and substituting . . . punched cards." As with Home Office mechanization, the changes in method at Scotland Yard had repercussions for the police officers who submitted the information: Hobson proposed replacing bound books with loose-leaf books for the initial recording of data. (In fact the more "advanced" Home Office solution of dual-purpose cards was chosen.) A secondhand Powers three-bank Printing-Counting-Sorter, fresh from use on the 1931 census, was bought (its availability was said to have "made the proposed scheme a practicable job"), and the mechanization of statistical production began at Scotland Yard in 1935.[97] Within a year and a half, 900,000 cards had been processed, and it was apparent that the two underpaid girls brought in to work the machines were "being overworked and getting practically no relief from the monotonous work of punching cards."[98] By 1936 criminal London was known, statistically, at a finer level than ever before.

During the interwar years crime and policing were both becoming more mobile and more international. Officers at Scotland Yard were regularly visited by their American counterparts, and vice versa. Captain Sillitoe, for example, visited the central bureau for criminal identification and investigation in Sacramento, the state capital of California, and was impressed by the centralized office where "the system of compilation is so up to date and elastic that it permits of the intimate study of information contained in . . . police reports in the shortest possible time." The achievements of Sacramento were made possible by the application of Hollerith techniques, imported, noted the inaccurate detective, from the "United States Bureau of Censors" (he misheard "Census").[99] Sillitoe's observations prompted the Metropolitan Police to consider whether cards could be used not only to produce statistics but "in trying to 'catch thieves on paper,'" although card experts in Scotland Yard, at Powers, and at the Ministry of Labour all rejected the idea.[100] Five years later, Mr. Coffey, an agent from the Federal Bureau of Investigation, visited and praised Hobson's "neat little machine plant" (he was particularly impressed by the dual-use cards). Again much exchange of information and experience occurred: Coffey informing Hobson of the Hollerith system used in Washington on which cards "containing coded descriptions [of] 12,000 really bad criminals" were quickly sorted; Hobson told Coffey about the Findex system which could sort "his 12,000 'bad hats' in a quarter of the time."[101] Chief Constable W. W. Foster of Vancouver, who witnessed Hobson's punched-card installation, was also struck by its possibilities, confessing to his counterpart Sir Philip Game: "Owing to a large foreign population, particularly the Orientals, over 30,000 strong in Vancouver, we have unusual problems to face. . . . I have every reason to feel grateful for the valuable information acquired."[102] The dream of police forces in London and North America, catching thieves by paper, was however much more tricky: Hobson in London spent much of the 1930s trying to mechanize the Criminal Records Office, with its extensive files and registers of modus operandi and fingerprints but with little success. Coffey sympathized: mechanizing the FBI, with 5 million fingerprints for example, was a daunting prospect. Not until the computerization of Scotland Yard, discussed in chapter 9, was this aim achieved.

The Metropolitan Police can be characterized as a body at the fringes of government but near the center of the state. It is important to note that the availability of mechanized data-processing methods, primarily punched-card machines, played a role in the remarkable growth of other organizations at the fringes of government. The Milk Marketing Board, for example, was a new sort of organization: non-profit-making, created by parliamentary statute, given state-backed monopolies, but owned collectively by milk producers. The Board was one of the first "quangos"[103] (indeed I have found a description of the Board as a "quasi-government organization" from 1945), and punched-card methods were "indispensable" to the Board's operation. After the Board's establishment in 1933, it was compulsory for milk producers to sell their produce to the Board in England and Wales, which was then obliged to market the produce to the dairy trade. Punched cards kept track of the many small transactions, for example payments to farmers, on which the Board's operation depended: the national flow of milk was mirrored by a flow of information.

The Milk Marketing Board put in BTM's "largest ever order," a significant one in many ways for the punched-card company.[104] The benefits to the dairy farmer, who had experienced grave economic difficulties after the First World War, was guaranteed purchase of milk, and the advantage to the consumer was state-guaranteed quality and hygiene standards. But a principle claim at the time was technocratic: that experts in charge at the Board would organize the industry, like a miniature Civil Service, in an "efficient" fashion.[105] This "typical British compromise" (like the BBC, which was established as a corporation at almost the same time) was the start of a burgeoning growth in bodies which were neither wholly public nor wholly private.[106] If cards were indeed "indispensable" to the Board then a clear link between the availability of data-processing techniques and changing styles of governance can be seen. Many of the British corporations, managing activities from television to postwar nuclear power (and even, arguably the original municipal bodies) were formed in response to technological change. Examples such as the BBC, the Central Electricity Board, the London Passenger Transport Board and the Atomic Energy Authority illustrate how large technological systems raised questions of organization and ownership: ownership by corporation formed a third way between private capitalism and full nationalization. The preservation of apparent independence did not mean the corporations did not act as state instruments: the Board for example was the tool through which the paternalistic Clean Milk Campaign was waged.[107] The Milk Marketing Board was an example of state-led, if not state-owned, centralization. Punched-card methods eased the process of centralization as the discussions surrounding the 1921 census illustrate.

The 1921 Census

> The great events of the decennium thus concluded cannot fail to impress a character of uncommon significance upon the results of this Census, whether regarded as vestigial records of the passage of the War itself or as a source of enlightenment upon the many problems which the War has bequeathed to us. For such enlightenment, at the very time when it is most sorely needed, the country has been, pending these results, unusually at a loss, since there are but few questions to-day upon which guidance can be sought of the last Census across the great gulf of War which lies between.
>
> —PRO RG 19/62. S. P. Vivian, Draft preliminary report of 1921 census, 1921

The 1921 census was, as Sylvanus Percival Vivian made plain in his report to Minister of Health Alfred Mond, an important one. The "great gulf of War" was an absence of information.[108] Just as the myth of the Belle Époque had rapidly grown after 1918 with regard to the apparent certainties of prewar social structure, so a similar sentiment could be found in discussions of the techniques of knowing. Before the war, people knew their place, and, through the census, the government knew the people. Now there was uncertainty.

The census of 1911 had been, as was shown above, an innovative one for Britain: the first use of punched-card machines connected with the attempt to generate masses of fertility statistics. However, ten years later, the fertility question—the duration of existing marriages and the number of children born of such marriages—was left off the schedule, the "first time in the history of modern census-taking in this country that any enquiry once introduced . . . has been omitted . . . on a subsequent occasion." This omission was not because

Figure 5.7
The Powers multi-counting sorter used in the 1921 Census of Population of England and Wales. This machine was probably shaped by negotiations between technically-competent civil servants and engineers from the Powers company. (source: National Archive for the History of Computing, University of Manchester)

the importance of the question had declined. Indeed the interest in eugenics in Britain was peaking in the decade after the First World War. Partly the reason lay in the sheer comprehensiveness of the 1911 statistics, the "long range of the 1911 enquiry and of the fact that the wealth of material which it provided had not been completely exhausted."[109] In chapter 4 it was argued that the British authorities realized that many interconnecting registers could perform the same job as the central register, which was more problematic to liberal values. Likewise, through judicious estimation of the long-lasting value of existing statistical information—in this case fertility statistics—government could refrain from appearing overly inquisitive. The second reason for dropping of the fertility question is just as interesting: because of the number of other questions being asked in the 1921 census was already straining the information technologies adopted only a decade earlier.

Three factors combined to put limits on the amount of information collected in a census. The first was the willingness of the public to answer both number and type of questions. Although the filling in of a census form could be enforced by law, this factor was still one the civil servants planning the census had to, and did, bear in mind, as Vivian despondently noted: "The limits of expansion of the Census Schedule appear to have been reached."[110] The second factor was technological: the finite size of the punched card meant that there was intense competition between government departments, each of which wanted different sorts of knowledge of the public, over the access to punched-card columns. Whitehall politics were therefore inscribed into the punched card itself (frustratingly, however, although the many draft cards have survived in the archive, the correspondence reflecting these negotiations has not).[111] Two new questions had been added: one on place of work, and one on dependency.[112] Some officials were certainly very unhappy about what they saw as a misallocation. "It seems to me," wrote one unhappy official, "that the space allotted to two new questions, place of work and dependency, is out of proportion. The card has 38 columns other than the seven allotted to identification and of these 13, or 34 percent, are allotted to these questions. Seeing that it has never been thought necessary to collect this information before in our census, or, so far as I know in any other, I cannot think that this allotment of space fairly represents their relative importance, and I fear that older and more important inquiries may suffer somewhat in consequence . . . but I know the Registrar General takes the opposite view."[113] This observer was particularly annoyed that a column devoted to "density" (the average number of rooms per person in family, related to the question of how many persons lived in the same dwelling, a tricky definitional problem for the census enumerators) might be rejected. Without the inclusion of a density column it could not be found out how "any section of the population distinguishable on the cards, as by age, sex, marital condition, orphanhood, occupation, industry, birthplace, etc., was housed." Considerable pressure, even at a time when there was a political battle over claims that "homes fit for heroes" would be built for the veterans, was required to reinstate density on the card. The outcome therefore was that work and dependency dominated the 1921 card, density was just retained, and fertility dropped. Of course, absence from the card did not mean that, so long as the questions had been included in the schedule, statistics could *not* have been obtained: they could have been worked out by hand, either in total or by sampling. However this work would have been expensive: if inclusion could not be justified on the cheaper card, it is hard to see how a case could be made for a pricier method.

One irony of this politics was that the total number of columns available was largely contingent. In 1920, British Tabulating Machines had politely intimated that it was not anxious to make their machines available for the forthcoming census, partly because of difficulties in obtaining quality card at a reasonable price, partly because of a rush of census orders from Australia, New Zealand, and Bengal.[114] Nevertheless, Desborough's office machinery committee asked HMSO to commence negotiations with both Powers-Samas and BTM over possible supplies of cards and machines.[115] By June, "after exhaustive re-examination," the Registrar-General stated the requirement for the 1921 census as being 170 key punches, 12 gang punches, 30 sorting machines, 16 counting machines, one tabulating machine, and 70 verification punches.[116] At this point, BTM withdrew, pleading that it could "only manufacture half the equipment necessary even if the Stationery Office advance a substantial portion of capital" and stating that there was "no possibility of obtaining paper for cards other than English at double the price of American."[117] The Treasury was unhappy with BTM's suggestion that 2 years' rent be paid before BTM would begin the order.[118] The contract therefore went to Powers, and their 45-column card, the paper secured after tough negotiations with a Prague-based firm.[119] Not everyone within government was pleased with this choice. The Superintendent of Statistics of the GRO in Edinburgh, for example, considered Powers machines "too delicate for constant work," the problem lying in "an essential part of the mechanism . . . a double wire constructed like that of a bicycle Bowden brake." It is interesting to note that punched-card engineering was *comprehensible* to non-specialists such as civil servants by analogy to familiar technologies: "Knowing the troubles arising from the use of such a wire on a bicycle, where only coarse movements are wanted, I feel that suspicions as to continued reliability for fine movements is very justifiable."[120] In following chapters we will see that making electronic computers comprehensible was, at least initially, a trickier matter. After much argument the Scottish Census retained its BTM machines. The Powers equipment for the English and Wales Census was installed at the Lambeth Workhouse in late 1920.[121]

Although I argue that the 45-column limit shaped the information collected in the 1921 census, and therefore the censal information of the British people, I do not argue that the constraint was deterministic. There were ways, for example, of squeezing more information onto a card, by double-punching in a single column.[122] Even the technology for managing the information was malleable. Powers did not offer a three-column counting-sorting machine—that is say, a machine that would enable a count to be taken of three different columns at the same time as sorting in a single passage of cards. Such strategies would save the 1921 census considerable time, allowing whole age groups to counted by orphanhood, education and Welsh language in one sort. The technical innovations to accomplish this feat, proposed by W. W. Wallis, a member of the Registrar-General's department with a "natural bent for matters mechanical" who was in charge of the 1921 census equipment, were retained by Powers—a good, if minor and if true, example of how government interests shaped information technology.[123]

Furthermore, expansion of information could always be bought. Before 1921 the Ministry of Labour, along with the Home Office and the Board of Trade, had considered how to improve the statistics of occupation and industry (in particular, to make them comparable with those generated by the Census of Production). A set of occupational and industrial classifications was adopted, the workplace question was included in the census schedule, and swathes of the punched card were devoted to the extra data. However, between October and December 1921, after the census had been taken, the Treasury began demanding that expenditures be reduced in line with the "Geddes cuts," a response to an ailing economy. Much to the Ministry of Labour's annoyance, one cut fell on the industrial tables by county, the information it wanted regarding the geography of amounts and sorts of industry.[124] The Ministry of Labour required the statistics "to make comparisons locally as well as nationally between the number of persons engaged in different industries and the numbers insured, and to this end the classification of industries for Unemployment Insurance Statistics was brought into line with that adopted for the Census."[125] Coordination had led to comparability and thence to certain momentum to produce the statistics. In early 1924 the Ministry of Labour agreed to fund the extra tabulation itself, at a cost of £1000, using Powers machines at the Ministry of Pensions. Therefore, extra information was available, but at a price.

Even before tabulation a complex series of negotiations had been accomplished, each of which entailed expense: a bill passed through Parliament, boundaries were reorganized, census areas were drawn on Ordnance Survey maps, occupations and other categories were defined and stabilized, the Schedule was designed and printed, enumerators were appointed and trained, enumerators' books were checked, and cards were debated, designed, and finally punched. In a breakdown of expenditures on the 1921 census (total £155,653), the punching of cards (£18,784) and machine tabulation (£26,726) were the two most expensive items. The cost was not merely rental of machinery from Powers, but also "programming": working out the algorithm whereby the raw stack of cards would be sorted and counted to extract the figures desired.

The expense of temporarily assembling people and machines, and the problems with the manufacturers of punched-card machines, had in the midst of organizing the 1921 census prompted Vivian to suggest a radical solution: since "plans must shortly be made for the manufacture of a large mechanical equipment for the collecting, organization and training of a large staff of coders, punchers, checkers, machine minders, tabulators, etc., etc., and for securing, adapting and fitting a large building to contain them," why not seek a way to make permanent use of them? Many government departments now had statistical departments, and most made some use of machinery.[126] But the small scale of departmental statistics led to problems: if they could only afford one machine, say, but needed to process a range of types of statistics, the machine would inevitably only be suitable for some of them. This limitation would be removed if statistical calculation was centralized. Vivian's vision in 1920 was a centralized data-processing center for government statistics, "a single big establishment well equipped with all kinds of machinery." With at least "equal efficiency and with enormously greater economy," a government center for statistical calculation would bring a further benefit: increased control over the manufacturers, or even nationalization of the means of calculation:

> A fairly large mechanical establishment in constant employment would enable the Government to be less dependent upon the existing firms of machine-makers than at present. It would permit of machines being built by or for the Government, or owned by the Government, and would thus enable the Government to take advantage of any progress in machine-designing, in whatsoever quarter it appeared.

It is not known why Vivian's scheme failed. The political context augured well, with the Chancellor of the Exchequer keen that statistical services be reorganized. Vivian's allies were enthusiastic. HMSO, for example, wrote in immediately to lend support, the officer responsible declaring "As you know,

I am a firm believer in the centralization of all kinds of mechanical and manipulative work."[127] There would certainly have been opposition from the Board of Trade, and smaller statistical departments, not merely because of loss of control per se, but because they held doubts that other parts of government would have the expertise to correctly produce their statistics. The objection anticipated by Vivian, that large statistical jobs might coincide and overwhelm a centralized statistical center, a problem potentially aggravated by powers to hold quinquennial censuses included in the 1920 Census Bill, was not regarded by him as insuperable (indeed a centralized center could more easily manage fluctuations of workload than many distributed units). Possibly there was just not enough time to set up a centralized statistical center before the 1921 census was upon them. Not until the Second World War would Vivian's scheme be realized.

The 1931 census did not raise any profound issues of organization, but there was a reversal in the choice of a supplier of punched-card machines. A tussle between British Tabulating Machines and Powers developed in the mid 1920s, and Vivian acted to assert the government's interest. Both companies were

Figure 5.8
The Powers Printing-Counting-Sorter machine used for the 1931 Census of Population of England and Wales. (source: National Archive for the History of Computing, University of Manchester)

Figure 5.9
The Powers Printing-Counting-Sorter machine used for the 1931 Census of Population of England and Wales. Note that an operator is shown, despite the fact that the P-C-S was described as "automatic." Operators within the Civil Service would have been classed as "mechanicals," so the elision would have been discursively justified. (source: National Archive for the History of Computing, University of Manchester)

told the GRO's opinion that "considerable administrative economies would be realized by the use of counting machines which automatically recorded the results," since "if feasible . . . machine and staff time [would be saved] by reducing the extent of machine stoppages and would eliminate some costs in checking."[128] Both manufacturers swiftly made this modification to their machines. In Vivian's view the Powers printing attachment was slightly superior to that on the BTM machine, but the latter Hollerith design was slightly cheaper. "Indeed," he informed Sir Russell Scott while thinking of the patriotic Buy British campaign then being waged by the *Daily Mail* and by the Tory politician Leo Amery, "both money and performance considerations appear to be so nearly balanced that the scale would probably be turned by any decisive advantage which either contractor might possess as regards British construction."[129] Both companies could claim "Britishness," but Powers-Samas

Figure 5.10
A Printing-Counting-Sorter (P-C-S) at the War Office. (source: National Archive for the History of Computing, University of Manchester)

was on more solid ground, and they were awarded the 1931 census contract.[130] The 1931 census was the first use of the Powers automatic Printing-Counting-Sorter—a device directly shaped by government interests and one which proved popular in other governmental applications.[131] By the time of the next projected (but aborted) census of population, 1941, Britain administrative energies were devoted elsewhere, although knowledge of the home population was not lost for the duration of the Second World War; indeed, the need for it intensified, and the P-C-S was a wartime workhorse.

An Expert Movement of Mechanizers

During the first half of the twentieth century, interest in mechanization in Whitehall departments grew. I will now present evidence that this interest can be found in a more extended form, and that indeed it is fair to talk of the existence of a community or culture of office mechanizers that increased in strength during the period. Some aspects of this culture are well known to historians; in particular, punched-card machine manufacturers in the United Kingdom have been exhaustively examined by Campbell-Kelly in *ICL*. Likewise, Croarken has provided an excellent account of how by the 1930s office machines had been turned by L. J. Comrie, among others, into means of scientific calculation, both for a government body (the Nautical Almanac Office) and as a private venture (Scientific Computing Service Ltd.).[132] Comrie's vision was to "spread the gospel of mechanical computation" as widely as possible.[133] But BTM, Powers, and the SCS can be placed in a wider milieus of interest in office mechanization. Evidence for this comes from three areas: an increase in specialist publications, specialist organizations of various types, and contemporary correspondence.

A number of books were published in the interwar period on office mechanization, mostly aimed at managers in private businesses, although some were targeted at public bodies such as local authorities and corporations. Examples include L. R. Dicksee's *Office Machinery and Appliances* (1917), Walter Desborough's *Office Machines, Appliances and Methods* (1921), Desborough's *Duplicating and Copying Processes* (1930), P. T. Lloyd's *The Technique of Efficient Office Methods* (1931), C. Ralph Curtis's *Mechanized Accounting* (1932), L. J. Comrie's *The Hollerith and Powers Tabulating Machines* (1933), Lloyd's *Research in the Office* (1935), Owen Sutton's *Machine Accounting for Small and Large Businesses* (1943), and Bernard Hazel's *Local Authority Accounting by Punched Card Methods* (1945).[134] Perhaps even more significant than individual books was the attention paid to the area by specialist presses—notably Sir Isaac Pitman & Sons, which made most of its money from guides to shorthand but which also published books on most other aspects of modern office work. The tone of many of these books was evangelical, promising a glorious future if only the managerial readers would convert. Desborough, for example, drew an analogy with manufacturing:

> The growth of offices makes organization imperative, since the success of a large business is now more dependent upon the smooth running and efficiency of the office staff than formerly. The attitude of British business men has practically become enthusiastic in favor of labor-saving machinery in the factory, but in the office little or no attempt is made to introduce machinery. . . . [But] the change from manual and mental to machine methods is bound to come in the office as it has in the industrial world.[135]

"Modern methods," the young Desborough wrote, "must necessarily be introduced into the office or the tide of progress will be arrested." The contrast between the traditional and the modern mechanized office was repeatedly drawn. In a lecture series organized by *The Accountant*, Desborough invited his audience to "compare the old-fashioned office with heavy duty cumbersome books, hard high stools, copying press, boiling can of hektograph jelly and pieces of paper for trial casting etc. with the modern mechanized office."[136] Of course direct competitive advantages were promised: ". . . the more highly organized the business the greater the amount of information required," while "enterprising" companies introducing "the most up-to-date machinery" into their offices would be "expediting their office work and amplifying the data and statistics concerning their manufacture, increase their business and probably their office staff." This latter remark shows how, as well as aiming to create a community of converts, modernizing office books and journals such as *The Accountant*, sought to reassure waverers (or even skeptics) that there were no bad side effects of mechanization. Much effort was expended showing that mechanization of clerical work would not lead to unemployment or drudgery. From census records, the number of male clerks rose from 687,121 in 1921 to 728,933 in 1931, while the number of female clerks and typists increased from 495,741 to 572,525. The number of clerks increased by 10 percent while the population as a whole rose by 5.16 percent—an indication of the growth of "knowledge workers." Such figures were mobilized to argue that no unemployment was being caused by mechanization, although, of course, these figure do *not* demonstrate that case). Unemployment was a particularly sensitive issue after the Great Crash and Depression in America inevitably had severe repercussions in Europe.[137] On the monotony of machine tending, Curtis maintained that "far from turning men into machines, the introduction of mechanical aids to book-keeping will lift the book-keeping profession out of the slough of drudgery into which the old-fashioned methods of the Victorian era precipitated it."[138] Desborough repeated the slightly strange argument of Stanley Rowland that office mechanization led to a need for *more* intelligent employees: "Any fool can keep books with pen and ink; but a fool easily discovers that the mute obedience of the machine soon proclaims the foolishness of the machine's master. In other words, the fool who controls machines soon gets things so tied up . . . that employers almost automatically discover the facts and fire them."[139] Note who this "automatic" argument was aimed at: middle management, in this case overseers of an accountancy office. If the audience was still not convinced, the hoary story of national decline was rehearsed again: "Our principal competitors in the world markets [America, Germany, even Japan]," Desborough warned, were "adopting mechanization of the office to a larger extent than in Great Britain."[140] In summary, office mechanization was presented in published works of the interwar period as a modernist ideology for consumption and conversion of middle managers in business in a manner that anticipated and assuaged anxieties.

If attention was restricted to the published works relating to office mechanization, it might be assumed that it was largely a movement in the private sector. However, this impression is an artefact of the publishers' market: the largest group who needed to go to books and journals for the modernizing message were middle managers in the private sector, predominantly accountants, and the published works obviously appealed to this constituency. Other groups learned the culture of office machinery through other routes, including the Civil Service (the largest organization in the United Kingdom). Mechanizers could read of new techniques in books and journals; more important, they could access the information internally (for example, through contact with Treasury investigating officers). And analysis of private correspondence illustrates another aspect of the culture: the role of the London gentlemen's clubs that encircled Whitehall. Treasury officers such as D. G. Robertson regularly attended the National Liberal club, also meeting fellow office mechanizers at the Reform Club, and there is evidence that experiences of mechanization in both the private and the public sector were shared in these spaces in the interwar years.[141] At other gentlemen's clubs, civil servants mixed with their equals in scientific and technical expertise: the Athenaeum in particular was one of the most important "trading zones" between British science and government through much of the twentieth century, a history which is unlikely to be given its due prominence because of the discreet reticence of these bodies (which was, of course, why they worked).

Further evidence of an office-mechanization movement is provided by the appearance and growth of organizations that marked the existence and the bounds of the more fluid and less visible network of contacts between people. The Office Appliances Trades Association was founded in 1911 and revived after the Great War; beginning in 1920, it staged Business Efficiency Exhibitions—regular gatherings of the movement, aptly described by one historian as "tremendously popular events, very much the forerunners of present-day computer fairs, at which vendors would announce their latest machine developments."[142] Desborough, who chaired the OATA before leaving the Treasury in 1931 to become managing director of Powers-Samas, boasted that the first thing he did with "corresponding members" (contacts in government departments responsible for transmitting Treasury guidance on mechanization) was "take 200 of them in small parties during ten days to the Business Efficiency Exhibition."[143] Such actions in the late 1920s, Desborough thought, had made possible the Treasury's Controller of Establishments Sir Russell Scott's reply to a Select Committee, in which he "justly claimed" that the Civil Service was "in the van of progress as regards office efficiency." Complementing the OATA was the Office Machinery Users Association, set up in 1912. The volunteers who ran these organizations were drawn from the manufacturing firms, from private business, from Whitehall, and from specialized consultancy or management study bodies, and they frequently changed jobs

Figure 5.11
The Accounting and Tabulating Corporation of Great Britain's stand at a 1920s Business Efficiency Exhibition. (source: National Archive for the History of Computing, University of Manchester)

and sectors. For example, Harry Ward worked as a gunner before joining the War Office, then worked for the National Institute of Industrial Psychology and for Management Research Group No. 1 (a mutual-aid research organization, founded in 1926 by 30 leading industrial businesses, that in 1942 became the Industrial Management Research Association—a government-industry cooperative venture); Ward then helped set up the consultancy Urwick Orr in the mid 1930s, and he regularly met with civil servants at the gentlemen's clubs.[144] Ward's Honorary Treasurer at Management Research Group No. 1, C. W. Reeve, was a managing director, and later chairman, of two firms, AEC and ACV, served for London Transport, and was an active member of the Office Machinery Users Association. From 1926 on, the Management Research Group No. 1 had a sub-body, the Office Committee, that specialized in office efficiency; in 1932 merged with the Users Association to form the Office Management Association, later renamed the Institute of Office Management. Finally, one of Ward's outfits, the National Institute of Industrial Psychology, founded in 1921, should be seen as promoting a goal very similar to what the Treasury mechanizers were to envision for government: "to consider the worker, the machine, and the task as one unit."[145] The pattern of people and organizations was therefore complex, but it should be understood as showing two things: that there was an extensive organized interest in office methods in interwar Britain and that they were run by a group—a group of potential technocrats—whose members moved easily between the private and the public sector.

Mechanization and the Female Civil Servant

I have discussed how work could be reorganized alongside the mechanization of government departments. One aspect I have not discussed fully up until now, however, is how mechanization was tied to changing patterns of the gendered division of clerical labor. The expansion of the Civil Service created demand for more and cheaper clerical labor. The small male-dominated Victorian office was transformed over a few decades into the large hierarchical Whitehall organization, with plenty of room for low-paid female labor and even small numbers of high-level generalist female civil servants. (The future Permanent Secretary and star of Crossman's *Diaries of a Cabinet Minister*, Dame Evelyn Sharp, was one such rare person, joining up in 1925.) The latter gained entry only after overcoming substantial resistance, the heart of the conflict being the contradiction between the supposedly meritocratic ideal of entry by open examination and the elite-preserving system of recruitment to the First Division as it operated in practice—a preference for testing subjects taught under Oxbridge classics triposes, for example.[146] As Zimmeck emphasizes, the common experience of the exam was the foundation of First Division esprit de corps (in the absence of significant movement between departments) and was of particular importance to the Treasury, which had first pick from the cadre of the successful candidates. Thus, it was at the Treasury First Division level that the contradictions of patriarchy and meritocracy would perhaps have been most keenly felt.

But the Treasury, in its establishment role, was also responsible for overseeing the provision of staff to the Civil Service, and increasingly sought to fill the increasingly routinized office positions with cheaper female labor and machines. Desborough's career should be seen in this context. He had emerged from the Home Office an expert in both machines and the associated employment of women in routinized work, and he had promulgated his message at London County Council evening classes. (Recall also that the London County Council's strategy of saving money by contracting out machine operation and therefore female employment to the Powers punched-card company was urged on Whitehall.) Desborough himself refused to draw a strict causal link but observed "office machines have certainly been largely responsible for the invasion of office work by girls." He went on to argue that the "same applies to industry generally and I do not think the continuity of quill pens and high stools would have kept girls out of offices."[147] Economies in salaries were not the only justification for the employment of female clerks. Punching cards was regarded as particularly suitable work for women. Indeed, in 1925 Sidney Downes, assistant general manager of the Acc and Tab (i.e., Powers) and a member of the executive committee of the OATA, wrote to inform Vivian that at an installation abroad a Head of Department had been instructed to replace the female punching operators "that we have been at considerable pains to train and who are now giving infinitely better results" with male government officials "who were originally put on the work"; fearing a "disaster" and for the "reputation of our machines as a consequence," Downes asked Vivian to state the "facts" about the 1921 census, and for "any information that you can give us with regard to the relative results obtained by men and girls." Downes's impression was that the Registrar-General was "fully convinced that female labor is more suited to this work than that of boys or men."[148]

In general, if (as Zimmeck argues) it was the case that, because of the threat of female employment, "from the turn of the century and more intensively after the First World War, top male civil servants acted in a shifty fashion," creating barriers from unequal pay to the marriage bar, then we might expect, since mechanization came with the employment of women, some of the anxiety to be transferred to attitudes against machines. This was not the case for two reasons. First, machines were not competing against First Division civil servants, at least not yet. Second, and more profound, there was a deep resonance between the values of mechanization and the values of the professional Civil Service, especially at the middle, executive officer levels. This points to a crucial question: Why did mechanization become a Treasury project?

Treasury Control and the Expert Movement of Mechanizers

In the early decades of the twentieth century, several individuals or groups operated as "investigators" in the public service, recommending mechanization in the name of efficiency. Ever keen to secure new contracts, manufacturers of office machinery also offered their services as investigators. In 1926, C. A. Everard Greene of BTM offered an investigation of HMSO—an invitation that was accepted since, Norman Scorgie of HMSO noted, it "would cost us nothing and might kill two birds with one stone."[149] Several govern-

Figure 5.12
A BTM 45-column punched-card subtracting printer displayed at His Majesty's Stationery Office in March 1930. (source: National Archive for the History of Computing, University of Manchester)

ment departments were growing their own expertise to cope with internal problems. The General Register Office's experience with mechanizing the 1911 census allowed them to develop and keep such skills. HMSO, in line with its responsibility for the material provisioning of Whitehall offices, regarded the addition of punched-card expertise as a natural extension of its duties. The growth of expertise was a result of a combination of pull by departmental interest and push from individuals: S. J. Hobson's articulation of mechanization schemes for the Metropolitan Police, for example, provided Scotland Yard with departmental expertise and Hobson with professional advancement for himself. Some departments, such as the Ministry of Labour, set up their own inspection branches, which pursued mechanization.[150] Departments in substantial direct contact with the public attempted to regularize and manage such contact through the intermediary of forms, and the redesign of forms was therefore a major and continuous, if relatively unsophisticated, focus of improvement. Taxation (Inland Revenue) and welfare (National Assistance Board and, again, the Ministry of Labour) provide two examples of organized expertise in form design.[151] However, the General Post Office was far and away the most important gateway of communication between public and

Figure 5.13
A typical government office of the early twentieth century. Notice the small range of information technologies: telephone, box files, desk trays, cupboards, pens and pencils. (PRO/STAT 20/391)

government via the standardized form. Postal surveyors began examining their own organization in terms of "efficiency" as early as the middle of the nineteenth century.[152] But the GPO's Forms and Office Methods Committee, formed in 1924, marked the British apogee in such paperwork. Since the committee's terms of reference explicitly called for the "utilization of modern office machinery" to be considered, form designers could and did become mechanization experts.[153] P. T. Lloyd, a member of this Committee, had already devised new office systems to pay separation allowances and pensions for the fighting forces during the First World War; subsequently he reorganized the National Savings Scheme at a time when the Post Office was the "largest administrative undertaking in the United Kingdom."[154] "Nature had blessed me or cursed me," Lloyd recalled, "with an inventive mind. It was a blessing to be able quite easily to help people with their difficulties but a curse to have your brain loaded with problems with no peace of mind until you had solved them." The Treasury coveted such engineering expertise, and in 1926 it hired the Post Office employee to join Desborough as an Investigating Officer.[155]

Figure 5.14
One of the more mechanized government offices of the early twentieth century: the Addressograph section of HMSO in 1920. Notice the female clerks, the large filing-card system at the back of the room, and the wartime posters. (PRO/STAT 20/417)

The Treasury became, under the guidance of its permanent secretary and head of the Civil Service Sir Warren Fisher, the foremost repository for information and expertise on mechanization in the 1920s, after its grip on the Civil Service was strengthened in the reorganization of 1919–1920. On 22 July 1920, an Order of Council had entrenched the Treasury's right to "make regulations for controlling the conduct of His Majesty's Civil Establishments, and providing for the classification, remuneration, and other considerations of service of all persons employed therein, whether permanently or temporarily."[156] Unification of the Civil Service under Treasury control led to standardization of bureaucratic technique and greater flow of information.[157] By grasping responsibility for mechanization from HMSO, the Treasury squashed a potential threat to this controlling role. Information was collected by accumulating, for example, assessments of all new calculating machines from the early 1920s onwards, as reviewed by authorities such as L. J. Comrie.[158] Expertise was embodied in the Treasury Investigating Officers. The project of mechanization was both an effect of increased Treasury power (it could reach further and justify intervention) and a cause of that power.

Histories of Civil Service mechanization written by civil servants emphasize the influence of a series of commission reports rather than appeal to departmental and individual interests, as I have done. Bunker's 1966 account (released to the public in 1999) is only the lengthiest internal historical summary; the rehearsal of the series of commissions—the MacDonnell Commission (1912–1914), Haldane's Machinery of Government Committee (1917–1918), the Bradbury Committee (1919), the Tomlin Royal Commission on the Civil Service (1931), and the May Committee on National Expenditure—is found in all whig justifications of the privileged place of the Treasury mechanizers.[159] Official reconstructions of history have a ritualistic element, ticking off the impact of commissions and reports and thereby ensuring formal bureaucratic respectability and justification. In such documents the democratic principle of politician-led or Parliament-led policy making followed by Civil Service implementation was apparently demonstrated and preserved. Against such an account I would stress the agency of Whitehall: a bottom-up history of civil servant actions rather than a top-down history led by the implementation of Committee reports. However, I would also argue that the commissions played an important supporting role, providing the language and examples to reinforce arguments and *retrospectively* justify action. Although the MacDonnell Commission, for example, concluded that "the administration of Government differs and must necessarily differ from the activities of the business world," it continued: "We do not contend that in some of its activities the Civil Service might not and ought not to become "more businesslike." Note the discursive flexibility: the same passage could be quoted by those attacking the Civil Service for not being like business and by those defending the same charge—it is for this reason such reports should not be cited as evidence, either way, of Civil Service backwardness.

However, Haldane and Webb's machinery-of-government report provides the most interesting example of a rhetorical resource. As I argued in chapter 2, the report was decisive in the translation of turn-of-the-century concerns about "national efficiency" into specific recommendations of the reformation of government, grounded in mechanical metaphors of administrative efficiency. The Haldane Committee had noticed the increase and routinization of "work performed by officers of ranks below the First Division" and, just as Partridge was writing in France at the same moment, that the "manipulation of this work involves considerations both of personnel and material":

> There are various mechanical arrangements to be considered such as the registering and custody of papers, the use of forms and statistical returns, copying, stationery, printing, office furniture and equipment, and labor-saving appliances. We think in all such matters progressive efficiency can only be secured by constant expert attention.[160]

Such a recommendation, carrying the name of a heavyweight politician and philosopher of organization, was a rhetorical gift that the expert movement of mechanizers was all too willing to accept. Furthermore, Haldane specifically called for an officer charged with systematic review of office procedure to be appointed in every department and recommended that in the Treasury "there should be a separate Branch specializing in this 'establishment' work and studying all questions if staff, recruitment, classification, etc., and routine business generally. . . . It would also keep itself acquainted with what was being done in business circles outside, and perhaps foreign countries." Haldane concluded that such a branch ought to possess the "necessary expert knowledge." The Whitehall department, overseen by experts, would become a self-recording machine: "All [large] Departments . . . should be made to keep continuous records of the amount of work done, the time occupied in doing it, and the cost incurred."[161] Haldane's general recommendations were fleshed out by the almost contemporary Bradbury Committee report (1919), which specifically called for "two or three specialists with expert knowledge" to be attached to the Treasury Establishment Division to add to the "ordinary calculating and addressograph machines" already in use in departments by the "more systematic investigation of the office methods adopted by the different departments and wider circulation of the information as to other machines for routine work." In 1920 the Treasury announced the existence of the Treasury Investigating Section, which would "advise the Establishments Department generally in office machinery, the keeping of registers, records and statistics, the employment of labor-saving machines etc. in the Public Service, and to conduct special investigations as required into methods, output, etc." As Bunker has noted, the language of this announcement appears to indicate the influence of the Haldane and Bradbury Committees in the decision to set up the section.[162] And, indeed, the language of Haldane was to be recruited and subtly redirected from discursive machinery toward mechanization projects. Metaphors of the government machine became justifications for mechanization. However, as I have shown, the formation of the section, if not officially announced, was well underway before the issuance of the committees' reports in the work of Partridge and Desborough and in the maneuvers of the Treasury. Indeed, it was the work of Executive Officer-level civil servants such as Desborough and Partridge to make the connection between their superiors' general flexible call for a cadre of experts and the specific concrete project to extensively mechanize Whitehall (a shift from Haldanian ideals to materiality). To achieve this, a distinction had to be drawn between old machines, which only assisted existed working patterns and did not require expert leadership, and the new machines, which had the potential to transform office work—so long as suitable experts were in charge. For example, examine closely this passage from Desborough's 1927 speech:

> Office machines have passed through one distinct stage of development, and are now well advanced into a second stage. In the first stage, they were designed to serve merely as adjuncts for facilitating the carrying out of existing processes. . . . On the other hand, the more recently designed machines, such as accounting and book-keeping machines, and statistical tabulating machines, belong to a different type entirely. They form a class the use of which necessitates an entire revision of existing office practice and methods. . . . This change ordinarily involves recasting the whole office organization.[163]

Such a revolutionary class of machines would have to be guided by experts: "The first essential in considering the possible introduction of machines into offices . . . is to study the organization . . . with a view to leading the operations into channels that will enable the machines to be used effectively," a study which "not an easy task" and therefore required experience, knowledge and training.

Appeal to the authority of reports such as Haldane's and Bradbury's gave the Treasury the power to gather to itself the right to investigate office methods, a right confirmed after a Whitehall turf war over the issue with the General Post Office in 1927.[164] By 1931, such investigators were quoting the Tomlin Royal Commission and the May Committee as evidence of their own good work.[165] In fact such praise was more an indication of how established the expert movement of mechanizers had become: Gerald May was also a deputy chairman of Powers, and his committee was therefore partly congratulating its own chairman when they "felt that the Civil Service compared very favorably with the Business world in the use of labor saving devices."[166] (In a further twist, May's report forecast a budget deficit of £120 million, leading to a withdrawal of foreign funds, a run on government securities, and the precipitation of a new "National" cross-party administration. "We have magneto trouble," Keynes wrote, calling for such efficient government. "How, then, can we start up again?"[167]) Keynesianism, in turn, would demand greater governmental powers of information collection and processing.

By 1939, four years into post-Depression recovery and on the eve of war, the Treasury possessed the right and the means to review Whitehall's office methods, often with a view to mechanization. Office modernization was therefore a cause and an effect of the strengthened Treasury control of the Civil Service. This view of the Treasury is in stark contrast to that found in the canonical historiography, where the myth of the "dead hand of the Treasury" is still common (and the idea of Treasury enthusiasm for expertise is anathema). But, as this and the following chapters show, increasingly through the middle of the twentieth century, if the Treasury hand was dead, it was also metal and active.

However, it was not until the Second World War that full use was made of the Treasury's power, and until the 1940s the staff of the Treasury Investigating Section was very small. But the Treasury was also a part, and a central part, of a network of office efficiency experts, a community given a rather amorphous form by a variety of organizations. But as late as 1943, according to one commentator, there was the feeling that among the Mechanizers "the right hand did not know what the left was doing."[168] Co-ordinating the hands and transforming this community into a full-fledged expert technocratic movement was an achievement of war. In a profound sense, warfare was paperwork.

6

An Information War

The Second World War is often presented, first and foremost, as a war of production in which American and Soviet manufacture of guns, ships, aircraft, and tanks were decisive. The prominent interventions of science, the Manhattan Project to build atomic weapons or penicillin on the medical front, were also largely achievements of engineering and mass production techniques rather than, say, "pure" science. However, it is the contention of this chapter that the conflict was also an "information" war—although a crude distinction cannot be drawn between the two—not only did the concept of information crystallize in the practical context of warfare, but also a string of new organizations emerged to collect, process and distribute it.

In this chapter the techniques and implications of government information processing in the Second World War are examined. Both radar and cryptanalysis—codebreaking—provide good, and now relatively familiar, examples of how prewar information systems were substantially deepened, expanded and mechanized. These systems were directed against the enemy. However less celebrated techniques on the home front were also transformed, although again by building on pre-1939 precedents: the bureaucracy of identity cards was re-introduced, enabling coordination of rationing, recruitment, and police surveillance, while the techniques of market research and advertising, which were largely a phenomena of private industry before 1939, became key government activities with propaganda, the Social Survey, and Mass Observation. It is argued that relatively unsung aspects of government work also changed, with important implications for the planning of war (and after): personnel and stores accounting records on punched cards, for example, allowed machines to keep track of people and objects. Reform in statistics—including the establishment of a Central Statistical Office—took place that, as was noted in chapter 3, proved impossible to achieve a few decades earlier. The calculating capacity of government deepened with the operation of bureaus such as the Admiralty Computing Service. Wartime developments in planning, operational research, statistical control, intelligence and aircraft control and reporting all shaped, and were shaped by, technical innovations. A class of government employees, experts in the management of machines and bureaucracy, became increasingly reflexive about their own work, with implications for science policy and the Treasury Investigating officers discussed in the preceding chapter. In particular, they became reflexive about "information." Finally, in the aftermath of the Second World War, different informational problems and opportunities arose. In general, I will argue that these apparently disparate innovations should be considered together as marking an important solutions to a perceived informational crisis in the 1930s.

Foreign Knowledge: Historiography

The historiography of radar and that of codebreaking share several similarities: both were projects surrounded by secrecy, credited with profound influence on the course of the Second World War, and have been celebrated as primarily technological achievements. The secrecy of radar lasted only until 1945 when official restrictions were lifted on major aspects of the work. Published accounts by leaders in British radar development soon followed. Superintendent at the Telecommunication Research Establishment (TRE) A. P. Rowe's slim *One Story of Radar* (1948) and Robert Watson-Watt's idiosyncratic *Three Steps to Victory* (1957) were published freely.[1] Since then a number of technical histories of radar, some penned by electrical engineers, have been published,[2] as has a popular, semi-scholarly history, *The Invention That Changed the World*.[3]

The secrecy surrounding codebreaking was enforced far more rigorously: those involved had to sign the Official Secrets Act and were told not to divulge any information on their contributions and to carry their secrets to the grave. This official attitude lasted intact until the mid 1970s, when the existence of the British codebreaking center at Bletchley Park was admitted and the first photographs of the electronic Colossus, a machine vital to the cracking of German coded teleprinter messages, were released. The change in attitude coincided with the publication by Group Captain F. W. Winterbotham of the first book to mention the top-secret Ultra decrypts produced by Bletchley Park and read daily by Churchill at the war's peak.[4] Bletchley Park appeared in the official history of British intelligence during the Second World War in the *British Intelligence in the Second World War* volumes overseen by F. H. "Harry" Hinsley and published by HMSO from 1979 through 1990. (Hinsley was at Bletchley Park.) However, the techniques of codebreaking remained shrouded, and even in the 1980s Gordon Welchman (who organized the network of intercept stations and the concentrated attack on the Enigma) was accused of causing "direct damage to security" by talking too freely after the publication of his account, *The Hut Six Story* (Allen Lane, 1982). Only after the end of the Cold War and the subsequent attempts by the intelligence establishment to forge a new rationale was the history of Bletchley Park seriously promoted rather than reluctantly admitted. The anxiety that too much knowledge would be given away was overcome by recognition of the public-relations advantages attainable by promoting the contribution of codebreaking to the Allied cause.[5]

Hinsley has argued that, although "we may at once dismiss the claim that Ultra by itself won the war," codebreaking was critical at three stages: by cracking an Italian shipping cipher and the German army Enigma in 1941 the tide was turned against Rommel in North Africa; by breaking the German naval Enigma from June 1941 to January 1942 and again from December 1942 millions of tons of North Atlantic ships were saved; and by cracking the Fish ciphers, Operation Overlord—the Allied landing in Normandy which depended on a "double-cross" feint at Pas de Calais—was made possible and successful.[6] However, public remembrance rather than official record proved a greater consequence of the lifting of restrictions. Often for the first time the staff of Bletchley Park and associated outstations, whose numbers topped 7,000 by 1944 and peaked at 8,995 in January 1945, could publicly reminisce about, remember, and place on record what they did during the war. The relief, for example evident in the stories told on the late-1990s landmark Channel 4 television program *Station X* celebrating the social history of Bletchley Park, was palpable.[7]

The emphasis in the histories of both radar and codebreaking has been either on technological innovation or on operational consequences. My interest lies in a slightly different direction: what were the changes in organization of information, and how should technological change be understood in this context? I will argue that codebreaking must be seen as part of the organization of information in the (bureaucratic) secret service, whereas radar drew on more immediately military and industrial sources.

Foreign Knowledge (1): Codebreaking

Britain had no signals intelligence (sigint) between the closure in the middle of the nineteenth century of the Decyphering Branch, which opened and decoded letters, and the First World War. In 1914, however, both the War Office and the Admiralty speedily established some sigint capability. After cables were cut, Germany was forced to use wireless telegraphy, and the government set up a network of listening stations, fourteen around the British coast, staffed by the General Post Office, as well as three overseas.[8] The Admiralty recruited apprentice cryptographers, including the young A. G. "Alastair" Denniston, and accommodated them in Room 40 (which became the name of the group) of the Admiralty's Old Buildings. In 1919 a peacetime cryptographic unit was formed by merging Room 40 with the War Office's equivalent, MI1b. Denniston was appointed to head the unit, which was named the Government Code and Cypher School (GC&CS). Though its public function was "to advise as to the security of codes and ciphers used in all Government departments and to assist in provision," its secret additional term of reference was "to study the methods of cipher communications used by foreign powers."[9] In April 1922 responsibility for GC&CS was moved from the Admiralty to the Foreign Office. Beginning in the mid 1920s, GC&CS became increasingly closely tied to the Secret Intelligence Service, popularly known in Britain as MI6, even sharing the same building (54 Broadway, London). The cryptanalysts had little success with German codes, but broke American ciphers from 1921, French from 1935 and had little difficulty with Japanese encrypted messages. But the main target was Soviet Russia. The Bolsheviks, unwilling to use old Tsarist codes they did not trust, nevertheless used encryption methods which GC&CS could attack successfully. However in 1927, decrypted Russian telegrams were read in Parliament by the Prime Minister, Stanley Baldwin, in an attempt to demonstrate the subversive activities of Soviet diplomats, and the Russians promptly introduced almost unbreakable codes. The consequences of this breach in secrecy—Britain was never able to read Russian messages as easily again—definitively shaped the culture of secrecy at GC&CS.

By the mid 1930s, GC&CS was, in its eyes, underfunded and suffering from poor morale. However, German rearmament was leading to a revival of interest in intelligence services, and GC&CS began recruiting again, usually through personal networks centering on King's and Sidney Sussex Colleges of Cambridge University. By 1939 the number of employees at GC&CS had grown to 100 and the Station had moved to a country house 50 miles north of London in Bletchley Park. Here cryptanalytical work initially remained largely pen-and-paper work, carried out by the linguists who dominated the staff. However, no progress could be made on the most important of the German codes, those encrypted by the Enigma machine.

Variants of the Enigma were used by German navy, army, air force, railways and Abwehr (secret intelligence service of German High Command) to code messages. It worked by passing an electric current through a series of rotating wheels and a wired plugboard, so that each letter was encoded: if "A" was pressed then "X" might light up, but if "A" was pressed again, one of the wheels would turn, and the new encrypted letter might be "Q." German cryptographers considered Enigma invulnerable. However, a remarkable stroke of good fortune transformed GC&CS work on Enigma. In 1931, a German traitor and bon-viveur, Hans-Thilo Schmidt had passed documents relating to Enigma, including diagrams of its internal mechanisms, to the French secret service. When the French concluded that Enigma remained unbreakable they had passed the documents to the Polish cryptographer Marian Rejewski. By 1933, Rejewski had succeeded in decrypting some Enigma messages, and his team spent the next few years developing their methods, including building an electromechanical device they called a bombe to assist in the deduction of the Enigma wheel settings. Only months before war would be triggered by the German invasion of Poland, in July 1939, the Polish intelligence service met a party of their French and British counterparts in the Pyry forest outside Warsaw and passed on their methods, a reconstructed Enigma and the bombe.[10]

Back at Bletchley Park recruitment continued apace. Gordon Welchman signed up his Cambridge college friend Stuart Milner-Barry and his fellow international chess-player Hugh Alexander. (Milner-Barry provides the link between the shrouded history of Bletchley Park and the postwar computerization of government, to which he brought "his matrix-analytical mind and astonishing memory" and the experience of "developing the "software" approaches to code-breaking"[11]). Against the sentiments of the older staff who regarded them as too narrowly focused, mathematicians began to be employed too.

Work was organized by "huts," first literally and then more figuratively. Hut 6 received the messages intercepted by the Y Stations, outposts which recorded high-speed German transmissions, of which three important ones were Y Group Beaumanor in the East Midlands, the Royal Air Force base at Chicksands in Bedfordshire and the police station at Denmark Hill in South London.[12] Hut 6 concentrated on the "Red" Enigma used by the German Air Force and exploited mistakes by German Morse operators or used cribs (guesses of likely words or phrases) to deduce the Enigma settings. Work was regulated by the 24-hour clock: the Enigma settings were changed at midnight and Hut 6 concentrated intensely until a solution was found (if possible). This effort was assisted by a growing number of bombes, machinery based on Alan Turing's successive improvements on the first Polish model, and constructed by British Tabulating Machines. Initially the bombes were operated by servicemen, working for BTM before their call-up, however with male conscription causing shortages of labor operating the bombes became women's work. By 1943 whole new outstations at Stanmore and Eastcote in North London contained arrays of bombes operated largely by Wrens—recruits in the Women's Royal Naval Service (WRNS). Once a key had been deduced, messages could be decrypted using modified British Typex cipher machines, which resembled typewriters. Hut 6 then passed the raw decrypted messages to Hut 3, where they were translated and their importance assessed. A member of the "watch," or team of translators, made the first parsing, which when complete was read by the head of the watch ("Number One") and reviewed by advisers, accumulating on the way extra meaning and interpretation. The finished product was then sent to London or the operational Commands.

The Bletchley Park attack on naval Enigma was organized in a parallel fashion. Hut 8, under Alan Turing, worked on decryption, innovating a series of new methods as naval Enigma became more sophisticated.[13] Decrypts were passed to Hut 4. Paper was ordered, sorted, stamped, and moved:

> As Hut 8's decrypts arrived in Hut 4, each group handled them as follows, exchanging jobs when necessary. A wire tray comes in, laden with decrypts in the form of sheets covered with tapes carrying the printed German text in five letter groups like those on the original cipher text. The sorter, often Number 2 of the group, glances at them, quickly identifies those important for the Admiralty, and hands them to Number 3; who rapidly writes out the German text in word-lengths, staples it on the decrypt, and hands it to Number 1; who translates it into English, stamps it with a number (e.g. ZTPG/4793), and passes it to a WAAF girl who teleprints it to the Admiralty, adding the initials of Number 1, e.g. WGE.[14]

While bombes were scarce, Hut 6 and Hut 8 had to compete to make use of them (though Hut 8—representing the war against the U-boats—had priority).[15] Bletchley Park therefore quickly displayed a division of labor, a compartmentalization greatly reinforced by strict secrecy rules. Despite an increase in staff, by October 1941 the codebreakers in Huts 6 and 8 felt that their work, and therefore the war in the Atlantic, was being severely hampered by lack of resources. Since previous complaints had failed to achieve their desired effect, four members of Huts 6 and 8 (Turing, Welchman, Alexander, and Milner-Barry) took the remarkable step of appealing directly to the Prime Minister, a voracious reader of Ultra. In their letter they complained of several "bottlenecks" and asked for more staff: clerks to run the Hollerith machines in Hut 8, typists to transcribe Luftwaffe wireless messages and Wrens to run the increasing number of Bombes.[16] This letter, and Churchill's reaction ("Action this day. Make sure they have all they want on extreme priority and report to me that this has been done") has a celebrated location in Bletchley Park historiography: it is used to underline the decisiveness of Churchill and the anti-hierarchical, but patriotic genius of the codebreakers. But this appeal brought in only a handful of extra staff compared to the massive expansion directed by the "normal machinery of allocations," as the four themselves called it. The analytical eye, in this case, should be kept on the organization rather than the individual: what is historically interesting about Bletchley Park was its transformation from collegiate, relatively undifferentiated group of codebreakers to one of the greatest centers of the industrialized production of information.

Let us look at where and how information was stored, and how this changed. The archetypal representative of collegiate, prewar GC&CS was Dillwyn "Dilly" Knox. Knox examined ciphers as a classicist scholar studied ancient, corrupted texts. The metaphors used to describe his methods are academic or puzzle-solving (especially crosswords). His labor was undivided: "Dilly was a lone hand (he always was) assisted by one secretary/assistant and enjoying a total lack of other facilities—though it is by no means clear that he could have used any."[17] After the cracking of Enigma (interestingly, Knox was one of the party that met the Poles) and the consequent flood of messages to be decrypted, translated and assessed, the methods of Knox became sidelined: not only was the labor of cryptanalysis divided on a finer and finer scale, but the *form* of information changed too. In rooms alongside the main huts of Bletchley Park great registers grew, some simple index cards, others punched and sortable by Hollerith machines. Historiographical attention on Bletchley Park has so often been on the eccentric characters and unique machines that the simple but powerful registries have been overlooked. A "fabulous index" of German scientific and technological terms was built up.[18] The "3N indexers—an ugly word for a talented group of loyal and lovely ladies [mostly] Wrens and WAAFs . . . were always on duty, keeping a record of every detail that might be needed for reference in solving some future conundrum."[19] Another index off Hut 3 kept in order information on the location of each German flying unit, and was updated as new decrypts came in: "the Military and Air Advisers . . . could not have performed their tasks without the elaborate indexes over which ATS, WAAFs, and civilian girls labored tirelessly, never more than a few hours behind the moving front of events, meticulously recording even the minutest details mentioned in Enigma decodes."[20] In Hut 7, Frederick Freeborn, the former director of the BTM factory at Letchworth, organized a team of women clerks to cross-reference details of the decrypts, so that any word could be quickly searched for and found.[21] More and more information was ordered and materially stored. Bletchley Park can be considered a total informational institution, no symbol was lost: there was even a group called Qwatch (a pun on "watch" and "Quatsch"—German for "rubbish") that kept track of the miscellaneous, initially worthless data.[22]

Not only was more information pushed into card store or registries, but the cryptanalytical process of searching for matches between cribs and coded messages became more mechanized. One simple example from the attack on naval Enigma was the punched-card machine minded by Turing's friend, Joan Murray (née Clarke):

> The Baby was a small special-purpose machine, made by the British Tabulating Machine Company at Letchworth, the firm which made the bombes: it was used to encipher a four letter probable word, *eins*, at all positions of the machine with the day's wheel-order and plugging, punching the results on Hollerith cards. The minder had to make regular checks, and set the Baby for a new start when a cycle was completed. By sorting and collating the encipherments of *eins* with the message texts, the starting position could be obtained for a good proportion of messages. . . .[23]

Punched-card methods complemented comparison of tapes by hand ("Bunburismus") and statistical analysis for regularities ("Yoxallismus"). Similar techniques proved relatively effective against the Fish, or encrypted non-Morse, traffic used extensively by the German army (a variant called "Tunny") and therefore of growing importance as the attention turned away from U-boats to the European land war. Maxwell ("Max") H. A. Newman, a member of Hut F (which was responsible for the attack on Fish), persuaded the director of Bletchley Park that high-speed machinery was needed for the job of comparing two enciphered messages. The first machines, called Robinsons, probably after Heath Robinson, the cartoonist of outlandish machines (and the British equivalent of Rube Goldberg), entered service in May 1943, and were designed by physicist C. E. Wynn-Williams at TRE assisted by electrical engineers at the Post Office Research Station at Dollis Hill.[24] However, it was clear to Newman that the work of the Heath Robinsons would be considerably speeded if some way was found of storing electronically the contents of one, or both, of the messages. This formidable electronic problem was tackled by a team of Dollis Hill engineers under T. H. Flowers, largely as a self-supported sideline to their other war work. The outcome of Flowers's labors by the end of 1943 was Colossus, the first mark of which contained 1,500 thyratron tubes, a number previously considered impracticable since any such machine would be unreliable. The trial of the Colossus on 8 December 1943 was a profound moment in the story of trust in the government machine: doubts about electronic cryptanalysis fell away as the machine correctly reproduced a set text three times, running for 8 hours without fault. The research was vindicated when a tightening of German security in February 1944 "threw the task almost entirely on to the machines" and meant that only such high-speed techniques were effective.[25]

Bletchley Park in 1944 was an industrialized enterprise: finely arranged division of labor, very high staff numbers, an emphasis on through-put, and innovative mechanization at bottlenecks. The factory metaphor recurs in reminiscences: "a society which began with something of a collegiate atmosphere of a common room was transformed into a bustling headquarters with multiple assembly lines."[26] Or again, at a lower level: "as befits a production unit, Hut 3 was set up like a miniature factory."[27] Those on top could view the organization as producing a science, intelligence was: "reviewing known facts, sorting out significant from insignificant, assessing them severally and jointly, and arriving at a conclusion by the exercise of judgment, part induction, part deduction."[28] Yet it must also be emphasized that it was a factory that worked on symbols and paper. And the direction symbols traveled was from uncertainty to certainty, culminating in the "unambiguous language of complete objectivity," as a Hut 3 officer described the end products of Bletchley Park.[29]

Unfortunately it is exceedingly hard to uncover how the structure of the GC&CS was represented in the 1940s, rather than how it has been described in recent published histories. The files of Bletchley Park released, finally, at the Public Record Office in the late 1990s are unhelpful: ragbag collections of telegrams, scribbled notes and unordered memoranda. They are almost certainly not the original files from the Park, but assembled at some point after 1945, the traces that remained after many selection processes: not only heavily weeded for security reasons, which they certainly are, but also the fraction of documents that survived the great bonfires of decrypts, ticker tape, and other papers made at the end of the war. This destruction of order is unfortunate for this historical project: the structure of the original files themselves often reveal much about organizations and associated information technologies (of which files, of course, are one). However, with radar much more of the material culture of bureaucracy has survived, and these clearly show how information, organization and technology were understood.

Foreign Knowledge (2): Radar

The organized development of radar began in Britain in the mid 1930s with the appointment of a Committee for the Scientific Survey of Air Defence, chaired by the chairman of the Aeronautical Research Committee, Henry Tizard, with two other London professors as members: physiologist A. V. Hill and physicist Patrick Blackett. The Director of Scientific Research at the Air Ministry, H. E. Wimperis, and his assistant (later Director of TRE), A. P. Rowe, also attended the meeting. Immediate encouragement was given to the work of Robert Watson-Watt and Arnold Wilkins (who, when asked by Wimperis to check the calculations on a proposed "death ray," wrote that although electromagnetic waves made poor weapons they might enable long-range detection of aircraft).[30] Following the successful demonstration using the BBC Empire transmitter at Daventry, showing that aircraft scattered enough radio waves to be detected on the ground, Watson-Watt's team moved to Orfordness on the East Coast of Britain and development began. This team concentrated on the development of devices for transmitting pulsed radio waves and receiving reflected echoes, and grew into the Telecommunications Research Establishment during the Second World War. Initially the focus was on early warning systems, producing the floodlighting Chain Home (CH) system, the first station of which was handed over to the Royal Air Force in 1937. Later, radar devices were developed for different functions: identification of aircraft (IFF), airborne interception of enemy aircraft (AI), tactical direction of aircraft from the ground (GCI), and many others.

But it is not the technical history of radar that concerns us. Although the technological innovations have been justly celebrated, it was the organization of air defense—of technology, persons and information—that proved crucial in, for example, the Battle of Britain in 1940. (Indeed, it was this organization, rather than technical superiority, that marked the difference between British and German radar.) The management of information was labeled "reporting and control." Before radar, reporting and control had reached quite a high level of sophistication: for example, an elaborate system had evolved against the threat of Zeppelin raids during the Great War. Britain (except North West Scotland) was divided into eight Warning Control areas, with a headquarters located at a key node in the telephone network, and each subdivided further into warning districts, roughly 30 miles in extension—the distance a Zeppelin crossed in half an hour.[31] Observers in each district spotted the Zeppelins either by using early wireless direction finding equipment to pick up transmissions or directly saw or heard the airship cross the coast. In each Control Area Operations Room a transparent map, lit behind by colored lights, displayed this information as it was telephoned in by observers, and passed on to the General Post Office (the GPO, which managed the telephone network). The Telephone Trunks manager at the GPO then warned the targeted district. Air-defense reporting and control organization was most sophisticated in the London Air Defence Area (LADA). Sean Swords in his history of radar reprints an excellent description of the LADA operation room, by its commander Major-General E. B. Ashmore in 1918, that is worth quoting again at length:

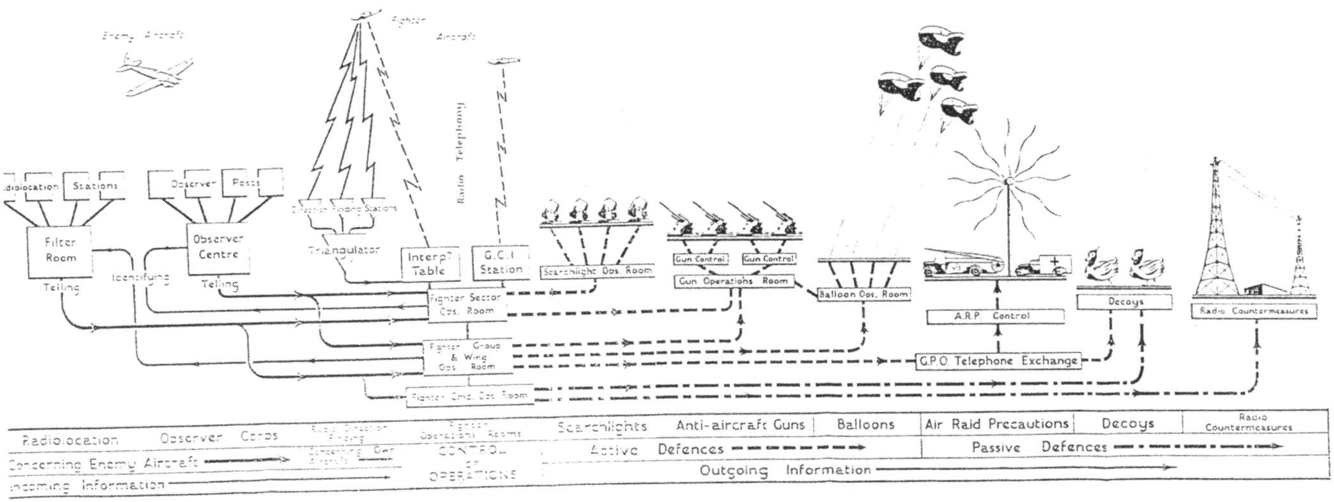

Figure 6.1
The organization of air defense as illustrated in An Outline of Air Defence Organization (Air Defence Pamphlet 1, February 1942). Note incoming and outgoing "information." (PRO AIR 10/3757)

> This central control consisted essentially of a large squared map fixed on a table, round which sat ten operators (plotters), provided with headphones; each being connected to two or three if the sub-controls. During operations, all the lines were kept through direct; there was no ringing throughout the system.
>
> When aircraft flew over the country, their position was reported every half-minute or so to the sub-control, where the course was plotted with counters on a large-scale map. These positions were immediately read off by a "teller" in the sub-control to the plotter in the central control, where the course was again marked out with counters. An ingenious system of colored counters, removed at intervals, prevented the map from becoming congested during a prolonged raid.
>
> I sat overlooking the map from a raised gallery; in effect, I could follow the course of all aircraft flying over the country, as the counters crept across the map. . . .[32]

From this position Ashmore could survey London and the airspace above it.[33] Information passed through this "central control," with orders directed outwards by telephone to anti-aircraft brigade. A direct command line connected Ashmore's deputy, also sitting in the gallery, to Biggin Hill, the air base south of London that led the defense of the city.

The air-defense organization of the Second World War was more complex than that of the First World War, but it fitted into this template. However, there were important differences: the extensive use of electronic devices, automation of some aspects of calculation and communication, the connected strict simplification and standardization of communicated knowledge, and the greater conceptualization of the process in terms of "information." These differences are best understood by considering the organization as a whole.

The air-defense organization was divided into two parts: the Raid Reporting Systems (marked by "incoming information") and the Operational Control Systems (marked by "outgoing information").[34] The Raid Reporting System performed six functions, each defined by different operations on information: "reading," "reporting," "filtering," "identifying," "telling," and "plotting."

"Reading" was the achievement of the radar stations and "Radio Direction Finding" ("radar" was a term invented by Americans in 1940), supplemented by visual sightings from the increasingly obsolete Royal Observer Corps. Around the coast Chain Home and Chain Home Low (CHL) stations, the latter a modification to detect low-flying aircraft using a beam of radio waves, by "reading outwards" provided "initial information about the quantity, height and position of aircraft approaching the defended areas." Inland from the coastal "chain," a radar "carpet" consisting of further modified Chain Home and Ground Controlled Interception systems provided inland knowledge and tactical capability. The radiolocation stations measured the range, bearing and angle of elevation of aircraft. The great importance of fresh, rapidly accessible information (the airplanes of 1939 were much faster than those used in the First World War) placed great emphasis on speed of calculation and communication. Because of the curvature of the earth, angle of elevation had to be converted to height above mean sea level before it was useful. This calculation was therefore done automatically, to save time. Other aspects of reading were more suitable work for humans rather than machines, estimating the number of aircraft from an echo, for example, was notoriously difficult and required skilled human operators. Even so large errors occurred, especially when more than 12 aircraft were being traced.

The raw information having been read, was now "reported" in a standardized format: "quantities and positions of aircraft, and, if the aircraft were seen visually, whether they were recognized as "Friendly" or "Hostile." The radiolocation information went first to Filter Rooms, an innovation on First World War practice. Here "the many separate reports as received" were "arranged in series and conflicting reports . . . reconciled." The accuracy of information from the CH and CHL systems could be quite poor, but errors were unevenly distributed: range was accurate to 1 percent (half a mile at 50 miles), but bearing errors ranged from 2° to 10°, and height was usually only accurate to 10 percent.[35] Since ranges were more accurate than bearings the technique of "range-cutting" was used to assign location: the adduced location of the aircraft was at the intersection of two ranges, rather than the intersection of two bearings.

Identification of aircraft also raised problems of errors. Some aircraft carried IFF equipment which responded to a radio beacon by emitting a message which identified the aircraft as friendly. Thus some identification could be mechanized. However, if the IFF set was malfunctioning, or not fitted, or being imitated by enemy equipment then human qualities were called on: a Filterer needed "good technical knowledge and sound judgment in assessing the weight to be attached to each station's reports." Unlike the calculation of height, therefore, the identification of aircraft was part human, part machine. Strict rules laid down when and where friendly aircraft could fly on non-operational flights—a means of reducing the amount of information that needed to be processed. The outcome of the "Raid Identification System" was the ascribing of "Friendly," "Hostile," or "Unidentified" to each aircraft. Each Filter Room had a Plotting Table Map around which the various staff of the Room—Filterers, Tellers and Reporters—clustered:

Filterers are responsible for estimating by range-cutting the assumed true plan-positions of the aircraft, and for placing a distinctive symbol at that point. Concentric range circles from RDF Stations are marked on the Map as a guide. . . . Other raid information and a Raid Designation are displayed alongside the plots. . . . In the Filter Room in a position overlooking the Plotting Table is a Teller with a Recorder alongside. The Teller "tells" by telephone simultaneously to all Fighter Operations Rooms concerned Raid Designations and full raid information. . . .[36]

Standard procedures of telling were strictly enforced: "The speed of aircraft allows no time for conversions from one nomenclature to another, or for checking back to ensure correctness."[37] There was a standard order for telling ten items of information; there was even a standardized manner of speaking, neither hurried nor too slow. The Operations Rooms also had a map, and the standardized simplified information told to them could be "displayed rapidly and in easily understood form" before the directors of operations. This plotting was, of course, itself standardized: each raid marked by a tower of numbered tiles with the passage of time marked by a color code (designed with help from the Psychological Laboratory of Cambridge University).[38]

The Raid Reporting System therefore acted by ruthlessly cutting down the large quantities of knowledge that was *potentially* available about incoming threats to provide a much reduced stream of standardized information to the Operations Rooms- a process known as "pre-processing" in computing. What is striking is how the systems became discussed, theorized and operated by a discourse of "information." For example, a 1936 summary of what an Operations Room was to be specified the following:

(a). It is a center at which information is collected by various means.

(b). The information so collected is required to be displayed in such a manner that it may rapidly and accurately be made use of by the Controlling Officer. . . .

(c). The final function is the issue of orders by the Controlling Officer and as a corollary some information that they have been received and carried out.

Stated briefly, then, the functions are the collection of information, the display of this information to a Controlling Officer, and means for the issue of orders by this Officer as a result of deductions he has made from the information displayed.[39]

The Operations Room of 1942 was still recognizably similar to that overseen by Major-General Ashmore in 1918. However, the increased complexity meant that new techniques were sought to represent the incoming information. There is evidence that the Air Ministry research scientists who designed the Operations Rooms looked around for similar cases from which to draw insight: large railway systems, in particular, "both for their traffic as a whole and for their marshaling and goods use in detail," but also underground railways, large electricity distribution networks, hydroelectric schemes and even police and fire brigade organizations.[40] One concrete example of imported methods were the "indicators" developed originally for stockbroker offices, which Ericsson Telephones Limited converted for Operation Room use.

Organization by information was also found in the other half of air defense, the Operational Control System: information passed out of the Operations Rooms to guide fighter aircraft, searchlights, anti-aircraft batteries, barrage balloons, and passive defenses such as air raid warning, decoy fires and fake airfields, and radio countermeasures. Operations Rooms were arranged in a hierarchy. At the top was Fighter Command, responsible for air defense over the whole "defended areas" (in total covering the island of Britain). In each air-defense area were Fighter Group (or Wing) Operations Rooms whose task was strategic control: "to order the disposition of the air forces on the ground and their states of preparedness; to give prior warning of impending enemy attack and to order sector aircraft off the ground in time and strength to meet it."[41] These Rooms also controlled large scale offensive combined operations by bombers and fighters. At the lowest level, the task of Fighter Sector

Figure 6.2
An interception table in a Fighter Sector Operations Room. "Air defence pamphlet. Number Five. The operational control of fighter aircraft," April 1942)

Operations Rooms—of which there were several per Group—was tactical control: "to order its fighter aircraft to fly in direction and at height and speed to intercept the enemy and join battle with advantages of sun and height and cloud." Communication was partially mechanized—prompting the Commander-in-Chief of Fighter Command to wonder if, one day, he too would be replaced by "a gadget."[42] Therefore, although each of the Operations Rooms at the three levels of hierarchy possessed maps which represented incoming information, only the Fighter Sector Operations Rooms plotted and guided the fighters directly. The organization of the Rooms was structured by how information moved, and vice versa: information was given meaning by the organization. Indeed, the whole began to be called an "Information System."

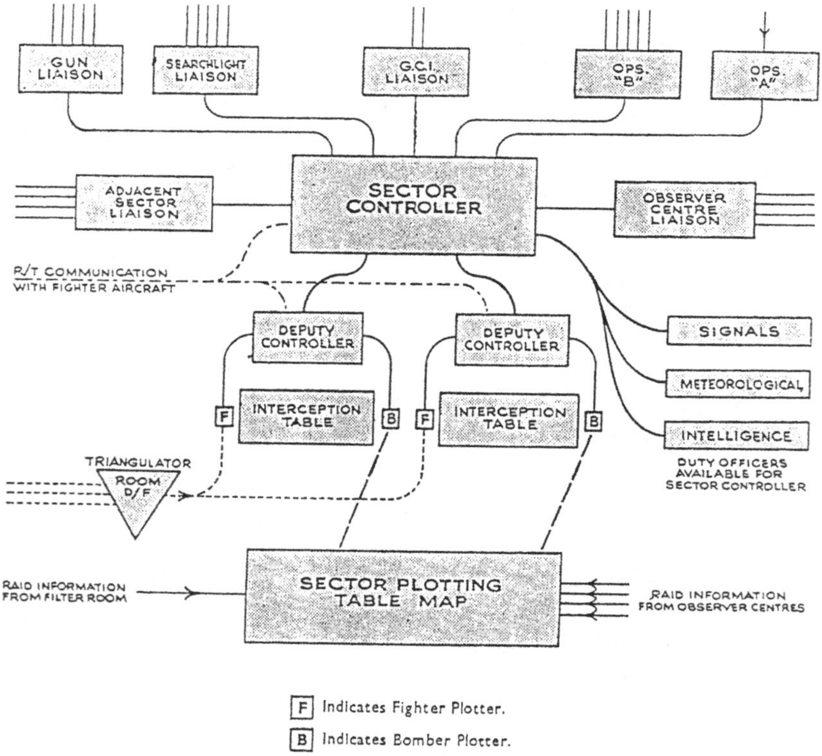

Figure 6.3

Information flow and functional organization of a Fighter Sector Operations Room. (PRO AIR 10/3761. "Air defence pamphlet. Number Five. The operational control of fighter aircraft," April 1942)

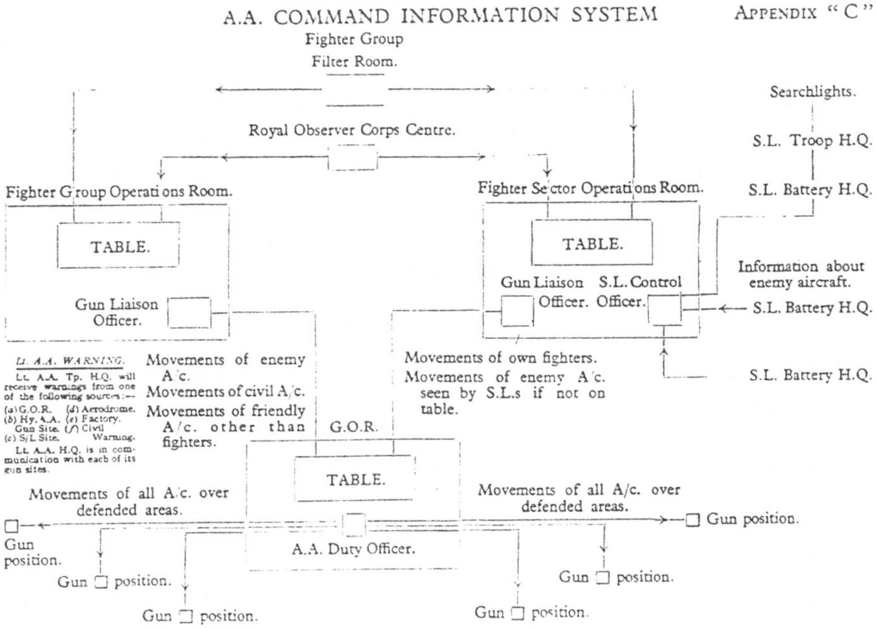

Figure 6.4
"Information system" used as a descriptive term. (PRO AIR 10/3762. "Air defence pamphlet. Number Seven. The operational control of anti-aircraft guns," 1942)

Foreign Knowledge: Significance of Infospheres

What is the significance of the complex informational organizations of cryptanalysis and radar for the arguments of this book? One straightforward answer is that the stored-program computer was materially realized by the combination of techniques worked on at Bletchley Park and Malvern, final home of the Telecommunications Research Establishment. At Manchester University in 1945 the paths of Max Newman from Bletchley and F. C. Williams from TRE crossed. Newman brought the project to build a computer, and Williams possessed the crucial technique needed to succeed: the means of storing and manipulating discrete electronic information. This encounter is further discussed in chapter 7. However, a central argument of this book is that the electronic stored-program computer should not be seen as a thing appearing de novo in 1948, and not just in the sense usually encountered in histories of computing that the concept of such a machine had already been described by the ENIAC team in the United States in 1945 or, indeed, as an entirely novel concept by Turing a decade earlier. To make such arguments is to retrospectively skew our historical understanding of Bletchley Park and TRE: they were not working toward a computer, but responding to the highly pressurized demands of warfare. What this context produced was a deepened and widened state infosphere: the increase in types and geographical extent of data collected, data increasingly discussed abstractly as "information." And it must be remembered that Bletchley Park was, first and foremost, a massive bureaucracy, albeit an increasingly industrialized one: what it operated on was symbols, its process depended on registers, card files and rules as well as famous machines. What it produced was "objectivity"—certain knowledge. This scientization of the process also occurred with radar: the science being named "operational research." As we shall see below, operational research became an expert movement within Whitehall, a military analogue of the work of the Treasury Investigating Officers encountered in the last chapter. Finally what this science concerned itself with was the efficient joint operation of humans and machines—and this way of thinking, although we have met it before with Partridge's memorandum in 1916, was spread by warfare. As Jack Good recalled of Colossus, "there was a close synergy between man, woman, and machine, a synergy that was not typical during the next decade of large-scale computers."[43]

Knowledge of the Home Front (1): The Rise and Fall (Again) of the National Register

Whereas Bletchley Park is now celebrated, if not perhaps as a mobilization of bureaucratic techniques, other large-scale projects are relatively unknown. The First World War National Register, as we saw in chapter 4, had collapsed as a useful bureaucratic technique, and it was largely forgotten outside Whitehall's War Book. However, a new National Register and accompanying identity card, for example, were implemented within days of the outbreak of war, this time under the command of the Registrar-General Sylvanus Percival Vivian, who was determined that it should enjoy greater success than its predecessor. During the interwar years the only pressure for a new national register had come from the military. The Committee of Imperial Defence (CID) argued in the mid 1930s that "in a Great War (as in the last) the nation would be compelled to call up its last man and comb and re-comb the classes previously passed over or disregarded. . . . A sound system [of National Registration] was most important."[44] Indeed, CID had proposed in the 1920s a universal registration system, as part of plans for "national service in a future war," consisting of an amalgamation of "the electoral registration system, the census organization, and the births, marriages and deaths registration system."[45] Although this scheme, like other systems of universal registration were deemed "impracticable," the debate did identify the crucial problem of any registration: the extreme difficulty of attaching official identity to individuals: "if it cannot be given enough real peace value of its own it must be given a borrowed and artificial peace value. . . . Its use and production and the quoting or recording of the number upon it must be made obligatory in regard to as many as possible of the organized activities in close touch with the life of the people. If it has not sufficient vitality of its own, it must derive a *parasitic vitality* from established national institutions and social organizations."[46] Vivian's proposed host was food: "Any system of [National Registration], as being an instrument of conscription, would obviously be received by the public with some reserve and suspicion, and in its actual administrative working, when established, would be exposed to a hostile bias on the part of the individual members of the public. By linking that system with the equally necessary system of registration for food rationing purposes . . . motives would be interlocked."[47] The linkage with the food rationing system worked: people kept their cards, and the Register was well maintained. However, while the public justification of the National Register emphasized the updating of the "stale" statistics of the 1931 census (indeed a continuous statistical picture was now available to the General Register Office), the fair distribution of food in a command economy, the assistance made possible to families split by the effects of war, and the identification of the dead after air raids, the main purpose of the system was conscription—to the armed services and the industrial work force.[48]

British identity cards were introduced swiftly for the second time. Registration took place on 29 September 1939, when buff-colored cards holding a very basic amount of information—name, address and official number—were issued to the citizenry. The Ministry of Health assumed overall responsibility, with local registers under the Registrar-General, and an innovation, a Central National Registration Office (CNRO) opened at Southport, north of Liverpool. At the CNRO, 7,000 transcript books contained the details of 40 million registrations, the Central Register alongside a book and card-based central indexes.[49] A large staff received and posted changes to the Register at a rate of 200,000 per week—a massive informational project—quite apart from the periodic extra 250,000–300,000 new entries as each age group was called up in turn. Vivian had had plenty of time to plan the organization of the CNRO, since he had seen the National Register adopted in the War Office War Book in the 1920s. He was also well aware of the technical opportunities: he was a

Figure 6.5
The Central National Registration Office at Southport. (PRO RG 54/3)

Figure 6.6
The Central National Registration Office at Southport. (PRO RG 54/2)

member of the Treasury Committee on Office Machinery—and therefore linked with Desborough's movement considered in the previous chapter—which kept him "*au courant* with the most recent developments in indexing and record-keeping methods and devices: indeed, I am in touch with some developments which are not yet even before the public."[50] (Vivian's sentiment remained to be explained by those who would accuse government departments in the 1920s of being technologically backward.) Vivian's decision to integrate modern card indexes with the older book methods had been taken more than 10 years before the 1939 implementation of the National Register. "The whole province of indexing, record-keeping and tabulating methods, devices and mechanism is making considerable progress at present," Vivian had noted, "and there is no reason why, when we know what purposes have to be served by the future National Register, we should not aim at providing it with the most efficient and convenient equipment (consistently with reasonable economy) which this progress may suggest."

While the personal card was kept simple, at the Central Register a mass of extra information could be stored: sex, date of birth, marital status, whether the individual had been called up for national service, or if the person was wanted, for example for desertion. The Register could also link up with other databases: those receiving family allowances, or the electoral register. A combination of sweeping Defence Regulations gave the police, in practice, the power to detain anyone who did not, when asked, produce their card.[51]

Local food and national registration offices were combined in 1943, when all cards were reissued, to knit the operations even closer.[52] This reissue was also designed to catch deserters and other evaders of national service. The paucity of information on the card, compared to that on the Central Register, was telling: a deserter with a forged or stolen card would have to guess a date of birth, which could then be cross-checked. It was the combination of a surprisingly simple card and a scrupulously maintained complex centralized listing that gave the National Register "so great a range of power."[53] Indeed, this counter-intuitive fact underlay the rejection of proposed card with photographic portrait (i.e., more information), except for use within Whitehall and sensitive military areas.

Sylvanus Percival Vivian's shadowy namesake, Lieutenant-Colonel Valentine Vivian, was the first to spot the dangers to Whitehall of anonymous civil servants. "There is possibly scope," the latter wrote in June 1940, "for evil activity by fifth columnists or parachutists in the diversity of departmental passes giving access to various buildings, such as the War Office or Admiralty."[54] Valentine, head of counter-espionage in the Secret Intelligence Service (vulgarly known as MI6), had spearheaded the tightening of security at the Rome and Berlin embassies before 1939.[55] (After the war, his reputation was tarnished with the revelation of the spy rings—he was, after all, head of counter-espionage, and Kim Philby was his protégé.) There is evidence, unfortunately fragmented, that the identity card and the National Register had extensive uses to the secret state, presumably arranged between the two Vivians.[56] Though the historical record is patchy—very few references to the secret services survive to appear in the ordinary files of the Public Record Office—Valentine's recommendation to Sylvanus, the Registrar-General, that new identification cards—with portrait photographs—should be issued to civil servants provides evidence of contact between secret and public bureaucratic worlds.[57] Sylvanus, with his long experience of bureaucratic systems, was actually more skeptical of the power of photographs than Valentine: "Those supporting [the photographic pass] overlook the fact that the affixing of a photograph, unless reliably authenticated from personal knowledge as that of a person to whom the card relates, is a free gift to the fifth column, since it enables the possessor of a stolen card to give it a fictitious validity by affixing his own photograph."[58] The photographic pass or "Green Card" was a remarkably late addition to Whitehall techniques, although as Sekula has shown photographs attached to files had a much longer bureaucratic history.[59] The Green Card was also a novelty for the background research that accompanied issue, as Sylvanus Vivian noted:

> This Identity Card is obtainable in exchange for the ordinary Buff Card, and it is evidence of bodily identity of the strictest kind. It bears a photograph, signature, and a statement of date and place of birth, and any distinguishing marks; and its made up according to technical Passport standards. . . . In addition to these strict safeguards the Green Card is issued after a test which has not previously been possible in any similar case in this country. The form of application states certain particulars about the applicant; and before the issue of the Green Card by the [CNRO] the stated particulars are checked against the independent return originally made in respect of that person.[60]

In other words, the Register could be used to check itself; at least, claims of identity made from checking the existing Register were held in equal regard as the claims of the applicant. In this way the power of registers increase through time.

However, for two reasons, technologies of control, such as the National Register system, did not confer power in merely one direction. First, the problem of fixing an official identity to an individual was, and is, an irreducibly difficult one. No matter what checks or extra information were added to the identity card or Register, no matter what extra incentives were given to the encourage the populace to carry the cards, there was always some slippage, either accidentally when cards were lost, or deliberately, when cards were forged and new identities created. Second, the power of the Register could be appropriated by the carriers: just as Vivian feared, a good forged card gave the fifth columnist or deserter even greater freedom to move than before. Public attitudes to the identity card ranged from docility to hostility, but there is also evidence that new crimes were made possible by the introduction of the card, showing that a small segment of the population could treat ID productively and creatively. Indeed the possibilities were apparent in official circles early on: "there will be an enormously enlarged field of "crime" opened and a corresponding necessity for official surveillance. The former result will be unfortunate, the latter both irritating and expensive."[61] What was regarded as criminal, in particular fraudulent, within Whitehall can also be seen as creative appropriation of official identities, a useful resource during harsh times. The evidence available for an underworld which played with official identity is refracted through bureaucratic categories, and does not reveal what the fraud meant to the perpetrators. Nor does the evidence indicate the exact scale of the phenomenon—except the crude indication that since civil servants regarded it as a serious problem for National Registration then the numbers could not have been negligible. Wartime investigations *using* the Register threw up diverse stories involving suspect cards: married women avoiding employment bars, under-age boys seeking to join the Royal Air Force, as well as bigamists, deserters and perpetrators of ration book fraud.

Of course successful impersonators could not be counted. But they could be categorized: drawing on the Ministry of Food's First World War experience, frauds were divided into two groups. The first was named "frauds of the lost or stolen Registration Certificate": the perpetrator presented someone else's card in order to gain extra ration books.[62] A quick check of the card's number against a blacklist revealed the fraud.[63] A variant was more tricky, since it was difficult pinning an identity on someone returning from war: "a person, having already a Registration Certificate, and having sold it or made use of it himself for his own purposes, alleges that he has never had a Registration Certificate, etc., owing to his [having] recently come into the country from Overseas or . . . been discharged from the Forces." Official identity could easily be denied. The second group was classed as "the frauds of the double life and the imaginary person." Frauds of the double life arose "through one person or a family obtaining two distinct sets of ration papers or cards under double personality, i.e. under different names." No complete remedy could be suggested against such a proliferation of identities. The hardest fraud to counter, however, was the "fraud of the imaginary person": a "householder, in making an application, simply overstating the number if his household," the simplest version being "to claim a child or children who has never existed or had died." Note that the proliferation of multiple identities was a *consequence* of an attempt to fix a unitary one.[64]

The creation of new official identities allowed new crimes: based on either pretending to be someone else, pretending to be more than one person, or pretending that someone else existed. Of course all these ploys predate identity cards, but the perpetrators now had a powerful extra resource: appropriating the authority of the state to support their claims. The state's answer was technical: better methods of sorting cards, and other cross checks—and therefore the appearance of such frauds constituted a pressure toward greater surveillance. However, it would be a mistake to write such history purely as a growth of such techniques: National Registration was not merely an extension of the state's ability to identify and track individuals, it also created a power that could be creatively appropriated that was not available before.

The related area of using the central register of identity card numbers for state purposes, such as welfare administration or criminal investigations, illustrates the extent made use of the increased surveillance possibilities. Although many of the documents relating to communication of information from the National Register remain closed, the policy that guided Second World War practice can be reconstructed. Theoretically, disclosure was confined to communication of information relating to serious crime or national security. In practice, requests from other government departments, or ones with government backing, were granted, except in debt cases when they were declined (unless the police "forgot" to mention what offense was being investigated). For example, wartime social surveys were built from National Register data, whereas school geography projects were rejected. Likewise, requests for addresses to trace missing tuberculosis cases were accepted once they had been routed via the Ministry of Health. No address was disclosed in inquiries from individuals about individuals, such as wives trying to locate husbands, although an offer to forward a letter was made if it was considered to be of "benefit to the person inquired after."[65] By the far the most publicized investigation was that of the murder of 3-year-old June Anne Devaney in Blackburn in 1948—although the press championed the heroic fingerprint search rather more than the use of the National Register.[66] The use of National Registration information illustrates the phenomena known now as "data creep": the 1939 act provided for three administrative applications (national service, security and food rationing), but 11 years later 39 government agencies made use of the records.[67]

By 1944, Sylvanus Percival Vivian, having witnessed five successful years of the National Register, wished to see his resurrected system continue, and he argued that a peacetime National Register would be an essential component of reconstruction. He envisaged a future state made of potentially interlocking organizations and portrayed the Register as the source of the all-important information that flowed between and held together the system:

> The National Register is in essence a form of identity registration; and its primary function is to absorb information, whether acquired under its own powers or from independent sources, to combine all information received in the record of the particular individual concerned and to relay the information wherever it is needed. The relations between the State and individual members of the community at all times require a number of large-scale administrative organizations which operate in isolation. Each of them needs to obtain from individuals the information necessary to the discharge of their respective functions; and many of them need the same information. In consequence, each department or organization is obtaining separately information which is also obtained by other organizations; and conversely, members of the public have to supply the same information on a number of occasions to different departments. It would thus be of advantage both to members of the public and to the body of public administration if the information, obtained once and for all from members of the public, is put at the disposal of all administrative consumers; and this is a service which . . . a National Register can supply.[68]

Vivian's vision was to "information" as sweeping, grand and comprehensive as Beveridge's was to "health"—it was a nascent National Information Service, born of war and collective action.[69] Not everyone in Whitehall was as keen as Vivian on a "new machine": even the Home Office, which might be expected to be solidly in favor of the identity card, did not believe "that the public opinion [would] stand for the retention of N.R. in its present form," although significantly "whether we like it or not, national registration of the resident population is bound to come in some shape or form if the Beveridge Scheme for universal social security comes into being."[70] During the war, opposition to the National Register was muted (although the *Daily Sketch*, for example, waged a campaign against identity cards even at the peak of the war). However, after 1945 there was no indication that the Register and accompanying identity card would be dropped, useful as it was to Attlee's administration as it continued food rationing and a control economy and built welfare state institutions. Opinion leaders in the press were divided by the Identity Card. Those in favor emphasized the Card's benefits. A *Sunday Times* op-ed piece by the trade unionist W. L. George was typical. First, the nation would have a better knowledge of itself "a continuous picture of the condition of the people." However, such administrative boons were not the most important. Second, identity cards made life more convenient for carriers. A card provided "an excellent evidence of identity. . . . There are many circumstances such as the receipt of registered letters, recovery of luggage, elections, disturbances, where evidence of identity saves the public much annoyance."[71] Indeed, George went further and presented a vision more akin to Pemberton Billing's national book-keeping of morals:

> I should like to see this idea of citizen identity carried much further, and to have the registration card incorporated into a system of personal history, rather akin to the medical history of each recruit that now stands on the War Office file. Registration would enable us to set up an *état-civil* of each individual, showing where and when he was born and married, whether convicted, sent to an asylum or home for inebriates, and what is very important, *whether and how he had been treated for infectious diseases.*

Such a inquisitorial system was justified by a simple appeal that recurs in almost every argument for an identity card system: "We must fasten to this: have nothing to hide and you need hide nothing." Only the guilty need be afraid; indeed; for George "secrecy is hateful; it breeds evils, and I would that all houses might be made of glass." George, like a surprising number of other supporters of the Card, emphasized how official unitary identities combated bigamy, a moral panic of the aftermath years—an obsession that (I have argued elsewhere) lay in conceptions of threats to the social order presented by multiple identities.[72]

The argument of the anti-Card lobby rested on two premises: that the Card was only meant to be a wartime measure and that the Card was counter to British national identity. For example, the *Daily Express* ran the following article in 1945—a prose poem of nationalism, snobbishness, and anti-bureaucracy:

> *Identity*
>
> The result of the *Daily Express* Center of Public Opinion investigation shows that there is a need for clear explanation of the menace of identity cards. Except as a wartime measure the system is intolerable.
>
> It is un-British.
>
> It opens the way to an unnecessary check on the daily life of every person in the State.
>
> It turns every village policeman into a Gestapo agent.
>
> It can put the law-abiding citizen in the same row of filing cabinets as the common thief with a record.
>
> It has already created a new underworld industry of faking, stealing and selling identity cards.
>
> It eases the path of those who seek compulsory direction of labor.
>
> *Talk it over*
>
> It will bring the law into contempt, because the British people do not tolerate bad laws.

> Continue this sort of thing after the war? Create a vast, costly and wasteful administration to check and file identity cards, in a country that needs very hard to be occupied? No.
> *Daily Express* readers, who constitute one in four of the national morning newspaper public, should discuss this issue with their friends and neighbors—especially those who are not readers.[73]

Despite efforts like that of the *Express*, the Card lasted for seven postwar years. After a legal challenge brought in 1951 by Clarence Willcock, seven law lords ruled (while convicting Willcock, but giving him the minimum possible punishment for refusing to hand over his Card to the police) that "to demand registration cards of all and sundry—from a lady leaving her car outside a shop longer than she should for instance—is wholly unreasonable. . . . We have always prided ourselves on the good feeling between the police and public, but this tends to make people resent the acts of the police, to obstruct instead of assist them."[74]

British identity cards and the National Register ended in 1952. However, it has continued under a different—and not apparently universal—guise. The bureaucracy of the National Health Service, launched under Attlee's postwar administration, needed some form of registration to keep track of patients' files. A universal registration scheme could therefore continue to be justified, now under the auspices of health. Combined medical, insurance, and NR cards were planned.[75] However, when National Registration collapsed in February 1952 after the Willcock decision, British identity cards also ended, much to the frustration of Whitehall. The National Health Service Central Register (NHSCR) was therefore constructed, on the recommendation of Treasury O&M, before the CNRO was dismantled, by duplicating the Central National Register.[76]

Knowledge of the Home Front (2): The Wartime Social Survey

National Registration gave the state the means to know the location of individuals. It did not give information about the opinions, problems, wishes and morale of groups, and this was precisely the sort of knowledge needed in a war that mobilized the population as a whole. The state therefore turned its attention to other techniques. In chapter 3 we saw how statisticians wrestled over whether the state should or should not be a producer of "informative" statistics, quantitative knowledge that went beyond administrative need. In the Second World War the production and dissemination of "informative" statistics, like propaganda, was wholeheartedly embraced.

Organized market research had begun around the turn of the century and had professionalism in the United States by the 1930s. Market research techniques were, as Beniger has shown, crucial "feedback technologies," allowing the alignment of mass consumption to mass production.[77] One technique was sampling and taking the responses of a segment of a population as indicative of that of the whole. The difficulty was over justification, and statisticians such as Arthur Bowley in First World War Britain and Morris Hansen at the United States Census Bureau in the 1930s worked hard to convince skeptics that the errors introduced in sampling could be known and controlled. Market survey techniques crossed the Atlantic and were slowly taken up by the British private sector in the 1930s. Its first British applications were surveys conducted by newspapers—vital in order to win advertising revenue, and soon covered the whole field of consumer spending by the late 1930s. Public opinion polling also arrived in Britain late: George Gallup opened a London office in 1938, selling exclusive rights to his polls to the *News Chronicle*. Government departments made very little use of surveys before 1939, with one or two exceptions, such as John Hilton—who had been encouraged by Bowley—at the Ministry of Labour.[78] Hilton had a remarkable life: in the 1890s he was an apprentice mill mechanic taking evening classes at Bolton Technical School. After rising to the position of manager at an engineering works near Manchester, he moved to Tsarist Russia to study, before pursuing a career that took in journalism, the Civil Service (as Assistant Secretary and Director of Statistics at the Ministry of Labour between 1919 and 1931) and finally, from 1931, a Professorship of Industrial Relations at the University of Cambridge. For a year after the outbreak of war Hilton moonlighted as Director of Home Publicity at the Ministry of Information—the newly set up department under the politician Duff Cooper, responsible for propaganda, public relations and, as we shall see, knowledge of the population. Hilton pressed successfully within the Ministry for a Home Intelligence Division—experts able to organize incoming knowledge of people in Britain. The most significant outcome was the establishment of the Wartime Social Survey, first under largely academic control in 1939 and then, a year later after vituperative attacks by the press on "Cooper's Snoopers," reorganized as a direct responsibility of the Ministry of Information.

The Wartime Social Survey drew staff from the two traditions of British social investigation: market researchers (such as its director, Louis Moss, from Marketing Survey of the United Kingdom and also the BBC's Survey of Listening), but also from philanthropic investigative organizations such as Rowntree. Staff numbers grew until more than 50 interviewers were in the field by the end of 1941, one half fixed in towns so that a continuous and consistent study of levels of public opinion could be obtained, the other half mobile so that new specific surveys could be rapidly launched. Many of the surveys were on shortages of goods (for the Board of Trade) or food and nutrition (for the Ministries of Health and Food—the latter also had to hand a Wartime Family Food Survey commissioned by the Committee of Imperial Defence from the commercial London Press Exchange), although an extremely broad range of other topics was also covered. The reason for this emphasis was because, from 1939, the United Kingdom had essentially become a directed, not a market, economy, and formal information production substituted market mechanisms. Informational replacements for the market had to be developed quickly: "those who found themselves in 1939 responsible for the conduct of the country in the rapidly changing conditions of war—when facts were more important than precedents—had very little to help them."[79]

It is interesting to note that these same "facts" would not have had that high status before the war, when sampling was contested. Here the resources of the state smoothed the path to objectivity: the National Register, for example, was employed by the Wartime Social Survey to generate names and addresses for random sampling—a robust but difficult method.[80] Less robust was "quota sampling," also used by the Wartime Social Survey and which worked by selecting a portion of the surveyed population by quotas of subgroups (a certain number of women, a certain number of poor, a certain number of young persons, and so on). Random sampling needed a register from which names could be randomly selected. Quota sampling did not, but had to rely on the interviewers' judgments as to the age, sex, and wealth of the interviewee.

Like National Registration, the Wartime Social Survey—aside from the Cooper's Snoopers accusations in 1939—was largely accepted, although, unlike NR, not just as a necessary wartime evil. For example the *Times* in 1942 ringingly endorsed the work of the Survey, it was "one of the most interesting wartime social innovations," research "on this scale is something new in sociology. It is concrete evidence of the advance of democracy . . . a new and quantitative bridge between the central Government departments and the people of the country. It looks as though the wartime Social Survey has come to stay."[81] The Social Survey, by making visible the feelings of the people, might have contributed to democracy, but it was democracy mediated by experts rather than by direct election. The Social Survey helped shape the state in a second way, the construction of a "new center" to British politics, which is best discussed after considering another organization which generated knowledge of the people, using a radically different methodology, Mass Observation.

Knowledge of the Home Front (3): Mass Observation

The popular information-gathering movement that was called Mass Observation began in the confusion that surrounded the abdication of King Edward VIII in 1936. Edward had abdicated in order to marry an American divorcee, Mrs. Simpson. When the self-censorship imposed by the British press during the abdication crisis became apparent, the effect was to reinforce a growing anti-Establishment sentiment among sections of the population. In particular, the intellectual middle-class Left thought that the working classes were not being "given the facts," while government was seen as inscrutable or untransparent. This argument motivated many informative enterprises of the late 1930s: the publication of cheap, mass market non-fiction paperbacks (such as the extremely successful Penguin Specials), the documentary film movement, the documentary newspaper *Picture Post*, Victor Gollancz, John Strachey, and Harold Laski's Left Book Club (which had 57,000 members at its peak in April 1939), and Mass Observation. The latter started after a chance encounter on the letter pages of the *New Statesman* in early 1937. In London, the "moderately well-known leftist poet and . . . frustrated journalist" Charles Madge, working with documentary filmmaker Humphrey Jennings, wrote a letter to the *New Statesman*:

> Mr. Geoffrey Pyke suggested in your columns the other week that the constitutional crisis [sparked by the abdication] had begun to produce material for an anthropology of our own people.
>
> Some days before the precipitation of the crisis, a group was formed for precisely this purpose. English anthropology, however, hitherto identified with "folk-lore," has to deal with elements so repressed that only what is admitted to be a first-class upheaval brings them to the surface. Such was the threatened marriage of the new "Father-of-the-people" to Mrs. Ernest Simpson, i.e. the collection of evidence of mass wish-situations, has otherwise to proceed in a far more roundabout way than the anthropologist has been accustomed to in Africa or Australia.[82]

The "real observers" of the abdication crisis, Madge continued, were "the millions of people who were, for once, irretrievably involved in the public events. Only mass observations can create mass science." The London group around Madge were already "engaged in establishing observation points on as widely extended a front as can at present be organized," and Madge invited "voluntary observers" to contact him. One who did was Tom Harrisson, the son of an Argentine railway operator who had pursued anthropological and ornithological studies in the New Hebrides before returning to Britain to anthropologize the working classes of Bolton.[83] By chance Harrisson had a poem published alongside Madge's letter. Whereas Madge's vision of mass observation was inspired by surrealism and psychoanalysis (encouraging, for example, the submission of personal diaries) Harrisson pursued a much more "objective" agenda, favoring the use of teams of eavesdropping documentarists working pubs and streets and anonymously noting down conversations. However, the London and Bolton groups combined to formally launch "Mass Observation" in February 1937. Harrisson, Jennings and Madge claimed to already have 50 observers at work on two "sample problems" but listed the possibilities for research if 5,000 volunteers could be recruited:

Behaviour of people at war memorials.
Shouts and gestures of motorists.
The aspidistra cult.
Anthropology of football pools.
Bathroom behaviour.
Beards, armpits, eyebrows.
Anti-semitism.
Distribution, diffusion and significance of the dirty joke.
Funerals and undertakers.
Female taboos about eating.
The private lives of midwives.[84]

Mass Observation's aim was complete knowledge—"it does not presuppose there are inexplicable things"—accessible to all (in particular, of course, the working classes): "it does not set out in quest of truth or facts for their own sake, or for the sake of an intellectual minority, but aims at exposing them in simple terms to all observers, so that their environment may be understood, and thus constantly transformed."[85] As its historian Tom Jeffrey has pointed out, Mass Observation was therefore conceived as a democratic science, knowledge made by the people for the people.[86] No longer would the general public suffer because of censorship of the press, or indeed because of advertising: adverts worked because organizations "employed the best empirical anthropologists and psychologists" to target superstitions; with the superstitions revealed through democratic science, the public could no longer be exploited.[87]

Four hundred observers were recruited in 1937. Jeffrey has made an excellent case to explain the motivation of the volunteers. He points out that there were many similarities between Mass Observation and the Left Book Club: both aimed to inform a "public ignorant and unaware," both were overseen by energetic, indeed somewhat "authoritarian" "cultural entrepreneurs" (Harrisson and Gollancz, respectively), both appeared in the context of the crises of the late 1930s, and both attacked the established media. Also, more significant, both offered the intellectual middle class the chance to participate in the resolution of the crises, and therefore helped build a new concept of "national unity" based on an alliance of "all people of goodwill"—a popular front to be contrasted with the National Government of the 1930s.[88] The attractions were social: organized sports, rambles in the countryside, lectures, even relatively expensive Summer Schools. Perhaps most important were the social benefits of correspondence: the observers communicating with the London Mass Observation office, and thereby building a culture of involvement.

In prewar Britain, the Left Book Club was a resounding success; Mass Observation remained small. In both cases it was their response to war which determined their futures. The Left Book Club, with its ties to the Communist Party, lost disillusioned members in droves with the announcement of the Nazi-Soviet Pact. Mass Observation, however, became a tool of government. Negotiations with the Ministry of Information began in 1939 via intermediaries and friends of Mass Observation, Mary Adams and Richard Crossman. Mass Observation soon proved its worth: the Ministry had made a disastrous start, reflected by the poster campaign "Your Courage, Your Cheerfulness, Your Resolution Will Bring Us Victory"—the implication being that there was a separate "you" (the people) and "us" (the state). Mass Observation feedback changed the Ministry's sloganeering toward inclusivity.[89] The period of grace known as the "phony war" meant that the Ministry could afford to make early mistakes. Mass Observation moved closer to government: it briefed Duff Cooper for his misleading House of Commons statement on the "Cooper's Snoopers" allegations—hardly the act of a popular front. First Jennings, then Madge, left the organization, leaving Harrisson in charge. However, with state-funding Mass Observation expanded, and published a series of important books and pamphlets during the war, including *War Begins at Home* (1940), *People in Production* (1942), and *The Pub and the People* (1943). Alongside work for the Ministry of Information, Mass Observation was also recruited by the Director of Naval Intelligence to feedback findings on morale in ports.[90] The busiest period for Mass Observation was the summer of 1940:

> The period from the invasion of Belgium to Dunkirk was the most intensely active of MO's existence. Detailed records of people's reactions to the news were kept daily, both through the direct method of questioning and by recording all sorts of overheard remarks and conversations in the street, in pubs, cafes and buses. People were observed in their homes listening to the news on the radio, their day-to-day and sometimes hour-to-hour expectations and fears were recorded and through the diaries long records of their private conversations and actions were collected. Rumor, includ-

ing the first version of the parachutist-nun with hairy hands, which persisted for many months later in various forms, were carefully collated and sifted each day. In March MO began asking "What do you think of the news today"?—a standard question which was asked at least two days a week for the whole war period. Analyzed in a standard scheme, answers to this question give one index to the blend of hope, expectation, interest, and forward looking which help to make up the elusive quality "morale."[91]

Mass Observation therefore contributed to the political constitution of Britain in two ways: by providing information about "the people," but also (along with other "radical fact-finding and fact-disseminating populist movements") by enrolling the left-wing intellectual middle class. Mass Observation helped form a "new center" of British politics that came to power during the war. Versions of this argument can be found in the histories by Angus Calder, Paul Addison, Arthur Marwick, and Tom Jeffery.[92] Likewise the Social Survey, although radically different from Mass Observation in methodology (statisticians were fiercely critical of MO's qualitative approach), can also be seen as instrumental in the building of the new center and its New Jerusalem project: the planned Welfare state covering British subjects "from cradle to grave." By far the most important project of the Social Survey was the Survey of Sickness which began in 1943 and provided a continuous statistical picture of the nation's health. The organization of such information was crucial to the operation—and articulation—of the National Health Service, announced in a white paper in 1944 and introduced under Clement Attlee's postwar Labour administration.

The techniques deployed by Mass Observation were relatively unsophisticated: qualitative collection. For example, there were no mechanically sortable lists of keywords or registers of all information. However, Mass Observation demonstrated the growing interest in data collection that meshed with the top-down, more mechanical information systems innovated by central government. This convergence was the foundation of subsequent welfare-state information systems.

Though this section has concentrated on the collection of information, a brief mention should be made of the dissemination and control of information that were equally important. British censorship, for example, has a long and complex history, and was, of course, of particular importance during wartime.[93] Censorship can be considered as "negative propaganda": the prevention of information being circulated by the introduction of restrictions on sources. "Positive"—normal—propaganda had many audiences, and merged at one end with the techniques of advertising and marketing. The British government made use of advertising techniques relatively early, compared, say, to the surveying discussed above (although the career of W. H. Smith, who introduced the concept of leasing the blank walls of railway stations for advertising in the 1850s, and later became Secretary to the Treasury, is an exceptional one).[94] The recruiting posters of the Great War featuring Lord Kitchener are a cliché. The Empire and Milk Marketing Boards employed skilled artists in their effective campaigns of the 1920s and the 1930s. Good histories exist of advertising and propaganda.[95]

Techniques of Bureaucracy in the War Machine

The "vital urge for topical information" led to a "mass of information collected by Ministries [being] analyzed and summarized in considerable detail to provide the planning authorities with current information on a wide range of subjects."[96] The surge in data processing is illustrated by the jump in expenditure on office machinery (table 6.1). The expenditure on punched cards in 1945–46, for example, was 10 times as much as was spent in the late 1930s.

Private industry was mobilized in the information war: British Tabulating Machines, one of the two British punched-card companies and the one which

Table 6.1
Expenditures (£) on office machinery items through HMSO. Source: T 222/915. Table, "HMSO: Expenditure," 1948.

Financial year	Tabulators (rent)	Cards	Total, cards + tabulators	Typewriters and duplicators	Other	Total
1927–28	12,235	10,515	22,750	35,296	13,833	71,879
1930–31	12,445	6,933	19,378	74,323	27,044	120,745
1933–34	24,990	8,583	33,573	56,335	29,486	119,394
1936–37	31,374	11,325	42,699	124,840	59,301	226,840
1939–40	59,289	17,486	76,775	498,414	144,651	719,840
1942–43	232,876	97, 664	330,540	1,090,844	383,479	1,804,863
1945–46	495,942	111,978	607,920	872,836	439,856	1,920,612
1946–47	360,003	60,736	420,739	378,689	467,986	1,267,414
1947–48[a]	375,000	50,000	425,000	390,000	245,000	1,060,000
1948–49[a]	440,000	50,000	495,000	395,000	255,000	1,145,000

a. estimated.

built the Bletchley Park bombes, set up a Government Service Bureau in 1940 at Cirencester, probably using on the Milk Marketing Board's machines, to process data for government departments that did not have their own punched-card installation.[97] (For an example of BTM propaganda, see figure 6.7.) The experiment in outsourcing did not last. In 1941 the Production Executive set up a Sub-Committee on the Supply and Requirements of Office Appliances. This Sub-Committee invited the Treasury Investigating Section to assume "responsibility for planning and coordinating the flow of work to the Bureau."[98] The Bureau was used extensively. However, the Supply and armed service departments in particular installed machines under their direct control to cope with the increased demand for processed information.

Why was there such a dramatic increase in the use of information technologies, especially office machinery? First and foremost, the Second World War presented massive problems of managing highly extended technological systems. People and matériel had to be organized at immense distances: in the British case this network might stretch from Command headquarters in London, via the devolved military hierarchy, to tank campaigns in North Africa or anti-U-boat activities in the North Atlantic, and further afield. Moreover, the operation was akin to a planned economy, with the consequence that much of the information processing normally borne by the market had to be done explicitly. Finally, speed—of decision making, calculation, and data handling in particular—was at a premium. Indeed, the great demand for office machinery created severe problems for its British manufacturers, BTM and Powers.[99] Indeed, some applications of Hollerith techniques to government work, even within the military, were delayed until after the war because of the apparent scarcity of machines.[100]

We have already seen that this context led to mechanization, automation, use of electronics, and standardization of communication. The widespread application of punched-card equipment to government work had consequences in four areas: for the level of detailed knowledge of the home front, a deepening of the capacity for calculation, and the ability to track objects and people within the "war machine."[101] An example of the first of these was the Social Survey, discussed above, which was dependent on teams of Hollerith staff to process its data.[102] The following three consequences will be examined in more depth below by focusing on three examples: the Admiralty Computing Service (deepened capacity for calculation), Royal Air Force stores accounting (tracking objects) and RAF personnel organization (tracking people).

Figure 6.7
BTM propaganda, 1942–43. The sequence of cartoons was the same as that of processing a card: punching, sorting, and tabulating, with optional interpreting. (source: National Archive for the History of Computing, University of Manchester)

The Admiralty Computing Service

War created intense demands for fast and accurate calculation. In the United States, this factor created the conditions which produced the massive ENIAC, with profound implications for the history of computing. In Britain, non-government and non-military centers of calculation were quickly requisitioned: Douglas Hartree's differential analyzer at the University of Manchester, and the University of Cambridge's Mathematical Laboratory, complete with a range of machines, were put to work by the Ministry of Supply, a new government department charged with producing weapons and defense technology for the army and air force. Comrie's Scientific Computing Service was also mobilized, the War Office making its first request—ballistic tables for anti-aircraft guns—within 3 hours of the declaration of war.[103] To fulfill its tasks, the SCS was offered use, when needed, of many of the Hollerith installations discussed in the previous chapter, such as that of the Milk Marketing Board.[104] A more radical change in the organization of government computation, however, occurred within the Admiralty.

The Admiralty Computing Service (ACS) grew from the work of the Nautical Almanac Office (NAO), a key interwar center of computation: the production of tables, predominantly values of mathematical functions.[105] The Admiralty's war effort depended on the effective development of new devices at a string of laboratories.[106] A bottleneck in this research was calculation. For example, ACS research subjects such as "behavior of the gas bubble formed by an underwater explosion in the presence of a target" (the "Taylor Bubble"), "problems arising from experiments on the high speed deformation of plastics," and "solution of a differential equation arising from a fire control problem" threw up tricky mathematical problems.[107] Some equations either cannot be solved analytically (that is, cannot be solved leaving a function for which values can be calculated in a straightforward manner) or require so much time to solve that the practical effect is the same. The solutions must therefore be found numerically by a process of estimating answers using a laborious but relatively simple iterative processes. Similarly, the values of some functions that are important to naval engineering must be found by the painstaking and repetitive summations. Mechanization using desk calculators was one solution to these problems. Punched-card machines could also be adapted for these purposes. Hollerith machines were, however, expensive, and the skills needed to use them for scientific computation were rare.

Therefore, there was a strong case for centralizing and concentrating the calculating capacity of the Admiralty. In 1943, John Carroll, then employed by the Admiralty's Directorate of Scientific Research and later a stalwart of postwar British defense research advisory bodies, argued that centralization would "not only lead to acceleration of results" but would also "make possible theoretical research involving calculations too lengthy to be tackled locally."[108] The NAO, with its expertise in computation, was able to handle work which was complex enough to warrant expert assistance but not so complex to require the most expensive equipment, as the following list shows:

1. All types of tabulation i.e. the calculation of a function for a large (preferably equal interval) number of values of the parameters concerned.
2. Calculations which, by their quantity, are capable of being systematized, in some way, even though they are for odd values of parameters.
3. Indirect calculations, i.e. the numerical solution of differential equations, which require a knowledge of numerical mathematics. In these cases it is desirable that the problem should be stated in precise mathematical terms.
4. Least squares methods and solution of normal equations, provided that the data are sufficient to warrant mechanical methods.[109]

"Mechanical" methods for the NAO merely meant the use of mechanical calculators—most often the Brunsviga 20, but also other machines such as the Marchant. (Brunsvigas were German and therefore in scarce supply.) The NAO had no Hollerith equipment in 1943. The ACS acted as a clearinghouse for naval calculation, with problems submitted by the research establishments and then sent out to the NAO or to individual experts (including members of the French Scientific Mission), with punched-card work put out to either the Admiralty's Scientific Research and Experiment Department (SRE) or the BTM Bureau at Cirencester. Though this arrangement was "by no means satisfactory as the establishment of a complete Hollerith Installation quickly," it did "allow the efficient use of Hollerith equipment without any undue delay."[110] The punched-card machines were used for the production of mathematical tables, but also for statistical work, such as analyses of casualties following torpedo attacks. The ACS also decided when it was necessary to build new machines to assist calculations, such as a Fourier transformer, an electronic differential analyzer for mine design, and a "rangefinder performance computer." The ACS issued more than 100 reports between 1943 and 1945.

Croarken dwells on the two-tier organizational structure of the ACS: "In order to use the service Admiralty establishments had to approach a small administrative staff at the SRE Department in Whitehall which then passed the work on to the NAO. . . . The ACS, therefore, operated on two levels: it was administered from Whitehall and the actual computational work was carried out at the NAO."[111] She notes the advantages and disadvantages of this system: prioritization decisions could be made, and experts managed and fitted into SRE's role as a general clearinghouse, while unfortunately sealing off the NAO from the users of the calculations. I merely add that the two-tier system should not be a surprise; it is just another example of the generalist-specialist split in Civil Service work.

The ACS, however, as Croarken writes, "did not operate on a large enough scale to run a fully equipped computing service. It was not economically feasible to install punched-card machines or a differential analyzer for example."[112] D. H. Sadler, head of the NAO, and John Todd, a SRE mathematician, proposed instead further centralization, recruiting John Carroll to present their argument. In their vision, expressed in a memorandum co-written with a scientific consultant to the Admiralty, A. Erdélyi, a National Mathematical Laboratory would be a comprehensive and permanent computing center, offering services to all of government, and extending its facilities to universities and industry. It would "carry out all types of computational work for any government department which needed assistance," "advise all government departments on the installation of computing facilities and liaise with the Treasury over such matters," and keep up to date with the latest technology through further liaison at home and abroad.[113] The proposal found allies, including the director of the National Physical Laboratory, Sir Charles G. Darwin, who had informally called for a similar body in 1943. The eventual watered-down outcome was the establishment of a new Mathematics Division at the NPL, which would be home to one of the first stored-program computers, Turing's Pilot ACE.

The work of the ACS, and the subsequent proposal for a national computing center, can be interpreted from several perspectives. First, they are evidence of the deepening capacity for computation and calculation during wartime. Second, they provide further examples of the influence of the generalist-specialist or generalist-mechanical split in the Civil Service (the proposed National Mathematical Laboratory was to inherit the ACS's two-tier structure). Third, the suggestion of liaison with the Treasury provided a hint of a conflict to come: a rivalry within Whitehall as to whether the NPL or the Treasury should be the pre-eminent adviser, controller, and even definer of computing machinery.

Mechanizing Logistics in the RAF

The Royal Air Force was faced with a formidable logistical challenge, especially after 1940 as operations intensified in continental Europe and North

Africa. Satisfactory maintenance, for example, meant that aircraft parts had to be labeled, tracked, transported, stored, and delivered across an increasingly wide geographical area. Such logistics were the responsibility of Maintenance Command, which had a pyramidal organization, with many Aircraft Equipment Depots (AEDs) under a Master Provision Office (MPO). Before mechanization the AEDs generated "Stores Records," hand-posted documents detailing the quantities of items in stock. At the MPO the Stores Records were duplicated and consolidated on Provision Control Record Cards. Also at the MPO were Contract Record Cards (the major postings being receipts of stores at AEDs or direct "Diversion" Issues from contractors to consumers), Statistics Cards (an abstract of data from the previous two Cards), and the Provisioning Schedule (which used the Statistics Cards to generate predictions of future needs, and which was shared with the Ministry of Aircraft Production). None of these cards were of the punched variety, and it was this change that was proposed in 1942. Four benefits were expected: standardization of stores accounting across 40 Group (Maintenance), greater geographical reach ("expansion with the hand method presents a very real problem to the Depots in this project"),[114] savings of human labor, and superior mechanical accuracy. "It is clear," one memorandum asserts, "that the operative factor in all these records is the stores movement. A card punched for each stores movement can therefore serve as a master for the mechanical preparation of all these records with considerable increased accuracy and a saving of labor. In this respect the problem presents itself as being most suitable for treatment by the punched-card method."[115]

The main question was whether to use Hollerith or Powers-Samas machines. Pressure was put on civil servants by Sir Joseph Burn, President of the Prudential insurance house, and by the Powers directors, to "buy British": ". . . they feel strongly that having regard to the critical position of shipping space, the dollar exchange on purchases and the subsequent remission of substantial royalties to America on all rentals. . . . It is not in the national interest that American or 'partially' American equipment of this character should be contemplated to do the work while machines of wholly British origin and manufacture are available."[116] However the civil servants supported Hollerith's 80 column card because of its "greater and more flexible capacity" compared to Powers's 65 column version.[117] The punched-card system was rushed into operation in 1943, more than 750,000 items of RAF stock being controlled. Using Hollerith cards, a master index was maintained covering every item of equipment held in the depots. As stores were received or issued, cards were punched to represent the movements, and these were sorted daily and associated using collators with the appropriate card from the master index.

A rolling total tabulator produced the required statistics, as well as punching new master cards. Using the punched-card system, the Master Provision Officer was able to maintain records of stock position of all items not more than 24 hours in arrears.[118] A level of stores accounting control was possible that, in the opinion of analysts in 1951, would not have been possible with hand methods.[119]

However, the introduction of stores accounting by punched card was not as smooth as this summary suggests. A comparison with interwar initiatives in the Army is helpful. The Ordnance Depots at Didcot (near Oxford) and Chilwell had introduced basic mechanization, based on National Cash Register machines, in 1934. Two years later the Treasury authorized an experiment with Hollerith machines. However, the War Office soon was complaining of technical breakdowns, the "cumbersomeness" of voucher preparation, the difficulty of finding trained operators, and "an ability, in times of rapidly varying expenditure to throw up items for review as promptly as required" (this was, after all, the time of hasty rearmament).[120] The Army first reverted to NCR machines, with Hollerith for centralized provisioning only, and then, in December 1938, dropped the mechanical component completely: Visidex, a system of "manually posted cards anchored in trays" was belatedly found to be adequate. Independently, Powers machines were tried out in regimental pay offices from 1934 until 1938, when they too were abandoned. The simple Visidex system lasted the war for the Army. What would explain this "failure"? First and foremost the armed services needed flexible stores accounting systems, which must be operable by staff with little training and at short notice. Hence, systems that depended on a reliable supply of expert operators were viewed with considerable suspicion. The War Office highlighted this difficulty, and the RAF was reluctant to adopt something the War Office had tried and rejected. The RAF, too, during the mechanization of the Aircraft Equipment Depots, complained that "frequent changes in staff resulted in loss of specialist knowledge in the management and operation of machines," and generally disliked mechanized methods that required special training.[121] The hasty introduction contributed to the dissatisfaction. The RAF officers responsible have been described as "babes in the wood" because of their lack of experience.[122] However, it must be remembered that the manual system was also severely strained by the time of its replacement, largely because of the sheer scale of the task: the stores accounting methods of big commercial firms (ICI, GEC, Vickers, STC) were examined, but "no mechanized system of the size and complexity of that in the RAF" was said to have been found.[123]

Mechanizing Personnel Records in the RAF

The problems presented by the management of human personnel in the RAF were just as formidable as that of matériel. The important difference was that punched-card techniques were championed over a long period by an insider, John Cordingley, eventually Air Vice Marshal and RAF Director General of Manning. In 1918, Cordingley initiated investigations into punched-card systems; these investigations culminated in the introduction of Powers machines between 1923 and 1929.[124] The personnel records section expanded enormously during wartime. A large building in Ruislip, Surrey, housed records of more than a million personnel—triplicate cards, at least, corresponding to each individual. The section maintained sixteen different indexes, stored on color-coded punched cards, and each in triplicate: a main series, which was always up to date, and second and third series (copies) used in alternate months to generate statistics. Like Bletchley Park, the work of Ruislip was conceived in terms of information flow: incoming forms were read by a Ringing Section and modifications to cards noted, mechanical Interpolators then extracted the cards to be amended. Staff in the Reproduction room then copied all the columns of the old card onto a new card, with the exception of the columns to be changed. The incomplete new cards were then punched, verified, and triplicated. After a final check the new cards were sorted into numerical order and re-filed using the Interpolator again. At its peak, this process, I estimate, involved more than 5 million card passages per week. Some of the largest data-processing jobs of the war occurred at its end, as demobilization created extra demands. A new index of 750,000 demobilized airmen had to be created at Ruislip. In 1947 the Board of Trade made its "largest pay-out ever," sending out 250,000 dual-purpose Powers punched card/payable orders to settle claims under the War Damage Act of 1943.[125] Figure 6.10 shows the basic airman's punched card, as held at Ruislip. One aspect to note is that the airman's official number (columns 1–7) was not related to the National Register number, and it is unclear how the two registers—two of the largest registers of personal information in mid-twentieth-century Britain—were interlinked.

Knowledge for a Planned Economy: The Central Statistical Office

The above examples of RAF matériel and personnel illustrate the mechanization introduced to process the massive quantities of information required during the Second World War. Many other examples could be given. In the rest of this chapter, issues of increasing generality are considered. The first is the establishment in 1941, after more than 50 years of lobbying, of a Central

Figure 6.8
RAF data processing. Above: "Sorting section where 24 sorters are kept continually busy." Below: "A view of the training room where new operators learn correct methods of manipulating the machines." (source: *Powers Magazine*, September-October 1947. National Archive for the History of Computing, University of Manchester)

Figure 6.9
"Personnel Statistics at the Record Office, Royal Air Force, Ruislip." (source: *Powers Magazine*, September-October 1946, National Archive for the History of Computing, University of Manchester)

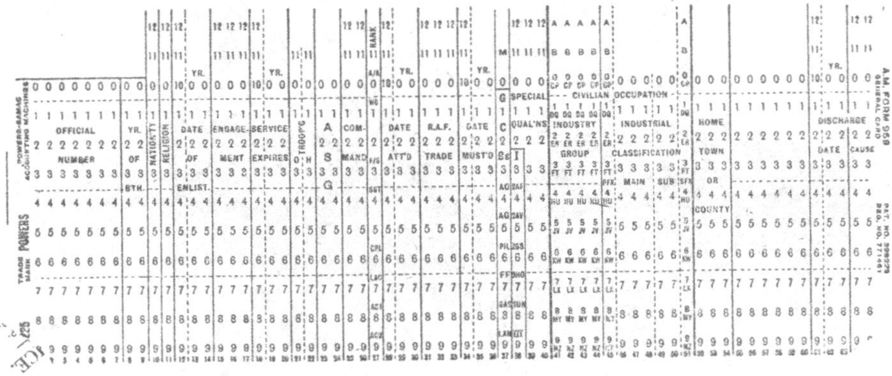

Figure 6.10
An airman's Main Index personnel record card, as held at Ruislip. (PRO T 222/811)

Statistical Office. In chapter 3 the lobbying was examined in detail and was located in a context where expert statisticians articulated new models of government in which they would play a central role. The only concrete outcome had been to set up the toothless Permanent Consultative Committee on Official Statistics (PCCOS) in the early 1920s. PCCOS drifted into inactivity, and last met in 1936. Yet within 5 years a full-fledged Central Statistical Office appeared at the center of Whitehall. What had happened?

The answer, unsurprisingly, was war. Beginning in 1939, Britain's government and economy were placed on a war footing. The diversion of scarce resources to the war effort led to the introduction of widespread controls and rationing. Shipping, imports, production, and manpower all became subject to central direction.[126] Issues of the relative allocation of resources among departments had to be decided at a high level (the War Cabinet), and the requirement to make these decisions created the need for large quantities of statistics, comparable across Whitehall. Likewise, progress of the directed programs could only be reviewed and guided through statistical measures. The new legal environment of warfare also smoothed the path of the statisticians. Previous arguments for a central statistical office had, on the surface, foundered on the technical constitutional argument over ministerial responsibility: a department might straightforwardly collect "administrative" statistics, but who would be responsible for the broader "informative" statistics which a central statistical office might want but the department might not? However, the Emergency Powers (Defence) Acts of 1939 and 1940 meant that such constitutional niceties could be overridden in the name of the war effort.[127] Propaganda had, too, pushed back the boundaries of acceptable "informative" knowledge produced by government. Furthermore, the use of the Cabinet Secretariat, expanded during the war, allowed the issue of ministerial responsibility to be finessed.

The Central Statistical Office was set up within the Offices of the War Cabinet in early 1941. Staff numbers were small but increased through the war: 7 in 1941, 12 in 1942, 17 in 1943, 18 in 1944, 17 in 1945, 21 in 1946.[128] The work was guided by an advisory committee of principal departmental statisticians, initially under the chairmanship of the Government Actuary, Sir George Epps.[129] The Central Statistical Office's remit emphasized the provision of an "agreed corpus of statistics," comparable across departments, which was quickly achieved. The influential position of the office—in the Cabinet Secretariat—meant that it soon dominated the statistical work of other departments. It was "frequently able to see more easily than a Department the inter-relations between the statistics collected by different Departments."[130] Furthermore, the Office advised the Cabinet Committees (the decisive center of government), even to the extent of writing white papers on National Income and Expenditure, on Statistics relating to the War Effort of the United Kingdom, and on Strength and Casualties of the Armed Forces and Auxiliary Services of the United Kingdom. A Central Statistical Office therefore occupied a real position of power, justified by expertise, just as the proponents in the early twentieth century had hoped and their opponents had feared. Finally, the insight from chapter 3 that the distinction drawn between "administrative" and "informative" statistics was a product of the debate over the rightful position of expert statisticians is confirmed by the fading of the distinction once the Central Statistical Office was formed. By 1946 this formerly fundamental distinction was described as "blurred." As the Central Statistical Office became a familiar part of the Whitehall landscape, the boundary disappeared.

When the war ended, the Central Statistical Office carried on. The planned, directed war economy was held to carry peacetime lessons, not least for Clement Attlee's Labour administration (a landslide winner in the general election of 1945). Nationalization of the coal industry and the railways followed, and Keynes's economic ideas, which depended upon continuous knowledge of key indicators, became orthodoxy. In this postwar context the Central Statistical Office—if understood primarily as a replacement for the informational mechanisms of the market—would continue to have strong relevance. "The continued existence of the Office now that the war is over," one member of the Office noted in 1946, "is justified by the general realization that any economic policy in the future will be dependent on the provision of a body of statistics which will make it possible to know the movements of the economic system as a whole, as well as in its several parts, clearly and constantly under review."[131]

Information Experts and War

The Central Statistical Office has already provided one clear example of the politics of expertise during the Second World War. Statisticians, in fact, were only one group among a number of such movements. This section continues the discussion by examining the emergence of Operational Research, the rise of scientific advisors, and the new strength and power of experts in the Treasury.

Operational Research

Operational Research appeared in late 1930s as the "meta-science" of radar. As we have seen, the Chain Home early warning radar raised questions about how the information gained should be used in the organization of Britain's air defense. These questions were answered by a series of experimental exercises in which aerial attacks were simulated and organizational reactions tested. The armed services could not develop these responses on their own, since the necessary expertise was in the possession of the radar scientists. Teams of RAF officers and scientists, on the suggestion of Henry Tizard, therefore monitored the experiments, beginning with one over Biggin Hill in 1936. The term "Operational Research" first appeared in descriptions of this teamwork in 1938 (the American "Operations Research" was a later invention).[132] The technique of "range cutting" and the design of Operations and Filter Rooms were achievements of the operational researchers. For the exercises in the summer of 1939, operational researchers were stationed in the Filter Room at the headquarters of the Fighter Command at Stanmore in North London. This team "produced such useful services" that Air Chief Marshal Sir Hugh Dowding appointed its members (civilians) permanently to this central location, and the team was renamed the Operational Research Section (ORS). By the early years of the war, each Command would possess an ORS.[133]

The promotion of the civilian operational research experts should not be seen as merely a recognition of their contribution to the efficient organization of defense. The collection of individuals soon developed a group self-identit as Operational Researchers and pushed for recognition, status, and promotion. Thus a central tenet of Operational Research emerged: that they could only make a maximum contribution if given access and influence at the top of the organizational pyramid. "Scientists at the Operational Level," an October 1941 memorandum by Professor Patrick Blackett (a member of the interwar Committee for the Scientific Survey of Air Defence and the instigator of operational research in Anti-Aircraft and Coastal Commands), provides the locus classicus of this claim: "The head of the Operational Research

Section should be directly responsible to the Commander-in-Chief and may with advantage be appointed as his scientific adviser."[134] The justification for this elevated position was expertise: "Very many war operations involve considerations with which scientists are specially trained to compete, and in which serving officers are in general not trained. This is especially the case with all those aspects of operations into which probability considerations and the theory of errors enter."[135] To underline the point, Blackett peppered his policy paper with mathematical formulas and argued that "the scientist can encourage numerical thinking on operational matters, and so can help to avoid running the war on gusts of emotion."[136]

By 1945 there existed an expert movement of self-proclaimed operational researchers cooperating at a high level in the armed services. The postwar development of Operational Research was mixed. Professional accoutrements appeared: an Operational Research Club (later Society), with a quarterly newsletter, for example, began in 1950. Its professionals promoted operational research as a tool for civil government and industry, moving away from its armed service roots. By the end of the 1950s operational research units could be found in such large industrial concerns as United Steel, British Petroleum, Shell-Mex, the National Coal Board, and BEA, and in the British Iron and Steel Research Association.[137] Ambitions were high, especially in the late 1940s. An enthusiastic civil servant claimed in 1948 that "the unit under investigation may be of any form. It may be an industry, or a single firm; it may be a social group, or a whole nation; it may be a military command, or a road safety system."[138] The civil National Physical Laboratory became an advocate in the early postwar years. The superintendent of the new NPL Mathematical Division, J. R. Womersley, returned from a visit to the United States, where he also saw the ENIAC and heard about the plans for the EDVAC, with news of American developments. His findings provoked the director of the NPL, Charles G. Darwin, to launch a civil initiative in the name of competition:

> The proposal is to apply for Industry methods which, under the name of Operational Research, have made important contributions to the military art, and by these methods to enable producers to learn how better to meet the consumer's demands. A similar project is at present being worked out in America, which, if it turns out as it promises, will give the Americans even greater advantages in the world's markets than they already possess.[139]

Darwin had in mind a new "Station" with a staff as large as 100, including "highly trained statisticians," using a "considerable amount of statistical equipment of the 'punched card' type."[140] However, despite teaming up with the

Board of Trade, and unlike his support in the proposal for a National Mathematical Laboratory, nothing emerged from his initiative. Indeed, operational research faded in influence, if not professional organization, during the 1950s. Early consultancy firms, such as SIGMA (a British subsidiary of the French Societé d'Economie et de Mathematique Appliquees led by Stafford Beer), were viewed with suspicion within Whitehall.[141] This diminution was due in part to the vagueness of operational research's claim to expertise. It was multi-disciplinary: "depending on the type of problem, social scientists, economists, medical scientists, or natural scientists might be included in the team," noted a civil servant in 1948, and all they needed to have in common was knowledge of "certain statistical techniques"—a shaky foundation for their claim.[142] In part, the 1950s decline was due to competition from other expert movements in government and industry. However, there was also a powerful political factor in the fortunes of operational research. It was no coincidence that operational research returned as a forceful and credible expert movement with the election of the next Labour government, under Harold Wilson, in 1964, after 13 years of Conservative rule. Blackett was a friend and adviser to Wilson, and became especially influential in the mid 1950s. As an illustration of the political sympathies of operational research, here is Lord Robens, Chairman of the National Coal Board writing to Secretary of State for Economic Affairs, Peter Shore:

> I can myself confirm that Operational Research in the Coal Board has become of considerable importance, and I would feel that the scientific, quantitative approach to problems has a very great deal to offer, even in situations which at first sight may seem intractable. In fact, if we as Socialists are to reject the market mechanism in many of its workings, we must offer something superior—and in my opinion there are many fields where this must involve powerful intellectual and computing powers such as those of Operational Research.[143]

The British deployment of operational research as part of a rejection of market mechanisms contrasts sharply with its uses in America, where, if we accept Mirowski's arguments, operations research bolstered the reformulation of neo-classical economics.[144]

This postwar diversion has been taken in this chapter for several reasons, the statement of which will serve as a conclusion on operational research. First, like the Central Statistical Office, operational research acted as a substitute for market operations, which explains its first appearance within the armed services and its adoption by protagonists of the directed economy. This aspect was what Robens explicitly appealed to in the letter quoted above. Second, operational research added to the number of expert movements—statisticians, economists, and mechanists—articulating technocratic visions of

Britain in the middle of the twentieth century. Last, operational research illustrates the rise in government of a particular form of expert: the scientific adviser.

The Rise of Science Advisers

The increase in influence of the scientific expert in government, exemplified by the Second World War careers of Blackett, Tizard, and Lindemann, is a well-known historical phenomenon.[145] My interest here is restricted to articulations of how the high-level scientist should relate to policy making, and, in particular, to some proposals put forward by Tizard in 1945. Tizard has already featured in this chapter through his involvement with radar development in the 1930s. During the war he continued to work as an adviser to government. He was entrusted with the scientific mission to the United States that brought the magnetron to American notice and led to the establishment of the Office of Science Research and Development (and indirectly, therefore, that of the postwar National Science Foundation).[146] In the United States and in Britain, Tizard insisted on the need for central strategic direction of scientific research, especially defense research. The 1945 proposals, written in the aftermath of Hiroshima and Nagasaki, summarized the lessons of the past 6 years and looked to how they should be learned in peacetime: "The atomic bomb has vividly impressed upon us all the tremendous influence of scientific progress on every aspect of national and international life. No long term policy of any kind can hope to attain its object, unless the Government has automatic access to the best scientific advice at all times."[147] The years of total war had blurred the lines between military and civil life, the "broad problems of war" could "no longer be separated from those of peace," and just as science had determined Britain's "ability to deter aggression and maintain . . . prestige and influence in world affairs," so "the same factor will have an equally profound influence on progress toward greater industrial prosperity and social welfare." The statisticians mentioned in chapter 3 had diagnosed afflictions of the political "head," and Tizard did likewise:

> The body of British science is healthy enough, and its physiology is quite appropriate, including the many local motor centers. But it has no head to control its overall rate of activity and growth, to guide its effort in the right directions, and to enable it to act as a fully informed and articulated adviser to the Government on the technical-scientific aspects of major policy issues—in a word, to formulate scientific strategy.

This "critical defect in our machinery" (note the slippage from body to machine metaphor) was to be corrected, as with operational research, by the permanent high-level influence of scientists on government: "Far more time and continuous thought, by scientists of considerable authority in the heart of the government machine, would alone ensure that the Chiefs of Staff [and, by force of argument, civil government] get scientific advice to guide their decisions." A "central scientific authority," beginning with defense research, should have, Tizard argued, "the right to know everything" and "the final say in what should be done in broad terms."

The immediate outcome of Tizard's arguments was the establishment of the Defence Research Policy Committee (DRPC). In practice the scientists, mostly government defense scientists, worked in close cooperation with the deputy Chiefs of Staff and research Controllers, in conditions of secrecy that have meant that its postwar contribution has, until recently, been underestimated.[148] Indeed, the influence of the DRPC was such that an anxious Treasury insisted on representation on the Committee in the mid 1950s, and it is to the wartime Treasury that I now turn. The argument above can be read as follows: The conditions of war necessitated an experiment with a directed economy based on controls and rationing. This expanded state gave expert movements the opportunity to claim more power and influence. The Treasury's response marked a decisive commitment to expertise in information handling. In this context the Treasury has to be considered on several registers: as the most powerful Whitehall department concerned about declining influence, as a model of bureaucratic action for Whitehall, as a center of both generalist and specialist expertise, and as the foremost body exercising financial control on public projects. An analysis of a fierce controversy at the highest level in the Civil Service will help us to understand this response.

Expertise and Treasury Control: The Origin of O&M

Stafford Cripps was, in the words of the historian of Whitehall Peter Hennessy, a "chemist turned lawyer, specializing in a highly technical brief, [who] believed in the possibility of scientific administration and, like the Webbs, saw it as part of the motive power of the forward march of British socialism."[149] It was Cripps's initiative, a campaign to review and reform the "machinery of government" (which he instigated immediately after his elevation to the War Cabinet in February 1942), that gave the Treasury its chance to re-stake its claim as the "center of the government machine."[150] In a bravura performance in the summer of 1943, the Treasury first seemed to concede all the criticisms leveled against the department:

> It is sometimes alleged against the Treasury, not so much that it interferes with the responsibilities of other Departments, as that it lacks this sympathetic understanding [of other departments, as Haldane put it]. It is said to be narrow in its conception of economy, to be instinctively and by long habit hostile to all increases in expenditure, to be negative and destructive where it should be constructive and helpful. It is the "dead

hand" chillingly restraining the Government machine as a whole from every desirable activity. It is pedantically disposed to make as much or more difficulty over the expenditure of small sums as of large ones. And finally, it is slow.[151]

But, the Treasury argued, either this sort of reaction was born of ignorance, or it was the inevitable lot of the central department, or it was a "bogey to hold up *in terrorem*," and in fact "much has been done, . . . particularly since the end of the last war, to remove the causes of criticism." The conclusions of the string of commissions examining the Civil Service since 1914 were listed: the MacDonnell Royal Commission (1914) had recommended, and the Select Committee on National Expenditure (1917) had confirmed, that "the Treasury should be strengthened for the purpose of establishing more effective control over the organization of the Civil Service." Critics were reminded of conclusions of the Haldane Committee (1918) and Sir John Bradbury's inquiry into the Organization and Staffing of Government Offices (1919) that "additions should be made to the Treasury Staff to enable the Department to study general 'establishment' questions relating to the Service at large and formulate the code which should govern the Service." Therefore—and this is fundamental to my argument—the Civil Service was, as articulated by the Treasury, a "general" "machine" governed by a "code."

The Treasury's grand wartime statement of purpose was circulated to all Permanent Secretaries, some of whom were effusive with praise. It was, wrote Sir Gerald Canny at the Inland Revenue, "masterly and convincing." Sir Alexander Cadogan at the Foreign Office thought it a "lucid document," with which Sir Donald Ferguson, Permanent Secretary of the Ministry of Agriculture and Fisheries expressed "entire agreement." Only a few quibbled. However, Lord Hankey, the linchpin of the interwar cabinet system and secretary to the Committee of Imperial Defence, was incensed. Maurice Hankey had been a Royal Marine artillery specialist before entering the Civil Service as a "temporary," but had radically reformed the organization as secretary in Lloyd George's war cabinet—the mushrooming "Cabinet Office" was their innovation in 1916. Hankey had survived Lloyd George's downfall, but only just (and against Treasury opposition), and became a scourge of appeasement during the 1930s.[152] All this background came to the fore in his response to the Treasury's statement. While calling it a "masterly exposition," Hankey was savage in his attack: "the tendency" was "towards a sublimation of a system, which, after all, had some share of responsibility for the deplorable situation in which this country found itself in 1939 for the second time in twenty-five years, and which brought us to the brink of disaster."[153] He continued:

There were of course many other causes for what happened—the overwhelming demand of public opinion for peace at any price regardless of future risks; the policy of disarmament, continued "to the edge of risk"; public insistence on too many and too costly social reforms, absorbing too great a share of available finance; disagreements between the Service Departments, now happily less pronounced, on their exact functions and mutual dependence; and the failure of successive Governments to educate public opinion through Parliament and to secure a proper perspective. But it is the business of Government Departments, which alone know all the facts, to educate their respective Ministers. The responsibility of the Official Treasury in this respect is especially heavy. . . .[154]

When it came to defensive preparation, the "'dead hand' of Treasury control fell on the whole machine." With intense irony, the failure of the machine was therefore one of information handling, knowledge, and control. If these failings were not recognized then, wrote Hankey, the consummate private and discreet civil servant, he would "with repugnance, publicly . . . criticize the present system."

In 1945 the Official Committee on the Machinery of Government concluded that "the present organization of the Treasury, the Cabinet Secretariat and the Secretariat at 10 Downing Street is well adapted to meet the needs of central coordination at the official level" and did not recommend "any substantial change in the organization or function of these three offices."[155] There was no apparent change—much, presumably, to Hankey's disgust. This "generally discredited" missed chance of reform is scathingly detailed by J. Michael Lee.[156] Indeed, in the narrow classic sense of machinery of government—the arrangement and hierarchy of departments—Lee is right. However, I argue, both below in this chapter and in chapter 8, that when expert movements, especially information experts and mechanizers, are added to the historical picture, it becomes far less true a representation. In particular I focus on the movement that grew out of Desborough's Treasury Investigating Section and was renamed Organization and Methods (O&M) in 1941. O&M emerges from Lee's account as a half-hearted adjunct of the machinery of government inquiry, a view that radically underestimates its significance and is certainly untrue regarding its postwar development. (Lee's account ends in 1952.)

The Investigating Section grew in numbers right from the start of the war, partly from recruits found via the Ministry of Labour's Central Register, C. P. Snow's list which was instrumental in organizing the British scientific war effort. The title "Treasury Investigator" created a "barrier of reserve" among investigated departments, so when a new term "Organization and Methods" began to circulate, probably following the addition to the Treasury of ex-Harrods and Ministry of Economic Warfare expert N. Baliol Scott, the

Treasury itself welcomed the change in name.[157] In 1941 the chartered accountant and Director of Vickers Ltd., the armaments and heavy engineering firm, James Reid Young, was called in to review the work of the Section. His report was quite critical: there was "little, if any, evidence of effective control or direction," a problem which stemmed from the relatively low rank of the head of the Treasury Investigating Section, who had difficulty in exercising control over newly recruited staff some of whom "have had considerable experience in responsible positions in industry."[158] The response to the Reid Young report was fourfold: a qualitative increase in status, a shift symbolized by the cementing of the new name "Organization and Methods," the establishment of a heavyweight Advisory Panel drawn from business, and the normalization of Treasury O&M at the center of a network of Departmental O&M Sections throughout Whitehall.[159] Although the conception of O&M changed over the years, its spirit was well captured by an introductory piece written in the mid 1950s:

> Under the first title, that of organization, must be included problems met at all levels of administration. At the highest levels O and M has on occasion been concerned with the main divisions of responsibility that enter the machinery of Government as a whole, that is the number of separate Ministries that carry out a Government's policy, the allocation of subjects and functions between them and the means for coordinating and harmonizing both the policies and activities of those separate Ministries. At lower levels O and M is concerned with, for instance, methods of filing papers or of managing and supplying the typing services. O and M work extends over an infinite variety of problems lying between these extremes of policy and process. The purpose [of O&M has been described as] "to secure maximum efficiency in the operation of the Government's executive machinery; and by the expert application of scientific methods to organization, to achieve economy in cost and labor."[160]

Treasury O&M was therefore a center of the expert movement of mechanists, with the wide-ranging capacity to review and recommend profound alterations to other government departments—in process, arrangement of functions, or even the material building, with all the attendant repercussions for hierarchy.[161] The four Treasury Investigating Officers before 1939 became a staff of 22 by July 1940, and a Treasury O&M Division of 46 by 1942, and 87 by 1949.[162] Though the center of O&M was the Treasury, it drew on the experience of large industry—an Advisory Panel of Businessmen met every 2 months from 1942—and, particularly in the postwar decades colonized other bodies: first, following Reid Young's advice, Whitehall departments had their own O&M units, beginning with the Admiralty, Air Ministry, Ministry of Aircraft Production, Ministry of Food and Board of Trade, and subsequently all large departments.[163] Such expansion was helped by the fact that O&M

responsibilities were devolved to departmental level—but the fact that each departmental O&M officer had to come to Treasury O&M for advice meant that the Treasury retained influence, and thus control.[164] The Whitehall O&Ms were followed by O&M units in private and nationalized industries and public organizations such as hospitals, police forces, and local government. O&M officers published textbooks and contributed to their own bulletin. O&M was therefore an expert movement of professionals. Attitudes to technique shifted in emphasis between 1945 and the 1950s. Although throughout O&M's influential life the "expert application of scientific methods to organization" meant a heavy commitment to mechanization, this commitment, present among Desborough's prewar Section, was deepened, widened, and made much more sophisticated in the early wartime years. Only later, however, as discussed in chapter 8, was the punched-card machine and the electronic computer the unproblematic tool and symbol of postwar O&M.

Immediately after gaining its new footing in 1941, O&M was the center of a great intake of specialist knowledge. Through contact with private consultancies (such as Urwick, Orr and Partners), O&M imbibed the techniques of the wide span of mid-century information experts: from the work of Sir Stephen Tallents (formerly of the Empire Marketing Board, subsequently director of public relations at the Post Office and BBC), to the Political and Economic Planning (PEP) think tank, to the London Press Exchange and the "Mass Observation crowd."[165] Lyndall Urwick himself, another product of Management Research Group No. 1 and the British celebrant and historian of American scientific management, joined the Treasury from the International Management Institute in Geneva in 1940, but clashed with Reid Young, complaining that he "found it quite impossible to reconcile the document with quite elementary principles of management."[166] However, Urwick's complaint that O&M was under-theorized was not quite correct, since, as we shall see, the external knowledge was combined with internal prewar experience, and synthesized into a guiding philosophy, most explicitly found expressed in the documents outlining the training of new O&M officers, written by I. James Pitman. Pitman, a gentleman and amateur athlete of considerable achievement, was born into a publishing family and served as chairman of Sir Isaac Pitman and Sons from 1934 to 1966, continuing and deepening the imprint's already strong back catalog in administrative science. (The British Library lists more than 10,000 works published by Pitman and Sons, including guides to the Civil Service, technical manuals, and the immensely influential primers on phonographic shorthand.) Between 1943 and 1945, Pitman was Director of Treasury O&M, while remaining also a

Director of the Bank of England. Crucially, Pitman was appointed at the Principal Assistant Secretary level—Administrative Class rather than mere Executive Class. Now, although the interests of O&M officers remained aligned to their rank in the middle-level Executive Class, the head of Treasury O&M could speak and act within Whitehall with First Division prestige, thereby lifting the status of O&M as a whole.[167]

The motif of Pitman's life's work, like that of his grandfather's, was the analysis of communication. The elder Pitman had devised phonography, or phonetics, celebrated by his biographer as "the first sign in modern times of a critical interest in language with a view to conscious control of it."[168] The efficient and controlled use of language was at a premium during wartime—recall the language of radar communication. The younger Pitman inherited the enthusiasm for the reform of the alphabet: he invented, for example, the "Initial Teaching Alphabet" which was designed for "the easier learning of literacy, oracy and the language in English," and assisted in the playwright and Fabian George Bernard Shaw's posthumous project of another new alphabet.[169] Likewise, Pitman's concern for the analysis of communication shaped his understanding of O&M, allowing him to synthesize the disparate wartime techniques, and then inculcate them in his recruits.

O&M staff were trained to follow several stages. First, they should be able to give a "precise definition" of their objective in any O&M study (Pitman's alphabets were also designed with precision and clarity as the main goal). Second, the objectives were divided up into different "duties," essentially components of the work at hand.[170] Third, among these duties the recruits would learn to spot familiar "common duties and procedures." Fourth, they would analyze them. Crucially, this analysis was structured by a sophisticated and complex informational typology, the "basic elements of communication." In the fifth and final stage, each element of communication was associated with the possible application of equipment and machines. The student was therefore led, by analysis, to consider mechanization as the route to efficiency and economy in clerical reform.

There were six "basic elements of communication," all ordered by actions on or with "information":

1. Collecting Information.
2. Checking Information and checking Recording for accuracy.
3. Making Information Conveniently Comprehensible.
4. Recording and reduplicating Information.
5. Storing Information.
6. Moving Information and/or material.[171]

Each of these elements had different aspects, each of which led to a device. For example, "recording and reduplicating information" led to "direct" methods such as printing, duplicating machines, typewriting with carbon paper or copying ink, photography, rolls from "adding and punched card machines, films, gramophone records," and to "intermediary" methods such as shorthand, dictating machines, rolls from teleprinters or punched summary cards. If the trainee was considering "moving information," he or she would be led to decide whether this information was to be sorted or delivered, if delivered whether it was to be recorded or not, and then on to the possible "methods" as solutions, many of which were mechanical. The end result was that O&M staff would possess together "a comprehensive knowledge of the whole field of communication" and individually "a specialist knowledge of at least one section of communicating." This theory should, wrote Pitman, be combined with a commitment to practice, to be achieved by "infusing interest, amounting to an almost religious fervor, for the worth-whileness of applying their talents": the trainee must get the practical "satisfaction of achievement and may make 'faith' a lasting part of his personal background, as St. Paul would say 'through works.'"

With Treasury O&M, as it developed through the Second World War and after, there was, at last, a British administrative science espoused by an expert movement which can be compared in relative size, influence, and theoretical sophistication to the management sciences found in early-twentieth-century America that have been described by Yates, discussed in the previous chapter.[172] Why did O&M appear in the Treasury, and why in the early 1940s? Like the cases of operational research or the Central Statistical Office, although not as directly, one factor was the shift to a directed economy—although in the Treasury the experts who made best advantage of the expansion of the state were the economists and statisticians (the latter were like "gold dust" during the war, writes Hennessy[173]). However, the answer does have to be sought in the context of wartime Whitehall. As I argued above, the Treasury was under intense pressure keeping its position as the "center of the government machine," and was threatened by the mushrooming growth of the free-spending Ministry of Aircraft Production, by the strengthening of the cabinet office as a rival central body, and by attempts, such as Hankey's, to place the department that had opposed rearmament expenditure among the guilty men of appeasement. O&M offered a synthesis of the informational techniques innovated in the "need to know" 1930s, a management science committed to mechanization (and therefore savings), and, in particular, an organizational self-understanding: general techniques for a general department, real machines for the "government machine," and a science of procedures for the department responsible for the Civil Service "code." Finally, and not insignificantly, O&M was evidence that the Treasury was "doing something."

Conclusion

The work of Bletchley Park and the Telecommunications Research Establishment extended what I have called the government "infosphere": the conceptualization of "information," the development of techniques to manipulate it, and an increase in the geographical extent of coverage. This was a bureaucratic expert achievement, not retrospectively a "computing" one. It was these experts who produced, in I. J. Good's words, "synergy" between human and machine—a vision anticipated by Sydney George Partridge behind the Western Front a quarter-century earlier. Moreover, the development of the government infosphere occurred across many fronts, both military and civil, as the informational gap of the "need to know" 1930s was filled by new enterprises: Mass Observation, the Wartime Social Survey, a new National Register, the Central Statistical Office, and Organization and Methods, as well as radar, operational research, and cryptanalysis. The fact that innovative informational organizations appeared across the entire state landscape raises an interesting question: Can a common cause be ascribed?

Once the informational innovations of the 1930s and the 1940s are analyzed comparatively, some simple explanations begin to look unconvincing. One emerging theme, for example in the discussions above of the Central Statistical Office, Operational Research, and even Nazi Hollerith accounting, was to see these phenomena as closely connected to the creation of the directed, or at least mixed, economy and the actions of a strongly interventionist state. The National Register preceded—and prefigured through the Central Register—the National Health Service. Certainly it could be argued that the expansion of the public sector eased some informational problems of the 1930s: with more industries under state control and more employees working in the public sector, the distinction between rulers and ruled became less clear, and therefore the "need to know" became less sharp. So can the expansion of the public infosphere be ascribed to the adoption of Keynesian economic policy? No. The appearance of the Central Statistical Office might initially be thought of as due to Keynesianism's insatiable greed for economic statistics, but the Office was clearly one of a number of informational institutions that appeared in a very short period of time, and Keynesianism cannot explain them all. Perhaps we are looking for an explanation "deeper" than Keynesianism, deeper than shifts in economic policy, however profound.

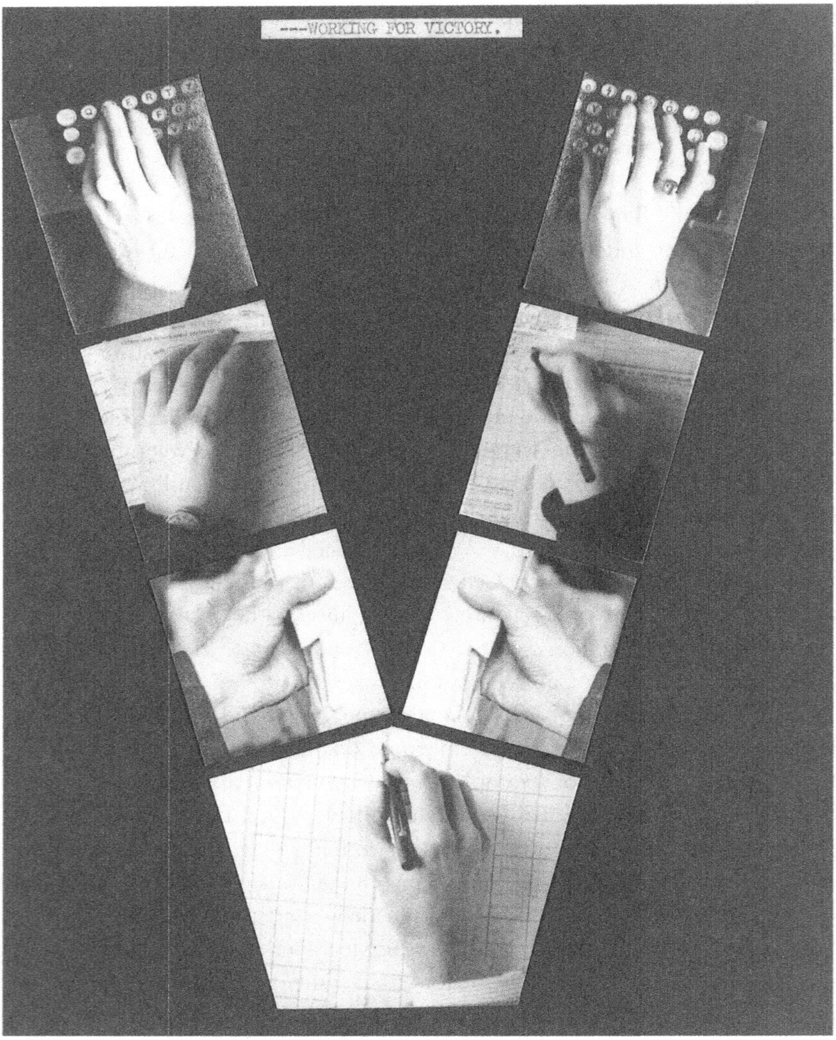

Figure 6.11
A page from a photo album put together by private individuals to illustrate daily life in the Chelsea tax office during the Second World War. (PRO IR 83/198)

Likewise, did the gap in the knowledge of the working classes, as perceived by the intellectual Left of the 1930s, cause the appearance of Mass Observation? No. Although the perception clearly motivated Harrisson, Madge, and Jennings, the same objection can be raised. What then might underlie the development of the extended infosphere? I will return to this question in the concluding chapter. However, the aspect of the Second World War's aftermath that has most direct relevance here, especially for chapter 8, was the reassertion of control by the bearers of the Civil Service "code," the Treasury, and the growth of an expert movement centered within that department: Treasury Organization and Methods.

7

The Military Machine?

The most devastating machine of the Cold War was fictional. In Stanley Kubrick's 1963 film *Dr. Strangelove, or: How I Learned to Stop Worrying and Love the Bomb*, President Merkin Muffley is horrified to discover that the Soviet Union has built a Doomsday Machine. The concept is explained by his advisor, Dr. Strangelove: atomic bombs of unlimited power are buried underground and connected to "a gigantic complex of computers," programmed to detonate if "clear and defined circumstances" occur. It is automatic: once triggered, the Doomsday Machine cannot be "untriggered." In the film, precisely such circumstances do occur—in an unforeseen, accidental way—and the world ends. Kubrick's satirical masterpiece has many targets: the rationality—or rather irrationality—of strategic planning, the capricious consequences of both rule following and personal initiative, and post-Second World War US-UK relations. I will look at some of these in detail later, but for the moment I will concentrate on the object at the film's center: the paragon of automation, the computer.

Computers enter Kubrick's story three times.[1] At the beginning we see a mainframe installation at a US Air Force base, where it is the backdrop to the scenes between the mad American Colonel Jack D. Ripper and the impotent British Group Captain Lionel Mandrake. At the end of the film, Dr. Strangelove includes the computer in his male-fantasy post-nuclear holocaust utopia to be established in one of the country's deeper mine shafts. The computer, he says, will pick a eugenic population on the basis of "youth, health, sexual fertility, intelligence, and a cross-section of necessary skills" (and including leading politicians and military men for their qualities of "leadership and tradition"). Significantly, this means that the president is relieved of making a difficult decision—who would be saved—with the effect that the computer, in this instance, replaces executive power. The trinity is completed by the central device, the Doomsday Machine itself. This is computerized because of a crisis of trust: "no sane man" could be trusted to operate it, nor could the Soviet

Union trust American actions, and vice versa. Kubrick's point is important. Mechanization—and here computerization—followed patterns of distrust. I noted this relation in earlier chapters, and in this chapter distrust again must be seen as an important factor guiding the political-technological developments of the Cold War. By the 1990s, the immense resources plowed into innovation in information technologies had led to digital superstructures underpinning military might, particularly in the West. (Arguably, these are unsuitable for a post-Cold War world.)

Electronic Stored-Program Computers

Many authors have noted that the development of the stored-program digital electronic computer was decisively shaped by military interests, not least through the massive financial resources made available during and justified by the Cold War.[2] Even the canonical history of the computer illustrates this involvement: the idea of a stored-program computer emerged from the team building the ENIAC, a behemoth constructed at the Moore School of Electrical Engineering at the University of Pennsylvania. The ENIAC was ordered by the United States Army, which was faced with a massive computational backlog in the calculation of the ballistics tables necessary to operate the armaments rolling out of the munitions factories. The celebrated émigré mathematician John von Neumann, who became associated with ENIAC in 1944, put his name to the Draft Report on the EDVAC, an architectural description of a projected stored-program computer based on serial processing of stored instructions and data. A series of summer schools, attended by British as well as American scientists, propagated the idea of an electronic stored-program computer and sparked the race to express the concept in material form. The race was won by a group at the University of Manchester.[3] In 1945, Max Newman, fresh from Bletchley Park and now in the university's mathematical department, had encountered the stored-program concept at Bletchley Park and had secured a sizable grant from the Royal Society to establish a computing laboratory. Newman was expecting to oversee the construction of a mathematical computer, using RCA's "selectron" components as memory units, but this project was overtaken by local developments. More or less independent of Newman, two electrical engineers arrived back at the University of Manchester from the radar project at the Telecommunications Research Establishment (TRE). F. C. Williams and his young colleague Tom Kilburn possessed the crucial technique needed to materialize the computer: a means of storing, manipulating, and retrieving electronic data using a cathode-ray tube (a "Williams Tube"). Williams had seen the ENIAC on a visit to the Moore School in 1946, after the suggestion of the Cambridge mathematician Douglas Hartree.[4] Kilburn had been expected to return to Cambridge, where he had completed a mathematics degree before his transfer to TRE. However, he was persuaded to complete his doctorate at Manchester while remaining, initially at least, attached to TRE. The link proved important, since TRE continued to provide components for the university machine.[5] Possessing the idea and the technique, Williams's team at the University of Manchester built and operated the first electronic stored-program by June 1948. Other machines quickly followed, in Britain and the United States.

Both Britain and the United States were therefore in position by the late 1940s and early 1950s to establish a computer-manufacturing industry. The explosive growth of this industry in the 1950s was due largely, on both sides of the Atlantic, to Cold War expenditures, but it was the difference in scale of this funding that largely determined the industrial dominance of American manufacturers, in particular IBM. The history of the influential Whirlwind computer, as part of the SAGE air defense system, provides a well-known paradigmatic example. Whirlwind, developed at MIT, has been described as the "single most important computer project of the postwar decade."[6] Although originally conceived as electronic aid to calculation, Whirlwind was recast by the opportunistic Jay Forrester as a command-and-control instrument and was sold as such to the military. IBM built 56 SAGE computers, receiving $30 million for each and $500 million in total through the 1950s, and thereby "obtained a lead in processor technology, mass-storage devices, and real-time systems, which it never lost and soon put to commercial use."[7] Such lavish support of both academic computing and the computer manufacturing industry could never be matched in Britain, which was struggling to cope with devastated industrial cities and economic crises and was diverting scarce resources into welfare provision, in particular the new National Health Service. However, the British computer manufacturing industry was also supported by government-military funding, with important consequences.

Despite the "invention" of the stored-program electronic computer, this first postwar chapter is very much a continuation of the earlier themes. In particular, the computerization of the United Kingdom's air defense organization dovetails with the account given in the last chapter. Computers were embedded in two large systems. The first (the joint air traffic and early warning system, eventually named Linesman/Mediator) was under exclusively British control, but the second raised thorny problems of national sovereignty: the Ballistic Missile Early Warning System (BMEWS) was an essentially American artefact, but the details of its software were shaped by conflicts between British and American foreign policy. Computerization was pursued most avidly by the

Royal Navy, and the contrast between naval systems such as CDS and ADA and rival Royal Air Force projects provides a window into the British institutional politics of military automation. Before these projects are discussed, an account of how military funding shaped the history of British computer manufacture should be given. This involvement forced the pace on a string of projects, from the first commercially available computer (the Ferranti Mark I, based on the Manchester machine), to the fast calculation devices demanded by the Atomic Weapons Research Establishment and other organizations in the British nuclear program, to more experimental or specialized computers. In general this is a story of relatively high spending and strong political commitment to the computer manufacturing industry. However, by the 1960s the British industry had fallen far behind the American.

British Computer Manufacture in the Early Cold War

In the late 1940s there were five experimental computer projects underway in Britain: the Williams Tube machine at Manchester, Maurice Wilkes's EDSAC (based on the description of EDVAC) at Cambridge University, the National Physical Laboratory's Pilot ACE (designed by Alan Turing), TRE's parallel machine TREAC (which also used Williams Tubes), and the small Automatic Relay Computer (built by Andrew Booth for the British Rubber Producers Research Association). Three of these, through collaboration with manufacturing partners, began lines of commercial computers. In Manchester, Ferranti built computers designed by the university. At Cambridge the EDSAC came to the attention of the management of the tea shop company Lyons & Co., a firm with a tradition of administrative innovation and interest in office machinery. The Lyons board were persuaded to support the construction of their own computer, based on the EDSAC, called the Lyons Electronic Office, or LEO for short. LEO was one of the first computers to find application in civil government work. The Pilot ACE interested the electrical engineering giant English Electric, and an engineered version of the computer called Deuce was on sale by 1955.

Turing, who had decided to work at the Mathematical Division of the National Physical Laboratory in mid 1945, arrived in October with his plans for an electronic stored-program computer well advanced. Yet he resigned less than 3 years later, moving first to Cambridge and then to Manchester and leaving a project that, had it been completed to his specifications, would have been the most radical and sophisticated of early computers. Historians, while agreeing on certain factors that delayed the NPL computer, such as inadequate support from the electronics experts at the Post Office, have offered divergent explanations to account for Turing's abrupt departure. Hodges suggests that Turing was not content to merely design a computer that could be built quickly, but was determined to use the project to investigate his developing ideas of machine intelligence. Such ambition was not received sympathetically by his NPL superiors—particularly the superintendent of the Mathematical Division, J. R. Womersley.[8] David Yates, on the other hand, argues that Hodges has been "too disparaging": "Womersley, though not in the FRS class for mathematical ability like several of his staff, did a solid job of establishing the Mathematical Division, and can hardly be blamed for not having the experience of electronics which would have enabled him to manage the ACE work more effectively. . . . Like an artist judiciously darkening part of a picture to emphasize the brightness of an adjacent highlight, Hodges may have inadvertently blackened Womersley and [H. A. Thomas, brought in to manage the project] the better to show off the undoubted brilliance of his hero Turing."[9]

I would like to offer an interpretation, based on the core argument of this book, which will help us understand why Turing's plans at the NPL were unlikely to be warmly received, and reconciles Hodges's and Yates's accounts. I argued in chapter 2 that Turing drew on features of British bureaucracy as a resource to articulate the range of operation of the universal computing machine, in particular recalling the generalist-mechanical split as an organizing principle at the center of a machine of general-purpose application. Had Turing had continued to follow this model, a design based on it would have been recognizable and acceptable to the civil servant officers of the National Physical Laboratory. In the next chapter, for example, we will find one of Turing's NPL colleagues, E. A. Newman, enthusiastically promoting the stored-program computer to a receptive Civil Service audience. Instead, Turing's new ideas willfully transgressed the distinction between the generalist and mechanical aspects of a computing machine. They did so in two ways. First, as Turing made clear in a talk to the London Mathematical Society in February 1947, though the ACE might start with a distinction between "masters" (the logical programmers) and the "servants" (the operators) of the machine, the distinction would be soon upset. Servants' work, being "mechanical," would be mechanized; more significant, the masters too would be "liable to get replaced because as soon as any technique becomes at all stereotyped it becomes possible to devise a system of instruction tables which will enable the electronic computer to do it for itself. It may happen however that the masters will refuse to do this. They may be unwilling to let their jobs be stolen from them in this way. In that case they would surround the whole of their work with mystery and make excuses, couched in well chosen gibberish, whenever any dangerous suggestions were made. I think that a reaction of this kind is a very real danger. This topic naturally leads to the question as to how far it is in principle possible for a computing machine to simulate human activities."[10]

Turing had recast the computer as a direct threat to generalist "masters." He was less interested in reaffirming existing orders as creating a challenge from within. The mechanical could spread through the organization, and (to borrow and extend Babbage's description) after Turing's revolution the legislative and executive would be under one mechanical—and intelligent—control. For the second aspect of his new ideas, building again from Turing's interest in the simulation of human activities, was that the machine would learn. Unlike the "von Neumann" model of the computer, or indeed Turing's own universal machines of the 1930s, the proposed ACE would be able to modify its own code as it went along. The rigid separation between order givers and order followers would be blurred. It is the transgression of hierarchical divisions that would have unsettled the Civil Service.

Certainly the scope of Turing's ambitious design went far beyond automating clerical work. In his 1945 design of the ACE, Turing had listed ten illustrative problems, from the calculation of range tables and the solution of simultaneous linear equations to the emulation of aspects of human intelligence: "Given a position in chess the machine could be made to list all the 'winning combinations' to a depth of about three moves on either side."[11] Several had direct military or cryptically cryptanalytical applications. Only one proposed task was clerical (to "count the number of butchers due to be demobilized in June 1946 from cards prepared from the army records") but such a simple application "would not be a suitable job for it. . . . Such a job can and should be done with standard Hollerith equipment." The Pilot ACE, engineered by the team that Turing left behind, ran its first program on 10 May 1950 and quickly became a computing workhorse for government research establishments, both civil and military.[12]

At Manchester, where Turing arrived in 1948, after the first program had been run, the story was one of close collaboration between the "imaginative developers of new techniques and ironmongery" at the university and another electrical engineering firm, Ferranti Limited.[13] Ferranti was a family-owned firm that had begun building electricity generators and supply technology around the turn of the century. By the 1940s it offered a range of electrical goods, and had a factory in Manchester. After the first program was run (in June 1948), the Manchester machine received some important visitors. In July, Sir Henry Tizard, now chairman of the Defence Research Policy Committee, saw it and "considered it of national importance that the development should go on as speedily as possible, so as to maintain the lead which this country has thus acquired in the field of big computing machines, in spite of the large amount of effort and material that have been put into similar projects in America."[14] However, support for a new industry was not the only factor driving early commercialization. Following Tizard to Manchester a few months later was the Chief Scientist to the Ministry of Supply, Sir Ben Lockspeiser. (The Ministry of Supply, it should be remembered, was the government department responsible for research and development for the Royal Air Force and Army, including at this time the atomic program, and therefore the most powerful agency of government support for science in Britain.) Lockspeiser, impressed by the Manchester experimental machine, immediately provided funding for Ferranti to produce an engineered version, beginning with £35,000 per annum over 5 years.[15]

The Ministry of Supply was interested in electronic digital computers because of postwar developments in three areas of defense. First, American-British nuclear weapon collaboration, which had flourished during the war with the transfer of Tube Alloys (the British bomb program) to the Manhattan Project, had ended abruptly when the US Congress passed the McMahon Act on 1 August 1946, terminating all foreign links, including, unwittingly, the British one. In reaction a British cabinet committee, chaired by Prime Minister Clement Attlee, decided to proceed with an independent British atomic weapon, a decision kept secret even from other members of cabinet, let alone parliament or the public, until 1950.[16] The design of atomic weapons was a voracious consumer of calculating power, a lesson learned well at Los Alamos, for example. Second, the air defense organization, though operating in 1948 largely as it had done on the last day of the Second World War, was being closely scrutinized and revised according to Cold War priorities. The Czechoslovakian coup and the Berlin blockade had clarified the postwar geopolitical pattern of East versus West, and henceforth the air defense organization was set against a Soviet threat. A number of technological factors also needed consideration. The introduction of high-speed, high-flying jet aircraft meant that early warning and response had to be much quicker and more effective than previously (possibly achievable through computerized automation). The development of guided weapons had implications both for early warning and air defense. Guided weapons design and defense, too, required access to high-speed calculation. These factors did not mean that the Ministry of Supply *inevitably* required electronic digital stored-program computers, since there were alternatives, for example analogue devices or even manual calculation using mechanical calculators such as the Brunsviga.[17] It does, however, explain why the ministry might want to be sure of the option of having computers available, and for this reason would be willing to fund development.

The collaboration between Ferranti and the electrical engineering department at the University of Manchester was a close one, with engineers and scientists traveling back and forth between factory and laboratory. The outcome was the Ferranti Mark I, first delivered to the University in February 1951 and subsequently offered for sale to other organizations. Though some financial support had also come from the Royal Society (whose grant was eventually spent on the building to house the Mark I) and from income from a large number of patents (held by individuals such as Williams and Kilburn, but also some by the Ministry of Supply—through the initial TRE connection—subsequently held by the National Research Development Corporation and made available to IBM for their 701 and 702 machines), the Ministry of Supply grants were the cement in the Ferranti-University partnership. In 1950 Brigadier Hinds wrote to Newman noting that "since the Ministry of Supply first placed the order with Messrs. Ferranti's for the High Speed Digital Computing Machine to be installed at the University of Manchester, the situation has now changed to the extent that we now have a number of computation problems of high service importance and great urgency awaiting solution on such a machine," and requested access.[18] The Ministry's Armament Research Establishment at Fort Halstead in Kent, a site of early atomic weapons development, quickly made use of the University of Manchester's Ferranti Mark I: in 1952 Fort Halstead bought 200 hours at the "economical" price of £10 per hour, operating the machine "when the normal working day comes to an end, and to run it until its efficiency . . . drops to an unacceptable level, or possibly until they (the Ministry scientists) get tired."[19] The same year Fort Halstead decided to purchase its own Ferranti Mark I, for general Ministry of Supply use.[20] Guided weapon calculations, beginning with "a series of calculations to estimate the effect of jitter on homing accuracy," were made with the machine for the Royal Aircraft Establishment (RAE), Farnborough. An odd order for the production of large quantities of random numbers was made in 1953.[21]

The Ferranti-University partnership continued through the 1950s and early 1960s: Kilburn's team's prototype Meg, completed in May 1954, was engineered as the Ferranti Mercury; the Muse project, begun in 1956, eventually became the Ferranti Atlas. The Ferranti Mercury sold well, and the University's own machine was available for hire, like the Ferranti Mark I, with large number of users registered between 1958 and 1962.[22] The Atlas was an explicit attempt to match the speed and performance of the top-of-the-range American computers, such as IBM's STRETCH. Two of the foremost potential users were thought to be the United Kingdom Atomic Energy Authority (a new corporation that had inherited the Harwell research establishment and

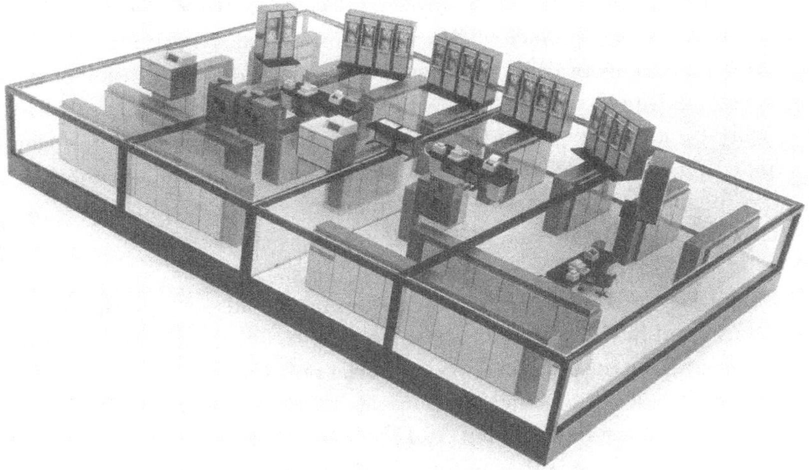

Figure 7.1
A model of the Atlas installed at the National Institute for Research into Nuclear Science (NIRNS) in Harwell. (source: National Archive for the History of Computing, University of Manchester)

other atomic laboratories, factories, and reactors in 1954) and the Atomic Weapons Research Establishment at Aldermaston. However, Aldermaston invoked pressing national security needs to order IBM machines immediately, rather than wait for the million-pound-plus Atlas. William Penney, who had directed Aldermaston before his appointment to manage UKAEA in 1959, chose to hire a STRETCH. As was noted in Whitehall: "Government has approved small scale experimental explosions in Australia in order to investigate the safety of atomic weapons. It is only by the use of a very large computer that the number of practical experiments is kept down, which is desirable both on political and financial grounds."[23] Such decisions taken against Atlas crippled the financial viability of the British project—and thereby adversely affected the British high-speed computer industry.[24] The Treasury attempted to force UKAEA to accept an Atlas but met with resistance. The compromise was the establishment of an Atlas Laboratory—running a single machine—as part of the new National Institute for Research into Nuclear Science (NIRNS), a common facility for academic scientists situated at the gates of Harwell. There is no doubt that, by 1960 specifications, Atlas was as powerful as any competing machine. Professor Nicholas Metropolis, of the University of

Chicago Computer Institute, reviewed the field: the Atlas was "the best computer in the world now under engineering development for commercial sale. . . . The drop in performance of Stretch . . . makes Atlas much more equal in performance and the price is much less. The design and sophistication of Atlas are well in advance of Stretch," with the University of Illinois's ILLIAC the nearest equivalent.[25] But Atlas was the end of the line. The next large computer prototype developed at the University of Manchester, the MU5, was not engineered into a commercial machine, although some ideas were recycled for ICL's 1905E, and the ICL 2900 series of the mid 1970s was also influenced.[26]

Competition with American manufacturers placed great strain on the numerous small British computer firms, with the resulting pressure, sometimes actively assisted by the government's industrial policy, to merge. As Campbell-Kelly describes it, this context was to lead to the formation in 1968 of International Computers Limited (ICL).[27] (I have little to add to Campbell-Kelly's account of the British computer manufacturing industry, except to note the interesting stance of the Government Communications Headquarters (GCHQ) as early as 1957. J. Morgan of GCHQ bemoaned the "shortcomings of the British effort on data processing, both in government and industry" in which the United Kingdom had lost the lead to the United States "irrevocably."[28] Morgan urged two industrial policies. First the creation of "an independent research and development organization consisting of at least one hundred graduates" to take a "positive lead in the development of computer techniques." Second, Morgan and GCHQ were in favor of laying down strict compatibility standards between UK computers, because "in a country as small as the United Kingdom" there was "not room for a diversity of manufacturers" or a diversity of incompatible types"; Morgan was in favor of "direct Government control of this development."[29] If this exceedingly rare appearance of GCHQ's opinions to appear in the public record is an indication of a cryptanalytical attitude toward policy on the British computer industry then an extra and potentially influential factor behind the formation of ICL can be added).

Alongside the growth and challenges of the British computer industry, the defense research establishments also built computers and investigated component technology. Naval laboratories such as the Admiralty Signals and Radar Establishment (ASRE) helped tweak Ferranti machines to suit their particular needs. The Royal Aircraft Establishment at Farnborough built TRIDAC, which began life as a simulator of guided weapons but was later modified to become a general-purpose computer. TRE, successively renamed the Radar Research Establishment and then the Royal Radar Establishment, continued its postwar role as a center for innovation in electronics, branching out into computing techniques. A. M. Uttley, a fascinating figure whose work ranged from electronics to cybernetics and cognitive psychology, oversaw the construction of the parallel TREAC, complete by early 1953. A second early computer, MOSAIC, derivative of the ACE designs, was also built.[30] These machines were experimental, with the emphasis on the investigation of new techniques and components. The RRE program accelerated during and after the Korean War with new systems placing great demands on the new electronic computing and data-handling techniques, by 1959 focusing on "the development of more sensitive infra-red detectors for use in homing eyes and the detection of ballistic missiles, the development of low noise receivers for use in air and ground radars and the development of micro-miniature components for use in airborne and guided weapon equipments," and computing for "airborne bombing navigation and interception equipments, in very complex data handling systems for air defense using fighters or guided weapons and . . . in an even more stringent form in any system of defense against ballistic missiles."[31] The old computers such as TREAC only met a tenth of the demand by the late 1950s, and RRE pleaded for more resources, arguing that "the computer . . . was as essential to the scientist today as the slide rule was to the engineer."[32] With the expertise on site a third one-off computer was built at Malvern, called the RREAC.[33]

The attitude toward solid-state electronics was, in the early 1950s, very cautious, and the armed services should not be seen retrospectively as enthusiasts for light-weight, low-power components, despite the apparent advantages in guided weapon and aircraft applications. For example, in 1953 a "radical review" of the research and development program by the Defence Research Policy Committee concluded:

> Transistors will be restricted to audio applications and switching devices in computers. This is a small part of the total electronic application of valves (which includes frequency power, mixers and power amplifications, etc.). This means that very few indeed of the valves in current and future types of Service electronic equipments could be replaced with transistors.[34]

Of course, as transistors became more reliable and cheaper through mass production, largely as a result of the massive American investment dating from the Korean War, and they did indeed replace valves in nearly all military and naval applications. Furthermore, the cautious attitude was uniform across the research establishments and armed service ministries. The politics of the former can be teased out by comparative study where two establishments clashed on the question of automation, but before this is examined we require an understanding of how the civil-military infosphere deepened and extended in the postwar years.

Ground Radar and Air Traffic Control

The previous chapter described the development of ground radar systems enveloping United Kingdom before and during the Second World War. The postwar history of this infosphere was tortuous, due mainly to an ever shifting political and economic context. It does not help to think of the Cold War as monolithic, especially for Britain. Although Western defensive alliances were stabilized after the formation of the North Atlantic Treaty Organization (NATO) in 1949, other factors contributed to a picture of instability and change. In the late 1940s a Labour government attempted to run a control economy, before retreating, defeated by economic crises, while at the same time postwar reconstruction, commitment to an independent nuclear deterrent and the construction of the National Health Service absorbed much effort. During the Korean War defense spending increased, but by Duncan Sandys's white paper on Defence, *Outline of Future Policy*, in 1957, such expenditure was seen as an over-commitment, and radical shifts in policy followed: national conscription ended by 1960, interdependence—essentially sharing the costs of research and development between NATO partners, especially the United States—encouraged, and the nuclear deterrent emphasized, paradoxically as a means of saving money. Further turmoil followed with the cancellation of the British ballistic missile, Blue Streak, in 1960, and adoption of American nuclear launch systems: first Skybolt (canceled by the United States in 1962), then the submarine Polaris. Against this background were commitments including new promises—for example British troops stationed on the Rhine—and older conflicts, notably colonial wars in Palestine, Malaya, Kenya, Iraq, and, most destructively of all for British prestige, the Anglo-French-Israeli debacle in Egypt in 1956, the Suez Crisis. Finally, thermonuclear weapons radically transformed what was considered as "defendable." Hydrogen bombs were as many times more powerful than fission weapons as the latter were over conventional explosive. The complete destruction an H-bomb could cause over a wide area meant there was little or no point defending "point" targets such as radar control centers or fixed rocket silos.

Planning a radar system in this context of rapidly changing priorities was therefore somewhat difficult. In the late 1940s there was little political commitment to changing the ground radar network inherited from the war.[35] Even the first development plan, code-named ROTOR for the United Kingdom network and VAST for overseas, consisted of a merely tidied-up wartime reporting and control system. Increased defense research and development expenditures in the early 1950s, however, quickly benefited RRE, where the invention of a powerful new prototype radar, Green Garlic, raised questions about how it should fit in to ROTOR and VAST. Green Garlic could be easily adapted to both reporting (replacing Chain Home) and control (replacing old GCI sets), part of a general postwar trend toward comprehensive systems in which the distinction between control and reporting became blurred. The appearance of thermonuclear weapons prompted a rethink of ROTOR and VAST before they were even complete: the new "1958 Plan" envisaged a computerized integrated control and reporting system based on "comprehensive master stations" built underground, a concept which passed relatively unscathed past the Sandys axe.[36] Although the search for cuts led to a slimmer version, Plan AHEAD in 1959, it was a political decision the following year that decisively shaped postwar ground radar. Prime Minister Harold Macmillan, on the recommendation of his chief scientific adviser, Solly Zuckerman, stated that the resources were only available for one joint military air defense–civil air traffic control system. Known as Linesman/Mediator, it combined Plan AHEAD (now Linesman, a sporting reference) and the civil ATC project (Mediator). Linesman/Mediator encountered the mid-1960s software crisis—where shortages of trained programmers struggled to write code for larger and more varied computers—and was not completed until the mid 1970s.[37] The outcome of these historical developments was a particular kind of infosphere, in which civil concerns were made to match defense models and interests.

The above thumbnail sketch is deficient on several accounts, most glaringly because it does not explain *why* automation was accepted in defense circles and how this military model extended to encompass civil arenas. In fact there were extreme tensions, which are particularly evident when the military and civil communities were forced to work together on the joint system. Therefore, to draw out some of these social and technological issues, we turn our attention to the arguments over automating air traffic control.

Prewar air traffic control (ATC) was limited to flight plan data filed by pilots before takeoff and radio contact between pilots and airport conning towers—and these only at the larger airports. The system, established in the United States in the 1930s, worked by ensuring a minimum separation between aircraft. With the increase in the number of flights and the speed of aircraft such a system became more difficult to operate. London Airport had 109,043 "air transport movements" in 1956 and expected more than 300,000 by 1970.[38] However, the response (manual systems—sophisticated information technologies in their own right—and teams of trained air traffic controllers) largely met these extra demands. The pressure for change came from the defense side, both governmental and industrial. The Ministry of Supply's Director General of Electronics Research and Development—the civil servant overseeing the work of RRE—approached the Ministry of Civil Aviation in 1953–54 with the suggestion of an experimental program on the computerization of air traffic control. Ferranti, which had already built computers for the Ministry of Supply and, as we shall see below, were constructing the Poseidon computer for the Navy, sought to acquire a contract that minimized further development of its military machines. The firm agreed to develop a computer, called Apollo, for the Oceanic Air Traffic Control Center to be established at Prestwick, Scotland. As was wryly noted in Whitehall: "Only firms dealing with radar data processing for military purposes have shown any real interest and this, it is believed, because they already had something on the shelf."[39]

The effect of this one-sided interest was that the military interest in information technologies and automation came to heavily shape how air traffic control was understood. By the mid 1950s the language used to discuss air traffic control had shifted. The metaphors were of information, data, and networks, with humans cast as inefficient data handlers. For example, a memorandum written within the Ministry of Transport and Civil Aviation in 1957 noted that the "ATC ground organization is . . . a large and complex communications network in which there are relatively few centers of executive action," and that "because of the inability of human beings efficiently to handle large quantities of data, and the precautions which have to be taken, much redundant information is transmitted, stored and displayed, while essential information remains inadequately collated. Therefore, if the accuracy of the basic information can be improved and the input rationalized, the ability of electronic computing techniques to organize and evaluate large quantities of data may be fully exploited."[40] In other words, the Ministry emphasized automation. A brief comparison of air traffic control as represented in figure 7.2 with the air defense information flow diagrams of chapter 6 underlines the fact that it was models of military origin that were being adopted. The head of the Air Traffic Control Experimental Unit, a civil body that investigated computerization but was skeptical of claims made for the effectiveness of full automation, recorded on extreme example and noted the military bias:

> With few exceptions this interest [in making ATC as automatic as possible] was found to be mainly concerned with the techniques of data processing rather than the presentation of the results to the extent that one visitor thought that a display was entirely unnecessary in an automatic system. He proposed that all information should be recorded by voice, as well as digital form, and that, in the unlikely event of human intervention being necessary, the Controller should select those parts of the tape record-

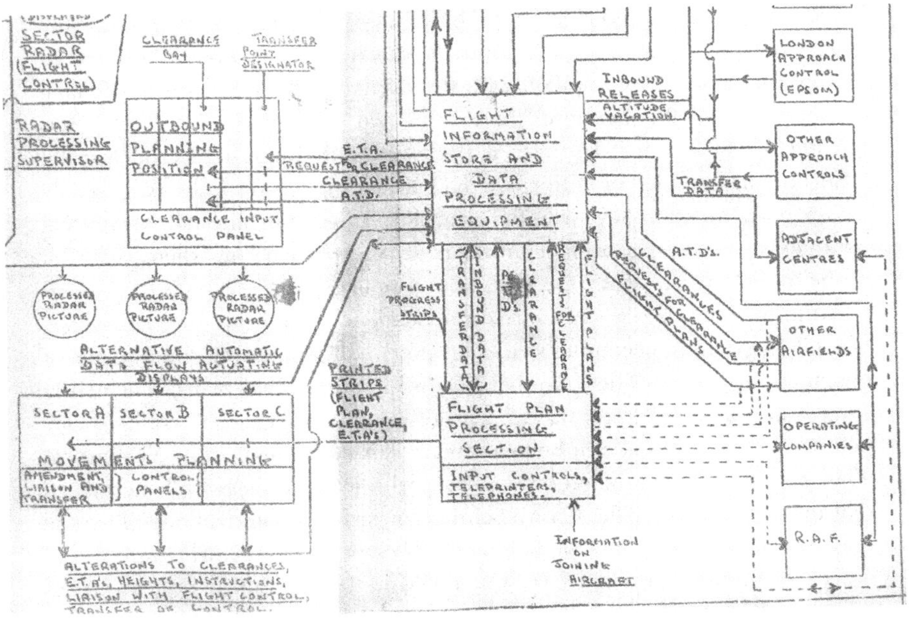

Figure 7.2
Air traffic control organized as an information system. (PRO MT 45/556)

ing to which he wished to refer and base his decision on this selective listening alone. A large number of visitors have also believed that the problems of ATC are identical with those of military interception with which, at first glance, they may have a deceptive similarity. Since many of them have often been familiar with the military requirements, this illusion has had a severe conditioning effect to their approach to the whole subject and more especially to that of the display of information.[41]

One partial exception to this story was the involvement of the Dutch firm, N.V. Hollandse Signaalapparaten (part of Philips). Signaal had already developed an ATC computer, but, unlike the British firms, placed great emphasis on the design and use of display devices—another example of British firms' relative indifference to peripherals development. In sympathy with the political policy of European interdependence, the general concept of Anglo-Dutch cooperation on ATC research was agreed in 1957, although the details were left vague. Financial approval for a research program was sought in September 1958 and achieved a year later. At this moment the American firm General Precision Systems caught wind of the proposals and argued that it, with its affiliate Decca Radar, should be allowed to tender for the computer.[42] Embarrassed, the government decided to put the development out to tender to industry generally, and received proposals from eleven firms by March 1960. After extensive negotiations the contract was awarded to English Electric to modify its Elliott 502 computer, with the displays sub-contracted to Signaal. By the early 1960s, therefore, there were two computerized ATC projects moving slowly forward: Ferranti at Prestwick, and English Electric/Signaal ("Euclid") in London. In both cases the guiding model was military.

The push for automatic air traffic control did not go uncontested. Most vocal opponents were the air traffic controllers themselves, who saw themselves not in the model of computer operators but more like pilots—responsible, executive and to some degree necessarily independent. (The irony was, of course, that pilots too were becoming written as potentially unreliable components of information systems). The controllers, on first hearing of the plans, vehemently complained that their "job was an art not capable of complete codification" (although they did possess a bulky manual of instructions[43]). The Ministry of Transport and Civil Aviation sympathized with its controllers while accepting that the increase in traffic density pointed toward computerization: "There is only one firm position that we hold at the present moment with regard to the use of computors," one civil servant noted in 1958, "that is that the ATC officer shall be an essential part of the system and that we should not attempt to design an ATC system which is entirely automatic."[44]

Air traffic control in the 1950s and early 1960s can therefore be seen as contested terrain, with opinions stretching from one extreme—full automation, a military ideal—to the other, ATC as a manual, human process. The commissioning of the Prestwick and London computers were turning points, not so much because greater roles were thereby given to machines rather than humans (although, of course, human involvement was never, nor could be, eliminated), but also because they marked the military remodeling of a civil area of governance. Nor did this process stop at Air Traffic Control: urban vehicle traffic problems—such as the West London Area Traffic Control Experiment (WLTCE), a prototype computerized control center project of the late 1960s—illustrate the further spread of the model into civil arenas.[45]

To Automate or Not?: Navy versus RAF

The politics of automation can be further analyzed by comparing work at the two biggest radar and electronics laboratories in the United Kingdom. The Admiralty Surface Weapons Establishment (ASWE, between 1948 and 1959 known as ASRE) and the Royal Radar Establishment, contrasted sharply in their attitudes to data handling for air defense systems. Both laboratories investigated three relevant areas of research: the manipulation of information gained from a radar system, techniques of display, and the command and control of guided weapon or manned fighter aircraft.

The early achievements of the Admiralty were precocious and remarkable, and largely the accomplishment of a team under Ralph Benjamin, a German Jewish refugee who had graduated from Imperial College in 1944 and subsequently joined the Royal Naval Scientific Service.[46] Benjamin conceived of encoding information digitally transmitted between ships, aircraft and weapons by high-frequency data links. The information, such as markers which together formed tracks, would be displayed on cathode-ray tubes, controlled by a joystick—a "mouse" was also considered.[47] Benjamin's project became known as the Comprehensive Display System (CDS) in the early 1950s. CDS can be thought of as like a wartime Operations Room, but with the table and counters replaced by electronics. Six trackers, each with a cathode-ray-tube display in front of them would use the joystick to select contacts from the raw radar image—the latter provided by the new and sophisticated Type 984 radar. A human tracker could manage eight tracks at once. The tracks were passed electronically to one of four analyzers, who would label the contacts and inject the information into an electromechanical-electronic store. Using this stored data an intercept computer, a program-controlled analogue device, could direct the engagement of a fighter aircraft with an incoming threat. A second computer used the data to advise on what weapons to use: gun, guided weapon or aircraft. The electronic data could be shared between ships within a radius of 100 miles using Digital Plot Transmission (DPT). The combined system was massive: CDS weighed 25 tons and occupied 2000 cubic feet in onboard volume, 60 cabinets contained 5000 valves.[48] However it was installed in ships from 1958, beginning with the aircraft carrier *Victorious*. That year, in a joint exercise to test CDS, American analysts were shocked to discover that the *Victorious*, with its analogue computer and digital data transmission, was for more capable of repelling attacking aircraft than their own ships.[49] CDS was subsequently fitted on some US ships, and the successor to DPT, Link 11, became the standard data link for all NATO navies.

Building on this lead, Benjamin's team began developing an all-digital system called Action Data Automation, or ADA. The analogue computers of CDS were replaced with three Ferranti Poseidons, digital stored-program computers similar to the Mercury, known jocularly within the Treasury as the "immortals on the Navy's side."[50] Ferranti Poseidons were fully transistorized and adapted by the company to the special demands of the naval data processing, in particular speed of processing to cope with the severity of threat from fast jet-powered missiles and aircraft:

> The general purpose computer POSEIDON has been designed for use with Naval data processing systems. The need is such that a fast machine with a fast access store is required. It is imperative that programs shall not be lost, and, as a result, a form of permanent storage for the program is necessary. The computer will be available for use in all types of ships of varying capability and it is necessary therefore that the computer should be one which can be a member of a suite of computers, the number of computers in the suite being dependent on the magnitude of the particular application. The system must receive information from, or transfer information to, peripheral equipments such as radar or sonar sources, data links, tape equipment, etc. It is essential that the system should be reliable, that it should be easy to maintain, that in the event of failure it should be easy to locate faults, and that while a computer is under maintenance alternative facilities—albeit of reduced capacity—should be available to the users.[51]

"Basically," summarized a Treasury civil servant, "a digital computer of high speed but relatively low storage capacity, . . . programmed to "know" (one cannot avoid anthropomorphism!) the capabilities of the weapons, the detection apparatus and the attack characteristics and react much faster than a team of highly trained specialists to the problem of which defense attack or retaliation button ought to be pressed."[52] Although ADA was only installed on one ship, the experimental HMS *Eagle* in 1964, the ASWE repeated the concept in more compact form in a series of automated data handling systems called ADA Weapon Systems (ADAWS) and Computer-Assisted Action Information Systems (CAAIS) which spread to link all ships in the modern Navy.[53]

Turning now to the Ministry of Supply (renamed Ministry of Aviation in 1959), and its laboratories at the Royal Radar Establishment, Malvern, we find that a similar specification provoked a different technological response. Despite the withdrawal from Empire, Britain in the late 1950s still had commitments to defend bases across the world. Akrotiri (Cyprus), Butterworth (Malaya) and Singapore presented particular problems. Cyprus was considered as a base from which British influence over the Middle East and Eastern Mediterranean could continue. The main threat, in the form of 24 Soviet divisions stationed in the Caucasus, was further complicated by the rise to power of the Egyptian nationalist Colonel Gamal Abdel Nasser in 1954. However, there was also local turmoil, as ultra-nationalist Greek Cypriots demanded *enosis* with their mainland, and, when Turkish paratroopers landed in response, a state of emergency was declared in 1955. Against this background scientists at RRE researched techniques capable of countering the increased speed of threatening guided weapons and jet aircraft. Like their Admiralty cousins, Malvern's proposal was a combination of local infospheres—linked radars, data handling technology and control rooms—and defensive guided weapons. A separate requirement, ASR2232, was therefore composed and approved by defense ministers. The defensive weapon was to be the Bloodhound II surface-to-air missile, originally designed to defend Blue Streak, (the UK ballistic missile nuclear deterrent, which never entered service), and the jet fighter, Lightning, armed with another missile, Red Top. When Blue Streak was canceled, the Air Ministry convinced its ministers that Bloodhound II should be kept and used at overseas bases. The problem was that Cyprus, Malaya and Singapore were thousands of miles from the early warning/air traffic control infosphere—Linesman-Mediator—enclosing Britain. "If," noted Air Marshal Ronald Beresford Lees, "the Bloodhound Mk II and the Lightning Mk III weapon systems were to work effectively overseas it was necessary to have an efficient means of transmitting information."[54] ASR2232 envisaged certain features:

(a) Ability to present a clear up-to-date picture of the air situation from the best source of radar information available at any given time.

(b) Means to coordinate activities of SAM [Surface-to Air Missiles] and Fighters and to allocate targets between them.

(c) Means to compute data of selected targets for transmission to, and for laying on, Bloodhound target tracking radars.

(d) Means to compute data on targets and fighters for purposes of efficient interception and fighter recovery.

(e) Means to coordinate air movement and track information, for identification purposes.[55]

What is significant is that RRE when faced with this requirement did not propose a fully computerized system—along the lines of ADA or SAGE—but insisted on the importance of manual extraction of tracks from the raw radar data. (Although a digital computer—built by Decca, since the Ministry did not want to "overload" Ferranti—would still store and process the tracks once extracted). Nine plotters, plus one supervisor, could manually track 72 aircraft. It did not escape the notice of politicians and the Treasury that two defense research establishments were developing data-processing and display systems—ASR2232 and ADA—for a similar purpose, and that the two proposed solutions were different. Their difference was captured by senior defense scientist and administrator Sir Robert Cockburn in 1962:

> The important issue was that two experienced establishments faced with meeting similar operational requirements in a similar time scale were depending on different technological solutions. We were in a period of transition from well-tried analogue techniques to more promising but risky digital techniques.[56]

However, partly manual (RRE) vs. automatic (ASWE) was not the only aspect of the difference. Intimately tied in to the difference was their respective attitudes to the capabilities of humans and machines. Admiralty senior scientist and administrator Sir John Carroll and Cockburn hastily set up a Working Party to review the situation. The Party found that RRE had not pursued manual systems out of ignorance Scientists at Malvern had been fully aware of ADA, SAGE, and STRIDA II automatic tracking systems, but had felt that automatic systems could not cope with jamming, where the discrimination of a human was needed. In the words of the Air Ministry: "The operational risks in adopting a fully automatic system [could not] be accepted."[57] However, such statements should not be read as incontestable technological "facts," for example ADA itself was touted as superior because the "human operator cannot sort this [jamming] out visually."[58] Instead the credibility of these statements can be related to the armed services' different attitudes to staff, less of a factor on the ground (for ASR2232) than on the sea (for ADA), and to other institutional interests. ASWE, for example, "had more faith in the system which they themselves were developing and they were keen to obtain the promised saving of shipboard manpower"—always a key consideration in naval systems. So behind the different styles of design were divergent attitudes to human operators, jamming, digital techniques, and understandable preferences for intramural development. Pressed to make savings, Cockburn and Carroll had to advise on some combination of ADA and ASR2232, and their proposal, that ASR2232 continue but an automatic system (SPADE) be added on top at a later date, was approved.

The comparison of ADA and ASR2232 is significant because it shows that full digital automation was not the only or best solution (indeed RRE was a center of expertise in digital computers yet still did not choose thorough automation). However the fact that ASR2232 was overruled illustrates some of the factors that can drive computerization, not the least of which was the acceptance within British defense *administrative* circles that systems such as SAGE or ADA were inevitable, a self-fulfilling prophecy. "It is agreed," summarized Carroll and Cockburn, "that the direction of evolution for ground radar is toward automatic systems and it would seem to be desirable to encourage this trend. There seems no doubt that the ADA is a step in the right direction and that further development along these lines in the direction of increased capacity and subtlety of tracking logic will ultimately provide a completely satisfactory solution."[59] Therefore, the significance of the ASR2232-ADA decision—on paper affecting only a few overseas bases, two of which a late 1960s decision had been taken to abandon—lies in its future effects. In 1962 the chief scientist, Solly Zuckerman, informed the Minister of Defence:

"We shall in the future be making use of data handling systems in an ever increasing range of military applications."[60]

Having raised the question of different attitudes toward automation in the Navy and the Air Force, I should note that a similar pattern occurred in the historical development of the coordination of statistical production within the armed services. The Army and Air Force both organized statistical work along similar lines, with analysis decentralized to Command level (in the RAF there were nine home Commands and three overseas Commands in the mid 1950s); statistical work in the Navy however was highly centralized, with nearly all statistical data sent directly to the Admiralty, with its "Central Nucleus" for analysis, although such work was diffused through that Whitehall department.[61] In both automation and statistical production, therefore, an institutional preference for centralization and control can be seen imprinted on Naval information-gathering and handling organizations.

US-UK Digital Relations: BMEWS and TSR-2

SAGE had been designed against the threat of massed attack by Soviet bombers. The launch of Sputnik in 1957, however, shockingly demonstrated Soviet capability in a more fearsome technology: the ballistic missile. Ballistic missiles traveled faster and further than any manned bomber, and any warning was likely only to give minutes to react and respond—a situation further complicated by the near impossibility of distinguishing the missile itself from decoys or separated rocket parts. Systems such as SAGE were helpless against ballistic missiles, and the United States therefore looked to a second radar network to provide early warning. The ground stations of the Ballistic Missile Early Warning System (BMEWS) had to be placed as near as possible to Soviet launch sites. One of the sites, Clear in Alaska, was in US sovereign territory, and a second, Thule in Greenland, could also be arranged unproblematically (in the political sense, not the climatic one). The third had to be in Europe, but where?

The first consideration was that the BMEWS station had to be near enough to receive the earliest possible warning of Soviet missile launch, but distant enough so that it would not be jammed by electronic counter-measures.[62] The station also had to be in a politically stable country, ideally with a history of cooperation with the United States over defense matters. All these factors pointed to the United Kingdom, which had postwar cooperative agreements concerning intelligence, chemical, biological, and guided weapons.[63] However, the advantages to the UK were not so clear cut: the information generated by BMEWS was barely sufficient to warn the United States, let alone Britain, so the primary purpose of BMEWS does not explain British cooperation. Instead the answer lies in less tangible benefits. First British scientists were in despair over the difficulties of resolving the incoming ballistic missile warhead from decoys, and suspected American research was more advanced.[64] Thus, noted the Ministry of Aviation, "in addition to being of value from an alerting point of view, construction of the station could be of great value to us in opening up collaboration with the Americans in the anti-BM field. The site is one of the things we have to offer in exchange for know-how and experience which the Americans already possess."[65]

Even given agreement that the third BMEWS sites should be in the United Kingdom, the precise location was an outcome of a balance of national interests. The further north the site, the quicker the detection of Soviet missiles heading over the polar latitudes. Hence the United States pushed for a location in Scotland. However, a Scottish BMEWS would fail entirely to spot ballistic missiles launched at low angle trajectories toward the United Kingdom, and was vetoed.[66] The UK Air Staff pushed for an Army exercise base near Thetford, a sparsely populated area in Norfolk, East Anglia—the War Office predictably objected, claiming its land was a valuable training area. In the event Thetford was rejected because of interference with the numerous nearby USAF and RAF air bases (the fact that a BMEWS radar, one of the most powerful in the world, presented a considerable microwave radiation hazard was not a decisive factor). The compromise was Fylingdales in Yorkshire, far enough north to satisfy the Americans and far enough south, just, to provide some useful early warning to the British.

A deal was hammered out. The United States would provide the hardware for Fylingdales: three AN/FPS-49 tracking radars, an electronic digital computer (an IBM 7090 was used) and the equipment to pass digital data across the Atlantic to the American control center, NORAD. The United Kingdom would provide the site, erect the buildings and provide the communications equipment necessary to feed the data into the British infosphere. Until the communications equipment—named Project Legate—was completed, with its own computer (an Elliott 803B), the British were entirely dependent on the Americans passing warnings back across the Atlantic. Meanwhile, "there could be significant delay in passing alarm levels to the UK because of the saturation of the work-load on the USAF duty personnel."[67] The hardware being a done deal, software became the focus for negotiation, indeed it is fair to say that the BMEWS software was extensively shaped by US-UK relations. First of all the details of the program would determine which geographical areas were covered—and remember that BMEWS was a system in which the margins of coverage were crucial. As Air Commodore F. E. Tyndall wrote to the directors of Operations (Air Defence) and Intelligence (Air):

> It is necessary to review the BM threat to the UK and the definition of a threatening missile in order that a satisfactory program for the computer at No 3 Site BMEWS may be evolved. When a response is received by the BMEWS it is subjected to a series of discrimination tests to eliminate satellites, meteorites, aurora interference and so on. Briefly these tests consist of determining whether the trajectory parameters fall within limits that have been worked out for all possible launch points and impact points for all likely types of missiles; there is a final test to determine whether if the predicted impact point lies within the UK target area. At the present time, programs have been worked out on the basis that there is no threat to the UK by missiles with a capability greater than 1600 [nautical miles] and that the target area is an irregular polygon closely circumscribing the British Isles, but excluding most of Ireland. Hence, if there is an interest in "near misses" or a threat of missiles of greater energy, there is a risk that these will be ignored.[68]

Confidence in BMEWS software was not raised by the widely leaked episode in October 1960 in which the Greenland computer had reported a "heavy missile attack," and that the report had been overridden manually minutes later when the culprit was found to be the moon. The programmers had thought lunar effects had been eliminated, but the scale of software for these new projects was such that "something had gone wrong."[69] It was doubly important, therefore, that British interests were served by the BMEWS software: "Since the Fylingdales installation is to operate as an Early Warning station for both the US and the UK," noted an RRE report, "an important British objective is to secure an operational philosophy giving the maximum degree of efficiency against missiles attacking the UK which is consistent with efficient operation against raids on the US. The functioning of the operation will ultimately be controlled by the program inserted in its main computer, and the advisory service has been concerned with the optimization of this program. This concentration of our effort is justified by the fact that, while the hardware for the station is almost completely designed, the computer program provides a point of flexibility where our suggestions can have real influence upon what is being prepared for our use by the US."[70] To make sure that "real influence" was secured, RRE posted staff to the United States for a number of years in the early 1960s, "the period in which work on the computer program will be mainly concentrated."

Finally, BMEWS, with its issues of UK-US cooperation and competition in digital techniques, can be compared to work on airborne computers. The very fact that computers were being considered for aircraft by the late 1950s, when the machines of the early years of the decade filled large rooms, demonstrated the remarkable achievements in miniaturization that the Cold War defense spending in the United States had produced. In Britain, airborne computers were first discussed as part of the radical new strike and reconnaissance multi-purpose aircraft, TSR-2. This was a deeply symbolic project, involving all three armed services ("vital to the Army in its strike reconnaissance role, to the Navy to strike against submarine bases, and the RAF abroad"), supporting the aircraft and electronics industry through valuable exports and direct grants, enrolling scientists through its innovation in almost every onboard system, and even demonstrating "to NATO that [the UK] intended to assist on other ways than maintaining the deterrent."[71] At its center was an American computer, the Verdan, handling several streams of radar and navigational data, controlling displays, communicating with ground bases, steering the aircraft on its terrain-following path, and guiding weapons. Not surprisingly, severe technical problems arose with integrating all the systems with the Verdan, although it was political and financial factors which caused the TSR-2 cancellation, with shattering effect on the British military-industrial complex, in 1965.[72]

Interest in airborne computers did not fade, indeed it intensified as the new Wilson administration, through its creation the Ministry of Technology, sought to boost and modernize British industry. As illustrated above, by the decision between ASR2232 and ADA, the Ministry of Defence had been converted to digital techniques—indeed the need to collaborate and therefore be flexible, imposed by involvement in organizations such as NATO, probably reinforced this conversion.[73] But in addition to this interest was a willingness from central government to support the computer industry through industrial policy. In 1965, a list of reasons to not buy American airborne computers was produced. Aside from the high dollar costs, and the problems experienced with Verdan, not buying British would mean "dropping out of a field which will have important applications in civil as well as military aircraft, and depriving ourselves and the computer industry of the general benefit of independent research in this field; various requirements inherent in the design of airborne digital computers, notably small size and extreme reliability, are likely to lead to further advances in technique which can have great value for future general computer design."[74] According to RRE, Britain was in the lead on digital processing for airborne radars, but "it would be difficult to withhold the results of our work from the Americans and once they had knowledge of the techniques they might overhaul us in exploiting them. It was therefore very important for consideration to be given to rapid exploitation by this country."[75] After due consideration, work at GEC

Stanmore (which was developing the digital "highway" concept of linking systems) and RRE directly benefited. Issues of industrial policy, especially with respect to American competition, were therefore important to airborne computer development, but they also shaped military automatic data processing more generally.

Dr. Strangelove

By the early 1960s, the secondary status of British to American digital technologies was clear to many informed observers. The relationship between the former great powers (Britain and Germany[76]) to the current superpower was one theme of Kubrick's *Dr. Strangelove*, a film by a British-resident but Bronx-raised director, made at Shepperton Studios outside London, for a Hollywood company (Columbia Pictures) for an American audience. The narrative is full of black humor. From the 1950s, the Strategic Air Command's B-52 bombers, armed with nuclear warheads, had been kept airborne continually as part of the policy of Mutually Assured Destruction deterrence. The system depended upon the meticulous, rational following of orders, since, for a deterrent to be credible, the opposing side had to believe that its use in response to a first strike was inevitable. But in *Dr. Strangelove* a peacetime exercise goes badly wrong when the bombers are ordered to begin their attack, code-named Plan R, by Colonel Jack D. Ripper, an American officer unbalanced because of Communist threats to his "precious bodily fluids." With Ripper at the Burpelson USAF base is an English exchange officer, Group Captain Lionel Mandrake of the Royal Air Force. The contrast is drawn between the mad (but, in the context of the system, rational) Ripper and the sane (but, in the context of the system, insubordinate) Mandrake. The impotence of Mandrake reflects Britain's position in the post-Suez world. On hearing the news of the attack, President Merkin Muffley calls the Soviet ambassador to the Pentagon War Room to explain what has happened. In the presence of President Merkin's scientific advisor, Dr. Strangelove, the ambassador confesses the secret of the Doomsday Machine. Meanwhile, Ripper commits suicide, nearly taking the recall codes with him. Mandrake breaks the code after noticing regularities in Ripper's doodles—"Peace On Earth," "Purity Of Essence." All the bombers but one are recalled, the last traveling on to drop its weapon and thus set off the Doomsday Machine.

There are two forms of "mechanical" action in *Dr. Strangelove*, and both are shown to be unreliable. The first is human, and includes both the following of military orders and the supposed rationality of grand strategy. Refusal to disobey orders adds tension to the film—when Mandrake, for example, is captured when the USAF base is stormed, the arresting officer refuses at first to let him contact the President, and only very reluctantly shoots the lock off a Coca-Cola machine to get enough cents for the phone-call (the regulations of Bell add another layer of rules). But unexpected deviation from procedure is also fatal: the final bomber is not recalled because the pilot has acted on—traditional—delegated initiative and changed course to attack another target. The point is that the human world works in a way that cannot be captured by the exhaustive description of scenarios—on which the rationality of mutually assured destruction depended.

But the interest of *Dr. Strangelove* to us is the mechanical action of both humans and machines. Indeed, as Kolker notes, "Mechanical failure or even "human error" are not the causes of Kubrick's apocalypse, but human activity imitating and surrendering itself to the mechanical."[77] Throughout the film, humans are operating as part of connected technological systems: the USAF base with its mainframe computers, the bomber above Russia and the Pentagon war room with its automated wall displays. The tragedy stems from the degree to which this mechanization has occurred, which is prefigured by the replacement of delegated military responsibility by a more rigid bureaucratic model. All decentralized information technologies—such as the personal radios, banned from the air base by Ripper because they might be used by saboteurs—are removed in the opening scenes. That leaves only the automatic machines, increasing the danger. The extent of the bureaucratization of the United States Air Force is made plain early on, with the air crew reading incoming code ("FFD135") on a device called a CRM114, and turning to an on-board safe, serving as a filing cabinet, and extracting Plan R.[78] The CRM114 is later destroyed, along with the radio, when the auto-destruct mechanism is accidentally set off. (Note again the darkly satirical joke being made about the dangers of automation, the fail-safe device that fails, a scene in miniature that echoes the arc of the entire film. Even then there is a slippage between human and machine: "the human element has failed us here," insists General Buck Turgidson to his President).

In *Dr. Strangelove* the rule-governed strategic world, when confronted by a plausible but unpredictable series of malfunctions and accidents, ends inevitably in the detonation of the Doomsday Machine. This device, though built by the Soviet Union because it could not afford the expense of the Cold War—a prophetic moment—is also conceived in America by Dr. Strangelove. He had commissioned a report on it from the BLAND corporation, an unsubtle jibe at the RAND Corporation. (Indeed Peter Sellers's Strangelove is based on an amalgam of Cold War advisors, including RAND boss Herman Kahn,

Henry Kissinger, H-bomb designer Edward Teller, and in particular the Nazi rocketeer-turned-American citizen, Wernher von Braun, a very visible public figure since the post-Sputnik debacle. Probably only the British audience world have spotted Sellers's nod to another scientist, the most famous in Britain at the time, Fred Hoyle, who shares Dr. Strangelove's haircut). The Doomsday Machine, a network of powerful atomic weapons linked to a "gigantic complex of computers," which if detonated would end all human and animal life on earth. Automatism is central to its operation, as it is to the theory of deterrence in general. Dr. Strangelove explains the importance of automation to President Muffley:

> Mr. President, it is not only possible it is essential. It is the whole idea of this machine, you know. Deterrence is the art of producing in the mind of the enemy the fear to attack. So because of the automated and irrevocable decision making process that rules out human meddling the Doomsday Machine is terrifying—simple to understand—completely credible and convincing.

Immune from human influence, the Doomsday Machine represents the fictional final end-point of the government as machine.

In this book I have traced the development of the government as machine, both as a metaphor and as a vision worked toward in practice, but always as political rather than cultural projects. However, in Kubrick's *Dr. Strangelove*, the ideal can be described in greater purity, and so the Doomsday Machine is a far more extreme, but recognizably similar, version of government as machine. My point is that the Doomsday Machine could only be imagined in a world framed by a long, influential history of government as machine. Its tie to non-fictional Cold War projects is not that important[79], although Norbert Wiener did discuss automated, learning machines in *God and Golem, Inc*::

> I certainly know nothing to contradict the assumption that Russia and the United States, either or both of them, are toying with the idea of using machines, learning machines at that, to determine the moment of pushing the atomic-bomb button which is the *ultima ratio* of this present world of ours.[80]

The machine that presses the button has, of course, become a cliché since then. It is important to remember that no organization is ever entirely automated, as the recent sociological studies by Harry Collins,[81] say, or the ethnomethodology-inspired Xerox group on air-traffic control again underline.[82] Histories of Cold War decision making, such as Twigge's, show plainly that humans continued to play their part, albeit in bureaucratically defined structures.[83]

Project Christchurch

In January 1965 the Cambridge molecular biologist and long-standing information-technology enthusiast John Kendrew, stepping it to chair a meeting of the Defence Research Committee, called for a synthetic review of military computing. The central Ministry of Defence, previously a small coordinating department between the three armed service leviathans, had just been expanded: now was the moment to force issues of standardization. The subsequent Working Party was called Project "Christchurch" and placed in the hands of the director RRE, G. G. Macfarlane.[84] The terms of reference of Project Christchurch were astonishingly broad: "to survey the possible field of application of general purpose digital computers in the period 1967–1980"; "to examine how far projected civilian designs of general purpose computers are likely to meet military with or without modifications"; "to propose the basic architecture of a compatible series or military computers, and to recommend how and when such a series should be brought into being"; to survey programming needs; to "propose a common user language"; to study peripheral equipment; and to examine requirements for research and development.[85]

Project Christchurch produced an interim report in September. Macfarlane predicted that the number of computers required for military purposes would be "large" ("250 by 1968, 1,700 between 1968 and 1975, and, more speculatively, more than 1,100 thereafter").[86] Almost all of these, he claimed, could be "met by a single series of machines, which is not yet available or projected at present but could be developed within a few years (1968–1970)," made possible by "the latest micro-electronic technique." Such a move would have radical implications for the British computer industry, at least the segments most concerned with defense applications—Elliott Automation, Ferranti, Plessey, and Marconi, only one or two of which could be awarded the prize. However, such concentration was in line with movements in the civil industry, where a pattern of merger had already appeared. The military series would have a standard interface and common instruction code. Protracted negotiations then began with the four firms—alongside Ministry of Technology efforts on the civil side. The manufacturers resisted this attempt to standardize their products, arguing that production would be disrupted and their products become less cost-effective. However, Project Christchurch forcefully urged the use of Ferranti Argus 400/500 or the Elliott 920M and 920C computers, and not the Plessey XL or Marconi Myriad.[87]

The second major recommendation of Project Christchurch also aimed at centralization, although the prompt was more economic: with one series of computers, programming language could be standardized. Indeed "computer language standardization could secure even greater savings than those which could result from computer standardization."[88] CORAL, developed for Linesman/Mediator, was suggested as the "first approved military programming language and that it should be used in as many systems as possible"—no military user employed high-level programming languages in 1965! Without the "discipline imposed by the structure of high-level language," programming for large-scale computer applications "could easily get completely out of hand." CORAL 66, a subset of Algol, got the nod over CORAL 64, a subset of JOVIAL. Finally, emerging from the Christchurch proposals was the conception of an ever more integrated defense organization: "there was at present little overlap between the Defence operational computers and the Defence administrative computers," but the Defence Research Committee envisaged a future of "an integrated computer network" connecting compatible machines via common interfaces. The next chapter considers administrative machines; chapter 10 examines the fate of networks.

Conclusion

Paul Edwards's argument that the computer shaped, and was decisively shaped by, its Cold War context makes sense in America where the form of both hardware and software were up for grabs. In the United Kingdom, defense computing became gradually more constrained. In the case of the Ballistic Missile Early Warning System at Fylingdales in Yorkshire, for example, the hardware exported from the United States was non-negotiable, and software became the "point of flexibility." The lines of BMEWS code were shaped by US-UK negotiations. It was suggested, but not proved, that digital systems may have been encouraged since their flexibility was desirable in a period of coalition building among Western allies (this would be a fascinating question to explore further). Also in agreement with Edwards's "closed world" thesis, I observed that models of controlled environments intensified in defense areas, and were transferred into civil arenas such as traffic control, although I would emphasize that, as the continuity between the last chapter and the present one, such "infospheres" did not depend on the availability of electronic digital computers, although they were certainly helped.

The story of British defense computing was therefore one of application rather than novelty. Much was borrowed from the United States, from hardware to programs for computerized war gaming.[89] Although startlingly innovative research was underway at laboratories such as at Malvern, and although the occasional system such as CDS or ADA could surprise in matters of sophistication, British defense computing was not especially exciting, as workmanlike surveys such as that commissioned by the Defence Research Committee in 1969 reveal.[90] As the encouragement given to automation by administrators in the debate over ASR2232 versus ADA hinted at, it is to the subject we now turn to, clerical work, that is most intriguing. Bear in mind that when the Ministry of Supply in 1951 had a director of "programming" it referred to the bureaucracy of planning for the armed services, not computers.[91]

8

Treasury Organization and Methods and the Computerization of Government Work

With the expansion of government in the Second World War, Treasury Organization and Methods (O&M) had also grown—to a staff of 35 by 1945. A new importance and a wider remit for the O&M expert movement had been confirmed by the Select Committee on National Expenditures (1941–1942) and the Select Committee on Estimates (1946–1947). Treasury O&M now was encouraged to go beyond merely advising departments on the improvement of "routine procedure," and tackle "more fundamental topics": advising on the re-organization of departments in the name of efficiency, and the structure of new departments. Though Treasury O&M never had executive powers to intervene, its position in the Treasury, which had regained its prewar dominance, made it powerful. O&M borrowed staff from elsewhere in Whitehall. "When these officers return to their departments," Lord Bridges noted, "they help spread the O and M outlook and habit of mind throughout the Service."[1] O&M officers were appointed in other departments, in nationalized industries, and even in the larger private corporations.[2] By 1955 there were 356 O&M officers in central government.[3] One aspect of "habit of mind" that diffused across Whitehall, was an association of mechanization with administrative efficiency.

To some extent, what we think of as Treasury O&M activities has been shaped by J. M. Lee's book *Reviewing the Machinery of Government*,[4] which charts the effort by a number of interlocking committees of insiders from the appointment of the Anderson Committee (1942) to the early 1950s in order to review the organization and the functional division of government departments. O&M emerges in this account as an adjunct to a "generally discredited" attempt at reform, and the diffusion of O&M as a rather half-hearted initiative by Bridges.[5] Although this may be an accurate picture of O&M in the austere early postwar years (Lee's account ends in 1952), it is misleading if extrapolated to later years. The intent to reform machinery of government waned as Treasury O&M placed more emphasis on a second route to efficient public administration. If the structure of departments was unyielding, then reorganization via technical change promised malleability. Moreover, the progressivist association of technology with efficiency provided a valuable resource for the promotion of modern office machinery and the persuasion of departments.

Before 1939 the introduction of punched-card machinery had been authorized "only where it could be shown that there would result some monetary economy" or where it seemed that the "operations could only be done by machines." In 1946, J. R. Simpson, who had taken over from Pitman as head of Treasury O&M, noted that the criteria had changed: mobilization during the Second World War meant that "machines were authorized where it could be shown that there would be an economy in manpower."[6] Though such changes demanded review by a Working Party, Treasury O&M was privately optimistic about future policy:

> It is probable that the view the Working Party will advance is that manpower should continue to be the criterion and that mechanization should be introduced to the greatest possible extent even in those cases where additional expenditure may be involved. It is obvious that there would have to be some balance between economy of manpower and increased expenditure, but the bias would be in favor of mechanization to the maximum possible extent.

Why was mechanization pursued by the government in the late 1940s? First, the personnel shortages of wartime continued into the period of reconstruction. "In view of the present manpower difficulties, which are likely to continue for an indefinite period," Simpson argued, "future policy should be to introduce office machines in all cases where some saving of manpower can be achieved."[7] However, the pressure for mechanization went beyond this economic rationale: "there are some grounds for going ever further and for contending that any routine processes which can be mechanized should be done by office machines in preference to their performance by such grades as Clerical Assistants and Clerical Officers." For large-scale operations the reason might be economies of labor, however for smaller-scale processes the important consideration was "not so much a net saving of manpower as the substitution of relatively unskilled labor for [skilled labor such as typists]."[8] Mechanization was justified as a partial replacement for relatively expensive skilled labor. However, a third reason was that mechanization expanded the range of the government's administrative capacities. Three examples illustrate this. The proposals to mechanize sick-leave statistics, promoted by Treasury O&M in 1946, were "not primarily . . . an economy measure, but because adequate statistics cannot be produced by existing methods."[9] The Census of

Distribution was also, according to Treasury O&M, "impossible to visualize . . . being done at all by hand methods," whereas "the calculation of value payments by the War Damage Commission and the preparation of payable orders and schedules would . . . have required an extra 400 or 500 staff over a period of six months if done by hand."[10]

Several factors weighed against mechanization. First, the Treasury had to deal with the two British punched-card firms (BTM and Powers), which did not produce the range of machines (nor the prices) of the American manufacturers. Purchase of American machinery meant the unwelcome expenditure of hard currency.[11] Second, departments might not be enthusiastic for several reasons, not least that the office machines represented the direct influence of Treasury experts. Departmental O&M therefore played a crucial intermediary role, since the individuals there were less obviously proselytizers of Treasury values and could claim the relative "neutrality" of expertise. "Tact" in recommending changes to senior administrators and a good "desk-side manner" were emphasized as good qualities for an O&M officer to cultivate if interdepartmental conflicts were to be avoided.[12] Treasury O&M officers ensured that they remained an obligatory passage point as the most expert advisers on mechanization projects. For example, a handbook produced in 1947 describing office machinery did not detail how an installation could be pursued:

> The handbook was not to explain the working of office appliances or to advise on the circumstances in which it would be right to use them but only awaken the staff of Departments to the possibilities of mechanization, and they were asked to make a special effort to come forward with suggestions which could be examined by the experts.[13]

What work had been mechanized through the installation of punched-card machines by 1948? Twenty-six government departments possessed or were planning punched-card installations.[14] Nearly 50 installations existed by March 1948, 80 by 1954.[15] Common uses included accounting, stores accounting, payroll, and the production of statistics. The Admiralty possessed Powers 65-column card machines at its Expense Accounts Offices at its Chatham, Devonport, and Havant dockyards. Stores accounting was also important in the Services: seven Air Ministry Maintenance Units installed Hollerith 80-column card tabulators. It is interesting to note that the armed service departments and the Ministry of Supply were relatively well endowed with punched-card installations, probably left over from wartime. Most departments had branches to make statistics for internal use; for example, Customs and Excise, Education, the Home Office, the Ministry of Labour, and the Board

Figure 8.1
Treasury O&M became an obligatory passage point for mechanization (and later computerization) of British government office work. Here is part of the Machine Demonstration Room at the Treasury in 1954. On the desk at the left are a Manifold Register and three varieties of typewriter. On the desk at center front are automatic, key-driven, and crank-operated calculating machines. Free-standing at center right and on desks at center rear are accounting machines. On desks along the wall at right are a ring binder, a strip index binder, a posting box, and other filing and indexing systems. There was also an "exhaustive index of office machinery . . . maintained by a staff of specialists who are able to keep abreast of current developments." (source: Treasury O&M, *Machines and Appliances in Government Offices*, revised edition, HMSO, 1954)

of Trade did. Government Communications Headquarters, now moved from Bletchley Park to Cheltenham, probably used its punched-card installation for the calculation of its payroll, in addition to the applications described in chapter 6. The production of statistics describing people and products made major use of punched cards: the Board of Trade's Censuses of Production and Distribution were now continuous, whereas the GRO's Census of Population occurred every decade. The 1950 Census of Distribution was an innovation, extending the spirit of the Production census to ask all commercial firms in the distributive trades questions on turnover, purchases, sales, stocks, profit, employees, wages, and commodities carried. The processing of the million forms generated was one of the tasks deemed "impossible" without punched-card mechanization.[16] The management of extra remuneration grants to specialists in the National Health Service (and subsidies paid to farmers), which was crucial to the Service's acceptance, was also greatly facilitated by the use of punched cards to handle the large number of small payments—a nice example of the interaction between available technique and administrative and political change.[17] The closest medical analogue to the Censuses of Production and Distribution was the similarly mechanized Oxford Nutrition Survey, the correlative statistical analysis of 95 different fields relating to 14,569 people in England and 3,325 famine-stricken Dutch, would have been hard to imagine without Hollerith cards.[18]

Treasury O&M, interested in promoting this mechanization but also aware that it had a remit to ensure that office machinery was introduced efficiently, reviewed the use of punched-card installations in 1948. Time spent idle through lack of work or breakdown was of particular concern. The reason for this was clear in Treasury O&M's subsequent recommendations for the centralization of government data processing in the London area.[19] During this period HMSO repeatedly argued for centralization. Presumably one benefit of a centralized punched-card installation would be an increase in the importance of HMSO. Treasury O&M's Report urged the setting up of an Inter-Departmental Study Group, and such a body was appointed in 1950 to consider the case for the merging of statistical installations.[20]

Nineteen London statistical punched-card installations, administered by 15 departments, were examined with a view to centralization. The work being done with these machines varied enormously: for example, the Meteorological Office's library used punched cards to record surface and upper air weather observations, whereas the Ministry of Transport used Powers machines to analyze road accidents and vehicle registration.[21] Even within departments the work could be very different—for example, in addition to the Meteorological Office's data processing, the Air Ministry had a library of punched cards at Stanmore recording sickness of RAF and WAAF personnel since the First World War. In December 1950, the Interdepartmental Study Group agreed that a pilot merger should be attempted, and six centers were chosen for centralization: the GPO's Accountant General's Department, the Ministry of Food's Common Services Division, the MAFF's Analysis of Statistics Section, the Ministry of Education's Statistical Branch, the Ministry of Supply's G9 (Central Statistics) branch, and the medical records of Air Ministry Central Statistical Branch 3.[22] However, the centralization of statistical branches meant a loss of control for the individual departments (affecting, for example, their ability to rush through important jobs), and all departments but Education initially objected. The Air Ministry agreed only on the conditions that its complete library of more than 2 million punched cards would be copied, that work could still be contracted out, and that the Treasury would guarantee immediate alternative data-processing capacity in the event of the central installation's destruction. (Stanmore, on the northern periphery of the capital, was considered safer than central London in a future war.) A centralized Combined Tabulating Installation, managed by HMSO, was set up in 1952.[23] In many ways it was a return to a similar arrangement to BTM's wartime Government Service Bureau. By the criteria of saved rental costs (£2,430 per annum) and reduced staff (84.5 compared to 92.5), the Combined Tabulating Installation was judged a success.[24]

At this point in the narrative I want to emphasize the achievement of an expert movement in recognizing aspects of government work as being open to explicit description in terms of a set of mechanical and mechanizable instructions. For example, in the census, what was labeled the "Machine Programme" was the description, action by action, of how a set of punched cards would be sorted and tabulated to produce the population statistics required.[25] The 1951 census was just too early for computerization: the first commercial machines had appeared that year, and planning for the census, of course, had had to begin much earlier; indeed, the General Register Office was no longer a radically progressive organization.[26] Powers-Samas's tender for the Powers's Universal Printing Counting Sorters was accepted in August 1950. Although these sorters were uniquely modified for census work, this was a relatively conservative choice.[27] Again the pressure on card space was high: the interest in extra "social group" information had to be shoehorned onto the larger 65-column Powers-Samas card. The volume of work at Southport (the same Lancashire town that was home to the National Register) to process the 50 million cards of the census generated complaints from the machine operators regarding poor eyesight, "appalling noise," headaches, and physical and "nervous" strain.[28] Such was the "drudgery" that was later to be emphasized in the debates over computerization. However, it is to the programmatic instructions for the 1951 census that I want to draw the reader's attention. The production of statistics is reduced to an explicit series of instructions, telling the machine operator at each stage what to punch or what to check; it is not a big step from "programmes" for humans and machines of the earlier type to programs for electronic computers, and indeed the production of census statistics was one of the areas in which the shift from punched-card machine to computer did not entail massive reorganization. However, the broader point I want to make is not specific to the census, since such programs would have had to be produced wherever government had substantially mechanized its work—and therefore had proliferated in Whitehall since the turn of the twentieth century. Having shown in previous chapters that the Civil Service was cast as a general-purpose, even universal "machine," I must now add the existence of programs.

Figure 8.2
Powers-Samas employees exhibiting the Universal Printing Counting Sorter (UPCS) in 1951. (source: National Archive for the History of Computing, University of Manchester)

Computerization

The last chapter described how the first handful of stored-program electronic computers were built and how they were applied to scientific and mathematical military tasks in Britain. Six years after the running of the first program at Manchester University in 1948, scientific and military computers had appeared at several government sites. The Pilot ACE was in operation at the National Physical Laboratory. The agricultural research laboratory at Rothamstead was running its Elliott 401 machine. The electronics experts of the General Post Office at Dollis Hill and the Ministry of Supply at Malvern had built experimental machines and had even supplied them to other users (including the War Office). The atomic weapon and atomic energy projects greedily bought up computing power—the weapons factory at Aldermaston, for example, had both a Ferranti computer and an IBM calculator on order,

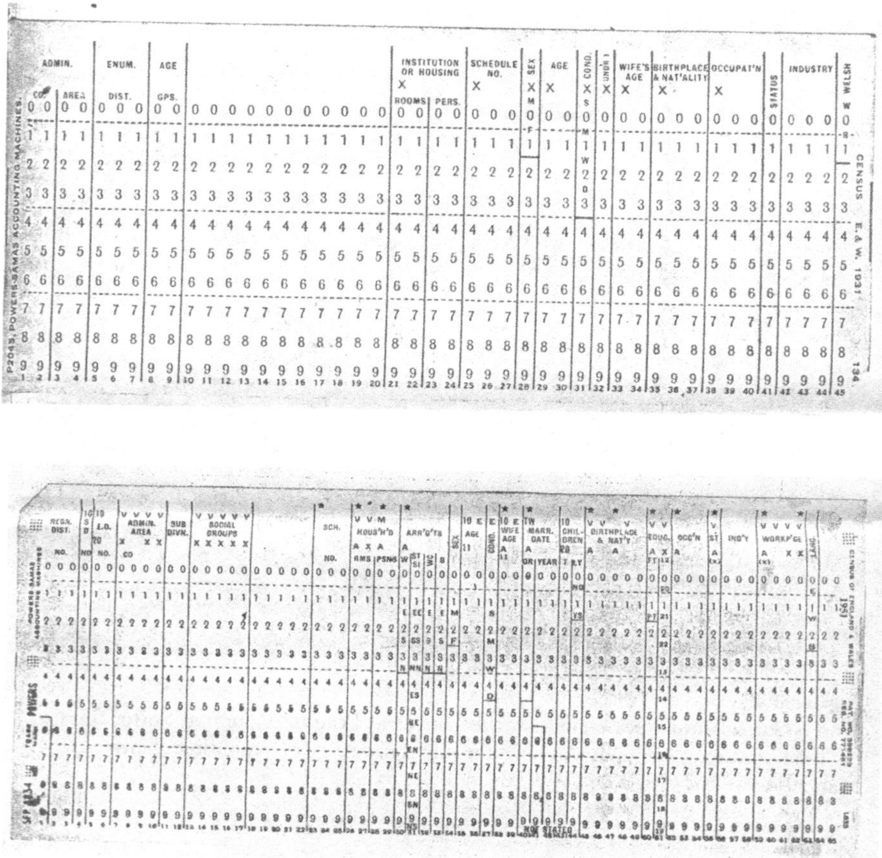

Figure 8.3
Punch cards for the Census of Population of England and Wales, 1931 (top) and 1951 (bottom).

the American machine a sign of future policy. By the end of 1954, five computers or electronic calculators were installed, fourteen were on order, and others were under consideration.[29] By April 1955, seven computers had been installed at government sites, more than were to be found in academia or industry.[30] None of these electronic computers, but a few of the electronic multipliers and calculators, were used for clerical work. By the late 1950s most of the government computers were clerical rather than scientific machines. How did the UK government come to understand this strange new technology as a device for the office rather than the laboratory? The answer can be found in the changing importance of advisors and experts in Whitehall.

In 1949 the first government committee to concern itself with electronic computers was set up. The Advisory Committee on High Speed Calculating Machines was a joint initiative of the Department of Scientific and Industrial Research and the Advisory Council on Scientific Policy, and became known as the Brunt Committee, after its chairman, meteorologist and Royal Society secretary and vice-president David Brunt.[31] Brunt's advice was highly influential in shaping British academic computer research. In particular, a research agenda oriented primarily toward scientific calculation rather than business data processing was confirmed.[32] However, away from academic centers, Brunt's Committee began to take an interest in the use of computers for business and administration in the early 1950s. Brunt invited T. B. Boss of the NPL's Mathematics Division to examine "in a general way whether any large scale punched card jobs in the Government Service offer some long-term scope for the use of computing machines."[33] Treasury O&M civil servants discussed large-scale punched-card installations but were not immediately enthusiastic about the application of large electronic computers.

Manufacturers of computing machinery also attempted to interest Treasury O&M. B. B. Swann of Ferranti, in the week following the well-publicized inauguration of their Ferranti Mark 1 computer in November 1951, wrote to Simpson:

> We are engaged in building other machines with a view to their use in statistical, accounting, etc. work, wherever this is on a sufficiently large scale to call for a machine of the large universal type. . . . It seems to me that there are some fields of Government statistical work in which the Electronic Computer could probably do a great deal of work which now occupies large numbers of clerks. . . .[34]

A subsequent meeting between Swann and the Treasury's Jack Dunkley led to a skeptical internal discussion within Treasury O&M about possible uses of computers in administrative work and the role the division could play.[35] There were at least four reasons for Treasury O&M's hesitant attitude. The first was technical. If computers were to take over punched-card work, various aspects of the computer's performance would have to be improved: the means of extracting data from documents (punching and verifying in the case of cards), the input of data into the machine, and the printing of results in a usable form.[36] Second, disciplines such as accounting highly valued accuracy, and it was not clear to the civil servants that "engineering and programming" could ensure and preserve this value. The accountants' and solicitors' legally driven high regard for permanent and stable records also raised questions of the output and automatic inscriptions of computers.[37] Third, computers were expensive. The Ferranti Mark 1s were sold at about £90,000 each. A switch from punched-card installations to electronic computers would have to be justified in the familiar economic terms of staff or money savings. This was unlikely while computers were regarded by Treasury O&M as merely a means of speeding up processing: "Government departments . . . stand little to gain from any new mechanism which does no more than speed up the operations of sorting. . . . The major problem was to find some way of either eliminating or reducing the amount of labor that goes into preparation for actually punching the cards."[38] Finally, nearly all the early designers, manufacturers, and users of computers regarded the devices as primarily scientific and mathematical objects, with the implication that attribution of expertise in computers followed scientific standing. For example, when it was suggested that a Treasury O&M "might take a more active part in the direction of development (and . . . experiment) and perhaps be represented on the Brunt Committee," one official's response was negative: "The Committee is made up of the leading professors, etc. in the scientific field and I would hesitate to agree that [a] member of the Branch should try to understand and contribute to discussions in this company."[39] However, the statement that computers were only regarded as scientific machines must be significantly qualified: there was also plenty of universalist rhetoric emphasizing the general-purpose character of stored-program computers. For example, an internal Treasury O&M note reported Lord Halsbury as stating to the Brunt group that "electronic calculators could do anything, including playing 'Annie Laurie' and winning a chess match."[40] However, the presumed requirement of scientific expertise, despite the claims for universality, powerfully contributed to the initial hesitancy of the Treasury.

In 1951, Boss reported to the Brunt Committee on the possible applications of computers to clerical work.[41] The committee, at a moment when only four computers existed in Britain, decided that a "detailed study" was needed.[42] They were already aware that Lyons had introduced its LEO computer to mechanize its office work, and Lord Halsbury, chair of the National Research Development Corporation and member of the Brunt Committee, had witnessed the US Bureau of Census's impressive use of a Univac.[43] The committee therefore warmly endorsed Boss's conclusions that the offices of the Ministry of National Insurance (MNI, later Ministry of Pensions and National Insurance, MPNI) at Newcastle offered "a very good opportunity to stage an experiment with an electronic machine."

These offices had been set up as a consequence of three acts of 1945 and 1946 dealing with family allowances, industrial injuries and national insurance. A staff of 8,000 kept the Central Records of the insured population (28 million people paid national insurance contributions), and 40 million payments by postal draft of sickness and other benefits had to be balanced each year. Boss's proposal was that an electronic computer could help three of the Newcastle office's jobs: the preparation of salary statements (including determination of PAYE income tax) for 20,000 MNI staff, the balancing of national insurance postal drafts, and the work of the MNI's Statistics Section.[44] In 1952 the income tax work was done with twelve Sundstrand accounting machines, and checking for accuracy was done by hand. The balancing of postal drafts was carried out by collating cards (sent by local Post Offices, one card punched for each draft) with a Powers machine, 220 employees using 130 punches, 20 sorters, and 14 tabulators and processing 800,000 drafts per week. Pneumatic tubes transported the cards around the buildings. The Statistics Section used Powers cards to analyze samples of the sickness, injury, and unemployment benefits paid, and reported the information to the Government Actuary, the Medical Research Council, and other interested bodies. Much of this information had been available only since the 1946 Insurance Act.

On the suggestion of S. Vajda of the Admiralty, the Brunt Committee appointed a subcommittee to study the Use of Electronics for Office Arithmetic. Vajda argued that the Working Party should examine whether the replacement of punched-card machines by computers was justified on account of "speed, elasticity and cost of performance" and what social "impacts" might accompany this change, whether alterations to existing computers was needed, and to what extent legal restrictions on "auditing and publicity" would necessitate the continuation of card records. Finally, the Working Party could consider questions of centralization: there seemed to be an economic case for combining the data-processing work of ministries, but both "security" and "political" reasons perhaps favored decentralization. Representatives of government departments, the NRDC, the Office Management Association, and Lyons (the only British manufacturer to concentrate on office computers) met in June 1952 under the chairmanship of Lord Halsbury (the chair passed to Vajda after the first meeting).[45] The group agreed on future membership (the Bank of England was invited to nominate a representative), although the Lyons members decided to decline official membership on grounds of confidentiality of patents, and its terms of reference:

(i) to consider whether it would be of advantage to the MNI or other offices doing a great deal of routine arithmetical or statistical work to supplement present methods with suitable high-speed computers.

(ii) to consider what ancillary equipment, and modifications in computer design, it would be reasonable to develop to make high-speed computers more suitable for such work.

(iii) to report to the Chairman of the ACHSCM [i.e. the Brunt Committee].[46]

These terms were more focused than Vajda's initial wish list: out went any explicit remit to consider the consequences of centralization. However, in the course of ten full meetings the subcommittee generated and considered many papers on the possibilities of office computerization. Attridge described the mechanization (without computers) of Bank of England work using Addressograph, Burroughs adding machines, Protectographs, and the three "prime Records": the registers, metal plates, and balance slips.[47] Computerization of clerical work using LEO was detailed by Thompson of Lyons, who in an upbeat conclusion reported that "programs can be prepared for many clerical jobs to be carried out by automatic calculators." Thompson also emphasized the need for reliable input/output systems and larger electronic stores, subjects that the NPL's E. A. Newman also reviewed in depth for the subcommittee.[48] These components comprised, following the terminology of the systems historian Thomas Parke Hughes, the reverse salients of the computerization of office work in the early 1950s: for example, a study of calculating a payroll for a factory of 3,500 employees found that numerical computation could be carried out in 48 minutes, but printing the payroll took 12–14 hours.[49] The salients were severe enough to discourage insurance companies such as Prudential, which had been in the forefront of punched-card mechanization, from adopting computers. Striking evidence of this wariness can be seen in the following account given by Greenall, the Brunt Committee's secretary:

> The Secretary of the Chartered Insurance Institute, whom he knew privately, had asked him to meet Mr. Menzler, President of the Institute of Actuaries, to talk about the Brunt Committee. Mr. Menzler had then written to Mr. Redington, Actuary of the Prudential; Mr. Beard, a machine enthusiast and Assistant General manager of the Pearl; and Mr. Bunford, Chairman of the Life Offices Association. The Prudential had invited him to lunch to meet these gentlemen. They had told him what, apart from the cost, they had thought were the shortcomings from their standpoint of the Ferranti machine: they had been unable to see how to get the best out of it, mainly because the "feeding" problems which they thought would largely offset the high speed of calculation.[50]

If well-placed "machine enthusiasts" located in companies with both the need for and the proven record of installing new information technologies were unwilling to invest, then the role of advocating and championing computers in offices could be taken up by government actors—an important shift of emphasis in the expert movement of mechanists.

For reasons that stemmed from their place in the context of Whitehall, it was to be members of Treasury O&M that, despite their initial reluctance, passionately adopted the cause of computerization. However, the Ministry of National Insurance (which began the first review) was not the site of the first government office computer. Although the DSIR's Brunt subcommittee continued the careful but protracted examination of MNI work with a view to installing a computer by 1960, Treasury O&M had successfully promoted the introduction of an office computer 3 years earlier.

"A Strong Section . . . Staffed by Engineers": Treasury O&M Takes the Lead

In 1952, Treasury O&M was ambivalent and hesitant about the use of computers in government offices. By 1957, the group had established itself as a "strong section" of experts and was enthusiastically promoting computers as a tool and a symbol of modern administration. Several factors lay behind the adoption of computers by Treasury O&M: the group's acceptance of the feasibility and economy of replacing clerks with computers, external pressure from manufacturers and the press, and internal pressures from within the Treasury and Whitehall more generally.

I noted above that in the late 1940s and early 1950s computers were regarded as mathematical or scientific devices, with the implication that only scientific experts could pronounce on their use. Therefore, scientific experts writing on the possible applications of computers in offices and employing concepts and arguments acceptable to Treasury O&M were crucial bridging agents. At an O&M evening meeting in early 1953, Edward Arthur "Ted" Newman (a member of the Pilot ACE team at NPL) made an explicitly economic case for the computerization of "semi-routine" clerical work.[51] Noting that "about two million clerical workers are employed in this country at a wage bill of over £1,000 million," Newman argued:

> It seems possible that in due course computers will do the country's routine clerical work, most of the work in fact of a deductive character. . . . When used for suitable purposes, and in particular for processes which are essentially serial, some automatic computers are very fast, up to 100,000 times as fast as man. Their potential power is thus very great.

However, what is most interesting is Newman's account of programming:

> It is unlikely that there will ever be any great reduction in the time needed for programming machines, since the organization of a complex job whether it is done by human clerks, by punched cards, or by high-speed computers is bound to be a long business, and *a program is only a coded form of this organization.*

For generalist civil servants, such an account was both reassuring (because it suggested that the their role of organizing and managing clerical work would be preserved) and empowering (because it presented what had been regarded as requiring technical expertise as something *familiar*: a homology between the program and the organization of clerks—indeed, in punched-card "programs" the connection was very close). The grasping of Newman's point was also a pivotal moment of self-awareness: if bureaucracy was the original rule-based, general-purpose machine, then this moment, in the British context, was when the civil servants saw past the unfamiliar technical guise and recognized their own mirror image.

Demonstrations of the application of computers to office work also helped to persuade Treasury O&M. Academics such as J. A. C. Brown's team at Cambridge University's Department of Applied Economics, and B. V. Bowden at Manchester College of Science and Technology (now UMIST) compared the use of computers and the use of punched-card installations to carry out statistical and accounting work.[52] These reports helped delineate for Treasury O&M in which areas the expense of electronic computers would be outweighed by savings. The success of the LEO at Lyons, first to produce the company's payroll and then to calculate 1955–56 PAYE tables for the budget of April 1955 (it had been set up to perform the same calculations in 1954, but the chancellor had not changed the rates), provided further displays of the applicability of computers to government work. The PAYE tables, in particular, marked a significant moment, being the first use of a computer to perform government clerical work. The trial was carefully planned. Because of the "chaos which a breakdown might have caused," two computers were used: Lyons's LEO and the NPL's DEUCE.[53]

However, persuasion that computerization was both feasible and justified by savings is not sufficient to explain why Treasury O&M adopted the strategy so enthusiastically. External and internal pressures also contributed. Externally, criticism from the press and lobbying by computer manufacturers made sure that Treasury O&M could not plead ignorance of developments and possibilities. On 17 November 1954, the *Financial Times* printed two reports on government use of computers, the leading article claiming that the government was reluctant to use the new machines. Two further *FT* reports followed within 2 days. The charge that the UK government was slow in installing computers was wrong when made against Treasury O&M by 1954, and had never been true for scientific Whitehall: five expensive computers were in place, and eleven on order. Companies such as Ferranti regularly wrote to Treasury O&M about new computer hardware, software, and techniques, helpfully drawing such things to the attention of the civil servants but also, of course, marketing their wares. Ferranti's C. B. Berners-Lee, for example, tried to interest Treasury O&M in linear programming computing techniques proven at Manchester and Cambridge universities.[54] Sometimes, media and manufacturer pressure combined: for instance, the Treasury suspected that the *FT*'s criticisms had been prompted by manufacturers to "put pressure on HMG."[55] Companies such as Ferranti used a carrot-and-stick approach: the carrot was in the form of tempting new techniques, the stick was the planting of critical stories in the press.

The most significant factors behind Treasury O&M's adoption of computerization were not external criticisms nor demonstrations of feasibility and economic savings; they were the realization that the strategy aligned closely with interests internal to Whitehall and a shift in industrial policy. Edward Playfair, a Treasury "high flyer" who later became the ill-fated chairman of International Computers and Tabulators (renamed ICL in 1968), expressed these factors powerfully in a Christmas 1954 note to Sir Alexander Johnston, Third Secretary of the Treasury and responsible for O&M. Playfair noted that his Overseas Finance division had a twofold interest in computers: as "a growing point in British industry and, in particular, British export industry . . . the kind of business which, in the postwar world, we are pretty good at" and as a means of "getting accurate and rapid information about our balance of payments."[56] Balance-of-payments information was obtained from the trade returns punched onto cards and sorted. But, Playfair, noted, "there are many cross-classifications and bits of information which are wanted and one of the problems of the present moment is a simple one of timing: different departments are queuing up to have cards run through the machine in different ways—and even the rapidest ones take too long." Rapid generation of trade statistics would, Playfair stated, be "an absolute snip for an electronic machine," *if* the problem of large electronic stores could be solved. Playfair then argued that existing government policy for computers had failed to deliver such machines (HMSO had "shrugged their shoulders," and the NRDC "made some tentative enquiries but went no further"), and contended that the "State" as a "potential large purchaser" had a choice: either the "pace is set by industry and followed by the Government," or "to decide that the Government's best interest lies in taking some risks to develop the industry—in short, to place development contracts." The most telling comparison for Playfair was to the aircraft industry, where the state's position as a large-scale customer (and defense interests), justified this practice.[57]

The importance of Playfair's arguments for this chapter lies not so much their relevance to the debate over the government's role in setting industrial policy as in their implications for the capacity of administration and in the shift in the locus of expertise if the policy were to be adopted. By Playfair's own admission, information processing by punched card could not generate statistical knowledge of the economy fast enough. Computers (with large stores) could produce that knowledge quicker, as well as new kinds of knowledge through different sortings. Changes in the organization of information collection and processing could expand and change the capacity to administrate. A second implication, if Playfair's suggestions were accepted, would be that the Treasury would need an indisputable center of expertise to advise on contracts and suggest sites of application. Playfair expressed this implication as follows:

> What I would like to see would be O&M and the Stationery Office [which bought machinery] setting up between them a strong section (of course it would mean manning it in part by scientists and engineers)—a strong but not a large one—with the deliberate object of trying out where the boundaries of technical knowledge could be enlarged, with Government offices as guinea pigs.

A strong Treasury group, staffed partly by specialists, with a powerful remit to modernize government work and to influence industry, runs counter to many preconceived notions of the "dead hand of the Treasury" in this period. Playfair's suggestions were not the cause of reorganization, but were an excellent and compact expression of its ideals.[58] Central government, because of O&M, was "extraordinarily well equipped to provide a field for experiment," and in this case Treasury interests (authority within Whitehall, increased power through increased knowledge of the economy) coincided with interests of specialists and experts.

Sir Alexander Johnston was already aware of many of the factors that Playfair indicated, and the argument that the move demanded a strengthened role for his Treasury O&M was not lost on him. However, the road to a strong Treasury O&M was not direct. Action followed four routes: circulation of information about computer applications, contacts with manufacturers, importing of expertise, and reformation of the committee structure. First, O&M built on their existing methods of drawing the attention of departments to information technologies: lectures, training courses, demonstrations, and the *O&M Bulletin* (circulated to all departments with O&M officers). As we saw in chapter 5, the information network reached outside Whitehall (the HMSO publication *Wage Accounting by Electronic Computer* was considered "an excellent case study" by *The Economist*).[59] Writing to Sir Thomas Padmore and Sir Edward Bridges in May 1955 to suggest a "child's guide on the type of work that the machines could do" for "wider circulation among senior civil servants," Dunkley noted that "the O and M division of the Treasury have had a great reputation as experts in the field of office machines, and it is important that we should retain this position in regard to electronic computers."[60]

All these measures to inform had a dual function: to increase awareness of the computer applications, and to reinforce Treasury O&M's position as the center for advice and expertise.

Although Treasury O&M's enthusiasm for government intervention did not quite match Playfair's, the group did favor awarding contracts for large memory stores, as the following internal argument illustrates:

> My dealings with the office machine trade have confirmed, what I think is general experience, that manufacturers are most effectively urged into speedy development by the knowledge that a market exists and that others are competing for this market. This view support's Mr. Playfair's proposal that suitably qualified people should be brought together to determine the needs in this field and to present them to the trade as a challenge to design, development and possibly experiment in selected government offices.

P. S. Milner-Barry, formerly Bletchley Park's master of procedure and now head of Treasury O&M, sent letters to computer manufacturers, saying that the government was reviewing its use of electronic computers, and inquiring about machines with very large memories. The first version of the letter (sent to IBM(UK), Plessey, English Electric, Elliott Bros., Decca Radar, BTM, Ferranti, and Powers-Samas) was more forthcoming than the second (sent to EMI Engineering, National Cash Register, and three other American firms: Burroughs Adding Machines, Remington-Rand, and Underwood Business Machines). Government laboratories, such as NPL, also experimented with large electronic stores in the mid 1950s.

The formation of a group of "suitably qualified people" to consider tenders depended on two developments: the import into O&M of technical expertise and the establishment of a committee structure dependent on O&M staff. "Headhunting" began in late 1955. With the help of Lord Halsbury, James Merriman was appointed Deputy Director and head of the Office Machines branch of Treasury O&M. Merriman's appointment at the Treasury was highly symbolic of the willingness to engage seriously with the opportunities presented by rapidly changing electronic technologies. He had been trained as a radio engineer, studying for a master's degree under Edward Appleton before being recruited to the General Post Office's excellent Dollis Hill research laboratory in 1936. After a war spent applying his radio engineering expertise surveying London by radio-location techniques in search of German spy broadcasts and later building "Meacons"—a radio countermeasure—and early VHF communication links, Merriman had turned his hand to the development of early Cold War communications infrastructures.[61] In 1953 Merriman had moved from Radio to Organization Branch within the Post Office, his first move in the direction of O&M. Before starting this new job,

Merriman, up to this moment an expert engineer only, broadened his education considerably by spending a year at the Imperial Defence College, where he encountered an "immense" range of subjects:

The characteristics of the British constitution—the relationships between a permanent secretary and a minister—the art of authority in defense—social structures—the source of growth in a nation's economy—population growth—critical assessments of the strengths and weaknesses of alternative forms of government—communism and its characteristics—the tension centers in the world—and so on. Subjects such as these would be studied for a fortnight with lectures by men of eminence gathered on a world-wide basis all speaking their minds freely in the knowledge that confidences would be kept.[62]

The engineer, bearing a coating of generalist knowledge, could now move more freely in higher Civil Service circles. Back at the GPO's "O" Branch, Merriman witnessed an "extremely imaginative" early promotional film from IBM, which fired his imagination but also made him angry: the engineer inside him was dumbfounded to find out that the Post Office's Central O&M Branch—an outlying part of Treasury O&M's organization, which he associated with the mundanity of the "layout of forms"—was charged with considering the implications of computers for the Post Office. For Merriman it "almost seemed offensive" that such a body with "no knowledge of electronics or engineering processes" would be involved "in and with a highly technological innovation like an electronic computer." This response is understandable when we remember that the GPO rightly regarded itself as a cutting-edge electrical engineering organization. Yet it also serves to underline just how strange this historical moment was, when a Treasury group—albeit one of administrative experts—was taking the lead. Merriman fired off a provocative memorandum to the engineer-in-chief suggesting that Post Office Engineering was "running out of steam," that the much-vaunted possibilities in electronic telephone exchanges were "promising but somewhat limited," and that resources should be redirected to "a major, all out determination to make maximum use of electronic computing facilities as a means of reducing massively the numbers of staff involved in clerical processes" and increase "efficiency."[63] The intemperate memorandum did not place in Merriman in trouble. Instead, his O&M-style argument must have attracted the attention of Halsbury's headhunters. Very soon, Merriman was installed as Deputy Director of Treasury O&M.

The Treasury that Merriman walked into around Christmas 1955 was still a fairly small organization of fewer than 300 civil servants, kept lean and mean by an "impeccable" filing system and therefore a "minimum of paperwork." The modern Registry contrasted with the heavy sense of overlaying tradition that the old Treasury building itself embodied—"a redolent place to work in," remembered Merriman, "with its decaying floors (chalk marks on the floor 'do not put anything heavy here'), its winding back stairs up the attic (approached through an iron gateway) in which was to be found Queen Anne's hip bath—the silk brocaded room on the ground floor overlooking the quiet garden beloved by Winston Churchill and used by him as his executive office. . . ."[64] In a corner of this building was Treasury O&M. The exception to the general "open-door" rule was Milner-Barry's office, where during lunchtime "he would . . . sit with eyes closed, shoes off, and in stockinged feet on desk, prepare, in the mind, to play in his annual grand-masters tournament."[65] Merriman thought Milner-Barry "a lean ascetic man . . . very much the type of a classical administrator, a pillar of the Establishment, a product of Oxbridge, casual, apparently easy-going, well versed in 'wise saws and modern instances' and with an immense coterie of acquaintances within and without Whitehall, but principally in the Establishment." After the director, Merriman soon encountered the rest of the O&M staff: Bob Marshall (a meticulous re-drafter of documents), the rotund Bertie Oades (who looked "much more like a successful farmer than a lifelong administrator"), and Donal O'Donovan (a friend of Maurice Wilkes from whom Merriman took over direct responsibility for administrative computing with a remit to "tell us if there is anything in this business of computers in administration, and if so what we ought to do about it, and while you are doing that, see if you can get some sense into a national policy on automation."[66] (In fact, Treasury O&M already had a sense of the "business of computing"—the casualness of how Merriman remembers the order is perhaps best read as an illustration of how the ex-engineer was not overawed in his new position).

Working Milner-Barry's contacts and assisted by long-standing O&M staff such as the punched-card expert Jack Dunkley and the defense specialist G. H. S. Jordan, Merriman was soon undertaking his first task: a tour of Whitehall. "From these preliminary visits," Merriman has written, "we established a range of working contacts and formed, perhaps for the first time in Central Government a single, structured view of the logical character of both the administrative and the executive operations of Ministries and Departments together with their principal data flows and interrelationships"—a bold claim perhaps, but one firmly based in O&M methodology (and reinforced, if anything, by the engineer's background).[67] The survey, and the more detailed studies conducted in the ensuing months, served to convince Merriman that "the potential economies in Central Government were indeed large, but this could only be done by an entirely new approach in organization and strategy."

Furthermore, news from across the Atlantic suggested that American competition was heating up, and Merriman decided to take an extensive tour of the United States and Canada. Jordan had visited the United States in 1954 and established some useful contacts, but Merriman decided an engineer's eye was needed "so that the shape of things to come could be assessed by making a detailed appreciation of what was going on in research and development laboratories and allied organizations."[68] In September 1956, Merriman, accompanied by the young GPO engineer Murray Laver, flew out on a slow and noisy four-engine BOAC DC-6. Their pulses must have quickened when they witnessed the remarkable developments in computing technology underway in IBM's laboratories at Poughkeepsie, at NCR in Dayton, at Remington Rand in Philadelphia (where they met Grace Hopper), at the National Bureau of Standards and the Bureau of Census in Washington, at MIT and Caltech, in the Central Administration of the State of California at Sacramento, and at the US Post Accounting Center at Richmond, although none of the technical wonders of these familiar sites seems to have made an impression as telling as the "permanent deep scoring" on a drum store of an experimental real-time airline seat reservation system in Hartford. The emotional charge of the latter drum memory, some 6 feet in length, was its supposed capacity of 100 megabytes. The duo also witnessed small core memories at IBM. The problems of large-scale data storage, so important for business and governmental data processing, were clearly being attacked from many directions in the United States. The slow journey home on a Cunard ship, the *Caronia*, gave Merriman and Laver a chance to digest what they had seen on their six-week tour. "What this visit did convince us," recalls Merriman, "was that our formulating ideas about the relevance of Automatic Data Processing in office organization and administration . . . were on the right lines but if anything we had underestimated the force and character of the developments that were already apparent and beginning to be brought into everyday operation in America."

Back in London, Merriman immediately began work on a report for joint Permanent Secretary of the Treasury and head of the Home Civil Service, Sir Norman Brook. Merriman's report, completed in February 1957, contained a comprehensive survey of existing government data-processing projects (despite protestations that "the technique of automatic data processing is too fluid, too unresolved, and too little practiced as yet to enable estimates to be given with accuracy"), made a number of significant recommendations, and was well received.[69] Otto Clarke considered it "first class."[70] Merriman argued that the government should commit to a substantial program of computer installation, accompanied by a committee structure topped by a high-level

Standing Advisory Committee. A 10-year program was to be divided into two equal phases. In the first phase, automatic data processing would be used to perform "relatively conventional tasks . . . such as payroll, statistics, or stores processing." In the second phase, "some direct advantage may be beginning to be apparent in terms of staff savings, greater immediacy of statistical information, greater speed on stores processing etc. and detailed planning of major integrated processing systems, possibly on a supra-departmental scale, would start."[71]

Merriman envisaged, with a program expenditure of £10 million, a staff saving of between 10,000 and 15,000 posts and a net annual saving before the end of the 1960s of between £1 million and £3 million. The installation of computers in government departments involved major organizational changes, requiring the "application of considerable expert knowledge," with long-term consequences in terms of staff, finance and technique. These changes, Merriman argued, along with "the waning significance of Departmental boundaries in such [data-processing] systems," established the case for a "body, free of Departmental interest, to superintend and coordinate . . . planning." He continued:

> The effects of these [changes] seem more likely to be assessable in a unit having strong liaison with Treasury O and M; the fact-finding techniques used by Treasury O and M seem to be an indispensable part of the preliminaries to EDP [Electronic Data Processing] and at the highest level the association of Treasury O and M with the work of Machinery of Government makes for better appreciation of the major issues of a supra-departmental nature that seem very likely to arise from EDP studies.

A strong Treasury O&M Division would therefore provide functional servicing for the high-level committee, advise other Treasury Divisions and other departments, plan major installations, advise and assist departments on specific systems, organize relevant research and development, train staff, and provide information. Below Treasury O&M would be subcommittees: Long-Range Planning, Technical Development, and systems planning working parties for each project. Furthermore, since "successful deployment requires close and coordinated team work between technical experts and organization and methods experts," Merriman called for a technical support structure, although he left open its specific form.[72] Lobbying for a Technical Support Unit (TSU) under Treasury O&M control had actually begun in September 1956, as the Jephcott Committee report into the DSIR calling for reforms in interdepartmental reforms was being considered, and both the NPL and DSIR had new heads.

A meeting chaired by Second Secretary to the Treasury, Sir Thomas Padmore (to whom Milner-Barry, himself no hardware expert, had explained "in words of one syllable how an electronic computer works" 2 weeks earlier[73]), made a preliminary review of the Merriman report and approved the creation of a Steering Committee for Automatic Data Processing, and, although not possessing "direct executive power," it would be "policy making" and have "compelling powers of persuasion." The Joint Permanent Secretaries ratified this approval, and the ADPSC held its first meeting in May 1957 with Padmore in the chair and with Sir Harry Campion (Central Statistical Office of the Cabinet Office), Sir Henry Hancock (Inland Revenue), Sir Harry Melville (Permanent Secretary, DSIR), Milner-Barry, Sir Edward Playfair (now Permanent Under-Secretary of State for War), and Sir Gordon Radley (Post Office) among the attendees. Merriman was almost always present by invitation. In general, the Steering Committee acted to approve, comment on, or send back reports generated within Treasury O&M. The organizational "machinery" was completed by the formation of the ADP Advisory Committee, chaired by Alec Johnston and containing some of the brightest names in postwar office computerization outside the Civil Service, including James Pitman, John Pinkerton (of Leo), Vivian Bowden, and Maurice Wilkes.[74]

The reorganization that led to the ADPSC and TSU held benefits and drawbacks for Treasury O&M. One benefit of the deepening of technical expertise combined with the high-level means of steering change was that a clearer expression of government interests in foreseeable technological change was articulated. Such a policy stood greater change of being implemented. A report written in 1959 for the ADPSC pinpointed the "subjects on which further research [was] essential to the Government ADP program and on which little or nothing seems to be going on in this country."[75] Foremost was magnetic tape technology, on which Treasury O&M argued "many of the ADP systems coming into use in the next few years" were "critically dependent." It was therefore "vital" for the government to "ensure these systems work efficiently." However, while IBM and other companies were already bringing reliable magnetic tape peripherals to market, British industry was not. Indeed, it was Treasury O&M's view that such development work must be done by a "neutral, impartial body" and would be "best tackled by a Government research establishment—in conjunction with TSU" rather than by industrial firms or universities. Here again there were problems: the NPL had just redirected its research program, dropping its strand in clerical mechanization in favor of investigations in basic techniques, mechanical translation (primarily the Cold War dream of automated Russian-English translation), "learning" machines, and automatic pattern recognition.[76] The whole question of storage devices was central to government data-processing interests: a "cheap, large capacity, medium speed information store . . . capable of a change in stored information of about 10^8 bits per day," for example, "would greatly increase the scope of computers for Government work—particularly jobs involving the maintenance of huge files of information such as work in Patent Office, Inland Revenue and the Premium Savings Bond Office." "The development of such a storage medium would constitute possibly the biggest step forward in ADP for clerical work," yet again "so far as we know, no one is looking into this in the UK." Other areas clearly identified by Treasury O&M but hampered by such problems in industrial policy were data transmission and the ever-increasing cost of programming (£100,000 per year in direct salaries and "constantly rising"). The drawbacks to the reorganization were that there was still no direct control of industrial policy and that Treasury O&M's remit was beginning to narrow (for example, the more narrowly technical aspects were made the responsibility of the TSU).

To summarize: By 1957, Treasury O&M, which can be identified as a continuation of the prewar expert movement of mechanists, had established itself within Whitehall as a center of expertise in electronic data processing. While the National Physical Laboratory (and to an only marginally lesser extent the laboratories of the Ministry of Supply and the General Post Office) remained the experts in scientific computation and basic computing research, it was Treasury O&M—at its peak—that reviewed departmental needs and made recommendations for the mechanization of office work.[77] From the mid 1950s until the late 1960s, Treasury O&M participated in surveys of government departments, many of which led to the installation of office machinery and the partial replacement of clerks with computers. The technocrats of Treasury O&M championed mechanization and justified their claims using the rhetoric of modern management, economy, and efficiency.

The "Guinea Pigs"

By February 1958, seven departments had installed computers or were in the process of ordering computers, and a further 28 schemes were also under consideration, not including special-purpose operations (such as air traffic control), scientific computers, and hospital installations. The projects near the top of table 8.1 were the earliest ones and therefore the "guinea pigs."

By 1965, government departments had installed 45 computers, and under a planned acceleration of the program between 250 and 300 were envisaged within the decade. Departments varied enormously in their reactions to Treasury O&M's computerization proposals. The armed services were

Table 8.1
Program of government department clerical computer projects, as projected in February 1958. Sources: PRO T 222/1304. "General summary of major ADP systems in hand or being planned," February 1958. PRO T 222/1331. "Progress summary of ADP projects as at December 1960."

Department	Purpose	Delivery	Make and location
Board of Trade	Census of Production, Census of Distribution	1957	Elliott (later NCR) 405 Eastcote
Ministry of Supply and National Assistance Board	Payroll	1957	Hec (ICT 1201) Chessington
Inland Revenue	Statistics	1958	ICT PCC Canons Park
Ministry of Agriculture, Fisheries and Food	Fatstock and fertilizer subsidy payments	1958–59	Two ICT 1201s Guildford
General Post Office	Supplies Department	1958	Hec (ICT 1201) Studd Street, London
HMSO	stores accounting, payroll	1958	Hec (ICT 1201) London
General Post Office	Payroll, statistics	1958–59	Two Elliott (later NCR) 405s London
Admiralty	Dockyard accounting	1959–60	Two ICT PCCs each Portsmouth, Devonport, Chatham Dockyards
Ministry of Pensions and National Insurance	Payroll, statistics, accounting for postal draft	1959–60	LEO II Newcastle
General Register Office	Census of Population	1961	Ancillary equipment only (RAPC computer used for 1961 Census) Titchfield
Ministry of Agriculture, Fisheries and Food	Agricultural census	1960	Deuce Guildford
Agriculture (Scotland)	Agricultural census, fatstock and cereal subsidies, payroll	1960	ICT 1202 Edinburgh
War Office—Royal Army Pay Corps	Soldiers' pay	1960	IBM 705 Worthy Down

Department	Purpose	Delivery	Make and location
Customs & Excise	Overseas trade and navigation statistics, accounting, payroll, warehouse accounting	1960–1963	Elliott 405 (?) Southend
Ministry of Labour	Statistics, payroll	1960	EMI 1100 Watford
Ministry of Transport and Civil Aviation	Accounting, payroll	(1960)	Canceled after ministry split up
Northern Ireland	Accounting, subsidy, payroll	1961?	
War Office	Civilian payroll	1961?	
War Office—Royal Army Ordnance Corps	Stores accounting	1960–1963	EMI 2400 Chilwell[a] and Donnington
Ministry of Pensions and National Insurance	Graduated pensions scheme	1961	EMI 2400 Newcastle
Ministry of Works	Accounting, works costing, stores accounting, payroll, statistics	1962	ICT 1301 London
Air Ministry	Civilian payroll	1961	EMI 1100 Handforth
Air Ministry	RAF pay and records	1964	
Air Ministry	RAF equipment supplies	1962	AEI 1010[b] Hendon
Home Office, Metropolitan Police and Prison Commission	Payroll, statistics	1963	
Ministry of Education	Accounting, teachers' records	1962	Greater London
Inland Revenue	PAYE	1964	Scotland
Ministry of Supply—Royal Ordnance Factories	Stock control, production control	1962	
Admiralty	Naval stores	1961	EMI 1100 Copenacre

a. See PRO T 222/1087. Reports of interdepartmental working-party on application of EDP to stores work in the Army, 1957–59.

b. The AEI 1010 cost £1.3 million and was much criticized by Merriman, who blamed overly persuasive salesmen.

generally, in Merriman's opinion, "quick off the mark," but the Paymaster General's Office, "the central banking/accounting operation for all Government money transfers . . . a vast docket handling, paper handling machine," was not at all keen.[78] It took many years and much negotiation before that office, the Post Office Savings Banks, and the five biggest British private banks introduced standardized machine-readable check formats, the Inter-Bank-Research-Organization, and the "Swift" automatic-funds-transfer system. Several questions can be asked about this reorganization of administrative work: What sort of work was mechanized? Did the installations merely replace existing methods (punched card, or hand)? Was the program justified by economies in staff and increased efficiency? How did the changes in the capacity for administration relate to wider changes in the Civil Service? To answer such questions, it is useful to examine some important schemes in greater detail: the Chessington payroll installations, the centralization of statistical work, the shaping of the Royal Army Pay Corps computer, and the ambitious computerization of the Ministry of Pensions and National Insurance office at Newcastle.

Guinea Pig (1): The Civil Service Payroll

The Chessington project illustrates two of the recurring themes of mechanization: the replacement of human clerks and the tendency toward centralization. Three departments were initially included in the South London scheme to mechanize the payroll of 21,000 pay accounts (including 4,800 weekly wage payments): the Ministry of Supply, the National Assistance Board, and the Ordnance Survey. The existing method of payroll accounting was purely clerical in the cases of the Assistance Board and Ordnance Survey, whereas the Ministry of Supply made use of clerks and simple keyboard accounting machines to process a larger number of pay accounts.[79] The scheme retained the existing organization of work, the mechanized system being a direct mirror image of the clerical system. Chessington employed "Hec" hybrid machines (electronic punched-card installations with limited programmability) rather than a more experimental stored-program computer. The "Hollerith Electronic Computer" ("Hec"), made by British Tabulating Machines, was the less risky, immediately available option. Other departments also ordered Hecs in the mid 1950s to augment existing punched-card and clerical systems, usually to cut staff costs (the expected saving for the three Chessington departments was between £33,000 and £59,000). Completed in late 1957, Chessington was the first, simple application of programmable electronic machinery to routine government data-processing work. Later it provided the center for a centralized Civil Service payroll system. In common with other early computerization projects in government departments, such as the 1958 Census of Production at the Board of Trade, the process was imagined to be one of merely speeding up the existing organization.[80]

Guinea Pig (2): The Production of Statistics

Speed in the production of statistics was tied to broad issues in British economic policy. Recall from chapter 6 that mid-twentieth-century informational changes were shaped by the extent to which the British economy was to be directed. The 1944 white paper on Employment Policy, which had committed the United Kingdom to Keynesian demand management of the economy, noted the repercussions on statistics production:

> The success of the Government's policy . . . will depend on the skill which is shown in putting general ideas into day-to-day practice. It is therefore vital for them to obtain more fully and much more quickly than they have in the past, exact quantitative information about current economic movements. Without this, informed control would be impossible and the central staff which it is proposed to set up would be left to grope and flounder in uncertainty.[81]

In the wartime command economy, statistics could be generated as a by-product of the process of government. Legislative changes, such as the Statistics of Trade Act of 1947, gave the government greater powers to secure information from sources less easily controlled, such as private firms. Censuses of Production, previously held at lengthy and irregular intervals, were held in 1948 and then annually from 1950 on. A new full Census of Distribution was held in 1950. Although the decision was taken in 1951 to regulate the economy by monetary policy rather than attempt to continue the peacetime command economy, the government did not lessen its demand for statistical information. Indeed, some critics complained that gaps still existed, that the time lag between collection and publication was too long, that revisions were too frequent, and that analysis was insufficient, too cautious, and poorly presented.[82] In 1954 the internal committee under Verdon Smith had raised the possibility of the use of "electronic machines" as one means of speeding up statistical production, while the think tank Political and Economic Planning argued that the use of computers would help attract statisticians to government work (a constant postwar issue, given the relative salaries able statisticians could demand from commercial employment).[83] However, besides speed and human resources, computerization of statistical work also allowed questions of centralization to be raised.

Treasury O&M viewed the production of statistics, along with payroll work, accounting, and armed services stores control, as core applications of electronic computers. In this context, it is fair to say, they regarded computers primarily as faster punched-card installations. Government-produced statistics, however, have a special significance: as Miles and Irvine point out, "the data that official publications provide can be obtained nowhere else, for the state is the only institution in modern society with both the economic resources and political mandate needed to generate it in large quantities on a national scale."[84] As we saw in chapter 6, the Government Statistical Service and the Central Statistical Office (CSO) were set up in 1941 and grew in the next three decades, particularly under GSS head Claus Moser during Wilson's premiership. This period was also one of increasing mechanization: clerks were augmented by punched-card machines and later by electronic computers. Statistical knowledge of the nation multiplied as the use of computers amplified the work of the expanding CSO. However, statistical work was still dispersed widely across government departments. Although centralization was a major theme of the mechanization of statistics, in practice it proved very difficult. Separate and incompatible computer installations were already under consideration for use by the Inland Revenue, the Ministry of Labour, and the Board of Trade in 1955, when a Working Party of O&M officers met to consider the issue. The Working Party, after surveying government statistical work, produced an interim report for the second meeting of the ADP Steering Committee in June 1958.[85]

The Working Party's interim report raised the possibility of establishing a "Ministry of Statistics," on the American model, which would have "executive responsibility for the collection and production of Government statistics other than those derived as by-products of a Department's main work." (The proposal raised the same hackles as did the earlier one for a centralized, executive British Empire Statistical Bureau.) The "Ministry" would therefore be restricted to census type surveys: the Census of Population, the Censuses of Production and Distribution, the Agricultural Census, the Family Expenditure Survey, and the Retail Price Index. As an alternative to this major reorganization, the Working Party also outlined a "central processing installation" akin to HMSO's Combined Tabulating Installation. Individual departments distrusted these centralized schemes, since they involved a loss of control over speed and direction of statistical production, as well as raising problems of confidentiality. But the ADP Steering Committee, which regarded a measure of centralization as necessary, was persuaded by arguments such as the following from Sir Henry Hancock:

> However right it may have been to permit Departments a fair degree of freedom to establish their computer systems in the early days of development, the time was now

approaching when a more robust insistence should be made upon an increasing measure of shared use in those cases where Departments were not using, or could not justify the use of, a computer on a full-time basis. Care should be taken, however, not to act in any way that would suppress departmental enthusiasm and invention.[86]

Sharing of computers by two or three departments was as far as centralization extended: the War Office's Royal Army Pay Corps collaborated with the General Register Office for the 1961 census, but a joint Customs and Excise/Ministry of Labour and National Service/Board of Trade computer was scuppered by the argument that each department should have "complete and unfettered control over its own processing."[87] Therefore, even in the statistics field, where "the case for centralization was stronger . . . than in any other," strong departmental interests proved a considerable obstacle, and a plan for a government centralized processing installation was put on hold until the CSO and the Economic Advisers had completed a broad review of the possible use of computers as aids to long-term statistical forecasting. The Working Party's studies ended in December 1959. The creation of the ADP Steering Committee came slightly too late to significantly shape the fundamental structure of computerized government statistics production, as the Working Party had warned:

If a decision on centralization is delayed, the question will answer itself, because once the necessary programs for departmental jobs have been written for a variety of incompatible machines (at a cost of many man-years of work) and departmental pride in ownership has been built up, the prospect of work being centralized within the next decade would be remote.[88]

The significance of this outcome lies in its implications for the kinds of knowledge made available (for example, cross-referencing between different databases would produce novel statistical information) and for the distribution of power in Whitehall (e.g., the question of who would be gatekeeper of government statistical production would have been raised).

Guinea Pig (3): The Census and the Army Share an Expensive Resource

When Parliament was told in 1962 that the War Office's computerization of the payroll for the Royal Army Pay Corps was believed to be "the most complex system in operation on a computer anywhere," it was an exaggeration.[89] The American SAGE command and control system, for example, was complete and much more impressive. But the military context had justified importing the latest American machine (the IBM 705), and the project had been designed with capacity to spare. The reason for this can be found in

British foreign policy of the 1950s. When computerization of the RAPC's payroll work was planned, young men were still conscripted into a year's national service, and the country still held onto notions of Great Power status. The botched invasion of Egypt after Nasser seized the Suez Canal in 1956, and in particular the consequent US opposition to the escapade, soon brought such illusions of grandeur down to earth. In the years after Suez, the British Army's commitments were scaled down. But by then the RAPC computer had already been planned to handle the payroll of potentially millions of men. Under Cold War conditions, and with the possibility of emergency mobilization, this extra capacity could be justified. Therefore, when civil servants in the General Register Office began thinking about the mechanical arrangements of the 1961 Census of Population, they were very interested to hear about computing resources going unused.

The 1951 census had been considered too early for the application of an electronic stored-program computer. Instead the GRO had deployed Universal Printing Counting Sorters built by Powers to prewar designs. In September 1953, a GRO team gathered at the Southport tabulation center to consider the options. One of their number had stopped off in Manchester on his way up from London to visit the Ferranti Mark I at the University, but was not reassured by what he saw, remaining "unconvinced that conventional punched card methods can be eliminated by the 1961 Census."[90] Instead, the GRO team offered suggestions of technical improvements to Powers, including circuit diagrams, for the rickety old Universal Printing Counting Sorters.

But Ferranti got wind of the GRO's interest. Swann, one of the company's managers, expressed confidence that an electronic computer could do the job in 1961, and he had high hopes that by then the firm would have experience, having computerized the 1956 Census of the Irish Republic.[91] To this sales pressure must be added the influence of Treasury O&M, which by 1956 was leading government computerization. Despite views expressed within the GRO that the department would not be ready to computerize the census until 1971, Treasury O&M's confidence in the technology gave reassurance.[92]

The GRO now became ambitious, planning to complete the processing of census data in just 2 years. (Oddly, the Treasury—a different division than O&M—wanted to save money on hiring staff, and therefore dragging the processing period out.[93]) The 1961 Census of Population was, if anything, smaller than the one conducted a decade earlier. In 1951, the whole of the Schedules received were coded for Occupation, Industry, Birthplace and Nationality"; in 1961, it was "intended to apply this central coding to only 10 percent of the Schedules. . . ."[94] The Home Office fired back that due to the rise up the political agenda of immigration from the West Indies, full information on birthplace and nationality was required.[95] In general, however, the tabulation of 1961 was going to be very similar to 1951, and therefore, as was noted above, the punched-card "programme" became the computer "program."[96] So the first point to note is that the highly formalized instructions given to lower, mechanical staff were translated into lines of code. The second is that computerization proceeded despite the fact that the data-processing job was probably smaller than the previous census handled by punched cards.

The GRO tendered out specifications of the tabulation task to computer manufacturing firms. Nine tenders, including one from IBM, were received by February 1958. But the GRO had a peculiar difficulty in justifying the purchase of a computer, since processing the Census of Population data only happened on a cycle of ten years, and was therefore expensive relative to investment. At this moment, the Office became aware of spare capacity on the Royal Army Pay Corps IBM 705 computer at Worthy Down. The War Office intimated willingness to cooperate, so long as the census would be halted "in the event of a full-scale war." Registrar General, Sir George North, discussed project with Sir Edward Playfair (the Treasury O&M's ally) and Major General O. P. J. Rooney, the Paymaster-in-Chief and Inspector of Pay Services in September 1958, quickly reaching an agreement to share. Despite consequent tussles over machine time, and some delays, the arrangement was a success.

Some isolated but severe tensions seem to have arisen from part of the tabulation work contracted out to the computer services firm C-E-I-R (UK) Ltd. This new contract had been awarded after complaints were received from other government departments, in particular the Ministry of Housing and Local Government, that the delay of crucial information from the census was holding up key legislation, probably on the New Towns that were a feature of the 1950s and the 1960s. In 1966, the GRO was surprised to learn that the Greater London Council had a copy of a tape of census data, breaking laws on release of such information. The source was traced to C-E-I-R. It was first thought that individual data had been sold on. Later it emerged that the data was de-individualized. But John Boreham, chief statistician of population and censuses, wrote with alarm to his counterpart at the Greater London Council: "I need not explain to you how vitally important it is to us that everyone believes absolutely in the secrecy of what he writes on his census form. It follows from that that we must at all times keep a tight control on the use of individual data and that this 'leak' is potentially a great embarrassment to us."[97] C-E-I-R apologized, and the matter was not made public. But issues of privacy were much more sensitive in 1966 than even a few years earlier, and if the leak had reached the press there would have been a scandal. Oddly, it also came at a moment when the GRO was considering releasing individual data, albeit for "approved purposes, subject to fairly strict controls." A market for government information began to stir.

The computerization of the 1961 Census of Population of England and Wales demonstrated the easy translation of "mechanical" civil servant work to electronic data processing. It also showed the need to make best use of expensive technological resources—even if the technology was justified more by appeals to what a modern bureaucracy should be doing than by appeals to straightforward economies. Perhaps most important, the narrowly averted C-E-I-R scandal.

During the programming period of the 1961 census, there were calls to use the COBOL language, since it was thought that learning a new language would interest the staff and that it would be easier to transfer the programs to whatever machine was used in 1971.[98] It is not clear whether this happened, or if it was overtaken by work for the unexpected mini-census held in 1966. This mini-census, which involved a 10 percent sample of the population of England and Wales, is interesting to us because of arguments over which machine to use. There were four options: use the Royal Army Pay Corps computer again, purchase a second-hand IBM 705 from the United States, or hire a powerful computer and either write new routines or simulate the 705 and run the old programs.[99] The GRO came under considerable pressure to pursue the latter two options, making use of the London Ferranti Atlas, an ailing British flagship project. But since a public ministerial commitment had been made to complete the mini-census in under 2 years, the GRO was able to secure its preferred cautious option and to purchase its own IBM 705.

Guinea Pig (4): Transforming the Pensions Offices

The fourth case, the Ministry of Pensions and National Insurance (MPNI) offices at Newcastle, draws attention to a different aspect of computerization: the process does not always merely reproduce an existing organization of data processing. Unlike, for example, the Chessington payroll scheme, the MPNI project involved extensive rethinking and reorganization of the information system: the MPNI used a complicated system of ledgers to record insured contributors, and it was not a case of replacing punched cards with stored electronic data.[100] This root-and-branch approach made for delays: although it was the first office computer project begun, a machine was not installed until late 1959. However, complexity was not the only reason for the delays in the MPNI project. The chairman of the group examining the Newcastle office, F. M. Colebrook, died suddenly and was replaced by R. H. Tizard (head of the

National Physical Laboratory's Electronics Division and son of the paragon of scientific advice, Sir Henry Tizard).[101] The early stages of the project were also the responsibility of the NPL scientists, at a time when Treasury O&M was growing in influence. Initially, members of the NPL team thought of the project in their own terms, describing, for example, how the MPNI procedures could be carried out with an English Electric DEUCE computer—the commercial version of the NPL Pilot Ace. Tizard's insistence that computer chosen be completely British, and the fact that no British company yet made the magnetic tape storage systems demanded by the scheme, also led to delays, and to observations from Treasury O&M that the "people in NPL may be more protectionist than the Government."[102] (Tizard resigned in May 1956 and left the NPL for academia.[103]) Finally, it was certainly the suspicion of some that the NPL dragged its feet, and indeed the NPL dropped out of clerical mechanization work by 1960.[104] The deliberations over the choice of computer system were resolved when Lyons (who along with the NRDC had earlier encouraged the MPNI study) pushed for the installation of one of their LEO II computers.

The introduction of the LEO II to handle the department's payroll and process national insurance and benefits statistics was merely the start of a rolling program of computerization in a large and complex organization. The Newcastle Central Office grew to be one of the largest employers in the north of England (more than 10,000 people by the mid 1980s). Innovation in organization and technology went hand in hand, often prompted by shifting policies of welfare provision—policies that were only *allowed* by the innovations, a good example of the reflexive relationship between governmental and technological change. The LEO II was followed in 1961 by an EMIDEC 2400, "conceived to record graduated contributions, to identify persons approaching pension age, and to calculate graduated pensions. It did not replace an existing system and had the new scheme been done clerically, rather than by computer process, it would have been heavily staff-intensive" (and therefore, probably, too expensive).[105] In the early 1970s, large ICL 1906A batch-processing mainframes were installed to replace the EMI machine, converting to decimalization at the same time. In 1977 they were networked to centers at Reading (west of London) and Livingston (in Scotland). The clerically maintained General Index of national insurance contributors, more than 50 million accounts, was only computerized in 1982, using the next generation of ICL mainframes (twin ICL 2982s). There was a parallel program to reorganize benefit payments, gradually extending the range of computerization as the limited LEO II was replaced by four ICL mainframes (in 1968–69) and an ICL 2970 (in 1976)[106] This rolling process continued into the 1980s with the

Operational Strategy, the plan to "convert all existing systems and to introduce new ones all based on the concept of a Departmental network of computers whose data can be accessed directly from a corresponding network of Visual Display Terminals . . . situated in HQ, central and local offices." Routinely described as the "biggest and most widely embracing series of coordinated ADP projects ever undertaken in the UK," this real-time, networked project is discussed in chapter 10. I mention it here to show that Whitehall computerization projects could entail the overhaul of departmental organizations and could take decades to develop.

The four subsections above can be summarized as follows: Studies with a view to the computerization of some government work began in the early 1950s and led to a handful of "guinea pig" installations by the end of the decade, although there was a rush soon after. Some computer installations involved major reorganizations of work; others simply replaced the punched-card "programme" with a computer "program." Treasury O&M displaced NPL as the body undertaking these reviews and making recommendations.[107] After 1957, during Merriman's tenure, Treasury O&M even began to comment on proposals for scientific work in research establishments and defense projects.[108] However, some contingent effects curtailed Treasury O&M's influence—for example, the change in the committee structure that established the ADP Steering Committee, the TSU, and the strong Treasury O&M Division came too late to effectively push for centralization, a problem exemplified by the case of the production of statistics.

What Computers Can and Can't Do

So far I have analyzed the studies and projects that led to the introduction of the first computers in government departments. Before turning to the mid-1960s acceleration of the computer program, I wish to examine broader debates within Whitehall over the *limits* of possible computer application.

All bodies examining clerical mechanization cast the debate in terms of a choice "between automatic electronic machinery, punched card machinery and human operatives." However, there existed differences between the groups as to how they portrayed the human clerk. For an NPL scientist the differences lay in inherent technical characteristics. Ted Newman, for example, found four: speed of operation, storage available at operation speed, series or parallel operation, the ability to "size up the problem," and offered rough figures for comparative assessment: for speed the ratio between computer, punched card, and human was 100,000 : 50 : 1, whereas for storage the "brain wins easily" (5×10^5, 250, and 10^9 bits respectively).[109] Treasury O&M had only a slightly less technical and functional model of the Civil Service clerk: they were well aware, for example, that direct replacement of human with machine was never the case in practice since it was always accompanied by a redistribution of skill and expertise—more technical support and more management. Both groups, however, mobilized the quantified estimates of human-machine differences in making economic arguments for mechanization and in indicating rough limits to computer application. As an indicator that Treasury O&M largely agreed with Newman's drawing of the civil servant-machine boundary, his four differences were published in the *O&M Bulletin*:

(1) Man has a relatively large storage capacity.
(2) Man's time per unit operation is relatively slow.
(3) Man can do many operations in parallel.
(4) Man can carry out inductive processes.[110]

Opposition to the expanding province of machines in Whitehall came from organizations representing civil servants and from skeptics among the generalists. The concerns of the representative organizations had many parallels with the worries about automation generally, which peaked in public forums in the late 1950s and the early 1960s. Richard Hayward, Secretary General of the Civil Service National Whitley Council (Staff Side), began complaining in 1956 that "moves towards automation" should not be made without "adequate staff consultation."[111] Such pleas were forwarded to Sir Alexander Johnston and Treasury O&M, who formulated a response. The Treasury's strategy was threefold (and somewhat contradictory). First, the Treasury played down the similarities between routine Civil Service work and the operations of a computer. For example, whereas internal memorandums recorded that "it is already clear that most clerical work . . . can theoretically be performed by computing machines," the statement made to a meeting of Treasury, Whitley Council, and the Civil Service Clerical Association was mild: computerization was "unlikely to have revolutionary effects at any rate in the foreseeable future."[112] Also removed were suggestions that Civil Service work *was* largely information processing. Second, the Treasury argued that computerization was nothing new, and that the development of this form of mechanization in the Civil Service should be regarded as a natural sequel to earlier stages of mechanization. Finally, the Treasury suggested that, with routine clerical drudgery lessened, the quality of Civil Service work would rise. The Staff Side did not attempt to halt mechanization completely; it restricted its actions to requests for early consultation and unspecified "safeguards."

One reason why mechanization was difficult to resist was because it was tied to wide-scale reformations of the lower Civil Service. Prime Minister Anthony Eden had announced in January 1956 that he was seeking cuts in Civil Service numbers, and the hunt for cuts accompanied social changes in recruitment. The 1957 decision to allow products of Secondary Moderns as well as those of more prestigious schools to join the Civil Service was designed to "bring into better relationship the school-leaving potential and the recruitment needs of the Civil Service," but also "to make full and rapid use of improved office machinery." The class and gender assumptions of this reorganization are illustrated by the following passage:

> The best advice procurable suggests that when electronic computer units are installed the clerical work which more readily lends itself to treatment included pay rolls; stores accounting; billing; recording; check and order book payments and probably a good deal more. . . . The effect would be to take away a large amount of middle-range clerical work which can be programmed for electronic computers by good logical-minded clerical or executive types and then be processed by machine operators. The former calls for selective recruitment of men and women for the type of work, and the latter seems more suitable for women and girls who appear to be not only good at it, but like it.[113]

Views of what changes in Civil Service structure might accompany the introduction of computers ranged from the elimination of routine work, to the influx of new groups to act as machine operators, to reassuring visions of no change at all. In such circumstances it was natural that the Whitley Staff Side would express their concerns over the changes in Civil Service working conditions. However, it was also in the nature of Whitleyism to forge cooperative agreements rather than follow the union-management pattern of conflict: Merriman recalled, for example, how Hayward was in fact a "powerful ally" to the cause: "He perceived very quickly the importance and significance of 'computerization' to clerical unions and their members and together with the then General Secretary Leslie Williams, I was able to have many valuable informal discussions on points of sensitivity and how they could be overcome in the common good."[114]

Opposition, although of a very different kind, also came from skeptics among the higher civil servants. This time the reaction was not against proposals to mechanize routine work but against suggestions that computers might replace parts of management. Consider what is at stake in the following, otherwise amusing, Treasury O&M anecdote:

> "The days of 'steam O and M' are numbered—the future lies with ADP [Automatic Data Processing]." This view was expressed by a Senior Administrator some years ago.

It provoked the pert retort "As this assumes that the Computer will perform reasoning and judgment for Management presumably the days of the Administrator are also numbered."[115]

A telling illustration of the relationship between computers and management can be found in the outcome of a role-playing business game. IBM, the dominant American manufacturer of office machinery and lately computers, had constantly sought entry into the British market. IBM's often more powerful and relatively cheap products found buyers in the private sector, but various factors (not least the government's reluctance to spend dollars and its desire to protect the fledgling British industry) weighed against government expenditure on American machines.[116] As a means of demonstrating its wares, IBM (UK) Ltd. imported a novel method. IBM's Management Decision Making Laboratory was based on the Harvard Business Game, and essentially involved players managing competing companies, their decisions simulated and judged by an IBM 650 computer. In late 1958, Merriman of Treasury O&M took part, competing against academics and representatives from Rolls Royce, British Rail, and Shell. The experience impressed Merriman, who wrote "I feel convinced that there should be some appreciation of the relevance of these techniques to [Civil] Service problems."[117] The significance for Merriman lay in the use of the IBM computer to simulate a simplified economy and to judge strategies—work typically done by managers and high-level administrators. The reaction of Otto Clarke of the Treasury's Economic Section is worth quoting in full:

> Mr. Merriman's note is very interesting. I am not yet entirely convinced—it is good skull-drill (and as most of us suffer from chronic mental under-employment, very salutary), but is it much better than the Naval War Game, or for that matter, chess or croquet? I thought Mr. Merriman put his finger on the point when he said that this simulation of real life was meaningful only if real life situations could be expressed in mathematical and quasi-mathematical terms. But public administration does not throw up this kind of question (not nearly as much as business does). Mr. Merriman mentions the theory of games, which is essentially mathematical. But what we need is the theory of negotiation—how you find the course that appears mutually advantageous for everyone, and thus acceptable. This (alas!) isn't mathematical at all—the academic pundits derive from a wide range of disciplines. Indeed, I am inclined to think that Mr. Merriman is tending to over-estimate the importance of this mathematical kind of thinking throughout the service. The PO engineers have their quasi-economic problems . . . and it would no doubt help if they could perform their tasks better; but the real difficulty of the institution is that the whole basis of its criteria of profitability and accountancy is confused and riddled with woolly "social" ideas—better calculations on an erroneous basis may well lead to answers which are *more* misleading and wasteful, rather than less. . . . The existence of a clear objective and criteria for decisions in business contrasts so sharply with the multiple objectives and conflicting

criteria in the public service that the parallels which are often drawn are to my mind very superficial.[118]

So for Clarke the complex and open character of public administration precluded the quantifying approach of computer simulation—the ideal civil servant would still be arts-based, not automatic. However, it would be wrong to interpret Clarke—or, to the extent that Clarke's attitude was typical, the higher Civil Service—as technophobic. Clarke, for example, produced for Sir Norman Brook—at the behest of Lord Hailsham, who thought the subject might produce material for the Conservative Party manifesto—an important report on automation in June 1959.[119] Furthermore, in the same year he strongly endorsed the application of computers by the Economic Section to long-term forecasting. (The idea came from the Economic Section's W. A. B. Hopkin, who had attended the IBM game on Merriman's advice.[120]) Clarke's reaction here must be seen against the background of the Plowden Committee's highlighting of the importance of long-term surveys.[121] With the collaboration of the Central Statistical Office, and in particular the personal backing of Sir Harry Campion, computers were used to predict national income and expenditure from late 1959. This application is even more surprising insofar as the Economic Section generally distrusted complex economic modeling as a guide to long-term change.[122]

The skepticism of the generalists—the Permanent Secretaries and their immediate underlings—was overcome by what Merriman called "a year of indoctrination and implementation" in 1959. For 4 months, seminars were held in the magnificent rooms of Carlton House Terrace, overlooking the Duke of York Steps on the Admiralty Arch side. "It was not an easy matter," recalled Merriman, "persuading coldly logical [sic!] Permanent Secretaries, Deputy Secretaries, Under Secretaries and Assistant Secretaries of the power and potential of a new technological thing . . . but somehow we hit the right note." Perhaps the presence among Treasury O&M of "three or four talented members of the Treasury Amateur Dramatics Society helped," since (Merriman noted) "one technique of getting the generalists' attention was quarter-hour 'playlets' which 'sent up' traditional routine office work in an attempt to get across the utterly automatic routine nature of a large proportion of the work, the opportunities that existed for error and efficiency, and, as well, tried to develop in fairly simple terms some basic understanding of computers, control, automation, communications and logic."[123] Merriman found it "interesting and utterly absorbing to see the way in which the classical administrators, by the middle of the first afternoon, were seeing through our little charades, getting the cold logical point, and by the middle of the second morning were starting to expose the basic programming steps in problems that we were setting—indeed to the extent that by the end of that morning many were writing reasonably complicated logical programming sequences for a hypothetical computer situation."

By such charades—play-acting repetitive clerks like Capek's robots—the upper echelons of the British Civil Service learned to see their own organization in terms of the modern machine. They were thus well prepared when the Conservative regime of the 1950s and early 1960s was replaced by Labour when Harold Wilson's party won the general election of 1964.

The Acceleration of the Government Program

Computers aligned perfectly with the white-hot modernization rhetoric of the early Wilson years (perhaps too perfectly—see figure 8.7 for a satirical view). Since the link between efficiency and computers had been forged in the *public* mind through the automation anxieties of the early 1960s, Labour ministers appreciated the benefits of a managed display of government commitment to information technologies. On New Year's Day 1965, Chancellor of the Exchequer James Callaghan, impressed by the work of Treasury O&M, ordered "a quick review of the forward ADP [Automatic Data Processing] programs for Government departments," with particular regard to "the scope for accelerating and expanding the existing programmes" and to "the implications of this in terms of extra expenditure, extra staff etc. on the one hand and longer-term savings on the other."[124] A press release announcing the review was issued the following day.

However, as in other areas, Labour found that the outgoing Tory government had not in fact been lax: 45 computers were already installed, with a further 42 on order. The Plowden Committee had claimed in 1961 that the Civil Service was "in the forefront of national progress in the use of computers," a statement endorsed by the Estimates Committee in 1964. Treasury O&M estimated "terminal levels" of computers in government to be about 220—a figure that would probably be reached "around the early 1980s,"[125] although in another report O&M outlined the possibility of accelerating the computer program by ordering an extra 200 computers.[126] This was at a time when about 1,000 were installed across Britain.[127] Note, however, that this a period of particularly rapid change: whereas in 1958 comparison between the public and private sectors of the use of computers was relatively straightforward, the situation in the mid 1960s was much more fluid.[128]

INSTRUCTIONS FOR PUNCHING OF SAMPLE

Lower the Gang Punch levers on Columns 3 to 11 and 25 to 27; set skip stops on Columns 28, 36, 38, 49, 54, 56 and 63.

Card Columns

GANG PUNCH SETTING

3–6 Punch the Registration District number in Columns 3 to 5 and Sub-District number in Column 6 (as shown at the head of each form). Where the Sub-District number is ten or more, over punch V and the units figure. Check that the Number is unchanged when commencing each fresh form, revising the setting whenever necessary.

7–11 Punch the Area Code shown on the front cover of the volume. If several codes are shown begin with the first one; a blank sheet will be inserted to indicate the change of code and that re-setting is necessary.

NORMAL PUNCHING

Set the margin stop to begin at Column 25.

Forms E.6.
(Enumerator's Sample Extract)

25–27 For the first line of each schedule (see 1st column of Part III of E.6) punch the Enumeration District number shown at the head of the form in columns 25 and 26, overpunching V in column 25 to indicate 100 and X to indicate 200. Punch the hundreds of the Schedule number in column 27. Where the number is less than 100 punch 0 in column 27.

For subsequent lines of each Schedule depress the skip key in order to gang punch the same information as above for columns 25 to 27.

Forms A.6.
(Registrar's Sample Extract)

For each line punch the Enumeration District number shown in the first column in columns 25 and 26 and the hundred of line number in column 27.

Where the line number is less than 100 punch 0.

Where the line number exceeds 999 adjust the margin stop then punch the thousands in column 24 and, if necessary, the tens of thousands in column 23. When punching for that Enumeration District is completed re-set the margin stop to begin at column 25.

28–37 I – Private Households, i.e. all entries on forms E.6 for which the numbers in columns 2 and 3 of Part II have not been deleted.

(a) First line of each private household.

(28–29) Punch the number of Rooms from column 3 of Part II in columns 28 and 29, prefixing the number with 0 if under 10, and overpunch 0 in column 29 if the number includes a fraction.

NOTE. The number of Persons is entered in column 2 and the number of Rooms in column 3 on the forms E.6, whereas the appropriate columns on the cards are for Persons 30 and 31 and for Rooms 28 and 29. The Rooms in column 3 must be punched before the Persons in column 2.

(30–31) Punch the number of Persons from column 2 of Part II in columns 30 and 31 prefixing the number with 0 if under 10 and overpunching V in column 30 if the number of Rooms in column 3 of the E.6 is prefixed by V.

Figure 8.4

Part of a "programme" for mechanical punching, sorting, and tabulation. This one is for the 1951 Census of Population. Such explicit instructions would have had to be produced whenever government offices were extensively mechanized. (PRO RG 19/158. "Instructions for punching," 1951)

Computers as Aids to Management

Prepared by Merriman's role-playing games and encouraged by the promotion of computing under the technocratic Wilson administration (the prime minister himself was a trained economist), generalist civil servants embraced the computer, which was increasingly seen not as a specialist tool for scientists or as a replacement for mundane clerical work but as a device that even those in the upper hierarchies of organizations might utilize. I have argued that computerization in the mid 1950s was the achievement of specialists, such as scientists, or subalterns. O&M was an expert movement whose appeal was felt most strongly by ambitious middle-ranking male civil servants—executive officers located just below the generalist class. As these groups felt ever more secure in the 1950s and the 1960s, and the project of computerization spread, interest in the subject rose up the hierarchy. Two kinds of evidence can be raised to support this claim. First, the rise up the hierarchy might be embodied by individuals: the career of Edward Playfair, sketched above, provided one such illustration. The second area of evidence is the development of software packages marketed as aids to management.

We have seen how generalists such as Otto Clarke might be dismissive of suggestions that computers could aid their work ("the Treasury equivalent of space fiction," Clarke labeled it) Yet, starting in the computing and engineering industries, software packages such as Program Evaluation Review Technique (PERT) began to penetrate Whitehall. (The PERT program had been developed in 1958 by the management firm Booz, Allen & Hamilton for the US Navy's Special Projects Office to handle the development of the Polaris intermediate-range missile. Hughes and Hughes record that 1962, the "peak year for the introduction of PERT-like programs," came to be "known among aerospace firms as the 'Year of Management Systems.'"[129]) These software packages were still promoted by the civil servants at the executive officer level, but the results of PERT were targeted at senior management. PERT can therefore be seen as a further refinement in a campaign by expert movements (primarily O&M and Operational Research) for influence within Whitehall. The departments most closely connected with engineering were the first takers: the Ministry of Transport, for example, because it already had to oversee large complex construction projects such as the new motorways. Likewise the Ministry of Aviation—latterly the Ministry of Technology—was confronted with complex management problems within aerospace, not least that of managing the Concorde (the Anglo-French supersonic airliner).

Roads provide a useful illustration of the above changes. Roads through the twentieth century became an increasingly sophisticated, even "intelligent"

Figure 8.5
The ICT 1301 computer being installed at the Ministry of Works, probably in 1963. (source: National Archive for the History of Computing, University of Manchester)

information system. Initially bare or macadamized tracks, clusters of signs began to proliferate on the roadsides, especially in the interwar years, each transmitting tiny quantities of information to the motorist. By the 1960s, the automation of traffic signals had progressed to include control by electronic stored-program computers (indeed, the first major experiment of these systems, the West London Area Traffic Control Experiment, can be viewed as the transfer, in miniaturized civil form, of military methods of organizing information, innovated originally in the context of air defense.) Just as roads themselves became dense information systems, so did the management of their construction. By the mid 1960s, more than 1,000 miles of three-lane motorway were planned in the United Kingdom, a popular program that rapidly followed the opening of the first stretch of the M6, near Preston, in 1958. Furthermore, the massive postwar increase in car ownership had encouraged an even more extensive system of trunk roads providing fast direct communication between towns. Both programs, but the latter in particular, were complicated by the sheer number of local authorities involved, by the uncertainty over routes, and by the difficulty of estimating how delays at any point in the

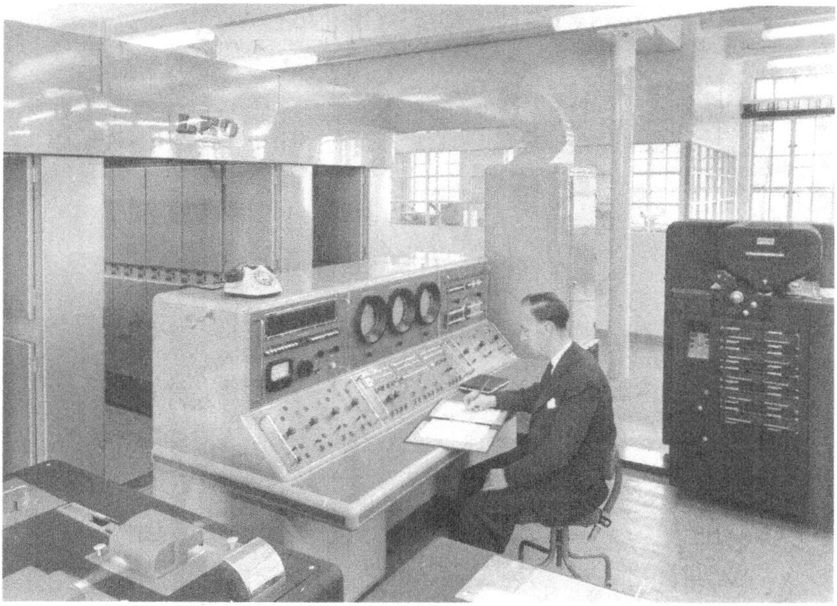

Figure 8.6
The LEO II computer. (source: National Archive for the History of Computing, University of Manchester)

schedule might impact affect the whole. By 1965 the Ministry of Transport was complaining:

> . . . at present the department was not exercising the right amount of control over the Road Program and there was a need to explore new management techniques, such as the use of PERT, to secure effective monitoring action of scheme progress and flow of payments from the time a scheme came into the program to the carrying out of construction work. The only fixed element in the Road Program was the annual financial ceiling. . . .[130]

The "enormity of [the] problem" meant that "neither the Ministry nor its agents were able to keep abreast of all the schemes in the program. This would grow with the further expansion. . . . The best hope of solving this problem was the use of PERT for the preparatory stages of highway schemes."[131] With PERT the generalist managers in Whitehall hoped to possess a controlling gaze: "more effective control over the flow of payments in the current and succeeding years," "the ability to monitor the progress of schemes," "the ability to forecast bottlenecks, for example an overload on the machinery for land

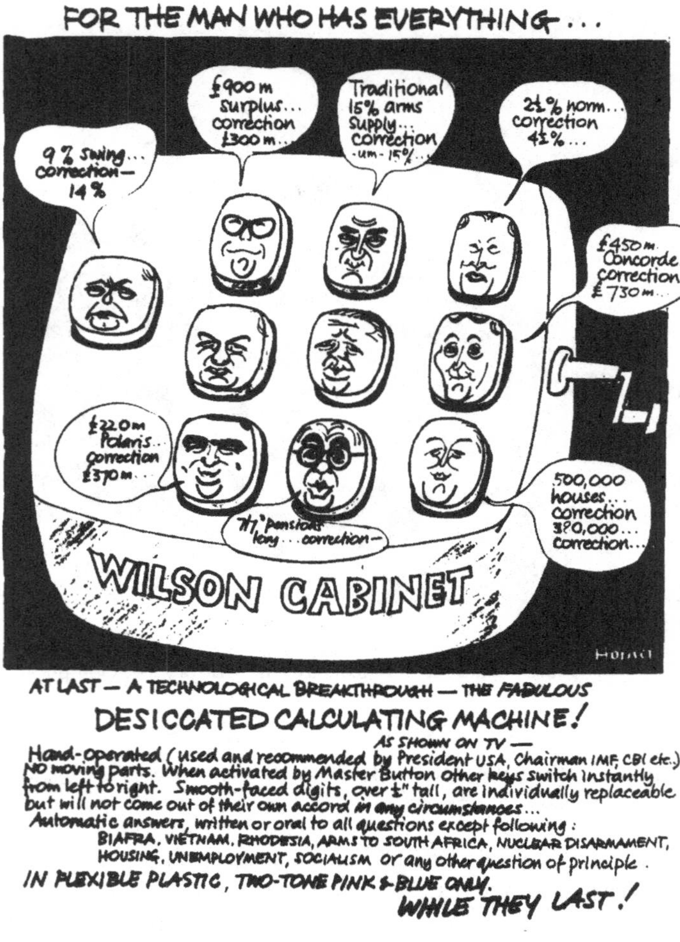

Figure 8.7

Harold Wilson's cabinet represented as a "desiccated calculating machine." The satirical point was that, although the answers the machine gave were automatic, they were also inaccurate or revised according to political expediency. (source: Centre for the Study of Cartoons and Caricature, University of Kent at Canterbury) acquisition," and "the ability to simulate results, through forward planning of the effects of, for example, slow or deferment of starts, or . . . the introduction of new factors by Ministry Headquarters."[132] The expectation had cybernetic tinges, measuring incoming against anticipated data, and then making adjustments: "we ought to be able to monitor scheme progress against expected progress and take any action that was open to use to put things right"—a government department acting like a gun predictor.[133] The episode is also a good illustration of the peculiar, and important, role played by central government: although the application of PERT to road construction was regarded, even by the Treasury O&M officers called in to review the proposal, as a marginal case for computerization, central government officials justified the expensive experiment in terms of gained experience. A pilot scheme involving roads near Durham was approved and was begun in mid 1966. However, within months, even before the experiment had been judged a "success," the Ministry of Transport was pressing for standardization: only central government was in a position to insist on compliance with centralized standards. Thus, the Ministry hoped the experiment would help "to explore the ways in which all highway authorities, whether as principals for classified road schemes or as agents for trunk and motorway schemes, can be brought to use PERT networks and then to feed the key products of these networks to us. . . ."[134] While senior management could not be expected to understand the complex network diagrams produced in the analysis, PERT did ease production of tables—which the senior managers did recognize, accompanied, presumably, by appreciation of the skills of the PERT expert who generated them. (Lower Civil Service grades' dislike of PERT was attributed by Treasury O&M management partly to ignorance and partly to time-consuming demands made by the system.[135]) PERT was subsequently promoted nationally, even before it had proved itself in the pilot scheme, because its centralizing tendencies appealed centrally, and its technocratic tendency appealed to the technocratic middle managers in their increasingly warm relationship with senior management.

The point to derive from the above is that, for various reasons, computerized aids to management became more acceptable by the mid 1960s. Both O&M and Operational Research could lay claim to PERT as their own. (PERT illustrates the shift in emphasis in the kinds of tool championed by these expert movements from hardware to software.) The spread of such techniques through local government (the giant Greater London Council adopted PERT in 1966), hospitals, and the nationalized industries helped popularize the notion of computers as management aids.[136] The spread helped further erode the notion of computers as the province of science. Computers as aids to the powerful prompted questions of what abuse of such power might be.

The language used to discuss computerization of management differed significantly from the language used to discuss computerization of clerical work. Both O&M and Operational Research emphasized the independence of decision making that remained: "In all this, management does not become a slave to the organization, but achieves increasing precision and refinement in controlling it."[137] Politicians need not feel threatened, one civil servant sought to reassure:

> I notice the view expressed in at least one department . . . that these techniques may not have much application where decisions are reached very largely on account of political considerations. This is largely misconceived; there will always be political decisions in the sense of decisions which are reached taking into account the whole variety of factors such as claims of pressure groups and so forth. This does not mean that OR or any other technique which shows the real cost of particular courses of action is useless. Ministers are always anxious to have the best and most accurate information available to them, and this enables them the better to weigh the cost of a "political" decision when this is something different from the one that, in terms of the ideal use of the available resources, would be "better."[138]

As technocrats moved closer to power, their rhetoric regarding computers became more neutral and instrumentalist. The inference can be reversed: such reassuring language can be equally read as evidence that political power increasingly accommodated the application of computers and the expert movements that promoted them.

Conclusion

In chapters 5 and 6 we saw the rise of an expert movement in the Treasury that promoted mechanization of work in government departments but was also part of a broad and diffuse community of management and machine experts. In this chapter we have seen how this movement, now named Organization and Methods, manifested itself, with a center in the Treasury and with branches in outlying departments, extending through hospitals and nationalized industries and even to large private firms, such as Shell. By the mid 1950s, Treasury O&M had been persuaded that the initially unfamiliar computer was in fact a machine that closely mirrored O&M interests. By 1960, more than 300 civil servants of executive officer rank or above were engaged on investigations into extending automatic data processing, mostly through computers, in Whitehall departments.[139] The short period 1948–1952, in which computers were regarded as specialist scientific and mathematical devices, therefore emerges as an aberration in the otherwise increasing Treasury commitment to the twin concerns of mechanization and Civil

Service control. By the early 1960s the scope of this technocratic movement was impressive. A program of extensive computerization was underway, and it provided a rare strong link between the upper echelons of the Civil Service (where the attitude of Permanent Secretaries shifted from suspicion to comfort and even enthusiasm) and the technical experts of the government physical laboratories. During the 1960s, "official visitors from overseas and from industry, commerce and local government came to O and M to learn what lessons had been distilled from O and M investigations."[140]

However, it is also correct to say that the influence of Treasury O&M declined after the mid 1960s. By the 1970s, Organization and Methods had retreated in influence, although (perhaps not unconnectedly) it also became a regular taught component in accountancy, management, and administrative science courses, spawning textbooks such as Anderson's *Organisation and Methods* (1973).[141] The retreat is difficult to explain, but was probably a combination of the transfer of knowledgeable personnel, the narrowing of Treasury O&M's scope for action, the unforeseen side effects of the reorganization of the Civil Service, and the formation of ICL.

To a minor extent the fortunes of Treasury O&M were affected by individual movements. Merriman had argued in 1960 that the expertise needed to comment on scientific and defense projects would be lost when he moved on, and he wanted his Treasury colleagues to be aware that although "TOM exercises . . . oversight for office computers" no one "appears to do it for scientific computers and you may wish to consider whether something should be done about it."[142] Following the Flowers Report, a Computer Board was set up to fulfill just this administrative function. In this and similar cases, Treasury O&M's remit was whittled away and it gradually lost its potential as an overall shaper of government mechanization. No organization that followed Treasury O&M had the same powerful combination of executive and administrative responsibilities. A set of smaller bodies with more narrowly focused agendas could not connect across the spectrum of Civil Service interests as Treasury O&M had done, nor could it thereby achieve the depth of research, evidenced by the "forward-looking" seminars on the "Mechanization of Thought Processes" jointly pursued by Treasury O&M and the National Physical Laboratory in the early 1960s, where everything from a new more profound National Register to the incipient "software crisis" were discussed. Merriman recalls:

> We looked at automatic translation. We looked at the possibility of codifying the basic logical processes of legal judgment taking, we looked at the possible implications of a single totally rationalized personalized data base for all legislative and administrative purposes, and we began to look at the possibilities of software language structure,

foreseeing the growing inability of programming forces to organize themselves to deal with tasks of mammoth and increasing complexity.[143]

Such seminars could bring together top NPL researchers with generalist future Civil Service high fliers—for example, Douglas Wass, later Treasury permanent secretary and Head of the Civil Service.[144] Such connections were broken with the decline of Treasury O&M.

In MacDonagh's account of experts in government, outlined in the first chapter, the nineteenth-century rise and flourishing of experts was ended when their influence was reined in and control reasserted around the turn of the century by generalists. I have already shown that a single rise and fall of experts is not an accurate historical picture: the rise and fall of many overlapping expert movements provides a better one. However, the pattern does therefore suggest one possible answer to the decline of Organization and Methods as an expert movement of influence: that other civil servants, jealous of O&M's technocratic claim to authority, actively sought to undermine the movement. I can find no evidence that this was the case. Indeed, the moment at which O&M's influence turned—the Wilson years of Mintech—seems, prima facie, to be one in which the prospects for O&M's continuing influence were good. Therefore, a simple answer along these lines must be rejected. But it was also certainly the case that a series of profound decisions having to do with the Civil Service's organization, taken in the mid to late 1960s, had the effect of breaking up the broad reach of O&M and replacing it by a more narrowly focused set of bodies. The 1968 report of the Fulton committee on the future of the Civil Service backfired in this respect. That report opened with a homily that the "Home Civil Service today is still fundamentally the product of the nineteenth-century philosophy of the Northcote-Trevelyan Report" and that "it is inadequate in six main respects for the most efficient discharge of the present and prospective responsibilities of government." Five of the items cited illustrate the centrality that issues of specialism and technocracy must have for the historical understanding of British executive politics:

(a) It is still too much based on the philosophy of the amateur (of "generalist" or "all-rounder"). This is most evident in the Administrative Class, which holds the dominant position in the Service.

(b) The present system of classes . . . seriously impedes its work.

(c) Scientists, engineers and members of the specialist classes are frequently given neither the full responsibilities and opportunities nor the corresponding authority they ought to have.

(d) Too few civil servants are skilled managers.

(e) There is not enough contact between the Service and the community it is there to serve.[145]

It might be thought that a major report framed in such a way, with its wish to increase the status of specialists and the management skills of civil servants, must have boosted the position of Treasury O&M. But two Fulton recommendations struck at its foundations. First, a new Civil Service Department was to be set up. No longer would the Treasury be so concerned with establishment (Civil Service personnel) issues: this meant that Treasury O&M, which thrived on the joint authority of the Treasury in matters of economy and personnel had its scope for action massively reduced. The broad church of Treasury O&M was replaced by the narrow technical sect of the Central Computer Agency. Politician-led alternatives, such as Edward Heath's Public Sector Research Unit or the Central Policy Review Staff, had less of a technocratic flavor. Second, the dissolving of boundaries between the administrative executive and clerical classes by the introduction of a "single, unified grading structure covering all civil servants" meant that O&M as an aspirational ideology of the middle ranks had lost its clear constituency. Such blows were not offset by other Fulton novelties, such as a Civil Service College to "provide major training courses in administration and management."

The establishment of ICL in 1968, at the end of a long series of mergers between British computer manufacturers, also marked a turning point. Once a "national champion" in the industry had been established, interventionist industrial policy could not go much further. The computer industry as a whole dropped down the government's agenda after 1968. And, although the career of Treasury O&M only occasionally intersected with arguments over industrial policy as they raged in the late 1950s and the 1960s, there is a sense in which computing as a whole became less visible to government, with repercussions of O&M-type activities in the 1970s. (Furthermore, Treasury O&M was always constrained by what was made available by British manufacturers, and therefore indirectly by the success of industrial policy.[146] Government purchases of computers were increasingly not a large enough proportion of sales to significantly shape the manufacturers' strategies, unlike, say, the cases of aviation or telecommunications.[147]) A similar argument, of relative levels of political interest, can also be made with regard to the relative heat of the Cold War. At its most intense periods (the late 1940s and the early 1950s, the late 1950s to the mid 1960s), there were corresponding influxes of resources into science and technology, benefiting computer science in particular. While in the United States resources continued to flow to research and development on the back of the Vietnam War, in the United Kingdom cutbacks in defense spending were a common feature of the 1960s. However, one idea that came out of Treasury O&M's links with the defense research advisors of Whitehall, "convergence," did have longer-lasting implications.

Members of Treasury O&M were by the late 1960s themselves reflecting on whether their movement had lost its way, and proffered diagnoses. One favored explanation was that attention to detail had distracted from the big picture which had once been in Treasury O&M's possession. Addressing his colleagues in the *O&M Bulletin* in 1969, Laurence Bunker, fresh from surveying O&M's history, turned to its present and future state, and made a plaintive plea:

> For several years O and M has been heavily engaged in coping with the day to day problems of Civil Service work. When some of you "come up for air" once in a while would it not be possible to take a fresh look at some of the fundamental issues so that there could be a leap forward? Failing that, might it not be possible to look beyond the details of methods and procedures and to make a fresh assessment of the direction in which management is going in the Civil Service? If O and M do not do it no one else will because the incentive must stem from a realization of needs and who better able to measure these than O and M? . . .
>
> When we have designed new forms and revised the procedures have we no wisdom to contribute to the wider issues of communication in general? Communication problems are those of human relationships every bit as much as problems of mechanics and sometimes even more. . . .
>
> It may seem an all too obvious comment to make that Civil Service work is done by people but one sometimes wonders to what extent management and O and M really acknowledges this truism.[148]

Truism or not, Bunker's plea for human understanding was indicative of an expert movement of mechanists in crisis.

9

Privacy and Distrust

Accounting for Privacy as a Political Issue

"By 1996 computing power should be used by everyone as casually as energy is today," the London School of Economics computer scientist John Laski wrote in *New Scientist* in September 1966.[1] Laski predicted a "monopoly that will supply computing power for bulk transformation, storage and retrieval of information and for diffusion of information, will depend the quality of life for every member of the community. And the nation that first makes available computing power to its citizens as a public Information Utility . . . will dominate the world economy as the steam engine allowed Britain to dominate the world throughout Victoria's reign." What is remarkable about Laski's article is the presumption that the audience would have few anxieties about a centrally controlled, hierarchically organized, governmental computer system reaching into every home. Compare Laski's upbeat tone against the tone of a second article published only 3 years later, also in *New Scientist.* Marshaling examples drawn from both sides of the Atlantic, but explicitly inspired by Alan Westin's *Privacy and Freedom*, Michael Stone and Malcolm Warner sought to shake British citizens out of their complacency and get them to recognize "a threat to individual privacy far more extensive than anything today": the computer.[2] The tone was now dark and suspicious: "How much freedom will be left to the individual in a fully data-banked society? How is he to know into whose hands both confidential and relatively innocuous, but still private, information is passed?"

Why did privacy, and in particular a perceived threat from government computers, suddenly become an issue in the United Kingdom between 1966 and 1969? (And it was particularly government projects that became a focus for concern, perhaps because the private data-bank schemes of the 1970s—such as the direct-mailing firms CCN and UAPT—could not operate without drawing on the tools provided by the state: postal codes and purchasable small-scale Census data.[3]) Colin Bennett, in his account of data-protection policies in Sweden, Germany, the United States, and the United Kingdom, while mobilizing a combination of five different factors to explain the convergence among these states on the principles behind legislation, presents a much simpler explanation of why privacy concerns had become an issue at all: "The increase in the number and complexity of policies that we expect the modern welfare state to administer has meant a quantitative increase in the amount of information collected from individuals"; meanwhile, "facilitated by information technology" a "qualitative . . . change [had occurred] in the nature of the information collected. As programs have become increasingly refined, more sensitive and discriminating information on the financial, employment, health, and educational histories of a citizen has been required."[4] This argument surely has much force: the projects discussed in this chapter were often connected to welfare provision (although equally so to policing matters), and were often on a very large scale. Furthermore, qualitative changes in the techniques available are undeniable. Witness the concern raised by the first free text retrieval software, and the emphasis given to improved software techniques in the last attempt by the UK government to significantly sponsor innovation in information technology: the Alvey program, launched in 1982.[5]

But this explanation for the sudden rise of the computer threat to privacy as an issue is not entirely satisfactory. One way of showing why is to examine attitudes toward privacy before and after the mid 1960s. The Oxford Record Linkage Study, which began in 1963, was not controversial until the refusal of some Buckinghamshire hospitals to join in 1973 suddenly made it so, yet the project itself had not changed. The Blackburn murder case, solved in 1948 partly by using the National Register, raised no concerns at all regarding privacy, yet the investigation into the more heinous Yorkshire Ripper case, in which the police were given access to DHSS records, sparked a public debate over confidentiality of government records.[6] The shift, I think, can be characterized as a movement from anxieties about threats to collective qualities to anxieties about threats to the individual. For example, opposition to the identity cards of the National Register invoked collective qualities such as the traditional liberties of the Englishman. After the 1960s, the concern seemed to be directed toward the threat of the collective to the individual. This was the language, for example, that framed the privacy panic of the 1960s, the debate over legislation in the 1970s, and the Data Protection Act of 1984. This shift, however, was not total. It is, of course, possible to find many examples of anxiety about threats to the individual from governmental information systems in the decades before the 1960s, and collective qualities are still invoked today.[7] My point is that the shift, though one of emphasis, was nevertheless profound.

Furthermore, I will show that it was just as social scientists began to articulate what an informationally fully rounded representation of a person might be like, and launch projects that might realize this simulacrum, that anxieties over threats to the individual peaked.

Although the National Register raised many emotions and arguments, it did operate for ten wartime and seven peacetime years in the United Kingdom, whereas in the 1970s and the 1980s even mere hints of a new Personal Identification Number were met with intense suspicion from some quarters. The following, written in inflammatory style by the journalists Duncan Campbell and Steve Connor, is a good example:

> The most threatening development in government databanks . . . would be the development of a central population register—probably accompanied by the introduction of a standard personal identification number. . . . But this is precisely what is now happening—not by sinister design as such, but in a series of steps intended to suit administrative convenience. . . . There will by the year 2000 be a government central computer network recording the name and number, current address, date of birth, sex, identity number, family relationships and many other particulars of virtually the entire population.[8]

Of course no such network existed "by the year 2000"; the point is that attitudes had shifted by the 1970s to the extent that such a prediction could seriously be made. Vincent offers a deeper historical explanation such changes, as part of a slow, long-term breakdown in the "honorable secrecy," the code of conduct that had governed civil servants in public. In the 1980s, for example, in the wake of the Rayner white paper *Efficiency and Effectiveness* (1982) and the subsequent Financial Management Initiative, civil servants became much more managerial, and in the 1990s many governmental bodies became independent. Civil servants were influenced by codes sourced from a wider business culture.[9] These were aspects of a sea change in the nature of public trust, and in a moment I will consider whether there were connections with changing information technology, but for the moment they should be understood as attempts to reconstruct trust in government on a second model, based on market-inspired ideas of contract and checked by audit. Was it merely an irony that this convergence of public bodies toward private models was underway at the same moment as electronically stored personal information held in the private sector overtook public sources in scale and sophistication? Vincent's arguments are directed toward explaining shifting attitudes to privacy and official secrecy. Yet the timing of the start of the privacy controversies—some time between 1966 and 1969—is so close to other profound shifts in social attitudes, especially toward the state, in the late 1960s, that a full historical account must surely draw on deeper factors still. Finally, perhaps it is to put the cart before the horse to try and explain the privacy controversies as a *reaction* to the scale of government computerization projects. Is there, instead, a sense in which computerization—like mechanization's earlier move to make the process of government more explicit—should be described as occurring *because* of the changing nature of public trust?

Driving a Police State?

Paper is as essential to running a modern car as petrol. As the use of automobiles increased in the early decades of the century, an immense quantity of paperwork was generated. In chapter 4, I discussed the early development of a key partial register. Two documents in particular were of interest: the vehicle register and the driver's license. These were components of largely separate systems until the possibility of convergence[10] was raised in the mid 1960s. At the same moment the operational capabilities of a central Police National Computer were being considered within Whitehall. This section traces the history and interaction between these two convergent information systems—one of the first "data banks," around which the privacy debate would center.

The pattern established by the 1930s, with vehicle licenses for policing and taxation reasons and driver's licenses justified on safety grounds—both produced locally—continued relatively unchanged through the Second World War until the 1960s. By then the continued growth of the vehicle and driver population, the former doubling every ten years, was subjecting the system to severe strain. Furthermore as town centers became more congested, police enquiries were expected to quadruple between 1963 and 1973.[11]

The Ministry of Transport ordered a full review of the system, and in 1963 brought together a joint Ministry/Treasury O&M group to begin it, and a Working Party to report in more detail. Unsurprisingly given Treasury O&M convictions, the review recommended that "the present system should be replaced by one authority operating on the basis of a central office . . . with a large computer system," although it conceded that it might be found preferable to have two central offices, one for vehicle licensing and registration and one for driving licensing."[12] Local outposts, including Local Taxation Offices and Post Offices, would renew licenses, pending confirmation by the central office. Centralization and computerization offered a vast resource to the police in particular, who would be able to deal directly with the central office. The proposal entailed massive organizational change—indeed the scale meant that O&M training was recommended for the managers, thereby spreading O&M philosophy even further—and much consultation, including visits to other large computer projects, followed. The proposal did not go unchallenged: an alternative was to have several regional computer systems, which was perceived to have three advantages. First, the central office was always conceived, as part of Labour Party policy, as being located in one of the poorer "Development Areas," and the fear was expressed that any future change of plans—for example full automation—would have an adverse effect on already high local unemployment.[13] Second, police work was strongly organized by region (especially by county) rather than nationally, and it was suggested that a regional computer system would better preserve these links. Finally, regional centers of computing fitted the policy proposed by the influential Flowers Report for academic and scientific research, and consistency was preached as a virtue.[14] Two of the large administrative computer projects then underway (the Post Office Savings Bank at Glasgow and the Post Office GIRO system at Bootle) were centralized, whereas two others (the Ministry of Pensions and National Insurance payments of benefits and Inland Revenue "pay as you earn" work) were regionalized, so Labour's policy seems only to have been selectively applied. A central system was confirmed at ministerial level: it was cheaper, but more important also made tax evasion and document forgery by dishonest drivers trickier. A "Development Area" was indeed selected for the office, and the Driver and Vehicle Licensing Center (DVLC) was built in Swansea, Wales, by the mid 1970s.

The surveillance possibilities of a centralized system were extolled by the joint Ministry/O&M team, it would "play a really effective part in assisting the enforcement staff": "One could envisage the computer examining the main file, at regular intervals, to ascertain those vehicles which have not been re-registered, say, within a month of the due date. Lists of vehicles, with names and addresses of last known owners, would then be printed out and sent to the local offices for follow up action by enforcement officers."[15] Centralization also facilitated, in principle, future exotic proposals, such as road pricing—still a contentious issue in the early twenty-first century.

The central office planned to collect seventeen separate pieces of information per vehicle and eleven per driver.[16] Among the latter were a "unique reference number," full name and address, sex, date of birth, details of previously declared diseases and disabilities, alongside the essential data on the state of the license—number of endorsements, when received, and so on.[17] The limit to the amount of information was set by estimations of the capacity of the central computer rather than by any explicit privacy concern. "It appears," noted one L. Grainger of the Ministry of Transport, "that the licensing project alone may approach the practical limits of a single computer."[18] By the mid 1970s, there were more than 20 million vehicle registrations and a similar number of drivers. DVLC constituted one of the largest "data banks" in the

United Kingdom. However, the path of the DVLC computerization project was far from smooth, indeed it has been called, against stiff opposition, the "most spectacular computer flop" of the 1970s, and it was only after the addition of two IBM 3083 computers in 1983 that it was quicker for the Swansea staff to check vehicle information on the Police National Computer, which we now turn to, than on DVLC's own system.[19]

From the paper-based system onwards, police access to the vehicle and driver information had always formed an important part of the registering and licensing system. To gain a better understanding, this use needs to be put in the wider context of police and Home Office data processing. Punched-card systems, developed in the interwar years and discussed in chapter 5, were computerized in the 1960s after O&M-type reviews in the late 1950s. The Home Office, responsible for law and order, policing, prisons and immigration, had for much of its history been presented with fearsome data-processing problems, often solved through extensive manual filing systems. Many of these were not considered for mechanization until the 1950s. For example, the Aliens Department, recorded the movement of foreigners into and out of the country using only a card index, sorting and filing landing and embarkation cards by hand—2.5 million per year (this power of surveillance had been granted to the police under the Aliens Act 1905). Although "a number of schemes of mechanization" had been "propounded from time to time," none were accepted until automatic data processing was introduced, an interim punched-card system followed by troubled computerization.[20] Much of the work for which the Secretary of State for the Home Office was ultimately responsible was decentralized, which raised the prospect of radical organizational change if centralizing ADP was introduced. The prisons, for example, relied on surveillance techniques not much different from the nineteenth century days of Bentham's brick-and-mortar panopticon—there was not even a central numbering system of prisoners, leading to confusion and forgetting as prisoners were moved around. The O&M team found the system "archaic": "There are surprisingly few machines or office aids of any kind in use throughout the Prison Service," and considered their desired "integrated data processing system," with a core of "centralized records of inmates," some years off.[21] Computerization was easiest in the parts of the organization that were already centralized, with the effect of reconfirming and strengthening that pattern: the Metropolitan Police at New Scotland Yard in London, remaining, for example, first among equals among the police divisions.

The cornerstone of the work of the Home Office and Metropolitan Police Joint ADP Unit (JADPU), formed in 1959 to coordinate the O&M studies, was a Police National Computer (PNC) based near London and connected by landlines to all police forces in the country. The PNC came together in a piecemeal fashion during the 1960s and the early 1970s. JADPU's first efforts had been devoted to administrative mechanization, first of the pay of the Metropolitan Police and then, after investigation and recommendations by the new Perks Committee, of Home Office statistical production. The demands made on statistical production had the effect of converging registers and statistical systems, as is apparent in the following changes outlined in the Home Office in anticipation of Perks's conclusions in 1965:

> It is clear that the kind of expansion in the scope and purposes of the criminal statistics . . . will require a radical overhaul of the present processing system, which came into force with the conversion from punch card methods to ADP in 1964. There will be additional data relating to crimes known, which have not previously been collected; there will be additional data relating to various forms of treatment of offenders, which either have not been collected hitherto, or, where they have been collected, have been maintained in clerically operated indexes; there will be new systems for linking categories of data which have not previously been linked; and by no means least in importance, there will be a need to operate the whole system at very much greater speed than appears likely ever to be achieved with existing methods. Speed will be especially essential [sic] for the achievement of the aim to provide a centralized statistical service to police forces.[22]

This shift to a more interlinked, comprehensive statistical system was, in the view of its proponents, the most important shake-up of criminal statistics for 70 years, although the many parallels with the 1930s innovations discussed in chapter 5 should be noted.

Attention then turned to computers as operational aids. Feasibility studies for a PNC, begun in the mid 1960s, recommended a first stage in which records relating to fingerprints, modus operandi, stolen vehicles, and criminal names would all be placed on the central computer and made searchable by police forces. Each of these tasks presented a formidable data-processing problems. The National Fingerprint Office at Scotland Yard, for example, contained nearly 2 million complete ten-fingerprint sets by 1968, a collection built up over the century. (The idea of universal fingerprinting was briefly floated in 1966, but then dropped.) JADPU anticipated that computerizing the fingerprint collection would reduce the need for skilled fingerprint officers by 80 percent, and it would also be made nationally available, via a picture transmission system. But it would take at least 3 years to convert the records, and even then would not be able to process single fingerprint (i.e., crime scene) requests.[23] In this instance computerization was shaped by changing public attitudes to convicted criminals: the introduction of parole in the 1960s necessitated more frequent identifications of criminals, for which speedier comparison with the ten fingerprint sets was required.[24] Modus operandi, the indexes of criminals distinguishable because of characteristic methods or descriptions, had previously been collected and held on a regional basis, leading to uneven geography of such information. Conversion to punched cards in the mid 1960s, with copies held nationally and by police force, meant that "searches can be national, local or [by] some intermediate area according to need." Likewise stolen car registers had been built up regionally or by local police forces and were often out-of-date. Criminal name indexes, however, were kept at all levels of police organization. The national index in 1968 contained 3 million names, built up over 70 years. Computerization of this national index was an enormous task involving "500 man-years of effort."[25]

Reacting to the formation of the DVLC, JADPU substantially modified and expanded its mid-1960s conception of a Police National Computer. Police forces had previously, of course, made great use of locally held information on drivers and vehicles. Now, via the DVLC, a central information source was available. Direct access to the Swansea computer via telephone lines was perfectly *politically* acceptable, but rejected in favor of duplication of the Swansea vehicle owner data, on the grounds of cost (£2 million compared to £4–6 million). Instead, data would be regularly transferred by transporting magnetic disks from Swansea in Wales to the Police National Computer located at Hendon, on the outskirts of London. In addition to data from the DVLC, the records held on the Police National Computer were expanded: to fingerprints, modus operandi, stolen vehicles and criminal aids were added registers of firearms, wanted/missing persons (on the insistence of Interpol, and, with stolen/suspect vehicles the aspect of the PNC which has drawn accusations of political bias), disqualified drivers, suspended sentences and various types of missing property.[26] Plans were also developed by 1968 for the eventual computerization of the criminal records files (the largest of all jobs, with conversion time estimated at "1,800 man-years), and scientists at the National Physical Laboratory were already investigating means of computerizing criminal intelligence on behalf of the Home Office.[27]

Initially it was thought that the PNC would consist of twinned ICT 1900 series computers, with the expectation that it would be replaced by the next generation, labeled Project 51, from the company in the late 1970s. (A brief digression is helpful to explore Project 51. Following the breakdown of talks to establish an Anglo-French large computer project, from July 1967, Treasury O&M and the computer manufacturer ICT met to discuss future industrial policy and the role of government support. ICT had recovered from a financial crisis in 1965 to lead the British electronic data-processing industry with its 1900 range.[28] The talks also involved most of the government agencies with an interest in high-performance computing: Ministry of Technology (via the two laboratories for which it had become responsible, National Physical Laboratory and the Royal Radar Establishment, Malvern), Home Office, Ministry of Transport, Ministry of Defence (via its Meteorological Office) and the Ministry of Social Services. Nine meetings and one month later, the government had concluded that its interests lay in the purchase of five computers of Project 51 specification, "provided that policy decrees that greatest use of computers should be made to further Research, Development and Administrative Efficiency."[29] The projects that were forecast as requiring the most advanced mainframes (3–10 times the power of an Atlas) were computerization of Police Records and possibly criminal intelligence for the Home Office, vehicle and driver licensing for the Ministry of Transport, weather calculation for the Meteorological Office, and research at the NPL and RRE.[30] Two more possible administrative applications were soon added, partly in anticipation of a "massive expansion of Government statistical services."[31] Only ICT among British manufacturers were regarded as capable of building a Project 51 machine, the alternative being an American firm such as Control Data Corporation. Although government support for Project 51 was partly motivated by a desire to bolster home-grown industry and an expectation that ICT—later ICL—would in fact provide the cheaper option, the civil servants also had in mind a strong vision of the benefits of compatibility.)

Three hundred local forces connected to the PNC via remote terminals and private wires provided by the Post Office. The location of the PNC in London attracted fierce criticism, but the police successfully resisted attempts to disperse it, like DVLC, to an economically deprived development area.[32] Instead of British computers, two Burroughs B6700s were installed in strengthened bunker-like buildings, complete with a stand-alone electricity supply, at Hendon in 1971, quickly followed by one more central processor, possessing in total 2,000 megabytes of disc storage.[33] The first applications (stolen/suspect vehicles and vehicle owners) went live in 1974. Four years later, the computers were replaced by the superior Burroughs B7700 machines; other Burroughs processors were added later to control the network and peripherals. By 1985, nearly 73 million enquiries per year were made by police forces across the country of the 47 million PNC records.[34]

Taken together, the DVLC and Police National Computer records constituted an impressive concentration of centralized information available to the police. However, it should be remembered that the kinds of information available did not radically change, since local arrangements had granted the police access to local authority vehicle and driver licenses, and the PNC records covered much the same categories as the local and regional antecedents. What

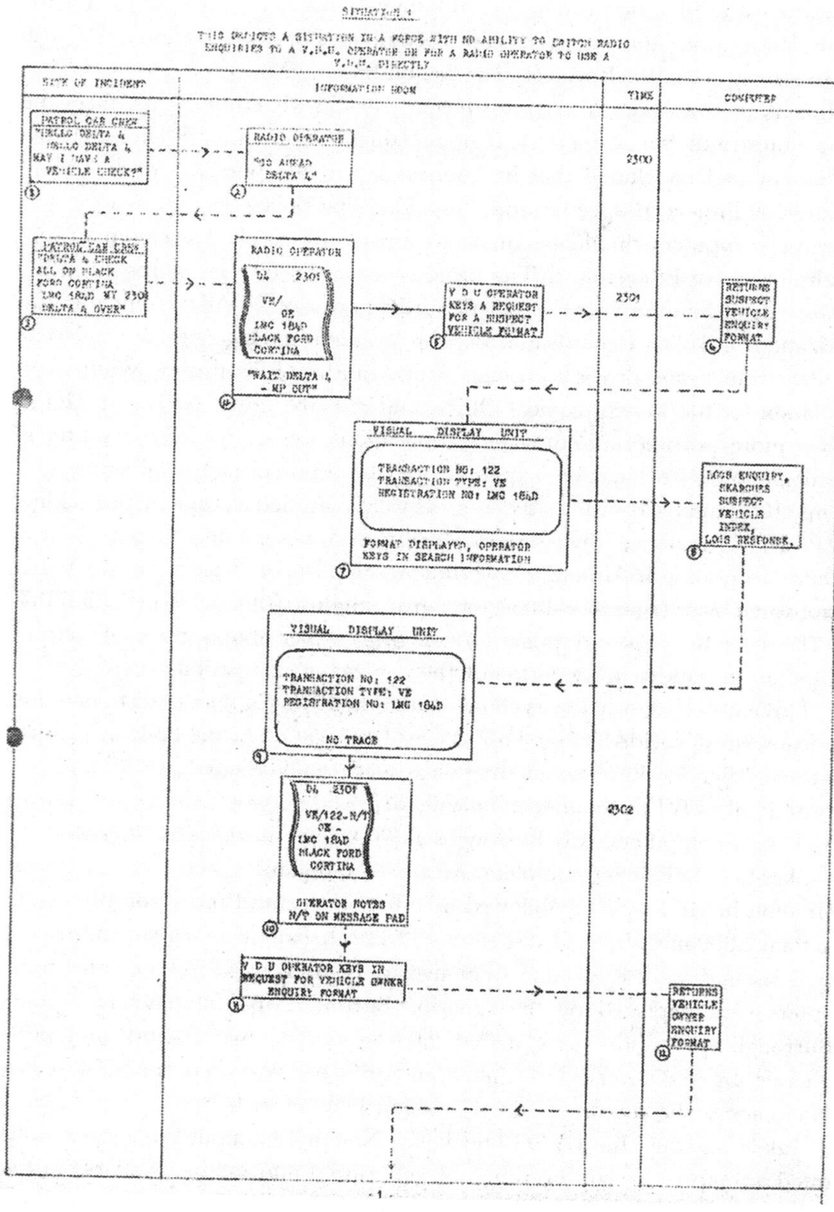

Figure 9.1
A flow diagram showing how a police patrol car, a police information room, and the Police National Computer would interact. (PRO/HO/287/1510)

centralization allowed was cross-referencing and interaction, made practicable because records were being processed by the same system.

Data Banks

In practice, but not in name, DVLC/PNC formed a "data bank," a concept imported from the United States, where it had provoked congressional hearings concerned with threats to privacy. The United Nations, with its proposal for a "data bank" of population censuses, also had promoted the idea.[35] In Whitehall civil servants rejected the word, well aware of the outcry across the Atlantic. However, it is clear that by the mid 1960s several data-bank projects were under consideration. One of these sparked another debate over universal personal numbers, which can be compared to those of previous National Registers examined in chapters 4 and 6.

As with National Registration, the General Register Office shaped ideas of universal numbers in the mid 1960s. This time, the role played then by Sylvanus Vivian was taken by Deputy Registrar-General Robert MacLeod. In a proposal launched in September 1967, MacLeod called for the creation of "Central Population Registers (one for England and Wales and one for Scotland)" and the assignment of "a personal identification number to each individual."[36] The difference this time was that the Register would be held on computer. Similar systems were already running in Israel, Denmark, Sweden, and Norway, and Whitehall's representatives to an International Symposium on Automation of Population Register Systems had reported back on them enthusiastically. However, "in this country," MacLeod considered, "it would seem that integration of the larger systems is out of the question." By this he meant not only that computer systems did not yet have the capacity necessary for a full-fledged national data bank, but also that it was not a politically feasible project, although the resistance centered around rights to individual privacy, rather than, as with National Registration, national liberty. As ever, technical and political factors were intertwined. "It may, however, be possible," MacLeod argued, "to introduce a greater measure of compatibility between the various systems if a personal number for each individual is brought into national use. . . ." His vision was of departmental data banks cross-referenced by universal personal identification numbers, with the GRO's Central Register, containing basic individual information (name, address, sex, date of birth, personal number, marital condition, maiden names, plus possibly the National Insurance number), at the center:

> It is desirable that the Register should be extended to incorporate material other than basic information. Any suggestion that it should be a data bank should be resisted

because under existing circumstances any such extension is likely to lead to serious difficulties having regard to the size of the population. This does not mean that there is no place for data banks, but their creation should be the responsibility of the individual departments.[37]

MacLeod's proposals were warmly received in parts of Whitehall, although the Ministry of Health was seriously concerned about "a possible allegation that we are running National Registration under the counter" through its NHS Central Register—the Ministry was not opposed to NR but thought that Ministerial approval should be sought, and therefore would welcome an initiative like MacLeod's.[38] Elsewhere, the Department of Education and Science, whose identification problem mainly consisted of tracking individuals through school, college, and university, enthused that "the establishment of a population register is a golden opportunity to lay the foundations of a really efficient computer system or systems throughout the country."[39] The system would enable a machine-readable identity card ("though heaven forbid we should use this term publicly"). But although they judged it "technically feasible," civil servants were aware that this benefit would have to be presented carefully: "We should discuss this when we meet and see if we can agree on what, if anything, should be said in the memo on the subject of confidentiality and the privacy of the individual." The Central Statistical Office provided valuable advice on this subject: a "proposal to set up a Population Register and allocate a number to each individual would be bound to remind many members of the public of National Registration in the last war and its association with identity cards, food rationing, mobilization, direction of labor, control of movements and so on." Therefore, the CSO recommended the abandonment of the sensitive identity card plan. Instead, "if the system were regarded as a natural extension of National Insurance and birth registration schemes" then "it may not be necessary to test public opinion" (although "there is no doubt that the Press could present any development for statistical purposes in an unsympathetic or even dramatic way").[40] A careful series of merged registry numbering systems therefore seemed the quietest path to secure a universal number. It was noted with pleasure that the new computerized PAYE taxation scheme would make use of another department's number, that of National Insurance (an epochal decision in its small way). Likewise in 1966 it was hoped that the National Health Service would share the format. However, in general, noted Rooke-Matthews of the GRO, "the biggest obstacle" was not the "practicability of the system" but "possible public and political objection to the whole idea." "For this reason," Rooke-Matthews continued, "it may be necessary to stress that to a degree the basic objections to population registration apply equally to some of the current individual proposals. Having dealt with the general question of acceptability of the register it could then be demonstrated that there were a number of practical advantages accruing if we are making fullest use of computer systems and other more modern ways of handling records of information."[41]

At this stage it was up in the air whether such a register—long a favored system within parts of Whitehall—would be re-introduced. Computerization, in this case, acted not as a drive determining political change, but certainly as an opportunity to resurrect preferred systems. However, such Whitehall maneuvers fed back and shaped what was expected of computing machines: "The establishment of a common register," argued the Board of Trade, underlined "the importance of establishing compatible computer systems in the various Departments serving and using it," which in turn reinforced government preferences for a single manufacturer, thereby shaping industrial policy.[42]

We have already seen that compatibility was one factor holding together the Project 51 proposals. Likewise, in the area of statistics, the vision of a data bank was a final cause that helped decide what should be computerized and how in the late 1960s. Thus, for example, the Director of the Central Statistical Office, Sir Claus Moser, considered it "an absolute requirement that the computers for the Ministry of Labour, the Board of Trade Census Office, [and a future business statistics office] should be completely compatible. At the present state of technical development this means that all must come from the one manufacturer."[43] Any future system "should so far as possible eventually include, on a compatible basis, all available industrial data," concluded the Cabinet Statistical Policy Committee, the highest decision-making body in official statistics: "it was essential that the new system to be set up should be compatible with the longer-term objectives of a data bank."[44] Though the technical choices varied according to circumstance (the bigger schemes needed machines of Project 51 specification, the smaller used ICT/ICL 1900 series computers), the effective outcome of industrial policy and a vision of data banks was a number of cross-departmental compatible systems—mini data banks. Family Expenditure Survey data, for example, was to be shared around the government statistical community.

The "Whole Person Concept" and Other New Objects of Science

As we have seen throughout this book, a considerable amount of information about individuals was collected by government departments primarily for use in fulfilling their administrative functions. A trend through the twentieth century was the use on a growing scale of this information for statistical and analytical purposes which often exceeded a strictly interpreted remit of individual departments. This phenomenon, whereby information collected for one narrow pre-defined purpose was subsequently made available more generally, known as "data creep," was not publicized.[45] The mid to late 1960s formed at a pivotal moment in this history: as computer store capacity grew, and compatibility between systems became encouraged, ever greater use of data was foreseen. "Substantially greater use," one civil servant noted, "could be made of the information from one Department if it could be linked with that from others, particularly as the rapid development of computers seems likely to remove the former technical obstacles to handling such data on a national scale. This would open the door for a substantial step forward, with the promise of wider-ranging and more detailed studies in the social and economic fields."[46]

I will take the Family Expenditure Survey as one example of such studies, since it shows how the new capabilities in data storage and manipulation facilitated the modification of objects of science. Each year the Social Survey, on behalf of the Ministry of Labour, selected 10,000 households across the United Kingdom, which were then visited in rotation during the year. These households were asked to maintain a detailed record of expenditures for fourteen consecutive days and gave the interviewer further information about the household, about incomes and certain regular payments. Such production of social knowledge was a continuation of the wartime Social Survey's methods, discussed in chapter 6. However, by the 1960s the FES was being used for many government activities—from calculating the retail price index to estimating national expenditure—and demand for FES-based knowledge was rising. In turn, the families were quizzed on an ever greater range of topics. The data-processing load swamped the small Emidec 1100 at the Ministry of Labour, and computing time was begged on the Ministry of Defence's LEO machines at the naval dockyards of Chatham, Portsmouth, and Rosyth. The load was sizable: 500,000 cards processed each year, with an additional regular production hundreds of thousands of cards in batches to supply to other departments. The effect of the combination of new technical capabilities and the political demand for information was a "rounding" of the family as a scientific object: each new question put a different perspective on the household under study. This rounding was later officially recognized as the "whole person concept," and developed within the Department of Health and Social Security as part of Operational Strategy, the biggest program of computerization in Europe (discussed below).[47] The "cross-analyses" permitted by such rounding were championed:

In the past administrative records have been the chief source of large scale statistics about individuals and aggregates of individuals. These relate to a limited number of characteristics and have not provided the kind of cross-analyses needed as a background to more sophisticated social security schemes, education, health, housing and transport policy and planning generally. Some of these needs have been met be extending the range of topics in the census of population and some by a proliferation of sample surveys on special topics. In the case of the Family Expenditure Survey, there has been mounting pressure from departments to cover more topics which can be related to each other, and to household income and size.[48]

The expanded FES configured new objects, such as the rounded family, in social science. In social and medical science, extensive cross-referencing of data enabled different questions to be asked, and thereby modified or even created scientific objects of study. The Oxford Record Linkage Study, which depended on continuous collection of records since 1963, and most famously the research under Dr. Richard Doll in which links were demonstrated between smoking and lung cancer, are good examples. Commenting on Doll's research, one proponent of the computerized Central Register noted: "Interest has tended to shift from acute conditions of short duration to more complex chronic conditions which require a study of the extended medical history of an individual involving linkage of records over long periods of time and from different parts of the country. . . . Large samples of data are needed."

Similarly, at the Ministry of Transport, scientists at the Road Research Laboratory shifted the direction of their work to make use of the new informational resources. Things such as driver behavior became objects of study largely because of the contingent availability of easily sorted and cross-referenced data. Furthermore, such scientists were in a position to request extra information be collected:

Centralisation of driver licensing work would produce the biggest increase in information for [the RRL] and that to help their research into driver characteristics it is desirable that the date of passing the driving test and the dates of any previous test attempts should be recorded. Their requirements would be for information on a sample basis. For sample surveys of drivers based on interviews it would be desirable to be able to use a central system to pick random samples for all licensed drivers by, among other qualifications age and experience and study the effect experience has on a driver's record. It is expected that approximately eight batches of five thousand driver records would be required each year. . . .[49]

Likewise, the Chief Psychologist of the Prison Commission anticipated a rapid intensification of statistical analyses of the prisoner population. The JADPU report accounted for the failure of previous efforts as due to a lack of computing power: "research appears to be severely hampered in two respects—the inadequacy of raw data and the lack of suitable means for processing the information which is available. These do not strike us as separate issues; we suspect one is largely a consequence of the other. If the processing facilities were at hand, we are sure that no further incentive would be necessary to secure the right kind of data"—a concise expression of the phenomena that data, means of handling the data, and scientific object (in this case prison population mapped on many axes) were produced together as a package.[50]

One of the most ambitious schemes to use computers to help reconstitute scientific disciplines was the Data Bank project in the social sciences: a pooling of survey data, contributed by and made available to academic and market researchers, such that, when combined with modern computing power, a new order of sophistication of statistical investigation could be reached.[51] If the Family Expenditure Survey was to give us the fully rounded statistical family, the Data Bank was a statistical "whole nation concept." Its proponents could point to several developments in the United States and Continental Europe to support claims that Britain was "lagging behind": an Inter-university consortium data bank at Michigan and the Roper Public Opinion Research Center at Williams College, both established in the 1950s, were the two most cited examples. (In 1965 it was just such a data-bank proposal, but this time a governmental one—a Federal Data Center—that sparked the storm of American protest against such projects as threats to personal liberties.) In 1963 and 1964 a group of social scientists met at Cambridge to begin to lobby for a British equivalent. After raising funding from academic, industrial and government sources, in 1965 John Madge of Political and Economic Planning was placed in charge of a feasibility study. By the following year Madge could show that many industrial market researchers, including Cadbury's, Mass Observation, Esso, ICI, and the Consumers Association, were willing to supply old data, and government departments displayed "almost universal willingness to cooperate."[52] The Data Bank was eminently achievable. Although Whitehall and the social science establishment wanted the data archive to be located in the capital at the London School of Economics, their wishes were thwarted by internal dissension within LSE. (Claus Moser at the LSE blamed "overwhelming space problems," but Bill Mackenzie at Manchester observed that, following its leader, the conservative philosopher Michael Oakeshott, "the whole atmosphere of political science in LSE" was "hostile to this kind of enterprise."[53]) Essex University, given a charter only a few years earlier, seized the opportunity. Promising dedicated time on the ICT 1909 machine at its Computer Center (run by R. A. Brooker, who had been trained at Manchester where he had helped design one of the first computer languages, Autocode), and acceding to all the restrictions laid down centrally, Essex brought the project to its Colchester campus, with the American-born Alan Potter in charge.[54] After the injection of government money, the Essex archive was named the Social Science Research Council (SSRC) Data Bank.

The centralized Data Bank produced two effects. First, just as with the Family Expenditure Survey and other "compatible" data sources, the combination of information from different surveys enabled new questions to be asked, as a introductory pamphlet to new users explained:

> The SSRC Data Bank is . . . the center for storing data from social surveys sponsored by government departments, commercial organizations and academic researchers, in order that the data can be analyzed by others besides the original sponsors. This secondary analysis will often involve more than one survey deposited in the Bank. The bringing together of data from surveys which would otherwise be scattered, or indeed destroyed after primary analysis, will therefore have a "multiplier effect. . . ."[55]

Second, since the SSRC was a major funder of social science in British universities, it was in a position to encourage standardization of methodology and format, and to ensure the use of—and contributions to—the growing Data Bank. In disciplinary terms the Data Bank therefore reinforced the dominant quantitative approach to sociology. Indeed, as the Data Bank project grew, proponents of this methodology became ever more bullish. In evidence to the Data Protection Committee in 1976, an official from the Public Record Office argued:

> . . . there has developed rather more recently and slowly an interest in quantitative data which can answer the same sort of questions about the past as economists and social scientists are asking about the present. This sort of historical research is called quantitative history. At present, quantitative historians are having to create their own machine-readable data from conventional paper records, but when the quantitative historian of the twenty-first century comes to study the 1970s he will expect to find an unrivaled source of government data already existing in machine-readable form which he can readily use to study the social and economic conditions of our time.[56]

Of course this raises questions about twenty-first-century historiography, but the sentiments are a good measure of the ambition of the Data Bank.

Who Is the "Necrophilist's Runner"? Privacy and Confidentiality

One serious obstacle to the SSRC Data Bank requisitioning all old government surveys was the assurance of confidentiality of information given to contributors, backed sometimes—such as with the Board of Trade's and the

General Register Office's censuses—by the force of law. The connected phenomena of data creep and data banks raised the questions of just how confidential such information was, or should be. The treatment of population census records provides a pithy example. We saw in the last chapter that the accidental leak of information from the 1966 mini-census caused a considerable scare within Whitehall. The fact that the GRO occasionally made copies of the punched cards from its Census of Population available for academic or other research made the department nervous, especially "from the public relations angle."[57] Legislation banned the divulging of individual records, but even cards stripped of individual signifiers might cause problems, since a combination of searches might soon reveal data on individuals. In a nutshell, "the only necrophilist's runner in the village may also be either the only Ph.D. or the only father of ten." Indeed, the hostility of the public reaction to the 1971 census, in which a higher than ever proportion of the population refused to fill out the schedules, caused great surprise and alarm in government circles. In many ways, this "biggest outpouring of public concern about privacy ever witnessed in that country" was to the United Kingdom what the data-bank proposals were to the United States in sparking concern over computers as a "threat to privacy."[58]

Thus, by the early 1970s the computer had become cast as a threat to privacy. In the United States the process of demonization can be dated to the reaction to the 1965 Federal Data Center proposal and the publication of Alan Westin's influential 1967 book *Privacy and Freedom*.[59] In Britain, some liberal groups and journalists picked up the issue and began organizing a campaign on similar lines, producing similar literature of conspiracy and outrage, such as Warner and Stone's *The Data Bank Society* (1970).[60] As a sample, typical in its fears and targets, here is part of the Trades Union Congress's evidence submitted to the Younger Committee on Privacy:

> . . . there is a considerable danger that civil liberties and in particular privacy could be seriously threatened by the growth of this massive and instant information service unless some means of public control over data-banks is introduced. Individuals could be placed on a national credit "black list" without ever knowing it. Together with an individual's credit rating can be stored his/her tax code, employer's assessment, political and religious views, medical history, trade union activities, family connections and any criminal convictions. In ten years time it is likely if no controls are introduced, that a customer of a private data bank, a Government department, or other public body will be able to easily obtain a dossier containing all relevant (and irrelevant) facts about almost any individual.[61]

How then was anonymity to be preserved? Without credible assurances of anonymity, public trust might be lost, surveys might become unreliable, and a crucial means by which the state gained knowledge would be damaged or even lost. One answer was legislation.

The first attempts in the early 1960s to introduce parliamentary bills to protect individual privacy focused on "behavioral" privacy—unjustified intrusion of the press or "paparazzi" into an individual's affairs—rather than on computerized data banks. However, the 1963 Profumo Affair (in which the press revealed an unseemly connection between a War Office minister and a model with links to a Russian attaché, severely tarnishing Harold Macmillan's Conservative administration), made it unpropitious to legislate against press interests. The climate changed somewhat with the election of a Labour government, under Harold Wilson, in 1964. By 1967 two organizations were lobbying for privacy legislation: Justice (a coalition of concerned lawyers led by the barrister Paul Sieghart) and the National Council for Civil Liberties. The bill, partly drafted by Sieghart and introduced by back-bench MP Brian Walden in 1969, was voluntarily withdrawn when the Wilson government, unwilling to publicly veto the bill, promised a Royal Commission to examine the area.[62] As David Vincent notes, this Commission on Privacy, chaired by Sir Kenneth Younger, "was and remains the only large-scale official study of privacy ever carried out" in the United Kingdom.[63] Vincent emphasizes that "the causes of the increasing disquiet about privacy, and many of the more powerful remedies, were located in forces well outside the political arena . . . stimulated by the growing pressures exerted by modern industrial society upon the home and daily life." The broad canvas of Younger's 1972 report and its recommendation of piecemeal protection did not satisfy the critics who insisted on targeting the computerized data base as the principal threat.[64] The greatest drawback to the Younger commission, however, was that public bodies were excluded from its purview. During the Conservative administration of Edward Heath (1970–1974) there was little expectation of movement, but when Harold Wilson returned in 1974, promising swift action, proponents of data-protection legislation were in high spirits. Two white papers, *Computers and Privacy* and a supplement, *Computers: Safeguards for Privacy*, were published in 1975.[65] (It is telling that the latter, the first substantial published survey of government computers, was framed by the contingent privacy debate.) However, hopes were set back again when a further Data Protection Committee was appointed, chaired first by Younger (who died in the post) and then by Sir Norman Lindop.

The evidence compiled by the Data Protection Committee shows the positions of government departments, local governments, and other bodies with respect to the recommendations of the white papers, but it also reveals the extent to which computers were in use, and for what purposes. (Before this material is analyzed, a word of warning: Many of the sources cited above and in earlier chapters comes from normal administrative files released to the Public Record Office after the statutory 30 years. The evidence presented to the Data Protection Committee in 1976–77 is of a slightly different nature: it consists of memoranda prepared specifically for the *public* purpose of persuading a committee to keep or modify parts of the white papers. They are more "political," and less candid, documents for this reason.)

Some 25 memoranda presented the attitudes of more than 50 departments—some departments which felt that the issue was relatively unimportant replied jointly. A similar quantity of material can be analyzed for the interests and positions of both public and private-sector industries. I will focus on six Whitehall bodies, all of which were concerned that data-protection measures might restrict their activities: the Central Statistical Office (on behalf of the broader Government Statistical Service), the Civil Service Department (within which the Treasury O&M rump—the Central Computer Agency—now resided), the Department of Health and Social Security, the Home Office, the Office of Population Censuses and Surveys, and, on the industrial side, the Post Office. Several of these departments had Scottish or Welsh equivalents, which, though important, closely parallel their English counterparts and are not considered here. (Other state bodies, such as the security services, obviously also had a strong interest in data-protection legislation, albeit not one expressed publicly.)

"Statistics are anonymous," Claus Moser boldly stated in the covering letter to the CSO's submission, the "objectives of data protection should only be specified and applied to statistical work bearing that in mind."[66] Indeed, the CSO quickly defined "privacy" and dismissed it as a problem:

> Privacy: ensuring that information is not so sensitive that it would be improper to ask individuals for it or to hold it for statistical purposes. This aspect is not further discussed here.[67]

Two other "aspects," the CSO held, were more important: security ("ensuring that the data collected are protected from unauthorized penetration") and confidentiality (the necrophilist's runner problem). On the latter the line proposed seems robust, but in fact was not: "Information about an identifiable individual should not be published or otherwise released outside government departments or their agencies unless the written consent of those providing it is obtained or there is independent approval that any disclosure would not result in harm to the individuals concerned." However, it was "virtually impossible to ensure that there is never any disclosure," and faith must be placed in mere "departmental rules." A similar stance was presented by the Office of

Population Censuses and Surveys (OPCS)—a body, formed in 1970, that succeeded the GRO in the areas of registers of births, deaths, and marriages, conducted the Census of Population, and maintained the NHS Central Register on behalf of the DHSS. The OPCS considered that only a "small but vocal fringe of the public" ever asserted that personal information was or could be used "improperly," and it welcomed the proposed Data Protection Authority since an "independent judgment . . . could be helpful in rebutting these attacks."[68]

The main public worry, which found expression in the 1975 white papers, concerned computerized records. Whitehall had reason to be concerned about some specific proposals.

First, the proposed legislation sought to make the transfer of information between agencies and the subsequent "linkage" of information systems possible only when sanctioned by law or by the agreement of an independent body. The OPCS objected that "the interests of an individual cannot be adversely affected by such transfers serving statistical ends provided . . . that the security of the receiving system is effective, that its statistical output does not reveal information about identifiable individuals, and that any follow-up surveys respect the privacy of the individual." However, it was the Department of Health and Social Security (DHSS) that was most concerned about disclosure of computerized records. The DHSS, on its own estimate in 1976, held more than 60 million fully identifiable records containing personal information about individuals: National Insurance alone accounted for 43 million, while pensions and Child Benefit added 9 million and nearly 8 million respectively. The "exceptional" circumstances when such information was disclosed without consent were actually quite large in number, although changes in disclosure policy were announced in Parliament.[69] It was not "practicable," argued the DHSS, to provide "print-outs" of an individual's personal information to check accuracy.

Second, a distinction was made between records held on paper and electronic forms (a distinction which implied assumptions of what was "electronic" and what was a "computer"). Only electronic records would be subject to data-protection legislation, so by not bringing traditional filing systems under the Data Protection regulations, much of Whitehall was left relatively unaffected. Furthermore, since the bureaucratic burden would fall on the growing proportion of computerized records, the effect might be to discourage further reorganization, since gains in administrative efficiency would be offset by the cost of data protection.[70] Some private firms, with less to lose, were vehement on this point. A director of the small computer salvage firm Galdor, for example, wrote: "How are we to define "Computer"? Manual information systems MUST be included. . . . [Any] definition finally arrived at has to be flexible to cope with future unforeseen data practices. This will prevent companies and the Civil Service using the year or two lag to re-vamp their data procedures outside any defined Info. System."[71] The only definition of a computer in an English statute had appeared in the Civil Evidence Act (1968): "any device for storing and processing information." Such a vague definition could prove troublesome in the event of a Data Protection Act.

The Central Computer Agency, now firmly cast as narrow technical experts, picked holes: even a more detailed definition, such as that provided by NATO would not do: "The Committee may . . . consider that such a technical definition, even if used to include, for example, equipment used to output information by microfilm techniques will not be appropriate. At the lower end of the scale the dividing line between computers and accounting machines/programmable calculators is so blurred as to almost non-existent. At this end of the scale, restrictions would be likely to prove a relatively heavy burden on operational efficiency."[72] The Post Office, "a large and complex organization, with a heavy commitment to data processing," supported this line, arguing that "too narrow a definition is likely to cause difficulties in practice by quickly becoming out of date" and that "a comprehensive registration and licensing authority" would be "expensive and unwieldy."[73] In particular, the Post Office (which, as we shall see, was a leading developer of networks in the 1960s and the 1970s) wanted to exclude "systems which are dedicated to the transmission of data (which may include personal information and short-holding-time storage) on behalf of other parties." So, again, the statutory definition of "computer" became shaped by institutional interests.

One sure way to escape these complications was to secure exemption from the Data Protection Act. National security files were exempted, and the Ministry of Defence attempted to gain similar privilege for defense contractors that held "national security information in their management computers."[74] Police and health records were nearer the borderline. The Home Office happily reassured the Data Protection Committee that many of its requests could be met (for example, the existence of the police information systems could be publicized, and people should have the right to know what purpose the information was used are who had access to it), but the right of someone to check the accuracy of information held on him or her was an obvious sticking point: "much of the information relating to individuals which the police have to record for the prevention and detection of crime particularly information on the activities of known or suspected criminals—stems from reports for whose accuracy the police cannot vouch. . . . It would clearly not be sensible to pass to the subject of the information."[75] In general, the Home Office sought, and secured in some cases, exemption of police files.

The exemption of health records was complicated by the fact that there existed many different kinds—the National Health Service (NHS) has always been an intensely bureaucratic structure. The OPCS maintained the NHS Central Register on behalf of the Department of Health and Social Security, while within the NHS itself doctors and other professionals held personal medical records relating to treatment and care of their patients. Furthermore, largely separate patient administrative records had many uses, from the management by a general practitioner of lists of registered patients to call-ups for immunization or periodic screening. The NHS also held statistical records, usually derived from personal health or administrative records and used for purposes of research. All except this last statistical group were manual records, not held on computer. The case for exemption on professional grounds was powerfully stated: "Confidentiality of information about patients and of patients' records is safeguarded by the ethics of the medical and dental professions . . . as enforced by the professional bodies concerned."[76] It was, in this view, the responsible doctor's clinical judgment that would guide what information should be released to the patient. Professional ethics prevented the disclosure of information to third parties without the consent of the patient, although statistical research blurred this rule.[77] The OPCS also pleaded professional grounds for exemption of its NHS Central Register:

> Information about individuals collected in the process of providing medical care in the widest sense should be subject to different rules from personal information collected from individuals through, say, their income tax returns. . . . The systematic collection and analysis of medical records has always been an important way of advancing medical knowledge, particularly of chronic diseases; and access to such records, whether identified or not, has customarily been granted to *bona fide* medical research workers without them having to obtain the express permission from the doctor in every case, let alone from the patients themselves. . . . In handling identifiable medical records (e.g. of cancer) we invariably get the prior approval of the Ethical Committee of the BMA.[78]

Any "print-out" generated during medical statistical research should, the OPCS recommended, be the concern of the "individual's doctor and *not* the individual himself." This professional solution to the problems of trust and threats to privacy was unavailable to most of the rest of the public sector, although social workers tried to follow the same path.

Norman Lindop's Data Protection Committee, when it finally reported in December 1978, recommended the establishment of an independent data-protection authority and a voluntary code of practice.[79] However, again a change of government caused (or appeared to cause) further procrastination, despite pressure from the Labour opposition and the National Council for Civil Liberties. Indeed, it was the interests of business that finally swung the issue: the computer industry and other firms in the service sector feared that unless data-protection legislation was introduced in the United Kingdom they would be penalized under a Council of Europe convention that sought to refuse the export of personal data to countries without data-protection safeguards.[80] The immediate prompt was the tabloid *Sun* newspaper's investigations into the background of Labour MP Michael Meacher. In a debate on the Meacher affair, new Conservative prime minister Margaret Thatcher announced the imminent introduction of a data-protection bill. This was apparently a complete surprise to the Home Office, the department concerned with preparing the legislation.

The bill passed Parliament and finally became the Data Protection Act in 1984. It was, as the Labour opposition contended, "the absolute minimum the government [could] get away with" that would satisfy Europe.[81] Critics of the Data Protection Act had many targets: manual records were exempt (which encouraged evaders of the act to "extrude" data from computerized to paper form, an interesting reversal); there was no code of practice; the Data Protection Registrar which the act established had very few strict responsibilities under the law beyond maintaining a register of users of electronic personal data (no duty of inspection, for example); many government bodies, especially any register connected with national security, were exempt.[82] The act was certainly rather strange in some of its features, and generally it filled more a symbolic than a practical role. Its purpose was largely to indicate that action had been taken. A much more detailed Data Protection Act, which preserved nearly all of the exemptions but extended coverage to paper records, was passed in 1998 and came into force on 1 March 2000.

10

Computers and Experts in the Hollowed-Out State, 1970–2000

The Fall from Power of the Expert Movement of Mechanizers

The large mainframe computer suited the large centralized departments that typified Whitehall, since the structure of the former mirrored that of the latter. But both underwent radical change, the beginnings of which can be detected in the 1960s and the 1970s but accelerated in 1980s and after. Attacks on the size, power, and inefficiency of the Civil Service led to troubled reform. In the same period, in a manner unprecedented in the history of technology, computers became much smaller and more powerful, and they came to be used in different (notably networked) forms. This raises the question whether there were links between the two transformations. Previously, such links had depended on critical social groups—the expert movements—that laid claim to technical expertise within government. After 1970, the power of the mechanizing expert movement was severely undermined by organizational change. This, I argue, had the effect of breaking the mirror. No longer was there a powerful group within government that could claim authority on the dual aspects of administration and technology, so the potentiality of small computers and networks went largely unrecognized because the skills were not in the right place to do so. This helps us understand why many government information-technology projects, from the 1970s until the end of the century, failed.

There is considerable irony in the fact that the fall of the expert movement of mechanizers was a by-product of initiatives that sought to remedy perceived problems of Civil Service expertise. The first wave of attacks on the competency of the Civil Service focused not on "big government" but on the "amateurism" of the administrative class—the top-rank of generalists. The Keynesian economist Thomas Balogh made this the main charge—accounting for no less than the decline of British power in the twentieth century—in his vituperative 1959 article "Apotheosis of the Dilettante." The "amateur

General Index........as it was.
General Index........as it is.

Figure 10.1
By April 1982, the manual paper-based General Index of National Insurance Contributors held in the Newcastle Central Office of the Department of Health and Social Security had been replaced by a computerized system based on individual keyboards and visual display units linked to a pair of ICL 2982 computers at nearby Washington. The General Index, which dated from before the First World War, was one of the great British registers. Even after computerization, the DHSS stated: "One of the biggest problems the Department has is that of identifying people and finding their correct NI numbers." (source: Department of Health and Social Security, Newcastle Central Office, 1986; copy in NAHC LEO/C155)

attitude" of the generalists was confirmed in the 1968 Fulton Report on "structure, recruitment and management, including training of the Home Civil Service," commissioned by Balogh's friend and ally Harold Wilson.[1] The Fulton hearings were dominated by accusations that technical expertise was undervalued in the Civil Service and by defensive replies from the generalists. Certainly there was stark evidence. In 1963, for example, there were only 19 economists in the whole Civil Service. Four years later there were only 106, and one member of the Fulton Committee "complained of economists and scientists being kept in back rooms and treated like plumbers."[2]

Wilson announced that the government accepted the broad conclusions of the Fulton Committee on 26 June 1968, but the 22 reforms recommended in the report were only ever implemented partially. Though the Northcote-Trevelyan split would have been removed had the recommendation that "all classes should be abolished and replaced by a single, unified grading structure covering all civil servants from top to bottom" been followed, in practice the generalist-specialist or generalist-mechanical split remained. A Civil Service College was opened in 1970 at Sunningdale, but it was a feeble creature compared to the French Ecole Nationale d'Administration. Most important for our story, the "pay and management" parts of the Treasury were transferred, combined with personnel matters, to create a new Civil Service Department in November 1968. As was discussed in chapter 8, Treasury Organization and Methods was moved and downgraded, an outcome at odds with the Fulton rhetoric of increasing the influence of specialists.

Margaret Thatcher became prime minister in 1979. After a faltering start, Thatcher's radical program developed considerable momentum, impacting the Civil Service. Her advisors on the right, such as Keith Joseph and Alan Walters (who was persuaded to return to Britain from Johns Hopkins University), were ideological followers of the monetarist economics of Friedrich Hayek and Milton Friedman. They were deeply antipathetic to state intervention, pursuing cuts in the public sector and privatization of state-owned bodies. The size of the Civil Service had peaked in 1976, but now fell further with the change in policy. In addition to "rolling back the state," Thatcher aimed to import private-sector management models into government departments. One of the first initiatives was "Raynerism," in which a new Efficiency Unit (led by Sir Derek Rayner, an ex-senior manager of Marks and Spencers) scrutinized departmental work, suggesting areas where savings could be made. Though it was championed as a new phenomenon, Raynerism in fact echoed O&M, but without the emphasis on computers. (For example, the abolition of 27,000 forms and the simplification with assistance from the Plain English Campaign of a further 41,000 was reminiscent of O&M's remit.[3] The difference was that, whereas O&M had aimed at efficiency through improved design of forms, Rayner aimed to cut what he saw as unnecessary forms altogether.) A new expert movement—a managerial, not a technical one—was in place.

Similarly, the introduction of "Information Systems" was heralded as an innovation inspired by private-sector practices. Michael Heseltine, then Environment Secretary and later an agent of Thatcher's downfall, championed MINIS, a ministers' information system, a "kind of bureaucratic Domesday Book itemizing every activity in the giant DOE [Department of Environment], the manpower and money devoted to it and the priority afforded it."[4] Despite an unenthusiastic response from other ministers and senior civil servants, once

Margaret Thatcher was convinced of the system's benefits, other departments had to follow. Departmental adoption of MINIS-type systems was enshrined in the Financial Management Initiative (FMI) announced in May 1982. Hennessy writes that it was "coupled with a Government announcement of a £35 million program in direct costs for the computer systems and the people to run them which the FMI schemes would require over the next two years."[5] This considerable investment in technology presumably involved the installation of small workstations connected to a central computer, or even personal computers (which were attracting popular interest at that moment), but technical details are hard to come by. MINIS certainly was a largely paper-based system, despite the technology in the background. What MINIS significantly marks is the recognition by politicians and the administrative class of the Civil Service that their departments could be understood and managed in terms of the movement of information. Again, this is reminiscent of O&M, especially the early articulation of an information science of government found in wartime O&M (discussed in chapter 6). The difference is that this interpretation had been adopted by high-profile politicians, in particular Michael Heseltine, and therefore came into public view.

The FMI encouraged ministers to view departments as consisting of interlocking *accountable* blocks: "Each department should . . . examine the scope for breaking its structure down into cost centers or responsibility centers to which resource costs can be allocated and for which, where appropriate, measures of output can be devised and measured."[6] This trend continued in the last shake-up of Civil Service organization I shall consider, the Next Steps initiative. The idea had been floated, but not publicized since it might have been seen as a criticism of earlier achievements, before the general election of 1987, which saw Margaret Thatcher returned for a third term as prime minister. In February 1988, a report titled Improving Management in Government: The Next Steps was published. Its central argument was that the core should be separated from the vast bulk of executive Civil Service work, the latter taking the form of agencies, managerially autonomous but accountable through performance measures. Hints of such a policy can be found in the Fulton report, although "in the late 1960s the financial management infrastructure (information, budgeting, accounting and computer systems) necessary to make the agency idea workable just did not exist."[7] (Despite this claim, a similar style of government by agency had been in place in Sweden. This raises questions about the necessity of a link between changing technical infrastructure and administrative style.) By the end of 1988, the first Next Steps agencies had been created, and HMSO had been made an agency. By 1994, 65 percent of civil servants worked in agencies, mostly carved out of the big Whitehall departments. Next Steps agencification went hand in hand with further privatization, and in particular the contracting out of many services—including computer services—provided to government departments. Such outsourcing was justified under the Market Testing regime, favored during John Major's Conservative government, and later the Private Finance Initiatives (PFIs), continued under Labour after Tony Blair became Prime Minister in 1997. A review process, which asks whether any activity should be abolished, privatized, contracted out, market tested, agencified, or remain in department, has become entrenched.

By the 1990s the much-changed remnant of O&M could be found in a Next Steps agency. After the dissolution of Treasury O&M in the early 1970s, its functions had reappeared in the Central Computer Agency, established within the new Civil Service Department on 1 April 1972. This brought together the rump of Treasury O&M, computer responsibilities inherited from HMSO and the Technical Support Unit—another former O&M body—that had languished briefly in the Department of Trade and Industry. It changed its name to the Central Computer and Telecommunications Agency in 1979. Though the CCTA passed back to the Treasury in 1981, it resumed none of its former influence, and any lingering technocratic impulses would have been completely at odds with the new climate inspired by Thatcher. In 1992 it became the Government Agency for Information Systems, under the model of Next Steps. Still known as CCTA, a small organization now resides in the Office of Government Commerce.

Having sketched important developments in the Civil Service, I can now analyze Whitehall computerization after 1970 in context, looking in turn at three aspects: large-scale projects that refashioned systems inherited from the O&M years, the introduction of small computers, and networks. (In what follows, I have not been able to access the primary material that I regard as essential to true historical research because of the 30-year rule restricting the release of government documents. Since my experience of writing about the government information systems before 1970 shows that a very different perspective is gained from reading such primary material, the account below of post-1970 developments is provisional and quite possibly misleading in crucial respects. But there is enough secondary material in the public domain, in particular reports by inquisitorial bodies such as the National Audit Office and the Public Accounts Committee, and monographs from a sociological or political science perspective, such as Helen Margetts's invaluable *Information Technology in Government*, that patterns of change can be outlined).

Contracting Out Expertise

Large-scale computerization projects in British government departments have been profoundly shaped by the new policy of contracting out. Encouraged to follow private-sector fashion, government departments chose to concentrate on "core competencies," which did not include computing. Furthermore, with the collapse of the O&M expert movement, competency had been eroded, with the result that more and more information systems have been developed and maintained by private-sector companies. For these companies, government departments were only one purchaser among many. But there was a lot of business to be done. By 1994 outsourced information-technology services formed a market of $12.7 billion in the United States, with Electronic Data Systems (EDS) securing a 40 percent share, followed by IBM, Andersen Consulting, and the Computer Sciences Corporation, each with more than 10 percent.[8] In the mid 1990s in the United Kingdom, the leader in a much smaller but growing market was Hoskyns (a British start-up, bought by Cap Gemini Sogeti), followed by AT&T, Istel, EDS, and Sema.

Contracting out could mean different degrees of private-sector involvement in government departments, from ad hoc consultancy, through project tendering or facilities management, to systems integration projects or even "strategic alliances" and "partnership agreements."[9] A few UK government contracts went to British firms, such as the computer manufacturer ICL, which was diversifying in response to a slump in hardware sales, and the consultancy Logica, contributing a sixth of the firm's turnover in 1994. Most contracts, however, went to non-British firms, such as Hoskyns, Sema, Bull, DEC, Coopers & Lybrand, Siemens Nixdorf, and EDS.[10] EDS, an American company founded by a former IBM salesman, H. Ross Perot, in 1962, had been one of the first companies to specialize in selling computer time, and other services, to government bodies. EDS grew rapidly on the back of Medicare work for federal government from the mid 1960s.[11] With the market established in the United States, Perot's company looked to expand by selling similar services to other customers. So, for example, when market testing identified information technology as promising area for the Department for Social Security to outsource, contracts for distributed systems were awarded to Sema and ICL, while EDS secured all "data center services." EDS has benefited as government has transferred parts regarded as non-core. The Department of Transport's information-technology arm was made a Next Steps agency in 1992 and fully privatized the following year. EDS bought the agency, along with its contracts. Likewise, when the Information Technology Office of the Inland Revenue was sold off in 1994, EDS won a ten-year contract worth £1 billion, making it Europe's largest data-processing outsourcing deal in either the public or the private sector.[12] EDS's position has been built up through aggressive marketing policies, providing, for example, system development at no cost to the contractor in return for share of the business gains, and, for government contracts bidding very low in the expectation that, once dependence had been built up, costs could be recouped at a later date. (EDS's bid for a benefit agency's contract was low because the company thought that it would develop into a lucrative identity card system.[13])

A familiar pattern emerges from these upheavals in the provision of computing expertise to government departments. Margetts notes that "EDS employees working on the Inland Revenue contract will be highly trained specialists, while the contract management team of the Inland Revenue will be generalists," and generally, she predicts, there "will build up a disparate concentration of specialists at the leading edge of technological innovation in companies like Electronic Data Systems, while the less well paid, less professionalized and less innovative will be managing contracts in Civil Service organizations." In other words, *the Northcote-Trevelyan split has survived*, but the locus of power—based in knowledge, competence, and expertise—has shifted out of Whitehall into private-sector specialists such as EDS.

As outsourcing companies pick up more business, their expertise grows. Correspondingly, as government expertise falls, government bodies become ever more dependent on companies to which business has been outsourced. The Central Computer and Telecommunications Agency, for example, was downgraded further in 1983 to become merely advisory, in principle to force individual Whitehall departments to be more self-sufficient in all aspects of information technology but in practice to increase their dependence on outside expertise. At the extreme, expertise can be lost to such a degree that great difficulties are encountered if the work ever needs to brought back or a if a supplier has to be changed. (Local government bodies in London, which contract out tax collection and benefits data systems, have nearly been bankrupted in this way.)

Contracting out of information-technology services was justified by a combination of an appeal to an ideological attack on big government and anxieties over accountability that have led to calls for greater "transparency." Privatized monopolies, such as water or the railways, have watchdog organizations to regulate the industries and, at least in principle, to make failings visible. Next Steps agencies have to produce and publish performance measures, which in turn demand intensive data processing. "Transparency," a very late-twentieth-century virtue, will be considered further in the concluding chapter, but here I will note that one effect of such accountability regimes has been that government computer projects have been far more publicly scrutinized than ever before. This visibility partially accounts for why many have been regarded as abject failures. (Private companies bury their failures, unless, for additional reasons, their computerization projects are peculiarly politically sensitive, as was the case in the London Stock Exchange's TAURUS debacle.[14])

Like many large-scale technological systems, major government computerization schemes have been prone to suffer from budget overruns that critics, retrospectively, attributed to poor project management. This problem, too, was shared with private companies' systems. In 1984, the Comptroller and Auditor General, the senior official of the National Audit Office, reviewed a sample of such projects and concluded there existed a "number of areas of common weaknesses in planning and control. There were significant penalties in terms of wasteful expenditure and delays in securing the financial savings and improvements in departmental operations originally expected," and that there was "evidence to suggest that similar experiences are found in the private sector."[15]

One of the NAO's case studies, one that provides a good illustration of the problems and complexities of late twentieth-century computerization of government work, was the colossal Department of Health and Social Security (DHSS). This department administered a range of welfare payments, which with the sharp increase in unemployment from the late 1970s absorbed more public expenditure than any other item. (By the late 1980s, for example, £45 billion *a year* was paid to more than 24 million beneficiaries and dependents, nearly half the population of the UK.) Attempts to cut the cost of benefit administration were therefore highly politicized. The administration of social security benefits in 1984 involved 83,000 employees in the DHSS central and local offices, and another 30,000 in the Department of Employment. The work of DHSS central offices and the payment of unemployment and associated supplementary benefits had been extensively, and largely successfully, computerized. So batch systems at the central computer centers at Newcastle, North Fylde, and Livingston held central records (with each benefit held separate), but there was no on-line access to local offices.[16] The 63,000 employees in 500 DHSS local offices continued to operate manual systems to handle the administration of other benefits. With the ballooning cost of benefits in general, it was hoped that computerization of this local office work would not only enable direct savings in the cost of transactions to be made but also "provide more effective cross-checking of benefit claims," or, in other words, to improve surveillance capacity.[17] In 1977, ministerial approval was given to a pilot scheme, the Computerization and Mechanization of Local

Office Tasks (CAMELOT), a nationwide system that was to be ready by 1986. By 1981, however, it was clear that CAMELOT was in trouble. Costs were spiraling upward, and the twin objectives of improved efficiency and tighter control were receding. One cause was weak project management, which allowed programs to increase in size until they were beyond the capacities of the hardware. A second was the flight of skilled programmers to better-paying jobs in the private sector—an ever-present problem, since the supply of trained programmers has never matched demand, but one which was exacerbated during relative boom years, such as the early 1980s when enthusiasm was stoked by inflated claims for home computers. Dependence on expensive consultants increased as internal staff numbers dropped. In December 1981, when many British children gratefully received Sinclair ZX81s for Christmas, the government announced that its high-profile computerization project, CAMELOT, was to be abandoned. Twelve million pounds had been wasted.

The DHSS, however, learned from the CAMELOT debacle. Its second report on the Operational Strategy tied the "whole person concept" to a long-term and massive computerization of the department's offices. "Experience on CAMELOT," the Comptroller and Auditor General noted approvingly, "has emphasized the conclusions in these reports that maximum gains are unlikely to be achieved unless individual projects are developed as part of an overall plan; and the latest strategy proposals envisage the coordinated development of some 14 major computer projects over a fifteen year period at an additional cost of £700 million. DHSS estimate the total potential savings from the projects over a 20 year period will reach some £1,900 million."[18]

The Operational Strategy was predicted to be the "largest program of computerization in Europe."[19] At its core was the computerization of the Departmental Central Index, which held records of benefit details of claimants, making them available on line to all offices. More than 33,000 visual display units would be installed in 450 local social security offices, connecting to centralized databases. In particular, a Local Office Project (LOP), costing more than £200 million and fully operational by 1991, would replace CAMELOT. In 1989, the normally critical Comptroller and Auditor General, reviewing the Operational Strategy, stated that the department had made "significant progress in developing the Strategy to replace costly clerical systems with on-line computerized system. This is a large and innovative undertaking at the forefront of new technology and information-technology management. Although the NAO investigation has identified some delays and substantial cost increases, many of these were due to the complexity of the tasks undertaken and . . . factors outside the Department's control."[20]

But, significantly, dependence on expertise sourced from outside government increased still further. In 1987–88, for example, the cost of consultants was "nearly five times that of equivalent in-house staff," although they were judged "good value-for-money."[21] A hint of problems in store, however, could be found in the 6-month slippage in the keystone computerization of the Central Index, when suppliers responded to a Departmental tender with proposals radically different from those expected. While the government machine was seemingly becoming ever more mechanical, the new systems were largely built to order by agents not under governmental control, and internal springs of expertise diminished.

In March 1989, on-line terminals were in use in local offices in a pilot scheme that was followed later in the same year by the beginning of the national roll-out of the Operational Strategy systems. It was completed in July 1991, by which time 35,000 terminals had been installed in 1,000 local offices. Sally Wyatt, who made a study of their introduction, is skeptical as to "whether or not the original aims of increasing efficiency, service quality and job satisfaction had been met." The "Operational Strategy became a tool for controlling costs and reducing jobs. This [was] partly due to the change in the wider political culture affecting public services in Britain," but also reflected "a coalition of interests, a solution to the different problems faced by a variety of groups; of the Treasury which wanted something in place so staff reductions could begin; of DSS management who wanted a strike proof structure and a structure that would enable them to abolish thousands of clerical jobs; of technical staff, internal and external, who wanted to keep mainframes; and, of project teams who wanted to develop their own projects." The result was an Operational Strategy that was "concerned neither with enhancing service quality nor with improving jobs through integrating benefits and allowing higher levels of contact between local office staff and claimants."[22]

CAMELOT had been the earliest in a series of high-profile public-sector computerization failures. Notorious examples from the 1990s involved new systems for national insurance, passport applications, immigration, and secret defense documents. I will say a brief word about each of these.

The story of the new National Insurance Recording System, NIRS2, provides a good illustration of the difficulties of managing large, complex technological projects within a hollowed-out state. By the 1990s, the collection of national insurance was not made by a central government department but by the Contributions Agency, a product of the Next Steps reforms.[23] This agency inherited one of the great welfare registers, the National Insurance Recording System (NIRS), computerized piecemeal since the 1970s, with 65 million accounts by the 1990s. After beginning to consider the question in 1992, in

May 1995 the agency decided to purchase a replacement system, NIRS2, under a Private Finance Initiative (PFI) agreement. PFI, in which private-sector bodies invest in and run a project in return for payments from government, was begun by the Conservatives but continued under Labour. Since a new system was beyond the capabilities of the rump of internal expertise, the contract was awarded to Andersen Consulting. While other competitors had bid high, Andersen Consulting offered to build NIRS2 for "no payment, other than for taking on responsibility for running the existing NIRS1 system, until the replacement system was operating satisfactorily, after which payments were to be based on usage. The Agency expected that the cost of the contract to them would be about £134 million."[24] Margetts notes that this was "startlingly cheap," an example of "penetrative pricing"—bidding low to secure the contract in the knowledge that if costs subsequently rise then the customer has little alternative but to pay up.[25] Despite promising complete delivery by February 1997, Andersen Consulting admitted problems by January 1996 and requested a new phased timetable. The Contributions Agency reluctantly agreed. In 1998 and 1999 the situation turned even worse, and the House of Commons Select Committee on Public Accounts, which had already been critical, counted more than 1,500 "unresolved system problems, many of which were crucial to full implementation."[26] David Davis, chairman of the Select Committee, opened the questioning of Andersen Consulting with the reminder that NIRS2 "impacts on almost every adult in the country" and listed with "dismay" the affects of delay: 17 million accounts not updated, and welfare benefits and an estimated 172,000 pensions, largely to people dependent on that income, underpaid as a result.[27] Another MP on the committee, Alan Williams, went further:

> Andersen are not exactly a tin-pot little back street firm, they are supposed to be—supposed to be—one of the major international consultants, yet here they are wanting desperately to get into a market which they knew they were being kept out of by other companies. I may say that EDS operates in my constituency, not that I have any great sympathy for them either but I had better make that point. They just made a bid that they could not deliver and very quickly had to try to get you to agree to a new form in the hope that over time they could make up for their technological inexperience and incompetence.

George Bertram, Chief Executive of the Contributions Agency, to whom this point was addressed, disagreed, but conceded that barely half the projected number of pensions had been paid out.

The similar problems that hit the administration of passport applications in 1999 caused an even greater political storm, perhaps due to the relative newsworthiness of irate summer vacationers. Again contracts, in this case to computerize the large passport offices at Liverpool and Newport, beginning in 1997, went to the private sector. Despite the new system supposedly mirroring the old, employees found it more difficult to use, and productivity fell. The cost of processing a passport increased to £15.50; the target had been £12.[28] By July 1999, the bureaucracy of issuing passports was close to collapse. Processing times hit 50 days, and anxious travelers had to turn up and queue. Only the addition of many extra employees and the cutting of corners in the examination of applications reduced the backlog. Inevitably, some illegal applications would have been approved.

Immigration—now under headlines referring to "asylum"—returned to political prominence in the 1990s. The Conservative opposition made "asylum seekers" a central component of its attack on the government. In response, the government had invested in more "integrated" systems with greater surveillance capacities. These systems were to use information technology intensively. In April 1996 Siemens had been contracted by the Immigration and Nationality Directorate of the Home Office to introduce information technology to handle casework generated at immigration control at ports and local offices by October 1998. But during a delay in implementation, the directorate underwent "business process re-engineering," with the unfortunate consequence that the new organization did not fit Siemens's system. The results were "severe disruption to the Directorate's services for [several] months, and a large increase in the backlog of cases" (76,000 asylum cases and 100,000 nationality cases, stoking the political temperature of the issue still further) and "considerable anxiety and hardship caused to thousands of applicants due to the failure to resolve their cases."[29] The project was criticized for being too "ambitious," although it could equally well be argued that if the Home Office, or Whitehall more generally, had possessed internal expertise in information technology, rather than relying so heavily on outside contracts, such a severe disjuncture between organization and technology would have been unlikely.[30]

The final notorious example is Project Trawlerman, and again a similar pattern can be spotted. The Ministry of Defence wanted a computer system to handle the large amounts of classified information for its Defence Intelligence Staff. A £32 million contract was agreed in 1988, but delays and increased costs soon set in. Although the department accepted the system in 1995, it did not by then meet the Defence Intelligence Staff's own changing requirements. In particular, by the mid 1990s a *networkable* system was deemed essential, but this facility had not been written into the original contract. In 1996 the unused Project Trawlerman was declared obsolete and £41 million was written off. A different system was purchased for just £6 million.[31]

So technological change had the effect that delays in public-sector computerization projects could prove costly. Furthermore, gaps in expertise made for cautious policy making with regard to technological innovation. The public sector has been inclined to be risk averse—especially in recent decades, with internal experts who could play the role of technology champions reduced in number and influence—and policies that have sought to tackle this problem (such as the Private Finance Initiative deals, which have had the stated aim of shifting risk to the supposedly more capable private sector) have had mixed results. The two main trends in technological change were to smaller and networked computers. Again, the documentary evidence currently available allows only a provisional review.

Small Machines

Government research establishments, like other laboratories, were fairly quick to make use of the "bench-top" minicomputers, such as DEC's PDP series, marketed in the 1960s. In the late 1970s and the early 1980s, government departments became increasingly interested in small personal computers applied in office environments, although they were very much followers rather than leaders in innovation. Many of the large systems discussed above, such as the Operational Strategy for social security, involved access to data via dumb terminals. Uptake of small computers for office tasks such as word processing seems to have been slow. This might seem odd, given that it is a core task of bureaucracy. The National Audit Office was right to note that "civil servants work with words. They use them to frame laws, advise Ministers, announce casework decisions, provide information to the public and communicate with one another. Much of their work would be impossible without the facility to process the written or dictated word into typed text."[32]

In chapter 2 we saw that the introduction of typewriters was connected to the employment of women of a "superior class" and the eradication of male copyists. Female employees were segregated, according to Victorian moral standards—a segregation that continued as typing pools, justified by appeals to early-twentieth-century managerial theory, developed. The typical divisions of labor within the Civil Service in much of the twentieth century were therefore as follows: ". . . . most headquarters typing [employees were] located in centrally controlled pools, partly close to authors and partly at remote locations (on the outskirts of London, where rents were cheaper), in total around 23,400 by 1989.[33] The "authors," mostly male civil servants, worked in Whitehall offices with fountain pen and paper. The segregation of women with machines from men with pens was preserved not only by subtle grade distinctions (e.g., between data-processing and typing employees) but also by office culture: departments did not encourage non-typing employees to use typewriters, since to do so would upset important distinctions. So from the 1870s to the 1980s, most civil servants had to produce text by pen and paper (a few used Dictaphones); typed copies—often improved—were then produced elsewhere by other hands. Technical change in text production was confined largely to the pools: electric typewriters in the 1930s; word processors from the mid 1960s; electronic typewriters, laser printers, word processors with spellcheck, personal computers, networked word processors, and rudimentary e-mail by the 1980s.[34] One effect was the widespread use of documents—such as letters and circulars—in standardized formats; another was the use of networked databases to insert specific details such as names and addresses into standardized forms. Nevertheless, this innovation was confined to pools.

But as word-processing skills spread, more and more entrants to the Civil Service were expected to be able to exploit them at work. (Curiously, this demand does not seem to have been so strong with typewriting skills, which were widely diffused in the first half of the twentieth century.) For example, drafting on screen, a feature of word processors as well as general-purpose personal computers, was seen by non-typing employees as desirable as well as more cost effective. Facilitated by the restructuring of secretarial grades, and by a merger of clerical and data-processing grades, so that "typists can do some clerical work, secretaries can perform minor managerial functions and clerical staff can routinely use computer equipment" (and print out e-mail), the demand for word processors began to break the distinction between small machine users and non-users in the Civil Service. One consequence was that many civil servants became direct authors of final texts for first time since the widespread introduction of typing pools. With the extensive introduction of personal computers, intranets, and e-mail, even very senior staff members have had to work at their own computers. The changes, however, could be slow: the last Cabinet Office typing pool disappeared in 2000.

Networks

The history of networking was also shaped by the transition from internal to external technical expertise. Indeed, the role of British government scientists in the early years of network development is now widely recognized. The reinvention of packet switching, this time in order to network computers, was made in the mid to late 1960s in the United States (where the Advanced

Research Projects Agency wanted techniques that would allow expensive supercomputing resources to be shared, and RAND wanted the same to be the basis of a communication system that could survive a nuclear attack) and in the United Kingdom (where computer scientists at the National Physical Laboratory were exploring the concept).[35]

In 1965, when Donald Davies proposed a national packet-switching network, the NPL was a part of the Ministry of Technology, a massive department that Labour Prime Minister Harold Wilson had created by merging the Ministry of Supply with the Department of Scientific and Industrial Research. However, unwillingness to disturb the boundaries between government departments disrupted the project. The historian of NPL computing writes: "The provision of telecommunication services was a monopoly of the Post Office, and they might reasonably ask why NPL, part of another Government department, was involving itself with matters that were not its concern. Davies's combination of professional expertise and political awareness successfully avoided this pitfall: it was understood that NPL would simply carry out research in the area, build an experimental local network on its own site, and would restrict public announcements to these technical matters. While it might make suggestions in UK telecommunications policy, responsibility for decisions in that area . . . lay solely with the Post Office."[36] An intranet linking buildings within the NPL followed, but the Post Office's Experimental Packet Switched Service—the prototype of a national network—was much delayed. (The Post Office, one of the major technical innovators of the first half of the century, was becoming ossified, a situation that was not to change until its partial privatization and the creation of British Telecom in the 1980s). At the 1967 Association for Computing Machinery meeting at Gatlinburg, Tennessee, fertile contact was made between ARPA and NPL. Larry Roberts of ARPA announced the requirement for a packet-switched network, and Roger Scantlebury of NPL provided a detailed design that fulfilled it. "ARPA accordingly adopted NPL's ideas enthusiastically," and the two groups cooperated.[37] The ARPANET, as is well known, was to evolve, after the introduction of new protocols, into the Internet. However, political commitments to assisting with the Post Office's network and a European Informatics Network meant that the NPL did not have the resources to pursue the simplest line of research into interconnection—which would have meant connecting the NPL network to the ARPANET.[38] Instead, the first British organization connected to the Internet was University College London. The choice of UCL rather than the more obvious NPL was the result of a political calculation of the balance of European and American relations: "A highly Europhilic Heath administration was preparing to lead the country into the Common Market. Any hint of a special relationship between the UK and the USA was to be avoided, and a UK national laboratory putting transatlantic links first was simply out of the question."[39] This political choice was reflected in NPL's support for different protocols: the European link led NPL to involvement with X.25, while participation—as national laboratory—in the International Organization for Standardization prompted enthusiastic backing for Open Systems Interconnection. Both of these top-down bureaucratic models would lose out to the Internet protocol, TCP/IP.[40]

The work of the NPL demonstrates that expertise in networking computers existed within British government in the late 1960s. But, to repeat again, from that time on the location of expertise shifted. The NPL was to become a Next Steps agency in 1990, but by that time innovation in government computer networking had already declined. One early proposal—GANNET, the first attempt at a "central government general administrative network," developed by ICL and the Central Computer Agency in the mid 1970s—was canceled (although it later formed the base of a network between North-West universities, and also of a Ministry of Defence network called GRIDFEST).[41] In 1986, four government departments (Inland Revenue, Social Security, Customs and Excise, and the Home Office), initiated a project to build a data communications system called the Government Data Network (GDN). Before GDN, individual departments had built small internal networks on an ad hoc basis. Most were poorly designed or poorly used, an example being the VIENNA system introduced in the Cabinet Office to link personal computers together. Eventually there were 115 workstations on the network. No overall "business benefits" justification guided the decision to build VIENNA, instead a "strategic decision was taken that networked industry standard systems were the future of office automation. VIENNA would therefore be an investment in the future through the provision of infrastructure and introducing staff to working with the technology."[42] Ethernet cabling was used, since British Telecom telephone lines could not cope. But the word-processing package (VIENNA WORD) was found to be unstable and the database program too complex. Already underutilized, VIENNA collapsed after the supplier was taken over by another company, which in August 1989 decided to discontinue service support.[43]

A rare success was the ambitious Edinburgh-London-Glasgow Information Network (ELGIN), piloted in 1982 and in full operation 2 years later. Consisting of IBM minicomputers linked by British Telecom, Mercury, and private Scottish Office lines, ELGIN connected personal computers in three cities, including those in the offices of all senior civil servants and ministers as well as those in typing pools.[44] But ELGIN, too, should be seen as a political project. Public opinion in Scotland in the 1980s was consistently hostile to Margaret Thatcher's Conservative administration. This antipathy would last until a separate legislative assembly was set up in Edinburgh in the late 1990s. Until then, Scotland was ruled from London. The ELGIN network, providing rapid, secure, and full transmission of documents between the two major Scottish cities and Whitehall in London, bolstered this power structure.

So ad hoc networks had limited success. The four departmental sponsors of the Government Data Network supposed that it would lead to single network, used by all, with each department benefiting from economies of scale. The Treasury ruled out a project developed in house, on the grounds that "no single department would have adequate financial or human resources," the political preference, anyway, would be for a private-sector solution.[45] Bids were invited, although the two largest providers of telecommunications services in Britain—British Telecom and Mercury—were excluded from leading bids or making bids on their own for reasons that are unclear but presumably connected to a wider political context of deregulation. Full tenders came from three consortia, one of which, Racal Data Networks Limited, a company with no previous experience in civil data networks, was successful.[46] It proposed the cheapest system, based on the X.25 protocol, compatible with Open Systems Interconnection. Racal Data Networks was to be paid by use. This contract made the company far keener on increasing the number of users than, it seems, were the four sponsoring departments. But users were not the focus of the design of the Government Data Network, an important cause of its subsequent failure. According to Sally Wyatt, Racal was "contracted to provide a network infrastructure. It was not charged with developing applications. No one was. Decisions about what data to communicate between whom were left to the users. For many civil servants, discovering a socket in their office walls was the first exposure they had to the miracle of data communication. Actual usage of the GDN was negligible. . . . "[47] Wyatt blames this state of affairs on the technologically determinist views held by the senior officials of the four sponsoring departments. It would also be true to say that a situation in which technical systems could be developed without considering civil servant users would have been unlikely in the earlier period when internal experts, such as O&M in the 1960s, led investigation and project design. A cross-Whitehall, extensively used network was not in place until the late 1990s, with the Government Secure Intranet, built by Cable & Wireless Communications, under contract from the CCTA. Forty departments (by no means all of Whitehall) were connected by this intranet by 2000; there were 120,000 users in all.[48]

Modern Government?

By 2000, riding on the galloping enthusiasm for all things Internet, networked government had become a keystone of wider moves to reform Whitehall. The emphasis was on exploiting network links between citizen and department, as well as on providing a technological carrier of departmental and interdepartmental reform. A bewildering array of new initiatives and jargon appeared, especially under the New Labour administration of Tony Blair. These included the appointment of an "e-minister" (responsible for the government's "e-agenda") and an "e-envoy" (following recommendations made in a report by the Performance and Innovation Unit of the Cabinet Office titled *e-commerce@its.best.uk*); the establishment in 1995—before Blair—of a Central Information Technology Unit (also within the Cabinet Office) responsible for developing the government's information-technology strategy and monitoring its implementation; the proliferation of web sites, brought under some control by the launch of a portal in 1995 (www.open.gov.uk, later

" The era of technomania is passing — and high time too." (Wedgwood Benn)

Figure 10.2
A cartoon by Nicholas Garland in the *Daily Telegraph* of 20 May 1969. The caption quotes Minister of Technology Anthony Wedgwood Benn, who is portrayed as a nihilistic robot: "The era of technomania is passing—and high time too." Note the computers at left and the Concorde overhead. (source: Centre for the Study of Cartoons and Caricature, University of Kent at Canterbury)

Figure 10.3
A cartoon by Steve Bell in the *Guardian* of 30 April 1998. Satirizing the simplistic reduction inherent in early e-government proposals, Bell turns the Book of Common Prayer into the tabloid *Sun*'s Book of Common Morality. (source: Centre for the Study of Cartoons and Caricature, University of Kent at Canterbury)

re-launched as www.ukonline.gov.uk). The white paper Modernising Government, prepared by the Cabinet Office, introduced targets and a distinctive language to the program.[49] The starting point may have been rather tired cyber-hype, as the following part of the "vision" suggests:

> Information technology is revolutionizing our lives, including the way we work, the way we communicate and the way we learn. The information age offers huge scope for organizing government activities in new, innovative and better ways and for making life easier for the public by providing public services in integrated, imaginative and more convenient forms like single gateways, the Internet and digital TV.

Fortunately, what followed in the main text of Modernising Government was more distinctive and substantive. The package of reforms offered included "joined-up government in action—including a clear commitment for people to be able to notify different parts of government of details such as a change of address simply and electronically in one transaction" and a "new target of all dealings with government being deliverable electronically by 2008."[50] (Although "electronically" meant by telephone or fax or e-mail.[51]) A

Figure 10.4
Wang word processors in HMSO's Basildon Reprographic Unit, 1982. (source: Public Record Office. PRO STAT/20/37)

"commitment" was made to "information age government": "We will use new technology to meet the needs of citizens and business, and not trail behind technological developments." Intentions were announced to "develop an IT strategy for Government which will establish cross-government coordination machinery and frameworks on such issues as use of digital signatures and smart cards, web sites and call centers" and to "benchmark progress against targets for electronic services." Modernising Government conceded that private companies had "used networked computing to refocus their activities on the customer. They have used IT to work more closely with their suppliers. They have made innovative use of information to become learning organizations. They have supplied new services, when, where and how the customer wants them. They have developed new delivery channels like call centers and the Internet. They have given their staff the support they need to use IT effectively," and government had "not kept sufficient pace with these developments." Minimum capabilities, promised by 2002, included citizens' being able electronically to book driving tests, look for work and be matched to jobs, submit self-assessment tax returns, get information and advice about benefits (but not to apply for and receive them), or get on-line health information and advice, while businesses would be able to complete VAT registration and make VAT returns, file returns at Companies House, apply for regional support grants or receive payments from government for the supply of goods and services. Perhaps most significant, the focus of service design would begin with the user, with the aim of "making sure that public service users, not providers, are the focus, by matching services more closely to people's lives." One-stop shops—or their electronic web site equivalent—would, in principle, make a citizen's business with government a less time-consuming affair. Companies lobbying for contracts under this new regime soon appropriated the language. In 2000, for example, Sun Microsystems (which boldly and briefly tagged itself "the dot in .com"), in conjunction with a consultancy known as Kable Ltd., produced a widely circulated leaflet titled Citizen Centric E-Government.

Such promises depended upon futurological assumptions. The white paper was unusually explicit as to what these "drivers of information age government" were. They included "household access to electronic services through developments such as interactive TV," "much more user-friendly, inexpensive, and multi-functional technology as TV, telephones and broadcasting converge," "less dependence on keyboard skills as remote control pads, voice command, touch screens, video conferencing and other developments make it easier for users to operate and benefit from new technology," "continuing dramatic increases in computing power, and in the power of networked computing," "wide scale take-up of multi-purpose smartcards, with which citizens can identify themselves, use services, safeguard their privacy and, increasingly, make and receive payments," "government forms and other processes which are interactive," and some less specific hopes such as "smarter knowledge management" and increased use of web sites. Some of these forecasts soon looked shaky (for example the promise of interactive TV receded significantly within the year). Others, which looked up to e-commerce models championed in the private sector, were severely shaken by the collapse of the dot-com bubble in 2000–2001. But despite these events, the Modernising Government vision survived.

Conclusion

Modernising Government reflected both continuities and changes in the long-term relationship between government and information technology. One of the key assumptions of the white paper was the continuation, and the continued importance, of a convergence of information technologies. Faith in the existence of such a convergence has guided information-technology policy since the 1960s. The enthusiasm for smartcards recalled the policy on peacetime identification documents, with voluntarism emphasized. The policy initiative of "one-stop shops" (and their virtual equivalent, the portal) is new in that the "shops" are designed from the users' perspective, so that from the outside government appears seamless, even if separate systems are maintained inside. They also mark a departure from the historical compromise on registers of welfare information: to have overlapping partial registers and not to keep them discrete. Against the culture of the Civil Service, information systems are becoming outward looking in appearance and as a policy aim, if not always in fact.

The authors of Modernising Government briefly discussed the issue of privacy. They acknowledged that there was "concern that information technology could lead to mistaken identity, inadvertent disclosure and inappropriate transfer of data" before promising that "government will address these concerns and will demonstrate our belief that data protection is an objective of information age government, not an obstacle to it." A string of by-now-familiar aims followed. In essence these were reassurances that existing data-protection legislation was adequate.[52] This rhetoric is interesting in its blandness. Despite concern that fears of data privacy were hampering e-commerce, the fact that no new actions were considered necessary was indicative that privacy was no longer conceived as a particularly important issue. In chapter 9 we saw concerns over threats to privacy from information technology come full circle, peaking in the late 1960s and the early 1970s. Curiously, this was the period in which the centralized database held on mainframe computers became less and less typical of government information-technology projects. David Burnham's 1983 book *The Rise of the Computer State* warned of "the widely acknowledged and heavily advertised ability of the computer to collect, organize and distribute information tends to enhance the power of bureaucratic structures." But such systems were increasingly in the hands, not of state bureaucracies, but of private-sector companies that picked up the business. The hollowing out of the state, and in particular the contracting out of computing services exemplified by the rise of companies such as EDS, was a trend that ran counter to concerns about the centralized-database state. If anything, the threat to privacy has increased, since private-sector companies are less publicly accountable than government.

These changes in technology and in the nature of the state were fundamentally linked to the social organization of expertise. No technology succeeds without a group to champion it. With the punched-card tabulator and the electronic computer, the relevant group was the expert movement of mechanizers, in particular the Organization and Methods movement based in the Treasury. The erosion of their power that began in the 1970s coincided with the breakdown of the hierarchical model of state action, with one trend shaping the other. In the 1940s and the 1950s, government action had led to the Colossus, the Ferranti Mark I, packet-switched networks, and many other achievements in information technologies and systems. By the 1980s, government computer projects were a by-word for exceeded budgets and failure. The last few years have seen a shift again. Government has been determined to identify itself with the *modernity* of information technology. Though it is too early to judge whether the shift in policy has indeed gone further than mere identification (Modernising Government, after all, was being composed while thousands had to queue for passports because of the latest system crash), this final stage of government computing features one similarity and two differences with the previous technocratic "golden age." The similarity was the concentration of initiatives in one strong department, albeit the Cabinet Office rather than the Treasury. One difference, of course, was the external location of much of the expertise: government was no longer a provider of technology. But the other, which will be examined in the next and final chapter, was how government championed the modern. The outward-looking emphasis on presentation in the 1990s contrasted starkly with the inward-looking modernity of the mid-century Civil Service.

Conclusions and International Perspectives

The Civil Service was a general-purpose "machine" governed by a code. The stored-program computer is a general-purpose machine governed by a code. Is this similarity a coincidence, or is there a profound connection? I think that the computer is indeed a materialization of bureaucratic action, but the connection between the two is far from simple. In particular, the relationship has had to be explored through a historical account of both the articulation of government as a machine and the achievement by social movements of the mechanization of the work of government. So not only have I tried to analyze developments in political thought; I have also sought to give accounts of mechanization within one of the most extensive (in space and time) organizations. In this final chapter I will attempt to summarize and to draw conclusions and (where possible) international comparisons. First, however, a historiographical point must be made.

How Do We Explain Mechanization?

In general, historians of technology have focused on the processes of invention and innovation, during which a technology might move from a small experimental setting to the market place.[1] For example, the pattern of development in the systems approach starts with invention and proceeds from there.[2] This being so, the factors that historians have discovered to be most important, at least in the non-internalist tradition, have been social or economic, which should not be too surprising: the moment of introduction is when social needs or wants have to be made plain.

But this emphasis makes most sense if mechanization is taken to refer to the introduction of *material* machines. The emphasis on introduction of technology makes less sense if we are interested in technology or the "mechanical" in both discursive and material forms (assuming, for the sake of argument, that the two can be separated at all). There are many reasons why we should be interested in discursive machines, not least because it is good historiographical practice to be attentive to the terms used by historical actors. So if, say, Goethe declared Frederick of Prussia to be like a "big old drum" governing a clockwork mechanism, we should presume his words were chosen well. Of course, when a historical actor deploys mechanical language, there is a spectrum of interpretative possibilities, from identity through metaphor to mere glancing analogy. My point is that the attribution of machine-like characteristics can be an important phase that is prior to and helps constitute any later project of mechanization. (In the scheme of table C.1, investigations of such attributions would be an example of type C.) An ontological choice lies between the "strong" and "weak" versions of argument (to employ the terminology of the Edinburgh school of sociology of science).[3] In the strong version, discursive and material technologies should be treated symmetrically. That is to say, mechanism should be accounted for, whether it be material or discursive, by appeal to the same kinds of factors, and a difference between the two should not be assumed. This has the effect of collapsing the distinctions between types A and C and between types B and D in table C.1. In a weak version, the presumption of a difference between material and discursive technologies is retained.

The question "How do we account for mechanization?" can, therefore, be broken down into two questions: (1) Why was something described as being like a machine? (2) Once described as being like a machine, why was it mechanized—in other words, what is the relationship between discursive and material mechanization? Answering questions of type 2, we enter fairly familiar

Table C.1

Four types of technology. Type A has been the traditional focus of history of technology. Social construction of technology, which insists on paying attention to the interpretative flexibility of material technologies, can be understood as a widening of the focus to include type B.[a] The transgression of the boundary between types A and B was one response. I am suggesing that historians of technology should pay attention to type C as well. I am not sure if type D is meaningful.

(A) Material technologies, referred to as mechanical	(C) Discursive technologies, referred to as mechanical
(B) Material technologies, referred to as non-mechanical	(D) Discursive technologies, referred to as non-mechanical

a. On this, see Wiebe E. Bijker, Thomas P. Hughes, and Trevor Pinch, "The social construction of facts and artefacts: or how the sociology of science and the sociology of technology might benefit each other," in *The Social Construction of Technological Systems*, ed. W. Bijker et al. (MIT Press, 1987).

historiographical territory, in which the most important factors will be social or economic or will concern the frame provided by preceding material technologies. So, in the parts of this book that have examined the mechanization of British government departments, the most important immediate influences were indeed such factors as economic judgments of savings of personnel or expenditure, or social judgments as to what sort of person should be a civil servant. But I have also tried to ask a question of type 1: Why was government, in particular the Civil Service, described as a machine?

In *War Machine*, Daniel Pick argues that the stress of the Great War brought forth claims, across a broad range of arenas, of the revelation of hidden mechanisms: the "deeper forces" of history made explicit, for example, or the previously occult mechanisms of the unconscious brought to light by shell shock and psychoanalysis.[4] On the principle of "better the devil you know," Pick's examples and arguments suggest considering mechanization as prompted by extreme stress and, in some cases, as a means of replacing perceived hidden mechanisms with real mechanisms. With this proposal in mind, let us consider a second argument put forth by Pick. He tells us that war, cast as a machine out of control, was a significant and durable image from the nineteenth century on. In the age of the rationalization of slaughter, the metaphor of the war machine fed into the conceptualization of humans; for example, the "masses" were prone to *derangement*, as of a machine. Finally, Pick records contemporary observations that the elite, notably the intellectual elite, were if anything *more* susceptible to collective derangement.[5] Putting the two argumentative parts together, one can make the following intriguing claim: Faced with derangement of the intellect under the stress of war, intellectual processes were made explicit through mechanization. I put this forward partly to help explain the spread of punched-card and statistical techniques during and after the Great War, as discussed in chapter 5, and to suggest what might help explain the otherwise troubling cluster of informational organizations that appeared in the middle of the twentieth century and which formed the subject of chapter 6. Recall, for example, this 1924 justification for the new Census of Production: "We need to see where we stand after the disorganization of a great war, which has made all previous standards antiquated."[6] However, should the general point that mechanization was a means of making processes explicit and open be disconnected from warfare?

One of the great transformations brought about by the First World War will serve as an example. The Haldane Lecture of 1942 gave the arch-bureaucrat Maurice Hankey the opportunity to reflect on a revolution in British government: the establishment in December 1916 of government by cabinet committees, producing *permanent records*. From that date, government debate and action at the highest level was made permanently legible. Hankey first related Lord Curzon's description in the House of Lords, on 19 June 1918, of the bad old days (note the machinery metaphors):

> There was no agenda, there was no order of business. Any Minister requiring to bring up a matter either of Departmental or of public importance had to seek the permission of the Prime Minister to do so. No one else, broadly speaking, was warned in advance. It was difficult for any Minister to secure an interstice in the discussion in which he could place his own case. No record whatever was kept of our proceedings, except the private and personal letter written by the Prime Minister to the Sovereign, the contents of which were not seen by anybody else. The Cabinet often had the very haziest notion as to what to its decisions were. . . . No one will deny that a system, however embedded in the traditions of the past and consecrated by constitutional custom, which was attended by these defects, was a system which was destined immediately it came into contact with the hard realities of war, to crumble into dust at once. . . . I do not think anyone will deny that the old Cabinet system had irretrievably broken down, both as a war machine and as a peace machine.[7]

Hankey then celebrated the change from Committee of Imperial Defence to War Council to Dardenelles Committee to War Committee: "Each Council or Committee was an improvement on its predecessor as we groped our way by the light of our experience to a better system." The final fusion of Cabinet and War Committee by the new prime minister, David Lloyd George, completed the revolution:

> This body inherited all the powers and authority of the Cabinet—over the whole range of Cabinet business, and not only over the conduct of the war, as sometimes stated—together with the machinery and procedure of the War Committee. For the first time in the history of the Cabinet a Secretary was present to record the proceedings and keep the Minutes of the Cabinet and of its numerous Committees, and orderly methods, based on those developed by the [Committee of Imperial Defence], were introduced including agenda papers, the distribution (in advance of meetings) of relevant memoranda and other material, the rapid communication of decisions to those who had to act upon them or were concerned in the second degree; and the knitting up to the War Cabinet, not only of Government Departments, but also of numerous Committees covering a vast range of inter-Departmental business.

I have discussed this revolution in cabinet government here for three reasons. First, it does seem to confirm Pick's argument that war had the effect of making things visible and explicit, and that one path this process could take was through the extensive use of mechanical metaphor. Under the "harsh realities of war," charismatic government would "crumble into dust" unless reformed to become based on rational bureaucracy. Second, politicians have rarely entered my account of the government machine. One reason is because, after the formation of recordable cabinet government, politicians were, bluntly, part of the system. Third, it was a short step from making government mechanically visible to taking this metaphor literally, the transition being the substance of this book.

But the reformers of the Civil Service discussed in chapter 2 had, in times of peace, a clear motive for casting government as a machine. The Civil Service was described as a machine because it was advantageous to certain people and groups to do so. In particular it settled certain issues of trust, revisited below. By likening certain parts of government to a machine, the intended reading was often that the actions of those parts were predictable. They provided a means of underlining that the rules of state administration should be made visible—to clear out patronage and replace it with a supposed meritocracy forged in the physical stress of examinations (even if, by this very contract, British bureaucracy henceforth was marked by opaqueness and discretion—the discursive formation of the Civil Service as a machine assisted this disappearance act).

I am not claiming that discursive mechanization leads irrevocably to material mechanization. There would be several counter-arguments to such a claim. For example, it would be arguable that some countries, such as Germany, were marked as much by an organic conception of state as by a mechanical one.[8] (Coleridge tried to import this tradition into British political thought but largely failed.) But German government offices mechanized at much the same rate as Whitehall, so international comparisons can rule out the simpler models that would suggest that discursive mechanization prompted early material mechanization. Indeed, it could be argued that discursive mechanization provided an obstacle to material mechanization, since it lent the organization attributes of speed and efficiency that may not have been deserved. Instead, my empirical work suggests that the link between discursive and material mechanization had to be appropriated, articulated, and developed by people, often in the form of interested social groups.

The making explicit of the "hidden" processes of government could be done in various ways, and each created different opportunities. Trevelyan's reform of the Civil Service by the introduction of exams opened opportunities for examiners and the public school system more generally. When A. V. Dicey attempted to reduce the "unwritten constitution" to a "partially written code," he was enshrining "the meaning of the constitution in a set of legal principles that only lawyers could dispute."[9] In particular, when the hidden links in government were portrayed as a machine, an opportunity was created for what I have called an expert movement of mechanizers. They would have taken Mortimer Taube at his word when he wrote: "We can mechanize insofar as we can make a formal rule." Discursive mechanization of administration was a resource: it helped Alan Turing to articulate a new theory of the universal machine, and it gave the expert movement of mechanizers an opportunity to advance themselves and their vision of state action.

State Typologies

Government has often been likened to a machine. Sometimes the machine appealed to is a particular one, sometimes not. Otto Mayr argued that a different particular machine formed the core metaphor for different styles of government: clockwork or automata for the enlightened despotism of Frederick II's Prussia or *ancien regime* France, and the balance for liberalism, primarily of English inspiration. Mayr ends his discussion with the liberal balances of the early nineteenth century. In chapter 1, I sought to build on Mayr's insight, and to ask what mechanical analogues mirrored new styles of government from the nineteenth and twentieth centuries. I suggested that the steam engine became a model for the more dynamic styles of government, where the "motive force" might be either the will of the people (in democratic thought) or sovereign power (in Bagehot's monarchical textbook), depending on the political locations of commentators.

The distinction between the legislative and executive parts of government, crucial to "balance" theories of political thought and foundational to American systems of government, was criticized by utilitarians in Britain. While they preserved the distinction, they attacked the separation of the legislative and the executive. James Mill insisted on proper checks, so that one would influence the other in a dynamical relationship. In India, the experiment was less constrained, and in the utilitarians' ideal model there was "mechanical" control of both executive and legislature. I suggested there were parallels between such "mechanical" political thought and Babbage's designs for his Analytical Engine. Babbage had accepted with enthusiasm the description of the Engine provided by Giovanni Plana: as a machine that "seems to give us the same control over the executive which we have hitherto only possessed over the legislative department." Plana recognized this attribute because the kingdom of Piedmont-Sardinia was leading the debate that was to culminate in Italian nation building. Control over the executive—kings, bureaucrats, state machinery—was everything. It is plausible to argue that Babbage accepted this political reading because building the Analytical Engine was only one of several attempts he made at direct political influence. If it had succeeded, Babbage's Engines would have been revolutionary in both familiar senses of the word, as a new technique and as a coup d'état. By taking Babbage's own best description of his most radical machine seriously, we can see his other activities, as statistical organizer or as failed parliamentary candidate, as parts of a coherent whole.

Of all the parts of government that have been likened to a machine, the most ingrained example (in Britain) has been the Civil Service. The "Civil Service machine" is such a familiar figure of speech that it is easy for it to pass by unremarked. But to describe the Civil Service as a machine is rather odd, not least because senior figures in the Service were gentlemen, and to describe gentlemen as machines runs counter the received wisdom concerning an opposition between English culture and the "industrial spirit." I argued that use of the mechanical metaphor in discussing the work of the Civil Service should be related to three contextual factors. First, it supported a distinction drawn between politicians (as the operators of the machine) and a supposedly interest-free, neutral Civil Service that would be trusted to operate identically under both Liberal and Tory governments. Whereas civil servants were cast in the Northcote-Trevelyan report as sickly, now they would share the mechanical characteristics beloved by Babbage: the "great advantage we may derive from machinery is from the check it affords against the inattention, the idleness, or the dishonesty of human agents," which in this case would also refer to the operators, the politicians.[10] Second, labeling the whole of the Civil Service a machine solved other acute problems of *trust*. The growth of government departments drew people into bureaucratic work that the gentlemanly elite could not automatically trust: lower class clerks and even women. While trust in the upper echelons was secured by the appeal to honorable secrecy and gentlemanly discretion, these new staff, including men of all classes and women, could be cast as "mechanical." By making them components of a "machine" helped resolve these issues of trust by extending to the lower echelons a metaphorical reliability. The third reason for the mechanical metaphor of British bureaucracy was that it could be interpreted literally by members of the expert movement of mechanizers.

For these three reasons, the political machine in the United Kingdom was the Civil Service. In the United States the political "machine" was and is the constitution, or, more often, a party organization.[11] This national difference can be directly related to the different national politics of central administration appointments. In the United States, for 40 years after the adoption of the Constitution the small federal bureaucracy was in many ways similar to that of Britain, with a political executive assisted by a class of permanent administrators. The two systems diverged in the nineteenth century. After the election of Andrew Jackson as president in 1828 introduced the two-party regime, the "spoils system" was institutionalized.[12] The senior officials became the political appointees of the incoming administration. (This was, of course, an aspect of two quite different democratic systems, far more local, state, and national positions being politically determined, either by election or appointment, in the United States.) In Britain, though patronage was common, a spoils system did not develop. (Indeed, since positions could be owned like property, to "deprive a man of his place seemed, therefore, only less shocking than to deprive him of his goods or land."[13]) Instead, administration was separated from politics, epitomized by the establishment of the permanent, neutral Civil Service. The word "machine" did different political work in the two countries. In Britain it underlined the neutrality of the Civil Service; in the United States it suggested the relentlessness and power of party organization.

However, I do not want to overemphasize national differences. In first approximation, bureaucracies tend to be rather similar (which was why Weber could describe an ideal type). National styles of bureaucracy have provided a recurring theme in writings from nineteenth and twentieth centuries. Mill, in *On Liberty*, drew contrasts between the bureaucracies of Russia, France, the United States, Britain, and China. The cases of (Tsarist and Soviet) Russia and China in particular recurred as extreme inefficient forms, and Prussia/Germany as an efficient form. (These countries became critical clichés of machine-like states, and, as I argued in chapter 1, when mobilized by nineteenth-century critics of the government machine, had the effect of further reinforcing the metaphor). Mill cited the "melancholy condition of the Russian empire" and noted that "the Czar himself is powerless against the bureaucratic body." Just before noting the Chinese mandarin, he argues of Americans that "no bureaucracy can hope to make such a people as this do or undergo anything that they do not like. But where everything is done through the bureaucracy, nothing to which the bureaucracy is really adverse can be done at all." China, as a nation shackled to bureaucracy, was of course an enduring image, reproduced in the twentieth century in, for example, Karl Wittfogel's influential 1957 book *Oriental Despotism*. Though many analysts' first concern has been to produce a typologies of government (those of Gaetano Mosca, Herbert Spencer, and Max Weber are all important examples), these were soon connected to national examples. This process has caused greater emphasis to have been placed on national differences than on broad international similarities of government.

The distinctive feature of British bureaucracy has been the hierarchical distinction within the Civil Service: a generalist administrative class, a large class of "mechanical" employees, and an uneasy order of Executive Officers mediating between the two. A split between managerial and non-managerial employees was, of course, already old by 1854. But as part of a state bureaucracy it was part of an organization of general application, relative to such hierarchies in private concerns, which must necessarily be directed toward business goals.[14] This split, partly described by Charles Trevelyan in the Northcote-Trevelyan report in 1854, was adopted piecemeal within the British and the Indian Civil Services over the following decades. The generalist-mechanical split distinctly marked the description given by Alan Turing of the operation of his own universal machine. Turing imagined a machine in which precise instructions, written and stored in one part of the machine, would be followed with clerical precision by another. In describing the capabilities and limitations of a universal machine, there was only one other general-purpose machine in Turing's world that he could look to. Though it was "merely" a metaphorical machine, Turing certainly knew the operation of the Civil Service well, insofar as it was literally a component of his familial culture. Again the links between "computer pioneer" and government are profound—although Turing, unlike Babbage, saw his plans materialize at the apogee of mechanical government: Bletchley Park.

Statistical Organization

I have already said that it was important in the nineteenth century for civil servants be cast as components of a machine partly so that trust could be extended to encompass women and lower-class men. One reason this mattered was because the state was becoming an ever-more-prolific producer of knowledge, and a mechanical Civil Service lent a mechanical objectivity to the knowledge produced.[15] Again we see why fashioning a "mechanical" Civil Service was important: it finessed a transfer from gentlemanly modes of justifying trust in knowledge to modes dependent on state-backed specialists.[16] But why was the state producing and underwriting so much knowledge? Ian Hacking has accounted for the nineteenth century's "avalanche of numbers" partly as a consequence of industrialization: "The avalanche of numbers, the erosion of determinism, and the invention of normalcy are embedded in the grander topics of the Industrial Revolution. The acquisition of numbers by the populace and the professional lust for precision in measurement were driven by familiar themes of manufacture, mining, trade, health, railways, war, empire."[17] Hacking has interesting things to say concerning both national styles and the privacy of statistical knowledge. Statistical laws, he says, "had in the beginning to be read into the data. They were not simply read off." Hacking draws a "gross, but convenient" contrast between "Prussian (and other east European) attitudes to numerical data, and those that flourished in Britain, France and other nations of western Europe. Statistical laws were found in social data in the West, where libertarian, individualistic and atomistic conceptions of the person and the state were rampant. This did not happen in the East, where collectivist and holistic attitudes were more prevalent."[18] Thus, Prussia had the first central statistical office, but the concept of statistical law emerged in the West. This attribution helps us understand the campaign for, and opposition to, a British central statistical office, which was traced in chapter 3, and also why the office could only finally appear under the cover of war—recall that the National Register, too, was a supposedly "Prussian" institution made British in wartime.

A different explanation for government as producers of knowledge, inspired by Michel Foucault, is given by the governmentality school. Their objective—to provide an "analysis of political reason, of the mentalities of politics that have shaped our present, the devices invented to give effect to rule, and the ways in which these have impacted upon those who have been the subjects of these practices of government," pursued via a mixture of "a history of political ideas and a sociology of technologies of government"—is clearly close in spirit to my own.[19] Their argument that interests us here concerns the relationship, following Foucault, between liberalism and the production of knowledge. Liberalism is taken to be a stance—a "restless and dissatisfied ethos of recurrent critique of State reason and politics," and the protection of a space of free action, in particular one in which freedom is a "kind of well-regulated and 'responsibilized' liberty."[20] To protect this space, there had to be a concomitant realization that "government could be its own undoing" that, in Foucault's words, "if one governed too much, one did not govern at all." Liberal government was therefore to be "cautious, self-critical," its deliberate self-constraint creating the room for "society."[21] In this move, the social sciences were born: "On the one hand, liberal political reason is the historical condition of the very object of their disciplines—'society.' On the other hand, liberal political reason establishes a field of concerns that are as much *technical* as they are political or ideological."[22] This is a remarkably fertile insight, accounting for both the rise of, among other forms of expertise, the statistical movements, but also the *distance* and *engagement* of experts in such liberal government: "The supposed separation of State and civil society is the consequence of a particular problematization of government, not of a withdrawal of government as such." This Foucault-inspired argument offers cause and justification to be concerned with technical matters of government.

One problem with the governmentality approach, however, is a direct consequence of another insight. Barry, Osborne, and Rose argue that "instead of viewing technology of expertise as distinct from politics, 'technical' terms themselves—such as apparatus, machine or network—best convey a sense of the complex relays and linkages that tie techniques of conduct into specific relations with the concerns of government"; but indiscriminate use of such terms, with unacknowledged slippage from analyst's to actor's categories, threatens to weaken their entire argument. I would insist that discursive relations are powerful and important, but also that they need to be analyzed with extreme sensitivity; to fetishize the theoretical technologies of government, as Foucault and his followers sometimes do, can unfortunately obscure the insights which are undoubtedly there.[23]

Furthermore, one does not need to start with Foucault to arrive at the conclusions of the governmentality school.[24] Nineteenth-century commentators had already noticed the topic of the relationship of liberal government at a distance and the production of knowledge. The increase in state intervention, in for example social policy, was opposed by some observers with arguments superficially similar to late-twentieth-century opponents of big government. The evolutionary philosopher Herbert Spencer, in *The Man Versus the State* (1884), railed against the growth in government, and was particularly incredulous that Liberal politicians were largely responsible: "They have lost sight of the truth that in past times Liberalism habitually stood for individual freedom versus State-coercion."[25] Spencer was witheringly skeptical of government as a producer of knowledge:

> Perpetually Governments have thwarted and deranged growth, but have in no way furthered it; save by partially discharging their proper function and maintaining social order. So, too, with those advances of knowledge and those improvements of appliances, by which these structural changes and these increasing activities have been made possible. It is not the State that we owe the multitudinous useful inventions from the spade to the telephone; it was not the State which made possible extended navigation by a developed astronomy; it was not the State which made the discoveries in physics, chemistry, and the rest, which guide modern manufacturers. . . . The world-wide transactions conducted in our merchants' offices, the rush of traffic filling our streets, the retail distributing system which brings everything within easy reach and delivers the necessities of life daily at our doors, are not of governmental origin. All these are results of the spontaneous activities of citizens.[26]

Even if one accepts Spencer's line as polemic, there is an immense irony here: It was precisely because the state was growing that its knowledge-producing capacities were also increasing in leaps and bounds. From national laboratories to official statistics, the government sponsored the production of new knowledge, underwritten by the social status of fit gentlemen under the Northcote-Trevelyan plan. The explosion in statistics was of particular importance. A second argument, closely connected to Spencer's concerns—if in contradiction to some of his anti-state claims—was also articulated during Victoria's reign: that the government, through its increasing inquisitiveness, posed a threat to liberties of the subject. As John Stuart Mill wrote in his conclusion of *On Liberty* (1859), the great liberal handbook to freedoms of the individual in relation to the state:

> To determine the [size of government needed] to secure as much of the advantages of centralized power and intelligence as can be had without turning into governmental channels to too great a proportion of the general activity—is one of the most difficult and complicated questions in the art of government. It is, in a great measure, a question of detail, in which many and various considerations must be kept in view, and no absolute rule can be laid down. But I believe that the practical principle in which safety resides, the ideal to be kept in view, the standard by which to test all arrangements intended for overcoming the difficulty, may be conveyed in these words: the greatest dissemination of power consistent with efficiency; but the greatest possible centralization of information, and diffusion of it from the center.[27]

Mill's points were that information and power should not be centralized in the same hands, and that the art of good government lay in a judgment of balance. Thus, in his example of municipal-central government relations, power should mostly reside locally, but should be balanced by "a central superintendence, forming a branch of central government. The organ of this superintendence would concentrate, as in a focus, the variety of information and experience derived from the conduct of that branch of public business in all the localities, from everything analogous which is done in foreign countries, and from the general principles of political science."[28] Such a "central organ of information" would have "the right to know all that is done," its efficiency stemming from its emancipation from the "petty prejudices and narrow views of a locality by its elevated position and comprehensive sphere of observation, its advice would naturally carry much authority." Mill therefore gave his sanction to government—elevated, objective, all-observing—as a guarantor of knowledge. Although Spencer denied that government could efficiently make knowledge at all, he agreed with Mill's dictum that "the mischief begins when, instead of calling forth the activity and powers of individuals and bodies, it substitutes its own activity for theirs." However, moving from political theory to political history, the state *did* increasingly substitute its own activity, while growing precisely the information-collecting roles described by Mill.

Registers

Very non-liberal states could also generate and depend upon vast quantities of statistical data. "The government of our Führer and Reichschancellor Adolf Hitler is statistics-friendly," wrote Friedrich Zahn, president of the Bavarian statistical office, while emphasizing the necessity to the Nazi state of "useful knowledge" alongside "physical fitness and people strong in character and discipline."[29] And Zahn was correct in his assessment. Statistical knowledge of the population was generated through censuses, Edwin Black has recently made compelling claims regarding the role in gathering such information of IBM's subsidiary in Germany, Deutsche Hollerith Machinen Gessellschaft (known as Dehomag). (The following can be read alongside Michael Allen's excellent, and independent, critique in *Technology and Culture*.[30]) "IBM," writes Black, "primarily through its German subsidiary, made Hitler's program of Jewish destruction a technologic mission the company pursued with chilling success, IBM Germany, using its own staff and equipment, designed, executed, and supplied the indispensable technologic assistance Hitler's Third Reich needed to accommodate what had never been done before—the automation of human destruction."[31] For example, Dehomag bid, with enthusiasm and success, for the contract to conduct the first census after Hitler's rise to power in 1933.[32] Census taking culminated in the massive census of population of 1939, which required an installation 400 electrical key punches, 10 gang punches, 20 summary punches, 300 key punch verifiers, 70 sorters, 50 tabulators, 25 duplicators, and 50 specially modified tabulators, in order to produce data within months.[33] Such an collection was probably more than equal to the entire Hollerith equipment employed in UK government at the time.

The census data seems to have been systematically combined and cross-referenced with existing registries of personal information. These registries, such as land registers, work books, and the records of local government, police and church, already gave a thorough bureaucratic representation of German individuals before 1933, but under Nazi government they were further exploited and expanded.[34] The aim, of course, was the generation of state knowledge of the names and addresses of individual Jews. Further cross-referencing reveals Polish-speaking Jews, the *Ostjuden* that were the first targets of the Holocaust.[35] Aggregate censal information would have been inadequate for this task, which required a register-type information system. Nazi racial science, pursued in many institutions, focused on ancestry, making distinctions between those who were fully Jewish, half-Jewish, quarter-Jewish, and so on. Such personal information could have been generated, very slowly, from the local registries. So, Black notes, as a "competitive, confusing and often overlapping network of governmental, private, and pseudo-academic agencies . . . sprang into existence. All of these were directly or indirectly dependent on Hollerith's high-speed technology to sort through the voluminous hand-written or manually typed genealogical records needed to construct definitive family trees."[36] For example, the Nuremberg regulations of September 1935, which deprived Jews of German citizenship, clearing the way for Jews (and half- and quarter-Jews) to be legally persecuted, "would be completely dependent upon Hollerith technology for the fast, wholesale tracing of Jewish family trees that the Reich demanded. Hollerith systems offered the Reich the speed and scope that only an automated system could identify not only half and quarter Jews, but even eighth and sixteenth Jews."[37]

The combination of punched-card census data with older local registry-based information produced a centralized information system that can justly be called a "universal register." I argued in chapter 4 that in Britain a distinct decision was taken that, although partial or local registers of personal information might be allowed to overlap, there was to be no over-arching system, during peacetime, such as a universal identity number, and therefore no universal register. In both Britain and Germany, visions of universal knowledge of individuals were entertained. The best example in Britain was Noel Pemberton Billing's scheme for bookkeeping the morals of the nation. In Germany, Black tells us, to "cope with the growing bureaucratic fascination with punch card records, senior Interior Ministry officials reviewed one fanciful proposal for a twenty-five floor circular tower of data to centralize all personal information . . . Each of the twenty-five floors in the imagined tower would be comprised of 12 circular rooms representing one birth year. Every circular room would contain 31 cabinets, one for each day of the month. Each cabinet would in turn contain 7,000 names. Registrations and updates would feed in from census bureaus. All 60 million Germans could then be organized and cross-indexed in a single location . . . ."[38] If Billing's scheme had been realized, a similar edifice would have had to be built. But the difference between Britain and Germany was that in Germany such fantasies of total knowledge were openly attempted and nearly realized, while in Britain the capacity was partly there, in decentralized *partial* registers, but concealed—in accordance with sentiments of national identity.

Black's *IBM and the Holocaust* has flaws. In his eagerness to nail IBM, Black's account of IBM boss Thomas J. Watson Sr. is an essay in demonization (albeit one that provides a welcome antidote to some other saccharine, uncritical portrayals). Watson is portrayed as a proto-fascist, the subject of a personality cult that had more than a few similarities with Hitler's. Into this monotone story, even German-born Herman Hollerith becomes a caricature and monster: he is accused of cat torture, for example.[39] A firm led by evil men must be evil is Black's conclusion: "The company whose first overseas census was undertaken for Czar Nicholas II, the company Hollerith invented in his German image, the company war-profiteering Flint took global, the company built on Thomas J. Watson's corrugated scruples, this company saw Adolf Hitler as a valuable trading ally."[40] To make the company culpable it is necessary for Hollerith to be shown to be essential to the bureaucracy of the final solution. This is in fact extremely difficult to show: in making the case Black tends to overstate the role of punch cards and underplay the importance of the extensive local registers which were just as important, especially in generating state knowledge of personal ancestry.

Furthermore, Black stretches the argument when he suggests that the German experience was crucial to the overall business success of IBM. In 1935 the United States Congress passed the Social Security Act, which necessitated the construction and operation of a centralized register of individual information on nearly 30 million Americans. Black writes that there was doubt that such a system was possible, but that to "the amazement of the bureaucrats, IBM was ready. The company was quickly able to unveil a so-called collator that could achieve precisely what the government had in mind: compare and cross-reference two sets of records in a single operation."[41] IBM won the contract, one "so substantial it permanently boosted IBM into a corporate class of its own." The "dress rehearsal" of what Watson called the "biggest accounting operation of all time" was, says Black, the 1933 Nazi census run by Dehomag. In fact, it is not clear that without the German experience the Social Security central file would have been impossible. Other census efforts by IBM subsidiaries, or affiliates such as British Tabulating Machines, were of comparable size and complexity.

If Black sometimes tips over into polemic, his central charge, I think, is clear and just: that Hollerith-based punched-card systems formed a central component of the information infrastructure of Nazi Germany. Punch cards not only revealed the location of Jews, but also speeded up the fingerprint searches of the police, tracked people and things to the minute degree found necessary under the economic policy of autarky, and even lent credence to that great fascist cliché: they made the trains run on time. As Germany invaded other countries, so the Hollerith systems—either indigenous or foreign—became an infrastructure of a greater German empire. But I would equally insist that punch card systems, based on Hollerith's, were infrastructural to British governmental action at the time, and Chandler and Cortada suggest the same for the United States.[42]

The war in Europe ended in a period of transition, with many millions homeless and Germany under provisional administration, divided by the occupying forces. What was "known" of past and future was under shocking revision, due especially to the discovery of the industrialized genocide in the concentration camps, and the appearance of the new frontiers of the nascent Cold War. It was the latter which drove the scramble for German rocket expertise, with the elite designers such as Wernher von Braun fleeing west to the Americans leaving the technicians and V-weapon factories to be seized by the Red Army and transplanted east. Less well known is the capture of German information systems, two examples of which are cryptographic machines and punched-card statistical data.

In 1945 a secret Anglo-American mission, the Technical Intelligence Committee (TICOM) was sent into Germany to capture cryptographic equipment ahead of the Russian advance.[43] Dropped onto the Austrian-Bavarian border the team moved south and found several Enigma and one Lorenz machines. More equipment was found at Hitler's retreat in Berchtesgaden and trucked back to Britain. However, it was at Rosenheim that TICOM made its most important discovery: captured German signals intelligence staff who had developed techniques to break Soviet codes. Equipment and operators were swiftly removed to a house near Bletchley Park, and from that moment on cryptanalytic effort began to be concentrated against Soviet rather than German targets.

The British and American capture of the German punched-card systems was not driven by competition with their erstwhile Soviet allies, but with the more immediate issues of disarmament and control of defeated Germany. The British body charged with organizing these issues was the Control Commission. Intense debates over the nature, extent and use of German Hollerith machinery raged in the Commission in late summer of 1944. "There is no doubt," wrote Brigadier Gueterbock, Chief Staff Officer of the Commissioner's Office, "that if these statistics can be seized after the occupation of Germany very great help could be derived from them, as they provide the basic data for many control problems."[44] Indeed it was soon realized that the matter of controlling Germany was inseparable from the country's administrative systems of knowing. A meeting of Foreign Office divisions called to draw up policy in this area concluded that "it would be useless to have an independent system from the Germans. The German Machine would have to be taken over and used by the Control Commission."[45] All the divisions drew up lists of the information they needed. Thus the Economics Division requested the seizure of Hollerith cards containing statistics of agricultural and industrial production, process, consumption, stocks, import and export and armed service supplies and stores. The Public Safety Branch wanted "technical Police Statistics which are maintained at the National Police Headquarters in Berlin," and the Displaced Persons Branch the "statistics and records giving the numbers, location and classification of all foreigners in Germany including stateless persons. Any records classifying these foreigners according to nationality, age and sex, political status (internees, deportees, prisoners of war, etc.)

are of value."[46] All these requests were included in the first order to be given under the draft Terms of Surrender.[47]

The problem, however, was ignorance of exactly where and what statistics were held on German Hollerith cards. In 1943 these questions were put by the British Foreign Office to the Security Service and the Federal Bureau of Investigation in Washington. Both routes turned up the same intelligence. The first stop for the FBI was the headquarters of IBM Corporation on Madison Avenue, New York, since it was known that German punched-card equipment was predominantly machines built under license during the interwar years by Deutsche Hollerith Maschinengesellschaft mbH of Berlin (i.e., Dehomag). The FBI agents emphasized the "importance of the question from the point of view of disarmament and of control of German industry," and extracted from IBM a 1937 listing of royalties containing details of the type and serial numbers of more than 1,200 punched-card machines.[48] With the approach of war the Nazi authorities had realized the potential sensitivity of such detailed information, and disclosure was banned in 1938, even to IBM from its licensed manufacturer. (Black argues that IBM merely pretended to be detached from Dehomag). A few other sources contributed to this limited intelligence. In May 1944, a US Naval intelligence officer interviewed J. W. Schotte, the General European Manager for IBM at Geneva. Schotte had seen a customer list for 1938 or 1939, but the identity of the 20 to 30 names was concealed by code. With direct intelligence restricted, the allies had to rely on wartime German newspaper articles. It was learned, for example, that in early 1942 Albert Speer had introduced, on Hitler's request for "greater rationalization," a standardized numerical code for firms and commodities, followed by a similar one for order forms and bills, with a view to extensive application of Hollerith machinery, especially at the Zentral stille für Maschinelles Berichtswesen—a central statistical office—in the Armaments and War Production Ministry, and the Statistisches Reichsamt of the Ministry of Economics. This intelligence of "the intensive development of mechanized statistics in Germany"—"highly centralized, functionally, as well as geographically"—gave the Foreign Office confidence "that further information will show many other directions in which the system is used."[49] The disappearance of the market in the Nazi economy and its substitution by material controls and price fixing had encouraged the development of a uniform and compulsory system of accounting and cost accounting—ideal for mechanization. The centralization and standardization possible under a totalitarian regime meant that punched-card mechanization was far more extensive in Germany than in Britain (or for that matter, the United States). When the British army occupied its zones of Germany in 1945, punched-card experts were taken too.[50]

The irony was that the information system of Germany in ruins, was, because of its thorough standardization under the Nazi regime, more developed than that of the United Kingdom.

The Expert Movement of Mechanizers

"The intellectual machines are neutral. They do not care if they are working for the Registrar of Births, Scotland Yard, the National Health Service, or the supervisor of some new Belsen."[51] When this statement by an anonymous journalist, writing in the *Manchester Guardian*, was picked up by the *Powers-Samas Gazette* in 1952, punched-card machines had been in operation for many decades. But I do not think the machines were "neutral" in their interests, or at least neutrality was an attribute not an essence. Indeed neutrality was precisely the attribute that made the machine attractive to a particular middle-ranking group within the Civil Service. This is because punched-card machinery were the emblems and key tools of an expert movement of mechanizers, a group with a distinctive technocratic vision of government. This British group of technocrats were based in the Treasury. Only Edgerton, of recent historians, has emphasized that British government departments should be called technocratic. His argument is that "the central bodies of state, including the Treasury, have pursued a policy of "liberal militarism" which required the creation of "technocratic" departments of state. He then focuses on the military supply departments.[52] My expert movement of mechanizers should be seen as an extensive, non-military, Treasury-based, discreet technocratic network, overlooked in—but complementary to—the liberal militarists of Edgerton's analysis.

We are assisted greatly in the international comparison of twentieth-century mechanizing movements by the existence of several good, reliable national studies. Jan van den Ende's and Dirk De Wit's portrayal of punched-card mechanization and computerization in the Netherlands, touches the British case in many points of similarity. De Wit's analysis of the Post, Telefoon en Telegraaf (PTT), for example, bears close comparison with Campbell-Kelly on mechanization in the Post Office Savings Bank.[53] Van den Ende's examples are even more intriguing for what they speak of national differences and similarities. Geographical differences, for example, counted: the long-term national Dutch project of land reclamation, especially the enclosure of the Zuiderzee, created a special interest in tidal calculation for which there was no British equivalent.[54] Furthermore, the presence of a centralized statistical organization, the Dutch Central Bureau of Statistics, provided a center for mechanization of calculation, becoming in 1916 the first Dutch organization to install a punched-card installation (choosing Hollerith over Powers, as well as the French Classicompteurs rejected by the British General Register Office).[55] We saw in chapter 5 that the 1911 Census of Population provided an arguably late entry of punched-card techniques into Britain, although it was in the same year as Denmark, a case Heide has discussed.[56] National economic and associated employment conditions again played a key part in understanding mechanization, although the main argument that the United States had the advantage of a large potential market and the spur of too few skilled—and therefore expensive—workers, should be tempered by cases that can be cited where the technological politics of skill seems to have been reversed: the introduction of dictating machines, for example, was faster in the United States compared to the United Kingdom because the latter had many trained stenographers.[57] In general, of course, the United States developed both the manufacture and the use of office machinery at a much higher rate than in Europe: in 1918, for example, His Majesty's Stationery Office bought for the whole of the Civil Service less than one-fourth of the number of Comptometers that just one American federal government department, inland revenue, had ordered.[58] However, although as historians such as Mounier-Kuhn, Cortada, Campbell-Kelly, and Heide have shown, industrial policy (often reduced to the fostering or reacting to American firms) shaped twentieth-century mechanization, I would rather emphasize the deeper similarities between mechanization in industrial countries: in general similar procedures were mechanized at, give or take a few years, similar historical moments. It was noted in 1924 that "in all the industrial countries of the world the need for more information regarding production [was] being felt and acted upon," and the point stands for other informational sectors too.[59]

But there is little doubt that the vision was first seen in the United States, where it was part of systematic management. An important vector transmitting the philosophy across the Atlantic were the reports of President William Howard Taft's Commission on Efficiency and Economy in the Government Service, which ran from 1911 to 1913. The Taft Commission's reports combined the interest in the two kinds of government machinery—structural organization and material technologies—that would be found in Britain when the expert movement of mechanizers reinterpreted Haldane. Taft had been granted by Congress $100,000 "to inquire into the methods of transacting the public business of the executive departments and other Government establishments," and to recommend improvements. No such "exhaustive investigation," he claimed, had "ever before been instituted concerning the methods employed in the transaction of public business with a view to adoption of the practices and procedure best fitted to secure the transaction of such business with maximum dispatch, economy, and efficiency."[60] Exhaustive it certainly was. Organization, personnel, business methods, accounting and reporting across government came under investigation. In particular, the use of "labor-saving office devices in the service" was made the subject of a special inquiry, and between 6 and 16 July 1911 an exhibition of labor-saving devices was held in Washington. A hundred and ten manufacturers and dealers participated, and more than 10,000 officers and employees visited.[61] The exhibition was merely one of a myriad of initiatives that enabled Taft to conclude that an "excellent beginning" had been made "toward the reorganization of the machinery of this Government on business principles." Or, in other words, that the principles of systematic management had been imported from the private to the public sector.

Taft's Commission was interpreted for a British audience by Henry Higgs, the friend of expert civil servants, such as statistician Robert Giffen, and a popularizer of the programs of both statistical and mechanizing expert movements. In his Newmarch Lectures of winter 1916 and his *National Economy* (1917), he reported Taft's evidence of savings after investigation: $88,500 per annum after the introduction of vertical filing, $200,000 per annum with the introduction of decimal classification.[62] Higgs approved of its principles of systematic management (the rejection of the "element of personal habit" and the introduction of machines), but also notes that the strength of the American Commission lay "in the fact of its personal local inspection of actual working instead of 'sending for persons, papers, and records' and taking merely oral evidence. Its experience is ocular and gets to bed-rock fact."[63] Higgs rounded off his summary of Taft with an exhortation:

> We cannot suppose the officials of the United States Government to be wicked above all other public servants, less receptive to new ideas, or less anxious to secure economy and efficiency. The moral is that even where the cost of labor is much lower than in America, great economies may be achieved by organized knowledge.[64]

The moral was not lost. In chapter 5 I presented evidence that Partridge, behind the trenches in France, must have read Higgs's lectures very soon after they were published. Certainly personal local expert inspection became the organizing principle of the Treasury investigating section, and therefore central to the expert movement of mechanizers and the stock from which Organization and Methods would emerge. To domesticate the American vision of systematic management to a British audience, the techniques had to be interpreted and championed within Britain. It is in this role that the expert movement mechanizers were crucial to the story.

In chapter 5, I reviewed the development of Hollerith techniques, and the experimental application of both Hollerith and Powers systems in British governmental work before the First World War. Other major applications could be found in the British Empire, the Egyptian census in 1917, for example, requiring 15 million punched cards. However, it was with the stress and experience of bureaucracy at war that the impetus was given to the expert movement of mechanizers in Britain. A witness behind the front, Major Sydney George Partridge provided the expert movement with a slogan that was directed at the British government and interpreted the language of the President Taft: it should be "the aim of every alert organization seeking efficiency and economy in office administration to strike the balance between the 'human' and the 'mechanical,' and the more efficiently a Department is organized the greater will be the tendency for 'mechanical' to encroach on 'human' territory."

Partridge's call to arms translated into the establishment of a handful of Treasury "investigators," charged with reviewing Whitehall departments and recommending, where justified, mechanization. What Winston Churchill called "Desborough's toys" were largely justified in terms of economy: machines were introduced where it was shown that expenditure would be saved. One question that is often immediately asked is: was the British government backward or forward in office mechanization, was it doing a lot, or not? The reason the question is asked is because the answer is often assumed to be relevant to the large literature that seeks to explain British economic "decline." The relevance is potentially twofold. First, taking the Civil Service as a large organization, the rate of its "modernization" might be an indicator of the spread of, and receptiveness to, new technologies. The rate of mechanization of government could be compared to that in business. Second, the Civil Service, and especially the Treasury, is of course no ordinary organization. Indeed, the Treasury has been repeatedly labeled as one of the guilty—a repository of old-fashioned attitudes, a "dead hand" on industrial policy, and a hindrance to economic progress.[65] The poverty of declinism as a historical framework is well illustrated by historians such as Edgerton.[66] However, the question of whether the pattern of, for example, office mechanization in Whitehall was late or advanced is still a legitimate one: Campbell-Kelly, in his account of the mechanization of the Post Office Savings Bank, opens his concluding discussion by stating that it "poses one overarching question: Why was the bank so slow to mechanize?."[67] Having set up the problem, Campbell-Kelly, as part of a sensitive and nuanced account, appeals to some of the factors that will be familiar to anyone who has studied the declinist literature, of for example Corelli Barnett or Martin Wiener: "bureaucratic inertia," an British cultural "resistance to mechanization" that was particularly ingrained in the Civil Service. The "late" introduction of punched cards to the Census (1911 compared to 1890 for the United States) and even the rather unedifying graphical evidence of government punched-card use presented in table 5.1 above, could both be recruited in the search for evidence, *if* a picture of Whitehall hostility to mechanization was wanted. But if a satisfactory explanation for the unmechanized 1901 Census can be found then the "late" introduction of punched-card machinery is somewhat dissolved in that case (only a year after Hollerith's innovation, 1891, would have been too soon). On the Post Office Savings Bank, any declinist reading would have to also explain Desborough's observation that although the Post Office Savings Bank was "the first to mechanize in 1926," that "this was accomplished by Treasury Investigations," and that only 2 years later Scott could completely credibly state that Whitehall was at the "van" of office mechanization, whereas in 1932 the Bridgeman Committee of Inquiry on the Post Office cited "well known business experts" as stating "we do not think it is going too far to say that the savings Bank is ahead of any comparable private concern in the adoption and development of office mechanization and labor-saving devices."[68] Likewise, American witnesses of pre-Second World war Home Office and police mechanization were impressed by what they saw. At the Old Age Pensions Office at Kew, West London, "many delegations from the USA could not believe so much could be done with so few staff."[69] Other contemporary observers were less sure that the "van" was reached until the developments in the Second World War discussed in chapter 6.[70] In my judgment, mechanization was patchy: advanced in some departments and slow in others.

What were the factors that encouraged the growth of the expert movement of mechanizers? One factor can be called, in homage to George Dangerfield, the digital death of liberal England.[71] The National Register, the first comprehensive listing of the names and addresses of men and women in the United Kingdom, was accepted as a wartime measure, although I have shown that a troubled bureaucratic interest in such schemes haunted interwar Whitehall. The National Register, and other such schemes, were instigated because key persons were convinced that even systematic statistical information did not provide, qualitatively or quantitatively, the knowledge to govern. (To the civil servants' fury, the Register was used to settle a brutal head count: How many men could be conscripted?) At the same time a highly illiberal argument from political writer and co-founder of LSE, Graham Wallas, justified by appeal to new psychological science, was circulating: the vast majority of people were irrational (compare with the liberal tenet that individuals followed their rational interests), and therefore must be led by the rational elite—the latter assisted by massive quantification.[72] Such sentiments helped justify technocratic movements, such as that of the mechanizers. Both the Register and Wallas's *Human Nature in Politics* can be read as prompted by a fear and ignorance of the mass population. (The temptation to relate this simplistically to a fear of Bolshevism should be avoided: in all the many documents I have examined there is virtually no evidence for such a connection, beyond characters such Major Hall-Dalwood.) In a by now familiar fashion, Wallas appealed to "efficiency": the "efficiency of political science" which he predicted to increase as it was brought under the influence of new science and the weight of statistics.[73]

But, more important, the expert movement of mechanizers greatest strength was that their headquarters was in the Treasury, the government office responsible both for finding economies and for personnel matters—an ideal, if for some unlikely, location for proponents of mechanization. Furthermore, the project of mechanization must be understood in the context of an organization ordered by the Northcote-Trevelyan distinction between generalists and mechanicals, a distinction, after all, instigated and managed by the Treasury. Partridge's credo of mechanization appealed to middle-ranking executive officers, uneasily placed between the higher-ranking generalists (such as the first and second secretaries to the Treasury) and the many mechanical grades below (such as the typists and other machine minders). Within an office that was seeking to extend and deepen *control* throughout the Civil Service, mechanization provided the middle rank with a strategy that pleased their masters (it saved money, it made other departments take in and rely on Treasury experts) while also making their masters reliant on these experts, thereby protecting their status against encroachment from the ranks below. One tactic used by the Treasury to secure control over the wider Civil Service was the introduction and explication of a "code" of Civil Service behavior. This interest in explicit description of work meant that the mechanizers task of specifying machine "programmes" for punched-card work also found a sympathetic institutional home. Thorough-going mechanization and "modern management" were therefore encouraged by the hierarchical structure and peculiar position of the Treasury.

Under secure, mechanical control by the Treasury, the state was allowed to expand. Here again mechanization contributed by providing the means to speed up the state's capacities in data processing, a solution, as I noted in chapters 1 and 5, that was facilitated by the prior characterization of the Civil Service as a machine. It also provided a further cover for the introduction of female labor into the Civil Service, as part of the machine. At a fine level, there was considerable interplay between technological change and state action. Seemingly minor matters, such as how many columns a punch card might have, became implicated in arguments over what information should be collected, which in turn were predicated on commitments to particular preferred directions of government action. Vice versa, new styles of government, from military personnel management by punched card to a Milk Marketing Board, were permitted.

Partridge's vision of alert mechanizing organizations was precocious and remarkable. But, it was not until the Second World War, an information war, when expenditures on punched-card machines jumped nearly 1,000 percent, that the Organization and Methods movement (the flag the expert movement now marched under) seized power, with a credo of mechanizing and later computerizing wherever possible. The subject of machines is nearly entirely absent in the voluminous literature on the history of the Civil Service and public administration, yet I argue that it is only through a history of the material practices of government can an understanding of the capacities and actions of government be gained. If there has been a distaste for the machine it has been among writers on government rather than in government itself. An important consequence for the history of technology for such an study was that the computing machine shaped and was shaped by bureaucracy: it was symbol and technique.

War and Information Innovation

Jack Good, who worked at Bletchley Park, felt that a "close synergy between man, woman, and machine" had developed during the second world war. In chapter 6 I showed that a cluster of new information systems appeared around the middle of the last century. At Bletchley, the British codebreaking effort had transformed from a collegiate to an *industrial bureaucracy*: an organization marked by an intricate division of labor, very high staff numbers, an emphasis on through-put, and innovative mechanization at bottlenecks, all directed to speeding up and making more efficient processes of manipulating symbols. I think this aspect of Bletchley has been overlooked in a historiography which, perhaps forgivably, emphasizes Ultra secrets and romantic genius. Likewise, I highlighted the organizational features of radar, and in particular how an attenuated, abstracted representation of the land was created, an organization by information. At particular centralized locations, knowledge of airspaces, above London or Britain as a whole, was whittled down—filtered—until a sparse and skeletal representation remained. In this way, complex and messy materiality was reduced to information. I coined a term, *infosphere*, which I hope captured some of this virtuality and spatiality.

If the inventions of Bletchley Park and Malvern were largely aimed at gathering knowledge of British enemies, there was also plenty of developments in collecting, processing and representing "information" of the home front. The National Register was launched, in a more comprehensive form, for the second time, providing a bureaucratic mirror of the population. Its "primary function," said Sylvanus Percival Vivian, was to "absorb information." The Register was to be a National Information Service, as bold a vision as that of contemporary William Beveridge for the National Health Service. They should be seen as twin peaks of the welfare state. The Register was complemented by other, more targeted, information systems: the wartime Social Survey and the remarkable popular Mass Observation movement which generated knowledge of opinions, problems, wishes, and morale. State surveillance even extended to a new and comprehensive survey of farms, while propaganda—the conventional government "information service" became ever more sophisticated.[74] Government departments reorganized and introduced more technology to help handle the influx of data. Expenditure on punch cards increased tenfold between 1936–37 and 1945–46. A Central Statistical Office was (belatedly, according to the expert movement of statisticians) created in 1941. Experts—statisticians, economists, operational researchers—in government proliferated.

In particular, the expert movement of mechanizers congregated under a new label: the name Organization and Methods (O&M) also appeared in 1941. Significantly, the movement not only continued its preference for the " 'mechanical' to encroach on 'human' territory," but, confronted by the many cases of abstraction of knowledge, began to articulate a "theory" of information. I. James Pitman, the head of Treasury O&M, and therefore a leader of the movement, was continuing a familial obsession with the analysis and efficient representation of communication that dated back to his grandfather. This was a tradition quite distinct from the information theory also being tentatively outlined in the United States. But for the expert movement of mechanizers, this theory was subordinate to practice: faith was found through works. As we saw above, in the aftermath of an allied victory and the struggle to rebuild Europe, the vital strategic and tactical importance of mid-twentieth-century information systems was all too apparent.

A cluster of information processing innovations can be found around the middle of the twentieth century, starting roughly with the first development of radar in the early 1930s and merging with a later wave of invention that followed the first stored-program computers of the late 1940s. James Beniger has offered a theory that accounts for clustering of new information technologies. Like many authors, he has noted that changing patterns of information technology use can be related to crises in the industrial societies, which I emphasize again were more similar than different. It is now a familiar argument that the sources of innovation are increasingly knowledge-based, and in the post-industrial world, knowledge and information are more important relative to traditional factors of labor and capital. Some authors, notably Beniger, have argued that what he calls the "control revolution," which he locates as starting in the late nineteenth-century, should be understood as a reaction to—and therefore not a new stage but a late stage of—the industrial revolution.[75] Thus, for example, Beniger argues that industrial developments, such as the railroads and Bessemer steelmaking, caused problems—indeed a "crisis"—of control, which was met by the innovation of information processing techniques, from improved telegraphy to central office rationalization, expansion and mechanization, among many others. Beniger's seems a convincing case for American history. However, it is very hard to understand the clutch of informational innovations in the United Kingdom, which cluster around the middle of the twentieth century and were discussed in detail in chapter 6, as being responses to crises of industrialization. I therefore offer the following as a sketch of a different theory of the emergence of the information society.

To summarize: Many have claimed that industrial societies and economies have moved recently into a new paradigm in which information is a, even the, crucial resource. Beniger, and others such as Mosco and Harvey agree, argue that this shift should be seen as a form of late industrial capitalism (the key variables therefore remaining labor and capital).[76] What has lurked behind much of my discussion of mechanization and computerization, and which I now state explicitly, is a third possible position: the computer should be seen as a materialization of a prior model of state action. The second world war was an almighty challenge to the orderly nation state, and in conditions of stress state action becomes more explicit, more mechanical—one result being a cluster of new mid-century information systems. This position can perhaps be most easily seen by using a language familiar to historians of technology: that of "shaping." What shapes technology? Marxists, and many of their critics, would state unequivocally that, in the last instance, the answer is "the economy." (Marx himself became livid at any suggestion that the state possessed an autonomous agency, despite coming close to such a position in *The German Ideology*.[77]) Sociologists and historians of technology have spilled much ink in recent years to show that social factors of many kinds shape technology. However, technologies are also reification of order, and government has been, in a secular world, the grandest register on which to imagine order. As Barry, Osborne and Rose note, "if technology is political, it is because technology always with it a certain 'telos' of operations, a certain directive capacity."[78] (The point, an interesting one, of whether the state can be considered as prior to society is one that can be left at this stage to political theorists.[79]) At this point we should recall the close parallel between the organization and language of government administration, in particular the Civil Service and that of computers: a general purpose machine, programs, codes, a "civil intelligence," and so on. I have argued that this connection was the achievement of expert movements of middle-ranking officials, what for much of the twentieth-century were labeled the "executive officers." These groups, too, were responsible for the mechanization and computerization programs that rebuilt capacities to govern. The computer should be understood as a reification of state administration, notwithstanding complementary claims of business and military shaping (examined below); after all Chandlerian corporations took after state models and the behind the convincing demonstration of Cold War influence on the electronic-stored-program computer was massive *federal* funding. So, *pace* such arguments such as Castells's of the reduced power of the state in the age of mass computing,[80] it would be equally valid to say that government has replicated, miniaturized and diffused. If it has disappeared, then it has also reappeared, in such unlikely locations as desks and homes.

Military Machines

The ENIAC and the Bletchley Park machines were, of course, products of war, and the computer as war machine is a significant thread in historiography of computing. Cohen, for example, writes "the electronic, digital, stored-program computer came into being with massive government support—largely, but not exclusively from military agencies. Wartime needs provided an enormous stimulus to the design and development of new machines for calculation and computing."[81] The decisive role of government and especially military funding has been exhaustively demonstrated by Flamm.[82] Not only was the stored-program concept rooted in the Second World War, but the subsequent Cold War legitimated historically massive levels of federal government spending on high technology, with, to just pick one example, the capacity of IBM to produce cutting-edge machines boosted enough to create and dominate the nascent computer industry. However recent historiography of computing has broadened the inquiry to ask whether the military funding of computers played a constitutive role in shaping what a "computer" was. The most sophisticated answer has been given by Edwards in *The Closed World*. For Edwards, the computer was not only a tool of the Cold War—enabling, for example, the early-warning systems which enveloped the west—the machine also provided the discursive icon of a closed, controlled system through which Cold War foreign policy could be, and was, described. The military influence on the computer therefore ran far deeper than mere funding, although the lavish resources made available are still a crucial part of the story: the very form of the computer shaped and was shaped by the military context in which it worked. Indeed Edwards persuasively shows that the closed world model, of which the computer was iconic, inscribed emergent disciplines such as cybernetics, cognitive psychology and artificial intelligence, and therefore colonized academia and medical sites too. One of the greatest strengths of *The Closed World* is Edwards's insistence that the computerization of the United States military had to be achieved, that it was contingent on its promotion by certain groups, and did not go uncontested. "The automation of command," he writes, "runs counter to ancient military traditions of personal leadership, decentralized battlefield command, and experience-based authority."[83] Centralized top-down command, or explicit rule-based authority, was—contrary to popular stereotypes—antipathetic to military culture, and Edwards shows that the disasters of the computerized "electronic background" from Vietnam onwards, stem partly from this switch when it was enforced. From where, then, did the United States military borrow the model which was so expensively and fruitlessly deployed in Operation Igloo White, the computerized surveillance of the Ho Chi Minh Trail? Whence did its promoter, Secretary of Defense Robert McNamara, claim authority? The crude answer is ambiguous: McNamara was a peerless product of mid-century American business culture, but he was also a bureaucrat, an expert in statistical control techniques.[84]

Edwards's case for understanding the computer as both tool and symbol of the "closed world" of the Cold War is made on three registers. First, computers both created and sustained Cold War discourse, the language game within which both technology and foreign policy was formed: computers "allowed the construction of central real-time military control systems on a gigantic scale" (e.g. SAGE), but they also "facilitated the metaphorical understanding of world politics as a sort of system subject to technological management," exemplified by General Douglas MacArthur's epigram "we defend every place."[85] Second, postwar scientific disciplines, especially the "cognitive" sciences of artificial intelligence, cybernetics, computer science and cognitive psychology, were given meaning within the contexts of the Second World War and the Cold War. Third, Edwards identifies a subjective component that crosses these disciplines and discourses into popular culture: from the nascent practical sociology of human-computer interaction, to the Turing Test, to the cinematic manifestation of robots and cyborgs, the discursive imagination of computers was as a "second self." Though this last emphasis is strikingly similar to the Great War vision of S. G. Partridge, it is the first of Edwards's claims which most concern us here. The computer is seen, first and foremost, as shaping and shaped by, military interests. How does this square with the thesis of this book, which in this case can be understood as the claim that the computer is, first and foremost, tool and symbol of bureaucracy? In fact the two arguments are not incompatible, as a key episode of the SAGE story illustrates. As Edwards rightly points out military automation contains a paradox: automation of command actually runs *counter* to armed forces traditions of personal leadership, decentralized battlefield command in which responsibility for an order is devolved and experience-based authority.[86] The centralized top-down structure of SAGE, for example, was therefore, in principle, antithetical to the Air Force which commissioned the system. Vocal opposition, rather than acceptance, could have been predicted. Furthermore there were alternatives to the centralized, machine-based system: a less automated system called ADIS had minority backing within the Air Force, while the Soviets, as was known through intelligence sources, had developed an air defense system which followed traditional patterns of military organization. How was this paradox resolved? Edwards's answer lies in his identification of a movement within the Air Force: the acceptance of SAGE depended on its promotion by radical and ambitious USAAF officers, technocrats whose apotheosis can be found in close cousins, such as Robert McNamara, in the Kennedy administration. This promotion helps explain the acceptance of computerized command-and-control, but note that the ideology being imported was a *managerial even an administrative* one.[87] With SAGE the United States of America Air Force was not only computerized, but also, to an even greater extent than before, bureaucratized. Though the stored-program computer was indeed a "military" machine, it is also true that the meaning of "military" had shifted radically. In this way, the thesis of Edwards's *Closed World* complements the argument of this book.

After the bureaucratization of the military, which in many respects predated the Cold War, data-processing techniques could, in principle, pass with greater ease between civil and military infospheres. The construction of new air traffic control systems, such as the joint civil-military Linesman/Mediator discussed in chapter 7, provides examples of this phenomenon. But it is important to note that this similarity was not recognized by everyone at the time, as the Treasury O&M investigator James Merriman and General Pete Thuillier agreed:

> [There was an] almost complete divorce between ADP work of a civilian or "commercial" character, and work of a defense character, even though the essential characteristics of the two might be identical. Data transmission was a typical example. Much Research and Development effort had been spent on data transmission for missile guidance and telemetry. This posed, in essence, identical problems to those found in data transmission for stores accounting. But little mutual knowledge existed of work in these apparently diverse activities and no machinery existed for (for example) seeing either that overlapping development was not initiated or that information on defense work was not unnecessarily restricted by security.[88]

Despite remarkable projects such as Ralph Benjamin's Comprehensive Display System, used to automate the Royal Navy, the inventiveness of British military research establishments in the Cold War became secondary to American developments. The balance between the old country and the new superpower had shifted irrevocably. British interests could barely shape the American infospheres which extended over Britain: the balance of foreign policy negotiations became inscribed into the software of the Ballistic Missile Early Warning System at Fylingdales, for example, because the American hardware was non-negotiable. An American standard for global air traffic positioning was imposed in Europe. Like Captain Mandrake in *Dr. Strangelove*, the British were adrift in a rule-governed strategic world not of their own devising.

Expert Movements and Computerization

Organization and Methods (O&M) was the flag under which the expert movement of mechanizers marched in the postwar years. Its headquarters was the Treasury, still the most powerful of government departments. However, until the early 1950s, Treasury O&M, while enthusiastically pursuing further punched-card mechanization of departmental work, was shy of the new electronic stored-program computer. From 1948 to 1952 the computer was understood to be a specialist scientific or mathematical instrument, and the only experts competent to pronounce on its use were academics or National Physical Laboratory scientists, such as those who made up the Advisory Committee on High Speed Calculating Machines. It was the NPL, not Treasury O&M, which was first invited to examine "whether any large scale punched card jobs" might offer "long-term scope for the use of computing machines."

I think there is a considerable irony in this hesitancy. Civil servants had to be taught to recognize something of themselves in the computer. Only then would a temporarily *specialist* machine become reclaimed as *universal*. Lord

Halsbury, the chair of the National Research Development Corporation, who had witnessed the use of a Univac at the US Bureau of Census, insisted that the computer was not merely a scientific device. It was, as Turing had predicted, a universal machine, capable of anything "including playing Annie Laurie and winning a chess match." In Britain a few projects investigating office automation were underway, in particular Lyons & Company's LEO, and the experiments of the maverick academic B. V. Bowden, editor of *Faster Than Thought* (1953), one of the first books to popularize the universal capabilities of the computer. But the mirror that showed the Civil Service itself in material form was held up by an NPL scientist, Ted Newman. In early 1953 he wrote in terms that were both reassuring and exciting that "the organization of a complex job whether it is done by human clerks, by punched cards, or by high-speed computers is bound to be a long business, and a program is only a coded form of this organization." (Note the implied interchangeability, an echo of Partridge, of the human and machine). The expert movement of mechanizers accepted the equivalence that Newman had drawn, and henceforth Treasury O&M could be called the center of an expert movement of computerization. With the middle-ranking expert core convinced, the next battle was to persuade their superior generalists, achieved in the "year of doctrination and implementation," 1959. Again there was a moment of hard-won *recognition*, when, as the impresario James Merriman relates, after hours of play-acting the "utterly automatic routine nature" of lower-order Civil Service work, the generalists saw through "our little charades," got "the cold logical point, and "by the middle of the second morning were starting to expose the basic programming steps." The "point" was that one general-purpose machine governed by code could recognize another. Already by 1959 several departments had become computerization "guinea pigs." The difference that winning the support of the highest Treasury mandarins made was that Treasury O&M became ever stronger and more influential. The period when the computer was interpreted as only a scientific machine can be seen as a blip.

Organization and Methods was a fairly pragmatic movement. Although its center was in the Treasury, there were officers in nearly all government departments, as well as nationalized industries and large private corporations. Empirical knowledge about mechanization and computerization was circulated through meetings, placements and journals. O&M was a successful, *discreet* movement. It was not secretive, but it did not see fit to shout about its achievements. In the United States, there was a parallel expert movement, with an altogether different dynamic concerning its public image. American mechanization and computerization was also a ideology of middle management, but self-identification with technocratic ideals was much more publicly acceptable.[89] The slide rule could be a managerial badge of honor in America in a way that was unlikely in Britain.

Publications provide one indicator of national difference. Though the American expert movements of mechanization and computerization formed a much larger market for publications, there was also a greater willingness to theorize, to publish and to purchase. It is impossible to imagine a British equivalent of Herbert A. Simon, for example. Milwaukee-born and Chicago-educated, Simon was only 25, "with minimal management experience," when his iconoclastic dissertation was published.[90] *Administrative Behavior* passed through many printings and editions after its first publication in 1945. It was an attempt to present a theory of administration concerned with "processes of decision as well as with the processes of action."[91] Though Simon declared his disciplinary affiliation—"the construction of an efficient administrative organization is a problem of social psychology"—he was in fact part of the broader interdisciplinary movement of cybernetics then gathering pace.[92] *Administrative Behavior* sets out an "anatomy" of the organization that is in fact a mechanistic analysis, breaking down the influences on group behavior or the organization's communication system into parts. Simon describes his approach as like "organizational biology," but if so, it was inspired by only particular aspects of biology (as cybernetics, for example, returned time and time again to the feedback loop). Simon explored the connections between administration and machine. With Allen Newell he developed the "Logic Theory Machine," a "decision-making mechanism capable of exhibiting certain complex human problem-solving behavior."[93]

By 1957, when the second edition of *Administrative Behavior* was published, Simon could look back on what was already a phenomenal career: "I suppose that I might claim some sort of prophetic gift in having incorporated in the title and subtitle three of the currently most fashionable words in social science—'behavior,' 'decision-making' and 'organization.'"[94] Though Simon was a subtle analyst, he increasingly drew more direct parallels between administration and computing machines. In *Administrative Behavior* the link was suggestive—he insisted on the organismic inspiration while writing as if that organism was artificial.[95] With Newell he had made real machines, and declared them similar to a human organizational decision maker. But by 1960, Simon was predicting, on the back of five years spent "close to machines—the kinds of machines known as computers," that within a few decades organizations would be a "highly automated man-machine system," and "we shall have the technical capability of substituting machines for any and all human functions in organizations."[96] Drawing on empirical studies of early automation, such as James R. Bright's *Automation and Management* (1958) and Samuel Lilley's

Automation and Social Progress (1957), Simon argued that not only blue-collar and clerical work would be computerized, but management too.[97] In this revolution, managers would "need, to work effectively, to understand their organizations as large and complex dynamic systems involving various sorts of man-machine and machine-machine interactions," so "persons trained in fields like servo-mechanism engineering or mathematical economics, accustomed to dynamic systems of these kinds, and possessing conceptual tools for understanding them, may have some advantage."[98] Or, in other words, Simon promised power to the well-placed expert.[99]

It is not, therefore, surprising that tens of thousands of experts bought Simon's books, and bought into his technocratic, cybernetic vision. My point here is fairly simple: although Simon was an innovative and subtle cross-disciplinary thinker, and his books written with admirable clarity, he was covering much of the same ground, drawing many similar conclusions, as the expert movement of mechanizers across the Atlantic. Both considered the organization, including public administration, as a place of information flow, both analyzed the organization into parts to be mechanized, in both there is a slippage between metaphorical and real mechanization, with explicit description an important mediating process between the two. A clear distinction between generalist decision makers and mechanical rule followers was essential to the Northcote-Trevelyan model of organization. This was why the British Civil Service was capable of recognizing the stored-program mainframe computer, eventually, as something like itself. The early Simon seems to reject the distinction: "The task of 'deciding' pervades the entire administrative organization quite as much as does the task of 'doing'—indeed, it is integrally tied up with the latter."[100] But the later Simon resurrects it in his contrast between "programmed" and "nonprogrammed" types of decision, making the two similar again.[101] The difference, was the extent that ideology that favored and promoted the mechanization of organization was considered something prestigious, to be celebrated in public. The movement of which I am using Simon as a figurehead was *open*, whereas Treasury O&M was *discreet*.

By 1959, a permanent secretary—the most senior grade within the Civil Service, could make a speech (drafted by Merriman of Treasury O&M), that in its very language would have been inconceivable only 10 years earlier:

> [Until the] intricacies and involvements of human systems and organizations . . . can be described in mathemetico/logical language, we have little hope of harnessing the power of technology to the needs of business and administration. A social change that must be expected in offices is therefore a greater attention to purpose, and how it is achieved; a heightening of interest in patterns of communication between individuals within the complex of a given organization; a weakening of the importance of

> the written record; a growing awareness of the need for and power of mathematical symbolism and perhaps, more than all these, a growing concern for precision and definition as opposed to intuition and hunch . . . As well, we must expect the power of digital data handling technology to help the determination of policy by enabling complex mathematical models of human situations to be resolved with an ease that hitherto has not existed. There seems no basic reason why, provided the mathematical model can be formulated, the national economy or important segments of it should not be simulated upon a large computer, and the possible results of projected changes to that economy evaluated. Before this is done, however, models of successively increasingly complexity will have to be formulated and validated. The results of experience have to formulated and fed into the system. Such a development could have exciting implications, both socially and economically! . . . What I am suggesting is that the businessman or administrator must firstly learn to use the devices that technology puts at his disposal and secondly to learn that the power of these devices can never be fully harnessed without an equally imaginative and scientific approach to the organization which they serve and which surrounds them. Technical developments applied in this way will enable management to see more clearly the fundamental issues facing it. Management will not be superseded; it will become more exact and precise because the complex mass of detail surrounding the business will be ordered and refined so that strategical decisions alone remain outstanding, clear-cut and provoking.[102]

Here we are again reminded of the official interest in making processes visible, explicit and measurable in order to be administered: "precision and definition as opposed to intuition and hunch." A remarkable act of ventriloquism had occurred: the generalist—previously the gentleman who did indeed manage by intuition and hunch—spoke the words of the technocrat. Visibility was an extremely important aspect of state action, but, as the quotation above suggests, it was something required of the external objects of action, not government itself, which chose not to open itself up for inspection. The opaqueness of British government in the 1950s was not sinister, but reflected matters of trust.

Discreet Modernism

A repeated pattern has emerged from this study of the British government machine. The Treasury, frequent target of accusations of anti-technical biases, was home to an important and *uncelebrated* technocratic movement. The most remarkable wartime flourishing of British bureaucracy, at Bletchley Park, not only produced an electronic logical machine, T. H. Flowers's Colossus, but managed to keep it *secret* until the 1970s. Packet-switching networks emerged *unsung* from the National Physical Laboratory. Something much more interesting was going on here than the supposed British failure to exploit inventions. The pattern was a combination of reserve and a discreet modernity identified with technological innovation.

Historians have recently shown that modernism was appropriated in different ways across Europe, particularly with regard to attitudes to technology.[103] Herf, for example, shows that "before and after the Nazi seizure of power, an important current within conservative and subsequently Nazi ideology was a reconciliation between the anti-modernist, romantic, and irrationalist ideas present in German nationalism and the most obvious manifestation of means-end rationality, that is modern technology."[104] This "reactionary modernism" was a means by which technology could be "converted from a component of alien Western *Zivilisation* into an organic part of German *Kultur.*" In particular, Herf's "reactionary modernism" pithily summarizes elite attitudes to technology in Weimar and Nazi Germany.

I suggest *discreet modernism* best describes the British official tradition. Precisely because it was discreet, this form of modernism has escaped notice, although more familiar forms—of lesser importance, but much greater *visibility*—have been described. For example, in the 1950s British art world the Independent Group stands out for youthful vigor and an intention to seriously examine the role of science and technology. In the words of their recent historian, Anne Massey: "Inspired by the philosophy of logical positivism and existentialism, the Group arrived at a new understanding of modernism which emphasized the history of science and technology."[105] Group member Richard Hamilton organized the Growth and Form exhibition at the ICA, taking inspiration from D'Arcy Thompson's book as well as from Siegfried Giedion's *Mechanization Takes Command,* and included x-ray images, microphotographs, and tracks of atomic particles. Another Groupie, Reyner Banham, celebrated 1950s London as a futurist spectacle, all machines and light, and wrote *Theory and Design in the First Machine Age,* implying, of course, that he was living in a Second Machine Age: a "Jet Age, the Detergent Decade, the Second Industrial Revolution."[106] The Group's work awaits serious consideration by a historian of science—there are nice links between the Group and UCL's Communications Research Center and Admiralty games theorists that are intriguing—but they don't really help our search for an important British modernism: their influences were self-consciously foreign, their work a protest against establishment values rather than a reworking of them. Catching the cybernetics buzz from America, for example, they invited National Coal Board cyberneticist E. W. Meyer to talk: they did not understand what was said, but one member did produce a collage celebrating the transistor.

British modernity of another visible form can be found in official projects. For example, *Presenting Modern Britain: Her Life and Institutions* (1966), a slim

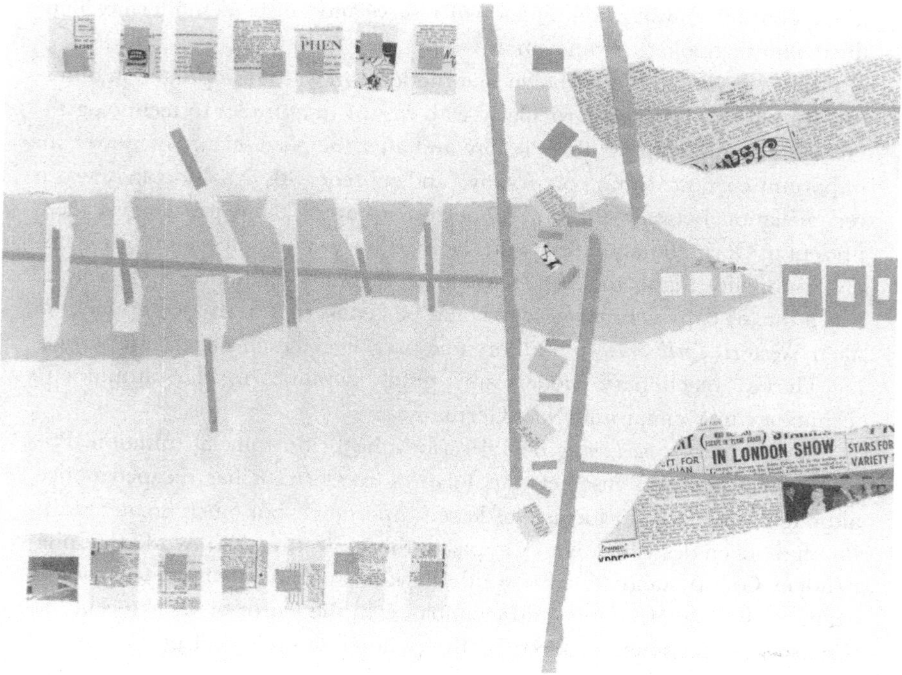

Figure C.1
John McHale, *Transistor,* 1954 (© Tate, London 2002).

volume whose declared aim was "to provide a picture of Britain and the British people today for those who live beyond the British Isles," has the dull familiarity of an official portrait, but note its contradictory modernity: "The past is important to Britain, but she does not live upon it, long and great as it is. Old-fashioned pomp and ceremony remain, but she is very much concerned with modern scientific and technological development. It is significant that she has led the way in radar, television, and the jet engine, to mention three fields of importance in this age."[107] The books summary, "Tradition and progress *go hand in hand* in modern Britain," could have been an official postwar slogan. But this was no botch job, a forced conjoining of opposites, since the contradiction did useful cultural work. The new was necessary in order to know that one was living in an old country. Nostalgia, Constable, and Pomp were highlighted by the contrast with Jet Engines, Radio Telescopes and Concordes, and vice versa. The Science Museum of London calls this visible, spectacular trope "defiant modernism."

But "discreet modernism" was quite different, and is more akin to what Peter Wagner has called "organized modernity." Wagner uses this term to characterize the technological response of business and government in the late nineteenth century: a "movement from an emphasis on the extension of the reach of human action to an emphasis on the control of social and natural spaces." Bureaucracy and control technologies were crucial. So far we are in familiar territory, as mapped by Weber, Chandler, and Beniger. "Discreet modernism" describes the organized modernity of the expert movement of mechanizers which began just before the First World War and peaked in influence during the 1950s and the 1960s. Unlike the French and American technocratic movements this one was not openly political. Since it was a movement centered in the Civil Service, the professional codes of honorable secrecy meant that they could not possess the public prominence of, say, the Veblenites in the United States, where, for example, technocrats ran for political offices. However, this low profile does not mean they were less important. We know that the Organization and Methods movement, as it was named by the 1940s, gained a powerful influence through the Treasury and its network extended through all major government departments and large industrial firms.

The Colossus, the centralized punched-card installation and the mainframe computer were all either produced or appropriated by government experts, and all remained hidden. Technologies are manifestations of ways of ordering nature and society. How they are talked about (metaphor, discourse) and the equally important visual equivalent (styling) are aspects of such "modes." In the 1950s and the 1960s the mode was the discreetly modern, untransparent machine, manifestations of technocratic government and of a society deferential to the expert. My favorite example of how trust in government and expertise intertwined during this period is ERNIE.

In June 1957 a machine was deployed to randomly choose winners of prizes among the holders of premium bonds. The machine—called ERNIE, for Electronic Random Number Indicator Equipment—was installed at Lytham St. Annes. Like Colossus, ERNIE was designed by T. H. Flowers, who was now Engineer-in-Chief of the General Post Office. (GPO engineering was closely allied with Organization and Methods.) Flowers's design consisted of two neon tubes generating a static output, essentially "two electronic roulettes, the output of which would be multiplied together to produce random numbers for selecting the bonds."[108] ERNIE itself was attached to a control console and teleprinters, an assemblage that was rather inscrutable:

> ERNIE is to be enclosed in lockable steel cabinets, and while this may appear impressive it is unlikely to satisfy public curiosity. The console associated with ERNIE will carry switches, indicator lights, monitoring equipment such as oscilloscopes, and the teleprinters which are to print the numbers. It is, therefore, likely to have greater public appeal than ERNIE proper; and while being intelligible to the initiated, likely to foster the public impression of "a modern scientific robot." Even so, the sound of the

teleprinters at work and the sight of their paper emerging from the console are the only indications which are likely to be associated in the public mind with the generation of numbers. Unofficial observers at the draw will undoubtedly desire some more tangible evidence that ERNIE is working and that the numbers which are emerging are random.[109]

It was decided that the "numbers emerging from ERNIE should not be disclosed completely or in any deducible form." The reason for this was that the numbers were to be passed to back rooms where humans would dig out the files and confirm a winner. The potential for human mistakes here was the source of anxiety. The Central Office of Information film *The Importance of Being ERNIE* sought to provide some reassurance:

Customer: Huh! I bought some o' those when they first came out. Must've had 'em six or seven years. Not a sausage. Stuck in the machine, I reckon—or lorst.

Postmaster: That's most unlikely.

[Film follows the procedure showing that nothing can go wrong]

Postmaster's voice: If they went astray, they'd find out.

Customer's voice: Who's "they"?

Postmaster: The people up at St. Anne's . . . check and double-check everything a dozen times over.

His last words are immediately followed by the clatter of a roomful of adding machines as we CUT TO . . . MACHINE ROOM.[110]

(Note the personalization of "they," but also the swift reassuring move from human to machine. In the film the "people" are visibly machines.) The film ended with a celebration of the uncontrollable ERNIE and caprice of lady luck:

COMMENTATOR: ERNIE generates bond serial numbers. The Post Office engineers who designed and built him had to devise a means for reproducing bond numbers in a way that would be completely uncontrolled and uncontrollable . . . ERNIE . . . was the result. He does it all of his own accord—nothing is fed into him—he's not like a computer—and he's been proved to be truly random.

[There followed a demonstration of neon lamps and counters and the procedure of digging out the winner's file (adjusted so that names are not shown).]

INT POST-OFFICE: CS Mrs. Mason "scrutinizing a 'London Gazette' list of prize-winners"

COMMENTATOR: "It might be one of hers."

CUT TO . . . gloomy customer:

COMMENTATOR: " . . . it might be one of his. It might be one of yours. Come to that it might be one of mine."

What to notice about ERNIE: First, the technology chosen was highly untransparent (hidden neon tubes, covered teleprinters). Second, what was remarkable was that apart from a brief flutter of worry in June 1957 when, with the story "has ERNIE got a blind spot? Gray metal ERNIE . . . stood accused on its red carpeted dais," journalists on *The Daily Express* and others pointed out that certain code numbers never appeared, there was remarkably little criticism of the procedure. In the 1950s ERNIE—and therefore the government expert—enjoyed considerable public trust. The bond holder had to, and largely did, accept faith in the closed verification procedure.

A contrast with the modern politics of transparent machines helps make my point. Consider ERNIE's 1990s equivalent: the National Lottery machines, Lancelot, Guinivere, and Merlin. These were see-through, low-tech devices. How could one doubt that the process is truly random when the viewer could see directly the bouncing numbered balls? By making the workings visible fairness was demonstrated, and transparency replaced trust in the expert. But Lancelot has only *apparent* transparency, yet it has attracted *more* suspicions of bias than ERNIE. Lancelot is a machine indicative of a culture in which there is a lack of trust: like the spread of the audit—another technique of transparency—the prompt was a *lack* or *failure* of trust rather than a real increase in accountability.[111] The modern transparent technology is widespread, other examples being the Dyson vacuum cleaner—look and you can *see* the dust, so it must be better, or the microbrewery where we are assured that the beer is real because we can see the pipes and barrels behind the glass.

I have little space to explain the history of transparent technologies, but knowing that computing machines are material metaphors for organization, I can point to some significant moments. First, we have already noted the peculiar history of explicit language in government. Within Whitehall it was a virtue, at least in the Treasury's eyes as it aided control. Outside Whitehall, from where government looked opaque, calls for clearer language were political projects. Sir Ernest Gowers's *Plain Words* (1948), or George Orwell's novels but particularly his famous essay on plain English prose, are foundational for British literary technologies of clarity and transparency.

These became part of a increasingly powerful transatlantic critique of opaque government. At the popular end of organization studies, a managerial-academic-journalistic movement, came critiques of the equivalence of the human and the organizational machine. William H. Whyte's 1956 best-seller *The Organization Man* was one such example. Another was Edinburgh professor of sociology Tom Burns who with psychologist G. M. Stalker in 1961 contrasted the lumbering "mechanistic" organization with the nimble "organismic" one. There is no doubting which of the two they held as morally and economically superior. Finally, three decades before the iMac, anti-corporatism was expressed through style by a new sort of computer. DEC's

PDP-8, marketed as a mini-computer to resonate with mini-cars and mini-skirts, demonstrated its difference by smoked plastic covering.[112] these were *transparent* machines designed for the *individual* not the organization. By its styling it announced a profound shift in values away from the opaque mainframe adopted by the expert movement of mechanizers.

The Great Change?

The aesthetics of organization and information technologies shifted in the 1960s and the 1970s, from a trusted opaqueness to a distrusted transparency. This change was one of many interconnected upheavals (including the peaking of privacy as a political issue, the increasing purchase of neo-liberal critiques of government, technological change that favored smaller, faster, networked computers, sometimes working in real time, as well as movements for civil rights, women's lib, and against Vietnam, and so on) which, though they are very difficult to analyze into causes and effects, form an impressive list. Many of these were the unintended consequences of state action. So, for example, smaller, faster and real-time computing was pulled by the demands of the federal space (and missile) program.[113] Big government might have produced the conditions which demanded the microprocessor, but the unpredicted and remarkable things done with the computer-on-a-chip were very much the achievements of entrepreneurs and small businesses. Computer networks, such as the military-academic ARPANET in the United States and the National Physical Laboratory's network plans for the United Kingdom, too, were clearly governmental projects, yet the later Internet was often cast (as were small computers) as a threat to hierarchy and to state action more generally.[114] The unexpected reaction to plans announced for a federal "database" marked the start of the privacy debate. In chapter 9 I emphasized that this debate, in Britain as in the United States, was unexpected since it was not as if government had become qualitatively more inquisitive, and in particular that similar databases (not least the National Register) had been built before. It was not a crisis caused by technological change, but it was a crisis of trust in *internal* technocratic expertise. I say "internal," because an outcome of the great change was not a lessening in quantities of data collected, since as quasi-autonomous audit bodies replaced departmental bodies, information was still collected and processed, but by external experts, and in a (distrustfully) transparent rather than discreet way.[115]

The fall of one collection of the experts, the expert movement of mechanizers in British government, was traced in chapter 10. The organizational vehicles of the movement were moved away from centers of influence. There is no evidence, as yet, that this was an intentional demolition of power of the movement—indeed, the first push came as part of the Fulton reforms of the Civil Service, which had the stated and contrary aim of empowering specialists. The fall of this particular brand of technocrat seems, in this case, to be an effect of wider changes in attitude toward hierarchy. Treasury O&M's rolling and ambitious program of mainframe computerization in the early 1960s was the peak of untroubled influence of the expert movement of mechanizers. As technology changed to become smaller there was no longer a match between the size of technology and the size of government. Personal computers were an awkward size to fit into Whitehall departments. Government computerization projects of the 1970s and the 1980s that called for networks of terminals, small and large computers, may have been extremely complex and expensive—the computerization of welfare benefit administration, called the Operational Strategy, was supposedly the "largest" project in the world at the time—but they were certainly not untroubled. The dire reputation in Britain of public service computerization, for budget overruns and failure to even operate, can be ascribed to the collapse in authority of the expert movement of mechanizers within government.

This collapse has seen the reciprocal growth of private contractors, companies such as EDS that have specialized in providing information-technology services to governments at a price, and which, as Margetts suggests, have created new dangers.[116] In America, the adjustment to small and networked computers has been smoother. Perhaps here the difference between Europe and the US may be speculated to be correlated to a difference in attitudes to ownership of machines. In Europe, including the United Kingdom, the model for much of the twentieth century for state action was public ownership, and when the scale of the government machine (i.e. the mainframe) mirrored the scale of government (i.e. the department) all was well. However, when the scale of the government machine changed (to small computers) deep anxieties and problems emerged. In the United States, a tradition of attitudes that privileged personal ownership of technology, held in defense of the individual against the state, meant that the relationship was different. This tradition might stretch from the constitutional right to bear arms, to the 1970s Californian culture of the computer "home brew" club and the famous advertisement of 1984 that contrasted the Apple Macintosh with the machinery of Big Blue/Big Brother.

The breakdown in hierarchical models can be found in many contexts. One surprisingly important one has been the information infrastructure of European high-energy physics. When Tim Berners-Lee presented his radical re-description of the information infrastructure of CERN, the European particle physics laboratory that is reflection of European governmental relations in miniature, it was inscribed by the move away from formal hierarchical organizations toward a flexible, non-hierarchical model. We are all familiar with Berners-Lee's proposal now—because it was the start of the World Wide Web.[117] What is significant about the Web, here, is that similar proposals had been made before, only by the 1980s the world had changed so that it was prepared for the Web. The Web did not succeed because it was a new idea, but because it was an idea that was now being articulated in a World that was ready.

The discreet modernism exhibited by the materialization of hierarchy of the mainframe favored by Treasury O&M, say, or the construction of the Colossus, is over. Early attempts to a base a new vision of government on networks, such as Karl Deutsch's 1963 book *The Nerves of Government*, either did not appeal to the old expert movement, or perhaps the expert movement of mechanizers were not flexible enough to shift allegiance to a new model.[118] In the last decade, however, another attempt to hitch reform of government to the application of modern technology has emerged in the form of e-democracy.[119] Again information technology has been presented as an agent for the transformation of government. The considerable modernist luster of such presentations formed parts of the distinctive governmental styles of Clinton and Gore's administration in America, and of New Labour in Britain. It is ironic that these initiatives are attempts to rebuild trust in government (increasing participation, for example), when it was a shift in attitudes to technocracy that formed part of the collapse of trust in the first place.

Notes

Introduction

1. Although it was historians in the United States and England (but not France) who provided the "cultural impetus" to establish the respective national archives. See Theodore R. Schellenberg, *Modern Archives* (Cheshire, 1956), pp. 6, 9. On Schellenberg, see Jane F. Smith, "Theodore R. Schellenberg: Americanizer and popularizer," *American Archivist* 44 (1981): 313–326.

2. In *Science and Spectacle* (Harwood, 1998) I argued that the crucial question facing radio astronomers was whether a particular signal was interesting.

3. Arthur L. Bowley, "The improvement of official statistics," *Journal of the Royal Statistical Society* 71 (1908): 459–495, at 463.

4. Linda Colley, *Britons* (Vintage, 1996), p. 305; Martin Campbell-Kelly, "Information technology and organizational change in the British census, 1801–1911," *Information Systems Research* 7 (1996): 22–36. For the standardized form used by the BAAS to award grants, see Jack Morrell and Arnold Thackray, *Gentlemen of Science* (Clarendon, 1981), p. 313.

5. John Brewer, *Sinews of Power* (Unwin Hyman, 1989), p. 221. "Growth in state power," Brewer continues, "is usually accompanied—either as cause or effect—by changes, in either the extent or the nature of a government's hold on social knowledge."

6. Schellenberg, *Modern Archives*, p. 10 (emphasis added).

7. For a detailed historical guide to this labyrinth, see M. H. Port, *Imperial London* (Yale University Press, 1995).

8. Dickens, speech to Administrative Reform Association, quoted in Emmeline W. Cohen, *The Growth of the British Civil Service, 1780–1939* (Allen & Unwin, 1938), pp. 50–51.

9. Martin Campbell-Kelly, "The Railway Clearing House and Victorian data processing," in *Information Acumen*, ed. L. Bud-Frierman (Routledge, 1994); Campbell-Kelly, "Large-scale data processing in the Prudential, 1850–1930," *Accounting Business and Financial History* 2 (1992): 117–139.

10. Roy MacLeod, "Introduction," in MacLeod, *Government and Expertise* (Cambridge University Press, 1988).

11. Oliver MacDonagh, "The nineteenth century revolution in government: A reappraisal," *Historical Journal* 1 (1958): 52–67, summarized in MacLeod, *Government and Expertise*, p. 4. The historical debate, in which MacDonagh took part, was centered for much of the twentieth century on the contribution of Benthamite thought to government growth, and was politically polarized since treatments of this topic were shaped by left-wing or right-wing attitudes toward state intervention in general.

12. See in particular the work of Christopher Hamlin, for example "Edwin Chadwick and the engineers, 1842–1854: Systems and anti-systems in the pipe-and-brick sewers war," *Technology and Culture* 33 (1992): 680–709.

13. MacLeod, *Government and Expertise*, pp. 15–16.

14. Ibid., pp. 16–17.

15. Three studies in MacLeod's edited collection confirm this downgrading of specialists: Jill Pellew, "Law and order: Expertise and the Victorian Home Office"; R. A. Buchanan, "Engineers and government in nineteenth-century Britain"; Gavin Drewry, "Lawyers and statutory reform in Victorian government."

16. "Expert movements" is an analytic (as opposed to an actors') category. I am using it to bring to the fore an interpretation of how specialists and professionals have fared within government while also remaining part of networks that lead outside government. Since it is not an actors' category, by definition, the people I discuss did not think of themselves as necessarily part of the same movement within which I place them, although they would almost certainly admit—and articulate—shared goals and assumptions. Because expert movements are a category of analysis, the issue of competition between movements is a complex one. I will sometimes claim that an expert movement supported, or conflicted, with another. Again, this support or conflict remains a term of analysis, although more often than not it will map on real shared interests or oppositions.

17. Rob Kling and Suzanne Iacano, "Computerization movements as the product of social movements, in *Microelectronics in Transition*, ed. Gordon (Ablex, 1985); Kling and Iacano, "Computerization movements and the mobilization of support for computerization," in *Ecologies of Knowledge*, ed. S. Star (SUNY Press, 1995). See also Rob Kling, ed., *Controversy and Computerisation*, second edition (Academic Press, 1996).

18. Note however that, although experts have a privileged role, they may not be pursuing such a technocratic state directly as a political goal; instead they may be pursuing it indirectly because of their interests as professionals.

19. Although the following point is sometimes made: "The work of a government department nowadays has the same proportions as an iceberg, one-third of it, if so much, is above water in the daylight world of party politics and public controversy, two-

thirds of it, if not more, is below in the dark important technical world which the public cannot see." (G. Kitson Clark, "'Statesmen in disguise': Reflections of the history of the neutrality of the Civil Service," in *The Victorian Revolution*, ed. P. Stansky (New Viewpoints, 1973), p. 87.

20. Even otherwise good analyses, such as that on pp. 98–101 of Theodore Porter, *Trust in Numbers* (Princeton University Press, 1995), are flawed in discussion of the British case by accepting Heclo and Wildavsky's assumption that the values of generalists stand for the values of the Civil Service as a whole. Hugh Heclo and Aaron Wildavsky's "anthropological" study of the Treasury (*The Private Government of Public Money*, University of California Press, 1974) is embedded in a 1970s critique of a closed Civil Service.

21. Richard A. Chapman and J. R. Greenaway, *The Dynamics of Administrative Reform* (Croom Helm, 1980). Peter Hennessy, *Whitehall* (Fontana, 1989), does, however, usefully list the management information systems of the major Whitehall departments.

22. Henry Higgs, interpreter of expert movements, asked what such a solution might look like (*National Economy*, Macmillan, 1917, p. 40): "Imagine an accounts department of one Chief Accountant and three Principal Officers each in a separate room, with 20 subordinates four to a room, the senior in each room receiving a supervising allowance. If the staff were all in one room, the Chief in a glazed enclosure, the Principal Officers on raised platforms enabling each of them to supervise six or seven subordinates, it might be possible to dispense with the five allowances, to diminish the number of messengers who fetch and carry between nine separate rooms, to speed up the circulation of papers, to economize space, fuel, artificial light, and cleaning expenses, and generally to improve business while reducing cost."

23. Robert Darnton, "An early information society: News and media in eighteenth-century Paris," *American Historical Review* 105 (2000): 1–35; Alfred D. Chandler and James Cortada, eds., *A Nation Transformed by Information* (Oxford University Press, 2000).

24. For this useful periodization, see Hennessy, *Whitehall*, p. 50.

25. JoAnne Yates, *Control through Communication* (Johns Hopkins University Press, 1989); James R. Beniger, *The Control Revolution* (Harvard University Press, 1986).

26. Harold Perkin, *The Rise of Professional Society* (Routledge, 1989). Though Perkin has his detractors, I think *Rise* is a remarkable synthetic work, with many interconnections with *The Government Machine*. Indeed, Perkin anticipates some of the directions of my argument. However, his analysis of expert movements (not his term) stops at the Fabians, and therefore misses the radical mechanizers of intellectual work such as Sydney George Partridge.

27. On Wallas, see Harold A. Innis, *The Bias of Communication* (University of Toronto Press, 1951), p. 191.

28. James C. Scott, *Seeing Like a State* (Yale University Press, 1998), p. 4.

Chapter 1

1. Otto Mayr, *Authority, Liberty and Automatic Machinery in Early Modern Europe* (Johns Hopkins University Press, 1986), p. 30. For evidence of how frustrating historical arguments concerning metaphor can be, see Jenny Uglow, "Introduction: 'Possibility,'" in *Cultural Babbage*, ed. F. Spufford and J. Uglow (Faber and Faber, 1996).

2. Thomas Carlyle, "Signs of the Times," reprinted in Thomas Carlyle, *Selected Writings* (Penguin, 1971), p. 70.

3. The argument concerns a correlation. It is, of course, possible to find examples of clockwork being used to make quite different political points. See e.g. the discussion of Robert Isaac Cruikshank's cartoon "The Time Piece" in Dror Wahrman, "Public opinion, violence and the limits of constitutional politics," in *Re-reading the Constitution*, ed. J. Vernon (Cambridge University Press, 1996).

4. Mayr, *Authority, Liberty and Automatic Machinery*, p. 199.

5. Peter Hennessy, *Whitehall* (Macmillan, 1989). The sample is taken from the first two chapters.

6. Christopher Hood, *The Tools of Government* (Chatham House, 1986).

7. James Boswell, e.g., used "mechanical" to mean simple (we would now use "routine"): ". . . for the mechanical part we employed . . . six amanuenses" (*The Life of Samuel Johnson*, 1791; quotation from 1973 Dent edition, vol. 1, p. 109).

8. Hennessy also mixes actors' and analytical categories.

9. D. G. Hale, *Body Politic* (Mouton, 1971).

10. Mill refers to himself in his most self-loathing patches as a machine, usually when recalling his most Benthamite early periods. For two or three crucial years of his life he was a "mere reasoning machine," a term often applied to the Benthamites (John Stuart Mill, *Autobiography* (1873), quoted from World's Classics edition, Oxford University Press, 1924, p. 92). Elsewhere, he expands "mechanical" as "mere force of habit" and again characterizes himself as "merely one wheel in a machine" (ibid., pp. 118, 72). Note how "mere" and "machine" seem inseparable. See also Stefan Collini, *English Pasts* (Oxford University Press, 1999), p. 121.

11. John Stuart Mill, *On Liberty* (John W. Parker, 1859), pp. 198–199.

12. Steve Woolgar and Keith Grint, "Computers and the transformation of social analysis," *Science, Technology, and Human Values* 16 (1991): 368–378.

13. For particularly important French case, see John V. Pickstone, "Bureaucracy, liberalism and the body in post-revolutionary France: Bichat's physiology and the Paris school of medicine," *History of Science* 19 (1981): 115–142.

14. José Harris, *Private Lives, Public Spirit* (Oxford University Press, 1993), p. 223; David Boucher, ed., *The British Idealists* (Cambridge University Press, 1997), pp. xx–xxi. J. A.

Hobson, in particular, wrote of the state as the "central organizing intelligence"; see Rodney Barker, *Political Ideas in Modern Britain* (Routledge, 1997), p. 31. The distinction continued to influence sociology through Durkheim, who distinguished between "organic" and "mechanical" forms of social solidarity.

15. In the case of the constitution this fluidity of metaphorical interpretation, not least because it was unwritten, was a key reason for its utility. See James Vernon, "Notes towards an introduction," in *Re-reading the Constitution*, ed. J. Vernon (Cambridge University Press, 1996), p. 2.

16. Samuel Taylor Coleridge, *On the Constitution of the Church and State According to the Idea of Each* (J. M. Dent, 1972), p. 91.

17. On the antiquity of "body politic," see Mayr, *Authority, Liberty and Automatic Machinery*, p. 102. See also D. G. Hale, *Body Politic* (Mouton, 1971). Another set of metaphors was that of the family, with head of state analogous to head of family; see David Lowenthal, *The Past is a Foreign Country* (Cambridge University Press, 1985). Another was the analogy to the Kingdom of Heaven.

18. Coleridge, *On the Constitution*, p. 70. However, Coleridge goes on to say "Nihil simile est idem"—Nothing similar is the same.

19. Coleridge to Rickman, 17 July 1812 (Orlo Williams, *Lamb's Friend the Census-Taker. Life and Letters of John Rickman*, Constable, 1912, p. 162).

20. Carlyle, "Signs," p. 71.

21. See e.g.: Leslie Stephen, *The English Utilitarians* (Duckworth, 1900), vol. 1, p. 19.

22. Ibid., pp. 129, 18–19.

23. Bacon does not even use the word "government" in his account of his scientifico-utopian state.

24. Jean Bodin, *Six Books of the Commonwealth* (Blackwell, 1955), p. 56.

25. Compare the cited passage with two earliest texts, both machine-less, the first from Bodin's 1576 Paris edition (*Les Six Livres de la Republique*, Jacques du Pays, 1576, p. 233) and the second from Richard Knolles's 1606 English translation (*The Six Bookes of a Commonweale*, G. Bishop, p. 199): "Or toute Monarchie est seigneuriale, ou royale, ou tyrannique. ce qui ne fait diversité de Republiques, mais cela provie[n]t de la diversité de gouver la Monarchie. Car il y a bien difference de l'estat, & du gouverneme[n]t: qui un secret de police qui n"a point esté touché de personne." "Now Monarchie is divided into three formes: for he that hath Soveraigntie is either lord of all: or else a king, or a tyrant, which maketh no diversitie of Commonweals, but proceedeth of the diversitie of the governour in the Monarchie: for there is great difference between the state, and the government of the state: a rule of pollicie (to my knowledge) not before touched by any man."

26. Mayr, *Authority, Liberty and Automatic Machinery*, p. 102.

27. Antonio Ponce de Santa Cruz, physician to the Spanish king, quoted in Mayr, *Authority, Liberty and Automatic Machinery*, p. 103.

28. Thomas Hobbes, *Leviathan, or the Matter, Forme, and Power of a Commonwealth Eccleasticall and Civil* (Andrew Crooke, 1651), p. 1. Hobbes (p. 176) urged would-be builders of the perfect political constitution to imitate good architects or engineers: ". . . as the art of well building is derived from Principles of Reason, observed by industrious men, that had long studied the nature of materials, and the divers effects of figure, and proportion, long after mankind began (though poorly) to build: So, long time after mankind have begun to constitute Commonwealths, imperfect, and apt to relapse into disorder, there may Principles of Reason be found out, by industrious meditation, to make their constitution (excepting by externall violence) everlasting."

29. For a revision of the relationship between political and natural philosophy, see Steven Shapin and Simon Schaffer, *Leviathan and the Air-Pump* (Princeton University Press, 1985). Compare Coleridge, "The Mechanico-corpuscular Theory raised to the Title of the Mechanic Philosophy, and espoused as a revolution in philosophy, by the actors and partizans of the (so called) Revolution in the state," in Coleridge, *On the Constitution*, p. 51.

30. For Hobbes (*Leviathan*, p. 19), a state was a machine made by men, whereas bodies were machines made by God. The "pacts and covenants, by which the parts of this body politic were at first made" were analogous to "the fiat, or the let us make main, pronounced by God in the Creation."

31. Penn, quoted in Mayr, *Authority, Liberty and Automatic Machinery*, p. 105.

32. Mayr, *Authority, Liberty and Automatic Machinery*, p. 105–109.

33. Goethe on his first and only visit to Berlin in 1778, quoted by Mayr, *Authority, Liberty and Automatic Machinery*, p. 109.

34. Mayr, *Authority, Liberty and Automatic Machinery*, p. 112. David Blackbourn (*The Long Nineteenth Century*, Oxford University Press, p. 25) records that mechanical metaphor for Prussian bureaucracy was widespread. Furthermore, the Prussian (and later German) army was likened to an automaton—see p. 98 re Metternich and the complaint of his "interfering with all the gears of the machine."

35. Mayr, *Authority, Liberty and Automatic Machinery*, p. 113.

36. Charles de Secondat, Baron de Montesquieu, *The Spirit of the Laws*, 1748, translated by Thomas Nugent, 1752), book 3.

37. Ibid., books 11–14.

38. David Hume, in his essay on the "Independency of Parliament" (1748), noted that the maxim that the "checks and controls of the constitution [should be framed so that] every man ought to be supposed a knave and to have no other end in his actions than private interest" was already a commonplace among political writers. One reason why the mechanical metaphor that guided the American constitutionalists is famous is that Woodrow Wilson revisited it in his 1912 presidential campaign: "The makers of our

Federal Constitution constructed a government as they would have constructed an orrery—to display the laws of nature. Politics in their thought was a variety of mechanics. The Constitution was founded on the law of gravitation. The government was to exist and move by virtue of the efficacy of its 'checks and balances.'" (quoted in Michael Kammen, *A Machine That Would Go of Itself*, Knopf, 1987, p. 19)

39. Kammen, *A Machine*, pp. 17–18. The book's title comes from an address by James Russell Lowell to the Reform Club of New York of 1888. From the turn of the twentieth century, organic metaphors for the constitution became popular. Many authors have explored the Newtonianism of the American constitution; see e.g. Stanley Pargellis, "The theory of balanced government, in *The Constitution Reconsidered*, ed. C. Read (Columbia University Press, 1938); Richard D. Mosier, *The American Temper* (University of California Press, 1952); Walter Lippmann, *A Preface to Politics* (University of Michigan Press, 1962); Richard Hofstadter, *The American Political Tradition* (Jonathan Cape, 1967); I. Bernard Cohen, "Science and the growth of the American republic," *Review of Politics* 38, 1976, p. 365. For a detailed examination, see Michael Foley, *Laws, Men and Machines* (Routledge, 1990). Foley's main contribution is to argue that the presidency has been understood in biological terms—vitality, evolutionism, etc.—but Foley's argument suffers from a failure to bring history of technology and political history together.

40. Peter Gay, "The applied Enlightenment," in *The Idea of America*, ed. E. Adams (Ballinger, 1977).

41. Alexander Hamilton, John Jay, and James Madison, *The Federalist Papers* (1787–1788).

42. The classic statement of Benthamism's impact on nineteenth century government is Albert Venn Dicey, *Lectures on the Relation between Law and Public Opinion in England during the Nineteenth Century* (Macmillan, 1905). For a counterblast, see Henry Parris, *Constitutional Bureaucracy* (Allen & Unwin, 1969), pp. 258–266.

43. Stephen, *The English Utilitarians*, vol. 1, p. 179.

44. Most of the subsequent publications were to be the work of disciples, including Dumont (through his *Traités de Législation de M. Jérémie Bentham*, 1802), Romilly, George Grote, and James Mill.

45. "The revolution, whatever else it might do, obviously gave a chance to amateur legislators. There was any amount of work to be done in the way of codifying and reforming legislative systems. The devisor of Utopias had such an opening as had never occurred in the world's history." (Stephen, *The English Utilitarians*, vol. 1, p. 196).

46. However, William J. Ashworth discusses the application of both of Bentham's ideas to the "Britain's largest industrial complex," the Royal Naval Dockyards, in "'System of terror': Samuel Bentham, accountability and dockyard reform during the Napoleonic wars," *Social History* 23 (1998): 63–79.

47. Stephen, *The English Utilitarians*, pp. 286–287.

48. "The end of Government has been described in a great variety of expressions. By Locke it was said to be 'the public good'; by others it has been described as being 'the greatest happiness of the greatest number.' These, and equivalent expressions, are just; but they are defective, inasmuch as the particular ideas which they embrace are indistinctly announced; and different conceptions are by means of them raised in different minds, and even in the same mind on different occasions." (James Mill, *An Essay on Government*, Cambridge University Press, 1937, p. 2).

49. Mill, *Essay on Government*, p. 26. In 1829, in the *Edinburgh Review*, Thomas Babington Macaulay attacked the essay for its Euclidean dryness. Macaulay's argument turned on whether Mill was following good scientific method; Bacon was invoked as the authority. An anonymous Utilitarian replied in the *Westminster Review*, sparking further exchanges.

50. The "object of desire" was an important, if undefined, term for James Mill.

51. Mill, *Essay on Government*, p. 25.

52. Ibid., p. 24.

53. Ibid., p. 29. Just in case there was any doubt, Mill hammered the point home on pp. 30–31: "In this doctrine of the simple forms of Government, is included the theory of the Balance among the component parts of a Government. By this, it is supposed, that, when a Government is composed of a Monarchy, Aristocracy, and Democracy, they balance one another, and by mutual checks produce good government. A few words will suffice to show, that, if any theory deserve the epithets of "wild, visionary, chimerical," it is that of the Balance."

54. Mill, *Essay on Government*, p. 34.

55. Note the body metaphor. Mill uses "machinery" only once, and even then it is derogatory: a system of selecting Representatives that only reflected the choice of a minority was "only an operose and clumsy machinery for doing that which as well might be done without it; reducing the community to subjection, under the One, or the Few" (*Essay on Government*, p. 44). In contrast, well-chosen Representatives were an "organ of Government" (pp. 59–60). Again we should remember that mechanism was attributed to the utilitarians by their enemies. Also note that Mill's elective body would be composed of men over 40 years of age owning an unspecified but not "little" amount of property.

56. Mill, *Essay on Government*, p. 72. It might seem contradictory that Mill, who took great pains to demolish Lord Liverpool's idea of the representation by estates, including the professional "clubs," should have placed such faith in the "wisdom of the middle rank."

57. Mill, *Essay on Government*, pp. 10–11.

58. Ibid., p. 65.

59. Stephen, *The English Utilitarians*, vol. 2, p. 34, using Graham Wallas's biography of the Radical tailor *Francis Place*, p. 91.

60. Mill, "Education," quoted in Stephen, *The English Utilitarians*, vol. 2, p. 82.

61. The implied link between Panopticon and political machine follows the hint in Stephen, *The English Utilitarians*, vol. 2, p. 83.

62. Eric Stokes, *The English Utilitarians in India* (Clarendon, 1959), p. 63.

63. Walter Bagehot, *Lombard Street* (H. S. King, 1873); *Physics and Politics, or Thoughts on the Application of the Principles of "Natural Selection" and "Inheritance" to Political Society* (H. S. King, 1872); *The English Constitution* (Chapman & Hall, 1867). Quotations from 1928 Oxford University Press edition.

64. M. Norton Wise with Crosbie Smith, "Work and waste: Political economy and natural philosophy in nineteenth century Britain" (three parts), *History of Science* 27 (1989): 263–301, 391–449, 28 (1990): 221–261.

65. Richard Holt Hutton, "Bagehot, Walter (1826–1877)," *Dictionary of National Biography* (Smith, Elder, 1885).

66. Bagehot, *The English Constitution*, p. 4.

67. As far as I am aware, the importance of engines to Bagehot has been missed, despite the intense scrutiny of *The English Constitution*. Stefan Collini, Donald Winch, and John Burrow (*That Noble Science of Politics*, Cambridge University Press, 1983) give a very good but static account of Bagehot. In general they take a far too limited context of explanation, for example accounting for Graham Wallas's famous epigram "The study of politics is just now in a curiously unsatisfactory state" as an attack on Oxford, whereas it was part of a wider concern for the state of the political neurology. Alison Winter (*Mesmerized*, University of Chicago Press, 1998, pp. 334–336) sees Bagehot's distinction between "efficient" and "dignified" in terms of reflexes.

68. Bagehot, *The English Constitution*, p. 203. Mill (*On Liberty*, p. 199) also used the metaphor of the "safety valve" (in a discussion of the Northcote-Trevelyan reforms), and it was a familiar analogy in politics of the franchise.

69. Bagehot, *The English Constitution*, p. 212. To complete the metaphorical structure, Bagehot (p. 237) conjured an image of "society"—meaning of course the ruling elite—as a body, energized by the dynamic monarch at its peak: . . . this wonderful spectacle of society, which is ever new, and yet ever remains the same; in which accidents pass and essence remains; in which one generation dies and another succeeds, as if they were birds in a cage, or animals in a menagerie; of which it seems almost more than a metaphor to treat as limbs of a perpetually living thing. . . ."

70. Bagehot, *The English Constitution*, p. 237.

71. John Stuart Mill, *Considerations on Representative Government* (Parker, Son, and Bourn, 1861), p. 1.

72. Mill, *Representative Government*, p. 2.

73. Ibid., p. 12.

74. Mill, *Representative Government*, pp. 114–115. In view of the postwar rise of the computer metaphor in cognitive psychology, and my arguments for the continuity of relations between metaphorical machines and the state, there should be a comparative argument here about nineteenth-century psychology and machines, both engines and state.

75. Thomas Reid, *Essays on the Active Powers of Man* (John Bell, 1788), p. 303.

76. Ibid., p. 308. It is this conception of the mechanical rule-following universe, common to other Newtonians, that later opens up for Babbage his *Bridgewater Treatise* argument that miracles must be understood as pre-programmed mechanical events.

77. And therefore "this grand machine of the natural world, displays the power and wisdom of the artificer" (Reid, *Essays*, p. 308). Demonstrators of natural phenomena in the eighteenth century reflected in this divine glory. See Simon Schaffer, "Natural philosophy and public spectacle in the eighteenth century," *History of Science* 21 (1983): 1–43.

78. Reid, *Essays*, p. 303.

79. Ibid., p. 304.

80. Ibid., p. 306.

81. Ibid., p. 303.

82. Steven Shapin, "The house of experiment in seventeenth-century England," *Isis* 79 (1988): 373–404; Shapin, "The invisible technician," *American Scientist* 77 (1989): 554–563.

83. Alexis de Tocqueville, *Democracy in America*, vol. 2, translated by Henry Reeve (Saunders & Otley, 1835), pp. 402–403. Only in the event of war, which "must almost compulsorily concentrate the direction of all men and the management of all things in the hands of the administration," would there be a reverse of this trend (*Democracy*, vol. 3, p. 220).

84. Perpetual-motion machines were popular objects of display and discussion in early-nineteenth-century American cities, especially Philadelphia. See Arthur W. J. G. Ord-Hume, *Perpetual Motion* (Allen & Unwin, 1977), p. 125.

85. The metaphor was present in the original French. "Ce qui frappe le plus l'Européen qui parcourt les États-Unis, c'est l'absence de ce qu'on appelle chez nous le gouvernement ou l'administration; en Amérique on voit des lois écrites; on en aperçoit l'exécution journaliere; tout se meut autour de vous, et on ne découvre nulle part le moteur. Le main qui dirige la machine sociale échappe à chaque instant." (Alexis de Tocqueville, *De la démocratie en Amérique*, vol. 1, Librairie de Charles Gosselin, 1835, p. 114).

86. Tocqueville, *Democracy*, vol. 1., p. 52. In French: "la machine agit par ses propres forces, et se dirige comme d'elle-même vers un but indiqué d'avance."

87. Henry David Thoreau, "Civil disobedience" (1849), reprinted in *The Portable Thoreau*, ed. C. Bode (Penguin, 1982), p. 109.

88. Ibid., p. 113.

89. Quoted from p. 113 of Thomas Carlyle, *Sartor Resartus* (Ward, Lock, n.d.).

90. Quoted from p. 122 of Thomas Carlyle, *Heroes and Hero-Worship* (Ward, Lock, n.d.).

91. Thomas Carlyle, "Signs," reprinted in Thomas Carlyle, *Selected Writings* (Penguin, 1971), p. 64.

92. On production: "Our old modes of exertion are all discredited, and thrown aside. On every hand, the living artisan is driven from his workshop, to make room for a speedier, inanimate one." On nature: "Even the horse is stripped of his harness, and finds a fleet fire-horse yoked in its stead. Nay, we have an artist that hatches chickens by steam; the very brood-hen is to be superseded! . . . We war with rude Nature; and by our resistless engines, come off always victorious, and loaded with spoils." On education: "Everything has its cunningly devised implements, its pre-established apparatus, it is not done by hand, but by machinery. Thus we have machines for Education: Lancastrian machines; Hamiltonian machines; monitors, maps and emblems." On religion: "We have Religious machines, of all imaginable varieties; the Bible-Society. . . . Has any man, or any society of men, a truth to speak, a piece of spiritual work to do; they can nowise proceed at once and with the mere natural organs, but must first call a public meeting, appoint committees, issue prospectuses, eat a public dinner; in a word, construct, or borrow machinery, wherewith to speak or do it." On science: "No Newton, by silent meditation, now discovers the system of the world from the falling of an apple; but some quite other than Newton stands in his Museum, his Scientific Institutions, and behind whole batteries of retorts, digesters and galvanic piles imperatively "interrogates Nature,"—who, however, shows no haste to answer." He goes on to trace the mechanical state of Science. His general point is that, although his contemporaries might have more methods and results, they did not have understanding: "we have more Mathematics than ever, but less Mathesis." (Carlyle, "Signs," pp. 64–68) Also (ibid., p. 75): "When we can drain the Ocean into mill-ponds, and bottle up the Force of Gravity, to be sold by retail, in gas-jars; then may we hope to comprehend the infinitudes of man's soul under formulas of Profit and Loss; and rule over this too, as over a patent engine, by checks, and valves, and balances."

93. Carlyle, "Signs," p. 70.

94. Ibid.

95. De Lolme is now the least well known of this trio. He was born in Geneva in 1745 and came to England a young man of 27. His constitutional analysis, first published in French in Holland, was translated and published as *The Constitution of England, or an account of the English Government; In which is compared with the Republican Form of Government, and occasionally with the other Monarchies in Europe* (T. Spilsbury, 1775. His next book, *The History of the Flagellants* (1783) was less well received, and he fell into poverty. Returning to continental Europe, he became a sub-prefect in Napoleonic Geneva,

before dying in 1807. *The Constitution* was a politically charged work, since it argued that the English constitution had survived because it had adapted—a warning to more ossified regimes. This was flattering to the English, and appealing to French reformers. The regard for de Lolme waned as he became less politically useful. Carlyle presumably attacked him because at times de Lolme reads like a proto-utilitarian, and for the mechanical metaphors of government found in *The Constitution.* For example, here is de Lolme (ibid., p. 169) on advantages peculiar to the English constitution: "We have seen, in former Chapters, the resources of the different parts of the English Government for balancing each other, and how their reciprocal actions and reactions produce the freedom of the Constitution, which is no more than an equilibrium between the ruling powers of the State." And again (ibid. pp. 311–312): "But when the moving springs of Government are placed entirely out of the body of the People, their action is thereby disengaged from all that could render it complicated, or hide it from the eye. As the People thenceforward consider things speculatively, and are, if I am allowed the expression, only spectators of the game, they acquire just notions of things; and as these notions, amidst the general quiet, get ground and spread themselves far and wide, they at length entertain, on the subject of their liberty, but one opinion. Forming thus, as it were, one body, the People, at every moment, has in its power to strike the decisive blow which is to level every thing. Like those mechanical powers, the greatest efficiency of which exists at the instant which precedes their entering into action, it has an immense force, just because it does not yet exert any; and in this state of stillness, but of attention, consists its true *momentum.*"

96. Stephen, *The English Utilitarians*, vol. 1, p. 250. Carlyle, "Signs," pp. 72–73. Certainly the "Codemaker" Bentham was on Carlyle's mind in that passage: "For the wise men, who now appear as Political Philosophers, deal exclusively with the Mechanical province; and occupying and estimating men's motives, strive by curious checking and balancing, and other adjustments of Profit and Loss, to guide them to their true advantage: while, unfortunately, those same "motives" are so innumerable, and so variable in every individual, that no really useful conclusion can ever be drawn from their enumeration." Also note the diatribe against "Motive-grinders and Mechanical Profit-and-Loss Philosophers" on p. 112 of Carlyle's *Sartor Resartus*.

97. For example, one cannot conclude whether inward mechanization was achieved. First Carlyle dismisses it, but later he suggests that it has had powerful and dreaded repercussions. Certainly, if one reads "Signs" as a critique of Benthamite Utilitarianism then Carlyle anticipates Foucault by a century: "Again, with respect to our Moral condition: here, also, he who runs may read that the same physical, mechanical influences are everywhere busy. For the 'superior morality' of which we hear so much, we too would desire to be thankful: at the same time, it were but blindness to deny that this 'superior morality' is properly rather an 'inferior criminality,' produced by greater love of Virtue, but be greater perfection of Police; and of that far subtler and stronger Police, called Public Opinion. This last watches over us with its Argus [ie all-seeing] eyes more keenly than ever; but the 'inward eye' seems heavy with sleep." (Carlyle, "Signs," p. 81)

98. Carlyle, "Signs," p. 84.

99. Carlyle, "Signs," p. 77.

100. Michael J. Cullen, *The Statistical Movement in Early Victorian Britain* (Harvester, 1975), p. 80. Doron Swade (*The Cogwheel Brain*, Little, Brown, 2000, p. 74) notes that Babbage was heckled concerning the money spent on the Difference Engine.

101. Quoted in Cullen, *The Statistical Movement*, p. 78. The change in Babbage's conception of the locus of power and influence is interesting. In 1832, he pointed his finger at the "commercial interests of the country" and urged the assembled members of the British Association for the Advancement of Science to cultivate them. In 1853 it was the civil servants, members of Parliament and men of public affairs; by the time of his autobiography (the 1860s) it included the "landed classes and the governing elite."

102. C. R. Saunders, *Carlyle's Friendships and Other Studies*, quoted in Martin Campbell-Kelly's introduction to Charles Babbage, *Passages from the Life of a Philosopher* (William Pickering, 1994), p. 13.

103. British Library Add. 37195, Babbage Correspondence, f. 80. Draft letter, Babbage to Lord Derby, 1 June 1852. This insistence on the necessity to reform through the invention of exact language can be compared to Bentham's project between 1802 and 1812 in the *Rationale of Evidence* to adopt a "substantive-preferring principle" (in effect, to employ nouns at the expense of verbs wherever possible) in his writings. "The ideal language would resemble algebra, in which symbols, each representing a given numerical value, are connected by the smallest number of symbols of operation, +, –, =, and so forth. To set such statements side by side, or to modify them by inserting different constants, is then a comparatively easy process, capable of being regulated by simple general rules." (Stephen, *The English Utilitarians*, vol. 1, p. 272)

104. The extension to thought is justified: Babbage himself wrote that the Analytical Engine was "of almost intellectual power." see William J. Ashworth, "Memory, efficiency, and symbolic analysis: Charles Babbage, John Herschel, and the industrial mind," *Isis* 87(1996): 629–653, p. 629: "Doing and observing operations on symbols . . . put the naked workings of the mind on show. Indeed the mind was rendered visible and open to empirical scrutiny. . . . The way was then opened to the possibility of artificially building the same kind of intelligence into a machine." Compare this with James Mill's opening of the mind's workings to visible scrutiny.

105. Charles Babbage, *Passages from the Life of a Philosopher* (Longman, 1864), quoted from pp. 97–98 of 1994 William Pickering edition.

106. Plana's summary of the power of the Analytical Engine, endorsed by Babbage, is both a statement about mathematics and a statement about politics. The mathematical sense is conveyed by Swade (*Cogwheel Brain*, p. 131): "The distinction is one we would now make between 'mathematics' and "computation"—between abstract generalized laws represented by formulae on the one hand, and the stepwise rules and techniques by which specific numerical values can be found on the other." But in making an analogy, the likening of something to something else, interpretation cannot be restricted only to one side. Both Plana and Babbage thought the analogy meaningful and profound about mathematics *and* politics.

107. Silvana Patriarca, *Numbers and Nationhood* (Cambridge University Press, 1996), p. 98, p. 104.

108. British Library Add. 37191, Babbage Correspondence, f. 501. Unsigned (Sismondi) to Babbage, 1840. "Si le Roi de Sardaignes m'avair conféré une décoration d'un rang supérieur, une telle marque de son approbation aurait sans doute fait beaucoup d'éffêt dans mons pays, et il est même probable qu'elle aurait ouvert le chemin à la construction de cette machine qui, comme Plana a écrit, comprend tout l'executif de l'analyse mathematique. Elle aurait aussi aidé à relever la science en angleterre; et j'espère de pouvoir ajouter que S. M. [?] même aurait de quelque manière ajouté à la gloire, étant le premier à apprécier et récompenser Signement un de découverte qui est destinée à changer l'aspect de [*la societé moderne*—crossed out] *l'analyse moderne.*"

109. British Library Add. 37191, Babbage Correspondence, f. 582. Babbage to Sismondi, undated (March 1841).

110. British Library Add. 37191, Babbage Correspondence, f. 501. Unsigned (Sismondi) to Babbage, 1840.

111. British Library Add. 37191, Babbage Correspondence, f. 582. Babbage to Sismondi, undated (March 1841).

112. British Library Add. 37195, Babbage Correspondence, f. 80. Draft letter, Babbage to Derby, 1 June 1852. Rosse found the opportunity to give Lord Derby the letter in mid July. Ditto, f. 108. Rosse to Babbage, 22 July 1852.

113. British Library Add. 37195, Babbage Correspondence, f. 95. Leger to Babbage, 17 June 1852. The phrenological reading of Babbage's skull used "Dr T. Leger's modification of Mr Rutter's Magnetoscope," and Leger's numerical results (on a standardized form) came with a surely disingenuous commentary: "I was in perfect ignorance of this character having constructed a calculating machine, but the chief qualifications of this examination point out immediately how and why such invention has been made by this person." Babbage's scores (probably out of 20) included: number 17, constructiveness 15, conscientiousness 14, comparison 14, adhesiveness 13, amativeness 12, cautiousness 12, ideality 12, time 12, causality 12, benevolence 11, . . . , wonder 4, destructiveness 1, imitation 0. The number of "organs" above par was 28, the number at par was 5, and the number below par was 3.

114. The result of the July 1852 election were 299 Conservatives, 315 Liberals, and 40 Peelites. Derby could not persuade the Peelites to join, but managed to cling on to power until December 1852. The lame Derby could not have offered Babbage anything.

115. British Library Add. 37195, Babbage Correspondence, f. 432. Trevelyan to Babbage, 16 January 1854. Trevelyan's letter is also interesting as representative of a subgenre of official writing: it was standardized and printed up, with inappropriate passages ruled out. Presumably many savants were consulted on the question of scales for the new maps. Ditto, f. 433. Draft letter, Babbage to Trevelyan, undated. Babbage made

an additional suggestion, possibly the basis of the innovation: "There is one point I wish *strongly* to press upon yours Lds attention": a scale showing both English feet and French metres should actually engraved on the map, since "every person who consults these maps may not have a foot rule within his reach but the scale itself will always be present with the map for whose understanding it is requisite."

Chapter 2

1. Sources of data: Colin Padfield and Tony Byrne, *British Constitution* (Heinemann, 1981), p. 152; Hennessy, *Whitehall*, p. 28.

2. Mary Croarken, *Early Scientific Computing in Britain* (Clarendon, 1990), p. 8.

3. Stephen, *The English Utilitarians*, vol. 1, p. 27.

4. Henry Parris (*Constitutional Bureaucracy*, Allen & Unwin, 1969, pp. 134–159) finds five types: patricians (often sons of the aristocracy), plebeians (gifted men of poor or obscure backgrounds, necessary because the patricians could not cope with the workload), zealots (Parris includes Charles Trevelyan and G. R. Porter), a few professionals, and the generalists.

5. The assault on sinecures had some successes. Besides Edmund Burke's act of 1782, intense (but not immediately successful) pressure was mounted toward the end of the Napoleonic wars, when British budgets were stretched to breaking point. Significant naval administrative reform took place in 1833, and some of the more grotesque sinecures, the Tellers of the Exchequer, were abolished the following year.

6. The early individualized system meant that with each new chief accountant a new account was opened, the old only being closed when all the transactions had been made. This led to famous cases of bad debt: in 1780 it was estimated that the country was still owed £27,611 from Viscount Falkland's 1680s tenure as Treasurer of the Navy. Lord Holland, a Paymaster-General, owed more than £400,000 until 1780, when half the debt was paid up. Debts rested with the heirs of the officer, since they were personal accounts, albeit arising from public service. Source: Emmeline W. Cohen, *The Growth of the British Civil Service, 1780–1939*, Allen & Unwin, 1941, p. 32.).

7. Cohen, *Growth*, p. 78.

8. Ibid., p. 81. The Mathematical Tripos was introduced in 1747; for decades it attracted few students.

9. "It is notorious that the examinations for Trinity Fellowships have, directly or indirectly, done much to give direction to the studies of Cambridge, and of all the numerous schools which are the feeders of Cambridge. What then, is likely to be the effect of a competition for prizes [i. e. appointment to the Indian Civil Service] which will be ten times as numerous as the Trinity Fellowships, and of which each will be more valuable than a Trinity Fellowship." (The Indian Civil Service, Report to the House of Commons, 1855, pp. 7–8) (See Cohen, *Growth*, p. 83.).

10. On India as a "laboratory" and as a "precursor" to the Northcote-Trevelyan reforms, see Thomas Osborne, "Bureaucracy as a vocation: Governmentality and administration in nineteenth-century Britain," *Journal of Historical Sociology* 7 (1994): 289–312.

11. Stokes, *English Utilitarians in India*, pp. 10, 13–14, 20.

12. Ibid., p. 51.

13. Quoted in ibid., p. 68.

14. C. A. Bayly, *Empire and Information* (Cambridge University Press, 1996), p. 8. Bayly adds that this was particularly true after 1830.

15. Stokes, *English Utilitarians in India*, p. 70.

16. Cohen, *Growth*, pp. 80–81.

17. Malthus had toured Sweden, Norway, Russia, Germany, France, and Switzerland to collect data for the heavyweight second (1802) edition of his epochal *Essay on Population*. The *Essay* is a good example of the checks and balances in political economy: the rise in the population is only checked by "misery and vice."

18. Evangelicalism was a new vigorous religious movement in the early nineteenth century. The evangelical Clapham Sect formed a link between the Cornwallis system and the utilitarians: evangelicalism inspired the missionaries that were crucial to the Cornwallis project of cultural transformation, and Charles Cornwallis was advised by two members of the Clapham Sect, John Shore and Charles Grant. Stokes (*English Utilitarians in India*, p. 54) has noted the parallels between the Clapham Sect and utilitarianism: both "sought to liberate the individual from the slavery of custom and from the tyranny of the noble or priest [i. e. from personal human authority]. Their end was to make the individual in society a free, autonomous individual." Furthermore, both problematized lack of knowledge: failure to attain happiness was the result of ignorance, and we have seen how this view validated for the utilitarians massive enterprises of fact collection and dissemination. Where the two differed was in the influential role that the utilitarians allocated to law and government.

19. G. C. B., "Charles Edward Trevelyan (1807–1886)," *Dictionary of National Biography*.

20. Cohen, *Growth*, p. 84.

21. Charles Edward Trevelyan, *Papers Originally Published at Calcutta in 1834 and 1836 on the Application of the Roman Letters to the Languages of Asia*, p. 24. He continued: ". . . the absence of which has always so much impeded the due administration of justice in this country, and stood in the way of our taking root in the affections of our subjects to the extent, which the rectitude of our acts and intentions might entitle us to expect."

22. Charles Edward Trevelyan, *Address to Conference on Society for Organising Charitable Relief and Repressing Mendacity on Systematic Visitation of Poor in their Own Homes as an Indispensable Basis of an Effective System of Charity*, 1870.

23. Humphrey Trevelyan, *The India We Left* (Macmillan, 1972), p. 56.

24. Cohen, *Growth*, p. 88.

25. *Minutes of Evidence of the Select Committee on Miscellaneous Expenditure, Parliamentary Papers*, 1847–48, 18, p. 151. Trevelyan suggestions to this committee (a split between superior and mechanical staff, a appointment after proven fitness "in some line of life") were an early version, applied to his home department, of those found in the Northcote-Trevelyan report.

26. Cohen, *Growth*, p. 88.

27. Stafford H. Northcote and Charles E. Trevelyan, "The Northcote-Trevelyan Report," reprinted in *Public Administration* 32 (1954): 1–16, originally signed 23 November 1853 and published as House of Commons Parliamentary Paper 1713 in February 1854. Northcote and Trevelyan also reported to the Treasury in 1853 in a paper—"The Reorganisation of the Permanent Civil Service"—that was published, along with a letter from Benjamin Jowett and criticisms of the paper, in 1855.

28. Ibid., p. 4.

29. Andrew Warwick, "Exercising the student body: Mathematics and athleticism in Victorian Cambridge," in *Science Incarnate*, ed. C. Lawrence and S. Shapin (University of Chicago Press, 1999).

30. Gladstone to Lord John Russell, quoted in Hennessy, *Whitehall*, p. 44. James Mill would have disagreed. In the Essay on Government, he remarks that "intellectual powers are the offspring of labor"; hence, idle aristocrats would be dim (Mill, *Representative Government*, p. 11).

31. Northcote and Trevelyan, "Report," p. 11. Inferior clerks were appointed, in many departments, usually after an in-house examination, not least to test handwriting, so the novelty of examination applies to superior class. Furthermore, some offices already held written examinations to test nominees (usually writing and arithmetic, but the Audit Office, e.g., demanded knowledge of double-entry bookkeeping and foreign exchanges, while other offices tested geography and history). But these tests were unstandardized, internal affairs.

32. Ibid., p. 12. As a fairly serious counterfactual speculative aside, the dropping of the common copying office idea was, contra Hennessy, the Northcote-Trevelyan Report's greatest flaw. Such a copying office would have formed a huge concentration of mechanical labor, and would surely have led to early mechanization with spinoffs in the development of office machinery. Hennessy (*Whitehall*, p. 40) argues that the decision to train young men internally rather than encourage for new blood by appointing "men of mature age" from outside Whitehall, was a "desperate flaw . . . one which built weakness into [Trevelyan's] entire structure and which will, in the end, be the undoing of his remarkably enduring creation. But as Trevelyan himself wrote in the report, external appointments were an established pattern in the pre-examination days of patronage, and had not led to a particularly efficient Civil Service.

33. Northcote and Trevelyan, "Report," p. 14. The *Morning Herald* poked fun at this proposal, imagining a world in which civil servants were encouraged to report one other's misdeeds: ". . . how comforting to the 16,000 clerks in her Majesty's Civil Service must be the knowledge that duplicate copies of the black books are to be kept . . . so that there is no fear that an indiscreet fire will deprive the future historian of this valuable mine of materials for composing these interesting biographies. Who, after our unqualified panegyric of this heaven-inspired scheme, will dare to insinuate that it smacks of Jesuitism either in its origin, its machinery, or its end?" See A Civil Subaltern, *Civil Service Reform* (William Edward Painter, undated).

34. Anthony Trollope, *The Three Clerks* (Oxford University Press, 1989; first published in three volumes by Richard Bentley, 1857), pp. 58–59.

35. Ibid., p. 124.

36. Ibid., p. 129.

37. Ibid., p. 325.

38. Ibid., p. 556.

39. For example, compare the following passage (Trollope, *The Three Clerks*, p. 556) with the passage quoted in the text above from the Northcote-Trevelyan report: "Many of a man's first years are spent copying, and the remainder of his official life can only exercise a depressing influence on him. He not only begins life with mechanical labor, but ends with it."

40. *Times*, 23 May 1859, p. 12.

41. Trollope's alternative plan for reforming the Civil Service entailed paying public servants more (to attract the "aspiring, energetic, and ambitious among British youths"), dissolving the boundaries between the Civil Service and the world of politicians, and ESTABLISHING a college for the instruction of government clerks. Trollope was therefore seeking to make the Civil Service akin to other professions, such as law.

42. George Otto Trevelyan, *Life and Letters of Macaulay*, vol. 2 (1876), pp. 375–376; Cohen, *Growth*, p. 104.

43. A Civil Subaltern, *Civil Service Reform*.

44. *Morning Post* editorial, republished in A Civil Subaltern, *Civil Service Reform*, p. 9.

45. *Morning Herald* editorial, republished in A Civil Subaltern, *Civil Service Reform*, p. 31.

46. *Daily News* editorial, republished in A Civil Subaltern, *Civil Service Reform*, p. 13. "Russia," "Prussia," "Austria," and even "China" are interchangeable in these attacks.

47. "They will draw up all bills—they will suggest, and probably write out, all motions—to them will be referred all proceedings to ascertain if they be according to rule—they will prepare all reports, even the reports of committees. This, in fact, is what

the civil servants aim at in proposing their pretended patriotic reform, and this is what, if they be established as a class with a technical education, they will accomplish. Supposing they did not, we should have them sulky and rebellious."

48. *Papers on the Reorganisation of the Civil Service, Parliamentary Papers*, 1854–55, vol. 20, pp. 244–245.

49. Samuel Best, *Thoughts on the Proposals for the Improvement of the Civil Service; and for the Granting of Diplomas through the Agency of the Institutions in Union with the Society of Arts* (Groombridge and Sons, 1854), p. 8. Best was in fact referring to a slightly earlier proposal to employ disaffected pupil-teachers in government offices, but it was his explicit view that the Trevelyan proposals carried on these advantages: that by creating a system in which talent could be "excited" and its "energy" trammeled to make the system work.

50. Hennessy, *Whitehall*, p. 48. For an analysis of the effect of the implementation of the Northcote-Trevelyan reforms, see Henry Roseveare, *The Treasury* (Allen Lane, 1969).

51. See e.g. Henry White, *Guide to Civil Service Examinations*, London, 1858; J. J. Adams, *The Note-Book of English History . . . for the use of officers and other gentlemen studying for Civil Service examinations* (J. W. Wakeham, 1896); Charles Henry Anderson, *The Intermediate Questions on Book-Keeping* (Stevens, Sons & Haynes, 1863); Herbert J. E. Barter, *A Handbook of Geography and History, for the use of Students preparing for Civil Service and other examinations* (Houlston & Wright, 1867); George Edward Skerry, *Skerry's Practical Papers in French* (Civil Service Press, 1899); Joseph Charles Parkinson, *Government Examinations* (London, 1860); John Hunter, *Civil Service Examinations* (Longman, 1882); John Keefe, *Civil Service Spelling and Dictation Book* (Simpkin, Marshall and Co., 1888). Skerry also offered mathematics; Hunter, a principal at the Uxbridge School, also offered a guide to questions on arithmetic and double-entry bookkeeping. Keefe also offered arithmetic.

52. For an advertisement for the King's College course, see Edward Stanford, *Handbook to Government Situations* (Edward Stanford, 1866).

53. For a critical view, see Hugo R. Meyer, *The British State Telegraphs* (Macmillan, 1907). For a more balanced history, see Jeffrey L. Kieve, *The Electric Telegraph* (David and Charles, 1973).

54. Harris, *Private Lives*, pp. 201–208; Gillian Sutherland, ed., *Studies in the Growth of Nineteenth-Century Government* (Routledge & Kegan Paul, 1972). For a convincing reassertion of the importance of considering taxation in understanding the growth of the British state, see James E. Cronin, *The Politics of State Expansion* (Routledge, 1991). Cronin, like Roseveare and many others, however, inherits the misleading negative model of the "dead hand of the Treasury."

55. For this summary of the LGB, see Harris, *Private Lives*, p. 198.

56. Cohen, *Growth*, p. 125. The press had been introduced by the Duke of Richmond, Master-General of Ordnance.

57. *Civil Service Inquiry Commission* (Playfair Commission), *Parliamentary Papers*, 1875, 23, p. 14.

58. Hilda Martindale, *Women Servants of the State, 1870–1938* (Allen & Unwin, 1938), p. 16.

59. Quoted in ibid., pp. 17–18.

60. Quoted in ibid., pp. 22–23.

61. JoAnne Yates, *Control through Communication* (Johns Hopkins University Press, 1989), pp. 39–41.

62. PRO T 108/6. Treasury book, 1874–1878. Entry for 1876. [Editor's note: Here and in similar notes, the convention of using periods—full stops—in listing PRO items has been followed. In such listings, a period does not mark a separation between two items.]

63. PRO T 108/6. Treasury book, 1874–1878. Entry for 1877.

64. PRO T 108/6. Treasury book, 1874–1878. Entry for 1878. PRO T 108/8. Treasury book, 1879–1883. Entries for 1879, 1881, 1883. In 1882 the Civil Service Commissioners undertook a comparative investigation "on the merits of various processes and awarding the palm to the Trypograph—[and produced a] statemt showing economy effected. . . ."

65. Martindale, *Women Servants*, p. 65. "In the afternoon to Coombe Wood, with my women typewriters from Somerset House," West noted in his diary in 1892 (*Private Diaries of the Rt. Hon. Sir Algernon West, G. C. B*, John Murray, 1922, pp. 39–40). "I was in later years glad to think that I had, after a battle royal with the Treasury, been successful in being the first head of a big department to advocate successfully their employment." See also Cohen, *Growth*, p. 151.

66. Report on the Royal Commission on Civil Establishments (Ridley Commission), Parliamentary Papers, 1888, 27, pp. 250–251; Cohen, *Growth*, p. 151.

67. David Abercrombie, *Isaac Pitman* (Sir Isaac Pitman & Sons, 1937), p. 2. See also Asa Briggs, *Victorian Things* (Penguin, 1990), p. 409.

68. Martindale, Women Servants, p. 66.

69. Ibid., p. 67. Martindale herself had been a civil servant in the Home Office and Treasury.

70. Figures from Dorothy Evans, *Women and the Civil Service* (Sir Isaac Pitman & Sons, 1934), p. 12.

71. For example, David Ricardo's political economy, which emerged from Utilitarian thought, alongside Malthus's, to become orthodox theory, was logically organized, and appealed to the analogy of "friction" in the system. Ricardo's opponents labeled it overly "mechanical" as well as abstract, materialistic, fatalistic and degrading. Stephen, *English Utilitarians*, vol. 2, pp. 216–220.

72. Take, e.g., Matthew Arnold, *Culture and Anarchy* (1869; Cambridge University Press edition, 1960), p. 75: "We have not the notion, so familiar on the Continent and to

antiquity, of the State—the nation in its collective and corporate character, entrusted with stringent powers for the general advantage, and controlling individual wills in the name of an interest wider than that of individuals. We say, what is very true, that this notion is often made instrumental to tyranny; we say that a State is in reality made up of the individuals who compose it, and that every individual is the best judge of his own interests. Our leading class is an aristocracy, and no aristocracy likes the notion of a State-authority greater than itself, with a stringent administrative machinery superseding the decorative inutilities of lord-lieutenancy, [etc.]. . . . Our middle class, the great representative of trade and Dissent, with its maxims of every man for himself in business, every man for himself in religion, dreads a powerful administration which might somehow interfere with it; and besides it has its own decorative inutilities of vestrymanship, [etc.] . . . and a stringent administration might take these functions out of its hands, or prevent its exercising them in its own comfortable manner, as at present. Then to our working class. This class, pressed constantly by the hard daily compulsion of material wants, is naturally the very centre and stronghold of our national idea, that it is man's ideal right and felicity to do as he likes." So, according to Arnold, no class welcomes administrative machinery. The point survived Arnold's wider project to replace the language of class with his alternative formulation of Barbarians, Philistines, and Populace.

73. Arnold, *Culture and Anarchy*, p. 74.

74. For example, in his satire on the Civil Service: "Because the Circumlocution Office went on mechanically, every day, keeping this wonderful, all-sufficient wheel of statesmanship, How not to do it, in motion" Charles Dickens, *Little Dorrit* (Penguin, 1967 (originally published 1857), p. 146. Arnold, *Culture and Anarchy*, p. 7: "The whole scope of the essay is to recommend culture as the great help out of our present difficulties; culture being a pursuit of our total perfection by means of getting to know, on all matters which most concern us, the best which has been thought and said in the world; and through this knowledge, turning a stream of fresh and free thought upon our stock notions and habits, which we now follow staunchly but mechanically, vainly imagining that there is virtue in following them staunchly which makes up for the mischief of following them mechanically."

75. David Vincent, *The Culture of Secrecy* (Oxford University Press, 1998), p. 34.

76. Ibid., p. 38.

77. Ibid., pp. 39–43.

78. For an interesting discussion of neutrality, see G. Kitson Clark, " 'Statesmen in disguise': Reflections of the history of the neutrality of the Civil Service," in *The Victorian Revolution*, ed. P. Stansky (New Viewpoints, 1973). Kitson Clark's point is that the "principle [of Civil Service neutrality] can be traced back into the nineteenth century without reference to the Trevelyan-Northcote reforms, or to their authors," indeed the pattern of the "responsible political minister and the non-political permanent secretary" was established by 1830.

79. Geoffrey R. Searle, *The Quest for National Efficiency* (Blackwell, 1971); citations from second edition (Ashfield, 1990).

80. Ibid., p. 54.

81. Daniel Pick, *War Machine* (Yale University Press, 1993), p. 102, p. 165.

82. Searle, *Quest*, pp. 60–67.

83. Ibid., p. 69.

84. Charles H. Wilson, *Haldane and the Machinery of Government* (J. W. Ruddock and Sons, 1957); *Report of the Machinery of Government Committee*, Cmd. 9230, 1918. Members of the committee were Haldane, Edwin S. Montagu, Sir Robert Morant, Sir George Murray, Secretary of the Treasury Colonel Sir Alan Sykes, J. H. Thomas, and Beatrice Webb.

85. Beatrice Webb on Wells: "A world run by the physical science man straight from his laboratories is his ideal: he does not see that specialized faculty and knowledge are needed for administration exactly as they are needed for the manipulation of machinery or natural forces." (Lovat Dickson, *H. G. Wells*, Pelican, 1969, p. 136) In *Modern Utopia*, Wells classified citizens into poietic, kinetic, dull, and base types and commented: "A primary problem of government was to vest all the executive and administrative work in the kinetic class, while leaving the poietic and legislature, controlling the base and giving the dull an incentive to kinetic effort." (ibid., p. 205).

86. "It would be out of place here to follow out further the kind of idealism that has throughout had hold of me. It is enough to say that its essence led me to the belief in the possibility of finding rational principles underlying all forms of experience, and to a strong sense of endeavour to find such principles as a first duty in every department of public life. . . . That has seemed to me to be as true of the Army and of the administrative services as it has seemed in the case of judicial duties." (R. B. Haldane, *Autobiography* (Hodder & Stoughton, 1929), p. 352).

87. Elizabeth Sanderson Haldane, *Richard Burdon Haldane, Viscount Haldane of Cloan*, DNB.

88. On Julius Turing's career, see Andrew Hodges, *Alan Turing* (Unwin, 1985), pp. 7–10.

89. Ibid., p. 544.

90. John Stuart Mill, *Autobiography*, p. 92.

91. Mill, *Representative Government*, chapter 5: "If followed that politics was an deductive science. It thus appeared that both Macaulay and my father were wrong. . . ." The philosophy of science that resulted from this attempt at reconciliation was expressed most fully in his *System of Logic*.

92. A. M. Turing, "On computable numbers, with an application to the Entscheidungsproblem," *Proceedings of the London Mathematical Society*, Series 2, 42 (1937): 230–265.

93. Hodges, *Turing*, pp. 93–96.

94. Turing, "On computable numbers," p. 231.

95. Turing calls the states "*m*-configurations" and represents them by $q_1, q_2, \ldots, q_R$, where R is finite. In a slightly confusing repetition, Turing uses "configuration" twice, but his meaning is clear in the statement "The possible behavior of the machine at any moment is determined by the *m*-configuration q_n and the scanned symbol. . . . This pair [*m*-configuration, scanned symbol] will be called the "configuration."

96. See Martin Campbell-Kelly and William Aspray, *Computer* (Basic Books, 1996), p. 9; Jennifer Light, "When computers were women," *Technology and Culture* 40 (1999): 455–483.

97. Turing, "On computable numbers," p. 253.

98. Ibid., pp. 253–254.

99. Hodges, *Turing*, p. 109. On the same page, Hodges remarks in passing on the relationship between Turing's and Babbage's machines: Turing "described his ideas to David Champernowne, who got the gist of the universal machine, and said rather mockingly that it would require the Albert Hall to house its construction. . . . Just south of the Albert Hall, in the Science Museum, were lurking the remains of Babbage's 'Analytical Engine,' a projected universal machine of 100 years before. Quite probably Alan had seen them, and yet if so, they had no detectable influence upon his ideas or language. His 'machine' had no obvious model in anything that existed in 1936, except in general terms of the new electrical industries, with their teleprinters, television "scanning," and automatic telephone exchange connections. It was his own invention." I agree that Babbage's engine did not have any direct influence, but suggest that both Babbage and Turing were influenced by models of administration.

Chapter 3

1. Martin Rein (*Social Science and Social Policy*, Penguin, 1976, p. 124) argues that "social data performs a leading part in the complex process by which society constructs its perceptions of reality, defines what its problems are and determines the goals and strategies it should adopt and what principles of intervention should guide its actions." This is quoted and discussed on p. 23 of Roger Davidson's *Whitehall and the Labour Problem in Late-Victorian and Edwardian Britain.*

2. G. Udny Yule, "Statistics of production and the Census of Production Act (1906)," *Journal of the Royal Statistical Society* 70 (1907): 52–99.

3. Arthur L. Bowley, "The improvement of official statistics," *Journal of the Royal Statistical Society* 71 (1908): 459–495.

4. Davidson, *Whitehall*, p. 207.

5. Ibid., p. 211.

6. Flux, in discussion after Bowley, "Improvement," p. 491.

7. Edward Higgs, "The struggle for the occupational census," in *Governments and Expertise*, ed. R. MacLeod (Cambridge University Press. See also Michael J. Cullen, *The*

Statistical Movement in Early Victorian Britain (Harvester, 1975), p. 10; D. V. Glass, *Numbering the People* (Heath, 1973). For a witty discussion on "statistics," see Ian Hacking, *The Taming of Chance* (Cambridge University Press, 1990), pp. 24–25.

8. Hacking, *Taming.*

9. On the disputed authorship of works attributed to Gaunt and Petty, see Cullen, *Statistical Movement,* pp. 4–5. Gregory King, a topographer and surveyor served as secretary to the commissioners of public accounts and calculated the income, expenditure and savings of households, published in *Natural and Political Observations upon the State and Condition of England* (1696).

10. Cullen, *Statistical Movement*; Glass, *Numbering*; Lawrence Goldman, "The origins of British social science: political economy, natural science and statistics, 1830–1835," *Historical Journal* (1983) 26: 486–616; Jack Morrell and Arnold Thackray, *Gentlemen of Science* (Clarendon, 1981); Mary Poovey, *A History of the Modern Fact* (University of Chicago Press, 1998), pp. 308–328.

11. For some of the complexities of this meeting, see Goldman, "Origins," pp. 591–600.

12. Quoted in Cullen, *Statistical Movement,* p. 79. See also Morrell and Thackray, *Gentlemen,* p. 292.

13. Cullen (*Statistical Movement,* p. 92) notes, and other authors have continued to note, that "Babbage was quick to lose his enthusiasm for statistics and became more and more involved in his calculating machine." My point is that as soon as one recognizes the political nature of Babbage's machines the shift becomes a continuity rather than a break.

14. For example, recommending keeping the religious and education questions in the 1861 census of population, and when they were dropped pressing again for their inclusion in 1871. The Society called for an industrial census in 1881, and for both 1881 and 1891 the institution of quinquennial rather than decennial census of population: Britain was lagging, the Society claimed, behind many countries that had followed this information-hungry path: the German empire (since 1866), Sweden (1805), France (1835), Finland (1875), and even parts of the British empire (New Zealand, Queensland, Manitoba, parts of the Northwest Territories of Canada). While the United States was decennial, fifteen states and territories took an intermediate census in 1885. The point being made is that while the Society seems to be acting as an external pressure group, calling on the government to reform, since the Society was composed of both official and non-official statisticians is should *not* be seen as external, but as a movement partly in and partly outside government. (The examples are from archives of the Royal Statistical Society, Minutes, Miscellaneous Committees, 1834–1901, B6.).

15. Witness, e.g., the reaction to Booth at the Royal Statistical Society in 1891, where the meeting had to be adjourned because of the overwhelmingly hostile reaction to his paper.

16. See Lorenz Krüger, Lorraine J. Daston, and Michael Heidelberger, eds., *The Probabilistic Revolution* (MIT Press, 1987); Theodore M. Porter, *The Rise of Statistical Thinking, 1820–1900* (Princeton University Press, 1986); Philip Mirowski, *More Light than Heat* (Cambridge University Press, 1989).

17. Cullen, *Statistical Movement*, p. 13. Cullen relates the appearance of national criminal statistics to the parliamentary campaign of Sir Samuel Romilly against inappropriate capital punishment.

18. Cullen, *Statistical Movement*, p. 11.

19. Hacking, *Taming*, p. 27.

20. Leslie Stephen, *The English Utilitarians* (Duckworth, 1900), vol. 1, p. 81. Stephen remarks on p. 79: "Sinclair was a man of enormous energy, though not of vivacious intellect. He belonged to the prosaic breed, which created the "dismal science," and seems to have been regarded as a stupendous bore. Bores, however, represent a social force not to be despised, and Sinclair was no exception."

21. Jacob, quoted in Cullen, *Statistical Movement*, p. 20.

22. "Porter, George Richardson (1792–1852)," *Dictionary of National Biography*, vol. 46 (Smith, Elder, 1896), p. 178. Auckland knew of Porter through membership of Henry Brougham's Society for the Diffusion of Useful Knowledge (SDUK). Porter turned his knowledge of sugar to good account in his *The Nature and Properties of Sugar Cane* and *The Tropical Agriculturalist* (Smith, Elder, 1833), which set out to be a colonial handbook on growing crops such as cotton, rice, coffee, cacao, vanilla, cloves, and nutmeg, besides sugar.

23. Jean-Michel Collette, *Empirical Inquiries and the Assessment of Social Progress in Western Europe* (United Nations Research Institute for Social Development, 2000), p. 25.

24. Ibid., p. 24; Paul Studenski, *The Income of Nations* (New York University Press, 1958).

25. Linda Colley, *Britons* (Vintage, 1996), pp. 304–305. According to Cullen (*Statistical Movement*, p. 12), this insight should be attributed to Professor D. V. Glass, who investigated proposals for the first census.

26. "By the eighteen-thirties, the English state had both a growing appetite for information and the means to gather that material on an unprecedented scale. Perhaps the most important consequence of this was a reconfiguration of power within the state. No longer was central government constrained by the capacity and willingness of local government to cooperate in investigation. Central government possessed machinery for amassing literally volumes of information without formal reference to the semi-autonomous agencies of local government." (David Eastwood, "'Amplifying the province of the legislature': The flow of information and the English state in the early nineteenth century," *Historical Research* 62, 1989: 276–294, p. 291) This, I feel, is right, although central freedom from local government did not mean freedom from non-official statisticians.

27. "Towards the illustration of these various points [i.e., the contents of *The Progress of England*], parliamentary and other official records will be used as far as practicable, and these records fortunately are sufficient in number, extent and variety, to afford data upon nearly all the subjects which it is proposed to embrace. The extensive inquiries that have been instituted from year to year by the Imperial Parliament, upon almost every branch of the national interests, have made available to our purpose an amount of testimony drawn from the most intelligent and experienced quarters, such as no other country or government in the world has ever brought together. Individual members of the legislature have likewise been accustomed to call upon our public departments for the production of various details, with the view of elucidating all matters that in any way affect either the interests of particular classes of their constituents, or those of the community at large. And recently, the executive government has established a department for the collection and systematic arrangement of information for the use of the legislature and the public, which has been instrumental in bringing to light and classifying a considerable amount of information upon nearly every topic that is connected with the apparent condition of society." (George Richardson Porter, *The Progress of the Nation*, vol. 1, Charles Knight, 1836, p. 4).

28. John F. W. Herschel, ed., *A Manual of Scientific Enquiry* (John Murray, 1849), preface (reprint of instructions from Lords Commissioners of the Admiralty).

29. George Richardson Porter, "Statistics," in ibid., pp. 465–484.

30. Frederick Morton Eden, *The State of the Poor* (London, 1797). The author was the eldest son of Robert Eden, Governor of Maryland. (Collette, *Empirical Inquiries*, p. 8).

31. Cullen, *Statistical Movement*, pp. 12–13; Higgs, "Struggle," p. 74. The 1831 census was the result of a struggle between the Tory John Rickman and "the Macculloch school of political economists" (Orlo Williams, *Lamb's Friend the Census-Taker*, Constable, 1912, p. 249).

32. Sylvanus Percival Vivian, *The Story of the General Register Office and Its Origins, from 1538 to 1937* (HMSO, 1937), p. 27.

33. "Rickman, John (1771–1840)," *Dictionary of National Biography* (Smith, Elder, 1896). Rickman has prepared an index to the statutes of the House of Commons in 1818, and organized the library. In addition to the Census of Population, he prepared annual abstracts of poor-law returns (1816–36). He "sympathized with Southey's conservatism, and with his hatred of Malthus and the economists."

34. Vivian, *Story*, p. 28.

35. Farr, "born in humble circumstances," benefited from a string of patrons before studying medicine in Paris and London. He contributed the essay "Vital Statistics" to McCulloch's Statistical Account of the British Empire, and joined the Registrar General's Office in 1838. His influence within the office grew with time, although not all his suggestions for the Censuses of Population were accepted. In 1879, when Major Graham retired as Registrar-General, Farr fully expected to be called to fill the post. When the politically more astute Sir Brydges Henniker was appointed, Farr resigned in disgust. ("Farr, William (1807–1883)," *Dictionary of National Biography*, Smith, Elder, 1889).

36. Cullen, *Statistical Movement*, p. 59.

37. The three were intimately connected, it being the conviction of many statisticians that widening education led to decreasing criminality. This was precisely why leading British statisticians were horrified by the Frenchman A. M. Guerry's heretical demonstration that education did not decrease crime. Not only did Guerry's conclusion strike at the heart of the statisticians' political convictions, but Guerry's continental statistics were highly sophisticated, with shaded maps and histograms. It took the combined efforts of W. R. Greg, Porter, Rawson W. Rawson (a central figure in the later Statistical Society of London), and Joseph Fletcher to repel the French threat. See Cullen, *Statistical Movement*, pp. 139–140.

38. Cullen, *Statistical Movement*, pp. 70–72.

39. Robert Dudley Baxter, *National Income. The United Kingdom* (Macmillan, 1868).

40. Collette, *Empirical Inquiries*, p. 35.

41. Davidson divides the historiography into "progressive" and "conservative" camps. The progressive view was that "a pluralist social policy-making process after 1870 had provided a powerful mechanism for affecting social transformation; that it reflected not simply the priorities of a capitalist elite but also embodied the values and interests of a range of progressive ideologies including those of the Labour Movement." A conservative interpretation was that welfare provision was social control rather than societal transformation, and was made from either a functionalist Marxist position ("social policy as primarily concerned with maintaining the efficiency and stability of the capitalist system"), or a more general interest-account theory ("fundamentally a product of the values and interests of dominant social groups within capitalist society"). Representative authors being Freeden and Emy for the progressive interpretation, and Gough, George, and Wilding and Mishra for the conservative. See Davidson, *Whitehall*, pp. 3, 11–12.

42. An "analysis of the rationale and scope of official statistics relating to the late-Victorian and Edwardian 'Labour Problem' clearly sustains an interpretation of social reform as primarily a means of social control" (Davidson, *Whitehall*, p. 255).

43. Industrial unrest can be linked to a downturn in the economic climate, due in turn to increased competition from Germany and the United States, which made employers more aggressive concerning costs; to changing relations of production stemming from increased mechanization, and therefore a shift in numbers of skilled, semi-skilled and unskilled hands; a new militancy in the labor movement, reflected in the phenomenon of New Unionism and the rejection of the mid-Victorian consensus that had tied union leaders to the bosses (i.e. the importance of thrift, self-help and the unity of capital and labor). The sense of crisis was palpable. Yet at the same time economic historians have shown that economic retardation was not severe, and Britain's ups and downs were shared by competitors. (Davidson, *Whitehall*, pp. 34–69).

44. Davidson, *Whitehall*, p. 79

45. Ibid., p. 81.

46. Stephen Inwood, *A History of London* (Macmillan, 1998), p. 512.

47. Davidson, *Whitehall*, p. 85.

48. Gareth Stedman Jones, *Outcast London* (Clarendon, 1971); José Harris, *Unemployment and Politics* (Clarendon, 1972. Statistical data on labor was disseminated through the Board of Trade's new *Labour Gazette*, a complement to the pre-existing *Journal*, which carried commercial information (Davidson, *Whitehall*, p. 98).

49. Davidson, *Whitehall*, p. 92. The 1892 election saw both parties appealing to working-class voters.

50. Davidson, *Whitehall*, p. 113.

51. Ibid., p. 119.

52. Ibid., pp. 120–121.

53. Donald A. MacKenzie, *Statistics in Britain, 1865–1930* (Edinburgh University Press, 1981); Davidson, *Whitehall*, p. 123.

54. A. L. Bowley, "Address to the Economic Section of the British Association," *Journal of the Royal Statistical Society* 69 (1906): 540–548. Quoted in Davidson, *Whitehall*, p. 124.

55. Davidson, *Whitehall*, p. 170.

56. Ibid., p. 185.

57. Cheysson, "The organisation of government statistical offices," *Journal of the Statistical Society of London* 45 (1882): 606–623. Also quoted in Charles Wentworth Dilke, "Presidential address," *Journal of the Royal Statistical Society* 70 (1907): 553–582.

58. Roy MacLeod, "Introduction," in MacLeod, *Government and Expertise*, pp. 15–16.

59. Frederick Purdy, "Suggestions upon the preparation and printing of Parliamentary statistics," *Journal of the Statistical Society of London* 34 (1871): 21–56.

60. See e.g. Dilke, "Presidential address," pp. 572, 574.

61. PRO CAB 139/5. See also (authorship uncertain but probably J. Stafford), "A note on statistical coordination in the United Kingdom," September 1946. The committee consisted of Childers, Colonel Romilly (Commissioner of Customs), T. H. Farrer (Secretary of the Board of Trade), Reginald Earle Welby (Treasury), Shaw Lefevre (a past President of the Statistical Society, now a member of Parliament and First Commissioner of Works), Arthur J. Balfour (then an MP, later prime minister), M. W. Ridley—replaced by Charles Thomson Ritchie (a conservative MP for the working-class London constituency of Tower Hamlets), and the inactive Sir John Lambert of the Local Government Board. See "Proceedings of the Statistical Committee of the Treasury," *Journal of the Statistical Society of London* 44 (1881): 269–367.

62. Giffen's evidence was reprinted verbatim. See *Journal of the Statistical Society* 44 (1881), pp. 337–364.

63. Quoted by Stafford. See also Parliamentary Paper 38 of 1881.

64. Quoted by Stafford.

65. Compare this with Latour's account of replication of laboratory conditions (Bruno Latour, "Give me a laboratory and I will raise the world," in *Science Observed*, ed. K. Knorr-Cetina and M. Mulkay (Sage, 1983).

66. James C. Scott, *Seeing Like a State* (Yale University Press, 1998), p. 80.

67. Stafford, "Note."

68. William Carr, "Farrer, Sir Thomas Henry, bart., first Baron Farrer 1819–1899," *Dictionary of National Biography* (Oxford University Press, 1995).

69. Dilke, "Presidential Address." Dilke (1843–1911) was a radical imperialist, a republican earlier in his career, eventually tamed enough for Gladstone to bring him into his cabinet in 1882 as president of the Local Government Board (Queen Victoria did not approve, apparently). He was rocked by a divorce scandal in 1885, and although returned again as a Member of Parliament in 1892, he stood aside from politics, but continued to travel and write. He invented the phrase "Greater Britain" for his first very successful book. He was tutored by Leslie Stephen. His father, grandfather, and son all had the same name.

70. Dilke suggested that a member of the public, in his case a farmer or trawlerman, filling in forms "may, perhaps, be less unwilling to make their returns to a department from which they may hope for aid"; financial interest therefore would encourage the public to contribute.

71. Davidson, *Whitehall*, pp. 199–200. Dilke's simultaneous pressing of the Select Committee on Income Tax for a Central Statistical Department provides further evidence that this was a coordinated campaign on behalf of the expert movement of statisticians.

72. Bowley, "Improvement," p. 461.

73. Ibid., p. 466. On "residuum," see Jones, *Outcast London*; José Harris, "Between civic virtue and Social Darwinism: The concept of the residuum," in Englander and O'Day, *Retrieved Riches* (Scolar, 1995). At issue was whether a distinction could be drawn between those unemployed but willing to work and those not. If repressive measures were aimed outside the residuum then, it was feared, the effect would be to further politicize the unemployed and contribute to social unrest.

74. In response to Bowley, Yule claimed: "No examination of a sample could possibly be a test of the adequacy of the sample in the real sense of the term, and there would always remain a doubt as to its really random and representative character." (discussion after Bowley, "Improvement," p. 488) On Giffen's attitude, and on his legacy at the Board of Trade, see Davidson, *Whitehall*, pp. 229–230.

75. Discussion after Geoffrey Drage, "The reorganisation of official statistics and a Central Statistical Office," *Journal of the Royal Statistical Society* 80 (1917): 31–64, p. 51.

76. Discussion after ibid., p. 55.

77. Henry Clay, "Sir Alfred William Flux," *Dictionary of National Biography* (Oxford University Press, 1995).

78. J. L. Garvin, Compatriots' Club lectures, first series, 1905, cited in Geoffrey R. Searle, *The Quest for National Efficiency* (Blackwell, 1971). Citations from second edition (Ashfield, 1990), p. 97.

79. Hector Leak, "Censuses of Production and Distribution," in Maurice G. Kendall and A. Bradford Hill, *The Sources and Nature of the Statistics of the United Kingdom* (Oliver and Boyd, 1952).

80. For this distinction, see W. H. Greenleaf, *The British Political Tradition* (Methuen, 1983 and 1987).

81. T. A. Coghlan, in discussion after Yule, "Statistics," p. 90.

82. Davidson, *Whitehall*, pp. 141–144.

83. Dilke, "Presidential address," p. 575.

84. Bowley, "Improvement," p. 460.

85. Clay, "Sir Alfred William Flux,".

86. Yule, "Statistics,".

87. PRO BT 11/2. "Census of Production Bill. Interview between the Rt. Hon. David Lloyd George . . . and Members of Parliament interested in manufactures," 25 October 1906.

88. A systematic Census of Manufactures began in 1899. For "census years prior to 1899 . . . quantity data [were] highly fragmentary" (Edwin Frickey, *Production in the United States, 1860–1914*, Harvard University Press, 1947, p. 4).

89. Department of Commerce, Bureau of the Census, *Census of Manufactures, 1914* (Washington: Government Printing Office, 1918), vol. 2., pp. 908–909, 1032–1033.

90. Yule, "Statistics," p. 82.

91. PRO RAIL 1059/56. *Census of Production. Final Report of the First Census of Production of the United Kingdom, 1907* (HMSO, 1912).

92. PRO BT 11/2. "Necessity for increase in the staff of the Commercial, Labour and Statistical Department," 27 November 1908.

93. PRO T 161/460. Flux, "Census of Production," December 1920.

94. Ibid.

95. PRO T 161/460. Internal note to Sir G. Barlow, February 1921.

96. PRO T 161/460. Sidney Webb to Snowden, 6 February 1924.

97. Anonymous, "The Third Census of Production. In respect of 1924," *Board of Trade Journal*, 28 February 1924, pp. 274–275.

98. PRO BT 70/46. Memorandum on history of Statistical Division, 1935.

99. Drage, "Reorganisation," p. 35.

100. Discussion after Drage, "Reorganisation," pp. 54–55.

101. Royal Statistical Society archives, Minutes, Official Statistics Committee, 1919, B14/1.

102. PRO HO 45/20284. F. C. Thomson asked Bonar Law on 14 July 1919 and received this answer: "I do not think that the suggestion . . . is practicable." Marriott asked two questions about the petition on 27 November 1919 and 11 December 1919, but only received confirmation that the petition had been received.

103. Stafford, "Note."

104. PRO HO 45/20284. "Memorandum by a Conference of the Official Statisticians of the Home Departments, upon a Petition to His Majesty's Government in regard to Official Statistics," April 1920.

105. PRO ACT 1/83. "First report of the PCCOS for the period 23 June 1921 to 31 December 1922." The following departments sent officers: Treasury, Admiralty, Air Ministry, Agriculture and Fisheries, Customs and Excise, Board of Education, Government Actuary's Department, Home Office, Inland Revenue, Medical Research Council, Labour, Health, Pensions, GRO, DSIR, Board of Trade, Transport, War Office, Scottish Office, Board of Agriculture for Scotland, Scottish Board of Health and GRO, GRO Dublin and Department of Agriculture and Technical Instruction for Ireland. The Irish representatives left in 1920 with home rule. A representative from the Mine Department was added in 1921.

106. J. Athelstane Baines, "Report on Census matters discussed at the St. Petersburg meeting of the International Statistical Institute 1897," *Journal of Royal Statistical Society* 61 (1898), p. 374.

107. Baines, letter to *Times*, 2 January 1909.

108. J. Athelstane Baines, "The population of the British Empire," *Journal of Royal Statistical Society* 69 (1906): 440–443.

109. PRO RG 19/45. Bellingham, "Memorandum in reference to the next census of England and Wales to be taken in March 1911," July 1908. No census at all had been taken in 32 colonies in 1901, several of them major colonies, including Northern and Southern Nigeria, North Rhodesia, Uganda Protectorate, Zanzibar and Pemba Island, Jamaica, Sarawak, Brunei, Barbados, and British Guyana, as well as the smallest, most remote colonies such as the Pitcairn and Christmas Islands.

110. Final report of the Dominions Royal Commission, Cd 8462, para. 676. Signed by Lord D'Abernon (chair), Sir H. Rider Haggard, T. Garnett, Sir W. Lorimer, J. Tatlow, Sir A. E. Bateman (for the UK), Sir G. E. Foster (for Canada), J. R. Sinclair

(for New Zealand), Sir J. E. S. Langerman (for South Africa) and Sir E. N. Bowring (for Newfoundland). (Note the presence of the imperialist novelist H. Rider Haggard.).

111. Note the parallels between my two camps of pragmatists and technocrats and the earlier two styles of Indian governance, the Munro and Cornwallis systems, discussed in chapter 2.

112. An analogy might be made to the case of imperial telegraphy. Telegraph networks were envisioned as forms of control, but distance made the imposition of control impossible, in practice. The tension was between dreams of the link between technology and centralizing power, and the performance of technologies in local contexts. On Australian telegraphy (including a brief appearance of Babbage's son, Benjamin), see Ann Moyal, "The history of telecommunications in Australia: aspects of the technological experience, 1854–1930," in *Scientific Colonialism*, ed. N. Reingold and M. Rothenberg (Smithsonian Institution Press, 1987).

113. G. H. Knibbs, *The Problems of Statistics* (Brisbane: by Authority of Anthony James Cumming, Government Printer, 1910).

114. PRO HO 45/20284. G. H. Knibbs, "Memorandum on the proposed conference of the statisticians of the British Empire," 25 February 1918.

115. "In some cases a considerable improvement in the work performed by local offices could be obtained by the use of mechanical devices and calculating machines. Typewriting machines with their several adjuncts are now so common as to require not more than mention. The usefulness of duplicating machines for the many purposes of statistical collection has not always received due recognition. It is unnecessary to say that machines for addition and subtraction or multiplication and division, should be used wherever the volume of work will warrant their purchase. Their use results in a distinct reduction of expense, a reduction of strain on the computer, and a corresponding increase in accuracy. . . . Whenever practicable, larger offices should contain devices for mechanical tabulation and an important service which an imperial bureau could render would be that of advising local offices concerning the latest devices of this and similar character." (ibid.)

116. PRO ACT 1/84. "British Empire Statistical Conference. Extract from Report of Proceedings of Meeting held on 13th February, 1920."

117. Ibid.

118. William Thompson, Registrar-General in Ireland from 1909, objected: ". . . it is one of the characteristics of Dublin, and of Ireland, no matter what their political feelings are, or their religious persuasions are, on social reforms we are all on the same platform." Watson dismissed this view, pointing out that the alleged lack of sympathy with the Irish people was a direct quotation.

119. Ibid. Vivian was specifically addressing a different paragraph to Watson, but one which seemed "to raise the point in an even more aggressive form."

120. PRO ACT 1/84. "Minority report on the proposals of the British Empire Statistical Conference," 19 May 1921.

121. Ibid.

122. PRO ACT 1/84. "Committee to consider the proposals of the British Empire Statistical Conference. Majority Report," 19 May 1921.

123. PRO ACT 1/84. Minority Report.

124. The Bureau would be under a Council consisting of "representatives of the Dominion Governments and of the Home Departments," with an Advisory Committee with power to co-opt "representatives of economic, commercial, industrial and financial interests in important parts of the Empire." The apoliticality came through comprehensive representation of interests, a surprising idea. That this was the technocratic position is confirmed by their approving quotation of a "well known publicist" that a "process of conference and counsel may be trusted to lead . . . to a "steadily increasing identity of purpose which, in the course of time, will discover its own sufficient instruments of policy. The principle of consultation adequately applied should do its most valuable work not in the solution of crystallized difficulties, but in the prevention of difficulties arising." (PRO ACT 1/84. Minority Report.).

125. On these bureaus, see Michael Worboys, Science and British Colonial Imperialism, 1895–1940, D. Phil. thesis, University of Sussex, 1979.

126. PRO ACT 1/84. Majority Report.

127. PRO ACT 1/84. Minority Report.

128. See e.g. Gill's map poster, reproduced in Stephen Constantine, *Buy and Build* (HMSO, 1989).

129. In "Pig" (in *Plain Tales from the Hills*, 1888), Rudyard Kipling related the story of the elaborate revenge taken by one civil servant on another. Pinecoffin had sold Nafferton an ill-trained horse, which nearly killed him. Nafferton then builds a spider's web of statistical requests to trap Pinecoffin. After 5 years of requests for information on the history, nature and economics of Indian pigs, before finally catching him out: writing to his superiors he complains of the "paucity of help accorded to me in my earnest attempts to start a potentially remunerative industry, and the flippancy with which my requests for information are treated by a gentleman whose pseudo-scholarly attainments should at least have taught him the primary differences between the Dravidian and the Berkshire variety of the genus *Sus*." Nafferton leaks the reply to newspapers back in England, and Pinecoffin is castigated as a "modern Competition-wallah" unable to grasp practical issues. Kipling's joke, of course, was that the prodigious system of Civil Service information gathering had become, in this instance, a tool of petty revenge.

130. This was the fulfillment of hopes that emerged from the Census of the British Empire of 1901. Bellingham wrote that it aimed to secure as far as possible "a uniform Census throughout the Empire on the next occasion. On this ground alone it is very desirable to scrutinize carefully the plans and procedure of the English Census Office in order to ensure that in the capital of the Empire Census methods are being employed which may serve as a model to the Statisticians of Greater Britain." (PRO RG 19/45. Bellingham, Report on the Census of the British Empire, 1901).

131. PRO RG 19/62. Vivian, draft preliminary report on 1921 Census, 1921.

132. MacKenzie, *Statistics in Britain.*

133. Quoted in Davidson, *Whitehall*, pp. 230–231.

134. Marshall to Bowley, 3 March 1901, quoted in Davidson, *Whitehall*, p. 235.

135. PRO HO 45/20284. Select Committee on Publications and Debates, Reports. Q. 232 (to Flux) and Q. 373 (to Houndle of the Local Government Board).

136. Compare Hacking's "avalanche" of printed numbers (*Taming*, p. 3).

137. Eastwood, "'Amplifying the province,'" p. 293.

138. For example, Patrick Colquhoun's *Treatise on the Police of the Metropolis* (first edition 1795, many subsequent editions) sold like hotcakes and provided reams of quotable facts: London, with a population of 641,000, contained 50,000 women supported by prostitution, had organized criminal gangs, and annual criminal turnover of £2,000,000. Colquhoun was a favorite citation of Bentham and his utilitarian allies on police reform.

139. For more on the "emerging scientific conception of the criminal" in the mid to late nineteenth century, see Martin J. Wiener, *Reconstructing the Criminal* (Cambridge University Press), pp. 231–232.

140. Coghlan, in discussion after Bowley, "Improvement," p. 486.

141. Mallet was particularly concerned that arithmometers were needed to generate statistics "for sanitary and other purposes involving very many calculations" (RG 29/4. Mallet to Treasury, 9 February 1910).

142. J. Adam Tooze, "Imagining national economies: national and international economic statistics, 1900–1950," in *Imagining Nations*, ed. G Cubitt (Manchester University Press, 1998).

143. Fréderic Le Play, one of the founders of French social studies, was motivated in his development of empirical sociology by a belief that, as one historian has summarized, "the chaos which he saw around him was a chaos of social ideas and, therefore, he stressed that all generalizations should be derived from a patient analysis of facts" (Collette, *Empirical Inquiries*, p. 12). According to his own autobiography, it was the shock of the July Revolution of 1830: launching a lifelong attempt to fill the hole left by monarchical order with sociological fact.

144. Bowley, "Improvement," p. 477.

145. Bowley, in discussion after Drage, "Reorganisation," p. 54. Josiah Stamp agreed (in discussion after Drage, "Reorganisation," p. 57): "The Central Office would keep constantly employed all the year round a skilled and well equipped staff with adding machines and calculating machines, which might properly and economically be adopted in such a Department."

Chapter 4

1. The Superintendent Registrar was also an authority with the Boards of Guardians for Registers of Marriage.

2. For the history of British government registries, see Theodore R. Schellenberg, *Modern Archives* (F. W. Cheshire, 1956). Also see PRO T 222/90. Sir George Murray, "Method of filing and arranging Treasury papers," 29 December 1904. PRO T 222/90. "The Treasury Registry," 1 December 1919, which contains a rare organic analogy: "The organization of the Treasury as a whole clearly owes its form to the relation in which the Department stands to the rest of the Home Service. A Registry system ought to follow to some extent the anatomy of the organism to which it belongs. It may be granted that the Treasury organism, owing to its comparatively small size, is best served by a single Registry. But if that Registry is to form part of a unity which is of necessity very complex, it must have its nerves radiating out into the Department. Otherwise there is bound to be organic trouble. In a word, there must be a number of local Registry outposts." (This could almost have been written by Haldane.) Finally, see PRO T 222/176 for a continuation of the Treasury Registry story.

3. Marjorie Caygill, *The Story of the British Museum* (British Museum Publications), p. 14.

4. Thomas Richards, *The Imperial Archive* (Verso, 1993).

5. On Le Queux, see Christopher Andrew, *Secret Service* (Heinemann, 1985), pp. 34–48.

6. PRO RG 28/110. Pemberton Billing to Addison, 7 December 1917.

7. PRO RG 28/110. Memorandum by Pemberton Billing, undated.

8. Quoted in Philip Hoare, *Wilde's Last Stand* (Duckworth, 1997), p. 58.

9. Andrew, *Secret Service*, p. 189.

10. PRO RG 28/110. Phillips to Hayes Fisher, 11 January 1918.

11. Keith Grieves, *The Politics of Manpower, 1914–1918* (Manchester University Press, 1988), p. 21.

12. Bill, *National Registration. A Bill for the compilation of a National Register*, Ordered to be brought in by Mr Long, Mr M'Kinnon Wood, Mr Birrell and Mr Hayes Fisher (HMSO, 1915).

13. Coincidentally, the *Times* took the title *Daily Universal Register*, for the first 3 years of its existence (1785–1788), and was planned to "facilitate 'channels of advertisements'; to record the principal occurrences of the times; and to abridge the account of debates of Parliament." See Harold A. Innis, *The Bias of Communication* (University of Toronto Press, 1951), p. 153.

14. "Organisation versus Fussiness," *Nation*, 3 July 1915, p. 436.

15. "A London Diary," *Nation*, 3 July 1915, p. 442.

16. PRO RG 28/1. Carruthers to Vivian, 20 July 1915.

17. PRO RG 28/1. "Memorandum on the National Registration scheme," by Vivian, 1 July 1915.

18. PRO RG 28/1. "Memorandum (2) on National Registration," by Vivian, undated (July 1915).

19. PRO NATS 1/127. Everard Greene to Chamberlain, 20 December 1916. Chamberlain was at this moment Lord Mayor of Birmingham.

20. PRO NATS 1/127. Letter to Atterbury, January 1917. A punched-card based National Register was suggested for a second time in 1935, see PRO RG 28/31, "Suggested scheme for Register of punched cards," 28 September 1935. Punched cards were, however, employed to extract statistical information from the NR returns, according to Desborough, *Office Machines, Appliances and Methods* (Isaac Pitman and Sons, 1921), p. 32.

21. PRO RG 28/1. Vivian to Carruthers, 21 July 1915. "Men available for military service in England and Wales," by Registrar-General, 6 October 1915. By "ju-ju" Vivian means voo-doo, and he is satirizing the fuss made of the figure once it had been conjured from the NR returns.

22. PRO RG 28/1. Carruthers to Vivian, 14 March 1916.

23. PRO RG 28/1. Vivian to Carruthers, 11 May 1916.

24. The Royal Commission on Venereal Disease called for confidential death certificates for this reason. State action on venereal diseases raised interesting issues of information provision, privacy and compulsion. See Roger Davidson and Lesley A. Hall, *Sex, Sin and Suffering* (Routledge, 2001).

25. PRO RG 28/7. Untitled memorandum, by Mallet, August 1916.

26. PRO RG 28/7. Untitled memorandum by Mallet, August 1916.

27. Administrative Counties, County Boroughs, and Metropolitan Boroughs.

28. PRO, guide to MI5 and MI6 records.

29. PRO RG 28/7. Untitled memorandum, by Mallet, August 1916.

30. PRO RG 28/7. Minutes of meeting at Local Government Board, 19 March 1918. The inclusion of occupation, and if so whether to make inclusion compulsory, was the most controversial suggestion.

31. PRO RG 28/7. "Canvass of representatives of local authorities as to local utility of a permanent national register," 18 December 1917.

32. PRO RG 28/7. Monro to Hayes Fisher and President, 22 September 1916.

33. Simon J. D. Green and R. C. Whiting, eds., *The Boundaries of the State in Modern Britain* (Cambridge University Press, 1996).

34. PRO RG 28/7. Note to Chairman, undated (1918).

35. PRO RG 28/110. Phillips to Hayes Fisher, 11 January 1918.

36. PRO HO 45/25014. Vivian to Ross, 9 October 1942. By "three years' experience" Vivian means 1939–1942 when he oversaw the re-introduction of National Registration (see chapter 6), but I introduce his comment here because of the continuity in the treatment of the national character and unobtrusive surveillance.

37. Bentham, *Principles of Penal Law*. For a discussion of the extreme difficulties of pinning an official identity on British subjects see Jon Agar, "Modern horrors: British identity and identity cards," in *Documenting Individual Identity*, ed. J. Caplan and J. Torpey (Princeton University Press, 2001).

38. PRO HO 45/25014. Vivian to Ross, 9 October 1942.

39. PRO RG 28/25. Sub-committees three of the Committee for Imperial Defence made the plans with regard to National Registration.

40. The difference is that a license is bought–as sum going to Inland Revenue as a tax, while a register, while compulsory, was in principle free. The 1903 Act is more usually celebrated as the legislation which ended the man carrying a red flag in front of automobiles, and for raising the speed limit from 4 to 12 miles per hour. For more on the relations between police and civil servants, see William Plowden, *The Motor Car and Politics in Britain, 1896–1970* (Pelican, 1971). Clive Emsley, "'Mother, what did policemen do when there weren't any motors?' The law, the police and the regulation of motor traffic in England, 1900–1939," *Historical Journal* (1993) 36: 357–381.

41. PRO MT 34 619. Procter-Gregg ("Tax on motor vehicles. Historical note, and explanation of changes," 1949) provides a record of taxation levels, which were not insignificant: From 1903 to 1920, the 1903 Act provided for a fee of 20 shillings to be paid on the registration of a car but in addition to that fee excise duty of £2 2s was payable annually plus a further £2 2s if the vehicle exceeded 1 ton unladen but did not exceed 2 tons or additional duty of £3 3s if it exceeded 2 tons. (Excise duty on "carriages" used on the roads, whether drawn by horses or mules or propelled by mechanical power, had been payable since at least 1860). From 1921 to 1934, cars were charged at £6 per annum if electrically propelled or up to 6 horsepower and £1 per horsepower; thereafter, no separate registration fee was charged. From 1935 to 1939, cars were charged at £4 10s per annum if electrically propelled or up to 6 horsepower and 15 shillings per horsepower thereafter. From 1940 to 1948, these rates were £7 10s and 25 shillings respectively. In 1947 a £10 flat rate was introduced.

42. See PRO HO 45/17778. Home Office. *Criminal Statistics 1928* (HMSO, 1930, for crime figures and their relation to the "incoming Motor Age."

43. PRO MT 34/67. Clark to Borough Treasurer, Eastbourne, 26 February 1929.

44. For a provocative history of police in interwar Britain, see V. A. C. Gatrell, "Crime, authority, and the policeman state," in *The Cambridge Social History of Britain, 1750–1950*, vol. 3, ed. F. Thompson (Cambridge University Press, 1990).

45. PRO MT 34/39. "Addendum to the Motor Car registration and licensing (England) Order, 1903," 1903.

46. PRO MT 34/67. Various letters, 1928–1931.

47. PRO MT 34/67. Hurcomb to Under Secretary of State, Home Office, 13 December 1929.

48. PRO MT 34/18. "Road Traffic (Driving Licences) Bill," 1936.

49. PRO HO 45/10636/203358 contains proposals for tests and records the official reluctance.

50. Sean O'Connell, *The Car in British Society* (Manchester University Press, 1998), p. 143.

51. Clive Emsley, *The English Police* (Harvester Wheatsheaf, 1991); David Taylor, *The New Police Force in Nineteenth-Century England* (Manchester University Press, 1997).

52. J. F. Moylan, *Scotland Yard and the Metropolitan Police* (Putmans, 1929), p. 189.

53. Ibid., p. 190.

54. PRO HO 45/12915. Habitual Criminals' Registry, *Instructions in the Method of Taking Finger Prints, with a Memorandum on the Working of the Finger Print System of Identification* (HMSO, 1909).

55. See discussion of Herschel in Allan Sekula, "The body and the archive," in *The Contest of Meaning*, ed. R. Bolton (MIT Press, 1989).

56. See e.g. Faulds's letter to Winston Churchill, which enclosed the former's pamphlet *How the English Finger-Print Method Arose*. PRO HO 45/12915. Faulds to Churchill, 3 March 1910.

57. Emsley, *English Police*, p. 141.

58. Moylan, *Scotland Yard*, p. 111.

59. Ibid., p. 60.

60. Ibid., pp. 174–175.

61. Ibid., pp. 75, 240–241.

62. PRO HO 45/22901. Hall-Dalwood, "Suggested scheme for the formation of a National Intelligence Service," 1 January 1917. Emsley notes that the interwar Chief Constable of Sheffield (alongside his Nottingham colleague) was a keen proponent of scientific forensic detection, working with biologists and pathologists in local universities. Emsley, *English Police*, p. 143.

63. Andrew, *Secret Service*, p. 229.

64. PRO HO 45/22901. Hall-Dalwood, "Suggested scheme for the formation of a National Intelligence Service," 1 January 1917.

65. PRO HO 45/12915. Prison Commission to Under Secretary of State, Home Office, 21 April 1913.

Chapter 5

1. Martin Campbell-Kelly, "The Railway Clearing House and Victorian data processing," in *Information Acumen*, ed. L. Bud-Frierman (Routledge, 1994).

2. Ibid., p. 68.

3. Daniel Nelson, "Scientific management, systematic management, and labor, 1880–1915," *Business History Review* 48 (1974): 479–500; JoAnne Yates, *Control through Communication* (Johns Hopkins University Press, 1989), p. 10.

4. Yates, *Control*, p. 10.

5. The definition of "information" was Henry Varnum Poor's. Poor was the subject of a 1956 biographicy by Alfred Chandler, Yates's historiographical mentor: *Henry Varnum Poor* (Harvard University Press). See also Yates, *Control*, pp. 7, 278, 279.

6. Yates, *Control*, p. 43.

7. Ibid., pp. 286, 48.

8. Ibid., p. 34.

9. Ibid., p. 48. Theodore R. Schellenberg (*Modern Archives*, F. W. Cheshire, 1956, pp. 82–83) notes that the "typewriter came into general use in Federal agencies late in the 19th century when its design was improved to permit the typist to view his product while operating the machine. It was not, however, immediately used for producing copies of documents. Early carbon papers were smeary and unstable."

10. Ken Alder, *Engineering the Revolution* (Princeton University Press, 1997).

11. Walter Desborough, *Office Machines, Appliances and Methods* (Isaac Pitman, 1921), p. 44; "Owing to the growth of direct mail advertising, the periodical issue of lists to customers and dividends to shareholders, the centralisation of the administration of large concerns and consequent necessity to write to the same person frequently, the question of addressing becomes a proposition which involves a large amount of clerical labor." Thus changes in the business corporation created more labor and a prompt for mechanization answered by the Addressograph and other machines.

12. Compare e.g. the typical prices to buy the machines I have listed, mostly as supplied by HMSO: slide rules (£3), calculating machines (£60), adding machines (£70–130), Wahl adders for use with typewriters (£70), cash registers (£250), typewriters (£18), rotary copying machines (£15), rotary duplicators (£15), Motabradors (£2), envelope-closing and franking machines (£90), electrical blue printers (£50–130), Gammeters (£160), Roneotypes (£50), dictaphones (£60), Linotypes (£700), printing presses (£40–200), litho presses and machines (£50–500), wire stitching machines (£30–50), guillotines (£20–100), Addressographs (£30–60), photostats (£285). Punched-card accounting and tabulating machines cost between £140 and £500

per annum to rent. Source: PRO STAT 12/23/3. Codling (Controller, HMSO) to Secretary (Treasury), 14 January 1918.

13. On Hollerith, see G. Austrian, *Herman Hollerith* (Columbia University Press, 1982).

14. James W. Cortada (*Information Technology as Business History*, Greenwood, 1996, p. 47) notes that the 1890 Census was seeking to obtain information on 235 topics per person, compared with 215 in 1880 and a mere 5 in 1870.

15. Martin Campbell-Kelly, *ICL* (Clarendon, 1989), p. 13.

16. Robert P. Porter, "The Eleventh United States Census," *Journal of the Royal Statistical Society* 57 (1894): 643–677; Herman Hollerith, "The Electrical Tabulating Machine," ibid.: 678–682. A discussion of these two papers appeared on pp. 682–689.

17. This early history of BTM is heavily based on pp. 16–20 and 24–46 of Campbell-Kelly, *ICL*.

18. Campbell-Kelly, *ICL*, pp. 34–35.

19. Ibid., p. 44.

20. Ibid., p. 45.

21. Ibid., p. 53.

22. Edward Higgs, "The statistical big bang of 1911: Ideology, technological innovation and the production of medical statistics," *Social History of Medicine* 9 (1996): 409–426. Campbell-Kelly records that Hollerith machines were given a trial at the Woolwich Arsenal, the state-run munitions factory, in 1904–05. The trial was not a success, attributed by Everard Greene, to what Campbell-Kelly (*ICL*, p. 19) calls "Luddism." See also Martin Campbell-Kelly, "Information technology and organizational change in the British census, 1801–1911," *Information Systems Research* 7 (1996): 22–36.

23. Michael Lindgren, *Glory and Failure* (Linköping University, 1987).

24. Stephen Johnston, "Making the arithmometer count," *Bulletin of the Scientific Instrument Society* (1997) 52: 12–12. Recall also from chapter 3 that Mallet insisted to the Treasury that arithmometers were essential to the production of new statistics.

25. Higgs, "Struggle," p. 418. Roger Davidson (*Whitehall and the Labour Problem in Late-Victorian and Edwardian Britain*, Croom Helm, 1985, pp. 193–196) describes the "conservatism" of the late-nineteenth-century GRO. A passage from the Royal Statistical Society archives confirms that cards were regarded as a possibility for 1901: "The Committee recommended that in Section 6 the direction that the enumerator is to copy each householder's schedule into a book provided for that purpose, should be so modified as to give the Registrar-General a discretion to dispense with such copying. Such a direction appears to the Committee to lay down a rigid rule for dealing with the documents upon which the compilation of the Census must be based, and they are of the opinion that it will be to the advantage of the administration if no rigid rule is laid down. It is a pure question of administration how the primary documents,

when once brought into existence, are to be utilized; and a hard and fast direction apparently tends to needless expense and delay in compiling the results. Were the department left quite free, it might or might not order copying into a book, and it would be free to substitute the use of cards for after-compilation, which is general in foreign countries." (Giffen, Second Interim Report to 1901 Census Committee, 1899, RSS Archives)

26. Simon Szreter, "The GRO and the public health movement in Britain," *Social History of Medicine* 4 (1991): 435–462.

27. PRO T 1/11243. Mallet, "Notes on Census of 1911," April 1910.

28. Edward Higgs, *Making Sense of the Census* (HMSO, 1989); *A Clearer Sense of the Census* (HMSO, 1996).

29. PRO T 1/11243. Stevenson, memorandum on machine tabulation, 18 July 1910.

30. PRO RG 19/45. "Memorandum in reference to the next census of England and Wales to be taken in March 1911," by Archer Bellingham, July 1908.

31. PRO T 1/11243. Stevenson, memorandum on machine tabulation, 18 July 1910.
PRO T 1/11243. Stevenson, memorandum on machine tabulation, 18 July 1910.

32. Ibid.

33. On distrust, the following is a quotation from early discussions of mechanization in the Post Office Savings Bank: re "the integrity of women clerks . . . I cannot think that a system which relies for security on the employment of a particular class of labor is a sound one." This can be read in several ways: as we saw in chapter 2, upper-class women were regarded as more trustworthy than working-class men, and the complaint could be that no system should be reliant solely on the class-credentials of those employed. Or, it could be read as a complaint that women were untrustworthy in themselves. PRO NSC 9/645. Smith to Controller, 7 June 1909.

34. PRO RG 19/45. "Memorandum in reference to the next census of England and Wales to be taken in March 1911," by Archer Bellingham, July 1908.

35. PRO RG 19/45. Billingham "Memorandum."

36. PRO RG 29/4. Mallet to Treasury, 3 November 1911. It is not known exactly what the Home Office and Board of Trade were after. PRO RG 19/45. Billingham "Memorandum." Memorial to the LGB, *Journal of the Institute of Actuaries* 25 (1900), p. 362. For more on the application of punched-card tabulation methods to the GRO's production of medical statistics after 1911 see PRO BT 70/46, "Births and deaths registration service," undated (1930s).

37. PRO MH 78/114. Stevenson to Mallet, 25 January 1920. Note: there are problems in using Stevenson's account to show this point (as Higgs does). Mallet was being pressured to leave and be replaced by Vivian. Mallet was obstructing furiously. As Sir Robert Morant wrote to his minister Mallet was "not playing the game" and it was Morant's "belief . . . that it is Dr Stevenson who presses Sir Bernard to make these

difficulties." At issue was the "Dr": should only medics be Registrar-Generals? PRO MH 78/114. Morant to Minister, 5 February 1920.

38. PRO RG 29/4. Mallet to Treasury, 11 July 1910.

39. This "latest type" of machine was almost certainly the automatic tabulators that Hollerith had introduced in the United States four years previously. On the automatic machines, see Campbell-Kelly, *ICL*, pp. 20–21.

40. PRO T 1/11293. "Why not threaten the company that we may put the Patent Acts in force?" 17 November 1910.

41. PRO T 1/11293. "Why not build for ourselves? 17 November 1910. PRO STAT 12/10/9, Newton to Murray, 23 November 1910.

42. PRO RG 29/4. Mallet to Treasury, 1 December 1909.

43. PRO RG 29/4. Mallet to Treasury, 4 November 1910.

44. PRO T 170/9. Mallet to Chambers, 23 October 1912: Bailey "thinks I forced the BTM Company on him. I certainly did, but only because I had no alternative as there was no other machine company in the world at that time which could give us what it was absolutely essential for us to have."

45. PRO MH 78/114. Stevenson to Mallet, 25 January 1920.

46. PRO STAT 12/25/5. Atterbury to Treasury, 25 June 1915. J. Atterbury (Controller of HMSO) accepted the invitation and sent three officers: W. R. Codling (HMSO Superintendent of Demands), A. L. Screech (HMSO Deputy Superintendent of Stores), and S. J. H. W. Allin (an actuary on the National Health Insurance Joint Committee). Campbell-Kelly (*ICL*, p. 37) records that the Prudential actuary Joseph Burn also attended, but his name was not listed by Atterbury.

47. A. I. Ogus, "Great Britain," in *The Evolution of Social Insurance, 1881–1981*, ed. P. Köhler et al. (Frances Pinter for Max-Planck-Institut für ausländisches und internationales Sozialrecht, 1982).

48. Martin Campbell-Kelly, "Large-scale data processing in the Prudential, 1850–1930," *Accounting and Business History* 2 (1992): 117–139.

49. PRO STAT 12/25/5. Everard Greene to Sir Rowland Bailey, 18 February 1913. Atterbury to Treasury, 25 June 1915.

50. PRO STAT 12/38/1. "Notes on some calculating and tabulating machines in use in public departments," June 1917.

51. PRO STAT 12/14/1. Beveridge to HMSO, 20 January 1915.

52. PRO STAT 12/25/5. Atterbury to Treasury, 25 June 1915.

53. For example, the Department of Applied Statistics at University College, London, performed calculations for the Department of Trade, the Royal Aircraft Factory at Farnborough, the Admiralty's Air Department, the Anti-Aircraft Section of HMS

Excellent, the Ordnance Committee, and the Ministry of Munitions. (Mary Croarken, *Early Scientific Computing*, Clarendon, 1990, p. 20).

54. Campbell-Kelly, *ICL*, p. 44.

55. They were in descending order, figures afterwards to the nearest million: the Egyptian Government (16), London and North Western Railway (10), Gas Light and Coke Co. (9), Lever Brothers Ltd (8), Central Argentine Railway Ltd (7), Chief Surgeon, American Expeditionary Force (7), Lancashire and Yorkshire Railway (6), City of Birmingham Gas Department (5), Hearts of Oak Benefit Society (5), Mobilisation Directorate (5), Shell Marketing Co. Ltd (4), Department of National Service (4), Pilkington Brothers Ltd (4), Ministry of Labour (3).

56. Henry Higgs, *National Economy* (Macmillan, 1917), p. 41.

57. Higgs, "Struggle," pp. 47–48.

58. PRO T 199/83. Partridge to Secretary, War Office, 18 December 1918.

59. PRO T 199/83, "On the necessity for the establishment of an Inspectorate of Office Administration," by Partridge, Scorgie and Grieve, December 1918.

60. Inquiry into the Organisation and Staffing of Government Offices (Bradbury Report), Cd. 62, paragraph 23, p. 6. Hennessy, *Whitehall*, p. 69.

61. PRO STAT 14/1156. Scorgie to Pitman, 8 April 1948.

62. PRO STAT 12/38/1. CB to Controller, 24 May 1925. Campbell-Kelly cites this quotation as evidence for the persistence of a "gentleman-and-player's attitude." However, it should be noted that the argument is being made in the context of presenting a case for supporting higher-status experienced mechanizers.

63. PRO STAT 14/1156. Desborough to Pitman, 15 July 1948.

64. The SO inspectorate was set up under Codling and included Stenson Cooke from the Ministry of National Service "to go round departments." He was loosely overseen by an Advisory Committee on Accounting Machines (A. T. V. Robinson, S. J. H. W. Allin, and J. P. Stevenson). Cooke's successes included the introduction of collating typewriters and an envelope saving scheme. PRO STAT 12/23/3. Codling to Treasury, 14 January 1918.

65. PRO STAT 14/1156. Desborough to Pitman, 15 July 1948.

66. PRO STAT 14/1156. Scorgie to Pitman, 8 April 1948. Scorgie continued: "The Establishment side of the Treasury had to sit up and take notice. The writing was beginning to get on the wall and they could not let a large part of their central control pass to a minor department."

67. PRO STAT 14/1156. Scorgie to Pitman, 29 July 1948. Strictly speaking the group was known as "Treasury Investigations" from 1919 with "Section" added in 1926. Between 1919 and 1926 the Office Machinery Committee still met, so there was a duplication of interest, if not necessarily effort.

68. PRO HO 45/17788. Notes in file "Statistical Branch. Application for a Staff Officer," and Farrant to Cave (Secretary of State for the Home Department), 17 April 1917.

69. PRO HO 45/17788. Farrant to Cave, 17 April 1917.

70. Ibid.

71. PRO STAT 14/1156. Desborough to Pitman, 15 July 1948.

72. PRO T 162/55. Memorandum from Comptometer Company, undated (October 1919).

73. Ibid. Sir Eric Geddes chaired a committee appointed by Lloyd George charged with recommending economies in government spending. The result, known as the Geddes Axe, symbolized a reversal of plans for post-war reconstruction.

74. PRO T 199/32. Rae to Allan, Vivian, Robinson and Hodgson, 24 February 1926.

75. PRO T 161/117, "The Royal Arsenal, Woolwich," 1921, e.g., gives details of requested machines "to enable the Management of the Royal Arsenal to be provided with the necessary information

76. PRO NSC 9/647. "Investigation carried out at the GPO Savings Bank Department, Blythe Road, Hammersmith," 1926. The massive building at Blythe Road is now a store for the National Museum of Science and Industry.

77. Martin Campbell-Kelly, "Data processing and technological change: the Post Office Savings Bank, 1861–1930," *Technology and Culture* 39 (1998): 1–32.

78. Ibid., p. 29.

79. PRO T 161/460. Desborough to Carr, 12 June 1929.

80. Croarken, *Early Scientific Computing*, pp. 30–32. Comrie used punched-card machines rented from BTM.

81. PRO T 161/460. Note by JC, 11 November 1930.

82. PRO BT 70/31. WWH (Powers), "Preliminary report to G. A. G. Stanley Esq. of the Board of Trade on the application of Powers-Samas Accounting Machines to the Census of Production 1930," 30 March 1931. A picture of a Census of Production card can be found in L. J. Comrie, *The Hollerith and Powers Tabulating Machines*, London, printed for private circulation, 1933, copy in British Library.

83. PRO BT 70/31. Powers brochure, "Use this key to disclose the hidden facts of your business," early 1930s. Note the appeal to science with the x-ray reference, a relatively late example, in fact. Government departmental users listed by Powers included: Customs Statistics (Imports and Exports)—Shipping Statistics; Births, Marriages and Deaths, Migration and Criminal Statistics, National Health Insurance Accounting; and Staff Records—Census.

84. PRO HO 45/16594. Banham to Kirwan, 21 July 1927, summarizing Report No. 1 by Desborough and D. G. Robertson on branch S. 4 (Statistical Branch) of the Home Office.

85. For early Home Office statistics, see James T. Hammick, "On the Judicial Statistics of England and Wales, with special reference to the recent returns relating to crime," *Journal of the Statistical Society of London* 30 (1867): 375–426. As noted in chapter 3, criminal statistics had been published by the Home Office since 1810.

86. PRO HO 45/17788. Farrant to Cave, 17 April 1917. After "drastically revising the whole scheme of statistics and the manner of their preparation," the Criminal Statistics Committee had in 1893 reported: "We think (1) that the Statutes of each Session should be carefully examined by the Statistical Branch with a view to note and provide for any new offences that may be created, or any changes in criminal procedure that may affect the tables; (2) that the Criminal Department should either have the general supervision of the Criminal Statistics, or should be consulted annually . . . ; (3) that all criticisms of the Statistics in newspapers and elsewhere should be noted, and should, if necessary be dealt with in the Introduction. Improvements in foreign statistics and discussions on International Statistics of Crime, should be studied and kept in view."

87. Ibid. For similar disciplinary regimes see Simon Schaffer, "Astronomers mark time: discipline and the personal equation," *Science in Context* 2 (1988): 115–145. Graeme Gooday, "The morals of energy metering: constructing and deconstructing the precision of the Victorian electrical engineer's ammeter and voltmeter," in *The Values of Precision*, ed. M. Norton Wise (Princeton University Press, 1995); Andrew Warwick, "The laboratory of theory, or what's exact about the exact sciences?" in *The Values of Precision*, ed. Wise.

88. PRO HO 45/17788. Farrant to Cave, 17 April 1917, my emphasis.

89. For example: "In England we have exceptional difficulties to deal with arising from the peculiarities of the English Criminal Law." (ibid.)

90. Ibid. This passage should be read with a pinch of salt in the context of Farrant's plea—for more money and resources for his department—although alternatively it could be argued that this context prompts Farrant to be explicit about what Home Office mechanization has occurred.

91. Campbell-Kelly, *ICL*, pp. 75, 76, 95.

92. PRO HO 45/17788. Lermon, "Report on card system of furnishing information regarding crimes and proceedings," 14 July 1938.

93. PRO MEPO 2/4994. BTM to Partridge, 10 January 1924. Note to Establishment Officer, 28 February 1924. This was the last appearance of Partridge. After serving in France until May 1919—receiving the Chevalier of Legion of Honour and being mentioned in despatches seven times—Partridge had worked in the Civil Aviation department for less than year before joining Scotland Yard (1920–1928). Retiring on pension in 1928 (presumably on grounds of ill health since he was only 47) he turned to writing.

His *Prisoner's Progress* (Hutchinson, 1935) examined crime and punishment in the nineteenth century. Partridge died in 1957.

94. PRO MEPO 2/5211. Stewart to Secretary, 8 October 1934.

95. PRO MEPO 2/5211. Hobson, "Review of the mechanised scheme for S2 Branch, with special relation to machine staff," 22 April 1936.

96. PRO MEPO 2/5211. "Commissioner's Office—Metropolitan Police. Outline of scheme for installing tabulating machinery in the Statistical Branch," undated (1934).

97. The transfer of punched-card machines from population census to work on criminal statistics was repeated in the 1950s when the "unique" Universal Printing Sorting Counters made by Powers for the 1951 Census were transferred to the Home Office Statistical Branch, see PRO HO 332/2.

98. PRO MEPO 2/5211. Hobson, "Review of the mechanised scheme in S2 Branch, with special relation to machine staff," 22 April 1936. A third girl was subsequently employed. The girls were underemployed by the Civil Service's own standards since the practice encouraged by Powers was accepted in which Powers rather than the Civil Service employed the machine operators who could then work for "less than the minimum scale for women clerks." This model was imported from the London County Council. "Summary of scheme for the partial mechanisation of the work of S2," October 1934. Examples of cards can be found in MEPO 2/5211.

99. PRO MEPO 2/4994. "Extracts as regards compiling police statistics on the Modus Operandi system of identification from Captain Sillitoe's report dated 13th September 1933, on his visit to America," undated (1933).

100. PRO MEPO 2/4994. Note, September 1933. Note by Stewart, 4 October 1933.

101. PRO MEPO 2/4994. Hobson, "Machines and crime detection," 17 January 1938.

102. PRO MEPO 2/4994. Foster to Game, 17 June 1938.

103. Bernard Hazel, *Local Authority Accounting by Punched Card Methods* (Gee, 1945), p. 12, is the source of both "quasi-governmental" and "indispensable."

104. Campbell-Kelly, *ICL*, p. 97.

105. This attitude is reflected in Stanley Baker's praise for the professional staff of the Board (*Milk to Market*, Heinemann, 1973), p. 34): "Just as Government would be wholly inept without a competent and incorruptible Civil Service, so would the milk producers' elected representatives be an ineffective body without a trustworthy machine whose wheels can be relied upon to keep turning without constant priming from a source of authority."

106. On the Board as "typical British compromise," see Baker, *Milk to Market*, p. 5.

107. Baker, *Milk to Market*, p. 86.

108. This was true just as much for statistics of industry as for Vivian's statistics of population. For example, here is the *Board of Trade Journal*: "We need to see where we stand after the disorganisation of a great war, which has made all previous standards antiquated. We need to have a datum-line from which we can measure afresh the progress on which we hope our industries are again entering. We need to ascertain what are the present relations between our home trade and our export trade, whether the structure of our industry as a whole is altering, whether the intensity of production is increasing or decreasing, and to all these questions only a Census of production can give an answer." ("The Third Census of Production," *Board of Trade Journal*, 28 February 1924, pp. 274–275)

109. PRO RG 19/62. Vivian, Draft preliminary report of 1921 census, 1921.

110. Ibid. Only a handful of people were prosecuted for refusing to provide information for the 1921 census. A note of July 1921 listed three cases dealt with, two definitely forthcoming, and potentially three more. Unfortunately there is little indication of the motivation of the delinquents. PRO RG 19/187. Talbot to Vivian, 21 July 1921.

111. Some of these cards merely rearranged the order of columns, or attempted to squeeze more information into one column to save space.

112. I have not been able to find out which departments wanted these questions included, and why.

113. PRO RG 19/62. Note to Mr. Derrick, 1921.

114. PRO STAT 12/28/2. T. H. C. Stevenson to Vivian, 29 April 1920. Note, therefore, that I disagree with Campbell-Kelly that the loss of the 1921 Census account was a serious blow to BTM. See Campbell-Kelly, *ICL*, p. 53

115. Indeed a third option an "invention" by Neil Williams (of the Aeronautical Department of Boulton and Paul aircraft works, Norwich) of a combined sorter and counter was considered. PRO STAT 12/28/2. Vivian, "Tabulating machines for the census," 19 April 1920. £300 was set aside by the Stationery Office to build Williams's experimental machine.

116. PRO RG 19/81. Registrar General to Stationery Office, 5 June 1920.

117. PRO RG 19/81. BTM to Stationery Office, 24 July 1920.

118. PRO STAT 12/28/2. Scorgie to Rose, 12 August 1920.

119. The company was Ignaz, Spiro & Sohne. This history is still unclear, since BTM did a 45-column card too. The key may be the *quality* of card available.

120. PRO STAT 12/28/2. Dunlop to Rose, 6 August 1920.

121. PRO BT 70/31. For illustrated descriptions of the 1921 census and description of the 1931 Census machinery, see "Powers-Samas machines and the Census," in *Powers-Samas Punch* (newsletter), May 1931.

122. PRO RG 19/81. Vivian to Everard-Greene, 15 October 1924: "This operation, though susceptible to improvement, saved us the necessity for some 93/4 million addi-

tional cards on which we should otherwise have had to record information for which there was no room on a single card."

123. PRO T 199/32. Vivian to Rae, 25 February 1926. PRO RG 19/104. Wallis, "Notes on the use of Powers Machines in connection with the English Census, 1921," 19 August 1923. The paucity of documents creates room for doubt also PRO STAT 12/28/2 suggests that three-bank sorters were used in 1911.

124. PRO RG 19/62. Vivian to Rose, 24 October 1921, lists four proposed "principal cuts": classification of families according to rooms occupied, subdivided according to number of children (the subdivision was dropped); tabulation of movements between residence and workplace at the fine level of civil parishes and wards (a coarser area was used); occupation and industry age statistics of employers, employees, etc. ; and a tabulation of the population by place of birth.

125. PRO RG 19/62. Ministry of Labour to the Secretary, Treasury, 7 February 1924.

126. PRO STAT 12/28/2. Vivian, memorandum, probably early May 1920.

127. PRO STAT 12/28/2. Codling to Vivian, 15 May 1920

128. PRO RG 19/81. "Note on the subject of tabulating machinery for the Census, 1931," 19 December 1929.

129. PRO RG 19/81. Vivian to Scott, 30 October 1930

130. Campbell-Kelly, *ICL*, p. 80, is therefore correct in surmising that "it seems likely that the awarding of the 1931 census to Powers-Samas rather than BTM was at least partially influenced" by the Buy British campaign.

131. PRO RG 19/81. "Machine equipment. Census 1931," undated (1933), lists the equipment used: 130 punches (all but 64 of which were subsequently distributed to other government offices), four gang punches, eleven counter-printer-sorters (eight three-bank, two two-bank, and one one-bank), ten sorters as well as eight Comptometers and two Burroughs calculators for arithmetic. 48,250,000 cards were delivered between July 1931 and January 1933. The subsequent trial of 1931 Census Powers punches at the Ministry of Health's Alteration Branch is discussed in T 222/419.

132. Croarken, *Early Scientific Computing*, 1990, pp. 22–46.

133. From the Royal Society obituary of Comrie by the British physicist and pioneer space scientist Harrie S. W. Massey, cited by Croarken, *Early Scientific Computing*, p. 40. Comrie certainly offered the benefit of his expertise to government departments, e.g., following his advice the Ballistics Research Department at Woolwich Arsenal installed a National Accounting Machine, while the War Office applied the Brunsviga Twin 13z calculating machine in the late 1930s (Croarken, pp. 41–42).

134. L. R. Dicksee, *Office Machinery and Appliances* (Gee, 1917); Walter Desborough, *Office Machines, Appliances and Methods* (Isaac Pitman, 1921); Desborough, *Duplicating and Copying Processes* (Isaac Pitman, 1931); P. T. Lloyd, *The Technique of Efficient Office Methods* (Gee,

1931); C. Ralph Curtis, *Mechanised Accounting* (Charles Griffin, 1932); L. J. Comrie, *The Hollerith and Powers Tabulating Machines* (printed for private circulation, 1933); P. T. Lloyd, *Research in the Office* (Gee, 1935); Owen Sutton, *Machine Accounting for Small and Large Businesses* (MacDonald and Evans, 1943); Bernard Hazel, *Local Authority Accounting by Punched Card Methods* (Gee, 1945).

135. Desborough, *Office Machines*, p. v.

136. Walter Desborough, "The merits of mechanical accounting," *The Accountant* Lecture Series No. 33 (Gee, 1934), p. 6. "The efficient office of the future," he concluded, "will be one that has been mechanized by a complete modern system," p. 8.

137. See, e.g., Curtis, *Mechanised Accounting*, p. v: "The principal objection to the introduction of office machinery has been that it involves a reduction in staff, which, at this period of national crisis, is anything but desirable. I maintain, however, that this should not be necessary." Curtis's solution was that "the men who are released by the introduction of machines should be put on to the production of those vital business statistics which should be at the disposal of all managing directors."

138. Curtis, *Mechanised Accounting*, p. v.

139. Desborough, Office Machines, p. 4.

140. Ibid., p. 7.

141. PRO T 222/1457. Ward to Bunker, 25 October 1965.

142. Campbell-Kelly, *ICL*, pp. 58–59.

143. PRO STAT 14/1156. Memorandum by Desborough, sent to Pitman, 15 July 1948.

144. PRO T 222/1457. Ward to Bunker, 25 October 1965. For more on Urwick Orr see chapter 6.

145. Robert Graves and Alan Hodge, *The Long Weekend* (Abacus, 1940 and 1995), p. 219.

146. Meta Zimmeck, "The 'new woman' in the machinery of government: a spanner in the works?" in MacLeod, *Government and Expertise*. Zimmeck shows that the few senior women who admitted tended to confine themselves, if they were to succeed, to the supposedly feminine separate sphere of "public housekeeping": "a sort of hypersensitive attention to duty, a bureaucratic punctiliousness . . . which] male mandarins hoped [would] lead senior women to be the gimlet eyes of the state in areas where gentlemen could not operate without distaste of embarrassment. Their insight of character "could discriminate the really deserving"." The women who most fitted were compliant, indeed in the case of Maude Lawrence "inactive as well as compliant."

147. Walter Desborough, "The merits of mechanical accounting," *The Accountant* Lecture Series, no. 33 (Gee, 1934), p. 6.

148. PRO RG 19/81. Downes to Vivian, 23 July 1925.

149. PRO STAT 14/1/1. Everard Greene to Scorgie, 6 January 1926. Note by Scorgie, 7 January 1926.

150. PRO T 222/1457. Bunker, "The origins and early history of O and M," undated (1966).

151. PRO T 222/1457. Desborough, "Office methods, operations and machines," talk to IPA, November 1927: "Statisticians, accountants, and actuaries when they design some of the very attractive forms which we as citizens have to fill up should bear in mind the work of the clerks who will later have to handle them. There are thus two considerations which must always be borne in mind in designing forms. Firstly, the forms must be so designed as to facilitate their completion. Secondly, the forms must be designed so as to present the information in the form which will best ensure efficient extraction."

152. N. O. Johnson, article in *Office Management*, 1961.

153. The full terms of reference of the Committee are of interest: "To undertake an examination of forms, stationery and printed matter. In connection with this examination the Committee should review the methods of work in the various Departments [of the Post Office] and should give special attention to the possibility of reducing routine clerical work by the utilisation of modern office machinery or in other ways."

154. PRO T 222/1457. Lloyd to Bunker, 10 November 1965. Bunker imports Lloyd's account more or less word-for-word into his historical account.

155. PRO T 222/1457. Lloyd to Bunker, 15 November 1965.

156. Quoted in Hennessy, *Whitehall*, p. 71.

157. Mariel Grant, *Propaganda and the Role of the State in Interwar Britain* (Clarendon, 1994), p. 47.

158. PRO T 222/1201 contains the reports and tests on calculators built by the following manufacturers: Mercedes, Monroe, Marchant, Muldivo, Brunsviga, Archimedes, Friden, Madas, Multo, Hamann, Remington-Rand, Peerless, Antares, Multisumma, Thales, Facit, Everest, Odhner, Sumlock, Wahler, Schubert, Badenia, Precisa, Stima, Famosa, and Numeria.

159. PRO T 222/1457. Bunker, "The origins and early history of O and M," undated (1966).

160. Haldane Report.

161. This conception is similar in some respects to Sir Norman Brook's O&M exercises of the 1950s and even the more recent "performance indicators," however the Haldane report insisted: "Such statistics would not of course be useful for any purpose of comparison between one Department and another, as the circumstances differ so widely, but would serve as a record from year to year of the transactions of the Department itself, and to be referred to as the occasion required."

162. PRO T 222/1457. Bunker, "The origins and early history of O and M," undated (1966).

163. PRO T 222/1457. Desborough, "Office methods, operations and machines," paper for IPA, 17 December 1927.

164. Ibid. The Post Office kept its own Investigating officers but conceded that they should "maintain direct communication and liaison with those of the Treasury"

165. From the Tomlin Royal Commission report: "The Treasury is already regarded as a clearing house for questions concerning improved organisation, labor-saving devices and the like."

166. For more on May at the Acc and Tab and Powers, see Campbell-Kelly, *ICL*, p. 77. For this quote from the May Committee on National Expenditure, see PRO T 222/1457. Bunker, "The origins and early history of O and M," undated (1966).

167. Graves and Hodge, *The Long Weekend*, pp. 255, 253.

168. PRO STAT 14/1156. Scorgie to Pitman, 8 April 1948.

Chapter 6

1. A. P. Rowe, *One Story of Radar* (Cambridge University Press, 1948); Robert Watson-Watt, *Three Steps to Victory* (Odhams, 1957).

2. Examples: S. S. Swords, *Technical History of the Beginnings of Radar* (Peter Peregrinus, 1986); Russell Burns, ed., *Radar Development to 1945* (Peter Peregrinus, 1988).

3. Robert Buderi, *The Invention That Changed the World* (Abacus, 1998).

4. Frederick William Winterbotham, *The Ultra Secret* (Futura, 1975).

5. In particular, as visitors to the recently opened Bletchley Park site, where the look and feel of wartime conditions are re-enacted, might pick up, there is a nationalistic edge to the promotion of this contribution.

6. F. H. Hinsley, "The Influence of Ultra in the Second World War," in *Codebreakers*, ed. F. Hinsley and A. Stripp (Oxford University Press, 1993).

7. Michael Smith, *Station X* (Macmillan, 1998). This is largely a summary of other literature leavened by some excellent, though unsourced, extracts from interviews with Bletchley Park staff. It is, however, occasionally unreliable.

8. Christopher Andrew, *Secret Service* (Heinemann, 1985), p. 87.

9. Andrew, *Secret Service*, p. 259.

10. Andrew, *Secret Service*, p. 450.

11. James H. H. Merriman, "A career in telecommunications," unpublished autobiography, BT Archives, HIC 002\012\0058. For more on Merriman and Milner-Barry, see chapter 8.

12. Derek Taunt, "Hut 6: 1941–1945," in *Codebreakers*, ed. Hinsley and Stripp. However note the entire lack of overlap with Smith's list of intercept stations (*Station X*, p. 24): Navy ones at Scarborough and Winchester; Army at Ford Bridgelands near Chatham, and RAF at Cheadle; alongside "a number" of GPO sites including Sandridge (Hertfordshire), Cupar (Scotland), and Brora (Scotland).

13. For more on these methods, see Andrew Hodges, *Alan Turing* (Unwin, 1985), chapter 4.

14. Alec Dakin, "The Z Watch in Hut 4, Part I," in *Codebreakers*, ed. Hinsley and Stripp, p. 52.

15. Stuart Milner-Barry, "Hut 6: early days," in *Codebreakers*, ed. Hinsley and Stripp, p. 96.

16. Hinsley et al., British Intelligence, vol. II, p. 655; Hodges, *Turing*, pp. 219–221.

17. Peter Twinn, "The *Abwehr* Enigma," in *Codebreakers*, ed. Hinsley and Stripp, p. 125.

18. Edward Thomas, "A naval officer in Hut 3," in *Codebreakers*, ed. Hinsley and Stripp, p. 44.

19. Ibid., p. 49. The worth of card indexes can be judged from the following recollection from Edward Green: "If we did strike a dud [person] it was my business to sell him or her. I am told that I once swapped a small but incompetent typist for a large and priceless card index." Quoted in Smith, *Station X*, p. 28.

20. Ralph Bennett, "The Duty Officer, Hut 3," in *Codebreakers*, ed. Hinsley and Stripp, p. 35.

21. Smith, *Station X*, pp. 86–87.

22. Taunt, "Hut 6," p. 109.

23. Joan Murray, "Hut 8 and naval Enigma, Part I," in *Codebreakers*, ed. Hinsley and Stripp, p. 114.

24. Jack Good, "Enigma and Fish," in Hinsley and Stripp, p. 162.

25. F. H. Hinsley, "An introduction to Fish," in *Codebreakers*, ed. Hinsley and Stripp, p. 143.

26. *Codebreakers*, ed. Hinsley and Stripp, p. vii.

27. William Millward, "Life in and out of Hut 3," in *Codebreakers*, ed. Hinsley and Stripp, p. 20.

28. Ibid. p. 17.

29. Bennett, "The Duty Officer," p. 34.

30. Swords, *Technical History*, pp. 84–85; Watson-Watt, *Three Steps*, pp. 78–83.

31. Swords, *Technical History*, p. 177. Much of the following section on First World War air defense organization follows Swords's description.

32. Swords, *Technical History*, pp. 177–178.

33. Such surveillance of London was of course resurrected in the Second World War, and was complemented by activities such as Merriman's radio direction-finding location of German spy transmissions (see chapter 8).

34. PRO AIR 10/3757. "Air Defence Pamphlet Number One. An outline of air defence organisation," February 1942. These pamphlets were issued "for the information of officers responsible for the organisation and conduct of defence against air attack."

35. PRO AIR 10/3758. "Air Defence Pamphlet Number Two. Radiolocation systems of raid reporting," April 1942.

36. PRO AIR 10/3758. "Air Defence Pamphlet Number Two. Radiolocation systems of raid reporting," April 1942.

37. PRO AIR 10/3760. "Air Defence Pamphlet Number Four. Telling and Plotting," April 1942.

38. Anonymous, *The Origins and Development of Operational Research in the Royal Air Force* (HMSO, 1963), pp. 18–19.

39. PRO AVIA 7/167. Barton, "Home defence, operations rooms and fighter radio communications," 28 April 1936.

40. Ibid.

41. PRO AIR 10/3757. "Air Defence Pamphlet Number One. An outline of air defence organisation," February 1942.

42. "A solution of the problem [of slow human transmission of information] was obtained, largely as a result of proposals by one of the Bawdsey [later TRE] staff, G. A. Roberts. An electrical converter was evolved, using automatic telephony technique, and known to the RAF as the "fruit machine," which enabled operators to press keys on their desks and so to transmit to the RAF control data covering grid position, heights and estimated number of aircraft. Dowding, on seeing the electrical converter, said it would not be long before the scientists replaced the Commander-in-Chief of Fighter Command by a gadget!" (Rowe, *One Story*, p. 26).

43. Jack Good, "Enigma and Fish," in Hinsley and Stripp.

44. PRO RG 28/27. Minutes of Vivian's sub-committee of the CID, February 1937.

45. PRO RG 28/25. "Subject matter of Sub-Committees on National Service," February–March 1923.

46. Emphasis added. For further discussion of "parasitic vitality," see Jon Agar, "Modern horrors: British identity and identity cards," in *Documenting Individual Identity*, ed. J. Caplan and J. Torpey (Princeton University Press, 2001).

47. PRO RG 28/28. Vivian to Foley, 14 February 1934.

48. PRO RG 28/261. Minister for Health in introduction of NR Bill to Parliament, cited in Report on CNRO, by John W. Foster, December 1947.

49. Eventually the transcript books contained 40 million registrations, with additional indexes: the card based birth index (those born after 1939), the "current register" (entries to country), the "Y register" (those who claimed their card was lost or stolen), a demobilization register, an alphabetical register (of those born post 1939), a record of service voters, a record of aliens and a record of persons who had changed their names.

50. PRO RG 28/25. Vivian to GG, 3 April 1923.

51. PRO CAB 103/396. "History of National Registration: Comments by GRO," May 1950.

52. Local registers were of four sorts: a maintenance register, a "dead register," the enumerator's schedules, and a reference leaf index (from ration books). Local offices kept information on: surname, first names, present full address, NR code and number, NR area, date of birth, and whether the holder was British or alien.

53. PRO CAB 103/396. Vivian to Acheson, 12 December 1948. Vivian thought this feature such a novelty as to justify (successfully, even now) keeping the detailed history of NR secret.

54. PRO CAB 114/2. V. Vivian to William Armstrong (the future Head of the Civil Service and unofficial "deputy Prime Minister" during Heath's tenure), 13 June 1940. Both Sylvanus Percival Vivian and Valentine Vivian were born in London in 1880.

55. Andrew, *Secret Service,* pp. 346, 405–406. The only published work by Valentine Vivian that I can trace is compilation he produced as Assistant Superintendent of Police in the Punjab. The extracts it contained were written by officers of the Indian police, their efforts assisted by the bureaucratic registration efforts that followed Criminal Tribes Act of 1871. V. P. T. Vivian, *A Hand-Book of the Criminal Tribes of the Punjab* (Punjab Government Press, 1912).

56. PRO CAB 103/396 contains all the references to the secret uses of NR of which I am aware. The file relates to S. P. Vivian's commissioned history for which he was instructed "to pull no punches and to disregard any security secrecy ban." Vivian therefore discussed both secret and non-secret aspects of the National Register and also lambasted the civil servants (Sir Wilfred Eady, Sir Ernest Gowers, Humbert Wolfe, and Sir Henry French) whom Vivian considers held "overriding opinions leading to a National Register in the First World War which was a miserable failure" and which "revived and very nearly wrecked NR in the Second World War." The secret elements, reading between the lines, included a special scheme for the Isle of Wight, a plan for new cards for all residents around the Kent and Sussex coasts, uses made of the Register by MI5, the link-up of the Green Card with passport office work, passages referring to the "suspected subversive activities of the IRA," and lastly a proposal for "Universal Photo-

bearing Cards" which "must obviously be relegated to the "Secret" class. Vivian's "secret history" has not been released at the Public Record Office, whether because of his fierce criticisms of fellow civil servants or because of the security aspects is unknown. (PRO CAB 103/396. Vivian to Acheson, 23 December 1948. Vivian to Johnston, 7 May 1949, and "History of National Registration. Comments by General Register Office," undated (May 1950)).

57. To reverse Andrew's complaint that historians too often ignore the secret services, historians of the secret services should be more sensitive to links with the public world beyond the familiar pattern of wise political action based on good intelligence, leaks, scandals and plots. As far as I am aware this book contains the first discussion of the relationship between Valentine and S. P. Vivian.

58. PRO CAB 114/2. Vivian, "The National Register System," undated (June 1940). He continued: "the plain fact is that if the whole population were on a photograph-Identity Card basis it would not tell the policeman or military patrol whether any particular person was disaffected or whether (on a different plane of values) the holder was or was not a person who ought to be allowed to pass or to move about in restricted areas or times as a person engaged on duties which are harmless and necessary in the public interest."

59. Allan Sekula, "The body and the archive," in *The Contest of Meaning*, ed. R. Bolton (MIT Press, 1989).

60. PRO CAB 114/2. Vivian, "The National Register System," undated (June 1940).

61. PRO RG 28/7. Sir H. Munro to Hayes Fisher and President of Local Government Board, 22 September 1916.

62. PRO RG 28/27. Draft report of sub-committee, undated (late 1938). Vivian's memorandum, "The National Register System," cited above, in its discussion and categorization of frauds, follows this interwar document closely.

63. This could be complicated when National Register officers themselves stole the cards, since they were in a position to change other records too. The corruption went further in some cases where policemen too were implicated. PRO MEPO 3/2353 contains details of a case where a plain-clothed policeman, PC Sidney Williams Nicholas procured from William Llewellyn Jones, an Assistant NR Officer, two identity cards for two deserters, Corporal J. White and Gunner H. White.

64. Sekula ("The body and the archive," p. 345) notices the same phenomena in nineteenth-century photography in his discussion of the "battle between the presumed denotative univocality of the legal image and the multiplicity and presumed duplicity of the criminal voice."

65. PRO RG 28/119. Application from probation officer for present address of woman under her Supervision who has failed to report, from "Note on applications for information from NR," 12 February 1947. PRO RG 28/122. North to Hale, 27 October 1947, however, illustrates how self-denying Whitehall could be: "once we allow info to be given from the NR for purposes of debt collection, even if the creditor is a

Government Department, we are well on our way down a slippery slope from which there is no recovery. Moreover I cannot see how we could justify discrimination in favor of the Crown."

66. Fingerprints were found on a "Winchester Quart" bottle near where the child had been snatched from hospital. Police first worked with the electoral register arranged in street order and took the fingerprint, name, address and NR number in a house-to-house check. Finger prints were taken to the Local Food Office and checked off with the alphabetically arranged records (food offices were integrated with the NR), this check revealed 100 persons whose names were not on the electoral roll and had not been fingerprinted. The subsequent visits led to the arrest of Peter Griffiths, the 46,253rd fingerprint taken in the investigation. (PRO RG 28/123. C. G. Looms (Chief Constable, Blackburn Police) to J. M. Ross (GRO), 9 November 1948).

67. PRO HO 25015. "Report, "Report of the Committee on National Registration," 1950. Three years earlier Treasury Organisation and Methods (O&M) had also noted the extra uses that NR information was put, including: routine police enquiries, applications for passports, opening Post Office Savings Bank accounts, entry into certain areas, collection of parcels from the Post Office, electoral registration, government departments verifying dates of birth (e.g. for pensions), and an anticipated demand for data from the National Health Service. PRO RG 28/261. Report by Foster (Treasury O&M), December 1947.

68. PRO HO 45/25014. Vivian, "The future of National Registration," September 1944. This is the most comprehensive, *publicly available* review of the National Register.

69. One direct medical inspiration for Vivian was the scheme suggested by Dr. Percy Stocks to link together medical histories, although as we have seen Vivian was also exposed to other earlier projects to link bureaucratically life histories. As Vivian noted: "the NR number will enable any data respecting individuals, however intermittent or diverse in origin, to be combined in a series of life histories from the aspect of the relevant class of circumstances for statistical or research purposes.

70. PRO HO 45/25014. Memorandum by Sir Ernest Holderness, 2 October 1944.

71. W. L. George, "National Registration: Why it should be maintained," *Sunday Times*, 6 April 1919.

72. Agar, "Modern horrors."

73. *Daily Express*, "Identity," 12 March 1945.

74. *Manchester Guardian*, "Identity card appeal lost," 27 January 1951.

75. PRO RG 28/116. Horn, "Combined NR/Medical Card," 19 September 1950

76. PRO RG 28/284. Simpson, "Health service records and National Registration," September 1950.

77. James R. Beniger, *The Control Revolution* (Harvard University Press, 1986), p. 378 and passim.

78. Louis Moss, *The Government Social Survey* (HMSO, 1991), p. 3.

79. Lord Woolton in his Presidential Address to the Royal Statistical Society in 1945, quoted in Moss, *The Government Social Survey*, p. 3.

80. Moss, *The Government Social Survey*, p. 22.

81. *Times*, 28 March 1942, quoted in Moss, *The Government Social Survey*, p. 7.

82. *New Statesman*, Jan 1937. The description of Madge is from Tom Jeffery, *Mass Observation* (Centre for Contemporary Cultural Studies, Birmingham, 1978), p. 3.

83. Harrisson also organized, at the age of 20, a pioneering ornithological study, coordinating 1,300 volunteers to observe the Great Crested Grebe (Jeffery, *Mass Observation*, p. 57). There are clear parallels between the Grebe enquiry and Mass Observation.

84. *New Statesman*, 30 January 1937.

85. Ibid. "The foisting on the mass of ideals or ideas developed by men apart from it, irrespective of its capacities, causes mass misery, intellectual despair and an international shambles."

86. Jeffery, *Mass Observation*, p. 21.

87. Charles Madge and Tom Harrisson, *Introductory Pamphlet: Mass Observation* (Frederick Muller, 1937), p. 20. Quoted in Jeffery, *Mass Observation*, p. 21.

88. Jeffery, *Mass Observation*, p. 17.

89. For a discussion of this Ministry of Information poster campaign, see Jeffery, *Mass Observation*, p. 38. See also Philip M. Taylor, *Munitions of the Mind* (Manchester University Press, 1995), p. 216.

90. Jeffery, *Mass Observation*, p. 40.

91. Bob Willcock, "Mass Observation," *American Journal of Sociology* 48 (1943): 445–456. Quoted in Jeffery, *Mass Observation*, p. 38

92. Jeffery, *Mass Observation*, p. 58. Angus Calder, *The People's War* (Cape, 1969); Paul Addison, *The Road to 1945* (Cape, 1975); Arthur Marwick, *Britain in the Century of Total War* (Bodley Head, 1968); Arthur Marwick, "Middle opinion in the Thirties," *English History Review*, April 1964.

93. Paul O'Higgins, *Censorship in Britain* (Nelson, 1972); Donald Thomas, *A Long Time Burning* (Routledge & Kegan Paul, 1969); James C. Crighton, *The Hidden Camera* (Routledge, 1989); Nicholas De Jongh, *Politics, Prudery and Perversions* (Methuen, 2000).

94. "Smith, William Henry (1825–1891)," by H. E. M., *Dictionary of National Biography* (Smith, Elder, 1898. W. H. Smith the elder, who founded the news agents, died in 1865, leaving W. H. Smith the younger in full charge of the lucrative concern. The latter became a Conservative MP three years later. Gilbert and Sullivan's *HMS Pinafore* mocked Disraeli's appointment of a mere London tradesman to the post of Secretary

to the Treasury. However, Smith was awarded with a promotion to First Lord of the Treasury in Lord Salisbury's second administration.

95. See e.g. Taylor, *Munitions*; John M. MacKenzie, *Propaganda and Empire* (Manchester University Press, 1984); Mariel Grant, *Propaganda and the Role of the State in Inter-War Britain* (Clarendon, 1994); Jeremy Hawthorn, ed., *Propaganda, Persuasion and Polemic* (Edward Arnold, 1987). See also Marjorie Ogilvy-Webb, *The Government Explains* (Allen and Unwin, 1965)

96. PRO T 222 915. "Punched card installations. Review of the usage of punched card machines in government offices during the year ended 31st December 1948," by Treasury O&M, March 1949.

97. PRO T 222 433. "Review of punched card agency of Service work," 1950. Martin Campbell-Kelly, *ICL* (Clarendon, 1989), p. 109. On the MMB at Cirencester, see Mary Croarken, *Early Scientific Computing in Britain* (Clarendon, 1990), p. 103.

98. PRO T 222 915. "Punched card installations. Review . . . ," March 1949.

99. According to Campbell-Kelly (*ICL*, p. 103), R&D stagnated and the postwar satisfaction of pent-up demand in home and export markets prevented the British office machinery companies from moving forward. Office machine production was coordinated after 1941 by its own Directorate (ibid., p. 110).

100. For example, a proposal by A. G. Pugsley and R. A. Fairthorne to use a Hollerith punched-card installation to solve large systems of linear simultaneous equations at the Royal Aircraft Establishment, Farnborough, was stopped because of "the intense pressures of the war and particularly the national shortage of punched card equipment" (Croarken, *Early Scientific Computing*, pp. 65–66). What is most interesting about this case is that a direct comparison can be made with Konrad Zuse's achievements in Germany, which were also prompted by the need to solve large systems of simultaneous equations generated by aeronautical research and development.

101. From the company archives there is little remaining data on government use of punched-card installations, beyond a list of some departments which possessed them (see e.g. Campbell-Kelly, *ICL*, p. 108), therefore the following is reconstructed largely from official sources and secondary sources based on official sources.

102. Moss, *The Government Social Survey*, p. 7.

103. Croarken, *Early Scientific Computing*, p. 62.

104. Ibid.

105. Ibid., pp. 61–73, provides an excellent account of the ACS. Croarken (ibid., p. 2) reserves the title of a "computing centre" to a body marked by nine characteristics relating to users, personnel, machinery, computing activity, advisory role, numerical research, computing machinery research, publications and library facilities. I use "centre" in a less strictly defined sense, believing that, e.g., somewhere can still be called a center of calculation even if it has a restricted set of users, or did not pursue research into numerical methods.

106. Admiralty's Scientific Research and Experiment Department (SRE), Admiralty Research Laboratory (ARL), Admiralty Signal Establishment (ASE), Mine Design and Development and Mining Establishment (MDD), Anti-Submarine Experimental Establishment (ASEE), MWD.

107. PRO ADM 283/34. "Department of Scientific Research and Experiment. Admiralty Computing Service. Seventh Report on Activities," undated.

108. PRO ADM 283/14. Carroll, "Admiralty Computing Service," 12 March 1943. On Carroll's postwar career, see Jon Agar and Brian Balmer, "British scientists and the Cold War: The Defence Research Policy Committee and information networks, 1947–1963," *Historical Studies in the Physical and Biological Sciences* 28 (1998), 209–252.

109. PRO ADM 283/15. "Computational facilities at HM Nautical Almanac Office," undated (1943).

110. PRO ADM 283/28. "Admiralty Computing Service: fourth report," 31 May 1944. The NAO finally received its own punched-card equipment, including one of the first IBM 602A calculating punches to be imported into the Britain, in 1949. Croarken, *Early Scientific Computing*, p. 111.

111. Croarken, *Early Scientific Computing*, pp. 69–70.

112. Ibid., p. 75.

113. Ibid., p. 77. Croarken is summarizing the arguments of the "Memorandum on the centralisation of Computation in a National Mathematical Laboratory," probably from 1944.

114. PRO T 222/420. Untitled memorandum on mechanization of AEDs and MPO, undated (1942?).

115. Ibid.

116. PRO T 222/420. Desborough to Robertson, 26 May 1943. Note the appearance of Desborough.

117. PRO T 222/420. Untitled memorandum on mechanization of AEDs and MPO, undated (1942?).

118. PRO T 222/420. Rees to Smith, 26 June 1946.

119. PRO T 222/420. "Development and control of mechanisation in the RAF supply system," 1951.

120. PRO T 222/420. "Brief note on Army Hollerith trial," undated.

121. PRO T 222/420. "Development and control of mechanisation in the RAF supply system," 1951.

122. PRO T 222/420. Foster, "RAF mechanised stores and provisioning," 17 September 1946. In Foster's view it was irresponsible of their superiors who "did not place the project with men of a suitable caliber and with a long service ahead of them to

work side by side with the late W/C Waharrad and Fl/Lt Keen. By so doing the could have ensured a thorough background knowledge of all the initial planning and the initial trials and tribulations of installing the machines . . . and this would have served them well in developing future phases of mechanization." Waharrad had subsequently joined BTM and was therefore compromised as an independent adviser.

123. PRO T 222/420. "Development and control of mechanisation in the RAF supply system," 1951.

124. NAHC. S/L S. J. Elvins, "Personnel statistics in the Royal Air Force," *Powers Magazine*, September-October 1947, pp. 2–7. Anonymous, "Personnel statistics at the Record Office, Royal Air Force, Ruislip," *Powers Magazine*, September-October 1946, pp. 4–5. The former records 1923, the latter 1929.

125. NAHC. "Editorial," *Powers Magazine*, July-August 1947, p. 1.

126. The career of Ely Devons, who worked at the CSO, suggests that models of planning transferred from industrial and technological organization to the economy. "Ely Devons," *Dictionary of National Biography*.

127. PRO CAB 139/5. "Central statistical organisation in the United Kingdom," May 1950.

128. PRO CAB 139/5. "Note on the origin, functions and future of the Central Statistical Office," 25 January 1947.

129. PRO CAB 139/5. "A note on statistical coordination in the United Kingdom," undated (1946).

130. Ibid., p. 5.

131. Ibid., pp. 5–6.

132. Anonymous, *The Origins and Development of Operational Research in the Royal Air Force* (HMSO, 1963), p. 6. Michael Fortun and Silvan S. Schweber, "Scientists and the legacy of World war II: the case of Operations Research (OR)," *Social Studies of Science* (1993) 23: 595–642. Erik P. Rau, "The adoption of Operations Research in the United States during World War II," in *Systems, Experts, and Computers*, ed. A. Hughes and T. Hughes (MIT Press, 2000).

133. On Coastal Command ORS, see C. H. Waddington, *OR in World War 2* (Elek, 1973). On other Commands, see Anonymous, *The Origins and Development of Operational Research in the Royal Air Force*, pp. 74–102.

134. The Blackett memorandum is reproduced in ibid., pp. 189–193, and can also be found in PRO ADM 219/16. For a discussion of "Blackett's Circus" at Anti-Aircraft Command, see PRO WO 291/887. Bayliss, "Army Operational Research Group Memorandum No. 615. The origins of operational research in the Army," 11 October 1945.

135. Ibid., p. 189.

136. For example, the chance that there were exactly *x* hits when the average number of hits in a given time was *m* was $e^{-x}mx/x!$ The use of such formulas in this memorandum was largely rhetorical.

137. PRO T 222/1442. "Some notes on Operational Research," 1960.

138. PRO T 222/1212. Robertson, "Advisory Council on Scientific Policy. Committee on Research and Productivity Working Party. The principles and practice of operational research," January 1948.

139. PRO DSIR 17/330. Darwin, "DSIR. Consumer standards of quality and the use of statistical methods in industry," 21 December 1945.

140. Operational researchers made some use of punched-card techniques during the war. See e.g. the illustration and discussion of the punched-card used to store information on attacks on U-boats in Waddington, *OR*, p. 183.

141. SIGMA's launch in October 1961 was met with indifference. "there is the usual cry that no one takes OR seriously or appreciates what it can do," wrote one civil servant dismissively. "I have heard Stafford Beer described by certain professional OR workers as the biggest charlatan in the business," wrote another. PRO T 222/1442. Crichton to Janes, 10 October 1961. Whyte to Lees, 2 December 1965.

142. PRO T 222/1212. Robertson, "Advisory Council."

143. PRO EW 1/64. Lord Robens of Woldingham to Shore, 6 December 1967.

144. Philip Mirowski, "Cyborg agonistes: Economics meets operations research in mid-century," *Social Studies of Science* (1999) 29: 685–718.

145. R. W. Clark, *The Rise of the Boffins* (Phoenix House, 1962); R. W. Clark, *Tizard* (Methuen, 1965). Philip Gummett, *Scientists in Whitehall* (Manchester University Press, 1980).

146. See Buderi, *Invention.* Computation crucial to the development of the magnetron was carried out on Hartree's differential analyzer while his laboratory was requisitioned by the Ministry of Supply. During this period the laboratory had a governmental name: SR(A), reporting to the Ministry's headquarters.

147. PRO DEFE 7/269. Tizard, "Chiefs of Staff. Central direction of scientific effort," 12 October 1945.

148. See Agar and Balmer, "British scientists."

149. Peter Hennessy, *Whitehall,* (Free Press, 1989), p. 129. Note the mechanical imagery, slipping from actor's to analyst's category.

150. On the machinery of government inquiry, see J. Michael Lee, *Reviewing the Machinery of Government, 1942–1952* (Birkbeck, 1977); Hennessy, *Whitehall*, pp. 128–130.

151. PRO T 199/78. "Machinery of government. The Treasury. The functions of the Treasury in relation to general financial control and to the control and management of the Civil Service," 27 August 1943.

152. Hennessy, *Whitehall*, pp. 60, 64–66.

153. PRO T 199/78. "Memorandum by Lord Hankey," 1943.

154. Ibid.

155. PRO T 199/78. "Cabinet, Official Committee on the Machinery of Government. The Centre of the Government Machine," June 1945.

156. Lee, *Reviewing the Machinery*, p. 150. The accusation is repeated in Richard Chapman and J. R. Greenaway, *The Dynamics of Administrative Reform* (Croom Helm, 1980), p. 135.

157. T 222/1457. Bunker, "The origins and early history of O and M," undated (1966). "Barrier of reserve" was in fact Reid Young's phrase. In a letter to Bunker an informant also notes that "Office Organisation and Method" was a chapter title in Edward Tregaskiss Elbourne, *Fundamentals of Industrial Management* (Macdonalds & Sons, 1934. PRO T 222/1457. Letter to Bunker, 10 November 1965. The 1934 usage was probably coincidental. Indeed Bunker's informant attributed the term to Pitman rather than Baliol Scott.

158. T 222/1457. Bunker, "The origins and early history of O and M," undated (1966).

159. Bunker, "Origins." On the naming of Treasury O&M, see also Raymond Nottage, "Organisation and Methods in the smaller public authority," *Public Administration* 32 (1954): 143–164.

160. PRO T 222/858. Simpson, "O and M in British Government Departments," 1956. Simpson was quoting the Fifth Report of the Select Committee on Estimates, Session 1946/47, HC143 (HMSO, para. 9, p. viii.

161. "I am quite convinced personally that very, very few of the higher level Civil Servants, to whom for hierarchical reasons these questions [of best use and organisation of space] are referred, have any grasp of the enormous difference which good lay-out and planning can make." PRO T 222/30. Urwick to Pitman, 30 September 1943.

162. PRO T 222/623. "Report of the Committee on Organisation and Methods," 9 July 1953, pp. 2, 4.

163. Seventeen departments by 1951.

164. D. G. Robertson, the Chief Treasury Investigating Officer allocated the respective responsibilities of Departmental O&M Sections and Treasury O&M Division as follows. The former were required to report monthly to the executive head of Treasury O&M (a) proposed programme of investigations with, if possible, approximate commencing dates (b) Progress of investigations in hand (c) Recommendations on investigations concluded and the position as to acceptance or otherwise. Whereas the Division's functions were (a) "to provide a pool of trained investigating staff, including specialists, for loan on a temporary or long term basis to departmental O and M Sections" (b) "Conduct investigations in departments which have not set up O and M Sections" (c) "Conduct extra-departmental or inter-departmental investigations" (d)

"Undertake investigations of 'Common Service' subjects" (e) "Co-ordinate the activities of O and M Sections" (f) "Maintain files of investigation reports, etc., indexed by subject and department" (g) "Scrutinize demands for office machinery, and appliances and recommend supply."

165. PRO T 222/30. Urwick to Pitman, 30 September 1943.

166. PRO T 222/1457. Bunker, "The chrysalis begins to form," undated (1966). The prolific Urwick's works included: *The Meaning of Rationalisation* (1929), *Committees in Organisation* (1937), *The Development of Scientific Management in Great Britain* (1938), *Personnel Management in Relation to Factory Organization* (1943), *The Human Factor in Management, 1795–1943* (1944), *The Elements of Administration* (1944), *The Making of Scientific Management* (with E. F. L. Brech, 1948), *Management Education in American Business* (1954), *Problems of Growth in Industrial Undertakings* (1960), and *The Pattern of Management* (1965).

167. T 222/1457. Bunker, "The chrysalis begins to form," undated (1966).

168. David Abercrombie, *Isaac Pitman* (Sir Isaac Pitman & Sons, 1937), p. 3. "Pitman, Sir Isaac (1813–1897)," *Dictionary of National Biography* (Oxford University Press, 1917). Pitman's "Stenographic Sound-Hand," a system of short-hand based on phonetic rather than orthographic principles, was published in 1837. His *Phonography* passed through many editions, especially after 1840 on the back of the penny post. The "phonographic crusade" extended to America and Australia.

169. Hugh Lawson Johnston, "Pitman, Sir (Isaac) James (1901–1985)," *Dictionary of National Biography, 1981–1985* (Oxford University Press, 1990. "Pitman, Sir (Isaac) James," in *Who Was Who*. Bernard Shaw's proposal to leave his money to further plan for a phonetic language that would save time and money. He wrote to the Royal Statistical Society arguing that "appropriate State departments may and should undertake and invent improvements in our national scripture just as they do in weights and measures, coinage, postal operations, traffic machinery, military and naval mechanization, building, sanitation, town planning, etc. etc." The statistician G. Udny Yule thought the idea a very bad one. (Royal Statistical Society (RSS) Archives. Shaw to various, 20 April 1944.) I. James Pitman was active in the Simplified Spelling Society of Great Britain, which was "recovering its early strength" in the prewar years, according to Abercrombie, *Pitman*, p. 24.

170. PRO T 222/30. Pitman, "Analysis of clerical procedures," 11 October 1943.

171. Ibid.

172. JoAnne Yates, *Control through Communication* (Johns Hopkins University Press, 1989. For a discussion of Yates, see chapter 5.

173. Hennessy, *Whitehall*, p. 102.

Chapter 7

1. Reportedly a fourth computer, which was to be a super-intelligent presence in the War Room, was cut (John Baxter, *Stanley Kubrick*, HarperCollins, 1977, p. 186). It was resurrected as HAL 9000 in Kubrick's 1968 film *2001*.

2. Kenneth Flamm, *Targeting the Computer* (Brookings Institution, 1987); I. B. Cohen, "The Computer: A Case Study of Support by Government, Especially the Military, of a New Science and Technology," in *Science, Technology and the Military*, ed. E. Mendelsohn et al. (Kluwer, 1988); Paul N. Edwards, *The Closed World* (MIT Press, 1996).

3. Simon Lavington, *A History of Manchester Computers* (NCC Publications, 1975; Lavington, *Early British Computers* (Manchester University Press, 1980), chapter 7; Special Issue: Computing at the University of Manchester, *Annals of the History of Computing* (1993) 15; Martin Campbell-Kelly, "Programming the Mark I: Early programming activity at the University of Manchester," *Annals of the History of Computing* 2 (1980): 130–168; Andrew Hodges, *Alan Turing* (Counterpoint, 1983).

4. Lavington, *A History of Manchester Computers*, p. 2.

5. Ibid., p. 5.

6. Edwards, *Closed World*, p. 74.

7. Ibid., pp. 101–102, 169.

8. Hodges, *Turing*, pp. 317, 366.

9. David M. Yates, *Turing's Legacy* (Science Museum, 1997), pp. 27–28.

10. Turing, talk to the London Mathematical Society, 20 February 1947, quoted in Hodges, *Turing*, p. 357. See also Yates, *Turing's Legacy*, p. 25. For the text of the talk, see pp. 106–124 of *A. M. Turing's ACE Report of 1946 and Other Papers*, ed. B. Carpenter and R. Doran (MIT Press, 1986).

11. Alan M. Turing, *Report to the NPL Executive Committee. Proposals for Development in the Mathematical Division of an Automatic Computing Engine (ACE)*, 19 March 1946. Also reprinted in *Turing's ACE Report*, ed. Carpenter and Doran. See also Yates, *Turing's Legacy*, pp. 21–22.

12. Yates includes the following examples of applications of the Pilot ACE: stress analysis of the catapult retardation structure on the aircraft carrier HMS *Ark Royal*, optimization of traffic signals for the Road Research laboratory, and "statistical work on stress measurement data from the Comet disaster investigation carried out by the Royal Aircraft Establishment." Yates, *Turing's Legacy*, p. 39.

13. The description of Williams and Kilburn is James Merriman's. PRO T 218/126. Merriman to Clarke, 22 March 1960.

14. Lavington, *Manchester Computers*, p. 15. This comment was reported by Newman in M. H. A. Newman, "A status report on the Royal Society Computing Machine Laboratory," 15 October 1948. NAHC MUC/C2.

15. Lavington, *Manchester Computers*, p. 15.

16. David Vincent, *The Culture of Secrecy* (Oxford University Press, 1998), pp. 199–200.

17. Early on there is often a choice, although manual methods would be time-consuming. For example, NAHC/MUC2/B7. Nice to Hoskin, 29 June 1953, notes that "22 solutions is a bit too much to do by hand [but] it is very small beer for the machine." Williams to Wass, 19 December 1951, notes that according Colebrook (NPL) one hour of computer production was equal to several "Brunsviga man years."

18. NAHC MUC2/B7. Hinds to Newman, 14 November 1950. Newman, in the name of "the best interest both of scientific studies in the University, and of prospective users of such machines on this country," replied that only during "periods left free by the research programme" would the Ferranti Mark I be made available.

19. NAHC/MUC2/B7. Williams to Corner, 19 December 1951. Corner to Williams, 29 January 1952. In the event the 200 hours were used by 1954, and the contract continued.

20. PRO DEFE 10/31. "MoD. DRPC. A high speed automatic calculating machine for the Ministry of Supply," by Chief Scientist, DRP/P(52)15, 20 February 1952. "The experimental establishments in the Ministry of Supply are today faced with computing problems of great magnitude and complexity. Without the services of an electronic computing machine, these computations would take hundreds of man-years. Most of this work is on projects of high priority such as GW, atomic energy and anti-aircraft artillery." The choice of the Ferranti Mark I was guided by the DSIR's Advisory Committee on High Speed Calculating Machines. £95,000 was granted for the computer, with £60,000 for housing it.

21. NAHC/MUC2/B7. Wass to Williams, 2 November 1951. Wass to Williams, 20 November 1951. Williams to Corner, 19 December 1951 also mentions the GW work. Reiners to Williams, 4 March 1953 relates to the purchase of computer-generated random numbers. Reiners was employed by the Ministry of Supply, section WR(D)1a—presumably Weapons Research, but there is a possible cryptographic connection here.

22. Government users of the University of Manchester's Mercury: Air Ministry, Air Ministry Meteorological Office, Armament Research Establishment, Atomic Weapons Research Establishment, Central Electricity Generating Board, DSIR Building Research Station, DSIR Hydraulics Research Station, Forestry Commission, Ministry of Supply, National Institute of Oceanography, National Physical Laboratory, Rocket Propulsion Establishment, Rothampstead Experimental Station, Royal Aircraft Establishment, UKAEA Harwell, UKAEA Dounreay Experimental Reactor, UKAEA Risley. Industrial users of Mercury included Atomic Power Constructions Ltd., Atomic Power Projects, A. V. Roe, British Nylon Spinners Ltd., British Shipbuilding Research Association, British Steel and Iron Research Association, C. A. Parsons Ltd., Constructors John Brown Ltd., CWS, David Brown Industries Ltd., Electrical Research Association Laboratory, English Electric Co. Ltd., Fairfield Shipbuilding & Engineering Co. Ltd., GEC, Hall-Russell Ltd., Hawker-Siddley Nuclear Power Co. Ltd., Henry Simon, ICI, J. & J. Colman Ltd., Joseph Lucas (Electrical) Ltd., The Nuclear Power Group, Robson Morrow, Rolls Royce, Shirley Institute (comprising the British Cotton Industry Research Association and the British Rayon Research Association), Simon-Carves Ltd., Vickers-Armstrong, and the Wool Industries

Research Association. Among the other users were CERN, Jodrell Bank, Kent Education Committee, North West Gas Board, Office of Naval Research, SHAPE, and the South Western Electricity Board. (NAHC/MUC2/B7).

23. PRO CAB 124/1906. "Large computer for AEA," 28 June 1960.

24. Jon Agar, "The provision of digital computers to British universities up to the Flowers Report (1966)," *Computer Journal* 39 (1996): 630–642. John Hendry, "Prolonged negotiations: the British fast computer project and the early history of the British computer industry," *Business History* (1984) 26: 280–306.

25. PRO CAB 124/1906. "Working Party on Expensive Research Equipment. American views on large computer development. Note of a discussion between Sir William Penney and Professor N. Metropolis," 18 October 1962. It is slightly unclear which Illinois project Metropolis was referring to.

26. Lavington, *Manchester Computers*, p. 41.

27. Campbell-Kelly, *ICL*.

28. PRO T 222/1304. Merriman, "Notes on discussion with Dr. J. Morgan, GCHQ on 25 February 1957," 26 February 1957.

29. PRO T 222/1304. Merriman, "Notes of discussion at Cheltenham on 11th March 1957 with Dr. J. Morgan and staff," 14 March 1957.

30. Yates, *Turing's Legacy*, p. 41–42. MOSAIC was started in 1947, and engineered for the Ministry of Supply by the Post Office research laboratory at Dollis Hill using Turing's theoretical plans. It was delivered to the Radar Research and Development Establishment (RRDE) in 1953. RRDE was a smaller sister laboratory to TRE, and the two merged to form RRE. On MOSAIC, see also: Eileen Magnello (with editorial advice from Graeme Gooday), *A Century of Measurement* (Canopus, 2000), p. 147.

31. PRO T 225/1181. Orchard to McKean, 1959.

32. PRO T 225/1181. Minutes of meeting held on 25 November 1959, 2 December 1959.

33. PRO AVIA 26/2070. D. A. H. Brown and T. R. Berry, "RREAC: the RRE Automatic Computer: main and modifier stores," RRE Technical Note No. 664, July 1963. RRE Technical Notes Nos. 691–699 describe the RREAC.

34. PRO DEFE 10/32. "MoD. DRPC. Radical review. Research and Development programmes. Report by the DRPC," DRP/P(53)45, 15 October 1953.

35. Jack Gough, *Watching the Skies* (HMSO, 1993), p. 42; Jon Agar and Jeff Hughes, "Open systems in a closed world: ground and airborne radar in the UK, 1945–90," in *Cold War, Hot Science*, ed. R. Bud and P. Gummett (Harwood, 1999).

36. Agar and Hughes, "Open systems," p. 232.

37. Within Mediator in the early 1970s the fiercest debate concerned which computer to use: to stay with the British Marconi Myriad 3 or to adopt an IBM machine as

approved by the US FAA. RRE Archives, "Programme 1971/72. Final Draft," June 1971. On the "software crisis," see pp. 196–200 of Martin Campbell-Kelly and William Aspray, *Computer* (Basic Books, 1996).

38. PRO MT 45/556. "Development plan for control of air traffic control in the UK national airways system," undated.

39. PRO MT 45/556. Veal to Hampden, 20 May 1959.

40. PRO MT 45/556. "The use of computing techniques in the air traffic control ground organisation," 30 November 1957.

41. Ibid. See also PRO MT 45/556, "The requirement for experimental automatic data processing equipment in ATC," undated, for more skepticism.

42. PRO AVIA 65/1600. "ATC experimental computer and display system. Historical aspects," undated (1960).

43. PRO MT 45/556. Merriman to Hampden, 28 May 1958. Merriman commented that this position was "in spite of the fact that they admitted a comprehensive manual of instructions."

44. PRO MT 45/556. Veal to Dalmahoy, 30 June 1958.

45. PRO MT 111/91 and 111/93 for more on WLTCE.

46. Eric Grove, "Naval command and control equipment," in *Cold War, Hot Science*, ed. R Bud and P. Gummett (Harwood, 1999).

47. Ibid., pp. 253, 260. Grove reports, and endorses, Benjamin's complaint that the patents describing the system, taken out in 1947, "are to this day the basis for all military Command-and-Control Information Systems, worldwide, and for all civil, air, sea or road traffic control systems and they are also the basis of the "mouse" cursor technique used on all modern personal computers. However I have no knowledge of the Crown having sought or received any royalties from them."

48. Grove, "Naval command and control equipment," p. 256.

49. Ibid., p. 258.

50. PTO T 225/2289. Dubery to Fraser, 13 March 1962. For an American perspective on ADA, see: David L. Boslaugh, *When Computers Went to Sea* (IEEE Computer Society, 1999), pp. 284–286, and for the influence of CDS on the US Navy, pp. 66–67.

51. PRO ADM 220/944. R. A. Ballard, "The general purpose computer POSEIDON: its facilities and system operation," ASWE Technical Note DX-60-6, 4 October 1960.

52. PRP T 225/2289. Dubery, "Note for file. ADA. Auto-detection and computers," 13 March 1962.

53. Grove, "Naval command and control equipment," pp. 259–260. CAAIS was the more fragile system, and acquired, Grove notes, the nickname "Can't Automate Anything Insufficient Software."

54. PRO DEFE 10/417. Minutes, DRPC, 28 February 1962.

55. PRO DEFE 10/490. "MoD. DRPC. Air Staff Requirement for a data processing and display system for use in air defence centres (ASR2232). Note by Air Ministry and Ministry of Aviation," DRP/P(62)16, 21 February 1962. ASR2232 is described in detail in appendix A of this memorandum.

56. PRO DEFE 10/417. Minutes, DRPC, 14 March 1962.

57. PRO DEFE 10/491. "MoD. DRPC. Air Staff Requirement for a data processing and display system for use in air defence centres—ASR2232 (Second Submission). Note by Air Ministry and Ministry of Aviation," DRP/P(62)57, 17 July 1962.

58. PRO T 225/2289. Dubery, "Note for file."

59. PRO DEFE 10/490. "Report of Working Party on ASR2232," 8 May 1962.

60. PRO T 225/1870. Zuckerman to Minister of Defence, 12 March 1962.

61. PRO CAB 139/175. CSO, "The organisation of statistical work in the services and service departments," 26 November 1956.

62. PRO DEFE 10/277. Minutes, DRPC, 18 November 1958.

63. Jon Agar and Brian Balmer, "British scientists and the Cold war: the Defence Research Policy Committee and information networks, 1947–1963," *Historical Studies in the Physical and Biological Sciences* 28 (1998): 209–252.

64. PRO DEFE 10/277. Minutes, DRPC, 2 September 1957; Agar and Hughes, "Open systems," p. 235.

65. PRO AVIA 65/1565. "BMEWS," January 1959.

66. In other words, the US concern was with intercontinental ballistic missiles, while the British worry was with intermediate-range and short-range ballistic missiles.

67. PRO AIR 2/16074. "BMEWS system," 8 December 1960. Project Legate, later called UK DIP, is described in PRO DEFE 10/491. "MoD. DRPC. Project Legate—UK display facilities for BMEWS (ASR2208)," DRP/P(62)56, 17 July 1962.

68. PRO AIR 2/16074. Tyndall, "BMEWS Site No. 3," 15 November 1960.

69. PRO AIR 2/16074. Salthouse to Private Secretary to Secretary of State, 28 November 1960.

70. RRE Archives, Malvern. RRE Annual Review No 5, April 1961.

71. PRO DEFE 10/277. Minutes, DRPC, 17 June 1958.

72. Agar and Hughes, "Open systems," pp. 238–240.

73. "The fundamental superiority of digital techniques in the solution of computation problems in modern aircraft is now established beyond reasonable technical doubt. Compared with an analogue computer a digital computer is inherently more flexible

so that the same basic concept may be followed in a wide variety of aircraft, either simple or complex. . . . The need for a versatile and flexible computer adequate to deal with navigation attack, control and flight management problems in future military aircraft has been formally recognized by the RAF, NATO and USAF. Only a digital solution is likely to be adequate. . . ." PRO DEFE 10/572. "MoD. DRC. Airborne digital computers research programme," DR/P(65)17, 4 March 1965.

74. Ibid.

75. PRO DEFE 10/624. Minutes, DRC, DR/M(66)9, 7 December 1966.

76. Germany is represented by Dr. Strangelove himself, whom we learn changed his name from Merkwürdigliebe to Strangelove. "A Kraut by any other name," remarks General Turgidson, caustically. According to Kolker, Merkwürdigliebe translates as "love of destruction and death." Robert Kolker, *A Cinema of Loneliness* (Oxford University Press, 2000), p. 121.

77. Kolker, *Cinema of Loneliness*, p. 126.

78. The interior of the B-52 was based on information from magazines such as *Flight* and *Jane's*. As Kubrick's designer, Ken Adam, recalled, when US Air Force personnel were invited to inspect the results, "They went white when they saw that CRM, so it must have been close. I got a memo from Stanley that said, "You better find out where you got your research from because we could be investigated." Basically, it was all from technical data in magazines." Vincent LoBrutto, *Stanley Kubrick* (Penguin, 1997), pp. 240–241.

79. Note, however, that it is well informed about contemporary American military technology. Edwards discusses the ties between fiction and non-fiction in *Dr. Strangelove*, in Edwards, *Closed World*, p. 319.

80. Norbert Wiener, *God and Golem Inc.* (MIT Press, 1964).

81. Harry M. Collins, *Artificial Experts* (MIT Press, 1990).

82. See, e.g., Lucy Suchman, "Technologies of accountability: of lizards and aeroplanes" and R. H. R. Harper and John A. Hughes, "'What a f-ing system! Send 'em all to the same place and then expect us to stop 'em hitting'" and "Making technology work in air traffic control," both in *Technology in Working Order*, ed. G. Button (Routledge, 1993).

83. M. Stephen Twigge and Len Scott, *Planning Armageddon: Britain, the United States, and the Command of Western Nuclear Forces, 1945–1964* (Harwood Academic, 2000).

84. Kendrew was basing his call on a report from a meeting held at the Signals Research and Development Establishment (SRDE) located in Christchurch on the English south coast. (PRO DEFE 10/570. Minutes, DRC, DR/M(65)1, 21 January 1965).

85. PRO DEFE 10/572. "Interim report on the automation of military data processing. Project 'Christchurch,'" 27 September 1965.

86. PRO DEFE 10/572. Ibid., covering note, 5 October 1965.

87. PRO DEFE 10/626. "Final report on the automation of military data processing (Project Christchurch)," 24 May 1967.

88. PRO DEFE 10/624. Minutes, DR 8th Meeting/67, 21 July 1967.

89. This seems to be implication from books such as Andrew Wilson, *War Gaming* (Penguin, 1970; first published as *The Bomb and the Computer* in 1968), and the limited references to computerized war games in PRO files, e.g.: DEFE 10/626, DEFE 10/624, DEFE 15/1001, and Merriman's comments in T 222/1305 and T 222/456.

90. PRO DEFE 10/629. "Ministry of Defence. Defence Research Committee. Report of the Scientific Computer Working Party," 1969, is interesting in that it attempts to define a measure of computer performance and predict future demand.

91. PRO AVIA 65/399. "Ministry of Supply. Organisation at July 1951," July 1951.

Chapter 8

1. Lord Bridges, 1964. *The Treasury* (Allen & Unwin, pp. 125–127.

2. O&M branches existed in the following departments: Treasury, Admiralty, Ministry of Agriculture, Fisheries and Food, Air Ministry, Customs & Excise, Inland Revenue, Ministry of Labour and National Service, National Assistance Board, Ministry of Pensions and National Insurance, Post Office, Ministry of Supply, Board of Trade, Ministry of Transport and Civil Aviation, War Office, and Ministry of Works.

3. PRO T 222/858. Simpson, "O and M in British Government Departments," 1956.

4. J. M. Lee, *Reviewing the Machinery of Government, 1942–1952* (privately printed, 1977).

5. Ibid., p. 150. Repeated in Chapman and Greenaway, *Dynamics*, p. 135.

6. PRO T 222/32. Note, Simpson to Kingdom, 29 May 1946. Simpson became Director of O&M (not O&M Division) a further increase in importance of Treasury O&M. In Bunker's opinion O&M "did not get a proper footing until JRS introduced a Civil Service discipline and it began to reveal an ordered organisation and not only in the Treasury but in the Service as a whole." T 222/1457. Bunker to Lees, 21 April 1966.

7. PRO T 222/32. Memorandum, "Organisation of the Civil Service. Working Party No 4. Business efficiency in departments," by Simpson, 29 June 1946.

8. PRO T 222/32. Memorandum, "Mechanisation to save manpower. Memorandum for the Financial Secretary to the Treasury," undated (1947). On de-skilling of clerical labor see Harry Braverman, *Labor and Monopoly Capital* (Monthly Review Press, 1974), pp. 293–358.

9. PRO T 222/32. Memorandum, "Organisation of the Civil Service."

10. PRO T 222/32. Memorandum, "Mechanisation to save manpower."

11. Ibid.

12. PRO T 222/858. Simpson, "O and M in British Government Departments," 1956.

13. "Mechanisation to save manpower." I have not found a copy of the handbook *Machines and Appliances in Government Offices.*

14. PRO T 222/915. Memorandum, "Punched card installations. Review. . . ." The departments were: Admiralty, Air Ministry, Board of Trade, Central Office of Information, Ministry of Civil Aviation, Customs and Excise, DSIR, Education, Food, Foreign Office (GCHQ), General Post Office, General Register Office, Health, HMSO, Home Office, Inland Revenue, Labour, Agriculture, Ministry of National Insurance, Ministry of Supply, Treasury, War Office, Ministry of Works, and three Scottish departments: Department of Agriculture, Department of Health and Registrar General's Office.

15. PRO T 222/915. Kingdom to various departments, 8 March 1948. Treasury O&M, *Machines and Appliances in Government Offices* (HMSO, 1954 (revised edition, first published 1947)).

16. After a competition between Powers and BTM the former, offering short-term savings, were granted the contract. See PRO T 222/424. Pollard, "Census of Distribution. Choice of punched card machines," 19 May 1950. Stout, "The first Census of Distribution," *O&M Bulletin*, March 1952.

17. PRO T 222/419. Woodlock to Mason, 20 January 1949.

18. PRO T 222/419. Sinclair, "Publication of results and conclusions of the Oxford Nutrition Survey," 26 January 1949.

19. PRO T 222/915. Report, "Punched card installations. Review of the usage of machines. Second report," August 1949.

20. Members were: A. R. Bunker (Treasury, chair), E. A. Allen (Board of Trade), B. S. Baker (HMSO), a representative of the Ministry of Food, C. W. Blundell (HMSO), J. E. Dunkley (Treasury O&M), F. A. Harmon (Ministry of National Insurance), N. O. Johnson (Post Office), E. Jones (Admiralty), E. H. Turner (Customs and Excise), and C. J. Hancock (Treasury, Secretary).

21. PRO T 222/433. Reports of punched card installations for statistics.

22. PRO T 222/433. Minutes of Interdepartmental Study Group on Punched Card Installations, PCI(50)3rd, 7 December 1950. PRO T 222/860. Memorandum, "List of installations selected as most suitable for a pilot merger," 1951.

23. PRO T 222/861. Minutes of Interdepartmental Study Group on Punched Card Installations, 31 January 1952.

24. PRO T 222/861. Report, "CTI. Report on the experimental merger of six selected installations recommended by the Interdepartmental Study Group on Punched Card Installations," by HMSO, 29 January 1953.

25. PRO RG 19/104 contains correspondence on the 1931 Census of England and Wales "Machine Programme," and "Notes on the use of Powers machines in connection with the English Census, 1921," 29 August 1923, a similarly programmatic set of instructions for the 1921 Census.

26. PRO T 222/813. Foster to Jefferies, 21 May 1949: "many months spent in the GRO convince me that the census is an event, talked about years before it is due, as something that only a major war could prevent. This outlook does not encourage objective thinking about the census in relation to present day national records and statistics of the population."

27. PRO T 222/813. Foster, "Some notes on probable requirement of HM Government in punched card machine development in relation to census work," 19 March 1947: "one of the next logical steps in the evolution of Census machinery [would be as follows]. Original machinery showed the totals on visible dials, then visible dials and hand transcriptions were replaced by the Printing Counting Sorter. What, so far, has been left entirely as a responsibility of the Operator—the human element—is to indicate in respect of "what" the counts were related. To my mind this is as great a "human element" gap to be filled as was the printing of the counts themselves." Also from Treasury O&M to Littlewood, 10 August 1950: IBM were considered but rejected because Treasury O&M decided it could not "advise on or recommend a machine which we have not examined or tested." PRO HO 332/2: The Powers UCPS machines were subsequently used by the Home Office to generate criminal statistics (see chapters 5 and 9).

28. PRO RG 19/158. Stewart, "Census 1951. Report on the punching process," 29 October 1953. "Census of Population 1951. Report on the Machine Room," undated (1952). The latter contains a fascinating conclusion: "In general, then, the ideal operator for Census work is male, physically fit, and free of any respiratory ailments or tendency towards nerves. He should have a strong practical side to his nature; the academic type invariably makes a poor machine operator. Female staff, if they must be employed, should have similar characteristics and they should be warned beforehand of the nature of the work." Apparently the "weight of a box of punched cards would surprise those who have never handled one, and the making of some hundred or so 'box journeys' daily between machine and storage racks, plus the tending and feeding of the machine, represents physical effort which no young lady who joins the Civil Service expects to encounter."

29. PRO T 222/1303. Dunkley to O'Donovan, 23 November 1954. The sites with machines installed listed by Dunkley were: National Physical Laboratory (Pilot Ace), Rothamstead (Elliott 401), "War Office Research Unit" (GPO built machine), HM Dockyards (Powers EMP), GPO Supplies Department (Hollerith 541). Sites with machines on order were: NPL (Deuce), Royal Aircraft Establishment, Farnborough (Deuce, Rascal), National Aeronautical Establishment, Bedford (Hec), Ministry of Supply (Ferranti Mk II), Aldermaston (Ferranti Mark II, IBM 626), Atomic Energy Research Establishment, Harwell (a "transistor machine"), AERE Risley (IBM 626), GPO Supplies Department (Hollerith 542), Board of Trade (Hollerith 550), Admiralty torpedo factory (Powers EMP), HMSO (Hollerith 542). Dunkley missed the Ordnance Survey computer, installed by April 1955. Note that little distinction was made between

fully programmable computers and the limited programmability of the souped-up punched-card machines—electronic multipliers, not computers—such as the Hollerith 542.

30. PRO T 222/1303. "Current developments in electronics," 25 April 1955. The seven listed here were at the Ministry of Supply, DSIR (i. e. NPL), War Office, Admiralty, Rothamstead and Ordnance Survey. Outside government, known to the author of this report (the small Booth machine at Birkbeck was, e.g., missed) were the two academic computers at Cambridge and Manchester, a Ferranti Mark I at Shell, the LEO and a prototype Elliott 402 which was available for hire. This report *does* separate stored-program computers from electronic multipliers and other calculators.

31. Members of the Brunt Committee were: Brunt (chair), three Royal Society nominees Douglas Hartree, Maurice Wilkes and F. C. Williams, S. Vajda (Admiralty), Brigadier G. H. Hinds and RAE's Stuart Hollingdale (Ministry of Supply), two DSIR nominees F. M. Colebrook and the NRDC's Lord Halsbury, and the DSIR civil servant P. D. Greenall as Secretary. The terms of reference were "(a) to keep under review the progress in the design, construction, and use of high-speed calculating machines in universities, industry and government departments. (b) to examine the main fields in which these machines are likely to prove useful. (c) to make recommendations to the Secretary, DSIR, on the most suitable types of machines with a view to promoting their construction and use."

32. On early computers as "mathematical" devices, see Campbell-Kelly, *ICL*, p. 163. For more on Brunt, see Jon Agar, "The provision of digital computers to British universities up to the Flowers Report (1966)," *Computer Journal* 39 (1996): 630–642.

33. PRO T 222/1303. Note, 31 October 1951.

34. PRO T 222/1303. Swann to Simpson, 19 November 1951.

35. Swann was quick to target government departments as potential customers. For the results of his research into likely demand, see Swann, "Machines in government calculations," in *Faster than Thought*, ed. B. Bowden (Sir Isaac Pitman & Sons, 1953).

36. PRO T 222/1303. Note, Dunkley to Simpson, 2 February 1952. The Brunt Committee agreed with this assessment. PRO DSIR 10 322. Report, "DSIR. ACHSCM. Second Report (October 1950–December 1951)," March 1952. As noted later, an informal inquiry by President of the Institute of Actuaries and other insurance representatives saw the same shortcomings in the Ferranti machine.

37. PRO T 222/1107. Robinson (Treasury Solicitor) to Merriman, 1 July 1959, and other notes in the same file discuss what is an "original" document and whether computer records or punched cards qualify. Compare also the troubled "biro" in Whitehall in the late 1940s.

38. Treasury O&M did not respond to Swann's argument that "the electronic machine scores because it can sense over a much wider range of factors and with its large memory can extract considerably more information in the one passage through the memory than is possible in the punched card procedure."

39. PRO T 222/1303. Note, Dunkley to Simpson, 2 February 1952.

40. PRO T 222/1303. Note, Dunkley to Simpson, 30 June 1952.

41. PRO DSIR 10 322. Memorandum, "DSIR. ACH-SCM. Survey of the scale of arithmetical work of the larger administrative government departments, and of the field for assistance by suitable electronic equipment," by Boss, H-SCM Paper 37, 23 November 1951.

42. PRO DSIR 10 322. Report, "DSIR. ACH-SCM. Second Report (October 1950–December 1951)," March 1952. The four computers were the Manchester Mark 1, EDSAC, LEO and the NPL Pilot ACE.

43. One other government body, the Joint Survey Advisory Board, was also examining the use of electronic computers, in this case to reduce data collected in big land surveys. The National Research Development Corporation (NRDC) was a government initiative launched by Harold Wilson in 1949 to encourage the development of science-based industries by providing loans and holding patents. Although deemed by historians largely a failure, it played an occasionally important role in shaping industrial policy for the British computer industry. See John Hendry, *Innovating for Failure* (MIT Press, 1989), Campbell-Kelly, *ICL*, pp. 166–167.

44. PRO DSIR 10/322. Memorandum, "DSIR. ACH-SCM. A survey of the possibility of the use of an electronic machine at the Central Offices of the Ministry of National Insurance, Newcastle-on-Tyne," by Boss, H-SCM Paper 45, 20 March 1952.

45. PRO DSIR 10/322. Minutes, "DSIR. Sub-committee on the use of electronics for office arithmetic," 20 June 1952. Present were: Halsbury (chair), Vajda, Dunkley, J. R. M. Simmons and T. R. Thompson (Lyons and OMA), A. Bradley (Ford Motor Co and OMA), H. Tetley (Government Actuary's Department), J. R. Jeffery and W. J. Littlewood (GRO), D. Newman and Miss C. H. Hampton (MNI), E. A. Newman and T. B. Boss (NPL), C. Strachey (NRDC), P. D. Greenall (DSIR, Secretary of Brunt Committee).

46. Ibid. The final subcommittee membership was Vajda (chair), Boss (secretary), Dunkley, E. A. Newman, Boss, Strachey, Greenall, Littlewood, D. Newman (MNI, Newcastle), Hampton (MNI, O&M), and L. J. Attridge (Bank of England).

47. PRO DSIR 10/322. Memorandum, "A summary of mechanised processes in The Bank of England, with particular reference to work in connection with the production of Dividend Payments," by Attridge.

48. PRO DSIR 10/322. Memorandum, "Input and Output for computing machines. part 1" and ditto "Part 2," by Newman.

49. B. B. Bowden's numbers, reported in J. A. C. Brown, H. S. Houthakker, and S. J. Prais, "Electronic computation in economic statistics," *Journal of the American Statistical Association* (September 1953) 48: 414–428.

50. PRO DSIR 10/322. Minutes, "DSIR. ACH-SCM," 8th meeting, 26 March 1952.

51. PRO T 222/1303. Draft paper, "The use and future of automatically controlled computers," *O&M Bulletin*, April 1953.

52. Brown et al., "Electronic computation."

53. PRO T 222/1303. Memorandum, "LEO," undated (July 1955). Lyons received £50 per hour for the use of LEO. See also David Caminer, John Aris, Peter Hermon, and Frank Land, *User-Driven Innovation* (McGraw-Hill, 1996). The NPL program had been written in 1954 for the Pilot ACE, but the DEUCE was delivered in time for the 1955 budget, and the program rewritten. On use of the DEUCE, see David M. Yates, *Turing's Legacy* (Science Museum, 1997), p. 39.

54. PRO T 222/1303. Berners-Lee to Simpson, 24 December 1953. PRO T 222/1086. Berners-Lee to Williamson, 24 December 1953: Berners-Lee also wrote on the same Christmas Eve to the Scottish office of Treasury O&M. In both cases he included the paper written by Ferranti Ltd on "Linear programming on the Manchester computer," 1953. The Scottish office followed up the suggestion.

55. PRO T 222/1303. Note, O'Donovan to Milner-Barry and Sir Alexander Johnston, 23 November 1954.

56. PRO T 222/1303. Note, Playfair to Johnston, 23 December 1954.

57. Another argument for computerization used by Playfair was related to dispersal: "There is no need at all why the big machines should be housed in London and, indeed, something to be said against it. Teleprinting facilities may be needed, but there is a good deal to be said for planning them safely outside the capital."

58. Playfair put his case with the enthusiasm of a convert: "I really believe this is a big thing and we can make it bigger if we try, to our own benefit and to the diminution of staff."

59. HMSO, *Wage Accounting by Electronic Computer*, June 1956. *The Economist*, 9 June 1956, p. 1021. Other means of extending the network outside Whitehall included periodicals such as *The Manager*, and conferences organized by Office Management Association and the British Institute of Management. Such conferences were an important site of technocratic computer enthusiasm. Sir Alexander Johnston recalled being "impressed at the [BIM] conference by the general acceptance of the notion that we were on the eve of a revolution in office and industrial techniques. No one thought it would happen overnight, but there was universal agreement, that these electronic developments would transform the scene in time." PRO T 222/1303. Note, Johnston to Milner-Barry, 7 November 1955.

60. PRO T 222/1303. Note, Dunkley to Padmore and Bridges, 4 May 1955. Padmore was Second Secretary to the Treasury, and Bridges was Permanent Secretary.

61. James H. H. Merriman, "A career in telecommunications," unpublished autobiography, BT Archives, HIC 002/012/0058, written c. 1987. The surveillance of London was conducted from fixed listening sites, mobile stations mounted on wooden cars and from the high-security prison, Wormwood Scrubs. "Meacons" (the name

echoed the Mekon of the *Eagle* comic books, and was a contraction of "Masking Beacons") were used in an attempt to hide broadcasting stations, such Radio Athlone in Ireland, which could be used as navigation aids by German bombers. Thirteen Meacons were operated by 80 Group RAF during the Battle of Britain.

62. Merriman, "Career."

63. Ibid.

64. Ibid. The Whitehall complex of buildings has a long history of repeated adaptation to shifting roles and uses, which, as with other British public buildings (old hospitals, e.g.) contributes to a peculiar architectural character and spatial feeling.

65. Merriman, "Career." Milner-Barry was at this moment the ranked second in the British chess team and regularly played in international matches.

66. Merriman is here recalling the directions given to him by Milner-Barry and Third Secretary to the Treasury, Alec Johnston. The friendship between O'Donovan and leader of the EDSAC team Maurice Wilkes was the route through which Treasury O&M found out about the Leo computer.

67. Merriman, "Career."

68. Ibid.

69. PRO T 222/1304. Report, "A preliminary appraisal of the place of automatic data processing systems in government service," by J. H. H. Merriman, February 1957.

70. PRO T 222/1304. Note, Clarke to Milner-Barry, 1 March 1957.

71. PRO T 222/1304. Report, "A preliminary appraisal of the place of automatic data processing systems in government service," by J. H. H. Merriman, February 1957.

72. Merriman suggested four possibilities: full reliance one either NPL or the Post Office, the coordination of the Post Office and NPL via a technical subcommittee, or the establishment of an "independent Computer Advisory and Research Unit possibly under direct control of TOM." It was unlikely that Treasury O&M would favor the NPL; as Boss of NPL reflected, there was a "'Royal Society atmosphere' [to] the place in which it was felt somewhat undignified to concern oneself with industrial business applications." PRO T 222/1304. Memorandum, "Note of a discussion with Mr. Boss, NPL on 10 September 1956," by Dunkley, 11 September 1956.

73. PRO T 222/1304. Note, Milner-Barry to Merriman, 22 March 1957.

74. Merriman, "Career." Other members were David Greensmith (Boots), Alastair Pilkington (Metal Box Co.), Gordon Radley (GPO), Dick Hayward (Chairman of the Staff Side of Central Whitley Council), and later Edward Playfair.

75. PRO T 218/126. "Specialist backing for the Government ADP programme," probably written by Merriman, December 1959.

76. Ibid. See also: Yates, *Control*, pp. 72–100.

77. PRO T 222/1203. Merriman to Armstrong, undated [January 1957] is a fascinating statement on where to "draw the line" between clerical and scientific computing: the "Ministry of Supply have the largest assembly of expertise on this subject in the country and, until recently, a HQ unit coordinating and examining proposals for new computers. Treasury O&M expertise resides in the field of application of principles of computers to clerical and office tasks. To question the use of computers in the field of science, mathematics and engineering is beyond the skill of Treasury O&M. We are not equipped to argue techniques with MoS and would not wish to be considered specialists or advisers to you on the development of computers for non-office jobs. In so far as it is difficult to draw the line between physical pieces of computing ironmongery used for scientific and for office work, we can, at times, but not always, make some comments on scientific proposals, but not out of any esoteric scientific capability." Merriman was speaking as an ex-engineer here: the more orthodox Treasury officials remained concerned that an expensive class of machinery should seem to be beyond Treasury (or even HMSO) control. No conclusion was reached on these boundary problems, the trickiest of which related to office machinery built into bigger scientific instruments.

78. Merriman, "Career."

79. PRO T 222/1313. Memorandum, "Application of punched card electronic computers to payroll work. Report of the "Chessington Scheme," by C. J. Hancock (TOM), 9 March 1955.

80. PRO BT 70/629. Watson, "Census of Production for 1958. Use of the computer in processing," 20 November 1959, puts the case against. Hinson, 3 December 1959, replies in favor of computerization, quoting comparisons of time taken by computer and manual methods to classify a return. Hinson had used a computer for part of the work on the 1957 Census of Distribution.

81. HMSO, White Paper on Employment Policy (1944), Cmd 6247.

82. PRO CAB 139/175 contains drafts of the PEP pamphlet "Statistics for Government," 1956, in which these complaints are made.

83. Ibid.

84. Ian Miles and John Irvine, "The critique of official statistics," in *Demystifying Social Statistics*, ed. J. Irvine et al. (Pluto, 1979).

85. PRO T 222/1091. Report, "Centralisation of statistical work. Interim report for the ADP Steering Committee submitted by the Inter-departmental Working Party on the application of ADP to Government Statistics," 22 May 1958.

86. PRO T 222/1091. Minutes, ADPSC, 2nd meeting, 25 June 1958.

87. PRO T 222/1091. Memorandum, "The possibility of a combined ADP installation for the statistical work of the Customs and Excise and MNLS. Report by the Study Group," 4 September 1958.

88. PRO T 222/1091. Report, "Centralisation of statistical work. Interim report for the ADP Steering Committee submitted by the Inter-departmental Working Party on the application of ADP to Government Statistics," 22 May 1958.

89. Hansard, "Supply: Report, Stationery and Printing," No. 79, Cols. 282–283, 20 March 1962.

90. PRO RG 19/316. "Notes of a meeting at GRO Southport on 17th September 1953. Informal discussion on possible machine requirements for the 1961 Census," undated.

91. PRO RG 19/316. Internal minute, Littlewood to Thorby, 5 April 1954. "All this I feel is looking to the electronic computer which personally I do not expect to see us using before 1971. However we do know (*confidentially* please note) that Ferranti's or at any rate Mr. Swann, think even now it might be a practicable proposition to do census on their machine (or rather type of machine)."

92. PRO RG 19/316. "Application of electronic machinery to GRO work. Note of a meeting on 20th December 1956," undated. The Treasury O&M officials present were Merriman and Jordan.

93. PRO RG 19/196. North to Campion, 23 August 1957.

94. PRO RG 20/311. "Provision of machines for the 1961 Census of Population of England and Wales," undated (September 1957).

95. Immigration into the United Kingdom from the Commonwealth, and in particular from the West Indies was of great cultural and political significance in 1950s. The following extract from a Home Office civil servant to the GRO, gives a taste of official concerns: "As you know, among my duties is that of keeping watch on the coloured population of this country and supplying Ministers with information on which to judge whether measures of control should be introduced over immigration from the Commonwealth. For this purpose, our statistical information about the coloured population of this country is far from complete. We have no accurate information of the age or sex distribution of these people, or where they are living, or what occupations they follow. We believe that they largely follow unskilled or semi-skilled occupations and it is alleged that, as compared with the emigrants from this country to other parts of the Commonwealth they come on the whole from a much lower social grade; we have no statistics with which to confirm or deny such allegations. It is also alleged that coloured people in this country breed much more rapidly than the native population . . . (The West Indian immigrants are more highly skilled, prosperous and adventurous than the average West Indian, and it may be that goes with a lower reproduction rate). We are also entirely ignorant of the extent of miscegenation." (PRO RG 19/195, J. M. Ross, HO, Nationality Division, to W. J. Littlewood, GRO, 2 August 1960).

96. The only major difference was that the end product of the 1961 Census of Population data processing was to be camera-ready copy. (PRO RG 20/311. "Provision of machines for the 1961 Census of Population of England and Wales," undated (September 1957).).

97. PRO RG 20/312. Boreham to Dr. Bernard Benjamin (Director of Statistics, GLC), 19 February 1966. Note Benjamin worked at GRO at the time of the 1961 Census.

98. PRO RG 20/311. Note to Benjamin, 15 November 1962.

99. PRO RG 19/494. "1966 Census. Further considerations of processing aspects," 12 November 1963.

100. PRO T 222/1303. Note, Dunkley to O'Donovan, 23 November 1954.

101. Tizard gives his account of computerization plans for national insurance in *New Scientist*, 9 May 1957, pp. 13–16. The *New Scientist* covered the subject of office automation again, more generally, in the issue of 13 June 1957.

102. PRO T 222/1303. Note, O'Donovan to Grant, 18 May 1955.

103. Tizard spent a 2-year fellowship studying the applications of control theory to economics at LSE, and, after a stint as a consultant, became a founding Fellow of Cambridge's new Churchill College in 1960 (Yates, *Control*, p. 310).

104. PRO T 222/1303. Playfair to Johnston, 16 June 1955. Playfair reported his interpretation of a conversation with Edward Bullard, the Director of NPL: "if HQ [i. e. DSIR] would not give him the staff which he wanted for things which he wanted to do, he would point the fact by saying that he had not got enough staff to do the things which they wanted him to do."

105. Department of Health and Social Security. *Newcastle Central Office*, Newcastle: NCO, 1986), p. 61. Copy in NAHC/LEO/C155.

106. Department of Health and Social Security. *Newcastle Central Office*, Newcastle: NCO, 1986), p. 63. Within the year the ICL 2970 was upgraded to a ICL 2980.

107. Note that the Post Office laboratory at Dollis Hill was also studying the Post Office Savings Bank with a view to computerization.

108. PRO T 225/1181. Merriman, "Computers for scientific work," 28 March 1960.

109. PRO DSIR 10/322. "DSIR. Sub-Committee on the Use of Electronics for Office Arithmetic. Factors affecting the economies of clerical mechanisation," by E. A. Newman, 15 May 1953.

110. PRO T 222/1303. "The use and future of automatically controlled computers," *O&M Bulletin*, April 1953.

111. PRO T 222/1320. Hayward to Abbot, 25 June 1956.

112. PRO T 222/1320. Memorandum, "Supplementary notes on possible effects of automation developments on Personnel problems," July 1956. Minutes, meeting of Johnston, five Treasury O&M officials, and seven Staff Side, including Haywood and George Green, General Secretary of the Civil Service Clerical Association. Compare with Playfair's enthusiastic comment on the "diminution of staff."

113. PRO T 222/1320. Memorandum, "Reorganisation of the clerical classes," 1957.

114. Merriman, "Career."

115. PRO T 222/1457. Bunker, "The next 21 years. Is O and M on a launching pad or a trampoline?," undated (1969).

116. The exceptions allowed were either very small computers (e.g. for the Welsh universities), or very large, e.g. the powerful computers requested by the nuclear laboratories. See Agar, "Provision."

117. PRO T 222/1305. Note by Merriman, 1958.

118. PRO T 222/1305. Note, Clarke to Robertson, 9 December 1958.

119. PRO CAB 124/1798. "Report on automation," 15 June 1959. Clarke argued that an alleged automation gap between Britain and the Superpowers was not the result of government inaction, but the unwillingness of the private sector to take risks. The political instigation of the report received rare explicit comment: "Sir Norman Brook's note of the 19th June and the report was produced at the request of the steering committee, a body more political than governmental in connection with the preparation of the Conservative Party Manifesto," from note, "Historical note," undated.

120. PRO T 230/456. Note, "Long term economic forecasting," Hopkin to Clarke, 11 November 1959, and Clarke's reply. The use of the computer is described in P. R., "Using a computer to forecast national income and expenditure: first results," 5 February 1960. A simple model, "A," with 84 equations, designed by Berman was used. Fittingly, computers for economic forecasting began to be a specialty of the London School of Economics: see PRO T 222/1331. "Specialist backing for the government ADP programme," ADPSC(60)5, 20 May 1960.

121. Hennessy, *Whitehall*, p. 179, for the description of Clarke as the Plowden Report's "theologian, its life-force and the man who made the report flesh."

122. PRO T 230/456. Note, "Longer-term economic forecasting," Sir Robert Hall to Clarke, 12 November 1959.

123. Merriman, "Career in telecommunications."

124. PRO T 222/1432. Note, Callaghan to Sir Laurance Helsby, 1 January 1965.

125. PRO T 222/1432. Memorandum, "The ultimate usage of ADP," January 1965.

126. PRO T 222/1432. Memorandum, "The acceleration of the Government ADP programme," by Murray Laver, 13 January 1965.

127. Estimated from information in *Computers '66* (Digest Data Books, 1966).

128. Not least because the computer industry and market was becoming highly complex. In 1958, a review of computers in the private sector could be restricted without loss to a handful of companies (ICI, Ford, Rolls Royce, Metal Box, etc.),

this was not the case by the mid-1950s. Compare PRO AVIA 65 1374, ADP Advisory Committee minutes, and the reports in PRO T 222/1432.

129. Thomas P. Hughes and Agatha C. Hughes, "Introduction," in *Systems, Experts, and Computers*, ed. A. Hughes and T. Hughes (MIT Press, 2000), pp. 10–11.

130. PRO MT 134/16. "Note of a meeting held on 2nd November 1965 to discuss the application of PERT to road programme management," 1965. For more on PERT, see David M. Stires and Maurice M. Murphy, *Modern Management Methods* (Materials Management Institute, 1963).

131. PRO MT 134/16. "Note of a meeting . . . ," 14 April 1966. This was not the first use of PERT. An earlier example was the employment of a PERT consultant in the transfer of the Post Office Savings Bank to Glasgow. British Rail employed a full-time PERT expert.

132. PRO MT 134/16. "Note of a meeting held on 2nd November 1965 to discuss the application of PERT to road programme management," 1965.

133. This late appeal to cybernetics is justified: only in the 1960s and the 1970s did there seem to have been an interest in cybernetics from the UK planning community. e.g. J. Brian McLoughlin, *Control and Urban Planning* (Faber, 1973).

134. Wood to Harris, 13 December 1966.

135. PRO MT 134/16. Alexander (O&M) to Ardley, 9 March 1966. "During the course of recent discussions on critical path networks with the Branches concerned I have been surprised and disturbed at the strength of the opposition to the use of network analysis within the Department. This is found generally in grades from HEO downwards. At Head of Branch level there is usually, but by no means always, acceptance that the system may be quite valuable. There is, however, no great enthusiasm for it and this would seem to be caused by two main factors:" 1) "There is a widespread ignorance of CPA procedure generally. Staff who have not yet been concerned with the pilot scheme do not understand network diagrams. . . ." 2) "monitoring of networks appears to the staff concerned to put further burdens on their already well-occupied time. This is resented by members of Divisions operating the PERT scheme who, by adopting a parochial attitude, can see no advantage to themselves in using critical path analysis."

136. For example, the King Edward's Hospital Fund for London and the London Teaching Hospital mounted a campaign in 1965 for a massive computer "comparable to the largest in the world," e.g. an Atlas, for medical applications in the capital. While senior computing advisers to government, such as Brian Flowers and B. V. Bowden were critical of the naiveté, the demand does illustrate how computers were seen by the mid-1960s as necessary adjuncts to large organizations. One anticipated application was PERT analyses. (PRO CAB 124/1476. "The application of computers to Hospital Practice," by Constable (Chair of the Study Group. Secretary, Teaching Hospitals Association), July 1965. Flowers to Bowden, 5 July 1965.) The campaign may have been encouraged by Donald Michie's description that hospitals and medical schools had been "invaded . . . by high speed computing machinery" in the early 1960s. (PRO UGC 7/626. Memorandum by Michie, undated.)

137. PRO T 222/1442. "The technique and uses of OR for organisational problems," by Management Services (General) Division, 1966.

138. PRO T 222/1442. "Survey of OR," S. P. Osmond to Lees and Baldwin, 31 May 1966.

139. PRO T 222/1369. Minutes of ADPSC, 26 May 1960.

140. PRO T 222/1457. Bunker, "The next 25 years," 1969.

141. R. G. Anderson, *Organisation and Methods* (Macdonald and Evans, 1980). The textbook was originally published in 1973 and went through four reprints before this second edition.

142. PRO T 225/1181. Merriman, "Computers for scientific work," 28 March 1960.

143. Merriman, "Career."

144. Wass later wrote of the effect of such contact to the NPL computing historian, David Yates: "I gained a great deal from the course which has stood me in good stead throughout my working life. What it gave me essentially was a sound conceptual framework within which to appraise the scope and limits of computerization of manual processes generally. As a result of this indoctrination, I have rarely felt ill at ease in looking at systems applications. . . ." From a private letter from Wass to Yates, quoted in Yates, *Turing's Legacy*, p. 55. Note Wass's echoing of Merriman's term, "indoctrination," which was presumably therefore used—jokingly—at the time.

145. Fulton report, Cmnd. 3638. Quoted in Hennessy, *Whitehall*, p. 195. The sixth respect was "(f) Personnel management and career planning are inadequate" and was of less direct relevance to Treasury O&M.

146. On the intertwining of military interests, industrial policy and Treasury O&M, see PRO T 225/1181. Merriman to Griffiths, 1 May 1959, and PRO T 218/126. Merriman, "Note of a meeting on high-speed calculating machine industry," 5 June 1959, and other notes and memoranda in that file.

147. PRO T 222/1331. "Limiting the number of types of ADP system in use for government work," ADPSC(60)3, 2 February 1960, noted that "government is the largest single purchaser of ADP equipment in this Country, but by no means dominates the market (our orders may amount to 15% of the whole, but could be less than 10%). We cannot therefore hope to exert a very big influence. . . ." The Ministry of Aviation procured enough aircraft and the GPO enough telecommunications to have a strong effect on the respective industries.

148. PRO T 222/1457. Bunker, "The next 25 years," 1969.

Chapter 9

1. John G. Laski, "Towards an information utility," *New Scientist*, 29 September 1966: 726–728.

2. Michael Stone and Malcolm Warner, "The computer's invasion of privacy," *New Scientist*, 1 May 1969: 238–239.

3. On CCN and United Association for the Protection of Trade (UAPT, despite its curious name also a direct-mailing business), see Duncan Campbell and Steve Connor, *On the Record* (Michael Joseph, 1986), pp. 55–58. Postcodes deserve their own lengthy history.

4. Colin J. Bennett, *Regulating Privacy* (Cornell University Press, 1992), p. 19.

5. For an example of concern over FTR, which to our retrospective eyes seems excessive, see comments on the "system whose potency scares many people" in Campbell and Connor, *On the Record*, pp. 42–46. On Alvey, see Brian W. Oakley and Kenneth Owen, *Alvey* (MIT Press, 1989); Ken Guy, *Evaluation of the Alvey Programme for Advanced Information Technology* (HMSO, 1991).

6. On the use of DHSS records in the Yorkshire Ripper investigation, see Campbell and Connor, *On the Record*, p. 111. Note the similarity of fears expressed in the opening quotation of this chapter.

7. The following is an excellent example of the former. In 1952 a journalist working for the *Manchester Guardian* was upset by a brochure for Powers-Samas punched-card machines: "'Take an imaginary citizen,' it says, 'whom we call John Smith.' He is born; he goes to school. Punched cards record these facts. He sits for examinations: his marks are analyzed by punched cards, though it appears that he still has to answer the questions himself. He starts work, he marries, he buys a house: the cards begin to shower round him as in the last page of 'Alice,' particularly when the mortgage and insurance transactions get busy. His rates, his gas and electricity bills, turn them into a deluge." So the life of John Smith goes on, riddled with holes in punched cards like a colander, though which his privacy has leaked away long before he is old enough to realize the fact. He becomes a father; he buys a car; he has an accident; he claims insurance benefit; he eats a meal in the train on his way to convalescence. He commits a crime, or he retires respectably on superannuation. The moral choice survives but the cards get him either way. "Finally," we are informed in language that no printing tabulator would dare employ, "Smith goes the way of all flesh. And his demise is recorded on a punched card." The fate of John Smith recalled that of his namesake, Winston Smith, in George Orwell's *1984*, published four years previously. Winston's relationship with the state was structured by information technologies, such as the two-way television screens by which Big Brother checked on his lowly siblings. Under such surveillance, the self becomes destroyed—or, more accurately, is transferred to the collective, merged with the state. Likewise the information held on John come to define John himself: the punched cards "turned to the eager task of plotting his life, being shot through with eloquent holes (each a bull's eye), sorted with the speed and unerring accuracy of a conjurer or card-sharper, and tabulated by the tell-tale machines which "sense" analyze, and record the facts or life or death, of buying or of selling, of good or of evil." Orwell's totalitarian dystopia, in which the privacy of the individual has become a crime, is a cliché in postwar discussions of the impact of the computer on government administration. Yet despite these two examples, even with the influence of a text so well known as Orwell's *1984*, such language, stressing the threat to individuals' private lives from

information technologies, was actually surprisingly rare, in Britain at least, before the 1960s. (Anonymous, "An organiser's heaven? Punches that plot life," *Manchester Guardian*, reprinted in *Powers-Samas Gazette*, November/December 1952, in NAHC photographic file).

8. Campbell and Connor, *On the Record*, p. 87–88.

9. Vincent, *Culture of Secrecy*, pp. 267–272.

10. A central concept in this story is "convergence." Indeed several different concepts of convergence are relevant to mid-to-late-twentieth-century history. First, there was the convergence between computing and telecommunications, which gave us "information technology" and increasingly became a commonplace in policy discussions. In the United States this convergence made most sense in the articulation of new forms of time-sharing and networking computers in the 1960s. In the United Kingdom, a formative moment was the meeting between the James Merriman of Treasury O&M, Solly Zuckerman, the foremost advisor on defense research, and Major-General Leslie de Malapert "Pete" Thuillier, a high-level military administrator—he was Director of Telecommunications at the War Office for three years in the late 1950s before joining the Cabinet Office in 1958. The "three of us," recalled Merriman, "spent some time in developing a policy that we called "convergence." The concept was that computers and computing would become increasingly interdependent. It seemed to us—more by intuition than by argument—that the functions of each could not be exploited to the full without the use of the resources represented by the other. We developed out of this industrial, managerial and administrative concepts." Such concepts, through Merriman's protégé Murray Laver, were imaginatively exploited during Anthony Wedgwood Benn's tenure at Mintech during the first Wilson administration. James H. H. Merriman, "A career in telecommunications," unpublished autobiography, BT Archives, HIC 002/012/0058, written c. 1987. The second conception of convergence was related to this first sense: a convergence of principles among American and European states that guided technical policy, including information technology and data protection. For this argument as it relates to the principles behind data protection, see Bennett, "The Duty Officer," especially chapters 3 and 4. For another technology, see Ronald Brickman, Sheila Jasanoff, and Thomas Ilgen, *Controlling Chemicals* (Cornell University Press, 1985). Also, as trivially illustrated by the Merriman-Zuckerman-Thuillier connection, there was a convergence between civil and military realms, which found technical expression in 1960s traffic control projects, most substantially in Linesman/Mediator discussed in chapter 7. Finally, but most directly relevant to this chapter's concerns the distinction between statistical systems, registers and other tools of administration began to become very blurred.

11. PRO MT 34/20. "Vehicle registration and licensing and driving licensing problems of the project," June 1966.

12. O&M interests, of course, centered on large mainframe computers, but also extended through the minutiae of office machinery. Recommendations for the central office included standardized filing systems, standardized ways of putting papers in files, the thorough application of the "Envopak" principle of transferring papers between

offices, and the extended use of devices such as envelope opening and sealing machines, and automatic staplers.

13. PRO MT 34/20. Back, "Vehicle registration and licensing and driving licensing. A regionalised computer system," July 1966.

14. Jon Agar, "The Flowers Report and the provision of computers to universities," *Computer Journal* 39 (1996): 630–642.

15. PRO MT 34/20. Back, "Vehicle registration and licensing and driving licensing. Policy aspects of vehicle registration and licensing," July 1966.

16. See James Rule, *Private Lives and Public Surveillance* (Allen Lane, 1973), pp. 97–121.

17. PRO MT 97/695. Fisher, "Organisation of the proposed computer system for the registration and licensing of vehicles and the licensing of drivers. Assessment of Departmental work to be included in the long term vehicle and driver organisation," 6 January 1967.

18. PRO MT 97/695. Grainger, "Computer licensing project. Assessment of departmental work, other than vehicle registration and licensing and driver licensing, to be included in the long-term vehicle and driver organisation," May 1967.

19. Campbell and Connor, *On the Record*, p. 184.

20. PRO HO 337/1. "Report of Working Party on feasibility of using automatic data processing in the Home Office," March 1958. Interestingly, one of the severe problems presented by searching the alien Traffic Index—the diverse ways of spelling phonetically similar surnames, coupled with international variations in name structure—was tackled through standardization. (The "Russell Soundex Code" allocated the same code, e.g., to "Johnson" and "Jonsen.") According to Campbell and Connor (*On the Record*, p. 157), the computerization of the Traffic Index, with system called INDECS, did not become operational until August 1980, and, although machine-readable passport trials began at Heathrow Airport in 1983, was "still not able to process details of all passengers arriving in or leaving the UK" in 1985.

21. PRO HO 337/4. JADPU, "Preliminary report on the feasibility of using automatic data processing in the Home Office, Prison Commission and New Scotland Yard," October 1959.

22. PRO HO 332/2. "The Criminal Statistics: the probable direction of change and its organisational implications (abridged paper)," 1965. The anticipated conclusions of the Perks Committee were: (a) "The inclusion of a considerable amount of factual information about crimes (relating to victims, types and values of property stolen, scene of crime, etc.) to supplement the present purely legal classification system (b) The incorporation of what may be called penal statistics (at present organized, in quite separate compartments, mainly on the basis of the indexes relating to inmates of approved schools, borstals, etc., and the projected prison index) into an integrated system of criminal statistics, in which data recorded at the "crime known" stage would be linked, where applicable, with the records of subsequent court proceedings and penal treatment."

23. PRO HO 337/80. JADPU, "April 1968 project review," September 1968.

24. This is a good example of the "never necessity" phenomena common to all mechanization projects in this book: at the moment that mechanization occurs it is always possible to continue using older method. Therefore it was never the case that, e.g., computers were a "necessity," and although social factors, in this case attitudes to parole, shape decisions they are never deterministic either. However successive mechanizations, because they tend to be infrastructural, build up and after a while it seems to contemporaries that a certain job was impossible without computers.

25. As with the Aliens Index, it was anticipated that more sophisticated routines to search the names would be developed: "Early name search programs will be relatively simple and require a greater degree of man-machine interaction than the more advanced systems which will later be developed involving weighting techniques and possibly, phonetics."

26. Campbell and Connor (*On the Record*, pp. 245, 248) noted in the mid-1980s that 39,300 persons on the wanted/missing index were under the PNC category of "Locate" and therefore "a major part of the index concerned people neither wanted nor missing, nor even suspected of any offence. The title of the wanted/missing index is a striking piece of Civil Service or police sophistry. Many entries on the index are neither wanted nor missing persons." Striking miners (as well as union officials and journalists) were added to the stolen/suspect vehicle index on the PNC during the bitter and highly politicized industrial dispute of 1984–85.

27. David M. Yates, *Turing's Legacy* (Science Museum, 1997), pp. 148–152.

28. Campbell-Kelly, *ICL*, p. 249.

29. PRO CAB 139/584. "International Computers and Tabulators Limited. Project 51," by J. T. Whittaker, 8 August 1967.

30. The vagueness in "Atlas power" is explained thus: the above source says "three" but Campbell-Kelly, an authority on the matter, lists "ten" (Campbell-Kelly, *ICL*, p. 249).

31. PRO CAB 139/584. Whyte to Laver, 15 August 1967.

32. PRO T 227/2682. Hartman, "National computer for police records," EP(68)1, 15 January 1968. This "difficult case" went to the Official Committee on Dispersal four times. The Police wanted the computer within 2 miles of the Criminal Record Office and Fingerprint Office at New Scotland Yard. Dispersal, it was claimed, "would involve the expense and risk [from sabotage] associated with long transmission lines."

33. Campbell and Connor, *On the Record*, p. 233.

34. Ibid., p. 235. In 1985, of 47.33 million records the bulk (35.61 million) were of vehicle owners, followed by 4.97 million criminal names, 3.51 million records in the fingerprint index, and 380,000 and 543,000 stolen/suspect vehicle registrations and engine/chassis numbers.

35. PRO RG 19/162. Murray to Davidson, 16 March 1965.

36. PRO RG 28/306. MacLeod, "Proposals for a population register system in Great Britain," September 1967.

37. Ibid.

38. PRO RG 28/306. Note to Registrar-General, 18 May 1966. The NHSCR was grossly inflated and now listed "103% of the population"!

39. PRO RG 28/306. Harvey to MacLeod, 4 October 1967.

40. PRO RG 28/306. Bishop, "A population register and common numbering system for Great Britain," 14 November 1967.

41. PRO RG 28/306. Rooke-Matthews to MacLeod, 14 October 1967.

42. PRO CAB 139/584. "Compatibility," 1967–1968.

43. PRO CAB 139/584. Whyte to Stafford, 29 December 1967.

44. PRO CAB 139/584. Minutes, Cabinet Statistical Policy Committee, 31 October 1967.

45. PRO RG 28/306. Note to Registrar-General, 18 May 1966, records: "as you know, the existing NHS Register in conjunction with our other records is being used for a number of purposes similar to those mentioned above [for the Central Register]. The usefulness of the register for these purposes falls far short of what would be expected from a complete national register. As you know the non-NHS uses of the Central Register have not been made the subject of particular public announcement."

46. PRO RG 28/306. Bishop, "A population register and common numbering system for Great Britain," 14 November 1967.

47. The computerization of the DHSS Central Index, the "biggest computerization programme in Europe," was guided by the department's Operational Strategy, and it is in the context of this document that the "whole person concept" emerged in 1977. Campbell and Connor, *On the Record*, p. 89.

48. PRO RG 28/306. Ibid.

49. PRO MT 97/695. Fisher, "Organisation of the proposed computer system for the registration and licensing of vehicles and the licensing of drivers. Assessment of Departmental work to be included in the long term vehicle and driver organisation," 6 January 1967.

50. PRO HO 337/4. "Preliminary report on the feasibility of using automatic data processing in the Home Office, Prison Commission and New Scotland Yard. Part B. The Prison Commission," August 1959, p. 9.

51. In early stages the Data Bank was to have included "ecological" data too.

52. PRO EY 2/34. Madge, "Progress report to advisory committee," 23 May 1966.

53. PRO EY 2/34. Moser to Young, 13 June 1966. Mackenzie to Young, 20 May 1966.

54. Other proposals by Political and Economic Planning and by the SSRC itself to run the Data Bank were dismissed, the former because they did not have the support resources and the latter on grounds of lack of "independence."

55. PRO PIN 47/174. Potter, "SSRC Data Bank," June 1967.

56. PRO HO 261/1. Roper, ""Computers and Privacy" and machine-readable public records. Evidence for the Data Protection Committee submitted by the Public Record Office," September 1976.

57. PRO RG 19/162. Note to Boreham, 11 May 1965.

58. Bennett, *Regulating Privacy*, p. 52.

59. Alan Westin, *Privacy and Freedom* (Atheneum, 1967).

60. Malcolm Warner and Michael Stone, *The Data Bank Society* (Allen and Unwin, 1970). A much more balanced enquiry is Rule's *Private Lives.*

61. PRO HO 261/4. "TUC. Memorandum of evidence submitted to the Committee on Privacy," 11 March 1971. Submitted unchanged to the Data Protection Committee in 1977.

62. Campbell and Connor, *On the Record*, p. 24; Bennett, "The Duty Officer," p. 85.

63. David Vincent, *The Culture of Secrecy: Britain, 1832–1998* (Oxford University Press, 1998), p. 235, citing *Report of the Committee on Privacy* (HMSO, 1972), p. 6.

64. Some of Younger's recommendations were adopted in the Consumer Credit Act (1974) and the code of practice of the British Computer Society. Campbell and Connor, *On the Record*, p. 25. Bennett, "The Duty Officer," p. 87.

65. Home Office, *Computers and Privacy* and *Computers Safeguards for Privacy* (HMSO, 1975). Bennett ("The Duty Officer, pp. 87–88) gives credit to the persistence of Sieghart and to Home Secretary Roy Jenkins and his junior minister Alex Lyon for pushing publication of these white papers. Lyon had previously (1967) brought one of the unsuccessful privacy bills to Parliament.

66. PRO HO 261/1. Moser to Jordan, 4 January 1977.

67. PRO HO 261/1. "Evidence from the Central Statistical Office in reply to the letter form the Data Protection Committee dated 5 August 1976," undated.

68. PRO HO 261/1. "Evidence to the Data Protection Committee from the Office of Population Censuses and Surveys," 22 December 1976.

69. PRO HO 261/1. "DHSS . . . Evidence to the Data Protection Committee," undated. Addresses were divulged: to courts, on request, for the purpose of maintenance proceedings; to the police on request in cases where more than trivial crime was involved; to local authority social service departments where parents had absconded;

to occupational pension schemes for the purpose of paying pensions as required by the Social Security Pensions Act 1975; to the Customs and Excise where they were investigating serious offences; to the Inland Revenue where they were seeking tax arrears which included arrears of National Insurance contributions; to Service departments in cases of desertion from HM Forces. Benefits information was passed to employing Departments and to the Social Service departments. Contributions information was passed to employers when dealing with NI contributions. Personal information was also used within the DHSS for "research and statistical purposes."

70. PRO HO 261/1. Sutherland to Secretary, Data Protection Committee, 27 October 1976, records the Department of Employment view which captures this latter point concisely: "Most computer data processing systems are a combination of computer and clerical records and legislation for the computer side may lead to undesirable anomalies and, perhaps, because of restrictions imposed on computer systems, clerical processing at greater cost and less effectiveness may persist where it should be replaced."

71. PRO HO 261/4. Fyfe to Secretary, Home Office, 27 October 1976.

72. PRO HO 261/1. Central Computer Agency, "Replies on behalf of a number of government departments to the questions in paragraph 2 of the letter from the Data Protection Committee dated 5 August 1976," October 1976.

73. PRO HO 261/3. "Post Office memorandum of evidence to the Data Protection Committee," November 1976.

74. PRO HO 261/1. Jaffray to Jordan, 16 November 1976.

75. PRO HO 261/1. "Home Office evidence about computer services available to the Police," undated.

76. PRO HO 261/1. "DHSS . . . Evidence to the Data Protection Committee. Part B: National Health Service and personal social services records," undated.

77. The DHSS's Mental Health Enquiry contained identifiable information which was used without obtaining doctors' or patients' consent on each occasion it was used. Similarly, Cancer Registry records were released to researchers who could show they were "reliable guardians of the data," that the project was approved by the BMA Ethical Committee, and that the research was necessary, and who undertook not to approach any patient without the permission of the clinician in charge.

78. PRO HO 261/1. "Evidence to the Data Protection Committee from the Office of Population Censuses and Surveys," 22 December 1976.

79. *Report of the Committee on Data Protection*, Cmnd. 7341 (HMSO, 1978.

80. Campbell and Connor, *On the Record*, pp. 28–29; Bennett, "The Duty Officer," pp. 90–91. The main evidence for this pressure comes from a published report from the Advisory Council for Applied Research and Development in 1980, and the first hints of a government inclination to introduce a bill was in Home Office minister Timothy Raison's speech to the British Medical Association in 1981.

81. Gerald Kaufman, quoted in Bennett, "The Duty Officer," p. 93.

82. *The Data Protection Act 1984. An Introduction to the Act and Guide for Data Users and Computer Bureaux. Guideline No. 1*, Wilmslow: Office of the Data Protection Registrar, 1985, lists some of the restrictions. For an especially critical review of the flaws of the act, see Campbell and Connor, *On the Record*, pp. 299–319. Bennett ("The Duty Officer," pp. 189, 192) points out that the Registrar was "expected to fulfill certain "ombudsman" functions, such as receiving complaints from the general public and investigating perceived trouble spots," but also notes that "the Registrar has only two positive duties under the law: to submit an annual report to the Parliament and to maintain the register."

Chapter 10

1. Kevin Theakston, *The Civil Service since 1945* (Blackwell, 1995), p. 89.

2. Ibid., p. 92.

3. Ibid., p. 128; Hennessy, *Whitehall*, p. 602.

4. Hennessy, *Whitehall*, p. 607.

5. Ibid., p. 611.

6. *Efficiency and Effectiveness in the Civil Service*, Cmnd. 8616.

7. Theakston, *Civil Service*, p. 133.

8. Helen Margetts, *Information Technology in Government* (Routledge, 1999), pp. 132–133.

9. Ibid., p. 126.

10. Margetts, *Information Technology*. Projects included the £250 million CHOTS for the Ministry of Defence, £41 million UKAir for the RAF and the £1 million Scottish Prison Service record system (ICL); air-quality systems for the Department of Environment, and, with IBM, the RAF's logistics system (Logica); £50 million for Iron systems integration for Inland Revenue (Bull); systems integration for the Royal Navy, a £52 million Home Office system, the National Unemployment Benefit System—Nubs2, with ITSA (Sema); NHS systems, the Bureau West computer centre for the Ministry of Defence, IT services to £20 million for the Department of Trade and Industry (Hoskyns); IT systems for the British Library (DEC); consultancy for the Department of Trade and Industry, alongside many other contracts across Whitehall (Coopers & Lybrand), and a warehouse and transport management system for the RAF (Siemens Nixdorf).

11. Paul Ceruzzi, *A History of Modern Computing* (MIT Press, 1998), p. 169.

12. Margetts, Information Technology, pp. 147–148.

13. Ibid., pp. 128, 156.

14. TAURUS, which stood for Transfer and Automated Registration of Uncertified Stocks, was to be the "paperless, computerized successor to the TALISMAN settlement

system." Begun in 1981, work was suspended in 1984 and resumed in 1987. Journalists satirized it as "Tortoise or Tortuous." In 1993 the project was halted at a cost of £400 million. David Kynaston, *The City of London*, vol. IV (Chatto & Windus, 2001), p. 742.

15. National Audit Office, *Report by the Comptroller and Auditor General. Administrative Computing in Government Departments*, HC 259 (HMSO, 1984), p. 2.

16. Sally Wyatt, *Technology's Arrow* (Universitaire Pers Maastricht, 1998), p. 81.

17. NAO, *Administrative Computing in Government Departments*, p. 5.

18. NAO, *Administrative Computing in Government Departments*, p. 5.

19. National Audit Office, *Report by the Comptroller and Auditor General. Department of Social Security Operational Strategy* (HMSO, 1989), p. 1. NIRS2 inherited this rather elastic claim.

20. Ibid., p. 5.

21. Ibid., p. 5.

22. Wyatt, *Technology's Arrow*, p. 91.

23. In 1990 much of the Department of Social Security was split up into five agencies: Contributions Agency, Benefits Agency, Child Support Agency, Resettlement Agency and the Information Technology Services Agency (ITSA).

24. House of Commons, Select Committee on Public Accounts, *Forty-Sixth Report*, Session 1997–1998. The tendering had two phases: an indicative bid and a final bid. Eight suppliers replied to the advertisement placed in the Official Journal of the European Communities. Eight were whittled down to three. Indicative bids were all similar: £242 million (Andersen Consulting), £241 million (CSC Computer Sciences) and £263 million (EDS/SEMA). But on the final bid Andersen Consulting (£134 million) went remarkably low, compared to £214 million and £235 million from the other two bidders, respectively.

25. Margetts, *Information Technology*, p. 156.

26. House of Commons, Select Committee on Public Accounts, *First Report*, Session 1999–2000. See also *Forty-Sixth Report*, Session 1997–1998 and *Twenty-Second Report*, 1998–1999.

27. House of Commons, Select Committee on Public Accounts, *Minutes of Evidence*, 25 January 1999. The figure of 172,000 comes from House of Commons, Select Committee on Public Accounts, *First Report*, Session 1999–2000.

28. House of Commons, Select Committee on Public Accounts, *First Report*, Session 1999–2000.

29. House of Commons, Select Committee on Public Accounts, *First Report*, Session 1999–2000.

30. The relatively new Central Information Technology Unit did advise on the contract. CITU at that stage was too small, with too weak an organizational memory, to act as an authoritative expert voice.

31. House of Commons, Select Committee on Public Accounts, *Eighteenth Report*, Session 1998–1999.

32. National Audit Office, *Report by the Comptroller and Auditor General. Text Processing in the Civil Service*, HC 85 (HMSO, 1989)

33. Ibid.

34. National Audit Office, *Report by the Comptroller and Auditor General. Text Processing in the Civil Service*, HC 85, HMSO, 1989. In fact, according to the Public Accounts Committee, "departments began using e-mail extensively only in 1998 several years behind private business and universities." House of Commons, Select Committee on Public Accounts, *Twenty-first Report. Government on the Web*, Session 1999–2000.

35. There are now some good accounts of the history of networking. See Janet Abbate, *Inventing the Internet* (MIT Press, 1999. Arthur L. Norberg and Judy E. O'Neill, *Transforming Computer Technology* (Johns Hopkins University Press, 1996). For brief overviews, see Martin Campbell-Kelly, *Computer* (Basic Books, 1996), pp. 283–300; Ceruzzi, *History*, pp. 295–298.

36. Yates, *Turing's Legacy*, p. 129.

37. Ibid., p. 130.

38. Ibid., pp. 139–144.

39. James Gillies and Robert Cailliau, *How the Web Was Born* (Oxford University Press, 2000), p. 52. The Conservative Edward Heath replaced Harold Wilson as prime minister in 1970.

40. See Abbate, *Inventing*; Yates, *Turing's Legacy*, pp. 145–146, 203–209.

41. Campbell and Connor, *On the Record*, pp. 189, 281.

42. National Audit Office, *Report by the Comptroller and Auditor General. Office Automation in Government Departments*, HC 314 (HMSO, 1991).

43. A second, better system, called COSINS, followed. The CCTA attempted to come to grips with such failures by producing project management methodologies: PROMPT (Project Resource Organisation Management Planning) from 1983, which was only used by four departments, and the enhanced PRINCE (Projects in Controlled Environments) from 1989.

44. National Audit Office, *Report by the Comptroller and Auditor General. Office Automation in Government Departments*, HC 314 (HMSO, 1991).

45. Wyatt, *Technology's Arrow*, p. 112.

46. The consortia were Racal with Scicon (subsequently Racal Data Networks Limited), Cable & Wireless (which owned Mercury) with ICL, and BT with Computer

Science Corporation (an American company with direct federal experience, having supplied a data network to the US Treasury).

47. Wyatt, *Technology's Arrow*, p. 139.

48. House of Commons, Select Committee on Public Accounts, *Minutes of Evidence*, 13 March 2000, Session 1999–2000.

49. Modernising Government, Cm 4310 (HMSO, 1999).

50. In 1997, Blair had announced that 25% of dealings with government should be capable of being done by the public electronically by 2002. Modernising Government therefore raised the target, to 50% of dealings to be capable of electronic delivery by 2005 and 100% by 2008. (Excluded from the figure were activities judged impossible to carry out electronically, e.g. operative surgery). The 2008 target was soon brought forward to 2005.

51. The Public Accounts Committee criticized this measure: "The Cabinet Office define "transactions" as any two way dealing between a government office and a citizen for instance just phoning a department for information or accessing a government Web site. We were surprised that a person telephoning a department was defined as an electronic transaction and was counted as contributing to the targets." The Cabinet Office promised to re-examine the matter. House of Commons, Select Committee on Public Accounts, *Twenty-first Report. Government on the Web*, Session 1999–2000.

52. Government would "work closely with the Data Protection Registrar to ensure that privacy implications of electronic service delivery are fully addressed"; "carry through our commitment to openness, so that the citizen has relevant information about our initiatives as they are developed and implemented"; "promote specific codes of practice, on a departmental or inter-departmental basis, for information age government"; "benefit from the Data Protection Registrar's powers to conduct independent assessments of the processing of personal data"; "deploy privacy-enhancing technologies, so that data is disclosed, accessed or identified with an individual only to the extent necessary"; "provide a proper and lawful basis for data sharing where this is desirable, e.g. in the interest of improved service or fraud reduction consistent with our commitment to protect privacy." Modernising Government, Cm 4310 (HMSO, 1999).

Conclusions

1. John M. Staudenmaier, *Technology's Storytellers* (MIT Press, 1985), p. 35.

2. Thomas P. Hughes, *Networks of Power* (Johns Hopkins University Press, 1983); Hughes, "'The evolution of large technological systems," in *The Social Construction of Technological Systems*, ed. W. Bijker et al. (MIT Press, 1987).

3. David Bloor, *Knowledge and Social Imagery* (Routledge & Kegan Paul, 1976).

4. Daniel Pick, *War Machine* (Yale University Press, 1993), p. 256.

5. Ibid. p. 215.

6. Anonymous, "The Third Census of Production," *Board of Trade Journal*, 28 February 1924, p. 275.

7. Lord Hankey, "The development of the higher control of the machinery of government," 11th Haldane Lecture, Birkbeck College, 22 May 1942. Lord Curzon's speech can be found in Parliamentary Debates: House of Lords, vol. 30, Col. 265.

8. The mechanical metaphor of government was, of course, widespread, but coexisted with an organic conception of government. (See chapter 1.)

9. James Vernon, "Narrating the constitution: the discourse of "the real" and the fantasies of nineteenth-century constitutional history," in *Re-reading the Constitution*, ed. J. Vernon (Cambridge University Press, 1996), p. 218. The argument is David Sugarman's.

10. The Babbage quotation is from *On the Economy of Machinery and Manufactures* (fourth edition, 1835); it also appears on p. 119 of Lorraine Daston and Peter Galison, "The image of objectivity," *Representations* 40 (1992): 81–128.

11. This generalization concerns tendencies. It is, of course, possible to find the mechanical metaphor being used to describe American administration. See, e.g., the following quotation from President William Howard Taft: "This vast organization has never been studied in detail as one piece of administrative machinery" (Message of the President of the United States on Economy and Efficiency in the Government Service, House of Representatives document no. 458. 62nd Congress, 2nd session, Government Printing Office, 1912), vol. 1, p. 4. On American constitutional machinery, see chapter 1.

12. Henry Parris, *Constitutional Bureaucracy* (Allen & Unwin, 1969), p. 29; Dorman B. Eaton, *Civil Service in Great Britain. A History of Abuses and Reforms and their Bearing upon American Politics* (Harper & Brothers, 1880; Ari Hoogenboom, *Outlawing the Spoils*, esp. pp. vii–ix; S. E. Finer, "Patronage and the public service," *Public Administration* (1952) 30: 329–360.

13. Parris, *Constitutional Bureaucracy*, p. 31.

14. Lane (*Venice*, Johns Hopkins University Press, 1973) records that there was a split between owners of capital and "mechanicals" in fourteenth-century Venice.

15. On "mechanical objectivity," see Daston and Galison, "The image of objectivity."

16. On gentlemanly modes, see Steve Shapin, *A Social History of Truth* (University of Chicago Press, 1994).

17. Ian Hacking, *The Taming of Chance* (Cambridge University Press, 1990), p. 5.

18. Ibid., pp. 3–4, 36.

19. Andrew Barry, Thomas Osborne, and Nikolas Rose, "Introduction," in Barry, Thomas, and Rose, *Foucault and Political Reason* (UCL Press, 1996), p. 2.

20. Barry, Osborne, and Rose, "Introduction," p. 8.

21. Michel Foucault, "An ethics of pleasure," in *Foucault Live*, ed. S. Lotringer (Semiotext(e), 1989), quoted in Barry, Osborne, and Rose, "Introduction."

22. Barry, Osborne, and Rose, "Introduction," p. 9.

23. Mitchell Dean, "Putting the technological into government," *History of the Human Sciences* 9: (1996) 47–68.

24. Nikolas Rose (*Powers of Freedom*, Cambridge University Press, 1999, p. 9) protests too much when he writes: "The kind of work undertaken under the sign of 'governmentality' has been splendidly varied: it is neither homogeneous school or a closed sect."

25. Herbert Spencer, *The Man Versus the State* (Watts, 1940; originally published 1884), p. 5. Another contemporary echo is Spencer's labeling of the Liberals as Tories in disguise.

26. Spencer, *The Man Versus the State*, p. 77.

27. John Stuart Mill, *On Liberty*, 1859. Reprinted in Mill, *Utilitarianism* (Fontana, 1962), p. 246.

28. Mill, *Representative Government*, p. 248.

29. Zahn writing in *Allgemeines Statistisches Archiv*, quoted in Edwin Black, *IBM and the Holocaust. The Strategic Alliance between Nazi Germany and America's Most Powerful Corporation* (Little, Brown, 2001), p. 47.

30. Michael Allen, "Stranger than science fiction," *Technology and Culture* 43 (2002): 150–154.

31. Black, *IBM*, p. 8.

32. Ibid., p. 55.

33. Ibid., p. 170.

34. Ibid., pp. 58, 103.

35. Ibid., p. 59.

36. Ibid., p. 90.

37. Ibid., p. 108.

38. Ibid., pp. 91–92.

39. "When too many cats scaled the top [of his fence] to jump into the yard, the ever-inventive Hollerith strung electrical wire along the fence, connected it to a battery, and then perched at his window puffing on a cigar. When a neighbor cat would appear . . . Hollerith would depress a switch, sending an electrical jolt into the animal." (Black, *IBM*, p. 28)

40. Black, *IBM*, p. 47.

41. Ibid., pp. 119–120.

42. Alfred Chandler Jr. and James W. Cortada, *A Nation Transformed by Information* (Oxford University Press, 2000), p. 19.

43. Michael Smith, *Station X* (Macmillan, 1998), pp. 173–174. This paragraph is drawn from Smith's unsourced description.

44. PRO FO 1032/1583. Gueterbock, "Statistics, recording machines, Hollerith system," 28 August 1944.

45. PRO FO 1032/1583. Minutes, 21 December 1944.

46. PRO FO 1032/1583. Notes from Lt. Col. A. F. Merry (Economics Division), 29 August 1944; Public Safety Branch, 20 August 1944; Displaced Persons Branch, 31 August 1944.

47. PRO FO 1032/1583. Note from Transportation Division, 12 September 1944.

48. PRO FO 1032/1583. "Memorandum for "I" Branch, Land Forces Division," October 1944.

49. PRO FO 1032/1583. Brigadier van Custen to Secretariat, 24 November 1944. Also, "Memorandum on statistical services in Germany," 1 January 1945.

50. Major G. E. Beynon, e.g., was taken because he was in charge of mechanizing the British Army pay system for the War Office, and had been engaged in the interwar years installing mechanized accountancy systems in large firms on the Continent.

51. Anonymous, "An organiser's heaven? Punches that plot life," *Manchester Guardian*, reprinted in *Powers-Samas Gazette*, November/December 1952, in NAHC photographic file.

52. David Edgerton, "Liberal militarism and the British state," *New Left Review* 185 (1991): 138–169, p. 140.

53. Dirk de Wit, *The Shaping of Automation* (Hilversum Verloren, 1994); Martin Campbell-Kelly, "Data processing and technological change: the Post Office Savings Bank, 1861–1930," *Technology and Culture* 53 (1998): 1–32.

54. Jan van den Ende, *The Turn of the Tide* (Universiteitsdrukkerij Delft, 1994), pp. 103–132. Geographical factors such as violent storms (and social factors such as reactions to violent storms) shaped how the tidal calculation project developed, e.g. p. 124.

55. Van den Ende, *Turn*, pp. 133, 137.

56. Lars Heide, "Punched-card and computer applications in Denmark, 1911–1970," *History and Technology* (1994) 11: 77–99.

57. PRO T 222/1457. Desborough, "Office methods, operations and machines," paper for the IPA, 17 November 1927.

58. PRO T 162/55. "Memorandum on supply of 200 Comptometers to the Inland Revenue for use in the offices of Surveyors of Taxes," December 1920.

59. Anonymous, "The Third Census of Production," *Board of Trade Journal*, 28 February 1924, pp. 274–275.

60. Taft, *Message of the President of the United States on Economy and Efficiency in the Government Service*, p. 4.

61. Ibid., p. 11.

62. Henry Higgs, *National Economy* (Macmillan, 1917), p. 44. On the Taft Commission's investigation of vertical filing, see *Economy and Efficiency in the Government Service. Message of the President of the United States Transmitting Reports of the Commission on Economy and Efficiency*, House of Representatives document no. 670. 62nd Congress, 2nd session, vol. 116, Washington: Government Printing Office, 1912), especially Appendix no. 7, "Memorandum of conclusions concerning the principles that should govern in the matter of handling and filing correspondence and preparing and mailing communications in connection with the work of the several departments of the Government, together with suggestions for the use of labor-saving devices in preparing and mailing letters, etc.," pp. 515–554.

63. Higgs, "National Economy," p. 45.

64. Ibid., p. 47. In 1911, the executive branch of the government of the United States employed more than 400,000, compared to 135,721 in the United Kingdom. Taft, *Message of the President*, p. 3. The US figure includes military and naval personnel. The UK figure does not.

65. On the Civil Service and British economic decline, see Hennessy, *Whitehall*, pp. 1–11, 170–172.

66. David Edgerton, *Science, Technology and the British Industrial "Decline," 1870–1970* (Cambridge University Press, 1996).

67. Martin Campbell-Kelly, "Data processing and technological change: the Post Office Savings Bank, 1861–1930," *Technology and Culture* 39 (1998): 1–32, p. 29.

68. PRO STAT 14/1156. Memorandum by Desborough, sent to Pitman, 15 July 1948. Experts to Bridgeman committee quoted in PRO T 222/1457. Bunker, "The origins and early history of O and M," undated (1966).

69. PRO T 222/1457. Bunker, "The origins and early history of O and M," undated (1966).

70. PRO STAT 14/1156. Scorgie to Pitman, 8 April 1948, intriguingly observes that "the modern (and justifiable) claim that the public service has been well in the van of progress in mechanization was never made years ago in the form that it intended and planned to be in the van." Note this assumes that the movement to the "van" was recent, but also "justifiable."

71. Part of a range of changes in which technological change has raised questions for liberal democratic government. Media technologies provide one set of example, but also information technologies such as forms: when information collection structures of government were small and/or unreliable greater emphasis had to made on more direct politician-public links. Therefore it could be argued that the increasing availability and sophistication of information collecting practices has allowed greater distance between politicians and people and subsequent problems for democracy.

72. Graham Wallas, *Human Nature in Politics* (Constable, 1929 (1909)), p. 98.

73. Ibid., p. 167: "the efficiency of political science, its power, that is to say, of forecasting the results of political causes, is likely to increase. I based my argument on two facts, firstly, that modern psychology offers us a conception of human nature much truer, though more complex, than that which is associated with the traditional English political philosophy; and secondly, that, under the influence and example of the natural sciences, political thinkers are already beginning to use in their discussions and inquiries quantitative rather than merely qualitative words and methods."

74. The plans for the National Farm Survey were begun during the months of the Battle of Britain, and required farmers to "fill up, without exaggeration, at least ten times the number of forms that even they were accustomed to and nearly every form at least twice as diabolical as any invented by Government Departments before the War," G. C. Hayter Hames, quoted in Brian Short, Charles Watkins, William Foot, and Phil Kinsman, *The National Farm Survey, 1941–1943. State Surveillance and the Countryside in England and Wales in the Second World War* (CABI, 2000), p. 230.

75. Beniger, *The Control Revolution.* Compare with Hacking on statistics.

76. Beniger, *The Control Revolution*; Vincent Mosco, *The Pay-per Society* (Garamond, 1989); David Harvey, *The Condition of Postmodernity* (Blackwell, 1989).

77. Martin Albrow, *Bureaucracy* (Macmillan, 1970), p. 70.

78. Barry, Osborne, and Rose, "Introduction," p. 15.

79. Christopher Dandeker's *Surveillance, Power and Modernity* (Polity Press, 1990) contains the materials for a movement in the direction of such a debate.

80. Manuel Castells, "The net and the self: working notes for a critical theory of informational society," *Critique of Anthropology* 16 (1996): 9–38.

81. I. Bernard Cohen, "The computer: A case study of support by government, especially the military, of a new science and technology," in *Science, Technology and the Military*, ed. E. Mendelsohn et al. (Kluwer, 1988)

82. Kenneth Flamm, *Targeting the Computer* (Brookings Institution, 1987); Flamm, *Creating the Computer* (Brookings Institution, 1988).

83. Edwards, *Closed World*, p. 71.

84. McNamara had joined the Kennedy administration from the Ford Motor Company. He had joined Ford after the Second World War (in which he had served in the Army). Through the promotion of statistical control techniques, he had risen rapidly, becoming president of Ford—the first not to be a member of the Ford family—in 1960. Within the year he was appointed Secretary of Defense.

85. Edwards, *Closed World*, pp. 7–8.

86. Ibid., pp. 70–73, 106.

87. Martin van Crevold, *Technology and War* (Brassey, 1991), p. 245.

88. PRO T 222/1305. Merriman, "Note for record," 23 December 1958.

89. See Agatha C. Hughes and Thomas P. Hughes, eds., *Systems, Experts, and Computers* (MIT Press, 2000), particularly Atsushi Akera, "Engineers or managers? The systems analysis of Electronic Data Processing in the federal bureaucracy." Akera makes the interesting comment that "once the technical community coalesced around the notion of a general purpose computer, it had opened up a flexible epistemological space that was subject to recurring questions of authority." Compare this with my discussion of "general-purpose."

90. Herbert A. Simon, *Models of My Life* (MIT Press, 1996), p. 86.

91. Herbert A. Simon, *Administrative Behavior*, fourth printing (Macmillan, 1949), p. 1. In particular it was a study of the effects of what Simon called the "bounded rationality' of humans. Put simply, this is the idea that individuals within organizations do not see the whole picture, and therefore do not have the means or resources to make rational judgments, and therefore opt for "subgoals" which might hamper organizational efficiency.

92. Simon, *Administrative Behavior*, p. 2.

93. Simon, *Administrative Behavior*, second edition (Macmillan, 1957), p. xxvi; Allen Newell and Herbert A. Simon, "The Logic Theory Machine," *IRE Transactions on Information Theory* 2 (1957): 61–79.

94. Simon, *Administrative Behavior*, second edition, p. ix.

95. Organization memory was "artificial." See e.g. Simon, *Administrative Behavior*, first edition, p. 166.

96. Herbert A. Simon, *The Shape of Automation for Men and Management* (Harper & Row, 1965), pp. 26, 27, 30. Part II of this book, from which these quotations are taken, was originally published as "Will the corporation be managed by machine?' in Melvin Anshen and George Leland Bach, *Management and Corporations, 1985* (McGraw-Hill, 1960).

97. Simon, *Shape of Automation*, pp. 44–47. "Managers are largely concerned with supervising, with solving well-structured problems, and with solving ill-structured problems . . . [The] automation of the second of these activities—solving well-structured

problems—is proceeding extremely rapidly; the automation of the third—solving ill-structured problems—moderately rapidly; and the automation of supervision more slowly."

98. Simon, *Shape of Automation*, p. 49.

99. Simon (ibid., p. 48) has his cake and eats it. He makes this claim only one page after stating that "we can dismiss the notion that computer programmers will become a powerful elite in the automated corporation."

100. Simon, *Administrative Behavior*, first edition, p. 1.

101. "Programmed" decisions were "routine, repetitive' and an "organisation develops specific processes for handling them' (including electronic data processing), while "nonprogrammed' decisions were "one-shot, ill-structured novel, policy decisions. Handled by general problem-solving processes." Herbert A. Simon, *The New Science of Management Decision* (Harper, 1960), p. 8.

102. PRO T 222/1305. Melville, Talk on "Possible developments in industrial technology over the next ten years with some statement of the consequences of the social and economic changes that may be expected," drafted by Merriman, 1959.

103. Michael Hà6rd and Andrew Jamison, *The Intellectual Appropriation of Technology* (MIT Press, 1998).

104. Jeffrey Herf, *Reactionary Modernism* (Cambridge University Press, 1984), p. 1.

105. Anne Massey, *The Independent Group* (Manchester University Press, 1995), p. 33.

106. Ibid.; Reyner Banham, *Theory and Design in the First Machine Age* (Architectural Press, 1960).

107. H. W. Howes, *Presenting Modern Britain* (Harrap, 1966).

108. PRO NSC 45/61. Minutes, "Premium bonds. Minutes of a meeting held at HQ on Saturday, 12 May 1956."

109. PRO NSC 45/51. Description of ERNIE.

110. PRO INF 6/113. Draft script, "The importance of being ERNIE," by R. K. Neilson-Baxter (Realist Film Unit), 24 June 1963.

111. For an excellent analysis of audit, see Michael Power, *The Audit Society* (Oxford University Press, 1997).

112. On the styling of the PDP-8 as a "mini," see Ceruzzi, *History*, p. 135.

113. On NASA and real-time computing, see Ceruzzi, *History*, p. 117.

114. This tradition extends from the counter-cultural pronouncements of the Californian "computer liberation' movement, through to claims that the internet erodes hierarchy, which can be found in both popular and academic forms.

115. Power, *Audit Society*, pp. 69–70.

116. Helen Margetts, *Information Technology in Government* (Routledge, 1999), p. 130.

117. James Gillies and Robert Cailliau, *How the Web was Born* (Oxford University Press, 2000), pp. 181–182.

118. Karl Deutsch, *The Nerves of Government* (Free Press of Glencoe, 1963). Deutsch saw government as being like a neural net. See also James A. Anderson and Edward Rosenfeld, eds., *Talking Nets* (MIT Press, 1998), p. 342.

119. For discussions, see Rob Kitchin, *Cyberspace* (Wiley, 1998), pp. 100–128; Brian D. Loader, ed., *The Governance of Cyberspace; Politics, Technology and Global Restructuring* (Routledge, 1997).

Index

Printed in the United States
By Bookmasters